McGraw Hill Education | create™

Annual Editions:
The Family, 40e

by Patricia Hrusa Williams
University of Maine at Farmington

http://create.mcgraw-hill.com

ISBN-10: 0078136202   ISBN-13: 9780078136207

Contents

Unit 4 129

Unit 5 227

Preface

The purpose of *Annual Editions: The Family 14/15* is to bring to the reader the latest thoughts and trends in our understanding of the family, to identify current concerns as well as problems and potential solutions, and to present alternative views on family processes. The intent of this anthology is to explore family relationships and to reflect the family's evolving function and importance. The articles in this volume are taken from professional journals as well as other professionally-oriented publications and popular lay publications aimed at both special populations and a general readership. The selections are carefully reviewed for their currency and accuracy.

In the current edition, a number of new articles have been added to reflect reviewers' comments on the previous edition. As the reader, you will note the tremendous range in tone and focus of these articles, from first-person accounts to reports of scientific discoveries, as well as philosophical and theoretical writings. Some are more practical and applications-oriented, while others are more conceptual and research-oriented. Together, they highlight the multidisciplinary nature of the study of the family and the myriad of influences that shape the family as a social structure and unit of socialization.

This anthology is organized to address many of the important aspects of family and family relationships. The first unit is an overview, looking at varied perspectives on the family. The second unit examines the beginnings of relationships as individuals go through the process of exploring and establishing connections. In the third unit, various types of relationships will be explored—including marriage, parent–child, sibling, and intergenerational relationships. The fourth unit is concerned with crises and ways in which these can act as challenges and opportunities for families and their members. Finally, the fifth unit takes an affirming tone as it looks at family strengths, ways of empowering families, and emerging trends within families.

Annual Editions: The Family 14/15 is intended to be used as a supplemental text for lower-level, introductory marriage, family, or sociology of the family classes—particularly when they tie the content of the readings to essential information on marriages and families, however they are defined. As a supplement, this book can also be used to update or emphasize certain aspects of standard marriage and family textbooks. Because of the provocative nature of many of the essays in this anthology, it works well as a basis for class discussion, debate, and critical thinking exercises about various aspects of marriages and family relationships. This edition of *Annual Editions: The Family* contains websites noted after each article that can be used to further explore topics addressed in the readings.

Editor

Patricia Hrusa Williams is an Assistant Professor in the Department of Early Childhood and Elementary Education at the University of Maine at Farmington. She received her BA in Health & Society and Psychology from the University of Rochester. Her PhD is in Applied Child Development from Tufts University. Dr. Williams's primary areas of interest are family support programs, parental involvement in early childhood education, service learning, and the development of writing and critical thinking skills in college students. She has authored, co-authored, or edited over 15 published articles in books, academic journals, and the popular press. Dr. Williams lives with her husband and three children in the mountains of western Maine.

Academic Advisory Board

Members of the Academic Advisory Board are instrumental in the final selection of articles for *Annual Editions* and ExpressBooks. Their review of the articles for content, level, and appropriateness provides critical direction to the editor(s) and staff. We think that you will find their careful consideration reflected in this ExpressBook.

William Michael Fleming
University of Northern Iowa

Josephine Fritts
Ozarks Technical Community College

Patricia Furnish
Blue Ridge Community College

Kathleen M. Galvin
Northwestern University

Teresa Gonzalez
Queens College

Gwendolyn Gordon
Connors State College

Rick Herbert
South Plains College

Dennis W. Johnson
Monterey Peninsula College

Diana Karol-Nagy
University of Florida

Debbie Keller
College of the Ozarks

Rhonda Korol Lyndon
State College

Leslie C. Lamb
Farmingdale State College

Carrie Lawrence
Indiana University–Bloomington

Larry LeFlore
Texas Women's University

Jeffrey Liew
Texas A&M University

John W. McNeeley
Daytona State College—Palm Coast

Kari Morgan
University of Wyoming

Michelle Morris
Northwestern State University

Patricia E. Neff Claster
Edinboro University of Pennsylvania

Catherine Norris-Bush
Carson-Newman College

Marcellina Offoha
Shaw University

Esther Onaga
Michigan State University

Hiromi Ono
Washington State University

Lauren M. Papp
University of Wisconsin—Madison

Sandra Prince
Delgado Community College

Frankie Rabon
Grambling State University

Mary Eva Repass
University of Virginia

Doug Rice
California State University—Sacramento

Frank A. Salamone
Iona College

Laurence Segall
Housatonic Community College

Barbara Settles
University of Delaware

Diana Shepherd
California State University—Chico

Leretta Smith
North Dakota State University

George F. Stine
Millersville University

James C. Stroud
Ball State University

Dianne Sykes
Gardner-Webb University

Bahira Trask
University of Delaware

Paula Tripp
Sam Houston State University

Kourtney Vaillancourt
New Mexico State University

Glenda Warren
University of the Cumberlands

Paul Wills
Kilgore College Troy University

Correlation Guide

The *Annual Editions* series provides students with convenient, inexpensive access to current, carefully selected articles from the public press. **Annual Editions: The Family 14/15** is an easy-to-use reader that presents articles on important topics such as *family composition, love and sex, family stressors,* and many more. For more information on *Annual Editions* and other *McGraw-Hill Contemporary Learning Series* titles, visit www.mhhe.com/cls.

This convenient guide matches the units in **Annual Editions: The Family 14/15** with the corresponding chapters in three of our best-selling McGraw-Hill Family textbooks by Lauer and Lauer, DeGenova et al., and Miller.

Annual Editions: The Family 14/15	Marriage and Family: The Quest for Intimacy, 8/e by Lauer/Lauer	Intimate Relationships, Marriages, and Families, 8/e by DeGenova et al.	Intimate Relationships, 6/e by Miller
Unit 1: Evolving Perspectives on the Family	**Chapter 1:** Marriage and Family in America: Needs, Myths, and Dreams	**Chapter 1:** Intimate Relationships, Marriages and Families in the Twenty-First Century **Chapter 2:** Gender: Identity and Roles	**Chapter 1:** The Building Blocks of Relationships
Unit 2: Exploring and Establishing Relationships	**Chapter 4:** Sexuality **Chapter 6:** Falling in Love **Chapter 7:** Selecting a Life Partner **Chapter 9:** The Challenge of Communication **Chapter 16:** Intimacy in Later Years	**Chapter 4:** Attraction and Dating **Chapter 5:** Love and Mate Selection **Chapter 6:** Qualities of a Successful Marriage **Chapter 10:** Sexual Relationships **Chapter 11:** Family Planning and Parenting	**Chapter 3:** Attraction **Chapter 5:** Communication **Chapter 8:** Love **Chapter 9:** Sexuality
Unit 3: Family Relationships	**Chapter 10:** Power and Conflict in Marriage **Chapter 14:** Separation and Divorce	**Chapter 6:** Qualities of a Successful Marriage **Chapter 7:** Marital Relationships Over The Family Life Cycle **Chapter 8:** Work, Family Roles, and Material Resources **Chapter 9:** Power, Decision Making, and Communication **Chapter 13:** Parent–Child Relationships **Chapter 14:** Parents and Extended Family Relationships	**Chapter 11:** Conflict **Chapter 12:** Power and Violence **Chapter 13:** The Dissolution and Loss of Relationships **Chapter 14:** Maintaining and Repairing Relationships
Unit 4: Challenge and Opportunities	**Chapter 13:** Family Crises **Chapter 14:** Separation and Divorce **Chapter 15:** Remarriage and Stepfamilies	**Chapter 8:** Work, Family Roles, and Material Resources **Chapter 9:** Power, Decision Making, and Communication **Chapter 15:** Conflict, Family Crises, and Crisis Management **Chapter 16:** The Family and Divorce **Chapter 17:** Coming Together: Remarriage and Stepparenting	**Chapter 11:** Conflict **Chapter 12:** Power and Violence **Chapter 13:** The Dissolution and Loss of Relationships **Chapter 14:** Maintaining and Repairing Relationships
Unit 5: Families, Now and into the Future	**Chapter 1:** Marriage and Family in America: Needs, Myths, and Dreams	**Chapter 1:** Intimate Relationships, Marriages, and Families in the Twenty-First Century	**Chapter 1:** The Building Blocks of Relationships

Topic Guide

Abuse and Neglect

Terrorism in the Home: Eleven myths and facts about domestic violence
Anguish of the Abandoned Child
We Are Family: When Elder Abuse, Neglect, and Financial Exploitation Hit Home

Aging

How to Stay Married
Sibling Rivalry Grows Up: Adult Brothers and Sisters Are Masters at Digs; Finding a Way to a Truce
The Accordion Family
Daddy Issues: Why Caring For My Aging Father Has Me Wishing He Would Die
We Are Family: When Elder Abuse, Neglect, and Financial Exploitation Hit Home
Family Members' Informal Roles in End-of-Life Decision Making in Adult Intensive Care Units

Bereavement

Family Members' Informal Roles in End-of-Life Decision Making in Adult Intensive Care Units

Biology

12 Rude Revelations about Sex
The Child's Advocate in Donor Conceptions: The Telling of The Story
There's No Such Thing as Everlasting Love (According to Science)
You Got Your Sperm Where?

Caregiving

Family Members' Informal Roles in End-of-Life Decision Making in Adult Intensive Care Units
Support Needs of Siblings of People with Developmental Disabilities
Supporting Siblings of Children with Autism Spectrum Disorders
The Positives of Caregiving: Mothers' Experiences Caregiving for a Child with Autism
The Coming Special Needs Care Crisis

Childcare/Childrearing

The Significant Dynamic Relationship between Globalization and Families
Matches Made on Earth: Why Family Values Are Human Values
Getting It Right from the Start: The Case for Early Parenthood Education
Parenting Wars
Why Chinese Mothers are Superior
Parental Responsibility and Obesity in Children
Anguish of the Abandoned Child
Behind Every Great Woman
The Coming Special Needs Care Crisis
Helping Children Endure Divorce
Relative Happiness
Back to the Dinner Table
The Child's Advocate in Donor Conceptions: The Telling of The Story

Children

Matches Made on Earth: Why Family Values Are Human Values
Parenting Wars
Why Chinese Mothers Are Superior
Parental Responsibility and Obesity in Children
Sibling Rivalry Grows Up: Adult Brothers and Sisters Are Masters at Digs; Finding a Way to a Truce
Supporting Siblings of Children with Autism Spectrum Disorders
Anguish of the Abandoned Child
Homeless in the Suburbs
The Coming Special Needs Care Crisis

Military Children and Families: Strengths and Challenges during Peace and War
Helping Children Endure Divorce
Strengthening Fragile Families
Relative Happiness
The Child's Advocate in Donor Conceptions: The Telling of The Story

Communication

Relationships, Community, and Identity in the New Virtual Society
Getting It Right from the Start: The Case for Early Parenthood Education
Helping Children Endure Divorce
Back to the Dinner Table

Dating

Relationships, Community, and Identity in the New Virtual Society
The Expectations Trap
Waiting to Wed
The End of Courtship?
Terrorism in the Home: Eleven myths and facts about domestic violence

Divorce

Are You with the Right Mate?
How to Stay Married
Why Do Marriages Fail?
Helping Children Endure Divorce

Family Forms

The Changing Face of the American Family
The Significant Dynamic Relationship between Globalization and Families
Matches Made on Earth: Why Family Values Are Human Values
The Polygamists
The Accordion Family
Behind Every Great Woman
Military Children and Families: Strengths and Challenges during Peace and War
Strengthening Fragile Families
Relative Happiness
The Child's Advocate in Donor Conceptions: The Telling of The Story
Meet My Real Modern Family

Family Interaction

Relationships, Community, and Identity in the New Virtual Society
Support Needs of Siblings of People with Developmental Disabilities
Sibling Rivalry Grows Up: Adult Brothers and Sisters Are Masters at Digs; Finding a Way to a Truce
Supporting Siblings of Children with Autism Spectrum Disorders
Terrorism in the Home: Eleven myths and facts about domestic violence
Building on Strengths: Intergenerational Practice with African American Families
Daddy Issues: Why Caring For My Aging Father Has Me Wishing He Would Die
Family Members' Informal Roles in End-of-Life Decision Making in Adult Intensive Care Units
Relative Happiness
Back to the Dinner Table
Family Unplugged
Meet My Real Modern Family

Fathers

You Got Your Sperm Where?
Strengthening Fragile Families
Meet My Real Modern Family

Unit 1

UNIT

Prepared by: Patricia Hrusa Williams,
University of Maine at Farmington

Evolving Perspectives on the Family

Our image of what family is and what it should be is a powerful combination of personal experience, family forms we encounter or observe, and attitudes we hold. Once formed, this image informs decision making and interpersonal interaction throughout our lives and has far-reaching effects. On an intimate level, it influences individual and family development as well as the relationships we create and maintain both inside and outside the family. On a broader level, it affects legislation, social policy, and programmatic supports developed and offered to couples, parents, and families. In many ways, the images we build and hold can be positive. They can act to clarify our thinking and facilitate interaction with like-minded individuals. They can also be negative, narrowing our thinking and limiting our ability to see how we can learn from others and to appreciate how other ways of

carrying out family functions have value. Interaction with others can be impeded because of contrasting views.

This unit is intended to meet several goals in exploring the evolving family: (1) to sensitize the reader to sources of beliefs about the "shoulds" of the family—what the family should be and the ways in which family roles and communication should be carried out; (2) to show how different views of the family can influence attitudes toward community responsibility and family policy; and (3) to show how changes in society are changing the nature of family life and patterns of communication. Issues to be considered in this unit include how historical, demographic, philosophical, and technological changes are influencing families and the nature of family life in the United States and abroad.

Prepared by: Patricia Hrusa Williams,
University of Maine at Farmington

Article

The Changing Face of the American Family

TIM STANLEY

Learning Outcomes

After reading this article, you will be able to:

- Explain the meaning and origins of the term "nuclear family."

- Describe shifts in family structure from 1900 to the present.

- Recognize differences in the ways the media have portrayed families from 1950 to the present.

On September 20th, 1984 a new sitcom aired on NBC. *The Cosby Show* starred Bill Cosby as Heathcliff 'Cliff' Huxtable, a middle-class, black obstetrician living with his wife and five children in Brooklyn, New York. It kicked off with a situation that millions of parents could identify with: Cliff's son, Theo, had come home with a report card covered in Ds. Theo's mother was deeply upset and Cliff was furious. But Theo said that his bad grades didn't bother him because he didn't want to go to college. His goal was to grow up to be like 'regular people' and, if Cliff loves his son, won't he accept him for what he is? The audience applauded. This was what TV had been teaching them for over a decade, that love and understanding were more important than competition and success. But, to their shock, Cosby's character didn't agree. 'Theo,' he said, 'that is the dumbest thing I ever heard! No wonder you get Ds in everything! . . . I'm telling you, you are going to try as hard as you can. And you're going to do it because I said so. I am your father. I brought you into this world, and I will take you out!' The audience's laughter was nervous at first, but by the end of the scene they were clapping wildly. Bill Cosby had just turned the liberal logic of TV Land on its head. 'Father knows best' parenting was back.

This scene is discussed in the PBS documentary *America in Primetime*, shortly to be shown by the BBC.

The programme makes the point that because the Cosbys are African-Americans, we might presume that the politics of the show are liberal—sitcoms in the 1970s had tended to use black characters to explore poverty and racism. Yet Cliff Huxtable's old fashioned parenting had much more in common with the optimistic conservatism of the 1980s presidency of Republican

Ronald Reagan. The Huxtables were wealthy, professional, churchgoers, dominated by a stern father. Alas, among black families their traditional structure increasingly made them the exception rather than the rule. In the America of the 1980s divorce and illegitimacy were rising fast. By 1992, when the show ended, 68 per cent of African-American babies were born out of wedlock. The last episode of *Cosby* coincided with riots in Los Angeles, the product of economic segregation and black fury at a brutal police force. The show might have started out as a healthy antidote to touchy-feely liberalism, but it ended as escapist fantasy.

The Cosby Show's huge viewing figures—among both blacks and whites—tell a confusing story. On the one hand divorce and illegitimacy were changing the character of the American family for good. Un-wed co-habitation was more likely; partners were more inclined to abandon an unhappy relationship; sex outside marriage was common. On the other hand Americans still held heterosexual marriage in high regard and wanted to watch shows that affirmed it. The big TV hits of the 1980s were all centred around traditional families— *Mr Belvedere, Who's The Boss?, Growing Pains*. Ronald Reagan's favourite show was *Family Ties,* which starred Michael J. Fox as a teenager who rebelled against his liberal parents by campaigning for Ronald Reagan.

The answer to this paradox lay in the enduring appeal of the nuclear family. America's nuclear unit wasn't around very long. It was forged by the unique economic and political circumstances of the 1950s, was undermined by social revolution in the 1960s and was revived as an ideal in the 1970s by a conservative movement with a deceptively rosy view of the past. But, while the nuclear family was only representative of how a number of people lived for a few years, its myth has hardened into an ideology. For many Americans it remains synonymous with the hallowed promise of the American dream.

Sitcom Suburbia

In 1957 CBS premiered a TV show called *Leave it to Beaver*. It starred Jerry Mathers as Theodore 'The Beaver' Cleaver, an inquisitive boy who lived with his parents June and Ward in a leafy suburb. The plot of every episode was the same: Beaver got in trouble, his parents reprimanded him and our hero would learn something about the realities of life.

In one storyline Beaver met the son of divorced parents and was jealous of all the presents he got from his estranged dad. But he quickly discovered that divorce also leads to insecurity and depression, so the episode ended with Beaver begging his parents never to part. Divorce wasn't the only model of social dysfunction that the show explored: spinsters like prim Aunt Martha were sexless harpies, while bachelors, like Andy the alcoholic handyman, were layabout bums. It was a world of conservative certainty, held together by a terror of nonconformity.

Today *Leave it to Beaver* is shorthand for the calm and luxury of American life before the storm of the 1960s. In fact the world that it depicted was a historical aberration; before 1950 things had been very different. In 1900 the vast majority of women went out to work and the US had the highest divorce rate in the world. Roughly one in ten children grew up in a single-parent household, hundreds of thousands of offspring were abandoned due to shortages of money and families were plagued with disease and death. Between 35 and 40 per cent of children lost a parent or a sibling before their 20s.

It wasn't until the 1950s that life began to get sweeter and more stable for the average American. The decade was characterised by a rising birth rate, a stable divorce rate and a declining age of marriage. In 1950 most married women walked down the aisle aged just 20. Only 16 per cent of them got a job outside the home and a majority of brides were pregnant within seven months of their wedding. They didn't stop at one child: from 1940 to 1960 the number of families with three children doubled and the number of families having a fourth child quadrupled.

Contemporary anthropologists dubbed this the 'nuclear family'. They meant nuclear as in a unit built around the nucleus of the father and mother, but the name also resonates with the politics of the Cold War. The family was on the front line of an existential conflict between communism and capitalism. On the communist side, the propagandists said, were collectivism, atheism and poverty. On the capitalist side was self-reliance, freedom of religion and a degree of material comfort unparalleled in US history. Science was eradicating disease, salaries were rising, household goods were alleviating drudgery and the nuclear family had a friend in big business.

The advertising agencies tried to create the model of the perfect housewife. A famous article in *Housekeeping Monthly* of May 13th, 1955 explained what perfection entailed:

> *Your goal: To try and make sure your home is a place of peace, order, and tranquility where your husband can renew himself in body and spirit. . . . Make him comfortable. Have him lean back in a comfortable chair or have him lie down in the bedroom. . . . Arrange his pillow and offer to take off his shoes. Speak in a low, soothing and pleasant voice. . . . Remember, he is the master of the house and as such will always exercise his will with fairness and truthfulness. You have no right to question him. A good wife always knows her place.*

Having popularised the ideal of a 'good wife', the advertisers recommended products that would put perfection within her reach. 'Christmas Morning, She'll Be Happier With a Hoover!' claimed one ad, which featured a housewife excitedly examining her new vacuum cleaner. Spending on advertising rose from $6 billion in 1950 to over $13 billion in 1963.

The efforts of advertising's Mad Men were central to the 1950s boom. Robert Sarnoff, president of the National Broadcasting Company, said in 1956: 'The reason we have such a high standard of living is because advertising has created an American frame of mind that makes people want more things, better things, and newer things.' He was probably right. Private debt doubled during the 1950s, driving up profit and productivity and returning much of it to the male wage earner. The economy grew by roughly 37 per cent, with low rates of inflation and unemployment. By 1960 the average family had 30 per cent more purchasing power than it had had in 1950. The nuclear unit was the engine of America's growth and the main beneficiary of its economic greatness.

The Sixties Swing Out of Control

But was everyone really as happy as the ads implied? In 1963 a book hit the shelves that claimed to expose all the oppression and misery that lay behind *Leave it to Beaver*'s white picket fences. Its author, Betty Friedan, described herself as a housewife and mother from the New York suburbs. In 1957 Friedan had been asked to conduct a survey of former Smith College classmates. The results depressed her. Girls who had studied and excelled at the arts and sciences were expected to surrender their minds and personalities to their roles as wives: 89 per cent of the Smith alumni who answered her survey were now homemakers. Intellectually repressed and lacking anyway to express themselves beyond cooking or sex, the housewife of the 1960s was suffocated by what Friedan called the feminine mystique. 'Each suburban wife struggles with it alone' she wrote. 'As she made the beds, shopped for groceries, matched slipcover material, ate peanut butter sandwiches with her children, chauffeured Cub Scouts and Brownies, lay beside her husband at night—she was afraid to ask even of herself the silent question—"Is this all?"'

The Feminine Mystique stayed on *The New York Times* bestseller list for six weeks and laid the groundwork for a feminist revolution that would redefine the nuclear unit forever. Friedan wanted women to take control of their lives and the shortcuts to liberation were contraception and employment. But the book wasn't quite the impartial account that its author claimed. Although she was technically a homemaker, Friedan was not an apolitical housewife who spent her evenings arranging her husband's pillow. She was active in socialist politics and had worked as a journalist for the United Electrical Workers union for a number of years after her marriage. Friedan probably hid all these details because she wanted to divorce feminism from radicalism and so make it more palatable to the average woman. More troublingly, she exaggerated the degree to which the women of Smith College were the passive victims of patriarchy. In fact most of the housewives who answered her survey said they were the happiest they had ever been—a majority expressed no desire to return to the world of work. But they did not buy the advertisers' myth of suburban fulfilment and many said that they felt frustrated that they could not use their intellect in more demanding ways. Instead they were channelling those energies into voluntary work and party political activism. Contemporary women were already finding ways to overcome the feminine mystique, while retaining their identities as wives and mothers.

Although Friedan and the women's liberation movement sometimes imagined that they masterminded the 1960s cultural revolution their role was actually to politicise social changes that were already happening. Just as science helped to forge the nuclear family, with better nutrition and disease control, so it created the conditions for its destruction. In 1960 the US Food and Drug Administration officially licensed the sale of the oral contraceptive known as the Pill. By 1962 an estimated 1,187,000 women were using it. Policy makers thought the Pill would strengthen the nuclear family by increasing disposable income via reduced pregnancies. What it did in practice was to weaken the links between sexual pleasure, childbirth and marriage. Sex before and outside marriage increased, while women who had married became more likely to seek work or stay in it.

The effects of such subtle changes in sexual practice were startling. Between 1960 and 1980 the divorce rate almost doubled. In 1962 only half of all respondents disagreed with a statement suggesting that parents who don't get along should stay together for the children; by 1977 over 80 per cent disagreed. In the early 1960s roughly half of women told pollsters that they had engaged in premarital sex. By the late 1980s the figure was five out of six. In the early 1960s approximately three quarters of Americans said premarital sex was wrong. By the 1980s that view was held by only one third of the nation. The most obvious legacy of shifting attitudes was the rocketing rate of births out of wedlock. In 1960 only five per cent of births were attributed to single mothers. By 1980 the figure was 18 per cent and by 1990 it was 28 per cent.

Both Left and Right were worried that America was coming apart. Although the 1960s were dominated by the struggles over Vietnam and Civil Rights, an equally big policy challenge was how to save the nuclear family unit. The Left concluded that the answer was greater government support. In 1965 the liberal sociologist Daniel Patrick Moynihan published *The Negro Family: The Case For National Action*. A study of poverty in the African-American ghetto, the so-called *Moynihan Report* argued that the underlying cause of inequality between black and white was not economics or race but family structure. Moynihan believed that the growing incidence of single motherhood was raising a generation of African-American males who lacked a model of self-reliance, discipline and authority. He advised Democratic President Lyndon Johnson that the solution was job training and education programmes that would empower black fathers to raise their family on a single salary. The welfare state would have to grow.

Johnson declared a 'War on Poverty' that created a plethora of entitlements to individuals. The use of government subsidies to buy meals (which had been around since the 1930s) increased dramatically under both Democrat and Republican administrations: the number of individuals using food stamps jumped from 500,000 in 1965 to 10 million in 1971. The overall effect was a fall in the proportion of Americans living in poverty from 19 per cent in 1964 to 11.1 per cent in 1973. But government generosity did nothing to stop the decline of the nuclear unit. Conservatives argued that it actually undermined the family by subsidising absentee fathers, educational underachievement, crime, drugs and a new, somewhat racialised, form of segregation between those in work and those on the dole. Moynihan's ambition to rescue the black family failed. While the median black family income rose 53 per cent in the 1960s, the rate of single parenthood also increased by over 50 per cent. Conservatives began to argue that the welfare state was not the solution but part of the problem. They claimed that the real goal of liberals like Friedan and Johnson was to create a world in which the nuclear family no longer existed.

Lost Age of Innocence

In 1976 America went to the polls to elect a new president. Its choice was Jimmy Carter, a former peanut farmer and one-term governor of Georgia. With his photogenic family and foursquare humility, the Baptist Carter felt like a throwback to the *Leave it to Beaver* spirit. In the mid-1970s America was experiencing a wave of nostalgia for the 1950s; movies like *Grease* and *American Graffiti* celebrated a lost age of innocence and certainty. Carter said that if he won the election he would hold a White House 'Conference on the Family' to discuss the best way of reviving some of those old values. It was exactly the kind of consensus-building, moral politics that Carter loved.

But after Carter's inauguration the White House announced a name change. The Conference on the Family would become the Conference on Families, reflecting the growing diversity of American family structures. Presidential aides pointed out that roughly a third of families no longer adhered to what they described as the 'nostalgic family'—their rather patronising term for the nuclear unit. One person who welcomed the rebranding was delegate Betty Friedan. In her 1981 book *The Second Stage* she wrote that she was pleased the conference recognised the most important shift in American life that had occurred in the last 20 years: 'women now work'. Indeed they did. In 1950 the proportion of married women under 45 who worked was just 26 per cent; by 1985 it would hit 67 per cent. The growing expectation—and need—for women to enter the labour market had a dramatic impact upon gender roles, child-rearing and patterns of cohabitation. Life for the Seventies woman was more independent and more complex.

Friedan hoped that the conference would continue the work of the Johnson administration in expanding government aid to individuals struggling to get by in the new social order. Recession made the task all the more important: 'With men being laid off in both blue-collar and white-collar jobs, with inflation showing no let-up, women's opportunity needed [legal] underpinning to insure the survival of the family.'

Friedan's manifesto was something that many European nations would enthusiastically embrace in the 1980s: accept that the family is no longer nuclear and build the welfare and employment opportunities necessary to strengthen its new incarnation. But this wasn't Europe and many Americans responded to social change with either resistance or denial. When the conference was finally held in 1980 it was dominated by polarising minorities of feminists and social conservatives.

America was undergoing a religious revival and the cultural Right was evolving into a well-oiled political machine. Its delegates to the Conference on Families believed that women's best hope of 'liberation' was found in marriage, where their compassionate instinct for motherhood formed a perfect union with their husbands' authority. To the feminists at the conference such views were the last gasp of an old, patriarchal order that was out of step with the unstoppable march of progress. Boasting superior numbers of delegates, the feminists were able to push through platforms endorsing abortion on demand and gay rights. Their success gave them the illusion of political momentum.

But the press and the public were rather more interested in the rhetoric of the conservative delegates, who staged a colourful walkout. Outside the conference, the anti-feminist activist Connie Marshner told the media that 'families consist of people related by heterosexual marriage, blood and adoption. Families are not religious cults, families are not Manson families, families are not heterosexual or homosexual liaisons outside of marriage.' Marshner's simple language articulated the feelings of millions of Americans that the sexual revolution was not just replacing the nuclear unit with something more complex—it was destroying the very concept of family itself.

Recognising that this view was gaining currency Carter tried to charm several televangelists at a White House breakfast in January 1980. The meeting was a disaster. When it was over, the preacher Tim LaHaye prayed 'God we have got to get this man out of the White House and get someone in here who will be aggressive about bringing back traditional moral values'. The religious Right decided that its best shot was Republican Ronald Reagan. When Reagan beat Carter by a landslide in November 1980 he captured two thirds of the white evangelical vote. Politics for the next 30 years would be dominated by the conservatism of Marshner, not the progressive ambitions of Friedan.

The Paradox of the American Family

Since the 1980s the American family has continued its inexorable evolution towards greater diversity and complexity. Yet America's popular culture, just like *The Cosby Show*, continues to celebrate a 1950s' vision of 'living right, living free'.

It is tempting to accuse conservatives of promoting paradoxical politics that are out of step with the modern world. In 2012 an estimated 19 per cent of gay people are raising a child in the US, yet every referendum on gay marriage has resulted in its ban. States like Texas offer abstinence promotions in place of sex education, yet people who take a chastity pledge are statistically more likely to get pregnant outside marriage than those who do not. And despite feminism's supposed grip upon the American imagination, voters are more anti-abortion than at any point since the 1980s. Against the European trend toward social liberalism the United States looks even more conservative today than it was when Bill Cosby first told his son to quit griping and start revising.

But the nuclear family endures as an ideal for good reason. For many middle-class whites the 1950s really were the Golden Age. At home families were large and stable and often kept by a single, generous wage. America was the workshop of the world, producing a flood of consumer goods that improved the lives of millions. Abroad the USA established itself as a model of the good life. The American Dream—meritocratic and capable of reaping great rewards—set an international standard for democratic capitalism. Never again would Americans tell pollsters that they were as content in their own lives or as confident about their country's direction. It was an age of innocence and sometimes that innocence blinded people to the realities of patriarchy and racism. But it will remain the yardstick by which Americans judge their country for a very long time.

Further Reading

David Allyn, *Make Love, Not War. The Sexual Revolution: An Unfettered History* (Little, Brown, 2000).

Mary Dalton and Laura Linder (eds.), *The Sitcom Reader: America Viewed and Skewed* (SUNY Press, 2005).

Daniel Horowitz, *Betty Friedan and the Making of The Feminine Mystique: The American Left, The Cold War, and Modern Feminism* (University of Massachusetts Press, 1998).

Dominic Sandbrook, *Mad as Hell: The Crisis of the 1970s and the Rise of the Populist Right* (Knopf, 2011).

Critical Thinking

1. Explain what the term "nuclear family" means and its origins.
2. There has been much debate about what kind of family structure is best for U.S. families. What structure do you view as most adaptive and why?
3. How have social, political, economic, and religious forces and scientific changes affected the structure, functioning, and expectations we have for families in the United States?
4. Do you feel that the media have portrayed the American family fairly and honestly? Why or why not?
5. How should we define what a family is in the United States today?

Create Central

www.mhhe.com/createcentral

Internet References

World Family Map
    http://worldfamilymap.org/2013
Australian Institute of Family Studies
    www.aifs.gov.au

Feminist Perspectives on Reproduction and the Family
http://plato.stanford.edu/entries/feminism-family
Kearl's Guide to the Sociology of the Family
www.trinity.edu/MKEARL/family.html

TIM STANLEY is associate fellow of the Rothermere American Institute, Oxford University. His documentary *Sitcom USA* will be broadcast on BBC2 on October 27th 2012 at 9 pm.

Article   Prepared by: Patricia Hrusa Williams,
                                             University of Maine at Farmington

The Significant Dynamic Relationship between Globalization and Families

BAHIRA SHERIF TRASK

Learning Outcomes

After reading this article, you will be able to:

- Describe the impact of globalization on families.

- Explain the impact of migration on families.

- Examine the impact of globalization on children.

Globalization is associated with profound changes for individuals and families in the United States and abroad. Some of these changes have been highlighted through the recent global economic recession. We are increasingly aware that economic downturns and governmental policies affect everyone's lives, often with unexpected consequences. Furthermore, rapid advances in communication and information technologies are changing the ways in which individuals connect, access information, and interact with each other. The farthest corners of the world now accessible, in ways that most of us were unable to imagine even just several years ago. All of these developments are related to globalization. Due to a number of factors however, in most people's minds, globalization remains primarily associated with economics and politics. In reality, globalization is closely related to both the major and day to day decisions that families make with respect to work issues, gender roles, the raising of children and care of the elderly, and moving and migration.

What Is Globalization?

Even though globalization is a complicated controversial phenomenon, there is some agreement that it refers to an economic and political process, and that it also entails a new form of connecting geographic and cultural distances. Globalization as a concept and a term, entered mainstream discussions in economics and political science from the mid-1990s onwards (Rodrik, 1997). With respect to globalization, of particular interest has been the flow of money and capital between countries, the changing role of governments vis à vis their citizenry, the increased movement and migration of individuals within and between countries, and the growth and expansion of multinational corporations and transnational organizations. However, despite the fact that individuals and families are affected by all of these issues, there has been remarkably little attention focused on the societal effects of globalization. This omission is important because it is specifically families, communities, and social life that are affected by globalization (Baars, Dannefer, Phillipson, & Walker, 2006).

Despite the lack of analyses of the effects of globalization on social life, individuals and families are directly and indirectly affected by globalizing processes all over the world. While family arrangements may vary, depending on place and time, some form of family or kin relationships characterize all societies. As individuals, families, communities, and societies increasingly become integrated into new complex globalized systems, their values, traditions, and relationships change (Parkin & Stone, 2004). Moreover, we often find that different groups of people react very differently to globalization. Globalization transmits new concepts about gender, work citizenship, identity, familial relationships, and women's and children's rights around the globe. In some cases, these concepts empower individuals and their families to change their lives, and in other cases, they are forced into situations that are disadvantageous and destructive. Also, in some places in the world, globalization is perceived as a form of enforced Westernization. The response to the assumption of dominance of Westernization is often nationalistic and fundamentalist. In an effort to preserve "traditional" values and beliefs, people turn back to what they believe are the authentic traditions and beliefs of their societies, sometimes even use violence to enforce their values.

Globalization and Migration

An important part of globalization is the movement of individuals within societies and across national borders. Migration is most commonly associated with seeking new work opportunities, but at times individuals and families migrate due to political and other social reasons. Specifically, international migration has led to a new type of family form, also known as transnational families. Transnational families are characterized by retaining roots in their home societies and simultaneously also creating new ties in their host countries. While proportionally to the world population, actual migration numbers are low (currently approximately 3 percent of the global population is on the move), modern migration has significant social effects. Most individuals migrate as families or in groups, and their residency in the new host society has a significant impact on both their country of origin, as well as the receiving society (Castles & Miller, 2003). For example, immigrants may be highly educated and possess important skills which benefit the receiving society but they also leave behind in their home countries what is commonly referred to as the "brain drain"—not enough highly educated people to take on important jobs that require education and skills, and could potentially improve the conditions in these countries. There are also other types of immigrants. For example, immigrants may be uneducated, poorer members of their home societies who leave and are then willing to take on the lowest level jobs in the host country. In either case, immigrants often send back extensive remittances (money to their relatives back home) that make a significant economic impact on their home societies.

Increasingly, transnational families are also associated with a phenomenon sometimes referred to as transnational mothering (Mortgan & Zippel, 2003). As service jobs in the industrialized world have multiplied, women from poorer countries are leaving their families behind in order to earn an income in other parts of the world. Women who leave their families to work abroad most often do this in order to help their families financially, and specifically to provide a future better life for their children. Many of these migrating women take on jobs associated with domestic labor such as cleaning houses and providing child and elder care. Most often women who migrate do so because there is a lack of economic opportunities in their home societies. However, this fact is often overlooked in political and academic discussions and analyses. Instead, because migrating women so often leave their children behind in their home countries, they are criticized and referred to as "negligent" or "uncaring" mothers by individuals in their host and home societies. Nevertheless, these women take on migration and its accompanying life styles and challenges and adapt their mothering styles with the hope of one day bettering the lives of their children. They usually make arrangements with their husbands (if there is a husband in the picture) and extended families to take care of their children while they are abroad. The growing phenomenon of transnational mothering illustrates that globalization can have significant impacts on family life that are not easily understood from a superficial perspective.

Globalization and Gender

As the migration example illustrates, globalization has had a profound effect on the lives of women, men, and children. It is worth noting that women as a group have been specifically and significantly impacted by globalizing processes. For example, for women around the world, there are today increasing chances for education, training, and work. In the West, specifically middle class women have seen new opportunities open up with respect to jobs, education, and equal rights over the last fifty years. Interestingly, in less developed countries, there has also been an increasing concern with the status of women. Some governments and international non-profits have set up training programs for poor and rural women in order to advance their lives. While these opportunities have not benefited all women, their very presence indicates that under the correct circumstances, globalizing forces can have positive effects on individuals' lives.

For the majority of women the world over, however, globalization has not necessarily improved their lives. Particularly in the developing world, but also in parts of the industrialized world, we are increasingly seeing what is termed as the "feminization of the labor force." This term refers to the growing number of women who are working outside of the home in paid employment. Most of the time, these women are working in employment that is more flexible than traditional U.S. 8–5 jobs and in informal types of work that are part time and come without benefits. Both in the U.S. and other countries, this trend has been accompanied by a decrease in the types of jobs that have regularly been held by men—full time jobs with benefits for the whole family (Safa, 2002).

As an increasing number of women take on this type of work, and as more men lose their role as the primary breadwinner, gender roles and relationships are changing. We see this particularly in the United States, Canada, Australia, and Europe, where there has been an increase in new living arrangements such as cohabitation, a rising divorce rate, and out of wedlock births. Moreover, cross-cultural research reveals that as economic bonds in families are changing with an increased number of women working in the paid labor force, the concept of marriage is shifting in response. For example, as women are able to earn their own living, they are less likely to stay in destructive and abusive relationships, or they may choose not to marry at all. These changes have results in a global rise in divorce and an increase in female-headed households. As women's roles are changing, diverse family structures are becoming more common even in places such South East Asia and the Middle East, where cultural beliefs about traditional roles in families have long played a significant role in preserving certain aspects of those societies (Moghadam, 2003).

In a discussion about the changing roles of women and men, is also important to remember that millions of women worldwide do not have the same freedom with respect to making choices about their marriages, working outside of the home, and having control over their money, such as those that are available to middle class Western women. For many women, especially rural and low-income women, working outside of the home in the formal and informal labor force has not bettered their lives. Instead, these women now carry the double burden of working for pay and having to take care of the home, the children, the disabled, and the elderly.

Globalization has also had a serious impact on the roles of men. As a significant number of men have lost their jobs and their primary role as breadwinner/provider, they have had to adjust to new roles in the family. For example, middle class American men today are more likely to be involved with home responsibilities and child care than men in previous generations.

However, these types of changes in family life have not necessarily occurred across the world. Instead, in some areas and in some cases, men have reacted with anger over the loss of what they perceive as their basic rights. In fact, there is some evidence that domestic violence rises in those places where men have been out of work for a significant period of time. Since most men the world over are raised to believe that men are to be the primary provider/breadwinner, when they lose that role, they may react in unexpected and at times violent ways. The clash of values that results from globalizing processes that draw women into the paid labor force conflicts with traditional values pertaining to the roles of women and men (Yan & Neal, 2006). Further, many of these conflicts are heightened through the spread of media and Internet images of the lives and rights of women in the West compared to those in other places.

Globalization and Children

While there is quite a bit of research on the relationship between globalization and women's changing roles, we know much less about the relationship between globalization and children. Globalization has produced and spread a popular vision of what childhood is supposed to be like, and what children should do with their time (Kuznesof, 2005). From a Western perspective, children need to be "protected" from harsh surroundings and complex situations, they should "play," and they ought to go to school. However, this concept of children and childhood does not fit neatly with the day to day realities of the lives of children in many parts of the world, raising complicated questions about universal concepts about the lives and rights of children.

Ideas about childhood and what children are like and what they are capable of are determined by the social context and the historical period in society in which they grow up. Historically, we have had very different beliefs about the capabilities of children. For example, during colonial times, children were raised very strictly and most children began learning a work related skill (usually through an apprenticeship) at a very young age (Malkki & Martin, 2003). In part, due to globalization, we have a very different situation today. Western, and specifically, American concepts about children and childhood are spreading to parts of the world where children live under very different conditions. For example, many contemporary children are growing up in war zones, areas ravaged by HIV/AIDS, and/or areas of extreme poverty. Under those conditions, children are unable to go to school and have no access to an easy, carefree childhood. Even here in the U.S., many children grow up in areas that are crime ridden and extremely poor. These conditions do not allow them to have the kind of childhood that is encouraged and promoted by so much of the current child pedagogy literature, raising complicated questions about the universal application of our ideas about children and childhood. What may be appropriate in one context, for example, for white middle class American children, may not befit in any way the lives of street children in Brazil. While this was also true in the past, in the contemporary context information flows more easily between societies and places. And since the West tends to dominate information flows, we are increasingly setting the standard for what is appropriate—or at least what we feel is appropriate when it comes to children and childhood experiences.

Another complex issue arising out of our globalized context is the disputed topic of children's rights. Children's rights are closely related to debates on human rights, which many feel have been, by far, one of the most important aspects of a growing system of globally shared values (Kaufman, 2002). The concept of human rights encompasses the idea that the world's most vulnerable individuals including minorities, women, children, and the disabled should receive equal protection under the law. This is based on the idea that all people have a shared humanity, irrespective of their nationality. For much of recorded history, children from many societies were not accorded the status of being "fully human" and were allowed to be sold and exchanged as if they were possessions. However, over the course of the last century, this situation changed and culminated in the global adoption in 1989 of the Convention on the Rights of the Child. This convention entails the protection of the largest single group (children) that any legal document with respect to human rights has ever dealt with. By signing on, countries take on a legal obligation to ensure the "best interests of the child" and work towards the survival, development, and protection of their nations' children. According to the Convention, children have certain basic rights that include the right to life, to their own name and identity, to be raised within their own families or cultural groupings, to express their opinions, to be protected from abuse, and to have their privacy protected. Currently, the only two countries in the world that have not signed on to the Convention on the Rights of the Child are the United States and Somalia. Much of the opposition in the U.S. comes from individuals who believe that there are some basic conflicts between the Convention and the Constitution and due to the resistance of some religious and political conservatives. Moreover, certain factions in the U.S. worry that by signing on to an international legal document, the U.S. will be bound to external international control over what are deemed as domestic policies.

Closely related to the issue of children's rights is the complicated topic of child labor. Current statistics indicate that child labor is actually increasing instead of declining. The International Labor Organization (ILO) (2002) estimates that approximately 352 million five- to seventeen-year-olds around the globe work in some form, and that out of this group about two-thirds of young workers are defined as "child laborers." Most of these children work, primarily on family farms, in their families' households, in small manufacturing businesses, and in mining. Some children are also involved with the production of carpets, garments, furniture, textiles, and shoes (French & Wokutch, 2005). Included in the statistics on child labor are a small group of children around the world who live on the street and participate in a wide range of legal or illegal activities or are involved in prostitution.

Globalization and engagement with the Convention on the Rights of the Child has raised awareness about the issue of child labor. Images of children working in sweat shops and hard labor move across the Internet and the media easily and have raised, in particular, concerns in the West about the lives of children in other parts of the world. Even people who would usually not be that concerned with social justice issues have spoken out publicly and led crusades banning "third world labor practices." This has led to international boycotts of certain brands and corporations who supposedly rely on this type of exploitive behavior for the production of their goods. What is rarely understood in these debates is that there is a great deal of controversy about what constitutes child labor, and to what extent enforcing a Western type of childhood would actually benefit these children. Often the children who are engaged in child labor are doing so to support their families and kin groups because there is no other way for them to survive. For example, in certain parts of Africa, many children have lost both of their parents to the HIV/AIDS crisis. The only way for them and their siblings to make any kind of a living is for some members of the family, or even for all of them, to work at whatever employment is available. This is only one example, but it points to the fact that we need to be more sensitive about the contexts in which children live, and we need to allow for some variation in their personal circumstances.

The complexity of child labor disputes is further heightened by the conflicts over what exactly constitutes "work." There are some types of jobs such as working in mines that are clearly harmful to children's health. However, it is unclear if helping on the family farm is really physically and psychologically damaging to a teenager. Critics of universal labor laws argue that if a family's survival depends on children's work, and if they are not being placed in harm's way, it may actually have social and personal benefits to not enforce a uniform approach to child labor. In other words, we should institute some basic laws that ensure the safety of all children, but that with respect to work, certain types of labor should be permitted. Moreover, gender needs to be taken into account in these discussions. Often, depending on cultural context, it is girls who are taken out of school and asked to take over domestic responsibilities such as cooking and child care, while their mothers work outside of the home and their brothers go to school. Statistics on child labor often do not include these employed girls, because their duties are not understood to be "real work." However, it is clearly these girls, life chances that become permanently constrained due to their lack of education. Again, this indicates that we need to think carefully about enforcing universal concepts such as the rights of children and the prohibition of child labor. An approach that universalizes the needs, beliefs, and rights of all children can have unintended detrimental consequences, thus it is imperative that local conditions also be taken into account.

The Continuing Significance of Families

While this article has raised awareness about some of the complex issues that are faced by individuals and families, in a globalized context, it has also highlighted the fact that there is a close relationship between globalization and families. In all parts of the world, individuals, be they children or adults, still make decisions in the context of those that they consider to be family or they have a close, family-like bond to. Families act as a buffer

between globalizing forces and the choices and challenges that individuals need to deal with (Edgar, 2004). However, globalization has varying effects and means different things depending on where people live and what their particular social, political, and economic situation is like. Globalization can allow individuals to be exposed to new ideas and resources; however, globalization can also mean that certain groups become poorer or are treated in a way that is not in synch with their particular culture or situation. Moreover, particularly in non-Western concepts the whole family often functions specifically as an economic unit (Kelly, 2001). Decisions with respect to who works, what they do, and if they work near their home or in a far away locale is closely tied to family decision making and often family survival. Globalization has provided the venue for many people to seek out new opportunities. But it has also limited the options of others. For example, it is now possible for an unemployed nurse from the Philippines to find work in Hong Kong and send money back to her family. However, a family father from a small mid-Western industrial town may find that after twenty years of devoted employment, he is permanently laid off from his manufacturing site, because his job has been outsourced to China. Both of these trends are related to globalization, making it difficult to speak about globalization as either just a positive or a negative force in individuals' and families' lives. We can also not assume that globalization will lead to all families having similar lives and sharing the same tastes despite increasing global exposure to similar messages and goods. Instead, we need to realize that people live in very varied circumstances and that these local contexts are an important component for how global messages and products are received. Maybe most importantly, it is critical to understand that globalization is related to fast, intense social change. None of us are immune to these changes but our experiences will vary depending on where we live and what our particular circumstances may be.

References

Baars, J., Dannefer, D., Phillipson, C., & Walker, A. (2006). Introduction: Critical perspectives in social gerontology. In J. Baars, D. Dannefer, C. Phillipson, & A. Walker, (Eds.), *Aging, globalization and inequality: The new critical gerontology.* (pp. 1–16). Amityville, NY: Baywood Publishing.

Castles, S., & Miller, M. (2003). *The age of migration: International population movements in the modern world.* New York: Guilford Press.

Edgar, D. (2004). Globalization and Western bias in family sociology. In J. Scott, J. Treas, & M. Richards (Eds.), *The Blackwell companion to the sociology of families* (pp. 3–16). Malden, MA: Oxford University Press.

French, J. L., & Woktuch, R. E. (2005). Child workers, globalization, and international business ethics: A case study in Brazil's export-oriented shoe industry. *Business Ethics Quarterly, 15,* 615–640.

Kaufman, N. (2002). The status of children in international law. In N. Kauman & I. Rizzini, (Eds.), *Globalization and children: Exploring potentials for enhancing opportunities in the lives of children and youth,* (pp. 31–45.) New York: Springer.

Kelly, R. M. (2001). *Gender, globalization and democratization.* Lanham, MD: Rowman & Littlefield Publishers.

Kuznesof, E. (2005). The house, the street, global society: Latin American families and childhood in the twenty-first century. *Journal of Social History, 38,* 859–872.

Malkki, L., & Martin, E. (2003). Children and the gendered politics of globalization: In remembrance of Sharon Stephens. *American Ethnologist, 30,* 216–224.

Moghadam, V. (2003). A political explanation of the gendered division of labor in Japan. In M. Marchand & A. Runyan (Eds.), *Gender and global restructuring: Sightings, sites and resistances* (pp. 99–115). London: Routledge.

Mortgan, K., & Zippel, K. (2003). "Paid to care: The origins and effects of care leave policies in Western Europe." *Social Politics: International Studies in Gender, State, and Society, 10,* 49–85.

Parkin, R., & Stone, L. (2004). *Kinship and family: An anthropological reader.* New York: Blackwell.

Rodrik, D. (1997). *Has globalization gone too far?* Washington, Institute for International Economics.

Safa, H. (2002). Questioning globalization: Gender and export processing in the Dominican Republic. *Journal of Developing Societies, 18,* 11–31.

Yan, R., & Neal, A. (2006). The impact of globalization on family relations in China. *International Journal of Sociology of the family, 32,* 113–125.

Critical Thinking

1. Describe globalization and how it impacts families.
2. If you were a mother who had to go to a different country to find work, would you be able to leave your children behind? What are your thoughts about the concept of transnational mothering?
3. Do you feel that globalization has had a greater impact on men or women?
4. Explain some of the human rights issues that were addressed in the article. If you were a policymaker, how would you address child labor?
5. What are some of globalization's impacts on families in industrialized nations such as the United States and poorer countries?

Create Central

www.mhhe.com/createcentral

Internet References

World Family Map
http://worldfamilymap.org/2013

Australian Institute of Family Studies
www.aifs.gov.au

Feminist Perspectives on Reproduction and the Family
http://plato.stanford.edu/entries/feminism-family

Kearl's Guide to the Sociology of the Family
www.trinity.edu/MKEARL/family.html

An original essay written for this volume. Copyright © 2010 by Bahira Serif Trask. Used by permission.

Article

Prepared by: Patricia Hrusa Williams,
University of Maine at Farmington

Matches Made on Earth
Why Family Values Are Human Values

Nancie L. Gonzalez

Learning Outcomes

After reading this article, you will be able to:

- Recognize the social construction of "family values" in families and society.
- Identify the impact of religion in how family values are constructed.
- Illustrate the diversity of family values.

The term "family values," the importance of which fundamentalist Christians have been preaching for decades, continues to permeate religious and political printed matter and discussions in the United States today. The conservatives' concept of family values is generally characterized by abstinence from sex until marriage, which is then entered into with a like-minded individual of the opposite sex and is thereafter permanent and free from adultery. It is also expected that children will ensue, either through birth or adoption. In line with these prescriptions, proponents of traditional family values foment prejudice and activism against divorce, abortion, homosexuality, single-parent families, and even the choice not to have children. The fact that their efforts have become more intensive and intrusive lately can be explained, I believe, by the increasingly tolerant and diverse sexual, racial, and religious views and behavior of the American public at large.

The problem isn't that some people espouse conservative ideals of family, but that they promulgate them as the only way to live, looking down upon and often demonizing those with other values. Indeed, the family values crowd often refers to any who oppose its agenda as having no values at all. They support their ideals as based upon divine "truth" by quoting the Bible and rejecting scientific evidence that supports a different set of explanations for the existence and history of humankind. They repeatedly argue that more general social acceptance of other ways to live will endanger their own. This fear has inspired efforts for decades to influence our school boards and our local, state, and national governments to change text books, curricula, and the law to reflect

socially conservative views. When these fail, parents turn to private schools or home schooling, and later enroll their offspring in one of the several conservative Christian colleges whose faculties and administrative personnel are vetted to make sure their values are religiously and politically "correct." The fact that some of these schools are admittedly training their graduates to seek public office or employment in state and national venues is further evidence of their intolerance, and their misunderstanding of the nature of society and culture.

Most of the idealistic family values held by conservative Christians today are not now nor have they ever been characteristic of the world at large. Statistics, as well as more informal evidence suggest that the so-called nontraditional behaviors they condemn are now common throughout the United States and much of the industrialized world, often despite laws forbidding them. Furthermore, such behaviors have existed in many parts of the world for centuries. The problem I see for humanists is to convince much of the conservative American public that these prejudices and fears are unwarranted on at least two grounds: 1) family values are the products of human sociocultural conditions, and cannot be attributed to either divine or biological imperatives, and 2) pluralism in marriage and family values should be expected in any large twenty-first century society as a result of technological advances that have made globalization both possible and perhaps inevitable.

If neither a deity nor our genes are wholly determinative, we must ask our conservative counterparts: what accounts for the vast panorama of intimate human bonding practices, either in the past, or today?

It may be useful to consider what social and biological scientists have concluded about the origin and nature of marriage and the family. All animals must struggle for self and species survival, which demands food, defense, reproduction, and care of newborns until they can care for themselves. Both genetics and learning are involved for all species, but only humans have created *social institutions* to help themselves in these endeavors. By social, I mean any kind of bonding with other humans to share in the food quest; to ward off environmental and other dangers; to reproduce, nurture, and educate the young; and to provide physical and psychological well-being for themselves, their children, and their neighbors. The specific characteristics of these institutions vary with the society; trial and error must have occurred over time, and some societies failed to persist. But those institutions that worked well became customary, "traditional," and thus value-laden. Children would be taught by example and by experience. But traditions change as cultural evolution occurs and as societies grow, develop new technologies, and increasingly influence each other. The young and the most pragmatically minded are likely to change with the times, yet there are always some who cling to the older ways—not that this is, in itself, dysfunctional, for the "old ways" still serve some purposes, and sometimes are reinstated or reinterpreted by succeeding generations.

Although marriage and the family have existed in all human societies and form the primary roots of all the particulars of family values everywhere, different societies have constructed their own definitions of incest; permissible marriage partners; appropriate sexual behavior before, during, and after marriage; "normal" and alternate sexual orientations; ideal post-marital residence; and composition of the ideal family and household, including what to do if too many children "appear," or if conception occurs at an inconvenient time. For example, marriages that we likely consider incestuous but others don't include marriage between first cousins, especially patrilateral parallel cousin marriage (where the children of two brothers marry) seen in some parts of the Middle East and Africa. Among some Bedouin cultures, there was even a stated preference for such a marriage. Similarly, cross-cousin marriage is widespread in many "tribal" societies, including the Yanomamo in South America.

Different societies have constructed their own definitions of incest appropriate sexual behavior, "normal" and alternate sexual orientations, and ideal post-marital residence.

Formal bonding or marriage rituals probably developed in very early human societies, since it was important then as now to confer legitimacy of the children in relation to membership in whatever social unit was pertinent (tribe, clan, patrilineage, matrilineage, nation-state, religious group, and so forth). Formal marriage also establishes rights of inheritance of property, as well as social position. In many societies, including our own, women, and to a lesser extent, men, are treated like adolescents until they marry.

Neither religious nor biological explanations for conservative family values take into account the fact that even the notion of two sexes is not, and probably never has been, biologically correct. We have no way to know whether prehistoric societies recognized inborn sexual variations, what the frequency of such variations might have been, or whether "different" newborns would even have been allowed to live. However, colonial travelers to America noted that some native cultures recognized the existence of some among them whose bodies, psyches, or

both weren't comfortable living in either of the two primary gender roles of male or female. They called these people "two spirits" and provided a socially acceptable niche for them.

Homosexuality of different types has been documented throughout Western civilization since at least the ancient Greeks. However, only in the current century has the recognition developed in Western societies that sexual orientation is not merely a matter of differences in genitalia, and that it isn't a mere matter of choice. The growing acceptance of the idea that sexuality and sexual identity should not alter one's basic humanity and civil rights has led to changes in the laws in many countries, including the decriminalization of certain sex practices and the legalization of same-sex marriage. At the time of this writing, five U.S. states as well as the District of Columbia now allow gay and lesbian couples to marry, and in three more states same-sex marriages are recognized but not performed legally. Nine other states recognize certain legal rights of same-sex couples through civil unions, domestic partnerships, or reciprocal beneficiary laws. Still, these arrangements are only gradually becoming acceptable to the general public, and since same-sex marriage hasn't been documented as legal in any society in history, we shouldn't be surprised that it is and will remain controversial for some time. Nevertheless, it should now be added to the evidence we have for different kinds of marriage and family institutions.

Studies of pre-agricultural and pre-industrial societies, as well as continuing historical research over the past century have documented such a variety of marriage customs and rules that a God hypothesis would almost have to suggest an anthropological deity who understood that no single practice should be imposed upon all. However, the following discussion focuses not on the supernatural, but the natural ways in which human pair bonding and family formation have occurred. These include *monogamy* as the permanent or lifetime union of two persons, usually, but not always, of opposite sex. This was probably the most common marriage form for Paleolithic foragers, as was the nuclear family. However, that small unit had affinal relatives (we call them in-laws), some of whom lived together in what anthropologists call a band. As the noted nineteenth-century anthropologist Edward B. Tylor suggested, early societies had to "marry out or die out." Institutions promoting reproduction and care of the young were crucial to social survival.

Polygamy is often confused with *polygyny—the* union of one man with several wives—but polygamy also includes *polyandry—one* woman with several husbands. All of these forms, especially polygyny, were more typical of larger, more advanced societies based upon pastoralism, agriculture, or both. The advantages were to enlarge the family unit by drawing in more nubile and fertile women, while at the same time providing care for those who might no longer have been able to bear children. If the sex ratio, for whatever reason, was unbalanced, as it was among early converts to the Church of the Latter Day Saints, polygyny also was a way for new single young women to be immediately drawn in to an existing family. The custom was formally abolished by the Mormons in the early part of the twentieth century, but the family values created more than one hundred years earlier have held on for some.

Polyandry has been fairly rare, practiced primarily in the Himalayan regions of Nepal, Tibet, India, and Bhutan. It has also occurred in the Canadian Arctic, Nigeria, and Sri Lanka, and is known to have been present in some pre-contact Polynesian societies, though probably only among higher caste women. Some forms of polyandry appear to be associated with a perceived need to retain aristocratic titles or agricultural lands within kin groups, and/or because of the frequent absence, for long periods, of a man from the household. In Tibet the practice is particularly popular among the priestly Skye class but also among poor small farmers who can ill afford to divide their small holdings. As to the latter variety, as some males return to the household, others leave for a long time, so that there is usually one husband present. Fraternal polyandry occurs when multiple brothers share a common wife. This occurs in the pastoral Toda community in Southern India. Similarly, among the Tibetan Nyinba, anthropologist Nancy Levine described the strong bond between brothers as essential in creating a strong sense of family unity and keeping land holdings intact, thus preserving socioeconomic standing.

Group marriage involving multiple members of both sexes has sometimes been averred to have existed; however, there appears to be no reputable description of it in the anthropological or historical literature. In recent years a movement has arisen that produces something very similar to the idea of group marriage; the term *polyamory* has been offered to describe plural simultaneous attachments between and among people, including lesbian, gay, bisexual, and transgendered individuals (LGBTs). From the perspective of this writing, this may or may not be new under the sun, but it doesn't (yet?) constitute marriage.

Serial monogamy is perhaps the most common type of marriage known in much of the world today. Individuals in such unions may have only one spouse but, shedding that one, they may contract any number later—again, usually only one at a time, except in those societies that still accept and approve polygyny. Serial monogamy depends on the existence of easy divorce laws or more informal practices, such as what is generally called "living together." *Domestic partnerships* by law may or may not be considered marriages. In the United States persons of both the same and opposite sex have for some time entered into such unions, but those of opposite sex partners have generally received greater social acceptance, even without the legal protections, status, or financial benefits society offers to married couples.

Why do some people choose not to abide by the marriage rules of their own society? Obviously, reasons vary. Some think a trial marriage to be a good idea; others simply don't care about rules of any kind. A few may be prohibited from marrying because one or the other is already bound by a previous, legitimate union which can't be formally dissolved. And while others have simply adopted a more individualized lifestyle, some are still convinced of the values of marriage in a previous age (as in polygyny). In short, the choice of whether and whom to marry has increasingly been seen as a personal, individual decision, and it is no longer important to the functioning of the modern industrial state that all persons marry, unless they wish the state to adjudicate property or child custody rights.

Co-residence of the partners and the creation of a household are usually, but not always, typical in any kind of marriage. Yet households vary enormously in both size and composition, and usually, but not always, include some kind of family. In societies in which men must find work through short or long term emigration, *consanguineal households* have arisen that contain no married pair. Such a household is most often headed by an elderly woman, together with some of her sons and daughters and their children. The marital partners of these co-residential adults live elsewhere—often with their own mothers. The United States today is also seeing an increase in extended families moving in together due to economic constraints, as well as "single" parents who live with a partner.

A study by the Pew Research Center released in November, titled, "The Decline of Marriage and Rise of New Families," revealed changing attitudes about what constitutes a family. Among survey respondents, 86 percent said a single parent and child constitute a family; 80 percent considered an unmarried couple living together with a child a family; and 63 percent said a gay or lesbian couple raising a child is a family.

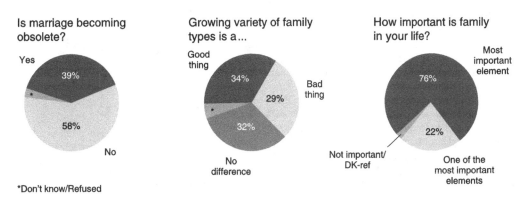

Is marriage becoming obsolete?
Yes 39%
No 58%
*

Growing variety of family types is a...
Good thing 34%
No difference 32%
29%
Bad thing
*

How important is family in your life?
Most important element 76%
One of the most important elements 22%
Not important/ DK-ref

*Don't know/Refused

Data from the Pew Research Center's 2010 survey, "The Decline of Marriage and Rise of New Families"

Obviously, the "traditional family" so highly valued by the religious right can't be considered as the typical American household today. Instead, the term "family" has taken on a much broader meaning to incorporate various combinations of persons of different genders, sexual orientations, and familial or non-familial relationships living together, as in the refrigerator magnet that proclaims, "Friends Are the Family You Choose for Yourself."

We still, and always will, value the need to bond with others. Kinship remains one major way to do so, but social and geographical mobility have lessened its role as the most important tie that binds. Today it may be similar age groups, vocations, or philosophical views on the nature of the universe or of the hereafter that form the basis of relationships. People will continue to find or invent ways to get together, live together, and share what is important in life with others.

Does this mean that marriage and the family as we know it will likely disappear in the near future as Focus on the Family fears? Does the fact that many young people of various genders and sexual identities choose not to marry or stay married, nor to form traditional households augur the demise, or even the diminution in value of these institutions in our society? Should the legal sanctioning of same-sex marriage in any way affect the dignity of opposite-sex couples joined by similar ceremonies? I think not. Society has, for the most part, already accepted the newer bonding patterns described above—at least for persons of opposite sex.

Taking away any social stigma, LGBT couples will likely experience the same joys and struggles in marriage as straight couples do, thus proving that sexual orientation is irrelevant when it comes to pair-bonding. Although the ethnographic and historical evidence doesn't confirm that true marriages were ever legally sanctioned between persons thought to be of the same sex, present-day reminiscences and folklore suggest that love, sex, and companionship were known and accepted among them, and that untold numbers of people have lived in happy unions with persons perceived to be of the same sex for perhaps hundreds of years.

Finally, what about love and companionship? It is only in modern Western society that these have become the very most important components of marriage. There is no evidence that these occur only between spouses of opposing sex or gender. The idea that sexual activity is only appropriate between members of the opposite sex is a product of our cultural conditioning, born of the thousands of years when it was important to keep people focused on finding a mate of the opposite sex to ensure continued reproduction. The need for population control, rather than survival of the species or of any specific society, makes this value irrelevant today, as it does for the idea that all marriages should produce children. Also, the extended family of yore is no longer functional in industrial society—today one does indeed marry the individual, not the whole family.

Sex is no longer seen as a major reward for contracting marriage, regardless of one's sexual orientation. Tests of virginity have disappeared as premarital sex with more than one partner has become more common and seems to be a largely irrelevant factor for many marriages, including the first. Yet, the fact that homosexual and lesbian partners engage in sexual activities without marriage is always seen as a disgrace, even for many of them who may share the traditional religious notion that unmarried sex is a sin.

As we continue to consider the nature and causes of the diversity of family values in the post-industrial, individualistic, global society in which we now live, I hope that the single set of specific rules of behavior promulgated by Focus on the Family and other such organizations comes to be seen as outmoded, even by the so-called moral majority. As the U.S. Constitution has always insisted, all citizens should have equal rights, so for those who find the "old ways" to their taste, we should wish them well, but plead with them not to damage the lives of those who choose to live or even to think differently, nor to forget that our nation was founded by outsiders and has continually accepted those from other cultures, and that we have, in fact, valued and profited by our diversity.

Critical Thinking

1. What are some of your family values? Where do your family values come from?

2. Do you feel that family values are a naturally occurring phenomenon or are they learned from society and culture?

3. After reading this article, are there some family values from your family of origin that differ now that you are in college?

4. What do you think about the author's question about "marriage and the family as we know it" disappearing?

Create Central

www.mhhe.com/createcentral

Internet References

World Family Map
   http://worldfamilymap.org/2013
Australian Institute of Family Studies
   www.aifs.gov.au
Feminist Perspectives on Reproduction and the Family
   http://plato.stanford.edu/entries/feminism-family
Kearl's Guide to the Sociology of the Family
   www.trinity.edu/MKEARL/family.html

NANCIE L. GONZALEZ is Professor Emeritus of Anthropology at the University of Maryland. She has conducted ethnographic and ethnohistorical research on marriage and family patterns in a number of societies, including the American Southwest, the Caribbean, Central America, China, and the West Bank and has published widely since the 1960s. She is presently working on a memoir dealing with changes in marriage and family patterns as revealed in letters and diaries from five generations of her own family. She lives in Richmond, Virginia.

Gonzalez, Nancie L. From *The Humanist*, January/February 2011, pp. 14-17. Copyright © 2011 by Nancie L. Gonzalez. Reprinted by permission of the author.

Article

Prepared by: Patricia Hrusa Williams,
University of Maine at Farmington

Relationships, Community, and Identity in the New Virtual Society

ARNOLD L. BROWN

Learning Outcomes

After reading this article, you will be able to:

- Describe the ways technology is used in the context of intimate and family relationships.
- Recognize the ways technology impacts communication and relationships.

As we spend more of our social lives online, the definitions of relationships and families are shifting. In India, where for centuries marriages have been arranged by families, online dating services such as BharatMatrimony.com are profoundly changing embedded traditions.

MyGamma, a Singapore-based mobile phone social networking site, has millions of users throughout Asia and Africa, giving social networking capability to people across continents—no personal computer necessary.

In China, individuals have been participating in wang hun (online role-play marriages). These gaming sites are causing actual married couples to get divorced on the grounds that this constitutes adultery—even though no face-to-face meetings ever took place.

And websites such as GeneTree.com and Ancestry.com, which offer inexpensive cheek-swab DNA tests, link up people throughout the world who have similar DNA, thus combining genealogy, medical technology, and social networking.

Clearly the Internet has radically reshaped our social lives over the span of just a couple of decades, luring us into a virtual metaworld where traditional interactions—living, loving, belonging, and separating, as well as finding customers and keeping them—require new protocols.

Relationships Take On a Digital Dimension

The future of falling in love may be online. Dating sites, once considered a gimmicky way to meet and connect with new people, have grown immensely in popularity, thanks in part to the convergence of information technologies and digital entertainment. Facilitating and managing relationships online is projected to become close to a billion-dollar industry in the United States in 2011.

In the new Virtual Society, we will see an increasing transition from basic matchmaking sites to sites that enable people to actually go out on online "dates" without ever leaving their desks. While face-to-face dating will never entirely disappear, the process—and even relationships themselves—will happen more and more in virtual space.

Especially for young people, relationships made in virtual space can be just as powerful and meaningful as those formed in the real world. Additionally, as more people gain access to broadband technologies, an increasing number are seeking social connectivity this way. There are already at least 500 million mobile broadband users globally. The speed and flexibility with which people communicate and socialize online will likely only continue to increase.

Technology doesn't just bring people together, though. As Douglas Rushkoff points out in Program or Be Programmed (OR Books, 2010), cyberspace creates a temporal and spatial separation from which it becomes seemingly easier to accomplish unpleasant interpersonal tasks. Hence, the techno brush-off: breaking up with a significant other via e-mail or text message.

This will increasingly be a dominant fixture of the global youth culture. Young people everywhere link up through IM, Twitter, blogs, smart-phones, and social networking sites that are proliferating at an accelerating rate. The emerging generation is part of what is, in essence, a vast new cross-border empire. It is marked by an instant awareness of what's new, what's hot, what's desirable—and what's not. This is the group that pollster John Zogby, in his book *The Way We'll Be* (Random House, 2008), calls the First Globals. His research shows that their expectations will be vastly. Young people will not, as their elders did, simply adapt to the technology. The new youth cyberculture will continue to find ways to adapt the technology to their needs and desires. For example, Ning, created in 2005 by Netscape co-founder Marc Andreessen, enables people to create their own individual social network—not join a preexisting world but actually build their own. A website called paper.li creates a personalized newspaper for you every day based on whom you follow on Twitter and whether or not they said anything particularly important in the last 24 hours (as measured by retweets). Your friend's brilliant blog post about last night's St. Patrick's Day party could appear directly next to Tim O'Reilly or Bruce Sterling's most recent missive on China's Internet policy. It's hard to imagine a local newspaper providing that sort of personalized content.

But online relationships are not exclusively reserved for young people. As the elderly become more comfortable with the Internet, they will increasingly turn to alternative spaces, such as virtual worlds, to find company or meet people with similar interests. By 2008, more than 20 million social networkers in the United States were over the age of 50, according to a study by Deloitte. There have been a slew of media reports playing up the fact that many seniors are joining Facebook and Twitter, as well as becoming an increasingly significant part of the growing commercial activity in virtual worlds.

Commercializing Communities

More and more people regard the virtual world as a place where they can establish and maintain safer, less demanding relationships on their own time. Ease, flexibility, and relative anonymity will continue to be three key components of dating online. Monetization will happen quickly, as virtual restaurants, movie theaters, concerts, and even wedding chapels are established.

In addition to using virtual worlds there will be a much wider variety of virtual products and services. Having these options would give a substantive feel to online relationships. The more real and satisfying these relationships can be made to seem, the more they will attract and hold people, and the more money they will generate.

Commercialized virtual venues such as upscale bars and coffeehouses could even be looked to as testing grounds to develop the social skills necessary to form meaningful human relationships. Businesses could use game applications like Mall World or Cafe World on Facebook as platforms to advertise various specials that occur in virtual space, ranging from coupons for those aforementioned simulations of bars and coffeehouses to discounts for two to "live" streaming concert events. Advertising boards could promote online activities and events—such as speed dating in a virtual nightclub setting. All this will dramatically change the nature of relationships.

As social researchers have pointed out, the Internet is programming us as well, starting at an early age. For example, there are combination social networking and gaming sites for children such as Disney's Club Penguin. Children are developing social skills within these virtual worlds. What this will mean in terms of how they will start, maintain, and end "real" friendships and relationships in the future is anyone's guess.

But the Internet can also strengthen family ties because it provides a continuously connected presence. In Norway, for example, one study showed that college students were in touch with their parents on average 10 times a week. Young people use mobile devices to Skype, text, upload photos and videos to Facebook, and more, with increasing frequency. Cyberspace enables families and friends to converse, in effect, as if they were in the same room. This is part of the reason that the Millennial generation reported feeling closer to their parents than did their older siblings during adolescence, according to the Pew Internet and American Life Survey.

So what does all this tell us? For one thing, the temporal and spatial "here-and-now" limitations that formerly characterized social interactions such as dating and family get-togethers have broken down. The composition of, and behavior in, relationships and households in the future will therefore change seriously. These trends are powerfully affecting how companies and organizations will design, sell, and market a wide range of products and services to consumers, with a growing emphasis on individualization and personalization. For instance, if relationships and families are more virtual, we should see an increase in the construction of new kinds of single-person housing units or dual sleeping quarters.

Family formation will need to be flexible and adaptive. The nuclear family was a response to the Industrial Age, in large measure replacing the extended family that characterized the Agricultural Era. It spurred vast economic shifts and led to new multibillion-dollar industries, from autos to washing machines to personal telephones. We are already seeing indications that the family is morphing into other forms as the Virtual Age approaches. Employers and governments will see their social, human resources, financial services, and benefits programs challenged, as the new economy takes great advantage of these multiple, newly unfolding personal relationships. For instance, should a "virtual spouse" be able to claim the Social Security benefits of a partner? The easy answer is, of course not. But what if it's the virtual spouse who is charged with monitoring the health of an aged parent remotely? What if he or she does the household bill-paying, or even contributes half of the household income? In other words, what if the virtual spouse performs many if not all of the tasks associated with a traditional spouse? And should the same polygamy laws applied to regular marriages also apply to virtual marriages? Should such marriages be subject to the same taxation laws?

With the advent of an electronic era, many social scientists and other "experts" decried what they saw as a loss of social capital—the so-called "Bowling Alone" theory—because people were supposedly decreasing their participation in such things as bowling leagues. The big mistake that the fearful always make is to equate change with destruction. The social turmoil of the 1970s was heralded by such observers as "the destruction of the family." But the family did not die; it just changed—and it is still changing.

Similarly, social capital is not going away; it is too intrinsic to human nature, although aspects of it may well be changing, and it is important that you view these changes objectively if you want to understand what they are and what they mean to you.

Social ties are being created, strengthened, and—yes—weakened in an almost unbelievable variety of ways. This has to entail, as well, the remaking and establishing of both a deeper and a shallower social capital. Someone with more than 3,000 Facebook friends probably has more than 2,000 shallow friendships, but there's a tremendous amount of variety in that number; some of these friendships are viable clients, others may be service providers, others may be long-term friend prospects, or secret crushes, or members of a social circle to which the person with 3,000 friendships wants access; some of them will be annoying people encountered only once at a party, begrudgingly given the status of "friend" to avoid seeming rude. All of these friendships have their own unique value. But Facebook sees little difference among them outside of how they are designated in privacy settings (some people can see more private posts than others). Outside institutions don't recognize any distinction among these virtual friendships, if they recognize such friendships at all.

Sociologist Richard Ling has labeled the new communication phenomenon micro-coordination—as people are constantly planning, coordinating, and changing plans because their cyber-connections are always on. University of Southern California sociologist Manuel Castells says that adolescents today build and rebuild social networks via constant messaging. This is helped by the fact that they have what he calls "a safe autonomous pattern," in that their parents are only a speed dial away.

Sociologists describe two kinds of social ties: strong ties of family members and those with shared values, beliefs, and identities; and weak ties to acquaintances and other people with shallower connections. According to some researchers, the Internet and, in particular, mobile devices are enabling the strong community ties to be reinforced, often at the expense of the weak ties. At a time when technology is being lauded for encouraging diversity and facilitating cross-cultural communication, there is, consequently, a strong and growing counter-trend: digital tribalism. Aside from strengthening ties to family and close friends, people are using the technology to find others with whom they share important affinities, ranging from genomes to beliefs to lifestyle choices. This digital form of tribalism is an unexpectedly strong trend, as observed by social critics such as Christine Rosen.

Information spreads electronically with speed and power. Maintaining the connection will require constant monitoring of the electronic tribal village and quickness to reposition or reinforce when required.

Bridal showers, for instance, can be attended by distant guests through Skype, and e-registries allow gift givers to view what others have bought. There is much room for innovation here, in terms of bringing people together who would not otherwise be in the same place for business meetings, financial planning, meal sharing, celebrations, and more. Associations might capitalize on online events for far-flung and numerous businesses, professionals, and friends and families of members. Employers might do the same for their employees' personal networks, perhaps offering discounts, education, job postings, and new products to all "friends of friends."

Expat workers and members of the armed forces might be more easily enabled to stay in touch with their families if their employers organized better around online communications and communities. This would ease the burden on relocated personnel, improve morale, attract more people, increase productivity, and spin the sale of products and service to these populations. This could also be true for alumni networks and other diaspora groups.

The Identity Industry

Social scientists make the distinction between a found identity and a made identity. The found identity is one created by your circumstances—who your parents were, your ethnic background, your religion, your sex, where you went to school, your profession, and all the other external factors that people use to categorize and describe you. The made identity, on the other hand, is the one you create for yourself. It is how you wish to see yourself and how you want others to see you.

In the past, people who wanted to escape what they saw as the trap of their found identity did such things as change their name or appearance. They moved somewhere else. Now, and increasingly in the future, technology will let you make and remake your identity at will—virtually. This extraordinary, even revolutionary, development will profoundly affect fundamental societal values such as trust and reliability.

In addition to engaging directly online with other individuals, you can also interact with them through avatars, the images that represent you (or an idealized version of yourself) in virtual worlds. Each virtual world requires a separate avatar, so in effect you can be as many different people as there are virtual worlds. In the future, you will be able to create avatars that will literally take on lives of their own. They will, once created, be able to "think" on their own, without further input from you. They may be able to perform intensive research tasks for you, start and even manage online companies, maintain your social relationships by reading your Facebook updates and blog posts and analyzing them for significant news so you don't have to. Increasingly, over time, distinctions between real and virtual identity will become less sharply defined, particularly for people who spend substantial amounts of time in the virtual world—or some enhanced combination of the real and the virtual. A company called Total Immersion combines 3-D and augmented reality technology, on the Internet, inserting people and physical objects into live video feeds. According to the company's website, "this digital processing mixes real and virtual worlds together, in real time."

All this could lead to growing confusion about identity. We will go from "Who am I?" to "Who, when, and where am I?" What in the twentieth century was seen as a problem that needed treatment—multiple personalities—will increasingly be seen in the twenty-first century as a coping mechanism, greatly affecting the evolving economy.

The future of business conferences? A virtual boardroom meeting in Second Life. Professional associations will hold more and more events and meetings in virtual spaces as well. Two avatars share a moment together in the virtual world Second Life. Could this represent the future dating experience (at least the positive side of it) as our social lives move increasingly online?

The Reality of Virtual Feelings

Advances in brain research and multisensory perception could play an important role in the development of virtual relationships. Neural devices already allow people to control electronic equipment such as wheelchairs, televisions, and video games via brain–computer interfaces. One day soon, avatars may also be controllable this way.

Virtual reality may become so advanced that it could trick the brain into thinking the invented images it is responding to are real—and human emotions would follow accordingly. Avatars will cause people to feel love, hate, jealousy, etc. And as haptic technologies improve, our abilities to respond physically to our virtual partners will also improve: Sexual pleasure may be routinely available without any inter-human stimulation at all.

If it becomes possible to connect virtual reality programs directly to the brain, thoughts and emotions may also be digitized, rendered binary and reduced to 0s and 1s. Feelings of satisfaction and pleasure (two key components in any relationship) could be created between avatars without any "real" stimulus at all. But would they be real or mimetic?

Once humans begin to perceive virtual social interactions as actually having occurred, it will greatly impact individuals, relationships, communities, and society as a whole.

Critical Thinking

1. Explain what the term "Virtual Society" means.
2. What do you see as similarities and differences in the relationships you've developed online versus in person?
3. What are some benefits of virtual or online relationships? What are some risks or concerns?
4. Does online communication strengthen connections or serve to undermine our ability to create "real" relationships and weaken our support networks?
5. What relationship skills can be learned online? Can or should they be learned exclusively online, or is experience in the "real world" still necessary?
6. How do you think technology and cyberculture will alter the development and maintenance of familial and intimate relationships in the future?

Create Central

www.mhhe.com/createcentral

Internet References

World Family Map
   http://worldfamilymap.org/2013
Australian Institute of Family Studies
   www.aifs.gov.au
Feminist Perspectives on Reproduction and the Family
   http://plato.stanford.edu/entries/feminism-family
Kearl's Guide to the Sociology of the Family
   www.trinity.edu/MKEARL/family.html

Unit 2

Prepared by: Patricia Hrusa Williams,
University of Maine at Farmington

UNIT

Exploring and Establishing Relationships

By and large, we are social animals—and as such, we seek out meaningful connections with other humans. John Bowlby, Mary Ainsworth, and others have proposed that this drive toward deep connections is biologically based and is at the core of what it means to be human. However it plays out in childhood and adulthood, the need for connection—to love and be loved—is a powerful force moving us to establish and maintain close relationships. As we explore various possibilities, we engage in the complex business of relationship-building. In doing this, many processes occur simultaneously. Messages are sent and received; differences are negotiated; assumptions are made; expectations are or are not met. The ultimate goals are closeness and continuity. How we feel about others and what we see as essential to these relationships play important roles as we work to establish and maintain relationships.

In this unit, we look at factors that underlie the establishment and beginning stages of relationships. Among the topics to be covered in this unit is an exploration of factors that influence how and why connections are built—including biology, emotion, sex, personality, and the context in which relationships are established and developed. Changing views and practices in dating, mating, marriage, commitment, family formation, and early family development are explored in an effort to understand the changing nature of intimate and family relationships in modern society.

Article   Prepared by: Patricia Hrusa Williams,
University of Maine at Farmington

12 Rude Revelations about Sex

ALAIN DE BOTTON

Learning Outcomes

After reading this article, you will be able to:

- Explain the science behind sex, sexual desire, and sexual behavior.
- Examine some of the major themes in the study of sex and intimate relationships.
- Understand sexual terms such as erotic and intimacy.
- Recognize the emotional and physical manifestations of sexual desire and behavior.

We have been led to believe, is as natural as breathing. But in fact, contends British philosopher Alain de Botton, it is "close to rocket science in complexity." It's not only a powerful force, it's often contrary to many other things we care about. Sex inherently sets up conflicts within us. We crave sex with people we don't know or love. It makes us want to do things that seem immoral or degrading, like slapping someone or being tied up. We feel awkward asking the people we love for the sex acts we really want.

There's no denying that sex has its sweaty charms, and in its most exquisite moments dissolves the isolation that embodied life imposes on us. But those moments are rare, the exception rather than the rule, says de Botton, founder of London's School of Life. "Sex is always going to cause us headaches; it's not something we can miraculously grow relaxed about." We suffer privately, feeling "painfully strange about the sex we are either longing to have or struggling to avoid."

If we turn to sex books to help us work out this central experience of our lives, we are typically assured that most problems are mechanical, a matter of method. In his own new book, *How to Think More About Sex,* de Botton makes the case that our difficulties stem more from the multiplicity of things we want out of life, or the accrual of everyday resentments, or the weirdness of the sex drive itself. Here are some of the most basic questions it answers.

Why do most people lie about their true desires?

It is rare to go through life without feeling that we are somehow a bit odd about sex. It is an area in which most of us have a painful impression, in our heart of hearts, that we are quite unusual. Despite being one of the most private activities, sex is nevertheless surrounded by a range of powerfully socially sanctioned ideas that codify how normal people are meant to feel about and deal with the matter. In truth, however, few of us are remotely normal sexually. We are almost all haunted by guilt and neuroses, by phobias and disruptive desires, by indifference and disgust. We are universally deviant—but only in relation to some highly distorted ideals of normality.

Most of what we are sexually remains impossible to communicate with anyone whom we would want to think well of us. Men and women in love instinctively hold back from sharing more than a fraction of their desires out of a fear, usually accurate, of generating intolerable disgust in their partners.

Nothing is erotic that isn't also, with the wrong person, revolting, which is precisely what makes erotic moments so intense: At the precise juncture where disgust could be at its height, we find only welcome and permission. Think of two tongues exploring the deeply private realm of the mouth—that dark, moist cavity that no one but our dentist usually enters. The privileged nature of the union between two people is sealed by an act that, with someone else, would horrify them both.

What unfolds between a couple in the bedroom is an act of mutual reconciliation between two secret sexual selves emerging at last from sinful solitude. Their behavior is starkly at odds with the behavior expected of them by the civilized world. At last, in the semi-darkness a couple can confess to the many wondrous and demented things that having a body drives them to want.

Why is sex more difficult to talk about in this era, not less?

Whatever discomfort we feel around sex is commonly aggravated by the idea that we belong to a liberated age—and ought by now to be finding sex a straightforward and untroubling matter, a little like tennis, something that everyone should have as often as possible to relieve the stresses of modern life.

The narrative of enlightenment and progress skirts an unbudging fact: Sex is not something we can ever expect to feel easily liberated from. It is a fundamentally disruptive and overwhelming force, at odds with the majority of our ambitions and all but incapable of being discreetly integrated within civilized society. Sex is not fundamentally democratic or kind. It refuses to sit neatly on top of love. Tame it though we might try, it tends to wreak havoc across our lives; it leads us to destroy our relationships, threatens our productivity, and compels us to stay up too late in nightclubs talking to people whom we don't like but whose exposed midriffs we wish to touch. Our best hope should be for a respectful accommodation with an anarchic and reckless power.

How is sex a great lie detector?

Involuntary physiological reactions such as the wetness of a vagina and the stiffness of a penis are emotionally so satisfying (which means, simultaneously, so erotic) because they signal a kind of approval that lies utterly beyond rational manipulation. Erections and lubrication simply cannot be effected by will-power and are therefore particularly true and honest indices of interest. In a world in which fake enthusiasms are rife, in which it is often hard to tell whether people really like us or whether they are being kind to us merely out of a sense of duty, the wet vagina and the stiff penis function as unambiguous agents of sincerity.

A kiss is pleasurable because of the sensory receptivity of our lips, but a good deal of our excitement has nothing to do with the physical dimension of the act: It stems from the simple realization that someone else likes us quite a lot.

What is the lure of sex in the back of an airplane?

Most of the people we come in contact with in daily life hardly notice us. Their businesslike indifference can be painful and humiliating for us—hence, the peculiar power of the fantasy that life could be turned upside down and the normal priorities reversed. The eroticism of nurses' uniforms, for example, stems from the gap between the rational control they symbolize and the unbridled sexual passion that can for a while, if only in fantasy, gain the upper hand over it.

Just as uniforms can inspire lust by their evocation of rule-breaking, so can it be exciting to imagine sex in an unobserved corner of the university library, in a restaurant's cloakroom, or in a train car. Our defiant transgression can give us a feeling of power that goes beyond the merely sexual. To have sex in the back of an airplane full of business travelers is to have a go at upending the usual hierarchy of things, introducing desire into an atmosphere in which cold-hearted discipline generally dominates over personal wishes. At 35,000 feet up, just as in an office cubicle, the victory of intimacy seems sweeter and our pleasure increases accordingly. Eroticism is most clearly manifest at the intersection between the formal and the intimate.

Is pornography a betrayal of humanity?

Pornography is often accused of being comfortingly "fake" and therefore unthreatening to the conduct of any sensible existence. But it is deeply contrary to the rest of our plans and inclinations,

rerouting rational priorities. Most pornography is humiliating and vulgar. Nobility has surely been left far behind when an anonymous woman is forced onto a bed, three penises are roughly inserted into her orifices, and the ensuing scene is recorded. Yet this poison is not easy to resist. Thousands of content providers have exploited a design flaw of the male—a mind designed to cope with little more tempting than the occasional sight of a tribeswoman across the savannah. There is nothing robust enough in our psyche to compensate for developments in technology. Pornography, like alcohol and drugs, reduces our capacity to tolerate ambiguous moods of free-floating worry and boredom. Internet pornography assists our escape from ourselves, helping us to destroy our present and our future with depressing ease. Yet it's possible to conceive of a pornography in which sexual desire would be invited to support, rather than undermine, our higher values. It could be touching and playful. It could show people having sex who like one another, or people like those we know from the rest of life rather than aberrations. No longer would we have to choose between being human and being sexual.

Why is "Not tonight, Dear" so destructive?

Logic might suggest that being married or in a long-term relationship must guarantee an end to the anxiety that otherwise dogs attempts by one person to induce another to have sex. But while either kind of union may make sex a constant theoretical option, it will neither legitimate the act nor ease the path toward it. Moreover, against a background of permanent possibility, an unwillingness to have sex may be seen as a far graver violation of the ground rules than a similar impasse in other contexts. Being turned down by someone we have just met in a bar is not so surprising or wounding. Suffering sexual rejection by the person with whom we have pledged to share our life is much odder and more humiliating.

Why is impotence an achievement?

There are few greater sources of shame for a man, or feelings of rejection for his partner. The real problem with impotence is the blow to the self-esteem of both parties.

We are grievously mistaken in our interpretation. Impotence is the strangely troublesome fruit of reason and kindness intruding on the free flow of animal impulses, of our new inclination to wonder what another might be feeling and then to identify with his or her potential objections to our invasive or unsatisfactory demands.

All but the least self-aware among us will sometimes be struck by how distasteful our desire for sex can seem to someone else, how peculiar and physically off-putting our flesh may be, and how unwanted our caresses. An advanced capacity for love and tenderness can ironically render us too sensitive to try to pester anyone else into having sex with us, although now and then we may cross paths with individuals who are not appalled by our longing for urgent and forceful sexual congress, and who see nothing disgusting in even the farthest erotic extremes.

Impotence is at base, then, a symptom of respect, a fear of causing displeasure through the imposition of our own desires or the inability to satisfy our partner's needs—a civilized worry that we will disappoint or upset others. It is an asset that should be valued as evidence of an achievement of the ethical imagination.

What do religions know about sex that we don't?

Only religions still take sex seriously, in the sense of properly respecting its power to turn us away from our priorities. Only religions see it as something potentially dangerous and needing to be guarded against. Perhaps only after killing many hours online at youporn.com can we appreciate that on this one point religions have got it right: Sex and sexual images can overwhelm our higher rational faculties with depressing ease. Religions are often mocked for being prudish, but they wouldn't judge sex to be quite so bad if they didn't also understand that it could be rather wonderful.

Does marriage ruin sex?

A gradual decline in the intensity and frequency of sex between a married couple is an inevitable fact of biological life, and as such, evidence of deep normality—although the sex-therapy industry has focused most of its efforts on assuring us that marriage should be enlivened by constant desire.

Most innocently, the paucity of sex within established relationships has to do with the difficulty of shifting registers between the everyday and the erotic. The qualities demanded of us when we have sex stand in sharp opposition to those we employ in conducting the majority of our other, daily activities. Marriage tends to involve—if not immediately, then within a few years—the running of a household and the raising of children, tasks that often feel akin to the administration of a small business and call on many of the same skills.

Sex, with its contrary emphases on expansiveness, imagination, playfulness, and a loss of control, must by its very nature interrupt this routine of regulation and self-restraint. We avoid sex not because it isn't fun but because its pleasures erode our subsequent capacity to endure the strenuous demands that our domestic arrangements place on us.

Sex also has a way of altering and unbalancing our relationship with our household co-manager. Its initiation requires one partner or the other to become vulnerable by revealing what may feel like humiliating sexual needs. We must shift from debating what sort of household appliance to acquire to making the more challenging request, for example, that our spouse should turn over and take on the attitude of a submissive nurse or put on a pair of boots and start calling us names.

The satisfaction of our needs may force us to ask for things that are, from a distance, open to being judged both ridiculous and contemptible so that we may prefer, in the end, not to entrust them to someone on whom we must rely for so much else in the course of our ordinary upstanding life. We may in fact find it easier to put on a rubber mask or pretend to be a predatory, incestuous relative with someone we're not also going to have to eat breakfast with for the next three decades.

Why are bread crumbs in the kitchen bad for sex?

The common conception of anger posits red faces, raised voices, and slammed doors, but only too often it just curdles into numbness. We tend to forget we are angry with our partner, and hence become anaesthetized, melancholic, and unable to have sex with him or her because the specific incidents that anger us happen so quickly and so invisibly, in such chaotic settings (at the breakfast table, before the school run) that we can't recognize the offense well enough to mount a coherent protest against it. And we frequently don't articulate our anger, even when we do understand it, because the things that offend us can seem so trivial or odd that they would sound ridiculous if spoken aloud: "I am angry with you because you cut the bread in the wrong way." But once we are involved in a relationship, there is no longer any such thing as a minor detail.

In an average week, each partner may be hit by, and in turn fire, dozens of tiny arrows without even realizing it, with the only surface legacies of these wounds being a near imperceptible cooling between the pair and, crucially, the disinclination of one or both to have sex with the other. Sex is a gift that is not easy to hand over once we are annoyed.

We are unable to rise above the fray and shift the focus from recrimination towards identification of the true sources of hurt and fear. Couples need to appreciate that their hostilities were shaped by the flow of their individual personalities through the distorting emotional canyons of their particular childhoods. We think we already know everything necessary about how to be with another person, without having bothered to learn anything at all. We are unprepared for the effort we must legitimately expend to make even a very decent adult relationship successful.

Why are hotels metaphysically important?

The walls, beds, comfortably upholstered chairs, room service menus, televisions, and tightly wrapped soaps can do more than answer a taste for luxury. Checking into a hotel room for a night is a solution to long-term sexual stagnation: We can see the erotic side of our partner, which is often closely related to the unchanging environment in which we lead our daily lives. We can blame the stable presence of the carpet and the living room chairs at home for our failure to have more sex: The physical backdrop prevents us from evolving. The furniture insists that we can't change—because it never does.

In a hotel room, we may make love joyfully again because we have rediscovered, behind the roles we are forced to play by our domestic circumstances, the sexual identities that first drew us together—an act of aesthetic perception that will have been critically assisted by a pair of terry cloth bathrobes, a complimentary fruit basket, and a view onto an unfamiliar harbor. We can see our lover as if we had never laid eyes on him before.

Why is adultery overrated?

Contrary to all public verdicts on adultery, the lack of any wish whatsoever to stray is irrational and against nature, a heedless disregard for the fleshly reality of our bodies, a denial of the power wielded over our more rational selves by such erotic triggers as high-heeled shoes and crisp shirts, by smooth thighs and muscular calves.

But a spouse who gets angry at having been betrayed is evading a basic, tragic truth: No one can be everything to another person. The real fault lies in the ethos of modern marriage, with its insane ambitions and its insistence that our most pressing needs might be solved with the help of only one other person.

If seeing marriage as the perfect answer to all our hopes for love, sex, and family is naive and misguided, so too is believing that adultery can be an effective antidote to the disappointments of marriage. It is impossible to sleep with someone outside of marriage and not spoil the things we care about inside it. There is no answer to the tensions of marriage.

When a person with whom we have been having an erotic exchange in an Internet chat room suggests a meeting at an airport hotel, we may be tempted to blow up our life for a few hours' pleasure. The defenders of feeling-based marriage venerate emotions for their authenticity only because they avoid looking closely at what actually floats through most people's emotional kaleidoscopes, all the contradictory, sentimental, and hormonal forces that pull us in a hundred often crazed and inconclusive directions.

We could not be fulfilled if we weren't inauthentic some of the time—inauthentic, that is, in relation to such things as our passing desires to throttle our children, poison our spouse, or end our marriage over a dispute about changing a lightbulb. A degree of repression is necessary for both the mental health of our species and the adequate functioning of a decently ordered society. We are chaotic chemical propositions. We should feel grateful for, and protected by, the knowledge that our external circumstances are often out of line with what we feel; it is a sign that we are probably on the right course.

Critical Thinking

1. The author states "few of us are remotely normal sexually." Do you agree or disagree? Why?

2. Describe some practical challenges sexual desires and impulses present in our daily lives.

3. Is sex more physical or emotional? Why?

4. What is a question about sex that has not been addressed in this article?

Create Central

www.mhhe.com/createcentral

Internet References

Go Ask Alice!
www.goaskalice.columbia.edu
The Kinsey Institute for Research in Sex, Gender, and Reproduction
www.kinseyinstitute.org
The Society for the Scientific Study of Sexuality
www.sexscience.org
The Electronic Journal of Human Sexuality
www.ejhs.org/index.htm

ALAIN DE BOTTON is founder of The School of Life, based in London.

Article

Prepared by: Patricia Hrusa Williams,
University of Maine at Farmington

There's No Such Thing as Everlasting Love (According to Science)

EMILY ESFAHANI SMITH

Learning Outcomes

After reading this article, you will be able to:

• Understand differences in theoretical, practical, and scientific definitions of love.

• Explain the science, biochemistry, and physiological components behind love.

In her new book *Love 2.0: How Our Supreme Emotion Affects Everything We Feel, Think, Do, and Become,* the psychologist Barbara Fredrickson offers a radically new conception of love.

Fredrickson, a leading researcher of positive emotions at the University of North Carolina at Chapel Hill, presents scientific evidence to argue that love is not what we think it is. It is not a long-lasting, continually present emotion that sustains a marriage; it is not the yearning and passion that characterizes young love; and it is not the blood-tie of kinship.

Rather, it is what she calls a "micro-moment of positivity resonance." She means that love is a connection, characterized by a flood of positive emotions, which you share with another person—*any* other person—whom you happen to connect with in the course of your day. You can experience these micro-moments with your romantic partner, child, or close friend. But you can also fall in love, however momentarily, with less likely candidates, like a stranger on the street, a colleague at work, or an attendant at a grocery store. Louis Armstrong put it best in "It's a Wonderful World" when he sang, "I see friends shaking hands, sayin' 'how do you do?' / They're really sayin', 'I love you.'"

Fredrickson's unconventional ideas are important to think about at this time of year. With Valentine's Day around the corner, many Americans are facing a grim reality: They are love-starved. Rates of loneliness are on the rise as social supports are disintegrating. In 1985, when the General Social Survey polled Americans on the number of confidants they have in their lives, the most common response was three. In 2004, when the survey was given again, the most common response was zero.

According to the University of Chicago's John Cacioppo, an expert on loneliness, and his co-author William Patrick, "at any given time, roughly 20 percent of individuals—that would be 60 million people in the U.S. alone—feel sufficiently isolated for it to be a major source of unhappiness in their lives." For older Americans, that number is closer to 35 percent. At the same time, rates of depression have been on the rise. In his 2011 book *Flourish,* the psychologist Martin Seligman notes that according to some estimates, depression is 10 times more prevalent now than it was five decades ago. Depression affects about 10 percent of the American population, according to the Centers for Disease Control.

A global poll taken last Valentine's Day showed that most married people—or those with a significant other—list their romantic partner as the greatest source of happiness in their lives. According to the same poll, nearly half of all single people are looking for a romantic partner, saying that finding a special person to love would contribute greatly to their happiness.

But to Fredrickson, these numbers reveal a "worldwide collapse of imagination," as she writes in her book. "Thinking of love purely as romance or commitment that you share with one special person—as it appears most on earth do—surely limits the health and happiness you derive" from love.

"My conception of love," she tells me, "gives hope to people who are single or divorced or widowed this Valentine's Day to find smaller ways to experience love."

You have to physically be with the person to experience the micro-moment. For example, if you and your significant other are not physically together—if you are reading this at work alone in your office—then you two are not in love. You may feel connected or bonded to your partner—you may long to be in his company—but your body is completely loveless.

To understand why, it's important to see how love works biologically. Like all emotions, love has a biochemical and physiological component. But unlike some of the other positive emotions, like joy or happiness, love cannot be kindled individually—it only exists in the physical connection between two people. Specifically, there are three players in the biological love system—mirror neurons, oxytocin, and vagal tone. Each involves connection and each contributes to those micro-moments of positivity resonance that Fredrickson calls love.

When you experience love, your brain mirrors the person's you are connecting with in a special way. Pioneering research by Princeton University's Uri Hasson shows what happens inside the brains of two people who connect in conversation. Because brains are scanned inside of noisy fMRI machines, where carrying on a conversation is nearly impossible, Hasson's team had his subjects mimic a natural conversation in an ingenious way. They recorded a young woman telling a lively, long, and circuitous story about her high school prom. Then, they played the recording for the participants in the study, who were listening to it as their brains were being scanned. Next, the researchers asked each participant to re-create the story so they, the researchers, could determine who was listening well and who was not. Good listeners, the logic goes, would probably be the ones who clicked in a natural conversation with the story-teller.

What they found was remarkable. In some cases, the brain patterns of the listener mirrored those of the storyteller after a short time gap. The listener needed time to process the story after all. In other cases, the brain activity was almost perfectly synchronized; there was no time lag at all between the speaker and the listener. But in some rare cases, if the listener was particularly tuned in to the story—if he was hanging on to every word of the story and really got it—his brain activity actually *anticipated* the story-teller's in some cortical areas.

The mutual understanding and shared emotions, especially in that third category of listener, generated a micro-moment of love, which "is a single act, performed by two brains," as Fredrickson writes in her book.

Oxytocin, the so-called love and cuddle hormone, facilitates these moments of shared intimacy and is part of the mammalian "calm-and-connect" system (as opposed to the more stressful "fight-or-flight" system that closes us off to others). The hormone, which is released in huge quantities during sex, and in lesser amounts during other moments of intimate connection, works by making people feel more trusting and open to connection. This is the hormone of attachment and bonding that spikes during micro-moments of love. Researchers have found, for instance, that when a parent acts affectionately with his or her infant—through micro-moments of love like making eye contact, smiling, hugging, and playing—oxytocin levels in both the parent and the child rise in sync.

The final player is the vagus nerve, which connects your brain to your heart and subtly but sophisticatedly allows you to meaningfully experience love. As Fredrickson explains in her book, "Your vagus nerve stimulates tiny facial muscles that better enable you to make eye contact and synchronize your facial expressions with another person. It even adjusts the miniscule muscles of your middle ear so you can better track her voice against any background noise."

The vagus nerve's potential for love can actually be measured by examining a person's heart rate in association with his breathing rate, what's called "vagal tone." Having a high vagal tone is good: People who have a high "vagal tone" can regulate their biological processes like their glucose levels better; they have more control over their emotions, behavior, and attention; they are socially adept and can kindle more positive connections with others; and, most importantly, they are more loving.

In research from her lab, Fredrickson found that people with high vagal tone report more experiences of love in their days than those with a lower vagal tone.

Historically, vagal tone was considered stable from person to person. You either had a high one or you didn't; you either had a high potential for love or you didn't. Fredrickson's recent research has debunked that notion.

In a 2010 study from her lab, Fredrickson randomly assigned half of her participants to a "love" condition and half to a control condition. In the love condition, participants devoted about one hour of their weeks for several months to the ancient Buddhist practice of loving-kindness meditation. In loving-kindness meditation, you sit in silence for a period of time and cultivate feelings of tenderness, warmth, and compassion for another person by repeating a series of phrases to yourself wishing them love, peace, strength, and general well-being. Ultimately, the practice helps people step outside of themselves and become more aware of other people and their needs, desires, and struggles—something that can be difficult to do in our hyper individualistic culture.

Fredrickson measured the participants' vagal tone before and after the intervention. The results were so powerful that she was invited to present them before the Dalai Lama himself in 2010. Fredrickson and her team found that, contrary to the conventional wisdom, people could significantly increase their vagal tone by self-generating love through loving-kindness meditation. Since vagal tone mediates social connections and bonds, people whose vagal tones increased were suddenly capable of experiencing more micro-moments of love in their days. Beyond that, their growing capacity to love more will translate into health benefits given that high vagal tone is associated with lowered risk of inflammation, cardiovascular disease, diabetes, and stroke.

Fredrickson likes to call love a nutrient. If you are getting enough of the nutrient, then the health benefits of love can dramatically alter your biochemistry in ways that perpetuate more micro-moments of love in your life, and which ultimately contribute to your health, well-being, and longevity.

Fredrickson's ideas about love are not exactly the stuff of romantic comedies. Describing love as a "micro-moment of positivity resonance" seems like a buzz-kill. But if love now seems less glamorous and mysterious than you thought it was, then good. Part of Fredrickson's project is to lower cultural expectations about love—expectations that are so misguidedly high today that they have inflated love into something that it isn't, and into something that no sane person could actually experience.

Jonathan Haidt, another psychologist, calls these unrealistic expectations "the love myth" in his 2006 book *The Happiness Hypothesis:*

> True love is passionate love that never fades; if you are in true love, you should marry that person; if love ends, you should leave that person because it was not true love; and if you can find the right person, you will have true love forever. You might not believe this myth yourself, particularly if you are older than thirty; but many young people in Western nations are raised on it, and it acts as

an ideal that they unconsciously carry with them even if they scoff at it. . . . But if true love is defined as eternal passion, it is biologically impossible.

Love 2.0 is, by contrast, far humbler. Fredrickson tells me, "I love the idea that it lowers the bar of love. If you don't have a Valentine, that doesn't mean that you don't have love. It puts love much more in our reach everyday regardless of our relationship status."

Lonely people who are looking for love are making a mistake if they are sitting around and waiting for love in the form of the "love myth" to take hold of them. If they instead sought out love in little moments of connection that we all experience many times a day, perhaps their loneliness would begin to subside.

Critical Thinking

1. What is your definition of love? What are some similarities and differences between your definition and the ones presented in the article?

2. Explain the love myth.

3. Do you believe that people can be trained to be more loving, as the article implies? Why or why not?

4. What are some advantages and disadvantages of defining love as "micro-moments" of positive feelings and emotions?

Create Central

www.mhhe.com/createcentral

Internet References

Go Ask Alice!
   www.goaskalice.columbia.edu
The Kinsey Institute for Research in Sex, Gender, and Reproduction
   www.kinseyinstitute.org
The Society for the Scientific Study of Sexuality
   www.sexscience.org
The Electronic Journal of Human Sexuality
   www.ejhs.org/index.htm

Article Prepared by: Patricia Hrusa Williams, University of Maine at Farmington

The Expectations Trap

Much of the discontent couples encounter today is really culturally inflicted, although we're conditioned to blame our partners for our unhappiness. Yet research points to ways couples can immunize themselves against unseen pressures now pulling them apart.

HARA ESTROFF MARANO

Learning Outcomes

After reading this article, you will be able to:

- Recognize cultural aspects of love and marriage.

- Identify personality characteristics which are important to dating success.

- Describe how culture impacts happiness within relationships.

Six years, ten months, and eight days into their marriage, Sam and Melissa blew apart. Everyone was stunned, most of all the couple themselves. One day she was your basic stressed-out professional woman (and mother of a 3-year-old) carrying the major financial burden of their household. The next day she was a betrayed wife. The affair Sam disclosed detonated a caterwaul of hurt heard by every couple in their circle and her large coterie of friends and family. With speed verging on inevitability, the public knowledge of their private life commandeered the driver's seat of their own destiny. A surge of support for Melissa as the wronged woman swiftly isolated Sam emotionally and precluded deep discussion of the conditions that had long alienated him. Out of respect for the pain that his mere presence now caused, Sam decamped within days. He never moved back in.

It's not clear that the couple could have salvaged the relationship if they had tried. It wasn't just the infidelity. "We had so many background and stylistic differences," says Sam. "It was like we came from two separate cultures. We couldn't take out the garbage without a Geneva Accord." Constant negotiation was necessary, but if there was time, there was also usually too much accumulated irritation for Melissa to tolerate. And then, opening a public window on the relationship seemed to close the door on the possibility of working through the disappointments, the frustrations, the betrayal.

Within weeks, the couple was indeed in discussions—for a divorce. At least they both insisted on mediation, not litigation, and their lawyers complied. A couple of months, and some time and determination later, they had a settlement. Only now that Sam and Melissa have settled into their mostly separate lives, and their daughter appears to be doing well with abundant care from both her parents, are they catching their respective breaths—two years later.

Americans value marriage more than people do in any other culture, and it holds a central place in our dreams. Over 90 percent of young adults aspire to marriage—although fewer are actually choosing it, many opting instead for cohabitation. But no matter how you count it, Americans have the highest rate of romantic breakup in the world, says Andrew J. Cherlin, professor of sociology and public policy at Johns Hopkins. As with Sam and Melissa, marriages are discarded often before the partners know what hit them.

"By age 35, 10 percent of American women have lived with three or more husbands or domestic partners," Cherlin reports in his recent book, *The Marriage-Go-Round: The State of Marriage and the Family in America Today.* "Children of married parents in America face a higher risk of seeing them break up than children born of unmarried parents in Sweden."

With general affluence has come a plethora of choices, including constant choices about our personal and family life. Even marriage itself is now a choice. "The result is an ongoing self-appraisal of how your personal life is going, like having a continual readout of your emotional heart rate," says Cherlin. You get used to the idea of always making choices to improve your happiness.

The constant appraisal of personal life to improve happiness creates a heightened sensitivity to problems that arise in intimate relationships.

The heightened focus on options "creates a heightened sensitivity to problems that arise in intimate relationships." And negative emotions get priority processing in our brains. "There are so many opportunities to decide that it's unsatisfactory," says Cherlin.

It would be one thing if we were living more satisfied lives than ever. But just gauging by the number of relationships wrecked every year, we're less satisfied, says Cherlin. "We're carrying over into our personal lives the fast pace of decisions and actions we have everywhere else, and that may not be for the best." More than ever, we're paying attention to the most volatile parts of our emotional makeup—the parts that are too reactive to momentary events to give meaning to life.

More than ever, we're paying attention to the most volatile parts of our emotional makeup—parts that are too reactive to momentary events to give meaning to life.

Because our intimate relationships are now almost wholly vehicles for meeting our emotional needs, and with almost all our emotions invested in one relationship, we tend to look upon any unhappiness we experience—whatever the source—as a failure of a partner to satisfy our longings. Disappointment inevitably feels so *personal* we see no other possibility but to hunt for individual psychological reasons—that is, to blame our partners for our own unhappiness.

But much—perhaps most—of the discontent we now encounter in close relationships is culturally inflicted, although we rarely interpret our experience that way. Culture—the pressure to constantly monitor our happiness, the plethora of choices surreptitiously creating an expectation of perfection, the speed of everyday life—always climbs into bed with us. An accumulation of forces has made the cultural climate hostile to long-term relationships today.

Attuned to disappointment and confused about its source, we wind up discarding perfectly good relationships. People work themselves up over "the ordinary problems of marriage, for which, by the way, they usually fail to see their own contributions," says William Doherty, professor of family sciences at the University of Minnesota. "They badger their partners to change, convince themselves nothing will budge, and so work their way out of really good relationships." Doherty believes it's possible to stop the careering disappointment even when people believe a relationship is over.

It's not going to happen by putting the genie back in the bottle. It's not possible to curb the excess of options life now offers. And speed is a fixture of the ongoing technological revolution, no matter how much friction it creates in personal lives. Yet new research points to ways that actually render them irrelevant. We are, after all, the architects of our own passions.

The Purpose of Marriage

Marriage probably evolved as the best way to pool the labor of men and women to enable families to subsist and assure that children survive to independence—and data indicate it still is. But beyond the basics, the purpose of marriage has shifted constantly, says Stephanie Coontz, a historian at Washington's Evergreen State College. It helps to remember that marriage

> ## Case Study
> ## Stephen and Christina
>
> Five years into his marriage, not long after the birth of his first son, most of Stephen G.'s interactions with his wife were not pleasant. "I thought the difficulties would pass," he recalls. "My wife, Christina, got fed up faster and wanted me to leave." He was traveling frequently and finances were thin; she'd gone back to school full-time after having worked until the baby was born. "Very few needs were being met for either of us. We were either yelling or in a cold war."
>
> They entered counseling to learn how to co-parent if they indeed separated. "It helped restore our friendship: At least we could talk civilly. That led to deeper communication—we could actually listen to each other without getting defensive. We heard that we were both hurting, both feeling the stress of new parenthood without a support system of either parents or friends. We could talk about the ways we weren't there for each other without feeling attacked. It took a lot longer for the romance to return."
>
> Stephen, now 37, a sales representative for a pharmaceutical company in San Francisco, says it was a time of "growing up. I had to accept that I had new responsibilities. And I had to accept that my partner, now 38, is not ideal in every way although she is ideal in many ways. But her short temper is not enough of a reason to leave the relationship and our two kids. When I wish she'd be different, I have to remind myself of all the ways she is the person I want to be with. It's not something you 'get over.' You accept it."

evolved in an atmosphere of scarcity, the conditions that prevailed for almost all of human history. "The earliest purpose of marriage was to make strategic alliances with other people, to turn strangers into relatives," says Coontz. "As society became more differentiated, marriage became a major mechanism for adjusting your position."

It wasn't until the 18th century that anyone thought that love might have anything to do with marriage, but love was held in check by a sense of duty. Even through the 19th century, the belief prevailed that females and males had different natures and couldn't be expected to understand each other well. Only in the 20th century did the idea take hold that men and women should be companions, that they should be passionate, and that both should get sexual and personal fulfillment from marriage.

We're still trying to figure out how to do that—and get the laundry done, too. The hassles of a negotiated and constantly renegotiated relationship—few wish a return to inequality—assure a ready source of stress or disappointment or both.

From We to Me

Our mind-set has further shifted over the past few decades, experts suggest. Today, the minute one partner is faced with dissatisfaction—feeling stressed-out or neglected, having

Case Study
Susan and Tim

Susan Pohlman, now 50, reluctantly accompanied her workaholic husband on a business trip to Italy believing it would be their last together. Back home in Los Angeles were their two teenagers, their luxurious home, their overfurnished lives—and the divorce lawyer she had contacted to end their 18-year marriage.

They were leading such parallel lives that collaboration had turned to competition, with fights over things like who spent more time with the kids and who spent more time working. But knocked off balance by the beauty of the coast near Genoa toward the end of the trip, Tim asked, out of the blue, "What if we lived here?" "The spirit of this odd day overtook me," recalls Susan. At 6 P.M. on the evening before departure, they were shown a beautiful apartment overlooking the water. Despite knowing no Italian, they signed a lease on the spot. Two months later, with their house sold, they moved with their kids to Italy for a year.

"In L.A. we were four people going in four directions. In Italy, we became completely dependent on each other. How to get a phone? How to shop for food? Also, we had no belongings. The simplicity forced us to notice the experiences of life. Often, we had no idea what we were doing. There was lots of laughing at and with each other." Susan says she "became aware of the power of adventure and of doing things together, and how they became a natural bridge to intimacy."

Both Pohlmans found Italy offered "a more appreciative lifestyle." Says Susan: "I realized the American Dream was pulling us apart. We followed the formula of owning, having, pushing each other. You have all this stuff but you're miserable because what you're really craving is interaction." Too, she says, American life is exhausting, and "exhaustion distorts your ability to judge problems."

Now back in the U.S. and living in Arizona, the Pohlmans believe they needed to remove themselves from the culture to see its distorting effects. "And we needed to participate in a paradigm shift: 'I'm not perfect, you're not perfect; let's not get hung up on our imperfections.'" But the most powerful element of their move could be reproduced anywhere, she says: "The simplicity was liberating."

a partner who isn't overly expressive or who works too hard or doesn't initiate sex very often—then the communal ideal we bring to relationships is jettisoned and an individualistic mentality asserts itself. We revert to a stingier self that has been programmed into us by the consumer culture, which has only become increasingly pervasive, the current recession notwithstanding.

Psychologically, the goal of life becomes *my* happiness. "The minute your needs are not being met then you appropriate the individualistic norm," says Doherty. This accelerating consumer mind-set is a major portal through which destructive forces gain entry and undermine conjoint life.

"Marriage is for *me*" is the way Austin, Texas, family therapist Pat Love puts it. "It's for meeting *my* needs." It's not about what *I do*, but how it makes me *feel*.

Such beliefs lead to a sense of entitlement: "I deserve better than I'm getting." Doherty sees that as the basic message of almost every advertisement in the consumer culture. You deserve more and we can provide it. You begin to think: This isn't the deal I signed up for. Or you begin to feel that you're putting into this a lot more than you're getting out. "We believe in our inalienable right to the intimate relationships of our choice," says Doherty.

In allowing such free-market values to seep into our private lives, we come to believe that a partner's job is, above all, to provide pleasure. "People do not go into relationships because they want to learn how to negotiate and master difficulties," observes Brown University psychiatrist Scott Haltzman. "They want the other person to provide pleasure." It's partner as service provider. The pleasure bond, unfortunately, is as volatile as the emotions that underlie it and as hollow and fragile as the hedonic sense of happiness.

The Expectations Trap: Perfection, Please

If there's one thing that most explicitly detracts from the enjoyment of relationships today, it's an abundance of choice. Psychologist Barry Schwartz would call it an *excess* of choice—the tyranny of abundance. We see it as a measure of our autonomy and we firmly believe that freedom of choice will lead to fulfillment. Our antennae are always up for better opportunities, finds Schwartz, professor of psychology at Swarthmore College.

Just as only the best pair of jeans will do, so will only the best partner—whatever that is. "People walk starry-eyed looking not into the eyes of their romantic partner but over their romantic partner's shoulder, in case there might be somebody better walking by. This is not the road to successful long-term relationships." It does not stop with marriage. And it undermines commitment by encouraging people to keep their options open.

Like Doherty, Schwartz sees it as a consequence of a consumer society. He also sees it as a self-fulfilling phenomenon. "If you think there might be something better around the next corner, then there will be, because you're not fully committed to the relationship you've got."

It's naïve to expect relationships to feel good every minute. Every relationship has its bumps. How big a bump does it have to be before you do something about it? As Hopkins's Cherlin says, if you're constantly asking yourself whether you should leave, "there may be a day when the answer is yes. In any marriage there may be a day when the answer is yes."

One of the problems with unrestrained choice, explains Schwartz, is that it raises expectations to the breaking point. A sense of multiple alternatives, of unlimited possibility, breeds in us the illusion that perfection exists out there, somewhere, if only we could find it. This one's sense of humor, that one's looks, another one's charisma—we come to imagine that there will be a package in which all these desirable features coexist. We search for perfection because we believe we are entitled to the best—even if perfection is an illusion foisted on us by an abundance of possibilities.

If perfection is what you expect, you will always be disappointed, says Schwartz. We become picky and unhappy. The cruel joke our psychology plays on us, of course, is that we are terrible at knowing what will satisfy us or at knowing how any experience will make us feel.

A sense of multiple alternatives, of unlimited possibility, breeds in us the illusion that the perfect person is out there waiting to be found.

If the search through all possibilities weren't exhausting (and futile) enough, thinking about attractive features of the alternatives not chosen—what economists call opportunity costs—reduces the potential pleasure in whatever choice we finally do make. The more possibilities, the more opportunity costs—and the more we think about them, the more we come to regret any choice. "So, once again," says Schwartz, "a greater variety of choices actually makes us feel worse."

Ultimately, our excess of choice leads to lack of intimacy. "How is anyone going to stack up against this perfect person who's out there somewhere just waiting to be found?" asks Schwartz. "It creates doubt about this person, who seems like a good person, someone I might even be in love with—but who knows what's possible *out* there? Intimacy takes time to develop. You need to have some reason to put in the time. If you're full of doubt at the start, you're not going to put in the time."

Moreover, a focus on one's own preferences can come at the expense of those of others. As Schwartz said in his 2004 book, *The Paradox of Choice: Why More Is Less,* "most people find it extremely challenging to balance the conflicting impulses of freedom of choice on the one hand and loyalty and commitment on the other."

And yet, throughout, we are focused on the partner we want to have, not on the one we want—or need—to be. That may be the worst choice of all.

Disappointment—or Tragedy?

The heightened sensitivity to relationship problems that follows from constantly appraising our happiness encourages couples to turn disappointment into tragedy, Doherty contends.

Inevitably, images of the perfect relationship dancing in our heads collide with our sense of entitlement; "I'm entitled to the best possible marriage." The reality of disappointment becomes intolerable. "It's part of a cultural belief system that says we are entitled to everything we feel we need."

Through the alchemy of desire, wants become needs, and unfulfilled needs become personal tragedies. "A husband who isn't very expressive of his feelings can be a disappointment or a tragedy, depending on whether it's an entitlement," says Doherty. "And that's very much a cultural phenomenon." We take the everyday disappointments of relationships and treat them as intolerable, see them as demeaning—the equivalent of alcoholism, say, or abuse. "People work their way into 'I'm a tragic figure' around the ordinary problems of marriage." Such stories are so widespread, Doherty is no longer inclined to see them as reflecting an individual psychological problem, although that is how he was trained—and how he practiced for many years as an eminent family therapist. "I see it first now as a cultural phenomenon."

First Lady Michelle Obama is no stranger to the disappointment that pervades relationships today. In *Barack and Michelle: Portrait of an American Marriage,* by Christopher Anderson, she confides how she reached a "state of desperation" while working full-time, bringing in the majority of the family income, raising two daughters, and rarely seeing her husband, who was then spending most of his week away from their Chicago home as an Illinois state senator, a job she thought would lead nowhere while it paid little. "She's killing me with this constant criticism," Barack complained. "She just seems so bitter, so angry all the time." She was annoyed that he "seems to think he can just go out there and pursue his dream and leave all the heavy lifting to me."

But then she had an epiphany: She remembered the guy she fell in love with. "I figured out that I was pushing to make Barack be something I wanted him to be for me. I was depending on him to make me happy. Except it didn't have anything to do with him. I needed support. I didn't necessarily need it from Barack."

Certainly, commitment narrows choice. But it is the ability to remember you really do love someone—even though you may not be feeling it at the moment.

Commitment is the ability to sustain an investment, to honor values over momentary feelings. The irony, of course, is that while we want happiness, it isn't a moment-by-moment experience; the deepest, most enduring form of happiness is the result of sustained emotional investments in other people.

Architects of the Heart

One of the most noteworthy findings emerging from relationship research is that desire isn't just something we passively feel when everything's going right; it develops in direct response to what we do. Simply having fun together, for example, is crucial to keeping the sex drive alive.

But in the churn of daily life, we tend to give short shrift to creating positive experiences. Over time, we typically become more oriented to dampening threats and insecurities—to resolving conflict, to eliminating jealousy, to banishing problems. But the brain is wired with both a positive and negative motivational system, and satisfaction and desire demand keeping the brain's positive system well-stoked.

Even for long-term couples, spending time together in novel, interesting, or challenging activities—games, dancing, even conversation—enhances feelings of closeness, passionate love, and satisfaction with the relationship. Couples recapture the excitement of the early days of being in love. Such passion naturally feeds commitment.

From Michelle to Michelangelo

Important as it is to choose the right partner, it's probably more important to *be* the right partner. Most people are focused on changing the wrong person in the relationship; if anyone has to change in a relationship, it's you—although preferably with the help of your partner.

> **Important as it is to choose the right partner, it's probably more important to *be* the right partner. We focus on changing the wrong person.**

Ultimately, "marriage is an inside job," Pat Love told the 2009 Smart Marriages Conference. "It's internal to the person. You have to let it do its work." And its biggest job is helping individuals grow up. "Marriage is about getting over yourself. Happiness is not about focusing on yourself." Happiness is about holding onto your values, deciding who you are and being that person, using your particular talent, and investing in others.

Unfortunately, says Margin family therapist and *PT* blogger Susan Pease Gadoua, not enough people today are willing to do the hard work of becoming a more mature person. "They think they have a lot more choices. And they think life will be easier in another relationship. What they don't realize is that it will be the same relationship—just with a different name."

The question is not how you want your partner to change but what kind of partner and person you want to be. In the best relationships, not only are you thinking about who you want to be, but your partner is willing to help you get there. Psychologist Caryl E. Rusbult calls it the Michelangelo phenomenon. Just as Michelangelo felt the figures he created were already "in" the stones, "slumbering within the actual self is an ideal form," explains Eli Finkel, associate professor of psychology at Northwestern University and frequent Rusbult collaborator. Your partner becomes an ally in sculpting your ideal self, in bringing out the person you dream of becoming, leading you to a deep form of personal growth as well as long-term satisfaction with life and with the relationship.

It takes a partner who supports your dreams, the traits and qualities you want to develop—whether or not you've articulated them clearly or simply expressed vague yearnings. "People come to reflect what their partners see in them and elicit from them," Finkel and Rusbult report in *Current Directions in Psychological Science.*

Case Study
Patty and Rod

Patty Newbold had married "a really great guy," but by the time their 13th anniversary rolled around, she had a long list of things he needed to change to make the marriage work. At 34, she felt depressed, frantic—and guilty, as Rod was fighting a chronic disease. But she had reached a breaking point, "I read my husband my list of unmet needs and suggested a divorce," even though what she really wanted was her marriage back. "I wanted to feel loved again. But it didn't seem possible."

Newbold has had a long time to think about that list. Her husband died the next day, a freak side effect of his medications. "He was gone, but the list remained. Out of perhaps 30 needs, only one was eased by losing him. I was free now to move the drinking glasses next to the sink."

As she read through the list the morning after he died, she realized that "marriage isn't about my needs or his needs or about how well we communicate about our needs. It's about loving and being loved. *Life* is about meeting (or letting go of) my own *needs. Marriage* is about loving another person and receiving love in return. It suddenly became oh so clear that receiving love is something I make happen, not him." And then she was flooded with memories of all the times "I'd been offered love by this wonderful man and rejected it because I was too wrapped up in whatever need I was facing at the time."

Revitalized is "a funny word to describe a relationship in which one party is dead," she reports, "but ours was revitalized. I was completely changed, too." Everything she learned that awful day has gone into a second marriage, now well into its second decade.

Such affirmation promotes trust in the partner and strengthens commitment. And commitment, Rusbult has found, is a key predictor of relationship durability. "It creates positive bias towards each other," says Finkel. "It feels good to achieve our goals. It's deeply satisfying and meaningful." In addition, it immunizes the relationship against potential distractions—all those "perfect" others. Finkel explains, "It motivates the derogation of alternative partners." It creates the perception—the illusion—that even the most attractive alternative partners are unappealing. Attention to them gets turned off—one of the many cognitive gymnastics we engage in to ward off doubts.

Like growth, commitment is an inside job. It's not a simple vow. Partners see each other in ways that enhance their connection and fend off threats. It fosters the perception that the relationship you're in is better than that of others. It breeds the inclination to react constructively—by accommodation—rather than destructively when a partner does something inconsiderate. It even motivates that most difficult of tasks, forgiveness for the ultimate harm of betrayal, Rusbult has shown.

It is a willingness—stemming in part from an understanding that your well-being and your partner's are linked over the long term—to depart from direct self-interest, such as erecting a grudge when you feel hurt.

The Michelangelo phenomenon gives the lie to the soul mate search. You can't find the perfect person; there is no such thing. And even if you think you could, the person he or she is today is, hopefully, not quite the person he or she wants to be 10 years down the road. You and your partner help each other become a more perfect person—perfect, that is, according to your own inner ideals. You are both, with mutual help, constantly evolving.

Critical Thinking

1. Describe some of the influences that culture has on happiness within marriages.
2. In the case study of Stephen and Christina, what do you think were some of the causes of the friction in their relationship?
3. What are some ways that couples can keep their relationships from becoming strained?
4. List some of the expectations that you have or had in a relationship. Did you see any in the reading?
5. Do you think that there is a trend in today's society that marriage should be perfect? Why or why not?

Create Central

www.mhhe.com/createcentral

Internet References

Love Is Respect
www.loveisrespect.org

Relationships Australia
www.relationships.org.au

Article

Prepared by: Patricia Hrusa Williams,
University of Maine at Farmington

Waiting to Wed

M ARK R EGNERUS AND J EREMY U ECKER

Learning Outcomes

After reading this article, you will be able to:

- Explain trends in coupling and the development of long-term committed relationships in young adults.

- Understand factors important to mate selection.

- Recognize the effects of commitment on sexual and emotional selves.

S ome outside observers look at the relationship scene among young adults and consider that it is entirely about short-term hookups and that the majority of emerging adults are avoiding lasting and meaningful intimate relationships in favor of random sex. While sexual norms have certainly changed, there's no evidence to suggest that emerging adults are uninterested in relationships that last, including marriage. In fact, they want to marry. Lots of studies show that nearly all young women and men say they would like to get married someday. We're not talking half or even 80 percent, but more like 93 to 96 percent. Most just don't want to marry now or anytime soon. They feel no rush.

The slow but steady increase in average age at first marriage—to its present-day 26 for women and 28 for men—suggests that the purpose of dating or romantic relationships is changing or has changed. Most sexual relationships among emerging adults neither begin with marital intentions nor end in marriage or even cohabitation. They just begin and end.

Reasons for their termination are numerous, of course, but one overlooked possibility is that many of them don't know how to get or stay married to the kind of person they'd like to find. For not a few, their parents provided them with a glimpse into married life, and what they saw at the dinner table—if they dined with their parents much at all—didn't look very inviting. They hold the institution of marriage in high regard, and they put considerable pressure—probably too much—on what their own eventual marriage ought to look like. And yet it seems that there is little effort from any institutional source aimed at helping emerging adults consider how their present social, romantic and sexual experiences shape or war against their vision of marriage—or even how marriage might fit in with their other life goals.

In fact, talk of career goals seems increasingly divorced from the relational context in which many emerging adults may eventually find themselves. They speak of the MDs, JDs and PhDs they intend to acquire with far more confidence than they speak of committed relationships or marriage. The former seem attainable, the latter unclear or unreliable. To complicate matters, many educated emerging adults are concerned about possible relational constraints on their career goals.

Since emerging adults esteem the idea of marriage and yet set it apart as inappropriate for their age, waiting until marriage for a fulfilling sex life is considered not just quaint and outdated but quite possibly foolish. Sex outside relationships might still be disparaged by many, but not sex before marriage. And yet creating successful sexual relationships—ones that last a very long time or even into marriage—seems only a modest priority among many in this demographic group. Jeffrey Arnett, a developmental psychologist who focuses on emerging adulthood, notes the absence of relationship permanence as a value in the minds of emerging adults:

> Finding a love partner in your teens and continuing in a relationship with that person through your early twenties, culminating in marriage, is now viewed as unhealthy, a mistake, a path likely to lead to disaster. Those who do not experiment with different partners are warned that they will eventually wonder what they are missing, to the detriment of their marriage.

Arnett's right. The majority of young adults in America not only think they should explore different relationships, they believe it may be foolish and wrong not to.

Instead, they place value upon flexibility, autonomy, change and the potential for upgrading. Allison, an 18-year-old from Illinois, characterizes this value when she describes switching from an older, long-term boyfriend (and sexual partner) to a younger one: "I really liked having a steady boyfriend for a long time, but then it just got to the point where it was like, 'OK, I need something different.' It wasn't that I liked him any less or loved or cared about him any less, I just needed a change." Many emerging adults—especially men—conduct their relationships with a nagging sense that there may still be someone better out there.

D espite the emphasis on flexibility and freedom, most emerging adults wish to fall in love, commit and marry someday. And some already have (more about them shortly). The vast majority of those who haven't married believe themselves to be too young to "settle down." They are definitely not in a hurry. In a recent nationwide survey of young men, 62 percent of unmarried 25- to 29-year-olds (and 51 percent of 30- to 34-year-olds) said they were "not interested in getting married any time soon."

While their reticence could be for good reasons, their widespread use of this phrase suggests a tacitly antagonistic perspective about marriage. "Settling down" is something people do when it's time to stop having fun and get serious—when it's time to get married and have children, two ideas that occur together in the emerging-adult mind. In the same national survey of men we just noted, 81 percent of unmarried men age 25 to 29 agreed that "at this stage in your life, you want to have fun and freedom." (Even 74 percent of single 30- to 34-year-olds agreed.) That figure would have been even higher had men in their early twenties been interviewed.

Trevor, a 19-year-old virgin from North Carolina, agrees wholeheartedly with this sentiment. He would like to marry someday. When asked if there were certain things that people should accomplish before they're ready to marry, he lists the standard economic criteria. But he also conveys a clear understanding that his best days would be behind him: "I'd say before you're married, make sure you have a place to live. Don't have a child before marriage. . . . Have a decent paying job because, I mean, it's only going to get worse."

A distinctive fissure exists in the minds of young Americans between the carefree single life and the married life of economic pressures and family responsibilities. The one is sexy, the other is sexless. In the minds of many, sex is for the young and single, while marriage is for the old. Marriage is quaint, adorable.

Thus a key developmental task for Juan, a 19-year-old from Southern California, is to have his fill of sex before being content with a fixed diet. His advice would be to "get a lot of stuff out of your system, like messing around with girls and stuff, or partying."

Likewise, Megan, 22, from Texas, doesn't conceive of parenthood as a sexual life stage, the irony of it aside. She captures what very many young men and women believe to be a liability of marriage: the end of good sex. The last omnibus sex study of Americans—issued in 1994—disputes Megan's conclusion, but the power of surveys and statistics is nothing compared to the strength of a compelling story in the minds of many people. We asked Megan whether married life would be less sexual than her single life:

Probably. [*Because?*] Just, as you age, your sex drive goes down. [*OK.*] I mean not because you want to be less sexual, that could be the case, but I won't know till I'm older. [*So some people say when you get married, you settle down, like it's literally a settling down. Do you look at marriage and married sex as being like, "That's off in the future; it might be a disappointment. Now I'm having a better time"?*] Yeah. [*Do you?*] Yes. [*Why?*] Why do I think it might be a disappointment? [*Sure.*] Um, just because of the horror stories of getting married. Nobody wants to have sex anymore. [*Where do you hear these stories?*] Movies, other people. . . . [*Like what? Can you think of one?*] Um, there's plenty. Like the movie that just came out—*License to Wed*—there's this one scene where the guy is sitting on top of a roof with his best friend talking about how his wife doesn't want to have sex anymore.

Although Megan enjoys sex for its own sake and predicts a declining sex life in her future marriage, it's not the presumed death of sex that frightens her about marriage: "It's living with a guy that freaks me out." Author Laura Sessions Stepp claims that today's young adults are so self-centered that they don't have time for "we," only for "me." They begrudge the energy that real relationships require. If that's true—and we suspect that's a journalistic overgeneralization—Megan should get together with Patrick. While so far he's slept with six women, Patrick informed us that he cannot imagine being married, and yet he too plans to do exactly that someday:

Well, I don't want to get married now. I guess, like, I do want to find a girl, but I just can't see myself being married. . . . [*And you can't see yourself getting married or being married because?*] I guess I just don't like the idea of being real tied down.

Patrick's current girlfriend is someone to hang out with, have sex with and generally enjoy the company of. Imagining more than that frightens him: "You sacrifice like so much stuff to be in a relationship that I guess I'm just not ready to make that huge sacrifice yet." Nor is 23-year-old Gabriela from Texas:

Once you get married, your responsibilities change. It's no longer, "Oh, I want to go to China next year. I have to save up money." No. Now you have to pay for the house—or you have a job and you can't just leave, because your husband can't get that day off. And things like that. It isn't just you, it becomes you and another person. [*So what do you think of that?*] I think that it's fine when I'm older. [*Which will be when?*] At least 30.

Devon, a 19-year-old from Washington, does most of his peers one better. Getting married—which he too eventually plans to do—is not just about "settling down" from the vibrant sex life of his late teen years. It signifies a death, albeit a scripted and necessary one. When asked what he wanted out of marriage, he said, "Just to have a good ending to my life, basically." Chen, a 20-year-old from Illinois, agrees: "I don't really plan on getting married for a while, or settling down for a while. I'd like to do all my living when I'm young. Like, save all the rest of life—falling in love and having a family— for later."

Such perspectives fly in the face of much empirical evidence about the satisfactions of marriage. That is, marriage tends to be good for emotional as well as sexual intimacy. Married people have access to more regular, long-term sex than do serially monogamous single adults. But that doesn't feel true to many emerging adults. Many perceive their parents as having modest or poor sex lives, and movie sex largely features singles.

Not every emerging adult pictures marriage as a necessary but noble death, of course. Elizabeth from New York likewise sees her twenties as about having fun. But her thirties (and marriage) would not be simply about settling down; they would be the time "when your life is really gonna kick into gear." We suspect that contemporary male and female perspectives on marriage, sexuality and fertility are indeed different, on average—that many men anticipate the institution as necessary and good for them, but with less enthusiasm for it than women express. For emerging-adult men, the single life is great and married life could be good. For women, the single life is good but married life is potentially better.

Ironically, after years of marriage, men tend to express slightly higher marital satisfaction than women. Moreover, marriage seems to be particularly important in civilizing men, turning their attention away from dangerous, antisocial or self-centered activities and toward the needs of a family. Married men drink less, fight less and are less likely to engage in criminal activity than their single peers. Married husbands and fathers are significantly more involved and affectionate with their wives and children than are men in cohabiting relationships (with or without children). The norms, status rewards and social support offered to men by marriage all combine to help them walk down the path of adult responsibility.

No wonder the idea of marriage can feel like a death to them. It is indeed the demise of unchecked self-centeredness and risk taking. Many men elect to delay it as long as seems feasible, marrying on average around age 28. That's hardly an old age, of course, but remember that age 28 is their median (or statistical middle) age at first marriage—meaning that half of all men marry then or later. Their decision to delay makes sense from a sexual economics perspective: they can access sex relatively easily outside of marriage, they can obtain many of the perceived benefits of marriage by cohabiting rather than marrying, they encounter few social pressures from peers to marry, they don't wish to marry someone who already has a child, and they want to experience the joys and freedoms of singleness as long as they can.

A good deal more is known about why people are not marrying in early adulthood than why some still do. And yet a minority marry young—and even more wish they were married—despite the fact that cohabitation and premarital sex are increasingly normative and socially acceptable. While the majority of emerging adults have no wish to be married at present, more than we expected actually harbor this desire. Just under 20 percent of unmarried young men and just under 30 percent of such women said they would like to be married now. Religious emerging adults are more apt to want to be married. And those emerging adults who are in a romantic or sexual relationship are nearly twice as likely to want to be married now than those who aren't in a relationship. Cohabiters are more than four times as likely to want to be married as those who are single. In fact, just under half of cohabiting young women and 40 percent of cohabiting young men said they'd like to be married right now.

Obviously, getting married introduces the risk of getting divorced. And that very specter remains a key mental barrier to relationship commitment among emerging adults. Six in ten unmarried men in their late twenties—who are already beginning to lag behind the median age at marriage—report that one of their biggest concerns about marriage is that it will end in divorce. Thus getting married young is increasingly frowned upon not just as unwise but as a moral mistake in which the odds of failure are perceived as too high to justify the risk.

This conventional wisdom is at work in journalist Paula Kamen's interview with a 24-year-old woman who claims she knows her boyfriend far better than her parents knew each other when they married. But would she marry him? No: "Like, are you stupid? Have you read the statistics lately?"

Emerging adults claim to be very stats-savvy about marriage. They are convinced that half of all marriages end in divorce, suggesting that the odds of anyone staying married amounts to a random flip of a coin. In reality, of course, divorce is hardly a random event. Some couples are more likely to divorce than others: people who didn't finish high school, people with little wealth or income, those who aren't religious, African Americans, couples who had children before they married, those who live in the South, those who cohabited before marrying and those who live in neighborhoods that have elevated crime and poverty rates. Lots of emerging adults have a few of these risk factors for divorce, but most don't have numerous factors.

And yet the compelling idea in the minds of many is that any given marriage's chance of success—however defined—is only 50–50, and worse if you marry early. In fact, most Americans who cite the statistics argument against considering marriage in early adulthood tend to misunderstand exactly what "early marriage" is. Most sociological evaluations of early marriage note that the link between age-at-marriage and divorce is strongest among those who marry as teenagers (in other words, before age 20). Marriages that begin at age 20, 21 or 22 are not nearly so likely to end in divorce as most Americans presume. Data from the 2002 National Study of Family Growth suggest that the probability of a marriage lasting at least ten years—hardly a long-term success, but a good benchmark of endurance—hinges not only on age-at-marriage but also on gender.

- Men and women who marry at or before age 20 are by far the worst bets for long-term success.
- The likelihood of a marriage (either a man's or a woman's) lasting ten years exceeds 60 percent beginning at age 21.
- Starting around age 23 (until at least 29), the likelihood of a woman's marriage lasting ten years improves by about 3 percent with each added year of waiting.
- However, no such linear "improvement" pattern appears among men.

The most significant leap in avoiding divorce occurs by simply waiting to marry until age 21. The difference in success between, say, marrying at 23 and marrying at 28 is just not as substantial as many emerging adults believe it to be. And among men, there are really no notable differences to speak of. While sociologist Tim Heaton finds that teenage marriage—and perhaps marriage among 20- and 21-year-olds—carries a higher risk of marital disruption, he too notes that "increasing the age at marriage from 22 to 30 would not have much effect on marital stability."

Still, to most of us, marital success is more than just managing to avoid a divorce. It's about having a good marriage. Sociologist Norval Glenn's study of marital success, in which "failure" is defined as either divorce or being in an unhappy marriage, reveals a curvilinear relationship between age at marriage and marital success. Women who marry before 20 or after 27 report lower marital success, while those marrying at ages 20–27 report higher levels of success. The pattern is a bit different for men. Men who marry before age 20 appear to have only a small chance at a successful marriage, while those who marry between ages 20 and 22 or after age 27 face less daunting but still acute challenges for a successful marriage. The best odds for men are in the middle, at ages 23–27. In a meta-analysis of five different surveys that explored marriage outcomes, researchers note that respondents who marry between ages 22 and 25 express greater marital satisfaction than do those who marry later.

In other words, the conventional wisdom about the obvious benefits to marital happiness of delayed marriage overreaches. Why it is that people who wait into their late twenties and thirties may experience less marital success rather than more is not entirely clear—and the finding itself is subject to debate. But it may be a byproduct of their greater rates of cohabitation. While relationship quality typically declines a bit over the course of marriage, the same process is believed to occur during cohabitation. If so, for many couples who marry at older ages, the "honeymoon" period of their relationship may have ended before they married, not after.

All these findings, however, are largely lost on emerging adults because of the compelling power of the popular notion in America that marriages carry a 50 percent risk of divorce. Consequently, marriage is considered off-limits to many emerging adults, especially those in the middle of college or building a career. Thus while research suggests that adults who are married and in monogamous relationships report more overall happiness and both more physical and more emotional satisfaction with sex, emerging adults don't believe it. Such claims just don't feel true. And why should they? When was the last time you watched a romantic film about a happily married 40-year-old couple?

Critical Thinking

1. What factors are important in mate selection? How have these factors changed over time?

2. Why do you think young adults are waiting to wed?

3. How do you think "settling down" affects your sex life?

4. What emotional sacrifices that come with commitment seem the most difficult to adjust to?

Create Central

www.mhhe.com/createcentral

Internet References

Love Is Respect
   www.loveisrespect.org

Relationships Australia
   www.relationships.org.au

MARK REGNERUS teaches at the University of Texas at Austin. **JEREMY UECKER** is a postdoctoral fellow at the Carolina Population Center at the University of North Carolina in Chapel Hill. This article is adapted from their book *Premarital Sex in America: How Young Americans Meet, Mate, and Think about Marrying,* just published by Oxford University Press. © Oxford University Press.

Prepared by: Patricia Hrusa Williams,
University of Maine at Farmington

Article

The End of Courtship?

ALEX WILLIAMS

Learning Outcomes

After reading this article, you will be able to:

- Identify how dating has changed due to generational, technological, societal, and economic factors.

- Understand the term "hookup culture."

- Explore the purpose and role of dating in relationship formation.

Maybe it was because they had met on OkCupid. But when the dark-eyed musician with artfully disheveled hair asked Shani Silver, a social media and blog manager in Philadelphia, out on a "date" Friday night, she was expecting at least a drink, one on one.

"At 10 p.m., I hadn't heard from him," said Ms. Silver, 30, who wore her favorite skinny black jeans. Finally, at 10:30, he sent a text message. "Hey, I'm at Pub & Kitchen, want to meet up for a drink or whatever?" he wrote, before adding, "I'm here with a bunch of friends from college."

Turned off, she fired back a text message, politely declining. But in retrospect, she might have adjusted her expectations. "The word 'date' should almost be stricken from the dictionary," Ms. Silver said. "Dating culture has evolved to a cycle of text messages, each one requiring the code-breaking skills of a cold war spy to interpret."

"It's one step below a date, and one step above a high-five," she added. Dinner at a romantic new bistro? Forget it. Women in their 20s these days are lucky to get a last-minute text to tag along. Raised in the age of so-called "hookup culture," millennials—who are reaching an age where they are starting to think about settling down—are subverting the rules of courtship.

Instead of dinner-and-a-movie, which seems as obsolete as a rotary phone, they rendezvous over phone texts, Facebook posts, instant messages and other "non-dates" that are leaving a generation confused about how to land a boyfriend or girlfriend.

"The new date is 'hanging out,'" said Denise Hewett, 24, an associate television producer in Manhattan, who is currently developing a show about this frustrating new romantic landscape. As one male friend recently told her: "I don't like to take girls out. I like to have them join in on what I'm doing—going to an event, a concert."

For evidence, look no further than "Girls," HBO's cultural weather vane for urban 20-somethings, where none of the main characters paired off in a manner that might count as courtship even a decade ago. In Sunday's opener for Season 2, Hannah (Lena Dunham) and Adam (Adam Driver), who last season forged a relationship by texting each other nude photos, are shown lying in bed, debating whether being each other's "main hang" constitutes actual dating.

The actors in the show seem to fare no better in real life, judging by a monologue by Zosia Mamet (who plays Shoshanna, the show's token virgin, since deflowered) at a benefit last fall at Joe's Pub in the East Village. Bemoaning an anything-goes dating culture, Ms. Mamet, 24, recalled an encounter with a boyfriend whose idea of a date was lounging in a hotel room while he "Lewis and Clarked" her body, then tried to stick her father, the playwright David Mamet, with the bill, according to a Huffington Post report.

Blame the much-documented rise of the "hookup culture" among young people, characterized by spontaneous, commitment-free (and often, alcohol-fueled) romantic flings. Many students today have never been on a traditional date, said Donna Freitas, who has taught religion and gender studies at Boston University and Hofstra and is the author of the forthcoming book, *The End of Sex: How Hookup Culture is Leaving a Generation Unhappy, Sexually Unfulfilled, and Confused About Intimacy.*

Hookups may be fine for college students, but what about after, when they start to build an adult life? The problem is that "young people today don't know how to get out of hookup culture," Ms. Freitas said. In interviews with students, many graduating seniors did not know the first thing about the basic mechanics of a traditional date. "They're wondering, 'If you like someone, how would you walk up to them? What would you say? What words would you use?'" Ms. Freitas said.

That may explain why "dates" among 20-somethings resemble college hookups, only without the dorms. Lindsay, a 25-year-old online marketing manager in Manhattan, recalled a recent non-date that had all the elegance of a keg stand (her last name is not used here to avoid professional embarrassment).

After an evening when she exchanged flirtatious glances with a bouncer at a Williamsburg nightclub, the bouncer invited her and her friends back to his apartment for whiskey and boxed macaroni and cheese. When she agreed, he gamely hoisted her over his shoulders, and, she recalled, "carried me home, my girlfriends and his bros in tow, where we danced around a tiny apartment to some MGMT and Ratatat remixes."

She spent the night at the apartment, which kicked off a cycle of weekly hookups, invariably preceded by a Thursday night text message from him saying, "hey babe, what are you up to this weekend?" (It petered out after four months.)

Relationship experts point to technology as another factor in the upending of dating culture.

Traditional courtship—picking up the telephone and asking someone on a date—required courage, strategic planning and a considerable investment of ego (by telephone, rejection stings). Not so with texting, e-mail, Twitter or other forms of "asynchronous communication," as techies call it. In the context of dating, it removes much of the need for charm; it's more like dropping a line in the water and hoping for a nibble.

"I've seen men put more effort into finding a movie to watch on Netflix Instant than composing a coherent message to ask a woman out," said Anna Goldfarb, 34, an author and blogger in Moorestown, N.J. A typical, annoying query is the last-minute: "Is anything fun going on tonight?" More annoying still are the men who simply ping, "Hey" or " 'sup."

"What does he think I'm doing?" she said. "I'm going to my friend's house to drink cheap white wine and watch episodes of 'Dance Moms' on demand."

Online dating services, which have gained mainstream acceptance, reinforce the hyper-casual approach by greatly expanding the number of potential dates. Faced with a never-ending stream of singles to choose from, many feel a sense of "FOMO" (fear of missing out), so they opt for a speed-dating approach—cycle through lots of suitors quickly.

That also means that suitors need to keep dates cheap and casual. A fancy dinner? You're lucky to get a drink.

"It's like online job applications, you can target many people simultaneously—it's like darts on a dart board, eventually one will stick," said Joshua Sky, 26, a branding coordinator in Manhattan, describing the attitudes of many singles in their 20s. The mass-mailer approach necessitates "cost-cutting, going to bars, meeting for coffee the first time," he added, "because you only want to invest in a mate you're going to get more out of."

If online dating sites have accelerated that trend, they are also taking advantage of it. New services like Grouper aren't so much about matchmaking as they are about group dates, bringing together two sets of friends for informal drinks.

The Gaggle, a dating commentary and advice site, helps young women navigate what its founders call the "post-dating" landscape, by championing "non-dates," including the "group non-date" and the "networking non-date." The site's founders, Jessica Massa and Rebecca Wiegand, say that in a world where "courtship" is quickly being redefined, women must recognize a flirtatious exchange of tweets, or a lingering glance at a company softball game, as legitimate opportunities for romance, too.

"Once women begin recognizing these more ambiguous settings as opportunities for romantic possibility," Ms. Massa said, "they really start seeing their love lives as much more intriguing and vibrant than they did when they were only judging themselves by how many 'dates' they had lined up."

There's another reason Web-enabled singles are rendering traditional dates obsolete. If the purpose of the first date was to learn about someone's background, education, politics and cultural tastes, Google and Facebook have taken care of that.

"We're all Ph.D.'s in Internet stalking these days," said Andrea Lavinthal, an author of the 2005 book *The Hookup Handbook*. "Online research makes the first date feel unnecessary, because it creates a false sense of intimacy. You think you know all the important stuff, when in reality, all you know is that they watch 'Homeland.' "

Dodgy economic prospects facing millennials also help torpedo the old, formal dating rituals. Faced with a lingering recession, a stagnant job market, and mountains of student debt, many young people—particularly victims of the "mancession"—simply cannot afford to invest a fancy dinner or show in someone they may or may not click with.

Further complicating matters is the changing economic power dynamic between the genders, as reflected by a number of studies in recent years, said Hanna Rosin, author of the recent book *The End of Men*.

A much-publicized study by Reach Advisors, a Boston-based market research group, found that the median income for young, single, childless women is higher than it is for men in many of the country's biggest cities (though men still dominate the highest-income jobs, according to James Chung, the company's president). This may be one reason it is not uncommon to walk into the hottest new West Village bistro on a Saturday night and find five smartly dressed young women dining together—the nearest man the waiter. Income equality, or superiority, for women muddles the old, male-dominated dating structure.

"Maybe there's still a sense of a man taking care of a woman, but our ideology is aligning with the reality of our finances," Ms. Rosin said. As a man, you might "convince yourself that dating is passé, a relic of a paternalistic era, because you can't afford to take a woman to a restaurant."

Many young men these days have no experience in formal dating and feel the need to be faintly ironic about the process— "to 'date' in quotation marks"—because they are "worried that they might offend women by dating in an old-fashioned way," Ms. Rosin said.

"It's hard to read a woman exactly right these days," she added. "You don't know whether, say, choosing the wine without asking her opinion will meet her yearnings for old-fashioned romance or strike her as boorish and macho."

Indeed, being too formal too early can send a message that a man is ready to get serious, which few men in their 20s are ready to do, said Lex Edness, a television writer in Los Angeles.

"A lot of men in their 20s are reluctant to take the girl to the French restaurant, or buy them jewelry, because those steps tend to lead to 'eventually, we're going to get married,'" Mr. Edness, 27, said. In a tight economy, where everyone is grinding away to build a career, most men cannot fathom supporting a family until at least 30 or 35, he said.

"So it's a lot easier to meet people on an even playing field, in casual dating," he said. "The stakes are lower."

Even in an era of ingrained ambivalence about gender roles, however, some women keep the old dating traditions alive by refusing to accept anything less.

Cheryl Yeoh, a tech entrepreneur in San Francisco, said that she has been on many formal dates of late—plays, fancy restaurants. One suitor even presented her with red roses. For her, the old traditions are alive simply because she refuses to put up with anything less. She generally refuses to go on any date that is not set up a week in advance, involving a degree of forethought.

"If he really wants you," Ms. Yeoh, 29, said, "he has to put in some effort."

Critical Thinking

1. Is courtship dead as the article suggests? Why or why not?
2. What is the purpose of dating?
3. How should the term "date" be defined?
4. What are the advantages and disadvantages of the post-dating or non-date culture? Does this culture promote or undermine the development of committed relationships?

Create Central

www.mhhe.com/createcentral

Internet References

Love Is Respect
www.loveisrespect.org
Relationships Australia
www.relationships.org.au

Article   Prepared by: Patricia Hrusa Williams,
                                         University of Maine at Farmington

You Got Your Sperm Where?

Tony Dokoupil

Learning Outcomes

After reading this article, you will be able to:

- Define reproductive terms including natural insemination and artificial insemination.

- Understand the reasons sperm donors offer sperm to individuals and couples trying to conceive.

- Recognize some of the ethical, political, social, medical, and family dilemmas created by reproductive technology and sperm donation.

For months, Beth Gardner and her wife, Nicole, had been looking for someone to help them conceive. They began with sperm banks, which have donors of almost every background, searchable by religion, ancestry, even the celebrity they most resemble. But the couple balked at the prices—at least $2,000 for the sperm alone—and the fact that most donors were anonymous; they wanted their child to have the option to one day know his or her father. So in the summer of 2010, at home with their two dogs and three cats, Beth and Nicole typed these words into a search engine: "free sperm donor."

A few clicks later, the couple slid into an online underground, a mishmash of personal ads, open forums, and members-only websites for women seeking sperm—and men giving it away. Most donors pledge to verify their health and relinquish parental rights, much like regular sperm-bank donors. But unlike their mainstream counterparts, these men don't get paid. They're also willing to reveal their identities and allow any future offspring to contact them. Many of the men say they do it out of altruism, but some also talk unabashedly of kinky sex and spreading their gene pool.

Curious, Beth and Nicole posted to a Yahoo Group, and within days they had more than a dozen suitors. "We got some weirdos," says Beth, a 35-year-old tech professional near San Diego. But most of the donors were "very nice and obviously well educated." After careful vetting—consisting of a home-made questionnaire, interviews, reference checks, and STD tests—the couple settled on a 30-something professional and arranged the donation.

Like most women in search of free sperm, Beth and Nicole asked for artificial insemination, or AI. As opposed to natural insemination (code for actual sex), AI typically involves injecting fresh sperm into the vagina, or loading it into a latex cup that fits on the cervix. Beth and Nicole had to work around three people's schedules and an ovulation calendar, so the venues at which they met their donor had a saucy impromptu feel: a hotel, the back of the couple's SUV, a camper trailer, a Starbucks bathroom. At Starbucks, the donor ejaculated in the bathroom in private, exited, and handed the sperm-filled latex cup to Nicole, who in turn entered the bathroom and attached the cup to her cervix. As nature took its course, the three sat down for coffee together. "It wasn't my highest moment," says Beth. They didn't conceive.

The couple is trying again with a new donor—and Beth has become a fervent believer in the strategy. In January, she launched the Free Sperm Donor Registry (FSDR), a sleek, user-friendly portal that works kind of like a dating site, only the women are listed as "recipients" and men as "donors." The homepage quotes Ralph Waldo Emerson: "The only gift is a portion of thyself." Six months in, FSDR has more than 2,000 members, including about 400 donors, and claims a dozen pregnancies. The first live birth is expected this fall.

Reproductive medicine is as close to miracle work as humans can muster: it has supplemented the stork with the syringe, creating thousands of new lives annually where none seemed possible. But in lifting the fog around infertility, doctors have moved nature's most intimate act deeper into the lab, and created a population of prospective parents—straight, gay, single, and married—who crave a more human connection. That need is now being met by sites like FSDR, which joins a global boom in the exchange of free, fresh sperm between strangers.

At least six Yahoo Groups, three Google sites, and about a dozen fee-based websites are dedicated to the cause. Most of them are in the United Kingdom, Canada, and Australia, where sperm banks have seen donations drop in the wake of recent laws that limit fees and, in some cases, forbid anonymity. The donor pool is still large in the U.S., where college kids can make as much as $12,000 a year from sperm banks for anonymous twice-weekly donations.

But sperm banks, though regulated by the Food and Drug Administration, carry risk. In recent years sperm with a host of serious diseases and disorders has been sold to hundreds of women, according to medical journals and other published reports. Earlier this year ABC News identified at least 24 donor-children whose father had a rare aorta defect that could potentially kill his offspring at any minute. And in September, *The New York Times* reported on sperm banks' creating 100-kid clusters around a single donor, raising questions about not only disease, but accidental incest.

Cost is also a concern. In many states, insurance won't cover donor insemination unless a woman can show that she hasn't been able to get pregnant. This makes it hard for lesbian couples and single women who don't have male partners. And all couples face insurance caps that can mean thousands of dollars in out-of-pocket pay.

Many women also believe their donor-conceived children have a right to know their fathers, something most sperm banks have resisted, fearing such openness would scare off potential donors. Even banks that do reveal dads' identities will do so only when a child turns 18.

As the first generation of donor-kids come of age, a growing number are expressing frustration at this closed-door policy. Confessions of a Cryokid and Anonymous Us are among the websites where they come to vent, airing unhappiness at feeling "half-adopted" and aching at the thought that their fathers could be anyone. "The system is severely broken," says Wendy Kramer, founder of the Donor Sibling Registry, a website that unites kids who have the same donor-fathers.

Of course, the market for free sperm raises its own set of questions. What if a donor sues for custody? What if he lies about an STD? Is he a potential threat to public health? What if his real motive is sex—and would that even matter? Just who are these guys anyway?

To find out, I registered at FSDR as a "just looking" member and spent two months following forum discussions, participating in chats, surfing through profiles, and interviewing more than a dozen donors and recipients. I also contacted donors who have set up personal websites or advertised on other sites. What I found was a universe that's often more lascivious than a Nicholson Baker novel, but somehow less bizarre and more relatable. Far from being overrun by sex-crazed "sperminators" and "desperate girls," the way British tabloids have portrayed the business, most of what I found was mundanely human.

Many of the women want to reproduce on their own terms, while they still can. Some have had miscarriages; others are widowed; still others, divorced. Some say they got pregnant when they were much younger and gave up the baby or aborted it, and now want another chance. Others have been busy with careers. Hope, a single 43-year-old zoologist, echoes most FSDR searchers when she says, "I really want to have a child, and I want to give that child the best shot at having a good life, which is why I chose this route."

As with traditional sperm banks, most of FSDR's users are lesbian couples or would-be single mothers. But the site does have an active cohort of straight pairs and married women, like a 37-year-old homemaker near Columbus, Ohio, who gave her name as Wendy. She says on a forum post that her husband—whose sperm count was diminished by a childhood case of the mumps—interviewed prospective donors with her. His

one condition: AI only. "It seems more 'our' baby if sex is not involved," she recalls him saying. Their son is due in January.

Donors on FSDR are a bawdier mix of high intentions and caveman dreams. One donor, whom Carissa, a 38-year-old divorcée in Fargo, N.D., was about to invite over for a "natural insemination" session, spooked her. "He wanted me to yell, 'Make me pregnant!'" during sex, she says.

It's a telling detail. Many donors say they are motivated not by sex so much as a desire to spawn as many children as possible. "I actually have little interest in even a stone-cold fox if she isn't going to get pregnant," says Ray, a 38-year-old who declined to give his real name. Ray, who already had two kids with his wife and claims to have two more via one-night stands, started donating sperm in 2009. He prefers to donate the natural way, which he says has a higher chance of success than AI (it doesn't), and he boasts of six births and six current pregnancies in attempts with about 40 different women. "I guess in some ways, helping lesbians, I am like an astronaut of inner space," he says, "going where no man has gone before."

One of the men who responded to Beth and Nicole, a married 29-year-old, said his IQ was in the 99.8th percentile ("note: results available") and said he would like to "propagate my genes, and help support the society of tomorrow by combating dysgenic reproductive trends." Translation: make babies as smart as he is. Down a few pegs on the pomposity scale, there's "Mongol," a 31-year-old Canadian who donates AI-style on both sides of the border. He arrives prepared, with a porn-loaded BlackBerry, headphones (to preserve the tranquillity of the moment), Hitachi-brand penis massager, and likes "the whole idea of having people out there related to you."

It's a motivation that flummoxes some sex researchers. Rene Almeling, a sociologist at Yale University and the author of a new study of the fertility market, *Sex Cells*, says that among the 20 sperm-bank donors she interviewed, the most common motives were money, spreading "amazing genes," as one guy put it, and helping women conceive. University of Nevada, Las Vegas, anthropologist Peter Gray, coauthor of *Fatherhood*, about the evolution of paternal behavior, says this drive to propagate reminds him of the ancient khan men of Mongolia—and of Moulay Ismail, the 17th-century emperor of Morocco—men who fathered as many as a thousand children, parenting none of them. "I'll have to think about this a bit," he says.

As the market for free sperm grows, regulators are keeping a watchful eye. Last December, Canada's public-health department issued an "information update," noting the rise of free-sperm websites and warning that "the distribution of fresh semen [for assisted conception] is prohibited." In the U.S., the FDA recently targeted at least one donor, citing his failure to comply with a 2005 law that requires donors to undergo STD and communicable-disease tests, reviewed by doctors, within seven days of every donation. (Commercial sperm banks use frozen sperm and test donors at the beginning and end of a six-month quarantine.) The case has emerged as a legal challenge for the alternative world, potentially slowing the market, since such tests can run up to $10,000, making donations cost-prohibitive.

It began in December 2006, when Trent Arsenault, now 36 and a bachelor outside San Francisco, began offering his sperm through Trentdonor.org, a website bedecked with shots of Arsenault as a cute toddler and hunky outdoorsman. Tall and blond, Arsenault works as an engineer at a tech company and is a former Naval Academy midshipman (he dropped out to move to Silicon Valley). His qualifications might make a sperm bank drool. But he prefers to work independently, he says, having already donated to about 50 women, mostly Bay Area lesbians. Perhaps thanks in part to his twice-daily "fertility smoothies" (a blend of blueberries, almonds, and other vitamin-rich fare), he has sired at least 10 children, he says.

His prospects came to a halt in September 2010, when FDA agents knocked on the door of his 700-square-foot bachelor pad. They interviewed him in his bedroom, and collected medical records and other material related to how he "recovers and distributes semen," according to the FDA investigation. The tone was cordial, Arsenault recalls. He even wrote a thank-you letter to the agency, complimenting "the professional and courteous attitude" of its agents.

But the following month, there came another knock on the door, this time from local police delivering an FDA order to "cease manufacture" of sperm, the first such order leveled against an individual citizen, according to a search of government records. Per the order, the agency considers Arsenault to be essentially a one-man sperm bank, referring to him as a "firm," and alleging that he "does not provide adequate protections against communicable diseases." If he engages in the "recovery, processing, storage, labeling, packaging, or distribution" of sperm, he faces a $100,000 fine and a year in prison. "I saved the FDA letter" Arsenault says. "It may be worth something someday on eBay."

In some ways, Arsenault is like other guys who are giving away their sperm, "fulfilling a needed role as women realize that anonymous biological fathers often deprive their offspring [of] a needed identity," as he put it in a letter to the FDA.

But he also finds the work gratifying in its own right. His only sexual activity, he says, involves masturbating into a cup and handing off the cup. "I describe myself as donorsexual," he says, "so my sexual activity is limited to donation." He jokes that in a few years he'll be "the 40-year-old virgin with 15 kids." He's appealed the FDA ruling on the grounds that free sperm donation is a form of sex, and thus not subject to government interference. The case is under internal agency review as officials decide whether Arsenault is trying to "skirt the law," as the FDA's lawyers have argued in documents sent to Arsenault, or if free sperm donation should be protected as a private sexual matter. The FDA declined to comment on the case.

Any attempt to limit private sperm donation is "preposterous," says Beth Gardner, the FSDR founder. "If it's legal to go to a bar, get drunk, and sleep with a random stranger, then it can't possibly be illegal to provide clean, healthy sperm in a cup." Still, she's the first to admit that not all donors are professional, and not all recipients make the most informed choices. She hopes FSDR will help change that, which is why it prohibits nudity, dirty talk, cruising for casual sex, and any behavior that other members deem harassing or inappropriate. There are also testimonials, how-to articles, cost comparisons, and legal materials.

Now Gardner says she has plans for expansion, adding an egg-donor section and recruiting bloggers. She may change the name to the Known Donor Registry because it's more "expansive." "The site is at the point now where I need to take it to the next level," she says. In August, page views topped more than 2 million—and, like its users, Gardner only hopes they'll multiply.

As for Arsenault, while he waits to hear about his reproductive future, he is enjoying the fruits of his past, posting pictures of his babies, and keeping up an active relationship with the five or six families who have requested one so far. Last month he visited with Keri and Amber Pigott-Robertson, a 30-something lesbian couple in Modesto, Calif., who found Arsenault through a Google search in 2009 and now have a 1-year-old daughter via his donation.

"When he saw her for the first time, his face just lit up," says Amber, who made peach pie for the occasion. "He was a perfect match. He gave us what we had been longing for, what we felt would complete us. So there's no expressing how much gratitude I have for him. People like Trent come once in a lifetime."

Critical Thinking

1. Describe the difference between natural and artificial insemination.
2. What are some reasons that a man may have for donating his sperm for free?
3. Describe some challenges or ethical dilemmas that may be created when individuals and couples become pregnant via serial sperm donors.
4. Should men be able to offer their sperm for free to those hoping to conceive? Why or why not?

Create Central

www.mhhe.com/createcentral

Internet References

The March of Dimes
　www.marchofdimes.com
Society for Assisted Reproductive Technology
　www.sart.org
Adelaide Center for Bioethics and Culture
　www.bioethics.org.au

Article   Prepared by: Patricia Hrusa Williams,
                                             University of Maine at Farmington

Getting It Right from the Start
The Case for Early Parenthood Education

Thomas G. Sticht

Learning Outcomes

After reading this article, you will be able to:

- List parental behaviors associated with school readiness and success.
- Identify core skills which may be taught as part of early parenting education efforts.

One hundred fifty-three thousand words per week. That's the difference between the 215,000 words per week that the average child in a privileged home hears and the 62,000 words per week that the average child in a family on welfare hears. I'll explain the research behind these numbers later; for now, just consider how staggering the difference is. And consider the implications. Hearing language is the first step in learning to read and write and make sense of the world.

The language gap that results in the achievement gap begins at home. Schools can and should do their part to close this gap, but parents, by reading to their children and interacting with them in positive and encouraging ways, need to do their part, too.

The idea that families need to provide enriching educational activities is not new. In 1908, Edmund Burke Huey, regarded as "one of the foremost leaders" in educating children with learning disabilities,[1] wrote, "The school of the future will have as one of its important duties the instruction of parents in the means of assisting the child's natural learning in the home."[2] This insight was just one of many in his classic work *The Psychology and Pedagogy of Reading*, a 500-page book so highly regarded that it was reprinted by the MIT Press in 1968 and again by the International Reading Association in 2009.

Today, a substantial body of scientific evidence supports Huey's call for the instruction of parents in the means of improving children's learning at home, and therefore their learning at school. Much of this evidence comes from the best research in early childhood education and, in particular one recurring finding: the most effective early childhood education programs include *early parenthood education*. The results of studies of major early childhood education programs suggest that some of the long-term academic and social outcomes of early childhood education result not so much from the direct education of the children, but rather from education provided to highly disadvantaged parents. Changes in parenting help explain why relatively short-term education programs for children could sustain them through school, and into adulthood. Better parenting provides a long-term educational intervention for children.

Before diving into the relevant research from effective early childhood programs, let's take a closer look at why Huey concluded that schools would need to teach many parents to facilitate learning at home. As Huey understood—and cognitive scientists have since demonstrated—literacy follows oracy, so parents who foster their young children's listening, speaking, vocabulary and knowledge are also fostering success in school.

The Intergenerational Transfer of Literacy

In *The Psychology and Pedagogy of Reading*, Huey reflected on the role of speech in reading. Drawing from the scholarly literature on reading and from teachers' observations, he concluded, "The child comes to his first reader with his habits of spoken language fairly well formed, and these habits grow more deeply set with every year. His meanings inhere in this spoken language and belong but secondarily to the printed symbols."[3]

Sixty-six years later, my colleagues and I recast Huey's statement as a simple three-part model of the development of literacy. We assert that:

1. People are born with information processing skills and the capacity for storing knowledge in memory.
2. By means of these information processing skills, when exposed to oral language people acquire the oracy skills of listening comprehension and speech, and use both to construct meaning and store knowledge.
3. With proper support in literate societies, people acquire the skills of reading and writing, which draw upon the same language and knowledge base that is used for listening and speaking.[4]

My colleagues and I call this the oracy-to-literacy transfer effect.

Of course, we developed this simple transfer model not based on Huey alone, but on a large body of studies. For example, the model is supported by research conducted in the 1960s by Walter Loban, whose longitudinal work on the development of language and literacy has been internationally recognized. He assessed children's oral language ability before they started first grade, and then tested their reading skills at grades 4 through 8. He found that those with high oral language skills before the first grade became high-ability readers and those with low oral language skills became low-ability readers.

Some 20 years later, Loban's work on the relationship of oracy to literacy was greatly expanded by researchers Betty Hart and Todd Risley.[5] Over two and a half years, they observed and recorded 42 families for an hour each month. At the beginning of the study, each family had a 7- to 9-month-old infant. Knowing that preschoolers from low-income families tended to have smaller vocabularies and overall weaker oral language than their peers from higher-income families, they wanted to see what happened before preschool—to determine the quality and quantity of language to which these children were exposed as they learned to talk. The 42 families spanned the income range, with 13 professional families, 23 working-class families, and 6 families on welfare. It took years to transcribe the tapes and analyze the data, but eventually they found extraordinary differences in the extent to which parents spoke to their children. Hart and Risley wrote, "Simply in words heard, the average child on welfare was having half as much experience per hour (616 words per hour) as the average working-class child (1,251 words per hour) and less than one-third that of the average child in a professional family (2,153 words per hour)."[6] Extrapolating these hourly findings to weekly totals (assuming 100 hours awake per week), they came up with the numbers with which I opened this article: 215,000 words heard by children in professional families and 62,000 words in welfare families. The weekly total for working class families was 125,000. Extrapolating these hourly findings across early childhood, they estimated that from birth to age 4, welfare children would experience some 13 million words of oral language, working-class children, around 26 million words; and children of professional parents, some 45 million words!

According to the oracy-to-literacy transfer effect, the children hearing the most words would develop the largest oral language vocabulary, and those hearing the fewest words would develop the smallest oral language vocabulary. Furthermore, once these children learn to decode, their oral vocabulary would determine their reading and writing vocabulary. Indeed, when Hart and Risley tested the children's oral vocabulary at age 3, the professional, working-class, and welfare children ranked highest, middle, and lowest, respectively. Six years later, 29 of the children were tested again, and their oral language skills at age 3 were highly correlated with their reading vocabulary and comprehension in third grade.

While we may hope that the early oral language gap would be closed in the first few years in school, the fact is that children spend very little time in school. The primary influence on their language development remains the home environment.

Moreover, by the time children start school—even preschool—the differences in the language experiences they have had are staggering. Huey was right: many parents need to be taught how to support learning at home.

The strong oracy-to-literacy transfer effects found by Loban and Hart and Risley (and many others) explain to a large extent the ubiquitous finding in industrialized nations that parents' educational level is a strong predictor of children's literacy level. Significantly, the oracy-to-literacy transfer effect suggests that it is not parents' education level per se that produces an intergenerational transfer of literacy, but rather what better-educated parents *do* with their children using oral language and literacy skills.

Discussing the ways children of educated parents may acquire a strong foundation for reading, Huey wrote: "The secret of it all lies in the parents' reading aloud to and with the child. . . . The child should long continue to hear far more reading than he does for himself. . . . Oral work is certain to displace much of the present written work in the school of the future, at least in the earlier years; and at home there is scarcely a more commendable and useful practice than that of reading much of good things aloud to the children."[7] Decades of research support Huey yet again: on average, children's listening comprehension surpasses their reading comprehension until seventh or eighth grade. Especially in the early years, and continuing up through middle school (and for some students, even into high school), learning through oral work is indeed essential.[8]

Listening to text read aloud is especially important: researchers have found that texts use much more advanced vocabulary and grammar than spoken language. A recent summary that research stated, "Regardless of the source or situation and without exception, the richness and complexity of the words used in the oral language samples paled in comparison with the written texts. Indeed, of all the oral language samples evaluated, the only one that exceeded even preschool books in lexical range was expert witness testimony."[9] Addressing the extraordinary differences that Hart and Risley found would not be as easy as encouraging low-income parents to read and speak with their children as much as possible—but that would be a good start.

The Intergenerational Transfer of Character

Literacy is not the only essential ability that is strongly influenced by parenting; character traits like motivation and persistence are also transferred from one generation to the next. And, like literacy, these traits have a substantial impact on student achievement. For example, researchers have found that "Parental beliefs, values, aspirations, and attitudes . . . are very important, as is parental well-being. . . . Parenting skills in terms of warmth, discipline, and educational behaviours are all major factors in the formation of school success."[10]

Hart and Risley's research provides some insights into how parents differ along these lines: not only were there large differences in the *quantity* of oral language in the 42 homes, but also in the *quality* of the language. Children in professional families heard far more encouraging comments, and far fewer discouraging ones, than children in families on welfare. Specifically, in a professional family, the average child heard 32 affirmatives and 5 prohibitions per hour; in a working-class family, the average child heard 12 affirmatives and 7 prohibitions per hour; and in a welfare family, the average child heard 5 affirmatives and 11 prohibitions per hour. Recalling the data on the quantity of language, we can see that children in professional families heard a lot of language—and much of it was positive. But children in welfare families heard relatively little language—and much of it was negative. These findings suggest that the feelings conveyed through oral language may influence the development of noncognitive traits such as motivation and persistence in learning.

While at first it may seem that intervening in the emotional aspects of parenting would be quite a challenge, numerous studies have found that the major outcome of adult basic education is improved noncognitive skills. Almost universally, studies of adult basic education report that adults feel better about themselves, overcome learned helplessness, and feel more motivated to succeed in life; importantly, these positive noncognitive skills often modify adults' behaviors with their children.[11]

In research with Wider Opportunities for Women (WOW), for example, Sandra Van Fossen (a research associate at WOW) and I found that mothers enrolled in basic-skills programs reported that they spoke with their children about school more, read to them more, took them to the library more, and so forth. In one visit to a single mother's home, the mother's second-grader said, "I do my homework just like Mommy" and thrust his homework into the researcher's hand. This type of emotional, noncognitive development in the child was obtained for free as a spinoff of an adult basic education program.[12]

Adult education focused on improving parenting can also be effective. Longitudinal research on the Prenatal/Early Infancy Project, for example, found many benefits for families in the control (nonintervention) group. This project studied two interventions, one more intensive than the other. In the more intensive (and more effective) intervention, young women were visited at home by nurses from about midway through their pregnancy until their children were 2 years old. The nurses addressed everything from prenatal care to child-rearing to employment. When the children were 15 years old, they were less likely to have been arrested, abused, or neglected. Similarly, their mothers were less likely to have been arrested, convicted, or incarcerated, and they reported many fewer episodes of impairment due to alcohol or drugs. Their mothers also had fewer subsequent pregnancies and went a longer time between births, which means they could devote greater attention to each child.[13]

Particularly strong benefits for character development have been found when child and parent education are combined. For instance, the HighScope Perry Preschool Program, a carefully studied preschool program that provided weekly home visits, mainly had character—not cognitive—benefits. Discussing Perry and similar programs, Nobel Prize-winning economist James J. Heckman downplayed their effects on children's cognitive skills, stating, "Enriched early intervention programs targeted to disadvantaged children have had their biggest effect on noncognitive skills: motivation, self-control, and time preference. . . . Noncognitive skills are powerfully predictive of a number of socioeconomic measures (crime, teenage pregnancy, education, and the like). . . . Kids in the Perry Preschool Program . . . are much more successful than similar kids without intervention even though their IQs are no higher. And the same is true of many such interventions."[14]

Parenting Power in Preschool Programs

While parent education appears to be an important part of highly effective early childhood programs, such programs have many components, and I have found no research that isolates the effects of the parent education component (or any other single component).* Yet, there are indications that some of the long-term cost-beneficial effects of early childhood programs result in part from the effects that the programs had on changing how the parents interacted with their children.

In a report for the Economic Policy Institute, Robert Lynch (an economics professor at Washington College) provided an analysis of several carefully studied early childhood education programs and concluded that they produce a considerable return on investment.[15] He found that investments in high-quality early childhood education programs consistently generated more than a $3 return for every $1 invested.

As an example of possible early parenthood education activities that may have influenced the preschool children's development, Lynch reports that in the well-known Abecedarian Early Childhood Intervention program, parents were given special educational materials to help them engage in educational activities with their children. Follow-up research showed that the mothers in the intervention achieved more education than those in the comparison group, and fewer of the intervention mothers had additional births than did the comparison mothers (which, again, means more time is available for each child).

The important role of parent education is supported by Lawrence Schweinhart, who is the president of the HighScope Educational Research Foundation and was the lead researcher on the Perry Preschool longitudinal study. Discussing what he sees as the key ingredients for achieving a good return on investment from early childhood programs, he recommended that such programs "have teachers spend substantial amounts of time with parents, educating them about their children's development and how they can extend classroom learning experiences into their homes." In addition, he noted, "All the programs in the long-term studies worked with parents. In fact, in the HighScope Perry Preschool program, teachers spent half their work time engaged in such activities."[16] This strongly suggests that some of the success of early childhood programs maybe dependent upon educational activities to improve the skills and knowledge of parents.

---

*Such research would be very helpful to program developers, but it is time consuming and expensive. To determine the effectiveness of each program component, a whole series of studies would have to be done in which one component at a time is changed.

It has been more than 100 years since Huey set forth a clear and effective path for supporting learning in the home. Educating those who are, or are about to become, parents offers the possibility of obtaining payoffs for future generations before conception occurs. And, if we focus our limited resources on reaching first-time parents, then one "dose" of parenting education could also benefit succeeding children. Given the intergenerational nature of literacy and character, that one dose could even benefit future generations. It is time that we move from thinking about education in terms of each child, to thinking about education from a multiple-lifecycles perspective. If we are really serious about attaining long-lasting increases in student achievement, we should look to both the school and the home: early parenthood education should take its place alongside early childhood education as a primary means of getting education right from the start.

Notes

1. See the "Psychological Bulletin" comment in John B. Carroll's foreword to Edmund Burke Huey, *The Psychology and Pedagogy of Reading* (Cambridge, MA: MIT Press, 1968).

2. Edmund Burke Huey, *The Psychology and Pedagogy of Reading* (Newark, DE: International Reading Association, 2009), 206.

3. Huey, *The Psychology and Pedagogy of Reading* (2009), 81.

4. Thomas G. Sticht, Lawrence J. Beck, Robert N. Hauke, Glenn M. Kleiman, and James H. James, *Auding and Reading: A Developmental Model* (Alexandria, VA: Human Resources Research Organization, 1974).

5. Betty Hart and Todd R. Risley, *Meaningful Differences in the Everyday Experiences of Young American Children* (Baltimore, MD: Paul H. Brookes Publishing, 1995).

6. Betty Hart and Todd R. Risley, "The Early Catastrophe: The 30 Million Word Gap," *American Educator* 27, no.1 (Spring 2003): 8.

7. Huey, *The Psychology and Pedagogy of Reading* (2009), 220–221.

8. Andrew Biemiller, "Oral Comprehension Sets the Ceiling on Reading Comprehension," *American Educator* 27, no. 1 (Spring 2003): 23.

9. Marilyn Jager Adams, "Advancing Our Students' Language and Literacy: The Challenge of Complex Texts," *American Educator* 34, no. 4 (Winter 2010–2011): 5.

10. Leon Feinstein, Kathryn Duckworth, and Ricardo Sabates, *A Model of the Inter-Generational Transmission of Educational Success* (London: Centre for Research on the Wider Benefits of Learning, 2004).

11. See, for example, Parkdale Project Read, *"I've Opened Up": Exploring Learners' Perspectives on Progress* (Toronto, ON:

2006), accessed April 15, 2011, www.nald.ca/library/research/openup/cover.htm; and Mary Beth Bingman and Olga Ebert, *"I've Come a Long Way": Learner-Identified Outcomes of Participation in Adult Literacy Programs* (Cambridge, MA: National Center for the Study of Adult Learning and Literacy, February 2000).

12. Sandra Van Fossen and Thomas G. Sticht, *Teach the Mother and Reach the Child: Results of the Intergenerational Literacy Action Research Project of Wider Opportunities for Women* (Washington, DC: Wider Opportunities for Women, July 1991).

13. Robert Lynch, *Exceptional Returns: Economic, Fiscal, and Social Benefits of Investment in Early Childhood Development* (Washington, DC: Economic Policy Institute, 2004).

14. James Heckman, interview by Douglas Clement, editor of *The Region,* Federal Reserve Bank of Minneapolis, June 2005.

15. Lynch, *Exceptional Returns.*

16. Lawrence J. Schweinhart, "Creating the Best Prekindergartens: Five Ingredients for Long-Term Effects and Returns on Investment," in *The Obama Education Plan: An Education Week Guide* (San Francisco: Jossey-Bass, 2009), 21–25.

Critical Thinking

1. What aspects of the home environment are important to future success in school?

2. What information do first-time parents need in order to help promote their children's literacy skills and traits important to later school success?

3. Do you think early parent education should be mandatory for all first-time parents? Why or why not?

Create Central

www.mhhe.com/createcentral

Internet References

Zero to Three
    www.zerotothree.org
National Association for the Education of Young Children
    www.naeyc.org

THOMAS G. STICHT is an international consultant in adult education, recipient of UNESCO's Mahatma Gandhi Medal, and author of hundreds of scholarly articles. Previously, he has served as the president of Applied Behavioral and Cognitive Sciences Inc., associate director of the National Institute of Education, visiting associate professor at the Harvard Graduate School of Education, and visiting noted scholar at the University of British Columbia in Canada.

Unit 3

UNIT

Prepared by: Patricia Hrusa Williams,
University of Maine at Farmington

Family Relationships

And they lived happily ever after. . . . The romantic image conjured up by this well-known final line from fairy tales is not reflective of the reality of family life and relationship maintenance. The belief that somehow love alone should carry us through is pervasive. In reality, maintaining a relationship takes dedication, hard work, and commitment.

We come into relationships, regardless of their nature, with fantasies about how things ought to be. Partners, spouses, parents, children, siblings, and others—all family members have at least some unrealistic expectations about each other. It is through the negotiation of their lives together that they come to work through these expectations and—hopefully—replace them with other, more realistic ones. By recognizing and making their own contributions to the family, members can set and attain realistic family goals. Tolerance, acceptance of differences, and effective communication skills can facilitate this process. Along the way, family members need to learn new skills and develop new habits of relating to each other. This will not be easy—and, try as they may, not everything will be controllable. Factors both inside and outside the family may impede their progress.

Even before we enter a marriage or other committed relationship, attitudes, standards, and beliefs influence our choices. Increasingly, choices include whether we should commit to such

a relationship in the first place. From the start of a committed relationship, the expectations both partners have of their relationship have an impact, and the need to negotiate differences is a constant factor. Adding a child to the family affects the lives of parents in ways that they could previously only imagine. Parenting is a complicated and often confusing process for which many of us have very little training or support. What's the "right" way to rear a child? There are a variety of different philosophies or approaches to parenting, many advocated through the popular media. We also have our own experiences of "being parented," which may influence our goals, choices, and ideals. These factors can all combine to make child rearing more difficult than it might otherwise have been. Other family relationships also evolve, and in our nuclear-family–focused culture, it is possible to forget that family relationships extend beyond those between spouses and parents and children.

This unit explores marital, parent–child, sibling, and intergenerational relationships within families. Among the topics explored are the characteristics of successful marriages, plural marriage, child-rearing philosophies, same-sex parenting, sibling relationships, and changes in parent–child relationships across the lifespan. A goal is to explore the diversity of structures and contexts in which couples, parents, children, and families develop and evolve.

Article

Prepared by: Patricia Hrusa Williams,
University of Maine at Farmington

Two Views of Marriage and the Falsity of the Choice between Them

JASON LEE STEORTS

Learning Outcomes

After reading this article, you will be able to:

- Identify the reasons for marriage in society.

- Understand legal considerations and perspectives in defining marriage.

- Explain the basis for opposition to gay marriage.

- Recognize the relationship between marriage and sexuality.

Our views about marriage are multifaceted, and the primary facets are two. On one hand, we think marriage has something to do with reproduction and its consequences; on the other, we think it has something to do with the experience of two people who are in love.

Opponents of same-sex marriage think the law should concern itself only with the first facet and must not define marriage other than in terms of its orientation toward procreation. I think the law has a legitimate interest in both facets and can reasonably address the public-policy considerations related to each.

I will call that position "traditionalist" according to which legal recognition of marriage should be restricted to unions of a man and a woman. The traditionalist holds that there is a pre-legal fact as to what marriage is, namely "comprehensive union" of two persons, and that only a "reproductive unit" can be a comprehensive union, although marriage qua comprehensive union is intrinsically valuable whether or not a couple reproduce. I use terms of Sherif Girgis and Robert P. George, both of Princeton, and Ryan T. Anderson, editor of *Public Discourse,* in their *Harvard Journal of Law and Public Policy* article "What Is Marriage?" They say that to exist as a person involves a bodily dimension as well as cognitive, volitional, emotional, etc. ones, and that any union which is not bodily will by that omission fail to be comprehensive. What unites the organs of a single person's body is their coordination toward achieving the biological purposes of the organism as a whole. When it comes to one such purpose—reproduction—the organism is naturally incomplete. Only a man and a woman, and not

two persons of the same sex, are able to join their bodies in such a way as to achieve this purpose.

Coitus achieves bodily union, traditionalists say, whether or not the couple intend to reproduce or are capable of reproduction. It is because any instance of coitus belongs to the kind of act that is reproductively oriented that the relationships of infertile couples, but not those of same-sex couples, are potentially marital. Traditionalists also say that it would be practically difficult and/or wrongly intrusive for the state to assure itself that a couple are fertile before marrying them.

Why does the law concern itself with marriage at all? A conservative might feel special force in the question, for a conservative wants the state at large removed from his life. The answer, as the editors of *National Review* have put it, is that the legal institution of marriage exists "to solve a problem that arises from sex between men and women but not from sex between partners of the same gender: what to do about its generativity." Sociology demonstrates that children are better off when raised by their two biological parents than when raised by single, cohabiting, or stepparents, although no methodologically rigorous research compares the former condition with that of being raised by two parents of the same sex. The norms of marriage—monogamy, fidelity, and thereby permanence—help bring it about that as many children as possible grow up with their biological parents. Legally recognizing marriage puts the force of the law behind the norms. It once did so by criminalizing behavior at odds with them and imposing a barrier to separation in the form of divorce. Today it is more permissive of liberty (libertinism?) and divorce, but its very existence reinforces the norms by focusing the public mind on the connection between sex, procreation, and marriage.

If the law called same-sex unions "marriages," it would obscure that connection and make the norms seem to have no purpose. Additionally, gay couples are statistically more likely to flout the norms than heterosexual ones, so we must worry that their inclusion would by example encourage rebellion.

Traditionalists see no injustice in excluding same-sex couples from the institution because to discriminate is to treat like cases differently, and same-sex couples, not being reproductive units, are unlike heterosexual ones. Same-sex couples are also mostly free to make whatever legal arrangements they wish concerning property, inheritance, medical care, etc. It is a hassle to make such arrangements piecemeal, and a same-sex couple is at greater risk not to have made them before times when they would be important, but some traditionalists meet this objection by endorsing civil unions.

I will call that position "revisionist" according to which the law should be willing to marry same-sex couples. The form of revisionism I will present agrees with traditionalism that there are pre-legal facts about what marriage is, but differs in its account of what the facts are and why the law should care about them.

The traditionalist finds a criterion of a certain intrinsic value in the simple fact that a married man and woman engage in the generative act. He cannot condition this value upon the *consequence* of reproduction, since he sees infertile heterosexual couples as candidates for marriage; nor can he condition it upon the *experience* of sexual intimacy as the bodily dimension of romantic love, since this would make candidates of same-sex couples. Contra this, the revisionist sees no difference of intrinsic value between coitus and the sexual acts of same-sex couples.

The revisionist may prosecute his view by challenging the traditionalist's claim that an infertile couple are a reproductive unit. A millennium or two ago, when the bodily means of reproduction were not well understood, every instance of coitus seemed to be of the same kind. But it is through instances that we see kinds, and we see more detail in the instances now, including physiological differences between fertile and infertile couples. These differences are natural facts no less than the macroscopic structures of sexual organs are natural facts, and when what is at issue is whether a couple are a reproductive unit, we will want our definition of that kind to overlap as precisely as it can with the facts about whether reproduction is possible. Confronted with the insistence that fertile and infertile couples are alike reproductive units, the revisionist might appropriate Bishop Butler's remark that "everything is what it is, and not another thing," and diagnose the traditionalist with descriptive myopia.

The more important point is that the traditionalist's "what it is" does not tell us why we should find value in "it." Let us ask the traditionalist: "Conceded, there are two kinds of sexual macro-structure, and a practice involving one of each that, depending on the instance, might or might not have the potential to generate children; would you now explain what good other than children or the hope or expectation of them, and other than the expression of a kind of love, depends on this practice?" Given that his judgment of value establishes no connection between the fact upon which it fixates and the experiences of human beings, what answer can the traditionalist make without turning his argument into a piece of dogma?

Against the traditionalist's "comprehensive union," the revisionist understands marriage as what I will call "maximal experiential union." This is two persons' sharing each other's lives—conceived not as the facts about their bodies plus the facts about their minds, but rather as the facts about their experienced unity of the two—as comprehensively and deeply as possible. It satisfies in the strongest way the desire to escape the condition of facing life alone. It necessarily involves, and is consummated by, sexual intimacy, for the reason Roger Scruton identifies in his essay "Sacrilege and Sacrament": "Sexual desire is not a desire for sensations. [Nor, I add, is it a desire for children, even if it is accompanied by that.] It is a desire for a person: and I mean a *person,* not his or her body conceived as an object in the physical world, but the person conceived as an incarnate subject, in whom the light of self-consciousness shines, and who confronts me eye to eye, and I to I."

Scruton thinks that, the sexes being different, the experience of homosexual desire is dissimilar—and, we are to assume, inferior—to the experience of heterosexual desire. This claim is separable from his insight about the nature of sexual desire, and I find it not very compelling. Presumably indeed the experience of homosexual desire is different from that of heterosexual desire, but this does not entail that the former is less directed toward or compatible with existential commitment, or that the categorical difference is greater than differences between couples of either category. No one can know for sure, since each of us is trapped in his own experience. But homosexual and heterosexual persons show the outward signs of finding in committed romantic love the same kind of value. If we grant that they do, we must conclude that the traditionalist indulges an untenable dualism about body and mind as these relate to value. He assigns to the body's reproductive function a fixed value for two classes of person between whom that function's fulfillment in experience differs greatly, yet for whom the value of sexual intimacy as the expression of love is the same. He thus conceptually detaches the body from the natural, body-with-mind reality in which a large class of human beings exist.

When a fertile couple have children, they realize an even greater intrinsic value than that of maximal experiential union as such, for they now share experiences with their children as well as sharing with each other the experience of generating and raising children. If one were free to choose to whom one is sexually attracted and with whom one falls in love, one could simply choose the greater value. But these are not choices, and for persons unattracted to the opposite sex, as for infertile persons, the greater value is not available. Depths of experiential union, and their corresponding categorical values, are lexically ordered such that any union of two persons who are in love is deeper than that of any two who are not, even if they have reproduced. This is so not just because lack of sexual attraction will undermine and destabilize a union, but more deeply because only in romantic relationships can persons fully and reciprocally share themselves.

The norms of marriage apply to maximal experiential union. If a couple's relationship is permanent, each party will share more of his or her life with the other than if they separate, and the expectation of permanence will give rise to a quality of no-holding-back.

Monogamy and fidelity contribute their own qualitative depth, thereby conducing to permanence. In a case of polygamy, polyamory, bigamy, or infidelity, at least one party holds part of himself in reserve for another no matter whom he is with just now, and because he might give himself more totally to anyone, his union with each is less than maximal. If they know this, it will probably dilute their disposition to give themselves fully to him.

It is only by deepening and enforcing experiential union that the norms achieve their child-welfare consequence. By ensuring that as many reproductive relationships as possible are maximal experiential unions, they ensure that as many children as possible are raised by their biological parents.

A final two norms. Maximal experiential unions should be of peers, for only peers can achieve mutual comprehension. One cannot form a maximal experiential union with another kind of animal or a child or a mentally impaired person.

Yet maximal experiential unions should be relationships of peers whose bodies/minds are complementary rather than overlapping. Part of what is stunting about facing life alone is the limitedness of one's resources of character and ability, and this is not helped by doubling up on what one has. This final norm goes some way toward explaining why incestuous relationships cannot easily attain the good of maximal experiential union. (There are independent and much stronger reasons, having to do with the nature of blood relations and the manner in which the intensity and possessiveness of sexual desire would destabilize them, to think incestuous relationships wrong or imprudent for the individuals themselves, as well as bad enough for society that the law should forbid them.)

What of the law? Has it any reason to concern itself with maximal experiential unions?

The revisionist, even if he is conservative, may say: The legal institution of marriage does not just protect children. It also protects the good of maximal experiential union. It does this by guaranteeing recognition of the couple as a couple in their commerce with the community. Sometimes this is not so important: *Will we get the couple discount at the dinner buffet?* But being in a maximal experiential union involves facing major life events jointly, even if this can mean no more than that one party makes decisions on the other's behalf, provides for the other's care, or, in the case of death, sees to it that the other's wishes are honored. Various social institutions play a role in deciding whether that is possible. We must ask whether, apart from considerations of child welfare, the state has any business requiring those institutions to recognize maximal experiential unions.

I think so. I think that even if human beings rose up fully formed out of lotus flowers, they would, if they felt romantic attraction and sexual desire, form maximal experiential unions and want the state to protect them. And if that is right, it is problematic—treating like cases differently, "separate but equal," discrimination—for the law to recognize homosexual and infertile heterosexual couples differently, even if, as under a civil-union regime, the difference is only of name.

Let us now write our positive marriage law on a *tabula rasa.* How will the foregoing considerations of pre-legal realities guide us?

We have seen that monogamous same-sex unions possess a value equal in kind to that of monogamous infertile unions, and that the norms of marriage make sense for all maximal experiential unions—so there is no reason in principle not to include same-sex along with infertile couples. The traditionalist might remind us that because the sociology of gay communities involves higher-than-average disregard for the norms of marriage, including gay couples would set a bad example for straight ones. As decisive against this, consider, first, that many heterosexual couples also flout the norms, and there is no principled standard as to what statistical deviance qualifies a group for exclusion. Second, the direct cause of the harm we wish to prevent is not childless persons who set a bad example, but persons with children who follow it. Finally, the law may enforce the norms upon all married couples, whether they have reproduced or not, to whatever extent we deem justified by the child-welfare consideration.

Yet this seems needlessly coercive of those who have not reproduced. It is true that the norms make sense for them, but if they flout the norms and destroy their unions the only parties to suffer will be themselves. Perhaps we must pour out a measure of liberty on the altar of child welfare, but why not set up a two-tiered system instead?

In the first tier, we confer on any maximal experiential union a group of rights more or less equivalent to those in civil unions. With one step common to all, couples secure recognition of their relationships in the laws governing property, health care, and other important pre-legal institutions. Marriages in this tier will be relatively easy to dissolve, along the lines of no-fault divorce.

A couple automatically pass into the second tier if they have children, biologically their own or not. (When it becomes clear how same-sex parenting affects children, we will apply this knowledge precisely via our laws governing adoption and fertility treatments, bearing in mind in the adoptive case that there is no option for the child to be raised by his biological parents, and in the case of fertility treatments that a person who comes into existence under less than ideal conditions may nonetheless prefer to exist and be valuable in his existence.) In the second tier, couples are not able to divorce as easily as in the first; a demonstration of fault and/or counseling could be required, and perhaps we should roll back the sexual revolution still further. We need not decide here to what degree the law should enforce marital commitments for the sake of children, but whatever the answer, the law could and should apply it to marital commitments involving children.

The virtues of such system are as follows. First, it does justice to the multifacetedness of our views of marriage by recognizing its experiential in addition to its reproductive dimension and creating appropriate legal categories for each. The law becomes a more precise instrument. Second and relatedly, it becomes more just, for it now treats nonreproductive maximal experiential unions equally. Third, it directly and vividly reminds heterosexual couples to think about their potentially reproductive acts as such. Last, it does this while honoring in the first tier that desire for freedom which motivated the sexual revolution. Note that merely adducing the facts about child welfare does not decide the conflict between wanting to avoid these consequences and wanting to maximize liberty; nor is there any clear way to decide, since the value of liberty cannot be expressed in terms of consequences.

Some couples may decline to enter the institution for fear of the second tier, but a single-tiered system of the type traditionalists favor would confront the same problem. In both cases, the solution is to impose on unwed parents strict obligations concerning such things as child support, so that not getting married does not appreciably shield them from risk.

A tiered system would not oblige us to recognize polygamous or polyamorous relationships, because these are not maximal experiential unions. On the other hand, if there is value in polygamous relationships, polyamorous relationships, or relationships of any other type, if legal recognition of some kind is needed to protect that value, and if we can confer it without causing unacceptable harm, then we have no grounds to withhold it. But let us at all times discuss these things directly—noting, for example, that polygamous unions tend to be exploitative for reasons intrinsic to their hierarchical structure, and that polyamorous unions are both reproductive and unstable. Everything is what it is and not another thing. When the traditionalist asks, "Once you allow same-sex marriage, how will you disallow such-and-such?" we should challenge him to explain why he would disallow such-and-such. If he can, he will have answered his own question, and if he cannot it deserves no answer.

It is all but impossible to separate judgments about marriage from judgments about sexuality. It is true that the traditionalist argument can be made without presenting any claim as to the value of same-sex relationships, but the traditionalist nonetheless holds that a special value inheres in a relationship between two heterosexual persons who are infertile but in love that cannot inhere in a relationship between two persons of the same sex who are in love. That is *just* what the revisionist rejects. He sees unique intrinsic value in maximal experiential union as such, and regards parental maximal experiential union—and the value that attaches uniquely to this subcategory—as its own kind of thing.

That the traditionalist's position involves a moral judgment about homosexual relationships is evident in the following passage from Girgis et al.:

> Because bodies are integral parts of the personal reality of human beings, only coitus can truly unite persons organically and, thus, maritally. . . . In this sense, it is not the state that keeps marriage from certain people, but their circumstances that unfortunately keep certain people from marriage (or at least make marrying much harder). This is so, not only for those with exclusively homosexual attractions, but also for people who cannot marry because of, for example, pressing family obligations incompatible with marriage's comprehensiveness and orientation to children, inability to find a mate, or any other cause. . . . What we wish for people unable to marry because of a lack of any attraction to a member of the opposite sex is the same as what we wish for people who cannot marry for any other reason: rich and fulfilling lives. In the splendor of human variety, these can take infinitely many forms. In any of them, energy that would otherwise go into marriage is channeled toward ennobling endeavors: deeper devotion to family or nation, service, adventure, art, or a thousand other things.

But most relevantly, this energy could be harnessed for deep friendship. Belief in [the assumption that meaningful intimacy is impossible without sex] may impoverish the friendships in which single people could find fulfillment—by making emotional, psychological, and dispositional intimacy seem inappropriate in non-sexual friendships. We must not conflate depth of friendship with the presence of sex. Doing so may stymie the connection between friends who feel that they must distance themselves from the possibility or appearance of a sexual relationship where none is wanted. By encouraging the myth that there can be no intimacy without romance, we deny people the wonder of knowing another as what Aristotle so aptly called a second self.

The first sentence is what you get when you stop short of saying anything about homosexuality: Only persons who have sex *like this* can unite bodily and only if persons unite bodily can their relationship possess the value of marriage. But then we realize that the authors—though surely no bigots—labor in blindness to the value of maximal experiential union as such, and to the fact that romance and friendship are different kinds of intimacy possessing different kinds of value. We detect no recognition that "those with exclusively homosexual attractions" can, while those who remain single for "any other reason" cannot, experience the value of committed romantic love. We get that quasi-reverential description of the possibility that a homosexual person might "harness[]" his or her "energy" for a platonic, Aristotelian friendship—the prescribed course, apparently. And we witness a special sympathy for persons who are afraid of sexual involvement, or even the false perception of it.

I think much of the public finds these attitudes quite alien. But the point is rather that they are of a piece with the judgment that the value of a relationship between two persons in love depends, intrinsically, on the structure of their genitals.

Critical Thinking

1. What are reasons that marriage, as an institution, exists in our society?
2. Is a desire to reproduce a necessary function of all marriages? Why or why not?
3. Why is the gender of partners in a marriage of concern?

Create Central

www.mhhe.com/createcentral

Internet References

The Pew Forum on Religion and Public Life: Gay Marriage and Homosexuality
www.pewforum.org/Topics/Issues/Gay-Marriage-and-Homosexuality

National Council of State Legislatures, Defining Marriage
www.ncsl.org/issues-research/human-services/same-sex-marriage -overview.aspx

Prepared by: Patricia Hrusa Williams,
University of Maine at Farmington

Article

The Polygamists

A sect that split from the Mormons allows multiple wives, expels "lost boys," and heeds a jailed prophet.

SCOTT ANDERSON

Learning Outcomes

After reading this article, you will be able to:

- Define polygamy.
- Identify the origins of polygamy in the United States.
- Explain the association between religious beliefs and polygamy.

The first church members arrive at the Leroy S. Johnson Meeting House in Colorado City, Arizona, at about 6 P.M. Within a half hour the line extends out the front doors, down the side of the building, and out into the parking lot. By seven, it stretches hundreds of yards and has grown to several thousand people—the men and boys dressed in suits, the women and girls in Easter egg-hued prairie dresses.

The mourners have come for a viewing of 68-year-old Foneta Jessop, who died of a heart attack a few days ago. In the cavernous hall Foneta's sons form a receiving line at the foot of her open casket, while her husband, Merril, stands directly alongside. To the other side stand Merril's numerous other wives, all wearing matching white dresses.

Foneta was the first wife.

Colorado City is a town with special significance for those of Foneta's faith. Together with its sister community of Hildale, Utah, it is the birthplace of the Fundamentalist Church of Jesus Christ of Latter-Day Saints (FLDS), a polygamous offshoot of the Mormon Church, or LDS. Here in the 1920s and '30s, a handful of polygamous families settled astride the Utah-Arizona border after the leadership of the Mormon Church became increasingly determined to shed its polygamous past and be accepted by the American mainstream. In 1935 the church gave settlement residents an ultimatum: renounce plural marriage or be excommunicated. Practically everyone refused and was cast out of the LDS.

At the memorial service for Foneta, her husband and three sons give testimonials praising her commitment to the covenant

of plural marriage, but there is an undertone of family disharmony, with vague references by Merril Jessop to his troubled relationship with Foneta. No one need mention that one of Merril's wives is missing. Carolyn Jessop, his fourth wife, left the household in 2003 with her eight children and went on to write a best-selling book on her life as an FLDS member. She describes a cloistered environment and tells of a deeply unhappy Foneta, an overweight recluse who fell out of favor with her husband and slept her days away, coming out of her room only at night to eat, do laundry, and watch old Shirley Temple movies on television.

At the conclusion of the service, most of the congregation walk over to the Isaac Carling cemetery for a graveside observance. I assume the enormous turnout—mourners have come in from FLDS communities in Texas, Colorado, and British Columbia—stems from the prominent position Foneta's husband holds: Merril Jessop is an FLDS leader and the bishop of the large chapter in West Texas. But Sam Steed, a soft-spoken, 37-year-old accountant acting as my guide, explains that elaborate funerals are a regular occurrence. "Probably between 15 and 20 times a year," he says. "This one is maybe a little bigger than most, but even when a young child dies, you can expect three or four thousand people to attend. It's part of what keeps us together. It reminds us we're members of this larger community. We draw strength from each other."

Few Americans had heard of the FLDS before April 2008, when law enforcement officials conducted a raid on a remote compound in West Texas known as the Yearning for Zion Ranch. For days after, television viewers witnessed the bizarre spectacle of hundreds of children and women—all dressed in old-fashioned prairie dresses, with elaborately coiffed hair—being herded onto school buses by social workers and police officers.

That raid had been spurred by phone calls to a domestic violence shelter, purportedly from a 16-year-old girl who claimed she was being sexually and physically abused on the ranch by her middle-aged husband. What lent credibility to the calls was that the residents of YFZ Ranch were disciples of the FLDS and its "prophet," Warren Jeffs, who had been convicted in a Utah court in 2007 for officiating at the marriage of a 14-year-old girl to a church member.

The raid made for gripping television, but it soon became clear that the phone calls were a hoax. And although authorities had evidently anticipated a violent confrontation like the 1993 shoot-out at the Branch Davidian compound in Waco—SWAT teams were brought in, along with an armored personnel carrier—the arsenal at the YFZ Ranch consisted of only 33 legal firearms. A Texas appeals court later found that authorities had not met the burden of proof for the removal of the more than 400 children, and most were returned to their families within two months.

Yet after interviewing teenagers who were pregnant or had children, Texas authorities began investigating how many underage girls might have been "sealed" to older men. (Plural marriages are performed within the church and are not legal.) The result: Twelve church members, including Warren Jeffs, were indicted on charges ranging from bigamy to having sex with a minor. The first defendant to stand trial, Raymond Jessop, was convicted of one charge last November. Trials of the other defendants are scheduled to take place over the coming year.

From the Bluff behind his Hildale home, Joe Jessop has a commanding view of the Arizona Strip, an undulating expanse of sagebrush and piñon-juniper woodland that stretches south of the Utah border all the way to the northern rim of the Grand Canyon, some 50 miles away. Below are the farm fields and walled compounds of Hildale and Colorado City, which Joe refers to collectively by their old name, Short Creek. "When I first came to Short Creek as a boy, there were just seven homes down there," says Joe, 88. "It was like the frontier."

Today, Short Creek is home to an estimated 6,000 FLDS members—the largest FLDS community. Joe Jessop, a brother of Merril, has contributed to that explosive growth in two very different ways. With the weathered features and spindly gait of a man who has spent his life outdoors and worked his body hard, he is the community's undisputed "water guy," a self-taught engineer who helped with the piping of water out of Maxwell Canyon back in the 1940s. He's had a hand in building the intricate network of waterlines, canals, and reservoirs that has irrigated the arid plateau in the decades since.

A highly respected member of the FLDS, Joe is also the patriarch of a family of 46 children and—at last count—239 grandchildren. "My family came to Short Creek for the same reason as everyone else," he says, "to obey the law of plural marriage, to build up the Kingdom of God. Despite everything that's been thrown our way, I'd say we've done a pretty good job."

Members of the faith describe the life that the Jessops and other founding families have built as idyllic, one in which old-fashioned devotion and neighborly cooperation are emphasized and children are raised in a wholesome environment free of television and junk food and social pressures. Critics, on the other hand, see the FLDS as an isolated cult whose members,

worn down by rigid social control, display a disturbing fealty to one man, the prophet Warren Jeffs—who has claimed to be God's mouthpiece on Earth.

To spend time in Hildale and Colorado City is to come away with a more nuanced view. That view is revealed gradually, however, due to the insular nature of the community. Many of the oversize homes are tucked behind high walls, both to give children a safe place to play and to shield families from gawking Gentiles, as non-Mormons are known. Most residents avoid contact with strangers. *National Geographic* was given access to the community only on the approval of the church leadership, in consultation with the imprisoned Warren Jeffs.

In keeping with original Mormon teachings, much of the property in Hildale and Colorado City is held in trust for the church. Striving to be as self-sufficient as possible, the community grows a wide variety of fruits and vegetables, and everyone, including children, is expected to help bring in the yield. Church members also own and operate a number of large businesses, from hotels to tool and machine manufacturers. Each Saturday, men gather at the meetinghouse to go over a roster of building and maintenance projects around town in need of volunteers. In one display of solidarity, the men built a four-bedroom home, from foundation to roof shingles, in a single day.

This communal spirit continues inside the polygamous home. Although living arrangements vary—wives may occupy different wings of a house or have their own granny cottages—the women tend to carve out spheres of influence according to preference or aptitude. Although each has primary responsibility for her own children, one wife might manage the kitchen, a second act as schoolteacher (virtually all FLDS children in Hildale and Colorado City are homeschooled), and a third see to the sewing. Along with instilling a sense of sorority, this division of labor appears to mitigate jealousy.

"I know it must seem strange to outsiders," says Joyce Broadbent, a friendly woman of 44, "but from my experience, sister wives usually get along very well. Oh sure, you might be closer to one than another, or someone might get on your nerves occasionally, but that's true in any family. I've never felt any rivalry or jealousy at all."

Joyce is a rather remarkable example of this harmony. She not only accepted another wife, Marcia, into the family, but was thrilled by the addition. Marcia, who left an unhappy marriage in the 1980s, is also Joyce's biological sister. "I knew my husband was a good man," Joyce explains with a smile as she sits with Marcia and their husband, Heber. "I wanted my sister to have a chance at the same kind of happiness I had."

Not all FLDS women are quite so sanguine about plural marriage. Dorothy Emma Jessop is a spry, effervescent octogenarian who operates a naturopathic dispensary in Hildale. Sitting in her tiny shop surrounded by jars of herbal tinctures she ground and mixed herself, Dorothy admits she struggled when her husband began taking on other wives. "To be honest," she says, "I think a lot of women have a hard time with it, because it's not an easy thing to share the man you love. But I came to realize this is another test that God places before you—the sin of jealousy, of pride—and that to be a godly woman, I needed to overcome it."

What seems to help overcome it is an awareness that a woman's primary role in the FLDS is to bear and raise as many children as possible, to build up the "celestial family" that will remain together for eternity. It is not uncommon to meet FLDS women who have given birth to 10, 12, 16 children. (Joyce Broadbent is the mother of 11, and Dorothy Emma Jessop of 13.) As a result, it's easy to see why this corner of the American West is experiencing a population explosion. The 400 or so babies delivered in the Hildale health clinic every year have resulted in a median age of just under 14, in contrast with 36.6 for the entire U.S. With so many in the community tracing their lineage to a handful of the pioneering families, the same few names crop up over and over in Hildale and Colorado City, suggesting a murkier side to this fecundity: Doctors in Arizona say a severe form of a debilitating disease called fumarase deficiency, caused by a recessive gene, has become more prevalent in the community due to intermarriage.

The collision of tradition and modernity in the community can be disorienting. Despite their old-fashioned dress, most FLDS adults have cell phones and favor late-model SUVs. Although televisions are now banished, church members tend to be highly computer literate and sell a range of products, from soaps to dresses, via the Internet. When I noticed how few congregants wore glasses, I wondered aloud if perhaps a genetic predisposition for good eyesight was at work. Sam Steed laughed lightly. "No. People here are just really into laser surgery."

The principle of plural marriage was revealed to the Mormons amid much secrecy. Dark clouds hovered over the church in the early 1840s, after rumors spread that its founder, Joseph Smith, had taken up the practice of polygamy. While denying the charge in public, by 1843 Smith had shared a revelation with his closest disciples. In this "new and everlasting covenant" with God, plural wives were to be taken so that the faithful might "multiply and replenish the earth."

After Smith was assassinated by an anti-Mormon mob in Illinois, Brigham Young led believers on an epic 1,300-mile journey west to the Salt Lake Basin of present-day Utah. There the covenant was at last publicly revealed and with it, the notion that a man's righteousness before God would be measured by the size of his family; Brigham Young himself took 55 wives, who bore him 57 children.

But in 1890, faced with the seizure of church property under a federal antipolygamy law, the LDS leadership issued a manifesto announcing an end to plural marriage. That certainly didn't end the practice, and the LDS's tortured handling of the issue—some church leaders remained in plural marriages or even took on new wives after the manifesto's release—contributed to the schism between the LDS and the fundamentalists.

"The LDS issued that manifesto for political purposes, then later claimed it was a revelation," says Willie Jessop, the FLDS spokesman. "We in the fundamentalist community believe covenants are made with God and are not to be manipulated for political reasons, so that presents an enormous obstacle between us and those in the LDS mainstream."

Upholding the covenant has come at a high price. The 2008 raid on the YFZ Ranch was only the latest in a long list of official actions against polygamists—persecutions for simply adhering to their religious principles, in the eyes of church members—that are integral to the FLDS story. At various times both Utah and Arizona authorities attempted to crack down on the Short Creek community: in 1935, in 1944, and most famously, in 1953. In that raid some 200 women and children were hauled to detention centers, while 26 men were brought up on polygamy charges. In 1956 Utah authorities seized seven children of Vera Black, a Hildale plural wife, on grounds that her polygamous beliefs made her an unfit mother. Black was reunited with her children only after agreeing to renounce polygamy.

Melinda Fischer Jeffs is an articulate, outgoing woman of 37, and she gives an incredulous laugh when describing what she's read about the FLDS. "Honestly, I can't even recognize it!" the mother of three exclaims. "Most all of what appears in the media, it makes us sound like we're somehow being kept against our will."

Melinda is in a unique position to understand the conflicting views of this community. She is a plural wife to Jim Jeffs, one of the prophet's nephews and an elder in the FLDS. But she is also the daughter of Dan Fischer, a former FLDS member who has emerged as one of the church leadership's most vociferous critics. In 2008 Fischer testified before a U.S. Senate committee about alleged improprieties within the FLDS, and he now heads an organization that works with people who have been kicked out of the church or who have "escaped." When Fischer broke with the church in the 1990s, his family split apart too; today 13 of his children have left the FLDS, while Melinda and two of her half siblings have renounced their father.

"And that is not an easy thing," Melinda says softly, "obviously, because I still love my father. I pray all the time that he will see his errors—or at least, stop his attacks on us."

If there is one point on which FLDS defenders and detractors might agree, it is that most of the current troubles can be traced to when its leadership passed to the Jeffs family, in 1986. Until then, the FLDS had been a fairly loosely run group led by an avuncular man named Leroy Johnson, who relied on a group of high priests to guide the church. That ended when Rulon Jeffs took over following Johnson's death. After being declared the prophet by the community, Rulon solidified the policy of one-man rule.

Charges that a theocratic dictatorship was taking root in the Arizona Strip grew louder when, after Rulon's death in 2002, the FLDS was taken over by his 46-year-old son, Warren. Assuming the role of the prophet, Warren first married several of his father's wives—and then proceeded to wed many more women, including, according to Carolyn Jessop, eight of Merril Jessop's daughters. Although many FLDS men have multiple wives, the number of wives of those closest to the prophet can reach into the double digits. A church document called the Bishop's Record, seized during the Texas raid, shows that one of Jeffs's lieutenants, Wendell Nielsen, claims 21 wives. And although the FLDS would not disclose how many plural wives Warren Jeffs has taken (some estimate more than 80), at least one was an underage girl, according to a Texas indictment.

Although the issue of underage marriage within the church has garnered the greatest negative media attention, Dan Fischer has championed another cause, the so-called Lost Boys, who have left or been forced from the community and wound up fending for themselves on the streets of Las Vegas, Salt Lake City, and St. George, Utah. Fischer's foundation has worked with 300 such young men, a few as young as 13, over the past seven years. Fischer concedes that most of these boys were simply "discouraged out," but he cites cases where they were officially expelled, a practice he says increased under Jeffs.

Fischer attributes the exodus partly to a cold-blooded calculation by church leaders to limit male competition for the pool of marriageable young women. "If you have men marrying 20, 30, up to 80 or more women," he says, "then it comes down to biology and simple math that there will be a lot of other men who aren't going to get wives. The church says it's kicking these boys out for being disruptive influences, but if you'll notice, they rarely kick out girls."

Equally contentious has been the FLDS restoration of an early Mormon policy of transferring the wives and children of a church member to another man. Traditionally, this was done upon the death of a patriarch so that his widows might be cared for, or to rescue a woman from an abusive relationship. But critics argue that under Jeffs this "reassignment" became one more weapon to hold over the heads of those who dared step out of line.

Determining who is unworthy has been the exclusive province of the prophet. When in January 2004 Jeffs publicly ordered the expulsion of 21 men and the reassignment of their families, the community acquiesced. Jeffs's diary, also seized during the Texas raid, reveals a man who micromanaged the community's every decision, from chore assignments and housing arrangements to who married whom and which men were ousted—all directed by revelations Jeffs received as he slept. He claimed that God guided his every action, no matter how small. One diary entry reads: "The Lord directed that I go to the sun tanning salon and get sun tanned more evenly on their suntanning beds."

In 2005 a Utah court transferred control of the trust that oversees much of the land in Hildale and Colorado City from the FLDS leadership to a state-appointed fiduciary; the church is currently waging a campaign to recover control of the trust. As for Jeffs, after spending over a year on the lam avoiding legal issues in Utah—and earning a spot on the FBI's Ten Most Wanted list—he was caught and is currently serving a ten-year-to-life sentence as an accomplice to rape. He awaits trial on multiple indictments in Arizona and Texas. The 11 other church members awaiting trial in Texas include Merril Jessop, who was indicted for performing the marriage of Jeffs to an underage girl.

Yet Jeffs's smiling portrait continues to adorn the living room of almost every FLDS home. In his absence, his lieutenants have launched a fierce defense of his leadership. While conceding that underage marriages did occur in the past, Donald Richter, contributor to one of the official FLDS websites, says the practice has now been stopped. As for the Lost Boys, he argues that both the numbers involved and the reasons for the expulsions have been greatly exaggerated by the church's enemies. "This is only done in the most extreme cases," Richter says, "and never for the trivial causes they're claiming. And anyway, all religious groups have the right to expel people who won't accept their rules."

Certainly Melinda Fischer Jeffs hasn't been swayed by the ongoing controversy. "Warren is just the kindest, most loving man," she says. "The image that has been built up about him by the media and his enemies is just unrecognizable to who he really is." Like other church members, Melinda has ready answers for most of the accusations leveled against Jeffs and is especially spirited in defending the policy of reassignment. According to her, it is almost always initiated at the request of a wife who has been abandoned or abused. This is debatable. In his diary Jeffs recounts reassigning the wives of three men, including his brother David, because God had shown him that they "couldn't exalt their ladies, had lost the confidence of God." One of his brother's wives had difficulty accepting the news and could barely bring herself to kiss her new husband. "She showed a great spirit of resistance, yet she went through with it," Jeffs records. "She needs to learn to submit to Priesthood."

Yet Melinda's defense of Jeffs underscores one of the most curious aspects of the polygamous faith: the central role of women in defending it. This is not new. In Brigham Young's day a charity rushed to Utah to establish a safe house for polygamous women seeking to escape this "white slavery"; that house sat virtually empty. Today FLDS women in the Hildale–Colorado City area have ample opportunity to "escape"—they have cell phones, they drive cars, there are no armed guards keeping them in—yet they don't.

Undoubtedly one reason is that, having been raised in this culture, they know little else. Walking away means leaving behind everything: the community, one's sense of security, even one's own family. Carolyn Jessop, the plural wife of Merril Jessop who did leave the FLDS, likens entering the outside world to "stepping out onto another planet. I was completely unprepared, because I had absolutely no life skills. Most women in the FLDS don't even know how to balance a checkbook, let alone apply for a job, so contemplating how you're going to navigate in the outside world is extremely daunting."

It would seem there's another lure for women to stay: power. The FLDS women I spoke with tended to be far more articulate and confident than the men, most of whom seemed paralyzed by bashfulness. It makes sense when one begins to grasp that women are coveted to "multiply and replenish the earth," while men are in extraordinary competition to be deemed worthy of marriage by the prophet. One way to be deemed worthy, of course, is to not rock the boat, to keep a low profile. As a result, what has all the trappings of a patriarchal culture, actually has many elements of a matriarchal one.

There are limits to that power, of course, for it is subject to the dictates of the prophet. After hearing Melinda's stout defense of Jeffs, I ask what she would do if she were reassigned.

"I'm confident that wouldn't happen," she replies uneasily.

"But what if it did?" I ask. "Would you obey?"

For the only time during our interview, Melinda grows wary. Sitting back in her chair, she gives her head a quarter turn to stare at me out of the corner of one eye.

On a sunny afternoon in March 2009, Bob Barlow, a friendly, middle-aged member of the FLDS, gives me a tour of the YFZ Ranch in West Texas. The compound consists of about 25 two-story log-cabin-style homes, and a number of workshops and factories are scattered over 1,700 acres. At the center sits a gleaming white stone temple. It is remarkable what the residents have created from the hardscrabble plain. With heavy machinery, they literally made earth out of the rocky terrain, crushing stone and mixing it with the thin topsoil. They planted orchards and gardens and lawns and were on their way to creating a self-sufficient community amid the barren landscape. All that ground to a halt after the 2008 raid.

"The families are slowly coming back now," Barlow says. "We'll come out the other side of this better and stronger than before."

I suspect he's right. So many times in the history of Mormon polygamy the outside world thought it had the movement on the ropes only to see it flourish anew. I'm reminded of this one afternoon in Colorado City when I speak with Vera Black. Now 92 and in failing health, Vera is the woman whose children were taken from her by Utah authorities in 1956 and returned only after she agreed to renounce polygamy. Within days of making that promise, she was back in Short Creek with her children and had renewed her commitment to the everlasting covenant.

Now living with her daughter Lillian, Vera lies in a daybed as her children gather around. Those children are now in their 50s and 60s, and as they recount the story of their long-ago separation—both from their mother and their faith—several weep, as if the pain were fresh.

"I had to make that promise," Vera says, with a smile, "but I crossed my fingers while I did it."

Critical Thinking

1. How do you view the FLDS communities and their beliefs on polygamy?
2. In your opinion, should government outlaw polygamy? Why or why not?
3. Does polygamy threaten traditional marriage?
4. Do you believe that law enforcement should investigate polygamist families?
5. What are some of the benefits of polygamy and the costs of polygamy?
6. In reading this article, how does polygamy impact children growing up in these families?
7. Thinking of the current media's portrayal of polygamy, such as *Big Love* and *Sister Wives,* does that make polygamy more acceptable?

Create Central

www.mhhe.com/createcentral

Internet References

Council on Contemporary Families
www.contemporaryfamilies.org

National Council on Family Relations
www.ncfr.com

Article

Prepared by: Patricia Hrusa Williams,
University of Maine at Farmington

Are You with the Right Mate?

REBECCA WEBBER

Learning Outcomes

After reading this article, you will be able to:

- Understand factors important to compatibility and marital satisfaction.
- Describe the personality characteristics associated with being a good mate or partner.
- Recognize reasons for growth and change in marital relationships over time.

Elliott Katz was stunned to find himself in the middle of a divorce after two kids and 10 years of marriage. The Torontonian, a policy analyst for the Ottawa government, blamed his wife. "She just didn't appreciate all I was doing to make her happy." He fed the babies, and he changed their diapers. He gave them their baths, he read them stories, and put them to bed. Before he left for work in the morning, he made them breakfast. He bought a bigger house and took on the financial burden, working evenings to bring in enough money so his wife could stay home full-time.

He thought the solution to the discontent was for her to change. But once on his own, missing the daily interaction with his daughters, he couldn't avoid some reflection. "I didn't want to go through this again. I asked whether there was something I could have done differently. After all, you can wait years for someone else to change."

What he decided was, indeed, there were some things he could have done differently—like not tried as hard to be so non-controlling that his wife felt he had abandoned decision-making entirely. His wife, he came to understand, felt frustrated, as if she were "a married single parent," making too many of the plans and putting out many of the fires of family life, no matter how many chores he assumed.

Ultimately, he stopped blaming his wife for their problems. "You can't change another person. You can only change yourself," he says. "Like lots of men today" he has since found, "I was very confused about my role as partner." After a few post-divorce years in the mating wilderness, Katz came to realize that framing a relationship in terms of the right or wrong mate is by itself a blind alley.

"We're given a binary model," says New York psychotherapist Ken Page. "Right or wrong. Settle or leave. We are not given the right tools to think about relationships. People need a better set of options."

Sooner or later, there comes a moment in *all* relationships when you lie in bed, roll over, look at the person next to you and think it's all a dreadful mistake, says Boston family therapist Terrence Real. It happens a few months to a few years in. "It's an open secret of American culture that disillusionment exists. I go around the country speaking about 'normal marital hatred.' Not one person has ever asked what I mean by that. It's extremely raw."

What to do when the initial attraction sours? "I call it the first day of your real marriage," Real says. It's not a sign that you've chosen the wrong partner. It is the signal to grow as an individual—to take responsibility for your own frustrations. Invariably, we yearn for perfection but are stuck with an imperfect human being. We all fall in love with people we think will deliver us from life's wounds but who wind up knowing how to rub against us.

A new view of relationships and their discontents is emerging. We alone are responsible for having the relationship we want. And to get it, we have to dig deep into ourselves while maintaining our connections. It typically takes a dose of bravery—what Page calls "enlightened audacity." Its brightest possibility exists, ironically, just when the passion seems most totally dead. If we fail to plumb ourselves and speak up for our deepest needs, which admittedly can be a scary prospect, life will never feel authentic, we will never see ourselves with any clarity, and everyone will always be the wrong partner.

The Way Things Are

Romance itself seeds the eventual belief that we have chosen the wrong partner. The early stage of a relationship, most marked by intense attraction and infatuation, is in many ways akin to cocaine intoxication, observes Christine Meinecke, a clinical psychologist in Des Moines, Iowa. It's orchestrated, in part, by the neurochemicals associated with intense pleasure. Like a cocaine high, it's not sustainable.

But for the duration—and experts give it nine months to four years—infatuation has one overwhelming effect: Research shows that it makes partners overestimate their similarities and idealize each other. We're thrilled that he loves Thai food, travel, and classic movies, just like us. And we overlook his avid interest in old cars and online poker.

Eventually, reality rears its head. "Infatuation fades for everyone," says Meinecke, author of *Everybody Marries the Wrong Person*. That's when you discover your psychological incompatibility, and disenchantment sets in. Suddenly, a switch is flipped, and now all you can see are your differences. "You're focusing on what's wrong with *them*. They need to get the message about what *they* need to change."

You conclude you've married the wrong person—but that's because you're accustomed to thinking, Cinderella-like, that there *is* only one right person. The consequences of such a pervasive belief are harsh. We engage in destructive behaviors, like blaming our partner for our unhappiness or searching for someone outside the relationship.

Along with many other researchers and clinicians, Meinecke espouses a new marital paradigm—what she calls "the self-responsible spouse." When you start focusing on what isn't so great, it's time to shift focus. "Rather than look at the other person, you need to look at yourself and ask, 'Why am I suddenly so unhappy and what do I need to do?'" It's not likely a defect in your partner.

In mature love, says Meinecke, "we do not look to our partner to provide our happiness, and we don't blame them for our unhappiness. We take responsibility for the expectations that we carry, for our own negative emotional reactions, for our own insecurities, and for our own dark moods."

But instead of looking at ourselves, or understanding the fantasies that bring us to such a pass, we engage in a thought process that makes our differences tragic and intolerable, says William Doherty, professor of psychology and head of the marriage and family therapy program at the University of Minnesota. It's one thing to say, "I wish my spouse were more into the arts, like I am." Or, "I wish my partner was not just watching TV every night but interested in getting out more with me." That's something you can fix.

It's quite another to say, "This is intolerable. I need and deserve somebody who shares my core interests." The two thought processes are likely to trigger differing actions. It's possible to ask someone to go out more. It's not going to be well received to ask someone for a personality overhaul, notes Doherty, author of *Take Back Your Marriage*.

No one is going to get all their needs met in a relationship, he insists. He urges fundamental acceptance of the person we choose and the one who chooses us. "We're all flawed. With parenting, we know that comes with the territory. With spouses, we say 'This is terrible.'"

The culture, however, pushes us in the direction of discontent. "Some disillusionment and feelings of discouragement are normal in the love-based matches in our culture," explains Doherty. "But consumer culture tells us we should not settle for anything that is not ideal for us."

As UCLA psychologist Thomas Bradbury puts it, "You don't have a line-item veto when it comes to your partner. It's a package deal; the bad comes with the good."

Further, he says, it's too simplistic an interpretation that your partner is the one who's wrong. "We tend to point our finger at the person in front of us. We're fairly crude at processing some information. We tend not to think, 'Maybe I'm not giving her what she needs.' 'Maybe he's disgruntled because I'm not opening up to him.' Or, 'Maybe he's struggling in his relationships with other people.' The more sophisticated question is, 'In what ways are we failing to make one another happy?'"

Now in a long-term relationship, Toronto's Katz has come to believe that "Marriage is not about *finding* the right person. It's about *becoming* the right person. Many people feel they married the wrong person, but I've learned that it's truly about growing to become a better husband."

Eclipsed by Expectations

What's most noticeable about Sarah and Mark Holdt of Estes Park, Colorado, is their many differences. "He's a Republican, I'm a Democrat. He's a traditional Christian, I'm an agnostic. He likes meat and potatoes, I like more adventurous food," says Sarah. So Mark heads off to church and Bible study every week, while Sarah takes a "Journeys" class that considers topics like the history of God in America. "When he comes home, I'll ask, 'What did you learn in Bible Study?'" she says. And she'll share her insights from her own class with him.

But when Sarah wants to go to a music festival and Mark wants to stay home, "I just go," says Sarah. "I don't need to have him by my side for everything." He's there when it matters most—at home, at the dinner table, in bed. "We both thrive on touch," says Sarah, "so we set our alarm a half hour early every morning and take that time to cuddle." They've been married for 14 years.

It takes a comfortable sense of self and deliberate effort to make relationships commodious enough to tolerate such differences. What's striking about the Holdts is the time they take to share what goes on in their lives—and in their heads—when they are apart. Research shows that such "turning toward" each other and efforts at information exchange, even in routine matters, are crucial to maintaining the emotional connection between partners.

Say one partner likes to travel and the other doesn't. "If you view this with a feeling of resentment, that's going to hurt, over and over again," says Doherty. If you can accept it, that's fine—provided you don't start living in two separate worlds.

"What you don't want to do," he says, "is develop a group of single travel friends who, when they are on the road, go out and flirt with others. You start doing things you're not comfortable sharing with your mate." Most often, such large differences are accompanied by so much disappointment that partners react in ways that do not support the relationship.

The available evidence suggests that women more than men bring some element of fantasy into a relationship. Women generally initiate more breakups and two-thirds of divorces, becoming more disillusioned than men. They compare their mates with their friends much more than men do, says Doherty.

He notes, "They tend to have a model or framework for what the relationship should be. They are more prone to the comparison between what they have and what they think they should have. Men tend to monitor the gap between what they have and what they think they deserve only in the sexual arena. They don't monitor the quality of their marriage on an everyday basis."

To the extent that people have an ideal partner and an ideal relationship in their head, they are setting themselves up for disaster, says family expert Michelle Givertz, assistant professor of communication studies at California State University, Chico. Relationship identities are negotiated between two individuals. Relationships are not static ideals; they are always works in progress.

To enter a relationship with an idea of what it should look like or how it should evolve is too controlling, she contends. It takes two people to make a relationship. One person doesn't get to decide what it should be. And to the extent that he or she does, the other partner is not going to be happy.

"People can spend their lives trying to make a relationship into something it isn't, based on an idealized vision of what should be, not what is," she says. She isn't sure why, but she finds that such misplaced expectations are increasing. Or, as Doherty puts it, "A lot of the thinking about being married to the wrong mate is really self-delusion."

Yes, Virginia, Some Mates Really *Are* Wrong

Sometimes, however, we really do choose the wrong person—someone ultimately not interested in or capable of meeting our needs, for any of a number of possible reasons. At the top of the list of people who are generally wrong for *anyone* are substance abusers—whether the substance is alcohol, prescription drugs, or illicit drugs—who refuse to get help for the problem.

"An addict's primary loyalty is not to the relationship, it's to the addiction," explains Ken Page. "Active addicts become cheaper versions of themselves and lose integrity or the ability to do the right thing when it's hard. Those are the very qualities in a partner you need to lean on." Gamblers fall into the same compulsive camp, with the added twist that their pursuit of the big win typically lands them, sooner or later, into deep debt that threatens the foundations of relationship life.

People who cheated in one or more previous relationships are not great mate material. They destroy the trust and intimacy basic to building a relationship. It's possible to make a case for a partner who cheats once, against his own values, but not for one who compulsively and repeatedly strays. Doherty considers such behavior among the "hard reasons" for relationship breakup, along with physical abuse and other forms of over controlling. "These are things that nobody should have to put up with in life," he says.

But "drifting apart," "poor communication," and "we're just not compatible anymore" are in a completely different category. Such "soft reasons," he insists, are, by contrast, always two-way streets. "Nobody gets all the soft goodies in life," he finds. "It's often better to work on subtle ways to improve the relationship."

A Critical Difference

There's a difference between fighting for what you want in your relationship and being in direct control of your partner, demanding that he or she change, says Real.

Firmly stand up for your wants and needs in a relationship. "Most people don't have the skill to speak up for and fight for what they want in a relationship," he observes. "They don't speak up, which preserves the love but builds resentment. Resentment is a choice; living resentfully means living unhappily. Or they speak up—but are not very loving." Or they just complain.

The art to speaking up, he says, is to transform a complaint into a request. Not "I don't like how you're talking to me," but "Can you please lower your voice so I can hear you better?" If you're trying to get what you want in a relationship, notes Real, it's best to keep it positive and future-focused.

In an ongoing marriage, he adds, "incompatibility is never the real reason for a divorce." It's a reason for breakup of a dating relationship. But when people say "she's a nice person but we're just not compatible," Doherty finds, something happened in which both were participants and allowed the relationship to deteriorate. It's a nice way to say you're not blaming your partner.

The real reason is likely to be that neither attended to the relationship. Perhaps one or both partners threw themselves into parenting. Or a job. They stopped doing the things that they did when dating and that couples need to do to thrive as a partnership—take time for conversation, talk about how their day went or what's on their mind. Or perhaps the real love was undermined by the inability to handle conflict.

"If you get to the point where you're delivering an ultimatum," says Bradbury, you haven't been maintaining your relationship properly. "It's like your car stopping on the side of the road and you say, 'It just isn't working anymore'—but you haven't changed the oil in 10 years." The heart of any relationship, he insists—what makes people the right mates for each other—is the willingness of both partners to be open and vulnerable; to listen and care about each other.

Although there are no guarantees, there are stable personal characteristics that are generally good and generally bad for relationships. On the good side: sense of humor; even temper; willingness to overlook your flaws; sensitivity to you and what you care about; ability to express caring. On the maladaptive side: chronic lying; chronic worrying or neuroticism; emotional over reactivity; proneness to anger; propensity to harbor grudges; low self-esteem; poor impulse control; tendency to aggression; self-orientation rather than an other-orientation. Situations, such as chronic exposure to nonmarital stress in either partner, also have the power to undermine relationships.

In addition, there are people who are specifically wrong for *you*, because they don't share the values and goals you hold most dear. Differences in core values often plague couples who marry young, before they've had enough life experience to discover who they really are. Most individuals are still developing their belief systems through their late teens and early 20s and still refining their lifestyle choices. Of course, you have to know what you hold most dear, and that can be a challenge for anyone at any age, not just the young.

One of the most common reasons we choose the wrong partner is that we do not know who we are or what we really want. It's hard to choose someone capable of understanding you and meeting your most guarded emotional needs and with whom your values are compatible when you don't know what your needs or values are or haven't developed the confidence to voice them unabashedly.

Maria Lin is a nonpracticing attorney who married a chef. "I valued character, connection, the heart," she says. "He was charming, funny, treated me amazingly well, and we got along great." But over time, intellectual differences got in the way. "He couldn't keep up with my analysis or logic in arguments or reasoning through something, or he would prove less capable at certain things, or he would misspell or misuse terms. It was never anything major, just little things."

Lin confides that she lost respect for her chef-husband. "I didn't realize how important intellectual respect for my partner would end up being to me. I think this was more about not knowing myself well enough, and not knowing how being intellectually stimulated was important to me, and (even worse) how it would tie to that critical factor of respect."

The Signal to Grow

It is a fact that like the other basic pillars of life, such as work and children, marriage is not always going to be a source of satisfaction. No one is loved perfectly; some part of our authentic self is never going to be met by a partner. Sure, you can always draw a curtain over your heart. But that is not the only or the best response.

"Sometimes marriage is going to be a source of pain and sorrow," says Givertz. "And that's necessary for personal and interpersonal growth." In fact, it's impossible to be deliriously happy in marriage every moment if you are doing anything at all challenging in life, whether raising children, starting a business, or taking care of an aging parent.

Disillusionment becomes an engine for growth because it forces us to discover our needs. Knowing oneself, recognizing one's needs, and speaking up for them in a relationship are often acts of bravery, says Page. Most of us are guarded about our needs, because they are typically our areas of greatest sensitivity and vulnerability.

"You have to discover—and be able to share—what touches you and moves you the most," he observes. "But first, of course, you have to accept that in yourself. Few of us are skilled at this essential process for creating passion and romance. We'd rather complain." Nevertheless, through this process, we clarify ourselves as we move through life.

At the same time, taking the risk to expose your inner life to your partner turns out to be the great opportunity for expanding intimacy and a sense of connection. This is the great power of relationships: Creating intimacy is the crucible for growing into a fully autonomous human being while the process of becoming a fully realized person expands the possibility for intimacy and connection. This is also the work that transforms a partner into the right partner.

Another crucial element of growth in relationships, says Givertz, is a transformation of motivation—away from self-centered preferences toward what is best for the relationship and its future. There is an intrapsychic change that sustains long-term relationships. Underlying it is a broadening process in which response patterns subtly shift. Accommodation (as opposed to retaliation) plays a role. So does sacrifice. So do willingness and ability to suppress an impulse to respond negatively to a negative provocation, no matter how personally satisfying it might feel in the moment. It requires the ability to hold in mind the long-term goals of the relationship. With motivation transformed, partners are more apt to take a moment to consider how to respond, rather than react reflexively in the heat of a moment.

In his most recent study of relationships, UCLA's Bradbury followed 136 couples for 10 years, starting within six months of their marriage. All the couples reported high levels of satisfaction at the start and four years later. What Bradbury and his colleague Justin Lavner found surprising was that some couples who were so satisfied at the four-year pass eventually divorced, despite having none of the risk factors identified in previous studies of relationship dissolution—wavering commitment, maladaptive personality traits, high levels of stress.

The only elements that identified those who eventually divorced were negative and self-protective reactions during discussions of relationship difficulties and nonsupportive reactions in discussing a personal issue. Displays of anger, contempt, or attempts to blame or invalidate a partner augured poorly, even when the partners felt their marriage was functioning well overall, the researchers report in the *Journal of Family Psychology*. So did expressions of discouragement toward a partner talking about a personality feature he or she wanted to change.

In other words, the inability or unwillingness to suppress negative emotions in the heat of the moment eliminates the possibility of a transformation of motivation to a broader perspective than one's own. Eventually, the cumulative impact of negative reactivity brings the relationship down.

"There is no such thing as two people meant for each other," says Michelle Givertz. "It's a matter of adjusting and adapting." But you have to know yourself so that you can get your needs for affection, inclusion, and control met in the ways that matter most for you. Even then, successful couples redefine their relationship many times, says Meinecke. Relationships need to continually evolve to fit ever-changing circumstances. They need to incorporate each partner's changes and find ways to meet their new needs.

"If both parties are willing to tackle the hard and vulnerable work of building love and healing conflict, they have a good chance to survive," says Page. If one party is reluctant, "you might need to say to your partner, 'I need this because I feel like we're losing each other, and I don't want that to happen.'"

In the end, says Minnesota's Doherty, "We're all difficult. Everyone who is married is a difficult spouse. We emphasize that our spouse is difficult and forget how we're difficult for them." If you want to have a mate in your life, he notes, you're going to have to go through the process of idealization and disillusionment—if not with your current partner then with the next. And the next. "You could really mess up your kids as you pursue the ideal mate." What's more, studies show that, on average, people do not make a better choice the second time around. Most often, people just trade one set of problems for another.

Boston's Real reports that he attended an anniversary party for friends who had been together 25 years. When someone commented on the longevity of the relationship, the husband replied: "Every morning I wake up, splash cold water on my face, and say out loud, 'Well, you're no prize either.'" While you're busy being disillusioned with your partner, Real suggests, you'll do better with a substantial dose of humility."

Critical Thinking

1. Is it "normal" to be discontented and disillusioned about your marriage and your partner?
2. What factors are most important to compatibility in relationships?
3. Does what bothers you about your relationship say more about you than your partner?

Create Central

www.mhhe.com/createcentral

Internet References

Coalition for Marriage, Family, and Couples Education
 www.smartmarriages.com

National Council on Family Relations
 www.ncfr.com

REBECCA WEBBER is a freelance writer based in New York.

Webber, Rebecca. From *Psychology Today*, January/February 2012. Copyright © 2012 by Sussex Publishers, LLC. Reprinted by permission.

Article

Prepared by: Patricia Hrusa Williams,
University of Maine at Farmington

How to Stay Married

ANNE KINGSTON

Learning Outcomes

After reading this article, you will be able to:

- Explain how men's and women's views and expectations for relationships and marriage differ.
- Describe the reasons behind women's adulterous behavior.
- Understand factors important to marital longevity.

Cynthia is a 68-year-old woman in a 45-year "committed marriage" who has figured out how to keep it that way. Every other month or so she goes out to lunch with her college boyfriend Thomas, who is also married and has no intention of leaving his wife. Usually their outings end in a hot and heavy "petting session" in his Mercedes. Sometimes, he rubs Jean Naté lotion, the scent Cynthia wore in college, onto her legs and compliments her beautiful feet. They've never consummated their relationship, nor do they intend to. Being with Thomas is "like a balloon liftoff," Cynthia reports, one that eases some of the tensions between her and her 74-year-old physics professor husband. "I'm a nicer, more tolerant person because of this affair," she says.

Cynthia's story is one of more than 60 confessionals from long-time wives that punctuate Iris Krasnow's new book *The Secret Lives of Wives: Women Share What It Really Takes to Stay Married*. And what their stories reveal is that marital longevity requires wives to establish strong, separate identities from their husbands through creative coping mechanisms, some of them covert. Krasnow spoke with more than 200 women, married between 15 and 70 years, who report taking separate holidays, embarking on new careers, establishing a tight circle of female friends, dabbling in *Same Time, Next Year*-style liaisons and adulterous affairs, and having "boyfriends with boundaries." Yoga and white wine also feature predominately.

The 58-year-old Krasnow, an author and journalism professor at American University, writes she was "stunned by the secrets and shenanigans" in her journalistic journey through American marriages. She comes to the subject from the vantage point of her own 23-year marriage to an architect she loves but admits to "loathing" occasionally. She credits summers spent apart, separate hobbies and her close relationships with male buddies for some of their marital stability.

It's a theory that builds on her previous books, *Surrendering to Motherhood* and *Surrendering to Marriage,* which extol the virtues of sublimating the self to a higher ideal.

Krasnow embraces the modern expectation that individuals experience perpetual personal growth and reinvention but dismisses the notion that partners must share each of these stages: "The reality is that for many wives, attaining longevity requires getting growth spurts elsewhere and experimenting with alternative routes," she writes.

First, however, women must lower their expectations of what marriage can provide, she advises: "Wives who don't rely on their husbands for happiness end up having the happiest marriages." Speaking on her phone from her home in Maryland, she echoes the sentiment: "You have to be partners on the level of the soul," she says of marriage. "But you are your own soulmate. Everybody needs a source of passion and purpose within. When you have that you can make any relationship work. You're not depending on anyone else to make you happy."

Krasnow paints a rosy picture of what a long-lasting marriage can provide women—better health, a rich shared history, the comfort of having someone who has your back, and personal and economic stability amid global uncertainty. Many of her testimonials suggest marriages can be regenerated over time, like a liver, with longer-married couples reporting the greatest happiness of all. There's also practical considerations, writes Krasnow, who admits online dating or disrobing in front of someone new horrifies her.

The book is destined to strike a nerve at a time when expectations of marriage and divorce are under scrutiny. Both the marriage rate and the divorce rate are dropping, with the exception of "grey divorce" among people over 50, embodied by Al and Tipper Gore who split after 40 years of marriage. We're in the midst of a divorce backlash, fuelled by the conservative-marriage movement and books like Judith Wallerstein's *The Unexpected Legacy of Divorce,* which raised consciousness about how divorce fractures families. Krasnow rejects the popular notion that divorce offers an opportunity for reinvention, as propagated by the booming divorce memoir genre. We should call it what it is: "a failure," she writes.

Yet it's clear the old script doesn't fit at a time women are increasingly out-earning their husbands and people are living into their 80s. "Women want to redefine how they navigate marriage," Krasnow says.

And the happily-ever-after prescription she offers will resonate. Many of the women Krasnow interviewed are like her—educated, smart, with enough disposable income to spend summers painting in Italy or travelling to ashrams. Most have financial autonomy: even a woman in a traditional arranged marriage has a thriving career and a helpful husband who gives her her own "space."

The directive that couples should give each other "space" for marriages to thrive is far from new, of course. Krasnow quotes from Kahlil Gibran's *The Prophet,* "Let there be space in your togetherness," published in 1923. In 1929, Virginia Woolf famously wrote of the need for women to have "money and a room of one's own" to create art. In 1954, Anne Morrow Lindbergh, wife of Charles Lindbergh, wrote *Gift From the Sea* on a summer retreat from her husband and children, which espoused the importance of solitude and self-reflection for women. It was an instant bestseller. And Johnny Cash attributed part of the success of his 32-year union with June Carter Cash to separate bathrooms: "The lady needs her space," he said.

Yet that sentiment runs counter to a popular culture in thrall to a "happily ever after" fairy-tale narrative and the "you complete me" message espoused in the movie *Jerry Maguire.* It's precisely the disconnect between the expectation that husband and wife be everything to one another and the reality of marriage that causes women to keep secrets, says Susan Shapiro Barash, a professor of gender studies at Marymount Manhattan College whose books include *Little White Lies, Deep Dark Secrets: The Truth About Why Women Lie.*

As time goes on, she says a lot of women feel trapped and that they've grown apart. "But because the culture so endorses marriage as a means and an end—children, a family, a partner for life (at least 60 per cent of the time). When it doesn't, "it's sometimes such a rude awakening for women they cover it up. Longevity does not lend itself to living happily as a wife."

That's a problem in a society in which women over 80 are the fastest-growing demographic.

Krasnow's examples indicate the wives most likely to live happily ever after into old age are those who can carve happily ever after out for themselves. It's the next iteration of the wife script that has traditionally called for a wifely sacrifice.

"We are the caregivers, the softies, the gender programmed to take care of the needs of everybody else before we care for ourselves," writes Krasnow. As a respite, she describes going out with her female friends for freewheeling bimonthly dinners where she can let loose as the "unmom" and "unwife."

Krasnow quotes 77-year-old sex and relationship therapist Marilyn Charwat, who says the American standard of sexual morality—that you marry one person and stay sexually and emotionally true and connected to that person—is "inhumane and impossible."

Yet the book reflects a broad view that sexual secrecy in marriage is rampant, from a woman buoyed by the memory of a furtive kiss with a neighbour to long-term sexual liaisons.

Not that Krasnow is advocating infidelity, though flirting is fine: "I say ride that hormonal surge straight to your own bedroom and initiate great sex with your spouse," she writes. Charwat's advice is more practical. She recommends women use vibrators, which releases them from relationship "tyranny."

The infidelity chapter, in which Krasnow spoke to 14 women conducting affairs, is coyly titled "Naughty Girls," a sensibility reflected in the cautionary references to 19th-century fictional heroines Emma Bovary and Anna Karenina. In one cautionary story, which reinforces Krasnow's theory that women should stick with their marriages, Lucy leaves her husband for a man she met on a plane and regrets her mistake.

Unlike husbands, wives are driven to extramarital affairs not as a way of exiting their marriage but remaining in them. One woman says her husband's sexual unresponsiveness justified her cheating. Mimi, a Lilly Pulitzer-wearing, 57-year-old conservative who's a secret swinger with her husband, practises an odd form of monogamy by saying he is the only man able to bring her to orgasm.

Shapiro Barash, who explored adultery in *A Passion for More: Wives Reveal the Affairs That Make or Break Their Marriages,* agrees unrealistic expectations usually fuel adultery. "The affair is always about what's missing from a marriage. I have rarely heard a woman speak of her lover being similar to her husband."

Krasnow's husband isn't a talker, so she craves extramarital conversation, not sex, a need sated by her various "boyfriends with boundaries." But seeking male friendship can be more fraught with peril than sexual affairs, the book reveals. One woman interviewed felt compelled to lie about her intense platonic relationship with a man; when her husband found out, he created a scene and demanded she never see him again. Krasnow admits there can be "danger zones": such as when participants text each other every 20 minutes. "Any man in my life, I immediately make sure my husband meets him."

What Krasnow is providing is a much-needed middle-aged fairy tale that begins years after the prince grows a paunch. Her prescriptions are both surprisingly banal and brilliant sound bites. "The real secret to staying married is not getting divorced," Krasnow writes, in a tautology. Save abuse or serial adultery, every marriage is salvageable with a big caveat that there's "trust, respect and intimacy, both emotional and physical."

As long as there's "a spittle of love," there's hope, she writes. Shelley, a woman whose marriage survived her husband's affair with her best friend, blames the woman more than her husband in a telling statement: "There's something sacred with the bond of women."

Then there's 48-year-old Julia, locked in a marriage "bound by the endless need" of her seriously ill daughter, who craves an "equal partner" but feels her husband is giving up. Her solution is to take up painting.

The focus on personal happiness would seem at odds with the notion espoused in Krasnow's other books. It's a perspective voiced by Phil and Pat Denniston, a happily married California couple even though they live and work together 24-7. They speak about the risks of separate directions and observe that marriages in which participants speak in terms of "me" not "us" are doomed.

In order to get to the happy "us," it's up to the wife to make the right choices from the get-go, Krasnow writes. She recalls she once asked Barbara Bush senior the secret to a happy marriage: "Pick the right husband in the first place."

The author agrees. "You should marry someone who's flexible, confident and trusts you: if you can't count on your husband or wife in a crazy unstable world then you're marrying the wrong person. But if you do marry the wrong person, you can always fall back on your secret life."

Critical Thinking

1. What do we hope to gain from getting married?
2. How do men's and women's views of marriage differ?
3. In *The Secret Lives of Women: What It Really Takes to Stay Married,* Iris Krasnow suggests that women need to lower their expectations of what marriage can provide. Do you agree or disagree? Why?
4. Is it a reasonable expectation in marriage to find someone who "completes you?"

Create Central

www.mhhe.com/createcentral

Internet References

Coalition for Marriage, Family, and Couples Education
www.smartmarriages.com
National Council on Family Relations
www.ncfr.com

From *Maclean's,* October 10, 2011, pp. 50–52. Copyright © 2011 by Macleans. Reprinted by permission.

Article

Prepared by: Patricia Hrusa Williams,
University of Maine at Farmington

Parenting Wars

Jane Shilling

Learning Outcomes

After reading this article, you will be able to:

- Recognize familial, societal, cultural, historical, and media influences on parenting.
- Understand child traits such as character and identity that are associated with positive developmental outcomes.

Recently I embarked on a long-overdue purge of my bookshelves. In the several dozen bin bags that made their way to the Oxfam bookshop (where the expressions of the staff slowly morphed from pleased gratitude, on my first visit, to unconcealed dread by the fifth) were two copies of the Communist Manifesto (*two?*); a formidable collection of works by Foucault, Sarraute, Perec and Queneau (I suppose I must once have read them—bookmarking postcards fell out of some of them—but if I did, no trace of the experience has remained); and all my parenting books. Penelope Leach's *Baby and Child,* Steve Biddulph's *Raising Boys* and *The Secret of Happy Children,* Kate Figes on *The Terrible Teens*—none of them, I realised, had been purchased by me: all had been acquired for some exercise in journalism— reviewing or interviewing, but never for private reading.

I don't know what made me think I could raise a child without an instruction manual, especially as I was the single mother of a boy, with no partner or brothers to consult about the mysteries of maleness. Sheer wilfulness, I suppose (and a certain bruised desire to avoid books that wrote of families as consisting of a child with two parents who were, in the days when I was doing my child-rearing, invariably assumed to be a mummy and a daddy). No doubt I should have made a better fist of it if I had been able to embrace Leach and Biddulph as my mentors, but my son is 21 now, and we are far into the territory for which no self-help books on parent/child relationships exist (unless you count D H Lawrence's *Sons and Lovers,* as a handy guide on what not to do).

As I began to inhabit my new identity as a mother and a lone parent, bringing up my child felt like an experience too personal and intimate to be trimmed to a template provided by experts. I was keen on babies and small children, and imagined that maternal instinct would cover the basics adequately. In this, I was faithfully replicating my own upbringing. My mother owned a copy of Dr Spock's *Baby and Child Care,* but it hadn't the air of a book that had been consulted frequently (though oddly enough I read it avidly as a child—so perhaps my son was, by default, a Spock baby).

My mother's maternal style must in turn have been modelled on her childhood, though my maternal grandmother was the youngest of a family of 13, so there would have been lots of people to offer advice on teething and potty training, a resource that my mother, an only child, and I, the first of my close friends to have a baby, both lacked.

I don't think that any of the women in my family took a conceptual or political view of child-rearing or parenthood. We were too absorbed by the day-to-day business of reading stories and wiping bottoms to find time to analyse what we were about. (I was the only one of us to combine work with motherhood throughout my son's childhood, and that wasn't a considered decision: as a lone parent, I had no choice.)

In my childhood—and, I think, my mother's—the visionary thinking came from my grandfather, who had spent his infancy and early childhood in the St Pancras workhouse and had, not coincidentally, strong views about the necessity for setting life goals and working towards them, preferably by getting an excellent education.

Even 20 years ago, my unprofessional attitude to bringing up a child was anachronistic; these days I suspect it would be regarded as borderline negligent. Mine was certainly the last generation in which one could allow oneself to muddle along without the assistance of the experts, treating parenthood as though it were analogous to friendship—a relationship that would grow and flourish of its own accord.

I might have done my best to ignore the fact, but as a single parent I was a fragmentary factor in what has grown into an urgent social crisis around the issues of childhood and family. If ever there was a time when one could raise children unselfconsciously, it is long past. Now every aspect of parenthood, from conception and birth to the forming of intellect and character, is the subject of anxious and often agonised scrutiny.

The crisis is both personal and political. On the one hand, as engaged parents, we feel that we are in some sense our children: their successes and failures represent us almost more vividly than our own achievements. And as the condition of youth becomes ever more extended, lasting in attenuated form until middle age and beyond, our children can help to feed our vision of ourselves as perennially young. (Whenever I hear a parent say that they are "more of a friend than a parent" to their son or daughter, I wonder what privately the child might think about that.)

The inevitable consequence of seeing our children as our alter egos and friends is the sense of dread that fills us when they become opaque to us. Children and adolescents need to have parenting from somewhere, and if it isn't offered by their parents they will seek it among their peers— a group that once might have included mainly the people in their year at school, but which now, thanks to social media and the internet, comprises a global community of "friends" and acquaintants, a world in which the most adhesive parent can find it difficult to stick with its offspring.

Beyond the family, there lies society—a construct composed, alarmingly enough, of other people and their children, many of them not as conscientiously raised as one's own. The media reports are dismaying; this is a generation disaffected and resentful, alienated from education, or unable to obtain the jobs that were promised them in return for their hard-won examination results, debarred by the lack of an income from buying their own home, the dependency of childhood uneasily protracted by having to return to living in the family home as adults after a taste of freedom at college. Despite our excellent intentions and our strenuous efforts, is this the world we have made for our children?

The confusion of western attitudes to parenting is reflected in a cacophony of contradictory images. Last year the cover of *Time* magazine featured a photograph of the 26-year-old attachment parenting advocate Jamie Lynne Grumet breastfeeding her son Aram, aged nearly four, who was dressed in military-style camouflage pants and standing on a small chair to reach the magnificently tanned breast protruding from her sexy black camisole top.

While Aram suckles in his miniature army fatigues, the infant literacy movement encourages parents to believe that it is never too early to begin learning to read, with initiatives such as Reading Bear, a free online programme for tinies whose editor-in-chief is Larry Sanger, the co-founder of Wikipedia. Not that a Tiger Mother-ish enthusiasm for prodigies of infant learning is an exclusively 21st-century phenomenon. Dr Johnson's friend Hester Thrale recorded in her Family Book of 1766 the achievements of her two-year-old daughter, Queeney, who later became the disaffected protagonist of Beryl Bainbridge's splendid novel *According to Queeney*:

> She repeats the Pater Noster, the three Christian virtues, and the signs of the Zodiac in Watts' verses; she likewise knows them on the globe perfectly well. . . . She knows her nine figures and the simplest combinations of them; but none beyond a hundred; she knows all the Heathen Deities by their Attributes and counts to 20 without missing one.

Eat your heart out, Amy Chua.

It is true that there has probably never been a time when parenting was regarded as the exclusive preserve of parents. In *Dream Babies,* her 1983 study of child-rearing advice to parents from Locke to Spock, Christina Hardyment notes that the history of childcare manuals is almost as old as that of mass publication. The original manuals were booklets written by doctors for use by nurses in foundling hospitals. "It is with great Pleasure I see at last the Preservation of Children become the Care of Men of Sense," wrote William Cadogan in his *Essay on Nursing* (1748). "In my opinion this Business has been too long fatally left to the management of Women who cannot be supposed to have a proper Knowledge to fit them for the Task, notwithstanding they look upon it to be their own Province."

The sentiment, if not the language, is curiously familiar from the plethora of modern parenting books which, even as they reassure anxious parents, cannot help but undermine their confidence with categorical but contradictory claims to know what is best for their offspring. Baby not sleeping? Gina Ford will fix that in no time. What a relief. Unless, that is, you happen to pick up Penelope Leach's most recent tome, *The Essential First Year: What Babies Need Parents to Know* (2010), from which you learn that leaving a distressed baby to cry can produce levels of the stress hormone cortisol (in the baby, that is, rather than the parent) that are toxic to its developing brain and may have long-term emotional consequences, as the anxiety of being left to weep unanswered pursues the beleaguered infant throughout childhood and adult life.

In short, you have a choice between inflicting brain damage and emotional distress if you leave little Magenta to cry herself to sleep; or an identical result if you rush to comfort her every time she wakes in the small hours and then—in an unforgivable, if perhaps understandable, episode of insomnia-induced rage—hurl her into her cot and lie on the floor beside it sobbing inconsolably and screaming, "I wish I'd never had a baby."

Still, let's not catastrophise. Somehow you and your child have both survived the essential first year, and even the essential first decade. Now you are entering the difficult hinterland of adolescence, and there are yet more things to worry about.

If you've got sons, there is the academic underperformance of boys in the overly feminised school environment, not to mention peer pressure to engage in all kinds of highly hazardous, not to say illegal, behaviour, and the long hours they spend closeted with their computer in their dark and malodorous rooms. For the parents of girls, there are problems of early sexualisation and their fragile relationship with their body image; nor is there any room for complacency about their examination results, which are likely to be affected by their desire not to be regarded as a nerd, neek, or anything other than one of the "popular girls".

For both sexes there is, besides the universal hazards of bullying and being mugged in the park for your cool stuff, the horrible complication of the way in which emergent adolescent sexuality is formed (or deformed) by online pornography.

Here, happily, Steve Biddulph the no-nonsense Australian family therapist and childcare guru can help, with his bestselling books *Raising Boys* and (most recently) *Raising Girls.* When it comes to bringing up daughters, a mother's place is invariably in the wrong, and Biddulph's warmth and wisdom will doubtless console many. Nevertheless, there is something about the spectacle of a middle-aged male expert issuing advice on raising girls that conjures a faint echo of Cadogan's conviction that the raising of children is best left to men of sense.

The happiness of children (as opposed to their moral education, which predominated in child-rearing manuals before the mid-20th century) is something to which a prodigious amount of expertise has been devoted over the past couple of generations.

Almost two decades ago, in 1994, Penelope Leach published a premonitory tract about the treatment of children in affluent western society. *Children First,* subtitled *What Our Society Must Do—and Is Not Doing—for Our Children Today,* was a scathing anatomy of the societal approach to child-rearing which saw parenting as "a universal hobby that is awkward because it cannot be shelved during the working week, interrupts important adult business and is hard on soft furnishings".

Some of Leach's most urgent priorities for a child-friendly society have been addressed in the intervening years. Yet her sunlit vision of a world in which children's needs have equal weight with those of adults remains dismayingly far from reality. In 2007, a Unicef study that assessed the well-being of children in six categories—material; health and safety; education; peer relationships; behaviours and risks; and young people's own perceptions of their happiness—placed the US second-to-last and the UK last in a league of 21 economically advanced nations.

In the introduction to his book *The Beast in the Nursery* (1998), the psychoanalyst Adam Phillips writes, "As children take for granted, lives are only liveable if they give pleasure." Yet the Unicef study suggests that despite our obsession with raising happy, successful children, many of them are trapped in lives that are, by Phillips's measure, unliveable.

So, what has gone wrong? In *Kith,* her strange, poetic book on the relationship between childhood and the natural world (to be published in May), the writer Jay Griffiths asks the intractable question: "Why are so many children in Euro-American cultures unhappy?" and concludes that, in the affluent west, childhood has become a lost realm.

Children's books are written by grownups, so it is unwise to call them in evidence when discussing styles of parenting. Nevertheless, it is striking that the fiction best loved by children—from Captain Marryat and Mark Twain, E Nesbit and Richmal Crompton to Jacqueline Wilson and J K Rowling—describes childhood as a state unencumbered by parental interference, in which children confront all kinds of challenges and dangers and survive by their own resourcefulness.

In modern America and Europe, Griffiths notes, children may read about the adventures of Huck Finn or William Brown but they are unlikely to share their experiences: "Many kids today are effectively under house arrest. . . . If there is one word which sums up the treatment of children today, it is 'enclosure'. Today's children are enclosed in school and home . . . and rigid schedules of time". Society, she adds, "has historically contrived a school system that is half factory, half prison, and too easily ignores the very education which children crave".

In *How Children Succeed,* the Canadian-American writer Paul Tough addresses the question of childhood unhappiness from a perspective that is the precise opposite of Griffiths's: her approach is lyrical, emotional and elegiac; his is logical, analytical and didactic. Nonetheless their theories converge on a single point—that, as a preparation for life, education is failing huge numbers of children.

Tough's book, as he writes, "is about an idea that is . . . gathering momentum in classrooms and clinics and labs and lecture halls across the country and around the world. According to this new way of thinking, the conventional wisdom about child development over the past few decades has been misguided. We have been focusing on the wrong skills and abilities in our children, and using the wrong strategies to nurture and teach those skills. . . ."

There is something very satisfying about an educational theory that denounces all previous theories. It seems to offer the possibility of a miraculous redemption of past errors and the hope of a certain path to a better future. The main mistake of recent years, Tough argues, has been to focus on measurable academic attainment by our children, to the exclusion of the more nebulous personal qualities (or "character") necessary to translate examination results into the kind of stable success that makes young people good citizens.

"Character" is a term with curiously Victorian overtones; the more formidable early child-rearing volumes that Christina Hardyment discusses in *Dream Babies* are keen on this quality. Yet the interdisciplinary school of thought that Tough describes,

Gurus of the Nursery

For 52 years after it was first published in 1946, **Benjamin McLane Spock**'s *Baby and Child Care* was the second-bestselling book after the Bible. A physician by training, Spock turned to psychoanalysis to examine child-rearing. His ideas were highly influential and encouraged parents to see their children as individuals.

The psychologist **Penelope Leach**'s *Baby and Child: from Birth to Age Five,* was published in 1977 and has sold more than two million copies. Much of her writing has focused on the drawbacks of childcare, a position that has attracted significant criticism.

Gina Ford, the author of *The Contented Little Baby Book* (1999), has long divided opinion, in part because she has no children (she bases her writing and advice on having looked after "over 300" babies as a maternity nurse). Some swear by her philosophy of strict routines, whereas others deplore the rigidity of her approach.

When *Battle Hymn of the Tiger Mother* was published in 2011, readers and critics were stunned at **Amy Chua**'s candid account of raising her two daughters. Chua, a Yale law professor, writes that "this was supposed to be a story of how Chinese parents are better at raising kids than western ones. But instead, it's about a bitter clash of cultures, a fleeting taste of glory, and how I was humbled by a 13-year-old. . . ."

Paul Tough is a journalist and former editor at *The New York Times* Magazine. In *How Children Succeed* (newly published by Random House), he analyses the character traits that help a child have a secure and happy future.

An endorsement by Bill Clinton gives some indication of the praise that has greeted **Andrew Solomon**'s latest book, *Far From the Tree,* in the United States. Solomon—who is also an activist and lecturer—spent years researching the work by interviewing families with diverse and challenging experiences of child-rearing.

which is based on the theories of Martin Seligman, a professor of psychology at the University of Pennsylvania, and the late Christopher Peterson of the University of Michigan, factorises the success trait into seven separate elements: grit, self-control, zest, social intelligence, gratitude, optimism and curiosity.

Armed with these attributes, the theory goes that children from all kinds of unpromising backgrounds, from the vastly affluent with no experience of character-forming misfortune to the underprivileged with a discouraging excess of "deep and pervasive adversity at home", can achieve both the academic qualifications that are the golden ticket to the security of regular employment and the qualities that will make them useful members of society.

On this side of the Atlantic, the case for character development as an element of education has been vigorously promoted by Anthony Seldon, the Master of Wellington College. In May last year, the University of Birmingham's Jubilee Centre for Character and Values was launched, with funding from the John Templeton Foundation, established by the American philanthropist.

Tough describes how the principle of teaching—and assessing—character as well as academic attainment was initially taken up by two schools, KIPP Academy Middle School in the South Bronx, whose students are mostly from low-income families, and Riverdale Country School, situated in one of the most affluent neighbourhoods of New York City, and where pre-kindergarten fees start at $40,750 a year.

KIPP was already something of a model institution after a programme of immersive schooling produced a startling improvement in its academic results. But the instigator of that programme, David Levin, a Yale graduate, was dismayed by how many of his high-achieving students subsequently dropped out of college. Meanwhile, the headmaster of Riverdale, Dominic Randolph, had begun to feel that "the push on tests" at high-achieving schools such as his was "missing out on some serious parts of what it means to be human".

For the students, the problems at both ends of the socio-economic spectrum were oddly similar: low levels of maternal attachment, high levels of parental criticism, minimal after-school adult supervision, emotional and physical isolation from parents and—in the case of the rich children—excessive pressure to succeed, resulting in anxiety, depression and chronic academic problems.

The evolution of the character development programme diverged sharply at the two schools during the course of the trial. At KIPP it leaned towards the practical and prescriptive; at Riverdale the emphasis was more moral and philosophical, on leading a good life rather than wearing the uniform correctly and paying attention in class.

As the programme has continued, the statistics on college dropout rates among KIPP students have seemed modestly encouraging. It is harder to measure the success of the experiment among Riverdale students, as their path towards academic success was always much clearer. Tough acknowledges that what he calls the "new science of adversity . . . presents a real challenge to some deeply held political beliefs on both the left

and the right". In the UK, Seldon concedes that "character" might be seen as a synonym for "middle-class" or "public-school" values. Yet both men appear convinced that it is the only means of enabling young people to alter what might otherwise appear to be a fixed destiny of failure and unhappiness.

While Tough proposes the formal exercise of grit and optimism as the key to personal success, Andrew Solomon's new book, *Far From the Tree,* is a study of families whose ideas about what constitutes "success" for their child have had to be recalibrated, sometimes very sharply. Solomon interviewed 200 families for his epic survey of identity and difference, which was a decade in the writing. Each chapter is devoted to the experiences of children and parents living with one of a dozen forms of "otherness"— deafness, dwarfism, Down's syndrome, autism, schizophrenia, prodigies, criminal children and those born of rape.

Solomon's theme is the development of identity. He argues that children acquire identity both "vertically", in the form of inherited traits such as language and ethnicity, and "horizontally", from a peer group. The greater the differences between the child and his or her parents, the more powerful the tensions between the horizontal and vertical identities.

The germ of the book sprang from an article on deaf culture that Solomon wrote in 1993 for *The New York Times.* He found that most deaf children are born to hearing parents, who often feel compelled to help their children "succeed" in a hearing world by focusing on the ability to communicate orally, often to the detriment of other aspects of their development. For such children, the discovery of a culture that celebrates deafness, regarding it as a state of being as vibrant and creative as the hearing world, often appears a liberation, a portal to an identity that does not have to be lived out against a contrasting "normality".

But within that experience of liberation lies the seed of a painful truth: that, for all children marked by difference, whatever its nature (Solomon is gay, and writes movingly about his experience of growing up in a straight family), their first experience of their otherness is almost invariably provided by their own family. He explores the complicated nexus of "normalities" which exists within the family of a child who is in some way different, and between the family and the outside world, with a dogged forensic elegance.

Solomon's account, like Tough's, is laden with anecdote, but while Tough uses his case histories to personalise his theories, Solomon's purpose in writing is narrative and exploratory, rather than ideological or didactic. Like Griffiths, he seeks the key to a universe of familial complexity, and finds it in the most obvious place of all. Love, he concludes, is all you need.

That was pretty much my guiding principle when I began my own experience of parenthood. And on the whole I'm not persuaded that the outcome would have been very different if I had spent more time consulting the experts. Which is not the same thing as feeling that I have been a success as a parent. Raising a child involves a circuitous journey of many branching routes that may lead, if parents and children are lucky, loving and tolerant, to a destination that everyone involved finds bearable.

Twenty years ago, or ten, or even five, if you had asked me whether I thought I was a good mother, I would have answered "good enough" with a degree of self-satisfaction. I had, after all, raised a kind, sane, personable grown-up with a decent clutch of exam results, an entrenched reading habit and an unusual ability to discuss with enthusiasm both West Ham's position in the League table and the nuances of female fashion; and I felt that I had done it largely contra mundum.

More recently, as my son and I have settled into our roles as adult equals and our accounts of the past have diverged, I have begun to understand that he has grown into the person he is as much despite me as because of me. My main aim as a mother had been to try to avoid the aspects of my own upbringing that had caused me pain. I thought that would be easy, but it was not.

Sometimes my son's narratives of his childhood (still so recent and fresh in his mind) make me think that almost everything I did was wrong. It is a melancholy reflection, to put it mildly. But it makes me think that perhaps the real work of parenthood is to learn to accommodate the stories that your children tell you about their upbringing.

Critical Thinking

1. Shilling's article discusses and reviews several different philosophies of rearing children. Which is closest to the style of parenting your parents used? Which style or attributes do you want to adopt as a parent? Why?

2. Why are modern parents believed to be more fearful and protective than past generations?

3. What is the single most important thing parents can do to help promote the healthy development of their children?

4. The article suggests that parents have over-emphasized academic success in children and under-emphasized character development. Do you agree or disagree? Why?

Create Central

www.mhhe.com/createcentral

Internet Reference

Health and Parenting Center
www.webmd.com/parenting

Tufts University Child and Family Webguide
www.cfw.tufts.edu

Positive Parenting
www.positiveparenting.com

The National Association for Child Development
www.nacd.org

Child Trends
www.childtrends.org

JANE SHILLING is the author of *The Stranger in the Mirror*.

Shilling, Jane. From *New Stateswoman*, January 2013, pp. 27–31. Copyright © 2013 by New Statesman, Ltd. Reprinted by permission.

Article

Prepared by: Patricia Hrusa Williams,
University of Maine at Farmington

Why Chinese Mothers Are Superior

Can a regimen of no playdates, no TV, no computer games, and hours of music practice create happy kids?
And what happens when they fight back?

Amy Chua

Learning Outcomes

After reading this article, you will be able to:

- Identify how culture influences parental expectations, goals, and behaviors.
- Identify how societal expectations influence parenting expectations, goals, and behaviors.
- Describe skills children need to be academically and personally successful.

A lot of people wonder how Chinese parents raise such stereotypically successful kids. They wonder what these parents do to produce so many math whizzes and music prodigies, what it's like inside the family, and whether they could do it too. Well, I can tell them, because I've done it. Here are some things my daughters, Sophia and Louisa, were never allowed to do:

- Attend a sleepover
- Have a playdate
- Be in a school play
- Complain about not being in a school play
- Watch TV or play computer games
- Choose their own extracurricular activities
- Get any grade less than an A
- Not be the No. 1 student in every subject except gym and drama
- Play any instrument other than the piano or violin
- Not play the piano or violin

I'm using the term "Chinese mother" loosely. I know some Korean, Indian, Jamaican, Irish and Ghanaian parents who qualify too. Conversely, I know some mothers of Chinese heritage, almost always born in the West, who are not Chinese mothers, by choice or otherwise. I'm also using the term "Western parents" loosely. Western parents come in all varieties.

All the same, even when Western parents think they're being strict, they usually don't come close to being Chinese mothers.

For example, my Western friends who consider themselves strict make their children practice their instruments 30 minutes every day. An hour at most. For a Chinese mother, the first hour is the easy part. It's hours two and three that get tough. Despite our squeamishness about cultural stereotypes, there are tons of studies out there showing marked and quantifiable differences between Chinese and Westerners when it comes to parenting. In one study of 50 Western American mothers and 48 Chinese immigrant mothers, almost 70 percent of the Western mothers said either that "stressing academic success is not good for children" or that "parents need to foster the idea that learning is fun." By contrast, roughly 0 percent of the Chinese mothers felt the same way. Instead, the vast majority of the Chinese mothers said that they believe their children can be "the best" students, that "academic achievement reflects successful parenting," and that if children did not excel at school then there was "a problem" and parents "were not doing their job." Other studies indicate that compared to Western parents, Chinese parents spend approximately 10 times as long every day drilling academic activities with their children. By contrast, Western kids are more likely to participate in sports teams.

What Chinese parents understand is that nothing is fun until you're good at it. To get good at anything you have to work, and children on their own never want to work, which is why it is crucial to override their preferences. This often requires fortitude on the part of the parents because the child will resist; things are always hardest at the beginning, which is where Western parents tend to give up. But if done properly, the Chinese strategy produces a virtuous circle. Tenacious practice, practice, practice is crucial for excellence; rote repetition is underrated in America. Once a child starts to excel at something—whether it's math, piano, pitching or ballet—he or she gets praise, admiration and satisfaction. This builds confidence and makes the once not-fun activity fun. This in turn makes it easier for the parent to get the child to work even more.

Chinese parents can get away with things that Western parents can't. Once when I was young—maybe more than once—when I was extremely disrespectful to my mother, my father angrily called me "garbage" in our native Hokkien dialect. It worked really well. I felt terrible and deeply ashamed of what I had done. But it didn't damage my self-esteem or anything like that. I knew exactly how highly he thought of me. I didn't actually think I was worthless or feel like a piece of garbage.

As an adult, I once did the same thing to Sophia, calling her garbage in English when she acted extremely disrespectfully toward me. When I mentioned that I had done this at a dinner party, I was immediately ostracized. One guest named Marcy got so upset she broke down in tears and had to leave early. My friend Susan, the host, tried to rehabilitate me with the remaining guests.

The fact is that Chinese parents can do things that would seem unimaginable—even legally actionable—to Westerners. Chinese mothers can say to their daughters, "Hey fatty—lose some weight." By contrast, Western parents have to tiptoe around the issue, talking in terms of "health" and never ever mentioning the f-word, and their kids still end up in therapy for eating disorders and negative self-image. (I also once heard a Western father toast his adult daughter by calling her "beautiful and incredibly competent." She later told me that made her feel like garbage.)

Chinese parents can order their kids to get straight As. Western parents can only ask their kids to try their best. Chinese parents can say, "You're lazy. All your classmates are getting ahead of you." By contrast, Western parents have to struggle with their own conflicted feelings about achievement, and try to persuade themselves that they're not disappointed about how their kids turned out.

I've thought long and hard about how Chinese parents can get away with what they do. I think there are three big differences between the Chinese and Western parental mind-sets. First, I've noticed that Western parents are extremely anxious about their children's self-esteem. They worry about how their children will feel if they fail at something, and they constantly try to reassure their children about how good they are notwithstanding a mediocre performance on a test or at a recital. In other words, Western parents are concerned about their children's psyches. Chinese parents aren't. They assume strength, not fragility, and as a result they behave very differently.

For example, if a child comes home with an A-minus on a test, a Western parent will most likely praise the child. The Chinese mother will gasp in horror and ask what went wrong. If the child comes home with a B on the test, some Western parents will still praise the child. Other Western parents will sit their child down and express disapproval, but they will be careful not to make their child feel inadequate or insecure, and they will not call their child "stupid," "worthless" or "a disgrace." Privately, the Western parents may worry that their child does not test well or have aptitude in the subject or that there is something wrong with the curriculum and possibly the whole school. If the child's grades do not improve, they may eventually schedule a meeting with the school principal to challenge the way the subject is being taught or to call into question the teacher's credentials.

If a Chinese child gets a B—which would never happen—there would first be a screaming, hair-tearing explosion. The devastated Chinese mother would then get dozens, maybe hundreds of practice tests and work through them with her child for as long as it takes to get the grade up to an A.

Chinese parents demand perfect grades because they believe that their child can get them. If their child doesn't get them, the Chinese parent assumes it's because the child didn't work hard enough. That's why the solution to substandard performance is always to excoriate, punish and shame the child. The Chinese parent believes that their child will be strong enough to take the shaming and to improve from it. (And when Chinese kids do excel, there is plenty of ego-inflating parental praise lavished in the privacy of the home.)

Second, Chinese parents believe that their kids owe them everything. The reason for this is a little unclear, but it's probably a combination of Confucian filial piety and the fact that the parents have sacrificed and done so much for their children. (And it's true that Chinese mothers get in the trenches, putting in long grueling hours personally tutoring, training, interrogating and spying on their kids.) Anyway, the understanding is that Chinese children must spend their lives repaying their parents by obeying them and making them proud. By contrast, I don't think most Westerners have the same view of children being permanently indebted to their parents. My husband, Jed, actually has the opposite view. "Children don't choose their parents," he once said to me. "They don't even choose to be born. It's parents who foist life on their kids, so it's the parents' responsibility to provide for them. Kids don't owe their parents anything. Their duty will be to their own kids." This strikes me as a terrible deal for the Western parent.

Third, Chinese parents believe that they know what is best for their children and therefore override all of their children's own desires and preferences. That's why Chinese daughters can't have boyfriends in high school and why Chinese kids can't go to sleepaway camp. It's also why no Chinese kid would ever dare say to their mother, "I got a part in the school play! I'm Villager Number Six. I'll have to stay after school for rehearsal every day from 3:00 to 7:00, and I'll also need a ride on weekends." God help any Chinese kid who tried that one. Don't get me wrong: It's not that Chinese parents don't care about their children. Just the opposite. They would give up anything for their children. It's just an entirely different parenting model.

Here's a story in favor of coercion, Chinese-style. Lulu was about 7, still playing two instruments, and working on a piano piece called "The Little White Donkey" by the French composer Jacques Ibert. The piece is really cute—you can just imagine a little donkey ambling along a country road with its master—but it's also incredibly difficult for young players because the two hands have to keep schizophrenically different rhythms. Lulu couldn't do it. We worked on it nonstop for a week, drilling each of her hands separately, over and over. But whenever we tried putting the hands together, one always morphed into the other, and everything fell apart. Finally, the day before her lesson, Lulu announced in exasperation that she was giving up and stomped off.

"Get back to the piano now," I ordered.

"You can't make me."

"Oh yes, I can."

Back at the piano, Lulu made me pay. She punched, thrashed and kicked. She grabbed the music score and tore it to shreds. I taped the score back together and encased it in a plastic shield so that it could never be destroyed again. Then I hauled Lulu's dollhouse to the car and told her I'd donate it to the Salvation Army piece by piece if she didn't have "The Little White Donkey" perfect by the next day. When Lulu said, "I thought you were going to the Salvation Army, why are you still here?" I threatened her with no lunch, no dinner, no Christmas or Hanukkah presents, no birthday parties for two, three, four years. When she still kept playing it wrong, I told her she was purposely working herself into a frenzy because she was secretly afraid she couldn't do it. I told her to stop being lazy, cowardly, self-indulgent and pathetic.

Jed took me aside. He told me to stop insulting Lulu—which I wasn't even doing, I was just motivating her—and that he didn't think threatening Lulu was helpful. Also, he said, maybe Lulu really just couldn't do the technique—perhaps she didn't have the coordination yet—had I considered that possibility?

"You just don't believe in her," I accused.

"That's ridiculous," Jed said scornfully. "Of course I do."

"Sophia could play the piece when she was this age."

"But Lulu and Sophia are different people," Jed pointed out.

"Oh no, not this," I said, rolling my eyes. "Everyone is special in their special own way," I mimicked sarcastically. "Even losers are special in their own special way. Well don't worry, you don't have to lift a finger. I'm willing to put in as long as it takes, and I'm happy to be the one hated. And you can be the one they adore because you make them pancakes and take them to Yankees games."

I rolled up my sleeves and went back to Lulu. I used every weapon and tactic I could think of. We worked right through dinner into the night, and I wouldn't let Lulu get up, not for water, not even to go to the bathroom. The house became a war zone, and I lost my voice yelling, but still there seemed to be only negative progress, and even I began to have doubts. Then, out of the blue, Lulu did it. Her hands suddenly came together—her right and left hands each doing their own imperturbable thing—just like that.

Lulu realized it the same time I did. I held my breath. She tried it tentatively again. Then she played it more confidently and faster, and still the rhythm held. A moment later, she was beaming.

"Mommy, look—it's easy!" After that, she wanted to play the piece over and over and wouldn't leave the piano. That night, she came to sleep in my bed, and we snuggled and hugged, cracking each other up. When she performed "The Little White Donkey" at a recital a few weeks later, parents came up to me and said, "What a perfect piece for Lulu—it's so spunky and so her."

Even Jed gave me credit for that one. Western parents worry a lot about their children's self-esteem. But as a parent, one of the worst things you can do for your child's self-esteem is to let them give up. On the flip side, there's nothing better for building confidence than learning you can do something you thought you couldn't.

There are all these new books out there portraying Asian mothers as scheming, callous, overdriven people indifferent to their kids' true interests. For their part, many Chinese secretly believe that they care more about their children and are willing to sacrifice much more for them than Westerners, who seem perfectly content to let their children turn out badly. I think it's a misunderstanding on both sides. All decent parents want to do what's best for their children. The Chinese just have a totally different idea of how to do that.

Western parents try to respect their children's individuality, encouraging them to pursue their true passions, supporting their choices, and providing positive reinforcement and a nurturing environment. By contrast, the Chinese believe that the best way to protect their children is by preparing them for the future, letting them see what they're capable of, and arming them with skills, work habits and inner confidence that no one can ever take away.

Critical Thinking

1. What does Chua see as the keys to raising successful children?

2. What do you think of Chua's advice? What are some strengths and weaknesses of her recommendations?

3. Are the skills children need to be academically successful the same as those needed to be happy and successful in life?

4. Do you think her perspective applies to all Chinese mothers? To what degree might her article promote negative stereotypes of Chinese mothers?

Create Central

www.mhhe.com/createcentral

Internet References

Health and Parenting Center
www.webmd.com/parenting
Positive Parenting
www.positiveparenting.com
Tufts University Child and Family Webguide
www.cfw.tufts.edu
The National Association for Child Development
www.nacd.org
Child Trends
www.childtrends.org

AMY CHUA is a professor at Yale Law School and author of *Day of Empire* and *World on Fire: How Exporting Free Market Democracy Breeds Ethnic Hatred and Global Instability*. This essay is excerpted from *Battle Hymn of the Tiger Mother* by Amy Chua, published by the Penguin Press, a member of Penguin Group (USA) Inc. Copyright 2011 by Amy Chua.

Article

Prepared by: Patricia Hrusa Williams,
University of Maine at Farmington

Parental Responsibility and Obesity in Children

Train up a child in the way he should go; and when he is old, he will not depart from it. (Proverbs 22: 6)
For I have told him that I will judge his house for ever for the iniquity which he knoweth; because his sons
made themselves vile, and he restrained them not. (1 Samuel 3: 13)

SØREN HOLM

Learning Outcomes

After reading this article, you will be able to:

- Define the term "best interests of the child."

- Identify factors contributing to the development of obesity in children.

Introduction

As the Old Testament verses above testify, attributing responsibility to parents for the behaviour and lifestyle of their children is nothing new. The question of when we can attribute such responsibility and what actions we can justifiably take on the basis of such attribution is, however still a very relevant question. It has recently been raised again in discussions about how society should tackle the so-called 'obesity epidemic', i.e., the rise in the proportion of persons with a bodymass index (BMI) above the conventional cutoff for obesity (currently BMI > 30). In the more and more alarmist media reporting of and political pronouncements concerning this 'epidemic'—now officially 'as bad as climate risk'—parents have again and again been berated for allowing their children to become obese.

In the present paper, I will first present a brief overview of current knowledge about (i) the link between parental behaviour and lifestyle and childhood obesity, (ii) the many other factors influencing overweight and obesity rates in children and (iii) the effectiveness of interventions in children who are already overweight and obese. On the basis of this, I will then consider to what extent it is meaningful to attribute responsibility to parents in theory and in practice. I will argue that although there is a sense in which many parents are causally and morally responsible for the obesity of their children, it is only infrequently that this parental responsibility justifies intervention in the family context by society on behalf of the children.

Throughout the paper, I will only be concerned with an analysis of the situation in industrialised, high-income societies and only with intervention within a public health frame. I will therefore not consider whether intervention is warranted in cases where a child is so obese that it has immediate health effects (i.e., the child is 'morbidly obese') and I will not consider the role of law, in general, in relation to childhood obesity (for an excellent and comprehensive discussion of this, see Alderman *et al.*, 2007).

The Best Interest Standard

To some, the topic of the present paper may initially seem rather quaint. In bioethics the currently most prominent debate about parental responsibility is about responsibility in procreative decisions, i.e., decisions about which, if any children to bring into the world. In that debate, a prominent position on the consequentialist side of the debate is that parents have strong obligations to choose the best child they possibly can (Savulescu, 2001). An extension of that argument seems to imply that parents have an obligation to provide their children with the best upbringing they can possibly do. Similarly, current legal theorising on decisions concerning children and a significant segment of the literature on children's participation in research often proceeds from the assumption that the interests of the child must be paramount in such decisions (Freeman, 1997).

Both lines of argument thus seem to lead directly to the conclusion that if obesity is bad for children, then parents have an overriding obligation to ensure that their children do not become obese (see below for more on the harm caused by obesity in children).

But I will persevere with the argument for two reasons. First, because procreative decisions differ from the parental decisions that we are considering here because of the possibility of replacement in reproductive decisions before conception.

Among the many children I could have, I will only have a few and it does not matter to any of these children *ex ante* which ones I bring into the world (there is no waiting queue of souls waiting to be ensouled or children waiting to be born). *Ex ante* it also matters little to me personally which child I get, since so many of its characteristics are undetermined. Decisions about the child I do have are radically different because they affect a determinate other person and affect me in quite different ways.

Second, because there is no way family decision-making can make the best interest of the child paramount in real life. The interest of other family members must almost always play a role and there is furthermore in many cases no clear answer to what the best interest of the child is. The decision made is part of forming that best interest. I have argued this point elsewhere so will not repeat it here (Harris and Holm, 2003, see also Holm and Edgar, in press).

The Causes of Obesity

Obesity has a multifactorial genesis in almost all cases except those involving rare genetic disorders like Prader–Willi syndrome, although the final common pathway is a long-term imbalance between energy intake and energy expenditure. This imbalance does not have to be large to lead to obesity in the long run and most obese people have not become obese by monstrous overeating. The fat tissue that the excess energy will eventually be stored in has an energy density of approximately 38MJ per kg. This means that a consistent positive energy balance of 104 kJ per day (i.e., considerably less than one ordinary glass of a non-diet cola beverage or one standard chocolate bar) will lead to a weight gain of 1 kg in a year, or 10 kg in 10 years, enough to move a nonobese 7-year-old girl into overweight or (depending on her height since BMI is height-dependent) obesity at the age of 17.

Among the factors predisposing to obesity, the most important is living in an obesogenic society. That is, a society where there is easy access to high-energy foods, no food insecurity and little need, incentive or opportunity to engage in physical exercise either at work or in leisure time. The main reason that widespread obesity has never occurred before in human history is that humans have never lived in a consistently obesogenic environment before. We are all genetically programmed to be energy conservers able to deal with periods of food scarcity and as one of the authors of a major UK report on obesity was reported as saying: '. . . in this environment, it was surprising that anyone was able to remain thin, and so the notion of obesity simply being a product of personal over-indulgence had to be abandoned for good.' Let us briefly describe some of the causal factors behind obesity. There are known genetic factors that increase the risk of obesity and it has been estimated from a range of studies that the minimum heritability for obesity is 0.4, showing that there is a significant genetic component even in 'ordinary' obesity (Bell *et al.,* 2005).

Early nutrition influences later food choice even as early as prenatally (Savage *et al.,* 2007) and many other family-related factors also influence the risk of child obesity. The most important factor is probably whether one or both of the parents are themselves obese (Whitaker *et al.,* 1997). Having two obese parents is a strong risk factor for early childhood obesity and a slightly weaker risk factor for obesity in adolescence. Parental obesity in itself is probably not a true causal factor, since it is difficult to imagine a mechanism by which parental obesity directly produces obesity in the child, but it is probably a proxy for a large number of genetic and environmental parent-related influences on child development. Some more specific factors linked to parental behaviour have also been identified. These include parental feeding style and parental modelling of physical activity (Savage *et al.,* 2007). There is also evidence that parental concern about overweight and obesity depends on whether the parents perceive the child to be overall healthy or not (Savage *et al.,* 2007; Wardle and Carnell, 2007).

Another very significant factor is socioeconomic status. Even after adjustment for all other known risk factors, low socioeconomic status is strongly associated with both childhood and adult obesity (Phipps *et al.,* 2006).

In a recent comprehensive report on the obesity problem for the British government's Foresight programme, more than 100 different risk or protective factors were identified and six sectors in society were identified as the sectors able to, and therefore in the report's view responsible for modifying these factors (the six sectors are: built environment, recreation and transport, education, food production and supply, health care and treatment options, macro-economic drivers, media, nature of work) (Butland *et al.,* 2007). To get an appreciation of the complexity of the causal network behind the development of obesity, it is well worth looking at Map 5 in the Foresight report (Butland *et al.,* 2007, pp. 84–85).

Causal and Moral Responsibility in the Context of Obesity

Each individual factor in the causal complex leading to obesity in the individual case is minimally what Mackie has called an INUS factor i.e., an insufficient but necessary factor in an unnecessary but sufficient causal complex (Mackie, 1980). It is not in itself sufficient to cause obesity, and it is not necessary in all causal complexes leading to obesity. If this is the case, removing one of the INUS factors will prevent the individual becoming obese, but if the specific causal complexes differ between individuals, we may, as a matter of public health policy, have to target a very broad variety of causal factors and each of these will be irrelevant in some individual cases.

The same will be the case if individual cases of obesity are overdetermined in the sense that removing just one causal factor would not have prevented the development of obesity. It is quite likely that many cases of childhood obesity, especially in older children are overdetermined and that no single causal factor can be identified as a necessary factor in the individual case (even in the INUS sense).

We can thus say that a parent is causally implicated in the obesity of their child if some parental action, inaction or more often sustained behaviour is involved in the causal complex that underlies the specific case of obesity.

This does not settle in which case a parent can be said to be the cause of the obesity. We first have to note with von Wright that when we try to determine 'the cause' of a complex event or state of affairs, it is always from some point of view and with a specific set of interests in mind (von Wright, 1971). Of the many elements in the causal complex, we fix on one because it is uncommon, linked to moral failure or duty, or believed to be open to possible intervention. And we constantly need to keep in mind that we are likely to identify the cause of childhood obesity quite differently at a population level than at the individual level.

Second, in cases of overdetermination where the causal complex is sufficient even after the removal of the parental elements, the parent is causally implicated but not the cause.

These considerations also influence the link between causal responsibility and moral responsibility. Let us, for the sake of argument accept an essentially consequentialist account of moral responsibility where agents are responsible for all foreseen and unforeseen consequences of their actions. On this account, parents would not be morally responsible if their contributions to an overdetermined causal complex were not necessary for the outcome. They would be responsible in cases involving INUS complexes, but so would all other actors implicated in the complex and there would be no specific reason to point out the parents as especially responsible.

Being causally and morally responsible is, furthermore not the same as being blameworthy or a legitimate target for other forms of punitive intervention. There is a complicated relationship between moral responsibility and blameworthiness. If we stay within a consequentialist approach that casts the net of moral responsibility very widely, there are still many acts for which an actor is responsible but not blameworthy, for instance most if not all of the class of acts where the bad outcome was not predictable at the time of action (or inaction). Even though a parent is thus causally and morally responsible, for instance because their feeding style is an INUS factor in the causal complex leading to obesity in their child, the parent may not be blameworthy if this consequence of the feeding style was not predictable or if the changing feeding style is practically impossible.

From Obesity Back to Normal Weight

Causal overdetermination also has implications for interventions to achieve weight reduction in already obese children. If there is overdetermination, interventions may have—at the same time—to reduce energy intake at meal times, reduce energy intake outside of meal times and increase energy expenditure both in school and in leisure time in order to achieve weight stabilisation and eventual reduction.

Even for current pharmacological interventions that affect appetite and satiety directly, it seems necessary to combine these with dietary and activity change to achieve optimal results. And no pharmacological interventions are currently recommended for children.

Because of this complexity, it is not totally surprising that we have no known interventions targeted at individuals and families

that lead to long-term sustainable reductions in obesity, despite the apparent simplicity of reducing energy intake and increasing energy expenditure (Brug and van Lenthe, 2005). There are a number of interventions that lead to short-term reductions in obesity, but as yet no interventions that can reliably sustain this short-term effect in the whole group (James et al., 2007).

Most of the effective interventions that are targeted at parents or families require considerable changes in the life of the whole family, changes in food preparation and meal patterns as well as changes in physical activities (Golan et al., 1998; Brug and van Lenthe, 2005).

The long-term success rate of targeted interventions can probably be improved if they are embedded within or supported by society-level interventions to modify the many factors contributing to the obesogenic environment. Many such interventions have been tried and the evidence seems to suggest that they have to target a range of different factors to have any effect.

Parental Responsibility for Obesity

What can we now say more specifically about parental responsibility in the context of childhood obesity? Let us initially distinguish between younger and older children. As long as the child is very young, the parents at least in theory have full control over its nutrient intake and possibilities for physical activity and are therefore fully causally responsible if their child becomes obese. We might, based on the analysis above think that this automatically makes them fully morally responsible as well, and in one sense that inference is true. Parents of young children are morally responsible for the effects of their feeding practices, but what they are responsible for are the total effects. Giving food and feeding has many other functions than providing nutrition. It provides bonding and social interaction, it adds to children's motor skills, etc. Feeding is also used to achieve specific short-term goals. Most parents will, for instance at some point in time, have used food to comfort their child or to keep the child occupied while the parent is engaged in other important activities. And most parents will have chosen to provide nutrition to their child in a certain way not only to achieve short-term satiety, but also long-term health and well-being goals, i.e., feeding the child what the parent perceives as a healthy diet.

It is also important to remember that parenting in humans is a learnt behaviour. Parents do not automatically know what or how to feed their children but are influenced by their own upbringing, by advice from grandparents and friends, by advice in magazines and books and by general and individual government advice. In most countries, parents get individualised feeding advice antenatally, immediately post-natally and during the first years of the child's life whether they want it or not. A parent who diligently seeks good-quality information and advice and follows it to the best of their ability is still causally implicated if the advice turns out to be wrong, and there are many examples of official parenting advice later found to be problematic. It would be appropriate for such a parent to feel regret that they followed the advice, as in the case of those parents who followed faulty advice about infant sleeping positions and whose child died from sudden infant death syndrome. But the parent in question is not blameworthy. He or she did their best and the outcome was not predictable. It is especially iniquitous if the entity that gave the problematic advice at a later point blames parents for the effects of following it, as is partially the case for parents who tried their best to get their baby's weight to follow the standard weight curves now believed to be set too high because they were based almost exclusively on data from bottle-fed babies (Victoria *et al.,* 1998; de Onis *et al.,* 2004).

For the older child, many more actors are actively involved in controlling its energy intake and expenditure. The child itself becomes increasingly involved, but the education system and groups running leisure activities are also directly involved, even in cases where schools do not provide school meals.

In the case of the older child, the number of actors indirectly involved in shaping the child's food and leisure preferences also multiply rapidly. The planning of the physical environment impacts on the possibility of outdoor leisure activities.

Unless parents very strictly control access to the media and the Internet, the child will be exposed to significant amounts of food and drinks advertising aimed specifically at children, and children are also susceptible to peer pressure.

But even for the older child, parents still have important responsibilities. They should as part of normal parenting monitor their child's health and well-being and take action if the child is moving towards becoming obese. What parents can do is, however still significantly influenced by the choices of other actors and by the advice available to them. If even the best designed programmes for achieving weight loss in children are of questionable efficacy in the long term, it is unclear exactly how much responsibility parents have if they and their child cannot achieve this either.

The Justification for Societal Intervention in the Family Context

We have now shown that some parents are, at least partly responsible for the development of overweight and obesity in their children. To get a complete justification for societal intervention in the family context, we do however need further justification. We need to show that (i) obesity in children is harmful, (ii) the proposed intervention is likely to work in the sense of reducing the harm caused by obesity, (iii) the intervention does not create significant harm in itself and (iv) the intervention does not infringe the rights or interests of those members of the family who are not the targets of the intervention (the parents or siblings).

There is little doubt that childhood obesity is harmful at a group level. Children who are obese are more likely to suffer from a range of health problems, they are more likely to have low self-esteem and low health-related quality of life, they are more likely to be obese in adulthood and do therefore on average have a lower life expectancy than their non-obese contemporaries as well as more disability (Schwimmer

et al., 2003; Alley and Chang, 2007, de Beer *et al.,* 2007; Flegal *et al.,* 2007). As with all other group attributes, it does not follow that every obese child is harmed in some way by being obese. Some may not be harmed at all, and while others might be harmed in a health sense (e.g. by living fewer years than they might have done), they may now or in adulthood be willing to trade off this harm against what they see as the benefits of their lifestyle. Second, it is not always clear how we should evaluate a given health outcome, or from what point of view in time it should be evaluated. This can be illustrated by the following two scenarios:

1. The parents choose to bring up their child in a way which will give it a healthy and enjoyable childhood and later life, but will increase its risk of disability or sudden death after the age of 60.

2. The parents choose to bring up their child in a way which will give it a healthy but slightly less enjoyable childhood and later life, but will increase its chance of living a disability-free life to the age of 80.

Seen from the point of view of the child at age 0, option 1 is probably preferable. It gives satisfaction now, and the price in health is only paid (if ever) 60 years from now. At the age of 60 option 2 is, for many people at least, much more preferable. (This is just the health version of the 'How I wish that my parents had forced me to continue piano lessons' syndrome that many including the present author suffer from).

Let us assume for the sake of the argument that the evidence of immediate negative effects of childhood obesity is so strong that option A can be discounted, because an obese child is unlikely to have an enjoyable childhood and that discounting of future harms therefore becomes much less relevant. At the public policy level, this will entail that preventing childhood obesity becomes a legitimate and perhaps even obligatory policy objective. A government which did not take active policy measures in this area would be negligent.

But this still does not entail that the goal of obesity prevention is an obligatory goal for each and every family. There may be children that are not disadvantaged in any way by being obese, and there may be families where other priorities legitimately outweigh the obesity priority. Before we move on to consider what these other priorities could be, let us just for the sake of completeness note that it is unclear whether the problem of low self-esteem in obese children is most effectively combated by targeting the obesity or by targeting the stigmatising social attitudes that create the low self-esteem. It is a common argument in bioethical analysis of reproductive decision-making that the fact that a child will be discriminated against in a specific society (e.g. by having lesbian parents or by being mixed race) is no reason not to have the child, but only a reason to fight the social prejudices at play.

What could possibly outweigh the interests of the obese child and make it morally legitimate for parents not to have obesity prevention or weight reduction as the main priority of the family?

This clearly depends on the degree to which the child's interests are affected. If the child is morbidly obese and there is an immediate risk of significant illness, then there will be very few situations where other factors can outweigh the child's interests, and a parent who did not act diligently to try to affect weight reduction would be responsible and blameworthy and might be a legitimate target for intervention from official bodies. In the more normal case of an overweight or obese child with no immediate health risk, the situation is quite different. Parents are not obliged to completely discount all of their own interests for the interests of their children and in families with more than one child the parents have a positive obligation to resolve any conflicts that arise between the interests of the individual children.

It should be uncontroversial that in cases where the changes in family lifestyle necessary to prevent obesity or affect weight reduction in one child impact negatively on another child in the family parents are not only allowed to, but must judge whether the benefits to the obese child outweighs the costs to the sibling. That judgement is obviously not infallible, but parents are in a better position than most outsiders to discern the interests of their children and an outside agency would need good justification to override the parental decision.

But what about the interests of the parents themselves? Could there ever be a parental interest that was sufficiently strong to outweigh an obese child's interest in weight reduction? Lotz argues that parental liberty interests are not strong enough to outweigh the interests of the child (Lotz, 2004). Her argument proceeds within a very narrow conceptualisation of this interest as an interest in being '. . . free from state intrusion in child rearing in order to protect family privacy.' (Lotz, 2004, p. 295). If that was the only parental interest at play, her argument for the permissibility of state intervention would probably go through. But parents have far wider liberty interests than that. They have interests in leading their own life in a way that is congruent with their values and preferences. Can these broader interests outweigh the interests of the child? To answer this question we again need to consider what is required to actually achieve weight reduction in an obese child. If there was a magic potion that parents could give to their child weekly and that would keep the child at normal weight, then no parental interests could outweigh the child's interest in getting that potion (as long as it was priced well within the affordability of all families). But such a potion does not exist. As noted above, long-term sustainable weight reduction requires significant changes in many aspects of lifestyle. Different foods have to be prepared; eating habits have to be changed, leisure habits modified and new physical activities engaged in. This is not an easy process and it is a process that will involve changes in the life of the whole family, not just of the obese child. Every family member will have to eat differently and modify other aspects of their own lifestyle because a large part of the influence of parental behaviour is chanelled through the child modelling its behaviour on the behaviour of the parent.

It is not inconceivable that the negative effects of the required changes may be so large for some parents that they are justified in not carrying them out, even after having given the interests of their child full and maybe even extra weight. This could for instance be the case where the parent has a condition that makes physical activity painful.

It is also not inconceivable that there are parents who, despite their best efforts cannot achieve the necessary changes because of structural factors affecting their lives. It is, for instance not uncommon for parents in low income families to have more than one job thereby significantly limiting the time available for other activities apart from rest and sleep (Abrams, 2002).

There are therefore situations where parents are fully justified in letting their interests outweigh the interests of the obese child. In those situations the state can still intervene if it does so in a way that is truly helpful, e.g., by providing the physical activity opportunities that the parent cannot provide. But the state has little justification for intervening in ways that imply that the parents are morally responsible and/or blameworthy.

Parents who are in that situation may further argue that it is not legitimate for official bodies to intervene in family life in a situation where the state is itself one of the actors that are both causally and morally implicated in creating childhood obesity. We have not belaboured the point above, but the state clearly has major responsibility for creating, or minimally allowing the creation of the obesogenic environment which promotes obesity and makes it much more difficult for parents to keep their children at normal weight. Before the state takes its own responsibility in this matter seriously, it can hardly claim any moral authority to intervene in the life of citizens. This point can be supported by considerations of the role of reciprocity in moral relationships but that is beyond the scope of this paper.

The Paternalism Parallel

In discussion about paternalism, it is commonplace to draw a distinction between hard and soft forms of paternalism. This distinction can be drawn in various ways and I am here following the line taken by Heta Häyry in her seminal book *The Limits of Medical Paternalism* (Häyry, 1991). According to Häyry, hard paternalism involves direct intervention with the actions of an agent whereas soft paternalism involves interventions that change the beliefs or attitudes of agents and thereby change the choices that agents make for themselves. Health promotion campaigns are paradigmatic examples of soft paternalism, and it is arguable that even exposing people to mandatory information (e.g., on cigarette packs) counts as soft paternalism.

Intervention in the family context in cases of childhood overweight or obesity is—in most cases—not strictly a form of paternalistic intervention. Its goal is to promote not only the interests of the child by changing the behaviour of the child but also of other family members. But considering the parallel with the different forms of paternalistic intervention may nevertheless be useful here. In the discussion above, it has implicitly been assumed that the interventions under discussion are towards the hard end of the spectrum involving direct intervention with the choices of parents. But what about softer interventions, e.g., providing all parents with weight information about their child combined with fairly generalised advice about healthy eating and physical activity or putting mandatory warnings on high-energy foods?

Nothing in the analysis above indicates that such softer interventions would be unjustifiable as long as they do not explicitly or implicitly claim anything more concerning parental responsibility than is warranted by the evidence. Such soft interventions also have the added advantage that their justification does not need to rely on correct analysis of the causal complex in any individual case. As long as a soft intervention targets a causal factor that is known to be present in many INUS complexes, it may be justifiable. Any health promotion message implying that 'you are responsible for your child's overweight' will, however still be too simplistic and is unjustifiably apportioning causal and moral responsibility as well as blame.

Conclusions

In this paper, I have argued that a parent has an obligation to give their child a good upbringing within the specific context of their own family. This will in many cases entail that they should try to prevent that their child becomes obese, and that they should intervene if their child becomes obese.

I have also argued that this does not mean that parents who have an obese child are necessarily bad parents. The changes that they would have to make to their way of living to prevent the child become or staying obese may be so great that they are not morally required, or they may not have sufficient control over their older child's energy intake or energy expenditure to effectively affect the child's weight.

Before the state is warranted to act in a way that interferes with family life, the state first have to have made reasonable efforts to change those risk factors for childhood obesity that the state itself controls.

References

Abrams, F. (2002). *Below the Breadline—Living on the Minimum Wage.* London: Profile Books.

Alderman, J., Smith, J. A., Fried, E. J. and Daynard, R. A. (2007). Application of Law to the Childhood Obesity Epidemic. *Journal of Law, Medicine and Ethics,* **35** (1), 98–112.

Alley D. E. and Chang V. W. (2007). The Changing Relationship of Obesity and Disability, 1988–2004. *JAMA,* **298,** 2020–2027

de Beer, M., Hofsteenge, G. H., Koot, H. M., Hirasing, R. A., Delemarre-van deWaal, H. A. and Gemke, R. J. B. J. (2007). Health-Related-Quality-of-Life in Obese Adolescents is Decreased and Inversely Related to BMI. *Acta Pædiatrica,* **96,** 710–714.

Bell, C. G., Walley, A. J. and Froguel, P. (2005). The Genetics of Human Obesity. *Nature Reviews Genetics,* **6,** 221–234.

Brug, J. and van Lenthe, F. (eds) (2005). *Environmental Determinants and Interventions for Physical Activity, Nutrition and Smoking: A Review.* Rotterdam: Erasmus University.

Butland, B., Jebb, S., Kopelman, P., McPherson, K., Thomas, S., Mardell, J. and Parry, V. (2007). *Foresight—Tackling Obesities: Future Choices—Project Report.* London: Government Office for Science.

Flegal, K. M., Graubard, B. I., Williamson, D. F. and Gail, M. H. (2007). Cause-Specific Excess Deaths Associated with Underweight, Overweight, and Obesity. *JAMA,* **298** (17), 2028–2037.

Freeman, M. D. A. (1997). *The Moral Status of Children: Essays on the Rights of the Child.* London: Brill.

Golan, M., Weizman, A., Apter, A. and Fainaru, M. (1998). Parents as the Exclusive Agents of Change in the Treatment of Childhood Obesity. *American Journal of Clinical Nutrition,* **67,** 1130–1135.

Harris, J. and Holm, S. (2003). Should We Presume Moral Turpitude in Our Children?—Small Children and Consent to Medical Research. *Theoretical Medicine,* **24,** 121–129.

Häyry, H. (1991). *The Limits of Medical Paternalism.* London: Routledge.

Holm, S. and Edgar, A. (in press). Best Interest—A Philosophical Critique. *Health Care Analysis.*

James, J., Thomas, P. and Kerr, D. (2007). Preventing Childhood Obesity: Two Year Follow-up Results from the Christchurch Obesity Prevention Programme in Schools (CHOPPS). *BMJ,* **335,** 762–764.

Lotz, M. (2004). Childhood Obesity and the Question of Parental Liberty. *Journal of Social Philosophy,* **35** (2), 288–303.

Mackie, J. L. (1980). *The Cement of the Universe: A Study of Causation.* Oxford: Clarendon Press.

de Onis, M., Garza, C., Victoria, C., Bhan, M. K. and Norum, K. R. (eds) (2004). The WHO Multicentre Growth Reference Study (MGRS): Rationale, Planning, and Implementation. *Food and Nutrition Bulletin,* **25** (supplement 1), S3–S84

Phipps, S. A., Burton, P. S., Osberg, L. S. and Lethbridge, L. N. (2006). Poverty and the Extent of Child Obesity in Canada, Norway and the United States. *Obesity Reviews,* **7,** 5–12.

Savage, J. S., Fisher, J. O. and Birch, L. L. (2007). Parental Influence on Eating Behaviour: Conception to Adolescence. *Journal of Law, Medicine and Ethics,* **35** (1), 22–34.

Savulescu, J. (2001). Procreative Beneficence: Why We Should Select the Best Children. *Bioethics,* **15** (5–6), 413–426.

Schwimmer, J. B., Burwinkle, T. M. and Varni, J. W. (2003). Health-related Quality of Life of Severely Obese Children and Adolescents. *JAMA,* **289,** 1813– 1819.

Victoria C.G., Morris, S. S., Barros, F.C., de Onis, M. and Yip, R. (1998). The NCHS Reference and the Growth of Breast- and Bottle-Fed Infants. *The Journal of Nutrition,* **128** (7), 1134–1138.

Wardle, J. and Carnell, S. (2007). Parental Feeding Practices and Children's Weight. *Acta Pædiatrica,* **96,** 5–11.

Whitaker, R. C., Wright, J. A., Pepe, M. S., Seidel, K. D. and Dietz, W. H. (1997). Predicting Obesity in Young Adulthood from Childhood and Parental Obesity. *New England Journal of Medicine,* **337** (13), 869–873

Wright, C. M., Parker, L., Lamont, D. and Craft, A. (2001). Implications of Childhood Obesity for Adult Health: Findings from Thousand Families Cohort Study. *BMJ,* **323,** 1280–1284

von Wright, G. H. (1971). *Explanation and Understanding.* London: Routledge and Kegan Paul.

Critical Thinking

1. What family and parental factors are associated with childhood obesity?

2. Using the standard of the best interests of the child, can parents be held morally and legally responsible for what their child weighs?

3. If a child is overweight, does it mean they have "bad parents?"

4. What should be the state or government's role in dealing with childhood obesity? Is a child's obesity a family matter?

Create Central

www.mhhe.com/createcentral

Internet References

Robert Wood Johnson Foundation, Childhood Obesity Area
www.rwjf.org/en/about-rwjf/program-areas/childhood-obesity.html

Let's Move
www.letsmove.gov

Positive Parenting
www.positiveparenting.com

Acknowledgments—This paper has benefited immensely from my participation in the EUROBESE project, directed by Professor Inéz de Beaufort and sponsored by the EU Commission, DG-Research and from discussions with colleagues at the Cardiff Institute of Society, Health and Ethics. The author is partly funded by the ESRC Centre for Economic and Social Aspects of Genomics (Cesagen). I gratefully acknowledge insightful comments on a previous version of this paper by the editors of the journal and by Mariette van den Hoven.

Sibling Rivalry Grows Up: Adult Brothers and Sisters Are Masters at Digs; Finding a Way to a Truce by Elizabeth Bernstein

91

Article

Prepared by: Patricia Hrusa Williams,
University of Maine at Farmington

Sibling Rivalry Grows Up
Adult Brothers and Sisters Are Masters at Digs; Finding a Way to a Truce

ELIZABETH BERNSTEIN

Learning Outcomes

After reading this article, you will be able to:

- Identify the impact of sibling relationships on an individual.

- Identify competition between siblings.

- Describe the influence of sibling relationships on individuals during adulthood.

Marianne Walsh and her sister, Megan Putman, keep track of whose kids their mother babysits more. They also compete with each other over parenting styles (Ms. Walsh is strict, Ms. Putman is laid back) and their weight.

Even after siblings grow up, rivalry and one-upmanship continue to crop up, Elizabeth Bernstein reports on Lunch Break.

"My kids play more instruments, so I am winning in piano," says Ms. Walsh, 38, the younger of the two by 13 months. "But she won the skinny Olympics."

Adult sibling rivalry. Experts say it remains one of the most harmful and least addressed issues in a family. We know it when we see it. Often, we deeply regret it. But we have no idea what to do about it.

Ms. Walsh and Ms. Putman have been competitive since childhood—about clothes, about boyfriends, about grades. Ms. Walsh remembers how in grammar school her sister wrote an essay about their grandfather and won a writing award. She recited it at a school assembly with her grandpa standing nearby, beaming. Ms. Walsh, seething, vowed to win the award the next year and did.

Ms. Putman married first. Ms. Walsh, single at the time, clearly recalls the phone call when her sister told her she was pregnant. "I was excited because this was the first grandchild. Then I got off the phone and cried for two hours," says Ms. Walsh.

Marianne Walsh and her older sister, Megan Putman, have worked out a way to end negative conversations based on rivalry.

Ms. Putman, 39 and a stay-at-home-mom in Bolingbrook, Ill., remembers that she too felt jealous—of her sister's frequent travel and promotions in her marketing career. "The way my parents would go on and on about her really made me feel 'less than,'" Ms. Putman says.

Ms. Walsh eventually married, had a son and named him Jack. Seven weeks later, Ms. Putman gave birth to a son and named him Jack. The discussion? "That was always my boy name." "I never heard you say that."

Sibling rivalry is a normal aspect of childhood, experts say. Our siblings are our first rivals. They competed with us for the love and attention of the people we needed most, our parents, and it is understandable that we occasionally felt threatened. Much of what is written about sibling rivalry focuses on its effects during childhood.

But our sibling relationships are often the longest of our lives, lasting 80 years or more. Several research studies indicate that up to 45 percent of adults have a rivalrous or distant relationship with a sibling.

Stop Fighting, Already

What siblings say indicating a rivalry is smoldering. Responses either make the rivalrous feelings worse, or defuse the situation.

People questioned later in life often say their biggest regret is being estranged from a sister or brother.

The rivalry often persists into adulthood because in many families it goes unaddressed. "Most people who have been through years of therapy have worked out a lot of guilt with their parents. But when it comes to their siblings, they can't articulate what is wrong," says Jeanne Safer, a psychologist in Manhattan and author of *Cain's Legacy: Liberating Siblings from a Lifetime of Rage, Shame, Secrecy and Regret*.

Dr. Safer believes sibling rivals speak in a kind of dialect (she calls it "sib speak"). It sounds like this: "You were always Mom's favorite." "Mom and Dad are always at your house but they never visit me." "You never call me."

"It's not the loving language that good friends have," Dr. Safer says. "It's the language of grievance collection."

It's hard to know what to say in response. "You are afraid that what you say will be catastrophic or will reveal awful truths," Dr. Safer says. "It's a lifelong walk on eggshells."

Sibling discord has been around since the Bible. Cain killed Abel. Leah stole Rachel's intended husband, Jacob. Joseph fought bitterly with his 10 older half brothers. Parents often have a hand in fostering it. They may choose favorites, love unevenly and compare one child with the other.

Dr. Safer draws a distinction between sibling rivalry and sibling strife. Rivalry encompasses a normal range of disagreements and competition between siblings. Sibling strife, which is less common, is rivalry gone ballistic—siblings who, because of personality clashes or hatred, can't enjoy each other's company.

Al Golden, 85, chokes up when he talks about his twin brother, Elliott, who died three years ago. The brothers shared a room growing up in Brooklyn, N.Y., graduated from the SUNY Maritime College in New York and married within a month of each other in 1947.

Yet Mr. Golden still remembers how their father often compared their grades, asking one or the other, "How come you got a B and your brother got an A?" He rarely missed a chance to point out that Elliott wasn't as good as Al in swimming.

When the boys were ready to get married, he suggested a double wedding. Mr. Golden put his foot down. "I shared every birthday and my bar mitzvah with my brother," he said. "I'll be damned if I am going to share my wedding with him."

Elliott Golden became a lawyer and eventually a state Supreme Court judge. Al Golden went into the mirror business, then sold life insurance. He says he always envied his brother's status and secretly took pleasure in knowing he was a better fisherman and owned a big boat. Once, Elliott asked him, "I am a lawyer. How come you make more money than me?" Mr. Golden says. "He meant: 'How come you are making more than me when you are not as successful?' But it made me feel good."

One day, Mr. Golden says, Elliott accused him of not doing enough to take care of their ailing mother. After the conversation, Mr. Golden didn't speak to his brother for more than a year. "It might have been the build-up of jealousies over the years," he says.

His brother repeatedly reached out to him, as did his nieces and nephews, but Mr. Golden ignored them.

Then one day Mr. Golden received an email from his brother telling a story about two men who had a stream dividing their properties. One man hired a carpenter to build a fence along the stream, but the carpenter built a bridge by mistake. Mr. Golden thought about the email then wrote back, "I'd like to walk over the bridge."

"I missed him," Mr. Golden says now. "I never had the chance to miss him before."

Dr. Safer says brothers' rivalries often are overt, typically focusing on things like Dad's love, athletic prowess, career success, money. Women are less comfortable with competition, she says, so sister rivalries tend to be passive-aggressive and less direct. Whom did Mom love best, who is a better mother now.

Brothers often repair their rivalries with actions. When women reconcile, it's often through talking. Ms. Putman and Ms. Walsh have learned to stop arguments using a trick from childhood. When a discussion gets heated, one sister will call out "star," a code word they devised as kids to mean the conversation is over. The sister who ends it gets the last word. "You may still be mad, but you adhere to the rules of childhood," Ms. Walsh says.

For some years, the two didn't socialize much. But when Ms. Putman's husband died last fall, Ms. Walsh, now a stay-at-home-mom in Chicago, helped plan the wake and write the obituary. Arriving at her sister's house one day before the funeral, Ms. Walsh found her in bed, crying, and climbed in next to her. The sisters said, "I love you," and Ms. Putman says she realized she was going to be OK.

"Lying there, I felt that if I've got my sister, I've got my strength," Ms. Putman says. "She is my backbone."

Putting a Stop to Sibling Rivalry

Fix the problem by addressing it head-on, says psychologist Jeanne Safer.

- The first step is to think. Who is this person outside his or her relationship with you? What do you like about your sibling? Remember the positive memories. Identify why you think the relationship is worth fixing—if it is.
- Take the initiative to change. It could be a gesture, like an offer to help with a sick child, a conversation or a letter. Be sincere and don't ignore the obvious. Say: "These conversations between us are painful. I would like to see if we can make our relationship better."
- Gestures count. Not everyone is comfortable talking about a strained relationship, especially men. But phone calls, invitations to spend time together, attempts to help should be seen as peace offerings.
- Consider your sibling's point of view. Try not to be defensive. What did childhood look like through his or her eyes? "You have to be willing to see an unflattering portrait of yourself," Dr. Safer says.
- Tell your sibling what you respect. "I love your sense of humor." "I admire what a good parent you are."
- And, finally: "It won't kill you to apologize," Dr. Safer says.

Critical Thinking

1. What factors are important to the development of healthy sibling relationships?
2. Is rivalry an inevitable aspect of sibling relationships?
3. When sibling rivalry exists, does it ever end?
4. What does sibling rivalry look like during adulthood?
5. What are some ground rules that should be established to promote healthy sibling relationships across the lifespan?

Sibling Rivalry Grows Up: Adult Brothers and Sisters Are Masters at Digs; Finding a Way to a Truce by Elizabeth Bernstein

93

Create Central

www.mhhe.com/createcentral

Internet References

Sibling Support Project
www.siblingsupport.org

Tufts University Child and Family Webguide
www.cfw.tufts.edu

National Council on Family Relations
www.ncfr.com

Article

Prepared by: Patricia Hrusa Williams,
University of Maine at Farmington

Support Needs of Siblings of People with Developmental Disabilities

Catherine K. Arnold, Tamar Heller, and John Kramer

Learning Outcomes

After reading this article, you will be able to:

- Identify the challenges adult siblings of those with developmental and intellectual disabilities face.

- Understand the support needs of adult siblings and aging parents of those with developmental disabilities.

Siblings of people with disabilities have been traditionally overlooked by parents, professionals, and researchers as a group with support needs and as potential advocates for their siblings with disabilities. Although the needs of people with developmental disabilities and their parents have been the focus of extensive research within the disability field, research on the needs of siblings is lacking (Hodapp, Glidden, & Kaiser, 2005). Much of the early research pathologized the experience of growing up with a brother or sister with a disability (Stoneman, 2005). More recent research on the sibling experience finds a mix of both positive and negative outcomes (Gallagher, Powell, & Rhodes, 2006). The support needs of adult siblings of people with developmental disabilities have received little attention from researchers up to this point. This study aimed to help fill this gap and give voice to the perspective of siblings so that their needs could be addressed by professionals and policymakers.

Siblings often become the next generation of caregivers when parents are no longer able to fill this role (Heller & Kramer, 2009). Sixty percent of people with developmental disabilities live with their families, and in 25% of these homes the primary caregiver is over the age of 60 (Braddock et al., 2011). As parents age and are less able to support their child with a disability, the involvement of siblings in the lives of their brothers and sisters with disabilities becomes more necessary. A review of the adult sibling literature found that most siblings anticipated taking on a greater supportive role in the future (Heller & Arnold, 2010).

The perspective of siblings of people with disabilities has not been looked at extensively in the research on families and disabilities, and the parent perspective is often incorporated, which is not always the same as siblings' self-reporting. However, a national survey of adult siblings by Hodapp, Urbano, and Burke (2010) showed siblings have service needs related to their struggle to balance care for their sibling with disabilities, their aging parents, and their own families. A study by Rawson (2009) interviewed siblings aged 17–23 years whose brothers and sisters with disabilities lived in a residential school for people with complex needs and found that siblings needed transition information, specifically on legal and financial planning, housing, and education. Siblings requested greater communication and wanted to be engaged in the decisions related to their brothers and sisters with disabilities. Also, Heller and Kramer (2009) surveyed adult siblings and found that the major support needs of siblings include the need for information, especially on planning for the future, as well as support groups both in person and online. The present study builds on the research done with siblings of people with disabilities and goes into greater depth with the perspective of siblings through a qualitative analysis.

Although support programs and services have been developed for individuals with developmental disabilities and their parents, supports for their siblings have been limited and mostly focused on children. There has been some intervention research that looks at the supports for siblings when they are children. Targeting nondisabled siblings for interventions to teach interaction skills and strategies was found to increase sibling play, communication, and successful interaction (Celiberti & Harris, 1993; Clark, Cunningham, & Cunningham, 1989; James & Egel, 1986). Sibling support groups for children were found to improve self-esteem, increase knowledge of their sibling's disability, and enhance interactions between siblings (Evans, Jones, & Mansell, 2001). Groups such as Sibshops provide "opportunities for brothers and sisters of children with special health and developmental needs to obtain peer support and education within a recreational context" (Meyer & Vadasy, 1994, p. 1). An evaluation of Sibshops by Johnson and Sandall (2005) suggests that providing support to siblings during childhood can have an enduring positive effect throughout their lives.

As siblings become more involved in the care of their brother or sister with a disability, their own support needs may increase. By understanding the needs of nondisabled siblings, parents

Support Needs of Siblings of People with Developmental Disabilities by Catherine K. Arnold, Tamar Heller, and John Kramer

95

and professionals can better empower and encourage siblings in supporting their brothers and sisters with disabilities. This study investigates the support needs of siblings of people with a developmental disability so they can be addressed by parents, professionals, and policymakers.

Method

Sample

The sample included 139 adult siblings of people with developmental disabilities. Adult siblings of people with developmental disabilities aged 18 and older were recruited through two strategies: an online Yahoo! Group listserv called SibNet and a statewide sibling conference. First, information about the research study was posted on SibNet, a listserv for adult siblings of people with disabilities. At the time of dissemination, SibNet had 485 members with unique e-mail addresses, yet only 426 of those e-mail addresses were valid. One hundred sixteen SibNet members responded, and eight respondents were excluded who were under 18 years old and therefore below the age of consent. The total number of respondents from SibNet in this study is 108 siblings. Second, surveys were handed out at a statewide sibling conference to 57 people. The survey was completed by 31 siblings who attended the conference. Combining the respondents from SibNet and the sibling conference, the overall corrected sample consisted of 139 respondents out of 483 for a response rate of 31%.

Demographics of respondents and their sibling with disabilities are shown in Table 1. The average age of all respondents is 37 years old with ages ranging from 18 to 62 years. The vast majority of respondents (92%) were female with no minority status (87%). Most respondents had an education level of some college or more (93%). Over half the sample was married, and 37% had between one and eight children. Sixty-nine percent of the respondents had family incomes over $40,000. For individuals with developmental disabilities, the average age was 34 years (range = 10–72 years). Sixty percent of siblings with disabilities were brothers. About 75% of siblings had an intellectual disability with the remainder having other developmental disabilities. The living situation of siblings varied, with 41% living at home with parents, 8% living with their nondisabled siblings, 24% living in a residential facility, 7% living with other family members, and 11% living with a spouse or independently.

Survey

The Supporting Siblings Survey included 59 questions that focused on respondents' sibling with a disability, their parents, their relationship to their siblings, and their family's future plans. Feedback on the survey was gathered from people with developmental disabilities, parents, and siblings. Pilot testing was done to help strengthen and finalize the survey. Most of the questions were close-ended with only the last four questions being open-ended. The open-ended questions captured descriptive information about the concerns and the support needs of siblings. For the focus of the research in this study, the two specific questions used to explore the support needs of siblings included: "What programs would you like to see targeted

Table 1   Demographics

Variable	n	%
Sibling respondent		
Gender		
Male	10	8
Female	120	92
Ethnic minority status		
Yes	19	13
No	128	87
Educational level		
High school or GED	8	6
Trade/vocational school	1	1
Some college	20	15
College	43	33
Some graduate school	14	11
Graduate school	45	34
Marital status		
Married	70	53
Not married	62	47
Children		
Yes	49	37
No	83	63
Income		
< $20,000	15	12
$20,001–40,000	24	19
$40,001–60,000	31	24
$60,001–80,000	25	20
$80,001–100,000	12	9
< $100,000	21	16
Sibling with a disability		
Gender		
Male	80	60
Female	54	40
Living situation		
Home with parents	55	41
In your home	11	8
Residential placement	32	24
Other family members	9	7
Living with spouse	2	2
Independently	12	9
Other	12	9

towards *families* of people with disabilities?" and "What programs would you like to see targeted towards *siblings* of people with disabilities?" These two questions provided space for siblings to write any thoughts and ideas that were relevant to their support needs.

Analysis

The responses to the open-ended questions were transferred from SPSS to a Word document with no identifiers. Two coders, both family members of people with developmental

Table 2 Support Needs of Siblings

Theme	Core variable	Definition
Include me	Sibling support	Sibling support services to connect siblings, share information, and provide support.
Include me	Inclusive family	A more inclusive definition of family that includes siblings and not just parents.
Start spreading the news	Education	Education and training opportunities such as conferences, workshops, and seminars.
Start spreading the news	Future planning	Information and support on planning for the future, such as financial and legal planning, guardianship transition, and estate planning.
Start spreading the news	System navigation	Information on how to navigate the system.
Start spreading the news	Disability awareness	Education of the public about people with disabilities.
Fix the mess	System improvement	Improvement of the support system such as shorter waiting lists, better service coordination, transportation, supported living services, better pay and career advancement for direct support professionals, and more.
Fix the mess	Funding	More funding sources or financial support.
Fix the mess	Respite	In-home and out-of-home respite services.
N/A	Anything	Anything at all.
N/A	Do not know	Do not know.

disabilities in the disability field, independently read through all the responses identifying overarching patterns and themes. The finalized coding frame (see Table 2) consisted of 11 core variables for sibling support needs. All coded responses were compared and showed 80% agreement. Any discrepancies were addressed until 100% agreement was reached for the coding of core variables to each response. A description of the support needs of siblings is highlighted in the results using quotes from siblings.

Results

The results of the present research captured the perspective of siblings and described the support needs of siblings. Of the 139 survey respondents, 120 shared their ideas for support needs. Quotations from the participants' open-ended responses highlighted the experience of siblings. The overarching themes that emerged from the data provided the framework for the support needs of siblings. Three overarching themes emerged that included 11 core variables. Table 2 shows the support needs of siblings. "Include me" emerged as a theme that encompassed two variables: *sibling support,* indicating the need for more sibling support services to connect siblings, share information, and provide support; and *inclusive family,* regarding the need for a more inclusive definition of family that includes siblings and not just parents. "Start spreading the news" was another primary theme related to siblings' need for information. Four core variables were captured within this theme: (a) education, indicating the need for education and training opportunities such as conferences, workshops, and seminars; (b) future planning, indicating the need for information and support on planning for the future, such as financial and legal planning, guardianship transition, and estate planning; (c) system navigation, regarding information on how to navigate the system;

and (d) disability awareness, for more education of the public about people with disabilities. "Fix the mess" was another major theme that included three variables: (a) system improvement, regarding the need for improvement in the support system, such as shorter waiting lists, better service coordination, transportation, supported living services, better pay and career advancement for direct support professionals, and more; (b) funding, for more funding sources or financial support; and (c) respite, for in-home and out-of-home respite services. Table 3 shows the frequency of sibling support needs. The top five support needs included sibling support (53%), education (35%), inclusive family (34%), future planning (31%), and system improvement (23%).

Table 3 Frequency of Sibling Support Needs

Core variables	N	%
Sibling support	63	53
Education	42	35
Inclusive family	41	34
Future planning	37	31
System improvement	28	23
System navigation	22	18
Funding	20	17
Respite	12	10
Disability awareness	5	4
Do not know	5	4
Anything	2	2

Note: The total number of respondents was 120.
Some numbers were rounded.

Support Needs of Siblings of People with Developmental Disabilities by Catherine K. Arnold, Tamar Heller, and John Kramer

97

Include Me

The overarching theme of "include me" highlighted siblings' yearning to be included in supports and services. Two core variables included sibling support and inclusive family.

Sibling support. Respondents were emphatic that they wanted more sibling support, making comments such as, "Group support with other siblings to enable open conversation about the many issues involved." They clearly wanted support "just like their parents!" as one respondent exclaimed. Numerous respondents shared the importance of targeting siblings as a group with support needs because they have felt neglected and desperately wanted to be included. One sibling wrote:

> More support for siblings. It felt like a guilty secret when I was a child and knew nobody in the same situation as myself. Also the professional people who spoke to my brother over the years never thought to ask me how I was.

Another sibling shared, "I think that a sibling support group would be appropriate. Sometimes, we as siblings tend to feel alone and isolated from others when we spend a lot of time caring for our sibling." And, another sibling said, "I think there need to be more groups for adult siblings. People tend to forget about the siblings anyway especially after they are adults." The need for sibling support was distinguished as an important way for siblings to "talk about their concerns" and get "advice/support with other adult sibs in my same situation." Sibling support can provide a space where siblings "can become empowered before crisis occurs." One sibling shared how an Internet sibling group "was my first introduction to feeling 'normal.'" Another sibling wrote how she had begun advocating for the creation of an adult sibling group with her local Arc.

Inclusive family. Another area of need is the notion of a more inclusive definition of family that includes siblings and not just parents. Siblings expressed their desire to be part of the services that are offered to families in general. Respondents wanted supports that included "the whole family—not just parents." They wanted to have their voice heard and be treated as people with a valuable role and perspective. One sibling shared, "I want to see more adult siblings being included in the 'Family' theory. I want us to be invited to meetings, and our thoughts and ideas respected." Another sibling wrote:

> I think there needs to be a focus on the family as a whole and creating programs that provide the opportunity for all family members to participate. There is not any consideration or emphasis on siblings being a valued part of the family and being included.

Start Spreading the News

The overarching theme of "start spreading the news" represented the respondents' need for information and education. The four core variables that made up this theme consisted of the following types of information gathering: (a) education and training opportunities, (b) future planning, (c) how to navigate the system, and (d) disability awareness education of the general public.

Education and training opportunities. Education was the second highest support need, with 42 siblings indicating the need for education and training opportunities such as conferences, workshops, and seminars. "I think siblings need information around many of the same issues as parents," stated one respondent. The siblings felt it was important to make "access to information more open" since much of their current experience is that "[w]e have to seek everything out for ourselves." Specific information topics were on "how to advocate for the rights of their siblings" and information "for sibling caregivers as their family member [with disabilities] and parents age."

Future planning. Siblings wanted "[f]amily programs so parents and siblings go through future family plans together." The primary aspect of future planning noted was to "[e]ncourag[e] families to talk about and plan for the future." Getting the dialogue started was a key aspect of future planning that helped to get families talking about their concerns and taking concrete steps to address those concerns and prepare for the future. The worry about what will happen when parents die could then be discussed, and families could begin the process of "making the transition of guardianship from parents to siblings."

System navigation. Siblings indicated a need for information on how to "maneuver within the system." Suggested information from respondents for navigating the system included the "rules/lingo/services to ask for," "how long waiting lists are," and "explanations of Medicaid programs." Another suggestion was "info on programs and how to apply" since this family "could have saved several thousands a year" if it had been aware of how to access certain services. "Easier ways to cut through the red tape of finding services appropriate to the sibling" was highlighted by one respondent. A suggested method for presenting information was "how-to guides on how to get/maintain services" and to give information so siblings felt "that they do not have to do everything on their own." There is a need for "programs that explain how to get services and what services are provided."

Disability awareness education. Disability awareness was a support need suggested by siblings as a means to educate the public about people with disabilities. Through increased awareness, one sibling hoped she would "see our society more inform[ed]." Suggested methods of educating the public included providing "information about disability issues in schools" and including "more positive things in the media with siblings of disabled people."

Fix the Mess

The overarching theme of "fix the mess" covered three core variables that focus on needs of siblings regarding the formal disability service system including (a) system improvement, (b) funding, and (c) respite.

System improvement. Siblings shared their frustration with the system and the need for great improvement in the system to better support their entire family. Different aspects of the system were mentioned, such as a "better system of checks and balance over group homes," "alternatives to supervised group housing," "better and consistent service coordination for people with disabilities," and "better pay and career advancement for direct care workers." One sibling articulated her needs by writing the following:

I need support and choices for residential living. As it appears now, I will have to have her live with me, which I don't believe will be the BEST thing for either of us. I would like to live close to her though and see her in a healthy residential group.

Another sibling shared that she felt the service system "doors are not sibling friendly. Service providers discourage, not encourage, involvement."

Funding. The need for funding sources and financial support was indicated by siblings. The current funding is not adequate for all families, and one sibling stated, "SS [Social Security] doesn't go far enough." One sibling articulated the need for the following:

A LOT more money for individuals on Social Security—at LEAST to the level of poverty; FULL medical care, meaning parity with services for the mentally ill. Caretaker siblings receiving financial compensation when they are caring for a sibling.

Funding is an important source of support for families of people with disabilities so that families "have more options about the care of their child."

Respite. Respite services were needed to give families "a break" and have time apart from the person with a disability to do other tasks and rest. One sibling described respite: "[S]omeone to watch the disabled individual while they go on vacation and small breaks throughout the week for an hour or two to get things done." Respite can be an important service that can help "families to stay together" instead of turning to residential facilities. It can alleviate some of the caregiving of families.

Discussion

The support needs found in this research study highlight the gap in meeting siblings' needs. Three overarching themes for sibling support needs include: (a) getting disability-related information, (b) getting support for their caregiving role, and (c) enhancing the formal support system to address sibling needs.

Information Needs

Siblings need information, just like parents and people with disabilities. Respondents articulated strong needs for education and training opportunities such as conferences, workshops, and seminars. Research that looks at families of people with disabilities shows that the needs of families include information

on housing options, financial planning, and guardianship as well as the need for case management, advocacy, and support groups (Heller & Factor, 1994). A model of a future-planning curriculum that includes siblings and has tested outcomes is The Future is Now (Factor et al., 2010; Heller & Caldwell, 2006). Families that participated in a future-planning training intervention took steps to plan for the future such as to develop a special needs trust, complete a letter of intent, and to take action on residential plans for their adult family member with developmental disabilities. Also, the intervention reduced feelings of caregiving burden and increased choice-making opportunities of people with disabilities (Heller & Caldwell, 2006). More future-planning programs should include both the siblings with and without disabilities in the entire process. And, more research needs to be done on the outcomes of future planning and the effectiveness of different training models.

One challenge is getting information to siblings. Although an extensive network of people with disabilities and parents exists through the formal disability support system, information is often not transferred from these established networks to siblings.

Inclusion of Siblings

A concept that resonated throughout the results was that siblings felt that their voices were not being heard and their needs were not being adequately met. The literature on siblings clearly shows how siblings provide critical support to people with developmental disabilities throughout their lifespan. Siblings have the inside story about their siblings' with disabilities habits and preferences, health care history, important relationships, and much more. As the people with the longest lasting relationships, siblings have a wealth of knowledge about their brothers and sisters with disabilities that could be invaluable to professionals and service providers. Therefore, parents and professionals should engage siblings as partners in planning to enhance the support of people with disabilities.

Along with being left out of research and services, siblings are also often left out of the disability advocacy movement. Siblings are an untapped constituency for policy advocacy that can increase the power in the disability advocacy movement. If there are over 3.7 million people with developmental disabilities in the United States (Fujiura, 1998; Larson et al., 2001; U.S. Census Bureau, 2010), and most of these people have at least one sibling, the number of potential advocates grows exponentially. Siblings with and without disabilities can support each other to get involved in advocacy together and learn how to help push the policy system. Also, sibling voices at the policy table may help to ensure more supports are allocated for their unique concerns and needs.

Formal Supports

The highest ranking need in this study, sibling support services, indicated that siblings want ways to connect with each other, share information, and provide support. The present study reinforced the results of the previous study that noted that siblings want support groups, workshops, and trainings for siblings and families (Heller & Kramer, 2009). An important source

Support Needs of Siblings of People with Developmental Disabilities by Catherine K. Arnold, Tamar Heller, and John Kramer

99

of information and networking for siblings is the online listserv called SibNet where adults who have a brother or sister with a disability can connect (www.siblingsupport.org/connect/the-sibnet-listserv).

The Sibling Leadership Network (SLN) is a national nonprofit with state chapters created to support siblings of people with disabilities and provide a stronger voice for siblings. The SLN's mission is "to provide siblings of individuals with disabilities the information, support, and tools to advocate with their brothers and sisters and to promote the issues important to them and their entire families" (Heller et al., 2008, p. 4). Siblings want a stronger voice at the policy table to balance the perspective of parents and to walk with their brothers and sisters with disabilities to effect change.

Siblings want to be included in supports that are provided to families. Although many programs and services publicize that they are open to "families," this typically means parents, and they are not always welcoming to siblings. Family support programs often do not consider the perspective of siblings or target siblings in their marketing. Currently, family support policy does not specifically include siblings. The SLN "believe[s] it is time to strengthen family support policy by explicitly including brothers and sisters of people with disabilities in federal family support program guidelines" (Heller et al., 2008, p. 13).

The SLN developed a policy white paper entitled "The Sibling Leadership Network: Recommendations for Research, Advocacy, and Supports Relating to Siblings of People with Developmental Disabilities" (Heller et al., 2008) that had key recommendations that can help address the support needs of siblings in the present research study. These included creating a national clearinghouse for sibling resources and providing information and education to siblings, parents, and professionals. The SLN white paper provides a road map for addressing the support needs of siblings.

Policy Implications

There is a lack of policies that support siblings of people with disabilities in the United States. Kramer's (2008) study of siblings pairs, including siblings with and without disabilities, showed that siblings "believed their efforts to change policy could enhance their support and lead to increased participation with their sibling with [intellectual and developmental disabilities]" (p. 107). As respondents highlighted, the formal disability service system is often difficult for siblings and their families to navigate. Policy advocacy is a key aspect of the SLN and is committed to creating an organization that works with people with disabilities. The SLN has partnered with the national Self Advocates Becoming Empowered (SABE) to ensure the sibling organization is truly advocating with people with disabilities since they are the true experts. This approach models how siblings can learn from each other and work together to improve the system for their entire family.

The Developmental Disabilities Assistance and Bill of Rights Act of 2000 (DD Act) is the legislation that created important programs for people with developmental disabilities and their families. The SLN is advocating for the specific inclusion of siblings in the definition of family on the reauthorization of the DD Act. Also, increased involvement of siblings in the developmental disabilities network programs is recommended such as sibling participation on the sister agencies' advisory councils. Involvement of siblings should be evaluated with specific outcome measures that include siblings in the participation of families (Heller et al., 2008).

With the impending long-term care crisis, policies must take into account the needs of caregivers without forgetting siblings of people with disabilities. Policy for family caregivers is severely lacking and significantly underfunded. There are only two federal programs designed specifically to support family caregivers. The National Family Caregiver Support Program was established in 2000 as the very first national initiative to address family caregivers directly. It was enacted under Title III-E of the Older Americans Act Amendments of 2000. It provides funds to states specifically to serve caregivers of adults age 60 or over and to grandparents providing care to children (Heller, Caldwell, & Factor, 2007; Levine Halper, Peist, & Gould, 2010). The Lifespan Respite Care Act was enacted in 2006 to provide inhome and out-of-home respite for caregivers to get relief to provide quality care to their loved ones. However, it was not funded until 2009, and then it received a minimal appropriation allocating only $2.5 million (Levine et al., 2010) of the total $53.3 million needed to fully fund the program (Heller et al., 2007). This allocation is very small in light of the $375 billion the government is saving because of the work of unpaid family caregivers (Family Caregiver Alliance, 2009). Recommendations for policies include fully funding the Lifespan Respite Care Act and the Family Caregiver Support Program. Along with funding these programs, the government also needs to target the unique needs of siblings. Additional recommendations include providing financial assistance to family caregivers and expanding the Family and Medical Leave Act to provide paid leave time to siblings. Since family caregivers are the bedrock of the long-term care system, with siblings being an especially underserved group, they need to be supported to continue to play an important role and become recognized partners in the solution to the long-term care crisis in the United States.

Limitations

Some limitations exist in this research. The study used a cross-sectional data set from only one point of time. Also, a convenience sample was used, capturing responses from siblings who were already connected to some sibling support, and the results may not be generalizable to siblings who are not connected to SibNet or sibling conferences. This may be a more involved group than is typical and may not represent siblings who are less involved in the lives of their siblings with disabilities and therefore not connected to any sibling support. The majority of the sample included women, yet this reflects the gendered nature of caregiving in the literature (Levine et al., 2010). Also, the sample of respondents was fairly educated, with few minorities. Additionally, the research was limited because it did not include the voice of people with disabilities and relied on self-reported information of siblings. However, this study is one of the first that really looked at the voice of siblings of people with developmental disabilities.

Future Research

Although this research study helps fill a gap in the disability sibling literature, additional research is recommended that includes the siblings with and without disabilities and examines family dynamics beyond just the sibling dyad to see how whole families interact to support each other throughout their lifespans. The sibling experience of people with disabilities is especially important to capture to gain insight into the benefits of supporting people with disabilities. Also, intervention research should examine successful ways to negotiate the transition of caregiving roles from parents to nondisabled siblings to foster positive outcomes for the entire family. Additionally, further research should be done to capture the experiences of siblings who are not already connected to sibling support programs, such as reaching siblings through provider and parent networks, as well as getting the sibling experience in other countries.

Conclusion

The results of this research provided descriptive information about the support needs of adult siblings of people with developmental disabilities. The study helped give voice to the sibling perspective. The hope is that this information will be used by parents, professionals, and policymakers to address these concerns and support needs. These findings have implications for future policy and research. More opportunities are needed for siblings of people with developmental disabilities to connect, network, and share information and resources. Family support services must include siblings so that they are supported to be involved in the care of their brother or sister with disabilities in whatever way they choose. Siblings are an important resource for the disability field as future caregivers and untapped constituents in the disability policy movement. Additional research on siblings is important to increase the understanding of the supports that benefit siblings and their entire families.

References

Braddock, D., Hemp, R., Rizzolo, M. K., Haffer, L., Tanis, E. S., & Wu, J. (2011). *The state of the states in developmental disabilities 2011*. Washington, DC: American Association on Intellectual and Developmental Disabilities.

Celiberti, D. A., & Harris, S. L. (1993). Behavioral intervention for siblings of children with autism: A focus on skills to enhance play. *Behavior Therapy, 24,* 573–599.

Clark, M. L., Cunningham, L. J., & Cunningham, C. E. (1989). Improving the social behavior of siblings of autistic children using a group problem solving approach. *Child Family Behavior Therapy, 11,* 19–33.

Developmental Disabilities Assistance and Bill of Rights Act of 2000, Public Law 106–402, 114 Stat. 1677 (2000).

Evans, J., Jones, J., & Mansell, I. (2001). Supporting siblings: Evaluation of support groups for brothers and sisters of children with learning disabilities and challenging behavior. *Journal of Learning Disabilities, 5*(1), 69–78.

Factor, A., DeBrine, E. J., Caldwell, J., Arnold, K., Kramer, J., Nelis, T., & Heller, T. (2010). *The future is now: A future planning curriculum for families and their adult relative with developmental disabilities* (3rd ed.). Chicago, IL: Rehabilitation Research and Training Center on Aging with Developmental Disabilities, University of Illinois at Chicago.

Family Caregiver Alliance. (2009). *2009 National policy statement.* Available at http://caregiver.org/caregiver/jsp/content_node .jsp?nodeid=2279.

Fujiura, G. T. (1998). Demography of family households. *American Journal on Mental Retardation, 103,* 225–235.

Gallagher, P. A., Powell, T. H., & Rhodes, C. A. (2006). *Brothers and sisters: A special part of exceptional families* (3rd ed.). Baltimore, MD: Paul H. Brookes.

Heller, T., & Arnold, C. K. (2010). Siblings of adults with developmental disabilities: Psychosocial outcomes, relationships, and future planning. *Journal of Policy and Practice in Intellectual Disabilities, 7*(1), 16–25.

Heller, T., & Caldwell, J. (2006). Supporting aging caregivers and adults with developmental disabilities in future planning. *Mental Retardation, 44*(3), 189–202.

Heller, T., Caldwell, J., & Factor, A. (2007). Aging family caregivers: Policies and practices. *Mental Retardation and Developmental Disabilities Research Reviews, 13,* 136–142.

Heller, T., & Factor, A. (1994). Facilitating future planning and transitions out of the home. In M. M. Seltzer, M. W. Krauss, & M. Janicki (Eds.), *Life-course perspectives on adulthood and old age* (pp. 39–50) [Monograph Series]. Washington, DC: American Association on Mental Retardation.

Heller, T., Kaiser, A., Meyer, D., Fish, T., Kramer, J., & Dufresne, D. (2008). *The Sibling Leadership Network: Recommendations for research, advocacy, and supports relating to siblings of people with developmental disabilities* [White paper]. Chicago, IL: Rehabilitation Research and Training Center on Aging with Developmental Disabilities, Lifespan Health and Function, University of Illinois at Chicago.

Heller, T., & Kramer, J. (2009). Involvement of adult siblings of persons with developmental disabilities in future planning. *Intellectual and Developmental Disabilities, 47*(3), 208–219.

Hodapp, R., Glidden, L. M., & Kaiser, A. P. (2005). Siblings of persons with disabilities: Toward a research agenda. *Mental Retardation, 43*(5), 334–338.

Hodapp, R. M., Urbano, R. C., Burke, M. M. (2010). Adult female and male siblings of persons with disabilities: Findings from a national survey. *Intellectual and Developmental Disabilities, 48*(1), 52–62.

James, S. D., & Egel, A. K. (1986). A direct prompting strategy for increasing reciprocal interactions between handicapped and nonhandicapped siblings. *Journal of Applied Behavior Analysis, 19*(2), 173–186.

Johnson, A. B., & Sandall, S. (2005). *Sibshops: A follow-up of participants of a sibling support program.* Seattle, WA: University of Washington.

Kramer, J. C. (2008). *People with disabilities and their siblings: Building concepts of support and transitions* (Unpublished doctoral dissertation). University of Illinois at Chicago, Chicago, IL.

Larson, S. A., Lakin, K. C., Anderson, L., Kwak, N., Lee, J. H., & Anderson, D. (2001). Prevalence of mental retardation and developmental disabilities: Estimates from the 1994/1995 National Health Interview Survey Disability Supplements. *American Journal on Mental Retardation, 106*(3), 231–252.

Levine, C., Halper, D., Peist, A., & Gould, D. A. (2010). Bridging troubled waters: Family caregivers, transitions, and long-term care. *Health Affairs, 29*(1), 116–124.

Support Needs of Siblings of People with Developmental Disabilities by Catherine K. Arnold, Tamar Heller, and John Kramer

101

Lifespan Respite Care Act, P.L. 109–442 (2006).

Meyer, D., & Vadasy, P. (1994). *Sibshops: Workshops for siblings of children with special needs.* Baltimore, MD: Paul H. Brookes.

Older Americans Act Amendments of 2000, Public Law 106–501, 114 Stat. 2226 (2000).

Patton, M. Q. (2002). *Qualitative research and evaluation methods, 3rd edition.* Newbury Park, CA: Sage.

Rawson, H. (2009). "I'm going to be here long after you've gone"— Sibling perspectives of the future. *British Journal of Learning Disabilities, 38,* 225–231.

Sarantakos, S. (1993). *Social research.* South Melbourne, Victoria, Australia: MacMillan Education Australia.

Stoneman, Z. (2005). Siblings of children with disabilities: Research themes. *Mental Retardation, 43*(5), 339–350.

U.S. Census Bureau. (2010). *Data finders: Population clocks.* Available at http://www.census.gov.

Weber, R. P. (1990). *Basic content analysis* (2nd ed.). Newbury Park, CA: Sage.

Critical Thinking

1. If you had a sibling with a developmental disability, what would be your greatest worries or concerns as your parents aged and you became an adult? How do you think having someone with a developmental disability in your family would alter family relationships?

2. What are some challenges and difficulties experienced by adult siblings when their brother or sister has a developmental disability?

3. Using information gained from this article, describe an intervention or support program that could be developed to facilitate positive family relationships, decrease caregiver stress, and aid in transition planning for families where an adult child has a developmental or intellectual disability.

Create Central

www.mhhe.com/createcentral

Internet References

Sibling Support Project
www.siblingsupport.org

Sibs
www.sibs.org.uk

Tufts University Child and Family Webguide
www.cfw.tufts.edu

Article   Prepared by: Patricia Hrusa Williams,
University of Maine at Farmington

Supporting Siblings of Children with Autism Spectrum Disorders

LING-LING TSAO, RANDY DAVENPORT, AND CYNTHIA SCHMIEGE

Learning Outcomes

After reading this article, you will be able to:

- Understand the characteristics of autism spectrum disorders (ASDs).
- Identify the challenges experienced by siblings when one has an ASD.
- Identity individual and family factors that promote healthy sibling relationships in families where a child has an ASD.
- Recognize supports needed by families when a child has an ASD.

Introduction

Autism is a pervasive developmental disorder. It affects essential human behaviors such as the ability to communicate ideas and feelings, imagination, and the establishment of relationships with others (National Research Council 2001). In a recent report, the Centers for Disease Control and Prevention (2009) estimates an average of 1 in 110 children in the U.S. has an autism spectrum disorder (ASD). Due to these alarming statistics, the topic of ASDs has become a nation-wide concern, prompting discussions among professionals and parents seeking the best possible intervention approaches to support families of children with ASDs (O'Brien and Daggett 2006). There are many unknowns about the most effective treatment strategy for children with ASDs. However, it is generally agreed that early intervention programs are crucial and effective. The National Research Council recommends that educational services begin as soon as a child is suspected of having an autistic spectrum disorder (p. 6, NRC 2001). Given the importance of early intervention for a child with an ASD, much attention is being devoted to the characteristics of effective educational interventions for children with an ASD.

In the family context, attention is typically focused on effective intervention for a child with an ASD. However, many parents, specialists, and researchers have concerns for other children in the family as well (Hastings 2007). Particularly,

there is concern about how best to support typically developing siblings of children with an ASD (Kilmer et al. 2008; Lock 2009; Schuntermann 2009). Consequently, the purpose of this paper is to review and synthesize the literature on support for siblings of children with an ASD. With this purpose in mind, this review focuses on approaches for supporting and fostering positive sibling relationships, with consideration of the family system where appropriate.

For the purpose of this paper, we refer to a child with an ASD as *the focal child,* and we refer to a typically developing sibling of a child with a disability or an ASD as *the sibling* or *siblings.* We focused on two basic questions about what it means to be a sibling of a child with an ASD: What is it like to grow up as a sibling of a child with autism? And what can we do to support siblings of children with autism? These questions helped guide us as we reviewed the literature, and we hope to address these questions throughout this review. Before discussing the available support for siblings, it is important to consider what has been researched and what is currently known about sibling relationships.

Sibling Relationships

One special characteristic of sibling relationships is that they share biological and affective ties with parents. Brothers and sisters can be a source of companionship, help, and emotional support. In their interactions with each other, siblings may acquire many social and cognitive skills that are central to healthy social development (Furman and Buhrmester 1985). Travis and Sigman (1998) suggested that siblings may be especially important for children with autism because they provide opportunities to socially interact with other children under maximally supportive conditions (Rivers and Stoneman 2008). Research suggests that children with ASDs need exposure to typically developing children to gain experience and learn about proper social interaction and relationships (Knott et al.1995; Tsao and Odom 2006). Typically developing siblings have great potential to influence children with ASDs, particularly in early development, and in the acquisition of social competencies.

Related to the discussion of sibling relationships is the discussion of what it is like to grow up as a sibling of a child with an ASD. McHale et al. (1986) interviewed 30 siblings of children with autism, 30 siblings of children with cognitive disabilities, and 30 siblings of typically developing children between the ages of 6 and 15. The children were asked questions about their sibling relationships, their attitudes, and their perceptions of their siblings. For both the group with siblings of children with autism and the group with siblings of children with cognitive disabilities, negative sibling relationships were associated with worries about the future of the child with a disability, perceptions of parental favoritism toward the child with a disability, and feelings of rejection toward the child with a disability.

Mascha and Boucher (2006) interviewed 14 siblings of children with autism between the ages of 11 and 18 and identified negative reactions, such as feelings of embarrassment related to the focal child's behavior problems (i.e., aggression or uncontrolled anger). Gold (1993) found siblings of boys with autism scored higher on the depression measure of the Children's Depression Inventory than siblings of typically developing boys. Thereby, siblings of children with autism may have potentially more internalizing symptoms particularly when they are moving into adolescence. (However, the researchers cautioned generalizing the finding due to a disproportionate number of adolescent siblings compared to the control group).

Compared to siblings of typically developing children, higher levels of attentional problems, loneliness, and problems with peers have been found in siblings of children with autism (Bagenholm and Gillberg 1991). Kaminsky and Dewey (2001) also found that in families with a child with an ASD, sibling relationships were characterized by less intimacy, less prosocial behavior, and less nurturance as measured by siblings' perceptions of their relationships on a sibling relationship questionnaire. This is consistent with another study by Knott et al. (1995), who reported that children with autism and their typically developing siblings spent less time together than typically developing sibling dyads.

In contrast to these potentially negative findings concerning sibling relationships, McHale et al. (1986) indicated that siblings with a good understanding of their brother or sister's disability, had positive sibling relationships when they perceived that parents and peers had positive reactions toward their sibling with a disability. Mates (1990) found that siblings of children with autism had high self-concepts, healthy academic performance, and healthy behavioral adjustment as rated by their parents and teachers. These positive findings are also in line with other similar research studies (i.e., Berger 1980; McHale et al. 1986). Although autism has doubtlessly had an impact on the family (e.g., Hastings 2003a; Hastings et al. 2005; Ross and Cuskelly 2006), these positive findings indicate that in some instances, siblings of children with autism seem to adjust well to their family situation, and occasionally perform better in some aspects of their social emotional development (e.g., the development of their mean self concept) than the normative sample (Mates 1990). Other positive impacts related to having a sibling with a disability may involve more acceptance (Roeyers and Mycke 1995), no deficits in social competence (Kaminsky

and Dewey 2002; Rodrigue et al. 1993), and greater admiration and less competition and quarrels (Knott et al. 1995).

Siblings with positive perceptions and experiences related to their sibling with a disability are likely to adapt successfully to the impact of having a disability on the family (Taunt and Hastings 2002). When siblings perceived their parents and peers as reacting positively to the child with a disability, they reported more positive relationships with their sibling (Petalas et al. 2009).

The impact of having a sibling with an ASD may vary among children; as Stoneman (2001) pointed out, the research on sibling relationships is often contradictory and difficult to interpret. Numerous researchers have found that the relationship between children with disabilities and their siblings is usually positive (McHale et al. 1986; Stoneman et al. 1987; Bagenholm and Gillberg 1991; Lobato et al. 1991). However, some negative impacts of ASD on sibling relationships have also been found (e.g., Bagenholm and Gillberg 1991; Kaminsky and Dewey 2001). Certain variables may directly or indirectly affect the adaption of typically developing siblings to their brothers or sisters with disabilities, such as gender, age, information, knowledge about the disability of the child with a disability, or age difference between the typically developing siblings and children with disabilities (Unal and Baran 2011). While there is little or nothing that can be done about the age of children, their ordinal position or the severity of the ASD, there are strategies that can be implemented to promote and facilitate positive relationships between typically developing siblings and their brother or sister with an ASD (Beyer 2009).

Supports and Approaches

Only a limited number of researchers have directly attempted to empirically validate support strategies for siblings that help them develop positive, mutually satisfying relationships with their brothers and sisters (Stoneman 2001). The lack of research on this topic is remarkable because intervention may help ensure that positive rather than negative outcomes of sibling relationship development occur (Mascha and Boucher 2006). Society has no greater task than to provide for the healthy, positive development of children; the ultimate goal is to support children with disabilities and their siblings in ways that enhance their chances of growing into psychologically healthy adults with firmly established positive interpersonal relationships (Stoneman 2005, p. 347).

Parenting

For a variety of reasons, parents may not treat all of their children identically. Not only is each child a unique individual, but parents also experience developmental changes over the course of parenting. This is perhaps particularly an issue for families with a child with a disability. For typically developing children, research has shown that differential parental treatment of siblings is linked to adjustment problems (Feinberg and Hetherington 2001). Many studies have also documented increased differential parenting in families with children with disabilities, generally favoring the child with a disability (Lobato et al. 1991; McHale and Pawletko 1992). Dunn and McGuire (1992) highlight an impressive consensus from the research that maternal differential treatment is linked to the quality of sibling relationships for typically developing children (e.g., Boer 1990; Brody and Stoneman 1987; Bryany and Crockenberg 1980, Dunn and Plomin 1990) and even for siblings of children with disabilities (McHale and Gamble 1989). When siblings are dissatisfied with differential parenting, the quality of the sibling relationship suffers (Rivers and Stoneman 2008). It is not simply a matter of poor sibling relationships and parental favoring that lead to increased psychological difficulties, but it is a more complex issue involving children who are sensitive to changes in the wider sibling context (Richmond et al. 2005; Schuntermann 2007).

Siblings may not always perceive differential parenting as favoritism—siblings' attitudes concerning how they perceive the differential treatment has much to do with their satisfaction with the sibling relationship. Children do not always object to being treated differently from their siblings, as long as they can find meaning in the difference and perceive the difference as being fair (Kowal et al. 2002). Similarly, McHale et al. (2000) found that differential treatment from parents does not always have negative implications for siblings; it is important to consider the subjective evaluation and the legitimacy of the differential treatment of the siblings themselves. Both children who have a sibling with a disability and children who have typically developing siblings experience a full range of feelings related to their brother or sister, their parents, themselves, and other people in general. Many siblings experience similar emotions. Some feel excitement, anger, frustration, and others might feel unfavorable or lonely.

Parenting Strategy: Communication

It is very important to acknowledge the impact of siblings' perceptions about parenting on their sibling relationship before trying to support siblings. Therefore, open communication is one way parents can provide support for siblings of children with autism. Gold (1993) stressed the benefits experienced by siblings when open communication was possible, especially when family members were free to communicate openly about the child with a disability. For more information on specific strategies for facilitating effective family communication (e.g., good listening skills for creating an atmosphere where siblings can feel free to reveal personal thoughts and feelings to parents), see Harris and Glasberg (2003).

In addition to good communication, it may be helpful for siblings to learn to label their emotions. This may help children understand their emotions by linking their own feelings or concerns about their sibling to their perceptions of their parents' emotional state (e.g., stress about care for every family member). Meanwhile, providing age appropriate explanations about what autism is can help siblings understand and manage their perceptions about why their sibling with an ASD receives extra attention and support (Harris and Glasberg 2003; Gallagher et al. 2006). Parents should do their best to understand what their typically developing children are saying concerning their sibling with an ASD. Furthermore, siblings will feel more supported when parents provide them with clear feedback that what they say has been received and taken into account by their parents. Acknowledgment of siblings' feelings will help them feel respected.

When determining how to best support siblings, it may be beneficial to consider not only good communication in general and education about autism, but also to consider the demands placed upon siblings as a result of having a brother or sister with an ASD. Do typically developing siblings of a brother or sister with an ASD take on more household and care responsibilities than siblings in families without disabilities? Interestingly, Gold (1993) found that siblings of children with autism report doing less domestic work than siblings of typically developing children. Perhaps this is due to parental fears and guilt about potentially burdening siblings by over-relying on them for help with childcare and a desire to not over-burden siblings with extra housework responsibilities.

Parental expectation about sibling responsibilities is one aspect of the parent–child relationship, which illustrates that the relationship between each child and parent can influence the sibling–sibling relationship. Such aspects of the parent–child relationship should be taken into account, and parental awareness of each individual child's needs in a family constellation can reduce sibling rivalry and bring the family members closer together (Cancro 2008). Bryant and Crockenberg (1980) found that parents who are responsive to their children's behavior are likely to foster prosocial behaviors between their children (Furman and Buhrmester 1985).

Support Group

Having a child with an ASD in the family not only has the potential to influence sibling relationships and the emotional well-being of siblings, it can also affect the emotional well-being of the parents. Research has found that parents of children with ASDs have higher rates of depression and stress compared to parents who have children with other disabilities and parents with typically developing children (e.g., Hastings 2003b; Hasting et al., 2005; Ross and Cuskelly 2006). Parents need a good support network. Having access to a support network and receiving specific support related to their child yielded great benefits for parents of children with autism (Guralnick et al. 2008). Parent support groups should involve meeting other parents of children with similar conditions. Such meetings offer parents the knowledge, understanding, and acceptance they seek (Banach et al. 2010). Through programs like a family support group or a parent-to-parent group, families have a place to share their joys and concerns, learn lessons to better support their child's needs, exchange information, and generally support each other.

Family support groups are good for parents and children. There is evidence that social support might moderate the severity of symptoms exhibited by the child with an ASD and might be related to adaptive coping and adjustment of siblings (Banach et al. 2010; Hastings 2003b; Law et al. 2001; Stoneman 2005). Many non-profit organizations provide support group services for families who have a child with autism, such as the Autism Society of America or the ARC of the United States at state and local levels. Some organizations also provide child-care services so that parents can attend without making baby-sitting arrangements—a potential challenge for many families with children who have disabilities. When parents have access to quality emotional and informational resources, they are bet-ter positioned to reach out for help and cope more effectively.

Parent Training and Support

Parental attitudes about support for each of their individual children are vital for promoting positive sibling relationships. Parents can act as both support agents and agent trainers; how-ever, before getting to this level, parents need the right informa-tion and training themselves. Support groups and community agencies are again likely to be a valuable source for these kinds of resources. A program focused on training parents to teach social skills to young siblings can not only promote positive, adaptive behavior, but can also capitalize on the powerful socialization effects of parents and siblings (i.e., parents and siblings are uniquely situated to make a profound impact on a child's development) (Tiedemann and Johnston 1992).

Parents may need assistance developing strategies to enhance children's social competencies. Programs exist to aid parents with the endeavor of creating their own intervention plan and can help parents create a custom intervention tailored to their families' specific needs. Programs such as these can also help parents understand different intervention approaches, which may help parents overcome the limitations of some existing interventions (e.g., limited ability to generalize from other interventions and maintenance issues; Tiedemann and Johnston, 1992). Parent training is necessary for teaching par-ents how to appropriately reinforce and maintain sibling efforts to positively interact with their brother or sister with an ASD (Petalas et al. 2009). For example, Lobato and Kao (2002) conducted an integrated sibling–parent group intervention for typically developing siblings of children with a chronic illness or developmental disability and their parents. When parents implemented good reinforcement and maintenance strategies, the authors found improved sibling connectedness and found that siblings had a better knowledge of the child's disorder and behavior problems (Petalas et al. 2009).

Sibling Play Intervention

Play provides the prime social context for children to create reciprocal roles, define power relationships, and facilitate mutual social exchanges (Stoneman 2001). Through trial and error informed by social feedback, typically developing chil-dren learn to accommodate their siblings' disabilities and facilitate social interaction (Stoneman 2001). However, the siblings' role as an agent for social skills training is not with-out challenges. Research indicates that it is more difficult for

typically developing siblings to create and lead play behaviors when their brother or sister's disruptive and negative behaviors are more severe (Bagenholm and Gillberg 1991; Knott et al. 1995; Mascha and Boucher 2006; Strain and Danko 1995). Therefore, an individualized play-based social intervention may be an effective strategy for supporting siblings' needs.

Tsao and McCabe (2010) provided a protocol for parents or early intervention specialists to develop a sibling play interven-tion focused on supporting proper interactions between a child with autism and a typically developing sibling. The interven-tion begins by observing the children's play and routines. Early intervention specialists and parents then search for opportuni-ties to use the focal child's preferred toys or activities to cre-ate play sessions with specific objectives for both children. The key to success for an intervention such as this requires taking the sibling's motivation into consideration (e.g., the specialist and parents should consider whether the sibling enjoys learn-ing new ways of interacting with the focal child). Motivated siblings can be a significant resource for the family, making the situation less difficult and allowing the family to cope more effectively.

Again, siblings can be successful social agents for chil-dren with autism. Siblings can facilitate initiations and learn to respond strategically to their siblings (El-Ghoroury and Romanczyk 1999; Tsao and Odom 2006). Siblings adept at selecting activities that actively engage both children will make more effective play partners than children who select activities that exclude one child or the other (Lobato et al. 1991; Stone-man et al. 1987). Through ongoing interactions, siblings with the social skills to appropriately understand and respond to the needs of their brother or sister with a disability can develop high quality sibling relationships (Stoneman 2005). Interaction training for siblings of children with ASDs may prove to be a valuable approach for an intervention. Such training could potentially enhance the social interactions and communica-tion between siblings and thus, reduce conflict. Continuity of training and periodic reassessment will ensure that siblings are provided with the necessary resources to meet the chang-ing demands as the sibling dyad develops and each child grows older (Petalas et al. 2009).

It is possible that skills siblings gain in intervention and sharpened through interactions with their brother or sister can generalize to contexts beyond the sibling–sibling relationship. (Mascha and Boucher 2006). For example, Colletti and Harris (1997) taught siblings of children with ASDs behavior modifi-cation techniques—techniques that could potentially be applied to other relationships and conflict management situations (e.g., relationships with friends and other children at school).

A few studies have begun to address the issue of support-ing siblings and providing them with the skills and resources they need to be powerful social skill trainers and models for their brother or sister with autism. For example, Celiberti and Harris (1993) taught typically developing siblings behavioral skills to engage their brother or sister in play. Tsao and Odom (2006) taught typically developing siblings how to play more effectively with their brothers (who had an ASD) and found that children with ASDs initiated more interactions with their siblings at the end of the intervention than at the beginning. They also observed more play behaviors between both children suggesting that the children were more socially engaged after the intervention. Parents also mentioned that children played like they were real siblings (e.g., played together and played more often). When siblings see their important role in helping their brother or sister, and see that they are making a positive impact, it is affirming. As a result, showing typically developing siblings how to best enhance their brother or sister's abilities and social skills can potentially boost siblings' self esteem, and help them form stronger relationships with each other (Mascha and Boucher 2006).

Sibling Support Groups

Given the importance of social support from family members, friends, neighbors, professionals, and parent groups, it is possible that social support specifically for siblings may also play an important role in the healthy and adaptive adjustment of siblings (Kaminsky and Dewey 2002). One well-documented program for supporting siblings is Sibshops (Meyer and Vadasy 2007). Sibshops resulted in increased positive feelings about the brother or sister with a disability and siblings acquired useful coping strategies (Johnson and Sandall 2005; Conway and Meyer 2008).

Bagenholm and Gillberg (1991) interviewed 60 children between the ages of 5 and 20 who had a brother or sister with autism, cognitive disabilities, or no apparent physical or cognitive disorders. They found that siblings of children with disabilities talked more about their brothers and sisters than siblings of typically developing children. Children in "ordinary" families do not talk very much about their siblings (p. 304). As a result, Bagenholm and Gillberg (1991) believed that if there is something to talk about—good or bad—it may be a relief for siblings to have the opportunity to talk about their experiences both at home and with friends and other supportive adults. Simply providing opportunities for siblings to express their feelings is a good start, but a more structured and clinical approach may be even better. Mascha and Boucher (2006) indicated that it might be beneficial to work directly with siblings by helping them explore their thoughts and feelings, including reflecting on their experiences with their brother or sister, their understanding of the disability, and the role of each family member within the family system. Therefore, it is often good practice to utilize a professional counselor when possible. Providing resources and appropriate support to siblings is essential, and can potentially have long-term benefits for both siblings. Siblings of persons with disabilities can their brothers and sisters live dignified lives from childhood throughout adulthood (Meyer and Vadasy 1997).

Discussion

The majority of brothers and sisters of children with autism function well (Ferraioli and Harris 2010). Research has shown that relationships between siblings when one child has a disability are not identical to the relationships that exist between typically developing siblings (Stoneman 2001). However, having a brother or sister with a disability does not cause maladaptation or pathology in children (Stoneman 2005; Rodrigue et al. 1993). Instead, siblings of children with disabilities engage in a rich and complex set of roles, such as that of teacher, caregiver, modeler, and confidant, which may promote developmental benefits (Stoneman and Brody 1982). Many siblings of children with disabilities successfully achieve mutually acceptable interactional role relationships, artfully crafted to fit their life contexts (Stoneman 2001, 2005). Certainly, this is in keeping with family theories that suggest that families define situations. The use of available resources and the important aspects of a good intervention, as identified in this review, can assist families to not only cope with a stressor event but also adapt and thrive with their unique challenge.

On the other hand, the behavioral problems frequently associated with an ASD (e.g., aggression or temper issues) can cause a variety of negative emotions for typically developing siblings. Therefore, there is a clear need for proper support of siblings of children with autism (Mascha and Boucher 2006). Siblings are an integrative component of the family system and are key players shaping the experiences and learning opportunities available to children with special needs (Kresak et al. 2009).

It is not always clear what the impact of a disability will be on sibling relationships. There are many factors (e.g., environmental factors) that make studying the effects of an ASD on the sibling relationships difficult (Beyer 2009). Because children on the autism spectrum vary in the severity of their condition, it is difficult to ascertain how the disability impacts a family. The extent of developmental delay could impact how much a family is affected by the disorder. These differences should be taken into account when making decisions about how to support siblings and what kinds of interventions are appropriate for individual families.

The role of siblings who have a brother or sister on the autism spectrum has been underexplored, despite the sibling's potential to significantly enhance family life and foster social skills in children with autism. Efforts should be made to raise parental and professional awareness of the potential issues faced by siblings to promote dialogue in families and between families and professionals. This may prove especially significant later in life, as sibling relationships are often long-lasting relationships. It is recommended that practitioners acknowledge and build on the positive views held by siblings. This may help siblings recognize their personal strengths and abilities, promote positive family relationships characterized by open channels of communication, and provide opportunities for families to bond. Additionally, increasing siblings' access to developmentally appropriate information and support that promotes positive perceptions and experiences may have lasting effects on sibling adjustment and sibling relationships (Petalas et al. 2009). Use of resources (e.g., material, informational, and emotional/social resources, etc.) can impact the dynamic functioning of a whole family, including typically developing siblings. Hence, future autism sibling studies should take a life course approach and consider the context of life stages (Beyer 2009), as well as the impact on the family system as a whole.

Conclusion

Each family member plays an important role in his or her own family system. Siblings are uniquely situated to help children with ASDs and other disabilities. The take-home message of this review is that empowering siblings to be effective intervention partners can potentially yield great benefits for the sibling, the child with a disability, and the greater family constellation. Parents need to utilize the resources and support networks available to them to help them cope with the potential challenges of having a child with a disability. With proper support and resources, parents can ensure the much-needed support of their typically developing children. Parents can also facilitate the training of typically developing siblings, thereby including siblings in the larger intervention plan for the child with an ASD or other disability. Asking what is it like to grow up as a sibling of a child with autism and what can we do to support siblings of children with autism, led to the identification of several important considerations for supporting siblings and designing effective interventions. These considerations included open communication, opportunities for siblings to express their feelings, utilization of support networks, parenting considerations, and training of both parents and siblings. Viewing the sibling in the larger family context and providing siblings with proper support are vital issues—the reward of which is too great to ignore.

References

Bagenholm, A., & Gillberg, C. (1991). Psychosocial effects on siblings of children with autism and mental retardation: A population based study. *Journal of Mental Deficiency Research, 35,* 291–307.

Banach, M., Judice, J., Conway, L., & Couse, L. J. (2010). Family support and empowerment: Post autism diagnosis support group for parents. *Social Work with Groups, 33,* 69–83.

Berger, E. W. (1980). *A study of self concept of siblings of autistic children.* Unpublished Dissertation, University of Cincinnati.

Beyer, J. F. (2009). Autism spectrum disorders and sibling relationships: Research and strategies. *Education and Training in Developmental Disabilities, 44,* 444–452.

Boer, F. (1990). *Sibling relationships in middle childhood: An empirical study.* Leiden: DSWO Press, University of Leiden.

Brody, G. H., & Stoneman, Z. (1987). Sibling conflict: Contributions of the siblings themselves, the parent–sibling relationship, and the broader family system. *Journal of Children in Contemporary Society, 19,* 39–53.

Bryany, B. K., & Crockenberg, S. B. (1980). Correlates and dimensions of prosocial behavior: A study of female siblings with their mothers. *Child Development, 51,* 529–544.

Cancro, R. (2008). Children with autism and their siblings. *Exceptional Parent,* December, 30.

Celiberti, D. A., & Harris, S. L. (1993). Behavioral intervention for siblings of children with autism: A focus on skills to enhance play. *Behavior Therapy, 24,* 573–599.

Centers for Disease Control and Prevention (CDC). (2009). Prevalence of autism spectrum disorders: Autism and developmental disabilities monitoring network, United States, 2006. *Morbidity and Mortality Weekly Report,* December 18, 58 (NoSS-10).

Colletti, G., & Harris, S. L. (1997). Behavior modification in the home: Siblings as behavior modifiers, parents as observers. *Journal of Abnormal Child Psychology, 5,* 21–30.

Conway, S., & Meyer, D. (2008). Developing support for siblings of young people with disabilities. *Support for Learning, 23,* 113–117.

Dunn, J., & McGuire, S. (1992). Sibling and peer relationships in childhood. *Journal of Child Psychology and Psychiatry, 33,* 67–105.

Dunn, J., & Plomin, R. (1990). *Separate lives: Why siblings are so different.* New York: Basic Books.

El-Ghoroury, N. H., & Romanczyk, R. G. (1999). Play interactions of family members towards children with autism. *Journal of Autism and Developmental Disorders, 28,* 249–258.

Feinberg, M., & Hetherington, E. M. (2001). Differential parenting as a within-family variable. *Journal of Family Psychology, 15,* 22–37.

Ferraioli, S. J., & Harris, S. (2010). The impact of autism on siblings. *Social Work in Mental Health, 8,* 41–53.

Furman, W., & Buhrmester, D. (1985). Children's perceptions of the qualities of sibling relationships. *Child Development, 56,* 448–461.

Gallagher, P. A., Powell, T. H., & Rhodes, C. A. (2006). *Brothers and sisters: A special part of exceptional families* (3rd ed.). Baltimore: MD: Brookes.

Gold, N. (1993). Depression and social adjustment in siblings of boys with autism. *Journal of Autism and Developmental Disorders, 23,* 147–163.

Guralnick, M. J., Hammond, M. A., Neville, B., & Connor, R. T. (2008). The relationship between sources and functions of social support and dimensions of child and parent related stress. *Journal of Intellectual Disability Research, 53,* 1138–1154.

Harris, S., & Glasberg, B. (2003). *Siblings of children with autism: A guide for families* (2nd ed.). Bethesda, MD: Woodbine House.

Hastings, R. P. (2003a). Brief report: Behavioral adjustment of siblings of children with autism. *Journal of Autism and Developmental Disorders, 33,* 99–104.

Hastings, R. P. (2003b). Behavioral adjustment of siblings of children with autism engaged in applied behavioral analysis early intervention programs: The moderating role of social support. *Journal of Autism and Developmental Disorders, 33,* 141–150.

Hastings, R. P. (2007). Longitudinal relationships between sibling behavioral adjustment and behavior problems of children with developmental disabilities. *Journal of Autism and Developmental Disorders, 37,* 1485–1492.

Hastings, R., Kovshoff, H., Brown, T., Ward, N., degli Espinosa, F., & Remington, B. (2005). Coping strategies in mothers and fathers of preschool and school-age children with autism. *Autism, 9,* 377–391.

Johnson, A. B., & Sandall, S. (2005). *Sibshops: A follow-up of participants of a sibling support program.* Seattle: University of Washington.

Kaminsky, L., & Dewey, D. (2001). Siblings relationships of children with autism. *Journal of Autism and Developmental Disorders, 31,* 399–410.

Kaminsky, L., & Dewey, D. (2002). Psychosocial adjustment in siblings of children with autism. *Journal of Child Psychology and Psychiatry, 43,* 225–232.

Kilmer, R. P., Cook, J. R., Taylor, C., Kane, S. F., & Clark, L. Y. (2008). Siblings of children with severe emotional disturbances: Risks, resources, and adaptation. *American Journal of Orthopsychiatry, 78,* 1–10.

Knott, F., Lewis, C., & Williams, T. (1995). Sibling interaction of children with learning disabilities: A comparison of autism and Down's syndrome. *Journal of Child Psychiatry, 6,* 965–976.

Kowal, A., Kramer, L., Krull, J. L., & Crick, N. R. (2002). Children's perceptions of the fairness of parental preferential treatment and their socioemotional well being. *Journal of Family Psychology, 16,* 297–306.

Kresak, K., Gallagher, P., & Rhodes, C. (2009). Siblings of infants and toddlers with disabilities in early intervention. *Topics in Early Childhood Special Education, 29,* 143–154.

Law, M., King, S., Stewart, D., & King, G. (2001). The perceived effects of parent-led support groups for parents of children with disabilities. *Physical & Occupational Therapy in Pediatrics, 21,* 29–48.

Lobato, D., & Kao, B. T. (2002). Integrated sibling–parent group intervention to improve sibling knowledge and adjustment to chronic illness and disability. *Journal of Pediatric Psychology, 27,* 711–716.

Lobato, D., Miller, C. T., Barbour, L., Hall, L. J., & Pezzullo, J. (1991). Preschool siblings of handicapped children: Interactions with mothers, brothers, and sisters. *Research in Developmental Disabilities, 12,* 387–399.

Lock, R. H. (2009). Examining the need for autism sibling support groups in rural areas. *Rural Special Education Quarterly, 28*(4), 21–30.

Mascha, K., & Boucher, J. (2006). Preliminary investigation of a qualitative method of examining siblings' experiences of living with a child with ASD. *British Journal of Developmental Disabilities, 52,* 19–28.

Mates, T. E. (1990). Siblings of autistic children: Their adjustment and performance at home and in school. *Journal of Autism and Developmental Disorders, 20,* 545–553.

McHale, S. M., & Gamble, W. C. (1989). Sibling relationships of children with disabled and nondisabled brothers and sisters. *Developmental Psychology, 25,* 421–429.

McHale, S. M., & Pawletko, T. M. (1992). Differential treatment of siblings in two family contexts. *Child Development, 63,* 68–81.

McHale, S. M., Sloan, J., & Simeonsson, R. J. (1986). Sibling relationships of children with autistic, mental retarded, and nonhandicapped brothers and sisters. *Journal of Autism and Developmental Disorders, 16,* 399–413.

McHale, S. M., Updegraff, K. A., Jackson-Newsom, J., Tucker, C. J., & Crouter, A. C. (2000). When does parents' differential treatment have negative implications for siblings? *Social Development, 9,* 149–172.

Meyer, D., & Vadasy, P. (1997). Meeting the unique concerns of brothers and sisters. In B. Carpenter (Ed.), *Family in context: Emerging trends in family support and early intervention.* London: Davis Fulton.

Meyer, D., & Vadasy, P. (2007). *Sibshops: Workshops for siblings of children with special needs* (revised edition ed.). Baltimore, MD: Paul H. Brookes.

National Research Council (2001). Educating Children with Autism. Committee on Educational Interventions for Children with Autism. In C. Lord., & J. P. McGee (Eds.), *Division of Behavioral and Social Sciences and Education.* Washington, DC: National Academy Press.

O'Brien, M., & Daggett, J. (2006). *Beyond the autism diagnosis: A professional's guide to helping families.* Baltimore, MD: Brookes.

Petalas, M. A., Hastings, R. P., Nash, S., Dowey, A., & Reilly, D. (2009). I like that he always shows who he is: The perceptions and experiences of siblings with a brother with autism spectrum disorder. *International Journal of Disability, Development, and Education, 56,* 381–399.

Richmond, M. K., Stocker, C. M., & Rienks, S. L. (2005). Longitudinal associations between sibling relationship quality, parental differential treatment, and children's adjustment. *Journal of Family Psychology, 19,* 550–559.

Rivers, J. W., & Stoneman, Z. (2008). Child temperaments, differential parenting, and the sibling relationships of children with autism spectrum disorder. *Journal of Autism and Developmental Disorders, 38,* 1740–1750.

Rodrigue, J. R., Geffken, G. R., & Morgan, S. B. (1993). Perceived competence and behavioral adjustment of siblings of children with autism. *Journal of Autism and Developmental Disorders, 23,* 665–674.

Roeyers, H., & Mycke, K. (1995). Siblings of children with autism, with mental retardation, and with normal development. *Child: Care, Health and Development, 21,* 305–319.

Ross, P., & Cuskelly, M. (2006). Adjustment, sibling problem and coping strategies of brothers and sisters of children with autistic spectrum disorder. *Journal of Intellectual & Developmental Disability, 31,* 77–86.

Schuntermann, P. (2007). The sibling experience: Growing up with a child who has pervasive developmental disorder or mental retardation. *Harvard Review of Psychiatry, 15,* 93–108.

Schuntermann, P. (2009). Growing up with a developmentally challenged brother or sister: A model for engaging siblings based on mentalizing. *Howard Review of Psychiatry, 17,* 297–314.

Stoneman, Z. (2001). Supporting positive sibling relationships during childhood. *Mental Retardation and Developmental Disabilities Research Review, 7,* 134–142.

Stoneman, Z. (2005). Siblings of children with disabilities: Research themes. *Mental Retardation, 43,* 339–350.

Stoneman, Z., & Brody, G. H. (1982). Strengths in sibling interactions involving a retarded child: A functional role theory approach. In N. Stinnett, B. Chesser, J. DeFrain, & P. Knaub (Eds.), *Family strengths* (pp. 113–129). Lincoln: University of Nebraska Press.

Stoneman, Z., Brody, G. H., Davis, C. H., & Crapps, J. M. (1987). Mentally retarded children and their older siblings: Naturalistic in home observations. *American Journal on Mental Retardation, 92,* 290–298.

Strain, P. S., & Danko, C. D. (1995). Caregivers' encouragement of positive interaction between preschoolers with autism and siblings. *Journal of Emotional and Behavioral Disorders, 3,* 2–12.

Taunt, H. M., & Hastings, R. P. (2002). Positive impact of children with developmental disabilities on their families: A preliminary study. *Education and Training in Mental Retardation and Developmental Disabilities, 37,* 410–420.

Tiedemann, G. L., & Johnston, C. (1992). Evaluation of a parent training program to promote sharing between young siblings. *Behavior Therapy, 23,* 299–318.

Travis, L. L., & Sigman, M. (1998). Social deficits and interpersonal relationships in autism. *Mental Retardation and Developmental Disabilities Research Reviews, 4,* 65–72.

Tsao, L., & McCabe, H. (2010). Why won't he play with me? Facilitating sibling interactions. *Young Exceptional Children, 13,* 24–35.

Tsao, L., & Odom, S. L. (2006). Sibling mediated social interaction intervention for young children with autism. *Topics in Early Childhood Special Education, 26,* 106–123.

Unal, N., & Baran, G. (2011). Behaviors and attitudes of normally developing children toward their intellectually disabled siblings. *Psychological Reports, 108,* 553–562.

Critical Thinking

1. If you had a sibling with an autism spectrum disorder (ASD), what would be your greatest worries or concerns? How do you think having a child in your family with a special need such as an ASD would alter family relationships?

2. What are some challenges and difficulties experienced by a sibling when their brother or sister has an ASD?

3. What are individual and family factors that are important for developing healthy sibling and family relationships when a child in the family has an ASD?

4. How might a typically developing sibling be able to assist in the treatment or education of a child with an ASD?

5. Using information gained from this article, describe an intervention or support program that could be developed to facilitate the positive development of siblings when a child in the family has an ASD.

Create Central

www.mhhe.com/createcentral

Internet References

Sibling Support Project
www.siblingsupport.org

Sibs
www.sibs.org.uk

Tufts University Child and Family Webguide
www.cfw.tufts.edu

Article

Prepared by: Patricia Hrusa Williams,
University of Maine at Farmington

Building on Strengths: Intergenerational Practice with African American Families

Intergenerational kinship and multigenerational families (three or more generations) have been a source of strength for African Americans. This article presents a culturally responsive intergenerational practice model for working with African American families that draws on this legacy. The model looks at intergenerational kinship and multigenerational families through an Afrocentric, intergenerational solidarity framework. It provides a means to understand and support the strengths and resource richness of intergenerational relationships; the Afrocentric paradigm's affirmation of family and cultural strengths; and the power of intergenerational kinship, family solidarity, and support across generations. Building on the six solidarity elements of the intergenerational solidarity framework, this model provides an empowerment-oriented approach for social work practice with African American families that takes into consideration cultural values and practices.

CHERYL WAITES

Learning Outcomes

After reading this article, you will be able to:

- Identify the strengths that African American families have as a result of intergenerational practice.

- Describe the resources that African American families have through intergenerational relationships.

- Examine how intergenerational family relationships influence cultural values.

Family networks, composed of several generations (three or more), have been a source of strength for African American families. Multigenerations providing support and care for family members and fictive kin (non-blood relatives) across the life course have been well documented (Billingsley, 1992; Billingsley & Morrison-Rodriguez, 1998; Hill, 1971, 1993, 1998, 1999; Martin & Martin, 1985; McAdoo, 1998; Schiele, 1996, 2000). Born out of African traditions and adaptation to a harsh environment, multigenerational families have persevered in the face of disparity and oppression spanning 400 years of slavery, years of "Jim Crow," and decades of segregation, marginalization, and intentional and unintentional racism (Christian, 1995). Despite these obstacles, people of African descent have a legacy of intergenerational kinship, resilience, spirituality, and hope (Bagley & Carroll, 1998; Denby, 1996). Multigenerational families and intergenerational

kinships have played a significant role in preserving and strengthening African American families.

As our society ages, multigenerational families will be more common, resulting in longer years of "shared lives" across generations (Bengtson, 2001; Bengtson & Roberts, 1991). It has been predicted that there will be almost equal bands of older adults, middle generation adults, young adults, adolescents, and children as we move deeper into the 21st century (U.S. Census Bureau, 2004). This statistic holds true for African Americans. The numbers of African American elders, age 65 and older, are increasing. Between 1980 and 1995, the number of African Americans increased from 2.1 million to 2.7 million (a 29 percent increase). This group is expected to expand to 6.9 million by 2030 and 8.6 million by 2050 (Miles, 1999). Individuals are now more likely to grow older in four, or even more, generation families; spend an unprecedented number of years in family roles such as grandparent and great-grandparent; and remain part of a network of intergenerational family ties (Bengtson, 2001; Bengtson, Rosenthal, & Burton, 1990; Hagestad, 1996; Riley, 1987). Kin, and non-kin, will be available to provide care and assistance to younger families (King, 1994; Silverstein, Parrott, & Bengtson, 1995) and caregiving for dependent elders (Bengtson et al., 1990). In view of the changing demographics, it is important to revisit cultural values regarding how families interact across generations.

Historically, cultural values, family practices, and strengths, such as special care for children and elders, kinship ties, and collectivism have been part of African American life (Barnes,

2001). Hill (1971, 1999) wrote eloquently about five strengths of African American families: strong achievement orientation, strong work orientation, flexible family roles, strong kinship bonds, and strong religious orientation. Hill and others have pointed to strengths that are linked to history, culture, values, and cultural adaptations and suggested that building on these strengths is a good strategy for working with African American families (Freeman & Logan, 2004; Logan, 2001; McAdoo, 1998; McCullough-Chavis & Waites, 2004; Staples, 1999). Strong kinship ties, intergenerational support, faith, and coming together during times of need have been effective resources for African American families.

Today's social environment, and the challenges individuals and families face, warrant use and revitalization of cultural strengths. Problems such as drug and alcohol addiction, overrepresentation of African American children in foster care, HIV and AIDS, health disparities, high rates of incarceration, unemployment, and poverty are severe and complex. Many individuals and families have demonstrated remarkable resilience; others have suffered. Effective strategies to help families as they contend with pressing issues are rooted in African American cultural strengths. Cultural values and practices that sustained families in the past can be used to empower families today. Use of the power of intergenerational kinships and multigenerational family support can serve to preserve and strengthen vulnerable African American families.

Over the past 20 years, a number of practice approaches have been proposed for culturally competent practice with African Americans and other ethnic and racial groups. Strengths-based, empowerment-oriented, ethnically sensitive, constructionist, Afrocentric, and social justice frameworks have been used to guide practice with African American families. Such frameworks provide models by which social problems are assessed and intervention strategies are outlined. Many recognize multigenerational and extended family strengths. However, there is a need for an approach that builds on and restores the strengths of multigenerational families and intergenerational kinship. This approach may include restoring the influence of the extended family's multigenerational network so that relatives and fictive kin are encouraged to remain involved with family members and step forward to provide support and care. An Afrocentric, intergenerational solidarity approach that acknowledges the family life cycle, as well as the values and traditions that have sustained people of African descent, is a mechanism for promoting family closeness and responsibility. Embracing the legacies and wisdom of past generations and the hope and promise of the future is a framework for best practice. This article describes an intergenerational model that can be used to understand and provide support and assistance to African American families. The model defines families of African descent from an Afrocentric intergenerational perspective. It highlights the history and interconnectedness of African American families and communities and takes into account the temporal nature of the family life cycle.

An Intergenerational Perspective: Theoretical Foundations for Practice

An intergenerational perspective is relevant to social work practice with African American families. It brings an awareness of and attention to kinship, intergenerational relationships, and multigenerational families. Strengths, values, and practices that are transmitted across generations, family life cycle stages, intergenerational support, and current cultural context are central to this perspective (Waites, 2008). It provides a framework for understanding the past, exploring the current environment, and using culturally relevant strategies and practices to empower families.

Intergenerational Solidarity

Family relationships across generations are becoming increasingly important. Changes in family age structures are creating longer years of shared lives (Bengtson, 2001). Bengtson stated that "intergenerational bonds are more important than nuclear family ties for well-being and support over the life course" (Bengtson, 2001, p. 7). With increased longevity, parents, grandparents, and other relatives can be available to serve as resources for younger generations. Kin, across several generations, will increasingly be called on to provide essential family functions; intergenerational support and care will increase over time.

Bengtson and his colleagues (Bengtson & Roberts, 1991; Bengtson & Schrader, 1982) provided a multidimensional construct for understanding intergenerational relationships. Derived from classical social theory, social psychology, and family sociology, their intergenerational solidarity model examines social cohesion between generations. The construct evolved from a longitudinal study consisting of a cross-sectional survey with more than 2,044 participants from three generational families. Data were collected at three intervals, including the great-grandchild generation. From this research, Bengtson and others (Bengston & Mangen, 1988; Bengston & Schrader, 1982; Roberts, Richards, & Bengtson, 1991) constructed an intergenerational solidarity taxonomy for understanding intergenerational relationships. These six elements provide a mechanism for understanding intergenerational relationships and are discussed later in greater detail.

Afrocentric Worldview

An Afrocentric paradigm fits nicely with the intergenerational solidarity framework because it affirms human capacities and family and cultural strengths and promotes intergenerational connections. It presents a worldview that highlights traditional African philosophical assumptions, which emphasize a holistic, interdependent, and spiritual conception of people and their environment (Schiele, 2001).

The Afrocentric paradigm affirms that there are universal cultural strengths and an African worldview that survived the generational devastations caused by the transatlantic slave trade and the oppression that followed. As a result, it is important to understand and respect the customs, practices, and values that are central to African American families and communities. These cultural strengths, as previously described, can be used in micro, meso, and macro interventions to enhance the lives of all people, particularly people of color (Schiele, 2000).

Family Life Cycle

Families are at the heart of the intergenerational perspective. Families have shared history and futures (Carter & McGoldrick, 1999); they move through time together. The sharing of history and futures and the moving through time together are often referred to as family life cycle stages. Theses stages have been identified as leaving home, single young adults, joining of families through marriage, the new couple, families with young children, families with adolescents, launching children and moving on, and families in later life (Carter & McGoldrick, 1999). Relationships with parents, siblings, grandparents, and other family members experience transitions as each group moves along the family life cycle. Multiple family units are formed (for example, families with young children and families in later life), and all are a part of the larger multigenerational family. In this respect, there is a temporal reality associated with multigenerational families, and the family life cycle provides some descriptive information regarding how families move across time.

The stages described by Carter and McGoldrick (1999) laid a foundation for understanding African American families and family life cycle stages. African cultural traditions, environmental realities, and the diversity of family forms—which evolved from cultural traditions and adaptations to hardships—are also relevant. They provide insights regarding intergenerational relationships and temporal stages. A legacy of strong intergenerational kinship, multi-generational families, and extended family networks is reflected in Hill's (1999) flexible family roles. For example, caregiving is an important value for African American families. Grandparents may step in to assist or raise a grandchild. A single parent may depend on support from parents, or grandparents, after a child is born. African American children raised by grandparents often feel filial obligations to care for parents and grandparents (Ruiz & Carlton-LaNey, 1999). Extended family may play important roles and provide support and care to young and older adult relatives. Multigenerations may live in the same residence and pool their resources. For African American families, the family life cycle stages have significant intergenerational patterns of assistance and care that are reciprocal over time. These intergenerational supports, in some cases, may be in need of validation, nurturing, and revitalization to strengthen and support troubled families (Waites, 2008).

Afrocentric Intergenerational Practice

The Afrocentric intergenerational practice model presented here builds on the solidarity construct and the Afrocentric paradigm. It acknowledges the diversity and flexibility of the family life cycle and brings attention to traditions and cultural influences, specifically, caregiving, kinship bonds, the interconnectedness of families, and extended families. It reflects an approach that respects and supports the strengths and resilience of intergenerational kinship. This practice model's basic principles promote a society that values all generations and

- recognizes that each generation has unique strengths—each person, young and older, is a resource
- recognizes the roles of youths, middle generations, and elders in families and communities
- acknowledges conflicts that may occur in inter generational relationships
- encourages collaboration and support across generations
- fosters intergenerational kinship and interdependence
- fosters public policy that recognizes and addresses the needs of all generations
- supports and nurtures family and cultural strengths.

This model is culturally responsive in that it uses strategies that are compatible with culturally competent practice and transforms knowledge and cultural awareness into interventions that support and sustain healthy family functioning (McPhatter, 1997; Waites, Macgowan, Pennell, Carlton-LaNey, & Weil, 2004).

Afrocentric Intergenerational Solidarity Model

The Afrocentric intergenerational solidarity model consists of six solidarity elements and provides indicators of intergenerational cohesion. The infusion of an Afrocentric worldview provides culturally relevant issues, questions, and empowerment-oriented strategies. The first element, *associational solidarity*, focuses on the type and frequency of contact between generations (see Table 1). Examining the amount and nature of intergenerational contact is at the forefront. Within an Afrocentric worldview, assessing family traditions and history regarding communication is important. Once information is obtained, a process of nurturing, reinforcing, and revitalizing contact and communication among family members can be undertaken. Intergenerational communication may go beyond phone calls; traditions such as Sunday dinners, regular family visits, family reunions, special events, and other celebrations are mechanisms for connections. Intergenerational communication can lead to strong supportive networks and enhance the amount and quality of intergenerational contact.

The second element, *affectional solidarity*, addresses the expressed closeness, warmth, and trust found in intergenerational kinships. The indicators call for the practitioner to look at emotional ties to family and community, signs of intergenerational conflict, and the overall reciprocity of positive sentiment among family members and across generations. With an Afrocentric view, affiliations with and sentiments toward the extended family, and the African American community as a whole, must also be explored. The goal is to assess and address the issues of affection, trust, and closeness and to support and nurture relational understanding and reciprocity across generations.

Table 1 Intergenerational Solidarity with an Afrocentric Worldview

Construct-Element	Definition	Indicators	Culturally Relevant Issues
Associational solidarity	Frequency and patterns of interaction in various types of activities in which family members engage	• Frequency of intergenerational interaction (that is, face-to-face, telephone, mail) • Types of common activities shared (that is, recreation, special occasion, and so forth)	• Family history, traditions, and practices regarding family communication patterns, and family gatherings and activities • Intergenerational family members' access to one another (that is, transportation, telephone, computer literacy)
Affectional solidarity	Type and degree of positive sentiments about family members, and the degree of reciprocity of these sentiments	• Ratings of affection, warmth, closeness, understanding, trust, and respect for family members • Ratings of perceived reciprocity in positive sentiments among family members	• Preeminence of close parent–child relationship, grandparent relationships, extended family relationships, and so forth
Consensual solidarity	Degree of agreement on values, attitudes, and beliefs among family members	• Intrafamilial concordance among individual measures of specific values, attitudes, and beliefs • Ratings of perceived similarity with other family members in values, attitudes, and beliefs	• Connections with Afrocentric values and practices (that is, respect for elders, special care for children and elders, kinship ties, spirituality, collectivism, and so forth) • Generational values, similarities, and differences
Functional solidarity	Degree of helping and exchanges of resources—giving and receiving support across generations	• Frequency of intergenerational exchanges of assistance (for example, financial, physical, emotional) • Ratings of reciprocity in the intergenerational exchange of resources	• Supportive behaviors and traditions (that is, role of children, parents, grandparents, extended family, the church, lodges and fraternal orders, and so forth in providing support and care)
Normative solidarity	Strength of commitment to performance of familial roles and familial obligations	• Ratings of importance of family and intergenerational roles • Ratings of strength of filial obligations	• Afrocentric holistic, collectivist orientation • Filial beliefs and responsibilities (that is, intergenerational support for at-risk youths, young families, and dependent elders) • Availability of aunts, uncles, children, extended family, church family, and other supports
Structural solidarity	Opportunity structure for intergenerational relationships reflected in number, type, and geographic proximity of family members	• Residential propinquity of family members • Number of family members • Health of family members	• Location of family and extended family members • Migration history • Transportation and travel distances and resources

Source: Bengtson, V. L., & Roberts, R.E.L. (1991). Intergenerational solidarity in aging families: An example of formal theory construction. *Journal of Marriage and the Family, 53*, 856–870.

The third element, *consensual solidarity*, looks at agreements of values and beliefs. The indicators call for an assessment of intrafamilial concordance. Assessing the transmission and agreement of Afrocentric values, beliefs, and traditions, as well as the cultural strengths, enhances the cultural relevance of practice. Understanding family members' generational differences and their willingness to build intergenerational respect, dialogue, and collaboration is also important. The model suggests that practitioners encourage the understanding and recognition of cultural strengths. In addition, attempts should be made to support family and extended family as they engage in history reminding, consciousness raising, and intergenerational understanding and respect.

The fourth element, *functional solidarity*, addresses the frequency of intergenerational exchanges of assistance and resources. The indicators direct the assessment of help giving and receiving and how families assist and support each other. The role of collectivism, extended family support, and community support from churches, lodges, fraternal orders, and so forth are also assessed. Mechanisms to support equable intergenerational care and the use of formal and informal resources are suggested. This may include extended family, fictive kin, church family, intergenerational programs, or other community resources.

Normative solidarity, the fifth element, looks at filial responsibility and obligations. The indicators are family roles and the strength of obligation to those roles. The Afrocentric worldview expands this sense of obligation not only to parents, grandparents, children, and grandchildren, but also to the extended family, fictive kin, and the community as a whole. Intergenerational family and extended family support, and the use of community programs and formal resources, are encouraged.

The sixth and last element, *structural solidarity*, highlights the opportunity for intergenerational interaction as it relates to residential propinquity. For example, some older adults reside with their children or grandchildren in coresidential situations or in the same community. This arrangement affords them great intergenerational access. Some families, however, may move far away and relocate due to employment opportunities elsewhere. Older adults may be unable to travel to family or community events due to distant locations, health issues, or limited access to convenient and affordable transportation. Both latter situations affect opportunities to maintain close contact. The empirical indicators focus on the residential proximity of family members, the number of family members, and health and disability issues. Afrocentric worldviews expand this element so that migration patterns, transportation issues, and travel distances are included. The empowerment strategy focuses on helping families rethink how to address structural proximity barriers. This could take the form of family members organizing and sharing transportation resources or establishing a family "home place" or location where family members can gather for respite, celebrations, and support.

Using This Model

This model is not complicated and can be used in harmony with other empowerment-oriented approaches. A culturally appropriate assessment of intergenerational issues and resources is conducted. Practitioners are directed to explore each of the intergenerational solidarity elements with family members using the practice strategies outlined in Table 2.

Associational solidarity is explored by asking family members questions about their family traditions and how they communicate and keep in touch with each other. Family solidarity is enhanced when there are traditions, activities, and history that serve to keep family members connected—for example, Sunday dinners at a relative's home, regular phone calls, church or religious service attendance, family reunions, birthday celebrations, or Christmas or other holiday activities. The practitioner can work with family members to use a variety of practice strategies (outlined in Table 2) to help family members improve their associational solidarity. This might include encouraging family members to plan and or participate in family events. Participation in family events can lead to more cross-generational communication and contact.

Affectional solidarity questions are posed to family members by first exploring whom they feel particularly close to and why. Helping family members understand their traditions regarding family roles and relationships and how they influence affectional solidarity is an important practice strategy. Affectional solidarity can be nurtured by encouraging a sense of intergenerational kinship—that is, affection for family and extended family members. It encompasses cultivation of intergenerational relationships. The practitioner role is to aid family members in identifying and developing closer ties.

Consensual solidarity is also important and can be explored by discussing family values and by affirming a shared vision for family life. Exploring family members' perceptions and generation differences and similarities provides information regarding family solidarity. Gauging the family's sense of cultural pride and their African American identify is also pertinent. Cultural pride can serve as a unifying force for family solidarity. History reminding to facilitate appreciation of family cultural strengths is appropriate as a practice strategy and might include providing information about cultural history, supporting family opportunities to share thoughts and information about cultural values and beliefs, and engaging family members in activities that will enhance cultural pride. Communities often have Kwanzaa celebrations, concerts, and religious-related programs; watch movies and videos; read books; or engage in culturally inspired storytelling activities. These resources can serve as activities and information that connect the generations and facilitate consensual solidarity.

Functional solidarity is assessed by identification of the "go-to" family members when someone needs assistance. It is also important to identify family roles and resources and how support and care are exchanged across the family and the generations. The practice strategy is to create or restore the family helping network and involves helping family members to embrace shared responsibility and intergenerational support and care for all family members.

Normative solidarity is assessed by exploring expectations regarding family roles. It is also crucial to discuss what happens when someone is not able to perform the designated role.

Table 2   Afrocentric Intergenerational Solidarity Model—Questions and Practice Strategies

Associational Solidarity Questions	Practice Strategies
• Tell me about your family's traditions (holiday celebrations, Sunday dinners, family reunions, special events, and so forth). • How do you participate? • How does your family keep in touch? How do you keep in touch?	• Encourage cross-generation communication, and contact. • Help family consider methods to communicate and to support each other. • Encourage family members to participate in family events (family reunions, and so forth) and efforts to remain connected.
Affectional Solidarity Questions • Tell me about the family members you feel close to. • What makes you feel particularly close to this person? • Tell me about your extended family and others who are like family. Do you feel close to them? • Are their certain relationships or duties that you must honor and respect?	**Practice Strategics** • Nurture relationship building, intergenerational kinship, and equable care. • Encourage supportive family and extended family closeness.
Consensual Solidarity Questions • Tell me about your family's history—your grandparents, great grandparents, and so forth. • What were/are important values, beliefs, and traditions in your family? • Do you and family members have similar values and beliefs regarding ___(sex, religion, education, drugs, etc.)? • Do you feel a connection and pride with the African American community? What type of cultural activities do you and your family participate in?	**Practice Strategies** • Engage family in history reminding to facilitate an understanding of cultural and family strengths. • Facilitate healing by engaging family in activities that will enhance cultural pride and self-esteem. • Encourage intergenerational respect and help family members acknowledge their shared visions. • Help family recognize intergenerational resources and strengths.
Functional Solidarity Questions • How does your family respond when one of its members needs assistance? • Who are the family members with resources (good, steady job; a home; savings; and so forth) in your family? Are they obligated to help out others in the family? Is there an exchange of resources? • Do older family members feel obligated to help out younger family members, and is this help reciprocal?	**Practice Strategies** • Support flexible family roles and intergenerational kinship. • Encourage reciprocal intergenerational support and care. • Assist family in using informal (extended family, church or faith based, and so forth) and formal support systems and recourses.
Normative Solidarity Questions • What roles do parents, grandparents, children, adult daughters and sons, aunts, uncles, and so forth play in your family? • In your family, what happens when someone is not able to function in his or her role as parent, son, daughter, caregiver, and so forth?	**Practice Strategies** • Encourage and support caregiving and other family commitments. • Develop multigenerational family support programs for grandparents, and other kin, raising children and for children caring for dependent elders. • Encourage the development of an extended family support systems.
Structural Solidarity Questions • Where do your family members live? • What led them to move to _____? Do you visit? • How do family members travel when they visit one another? Are there any barriers to visiting? • Does your family have a "home place," a residence where family members gather for special occasions?	**Practice Strategies** • Help family overcome travel and visiting-related barriers. • Help family members identity a plan for staying connected. • Develop community intergenerational programs.

What are the family norms for who should step in? The practice strategy is to affirm, strengthen, and formalize the family members' commitment to one another. This may take the form of encouraging the development of multigenerational networks where children, parents, grandparents, aunts, and uncles all play a role in supporting and caring for family members. Because this responsibility can be demanding, connecting families with community resources such as family support programs, support groups for caregivers, and other programs that serve to strengthen families and extended family helping is crucial.

Structural solidarity is explored by assessing family proximity. Some families use the home of a family member to gather for celebrations or other rituals: It is their home place. Other families do not have a central location, and some family members may live great distances from the family core of the home place. The role of the practitioner is to help family members explore proximity issues and overcome barriers to traveling and visiting with relatives. This help might include pooling of resources so that all family members can attend the family reunions, church or religious services, and health and wellness care. Providing assistance to families in the use of strategies to support involvement in family and extended family activities could help family members to visit and stay connected.

Use of this model involves the exploration of all solidarity elements. Family members and families may show strengths in a specific area. If not, the practitioner can then use one or all of the strategies suggested in the Practice Strategy sections of Table 2. To follow are three vignettes that present contemporary family issues and suggested strategies.

Vignette One

Denise is a 32-year-old African American single, divorced mother who is trying to cope with caregiving for both her son and her grandmother. Denise's nine-year-old son, David, has been referred to the school social worker due to excessive absences from school. Her 69-year-old grandmother had a stroke, six months ago, and is now residing with Denise and her son David and her 14-year-old daughter. Denise is distraught because her maternal grandmother was "the strong one in the family." All solidarity elements must be assessed. However, there is a pressing need for support and assistance for Denise and her family. This calls for focusing first on normative and functional solidarity. The worker can help Denise examine her current caregiving roles. It is also important for the worker to discuss Denises decision to care for her grandmother—What is her sense of obligation and commitment to this role? Once Denise has explored her caregiving values, beliefs, the realities of her situation, and her intentions, she and the practitioner can develop a plan. This might include exploring family resources, the availability of other family and extended family members for support and caregiving, and more formal resources.

Vignette Two

Mr. Brown is an 84-year-old African American, retired Navy civilian dock worker. His wife of 47 years died 14 years ago after a battling cancer for four years. His only son died in an accident 22 years ago. Mr. Brown has two granddaughters, ages 30 and 32, and one great-grandson, age 9. They talk on the phone occasionally, but his granddaughters and great-grandson live 2,000 miles away, and he has not been able to visit them. Mr. Brown reports that he is "lonely" and is considering moving into an assisted-living facility. He wants to reconnect with his family before he moves. All the solidarity elements must be assessed. Immediate issues appear to be Mr. Brown's expressed loneliness and his infrequent contact with his granddaughters and great-grandson. This calls for focusing on associational, affectional, and structural solidarity. The worker can help Mr. Brown make contact with his granddaughters and with other family members, especially those family members who have been supportive in the past. Mechanisms to maintain communication should also be explored. This may consist of organizing regular visiting, where transportation is arranged for Mr. Brown. It could also mean arranging regular phone contact, sharing pictures, and sending cards. Mr. Brown may also benefit from more contact with other family, extended family, and friends from church or any groups that he has participated in over his life course (for example, lodges, fraternal orders, church clubs, civic groups). Also, intergenerational programs, if available, may also be a good resource.

Vignette Three

Joan, a 41-year-old African American woman, is incarcerated because of a drug-related charge. She is in the second year of a three-year sentence and is now drug free. She has three sons, ages 19, 12, and 10. The two youngest sons reside with their paternal grandmother. Joan's oldest son has lived with her mother most of his life. Joan has not seen her sons in two years. The younger children's father died in a car accident; he was driving while impaired. Joan is very concerned about her sons and wants to provide a better life for them. She hopes to arrange visitation, and, so far, her younger son's grandmother has been uncooperative. Her 19-year-old son has refused to visit. Although all solidarity elements should be assessed first, this situation points to affectional and consensual solidarity problems. Joan must be aware that her addiction and past behaviors may have caused apprehension and skepticism on the part of her family. As the practitioner helps Joan to make contact with her children, it will be important for him or her to engage the family in forgiveness, relationship building, and reaffirming of a shared vision across generations for the health and well-being of the children and family. The kinship bonds are in need of revitalization.

Conclusion

In view of contemporary issues facing families and the significance of multigenerational families, culturally relevant models of practice are called for. African American multigenerational families have a legacy of resilience, spirituality, and hope that has served to fortify vulnerable members. As our society ages, the number of multigenerational families will increase, and intergenerational cohesion issues will move to the forefront. This demographic shift, and the opportunity for shared lives, can be an asset for families. An empowerment-oriented framework that provides a mechanism to build on cultural strengths, intergenerational kinship, and support processes by which generations can provide mutual assistance and care during times of need is indicated. This model is a good step in that direction. Many aspects of this model have been a part of culturally responsive work with African American families.

The Afrocentric intergenerational sodality model is a strengths-based approach that works to empower multigenerational families and intergenerational relationships. In this regard, there is an assumption that families and extended families have strengths and that some form of intergenerational kinship can be nurtured. A shortcoming of this model is that the full application of each solidarity component has not been systematically tested. I plan to apply this model to practice interventions and intergenerational programming.

The Afrocentric intergenerational practice model shows promise. Building on Bengtson and others' intergenerational solidarity construct, infused with an Afrocentric worldview, this model provides a culturally relevant approach for work with African American multigenerational families. It facilitates an understanding of how intergenerational relationships can be supported and provides multidimensional guidance regarding intergenerational relationships and multigenerational families. The intergenerational model considers generational transmission from a strengths perspective, looking not only at problems, but also at the assets that multiple generations may provide. It is a framework that taps into the power, resilience, and capital from past and current traditions and relationships. The three vignettes provide examples of how this model might be used. To fully examine this model, additional applications should be studied.

Application of the Afrocentric intergenerational practice model, in conjunction with other empowerment-oriented approaches, is a best practice method. Social workers are called on to work with African American and other families. This work is especially relevant for work with vulnerable African American families in need of nurturance and care. As our society ages, it will be increasingly important to understand intergenerational issues and develop resources that help multigenerational families navigate the complex and changing relationships and problems in our contemporary society. As we move through this century, this model may prove to be very relevant to the changing demographics of our aging society.

References

Bagley, C. A., & Carroll, J. (1998). Healing forces in African-American families. In H. I. McCubbin, E. A. Thompson, A. I. Thompson, & J. A. Farrell (Eds.), *Resiliency in African-American families* (pp. 117–143). London: Sage Publications.

Barnes, S. (2001). Stressors and strengths: A theoretical and practical examination of nuclear single parent, and augmented African American families. *Families in Society, 85,* 449–460.

Bengtson, V. L., (2001). Beyond the nuclear family: The increasing importance of multi-generational bonds. *Journal of Marriage and the Family, 63,* 1–16.

Bengtson, V. L., & Mangen, D. J. (1988). Family intergenerational solidarity, revisited. In D. J. Mangen, V. L. Bengtson, &

P. H. Landry (Eds.), *Measurement of intergenerational relations* (pp. 222–238). Newbury Park, CA: Sage Publications.

Bengtson, V. L., & Roberts, R. E. L. (1991). Intergenerational solidarity in aging families: An example of formal theory construction. *Journal of Marriage and the Family, 53,* 856–870.

Bengtson, V. L., Rosenthal, C. J., & Burton, L. M. (1990). Paradoxes of families and aging. In R. H. Binstock & L. K. George (Eds.), *Handbook of aging and the social sciences* (4th ed., pp. 253–282). San Diego: Academic Press.

Bengtson, V. L., & Schrader, S. S. (1982). Parent–child relationships. In D. Mangen & W. Peterson (Eds.), *Handbook of research instruments in social gerontology* (Vol. 2, pp. 115–185). Minneapolis: University of Minnesota Press.

Billingsley, A. (1992). *Climbing Jacob's ladder: The enduring legacy of African-American families.* New York: Simon & Schuster.

Billingsley, A., & Morrison-Rodriguez, B. (1998). The black family in the 21st century and the church as an action system: A macro perspective. *Journal of Human Behavior in the Social Environment,* (2-3), 31–47.

Carter, B., & McGoldrick, M. (1999). *The expanded family life* (3rd ed.). Boston: Allyn & Bacon.

Christian, C. M. (1995). *Black saga: The African American experience.* Boston: Houghton Mifflin.

Denby, R. W. (1996). Resiliency and the African American family: Model of family preservation. In S. L. Logan (Ed.), *The black family: Strengths, self-help, and positive change* (pp. 144–163). Boulder, CO: Westview Press.

Freeman, E. M., & Logan, S. L. (Eds.). (2004). *Reconceptualizing the strengths and common heritage of black families: Practice, research and policy issues.* Springfield, IL: Charles C. Thomas.

Hagestad, G. O. (1996). On-time, off-time, out of time? Reflections on continuity and discontinuity from an illness process. In V. L. Bengtson (Ed.), *Adulthood and aging: Research on continuities and discontinuities* (pp. 204–222). New York: Springer.

Hill, R. (1971). *The strength of black families.* New York: Emerson-Hall.

Hill, R. B. (1993). *Research on the African-American family: A holistic perspective.* London: Auburn House.

Hill, R. B. (1998). Understanding black family functioning: A holistic perspective. *Journal of Comparative Family Studies, 29,* 1–11.

Hill, R. B. (1999). *The strengths of African American families: Twenty-five years later.* New York: University Press of America.

King, V. (1994). Variation in the consequences of nonresident father involvement for children's well-being. *Journal of Marriage and the Family, 56,* 963–972.

Logan, S. L. (Ed.). (2001). *The black family: Strengths, self-help, and positive change* (2nd ed.). Boulder, CO: Westview Press.

Martin, J., & Martin, E. (1985). *The helping tradition in the black family and community.* Washington, DC: NASW Press.

McAdoo, H. P. (1998). African-American families: Strengths and realities. In H. I. McCubbin, E. A. Thompson, A. I. Thompson, & J. A. Futrell (Eds.), *Resiliency in African-American families* (pp. 17–30). London: Sage Publications.

McCullough-Chavis, A., & Waites, C. (2004). Genograms with African American families: Considering cultural context. *Journal of Family Social Work, 8(2),* 1–19.

McPhatter, A. R. (1997). Cultural competence in child welfare: What is it? How do we achieve it? What happens without it? *Child Welfare, 76,* 255–278.

Miles, T. P. (1999). Living with chronic disease and the policies that bind. In T. P. Miles (Ed.), *Full-color aging: Facts, goals, and recommendations for America's diverse elders* (pp. 53–63). Washington, DC: Gerontological Society of America.

Riley, M. W. (1987). On the significance of age in sociology. *American Sociological Review, 52,* 1–14.

Roberts, R. E. L., Richards, L. N., & Bengtson, V. L. (1991). Intergenerational solidarity in families: Untangling the ties that bind. *Marriage & Family Review, 16,* 11–46.

Ruiz, D., & Carlton-LaNey, I. (1999). The increase in intergenerational African American families headed by grandmothers. *Journal of Sociology & Social Welfare, 26(4),* 71–86.

Schiele, J. H. (1996). Afrocentricity: An emerging paradigm in social work practice. *Social Work, 41,* 284–294.

Schiele, J. H. (2000). *Human services and the Afrocentric paradigm.* Binghamton, NY: Haworth Press.

Silverstein, M., Parrott, T. M., & Bengtson V. L. (1995). Factors that predispose middle-aged sons and daughters to provide social support to older parents. *Journal of Marriage and the Family, 57,* 465–476.

Staples, R. (1999). *The black family: Essays and studies.* Belmont, CA: Wadsworth.

U.S. Census Bureau. (2004). *People and households.* Retrieved February 20, 2008, from www.census.gov/population/www/projections/usmterimproj/natprojtab02a.pdf.

Waites, C. (2008). *Social work practice with African-American families: An intergenerational perspective.* New York: Routledge.

Waites, C., Macgowan, M. J., Pennell, J., Carlton-LaNey, I., & Weil, M. (2004). Increasing the cultural responsiveness of family group conferencing. *Social Work, 49,* 291–300.

Critical Thinking

1. Building on the six solidarity elements of the intergenerational solidarity framework, how might this framework apply to other types of families?

2. Why is it important to take kinship into consideration when working with families?

3. If you were working in the social service field, how would you uncover individual culture within families?

4. Describe what an empowerment-oriented approach is and why it is useful in social work practice.

5. How does this article explain the importance of intergenerational relationships?

Create Central

www.mhhe.com/createcentral

Internet References

National Council on Family Relations
www.ncfr.com

Child Welfare Information Gateway, Working with African American Families
www.childwelfare.gov/systemwide/cultural/families/african.cfm

CHERYL WAITES, EDD, MSW, is associate dean, School of Social Work, Wayne State University, 4756 Cass Avenue, Detroit, MI 48202; e-mail: ccwaites@wayne.edu.

From *Social Work,* vol. 54, no. 3, July 2009, pp. 278–287. Copyright © 2009 by NASW Press. Reprinted by permission.

Article
Prepared by: Patricia Hrusa Williams,
University of Maine at Farmington

The Accordion Family

KATHERINE S. NEWMAN

Learning Outcomes

After reading this article, you will be able to:

- Identify factors leading adult children to live with their parents.

- Understand challenges for parents and their adult children living together.

Maria Termina and her husband, Alberto, live in the northwestern city of Bra in the Piedmont region of Italy. The people of Bra are traditionalists who struggle to hold the modern world at arm's length. Proud to be the hometown of Carlo Petrini, the founder of the Slow Food Movement, Bra hosts a biennial festival that celebrates artisanal cheeses from around the world.

Alberto, now 67, has lived in Bra almost all his life and worked for the same firm as an engineer for about 40 of those years. Maria is 57. They have three grown children, the youngest of whom, 30-year-old Giovanni, has always lived with his parents and shows no signs of moving out. (All the names in this piece, which is based on interviews, are fictitious to protect privacy.)

Giovanni graduated from the local high school but went no further than that and is content with his steady blue-collar job as an electrician. He works on construction sites and picks up odd jobs on the side. It's a living, barely. His wages are modest, the building trades go up and down, and—in all honesty— his tastes in motorcycles are a bit extravagant. Though he is a skilled worker, Giovanni knows he could not enjoy himself with his friends as he does if he had to support himself entirely on his own earnings. But because he pays no rent and can eat well at his mother's table, his living expenses are low, leaving money for recreation.

Of the three children born to Maria and Alberto, only Giorgio—Giovanni's twin brother—lives on his own. (Laura, divorced, and her 5-year-old daughter recently returned to the nest.) Giorgio completed a degree in economics at a local university and moved to Turin, where he works in marketing and statistics. He is the odd man out, not only in his family but also among many of his family's neighbors. More than a third of Italian men Giovanni's age have never left home; the pattern of "delayed departure" has become the norm in Italy. And while it was common in the past for unmarried men and women to remain with their parents until they wed, the age of marriage has been climbing in the last 30 years, so much so that by the time men like Giovanni cut the apron strings, they are very nearly what we once called "middle-aged." That has made the country an international butt of jokes about the "cult of mammismo," or mama's boys.

It is no laughing matter in Italy, particularly in government circles where the economic consequences are adding up. The former prime minister Silvio Berlusconi came out in support of a campaign against mammismo, having been elected on the promise of doing away with "those hidebound aspects of Italian life which 'inhibit dynamism and growth.'" In January 2010, Renato Brunetta, then a cabinet minister, proposed making it illegal for anyone over 18 to live with his or her parents. He made the suggestion on a radio show where he also admitted that his mother made his bed until he was 30, when he left home.

Why should government officials—including those whose own family lives are hardly worthy of admiration—care one way or the other where adult children make their home? The fact is that those private choices have serious public consequences. The longer aging bambini live with their parents, the fewer new families are formed, and the evaporation of a whole generation of Italian children is knocking the social policies of the country for a loop. Plummeting fertility translates into fewer workers to add fuel to the retirement accounts in an aging society. The private calculations of families like the Terminas, who wonder how long they can support Giovanni, are becoming the public problem of prime ministers.

Does his "delayed departure" worry 30-year-old Giovanni? Not really. Expectations are changing, and there is little pressure on him to be more independent. His family isn't urging him to marry, and he leans back in his chair and opines that "nobody asks you the reason [why you stay] at home with the parents at [my] age . . . nobody obliges me to move away."

Newton, Mass., is famous for its leafy streets, New England-style colonial houses, and well-educated parents who are professionals. The nearby universities—Harvard, MIT, Tufts—and numerous liberal-arts colleges, not to mention the concentration of health-care and computer-related industries, insures a steady influx of middle- and upper-middle-class families. Immigrants—especially high-tech professionals from Israel, India, and Russia—flock to this affluent community in pursuit of opportunity.

Newton boasts first-class schools from top to bottom; graduates of its high schools turn up regularly in the Ivy League. Poor black kids are bused in from inner-city Boston through the Metco integration program to partake of the town's exemplary educational facilities, but few poor families actually live within its boundaries. All but the fairly well heeled are priced out.

William Rollo and his wife arrived in Newton in 1989 after having lived in Seattle, Philadelphia, and Summit, N.J. A Brooklyn native, William married Janet at the age of 22 and set about completing a residency in podiatry. Their elder son, John, grew up in Newton and did well enough in high school to attend Williams College, one of the nation's most selective. Even so, he beat it home after graduating and has lived with his parents for several years while preparing to apply to graduate school. "A lot of my friends are living at home to save money," he explains.

Tight finances are not all that is driving John's living arrangements. The young man had choices and decided he could opt for more of the ones he wanted if he sheltered under his parents' roof. John is saving money from his job at an arts foundation for a three-week trip to Africa, where he hopes to work on a mobile health-care project in a rural region. It's a strategic choice designed to increase his chances of being accepted into Harvard University's competitive graduate program in public health.

John needs to build up his credentials if he wants to enter a program like that. To get from here to there, he needs more experience working with patients in clinics or out in the field. It takes big bucks to travel to exotic locations, and a master's degree will cost him dearly, too. In order to make good on his aspirations, John needs his parents to cover him for the short run.

On his own, John could pay the rent on an apartment, especially if he had roommates. What he can't afford is to pay for it and travel, to support himself and save for his hoped-for future. Autonomy turns out to be the lesser priority, so he has returned to the bedroom he had before he left for college, and there he stays.

John sees few drawbacks to that arrangement. His parents don't nag him or curtail his freedom. Janet wonders if they should ask him to pay rent, to bring him down to earth a bit and teach him some life skills, like budgeting. William is not so sure. He enjoys his son's company and was happy when John moved back into his old bedroom. Having a son around to talk to is a joy, particularly since John's younger brother is out of the house now, studying at the University of Vermont. That empty nest has refilled, and thank goodness, says William, rather quietly.

If John had no goals, no sense of direction, William would not be at ease with this "boomerang arrangement." Hiding in the basement playing video games would not do. Happily, that is not on John's agenda. William is glad to help his son realize his ambitions. He approves of John's career plans and doesn't really care if they don't involve making a handsome living. What really matters is that the work means something. It will help to remake the world, something William has not felt he

could contribute to very directly as a podiatrist. Having a son who can reach a bit higher—if not financially, then morally—is an ambition worth paying for.

And it will cost this family, big time. William and Janet have invested nearly $200,000 in John's education already. They will need to do more if John is going to become a public-health specialist. They are easily looking at another $50,000, even if John attends a local graduate program and continues to live with them. Whatever it costs, they reason, the sacrifice is worth it.

What is newsworthy, throughout the developed world, is that a growing number of young adults in their 20s and 30s have never been independent. In the United States, we tend to see a boomerang pattern in the affluent upper-middle class, with young people leaving for college and then returning home. Among working-class kids, the tendency is to stay put for the duration. Only one-quarter of today's college students are full time, living on campus, and largely supported by their parents. The norm is to live at home, study part time, work to pay your share, and shelter some of the steepest costs of higher education under the parental roof.

And in most countries—outside of the social democracies—there is far less investment in dormitories and other forms of transitional housing, meager government financial aid, and a historical pattern of pursuing university degrees wherever you grew up. With the labor market turning a cold shoulder to new graduates, simply staying at home seems the only option. Hence in Italy today, 37 percent of men age 30 have never lived away from home. Their counterparts in Spain, Japan, and many other developed countries are following a similar path: Millions are staying at the Inn of Mom and Dad for years, sometimes for several decades longer than was true in earlier generations.

In the United States, we have seen a 50-percent increase since the 1970s in the proportion of people age 30 to 34 who live with their parents. As the recession of 2008–9 continued to deepen, this trend became even more entrenched. Kids who cannot find jobs after finishing college, divorced mothers who can't afford to provide a home for their children, unemployed people at their wits' end, the ranks of the foreclosed—all are beating a path back to their parents' homes to take shelter underneath the only reliable roof available.

To some degree, that has always been the way of the private safety net. Families double up when misfortune derails their members, and the generations that have been lucky enough to buy into an affordable housing market, that enjoyed stable jobs for decades, find they must open their arms (and houses) to receive these economic refugees back into the fold. Blue-collar working-class families and the poor have never known anything different: Their kids have no choice but to stay home while they try to outrun a labor market that has become increasingly inhospitable.

Their parents have had it hard as well, as layoffs have spread through the factories of the Midwest and the South; pooling income across the generations is often the only sensible survival strategy, even if the climate becomes testy.

Until relatively recently, the middle class in most prosperous countries did not need to act as an economic shock absorber for such a prolonged period in the lives of their adult children. Their households might have expanded to take in a divorced offspring or support a child who had taken a nonpaying internship, but the norm for most white-collar parents was to send young people out into the world and look on in satisfaction as they took their places in the corporate world or the professions, found their life mates, and established their own nests.

Why, in the world's most affluent societies, are young (and not-so-young) adults unable to stand on their own two feet? Is it because we have raised a "slacker generation" that is unable or unwilling to take the hard knocks that come with striking out on their own? There are questions of taste lurking here: Young people in the middle class want jobs that are meaningful, rather than a means of putting a roof over their heads. They are not as eager as the "60s generation" of yore was to sleep on floors and wear clothes with holes in exchange for their independence.

And it is not especially painful for many of them to stay at home, because they share a lot of interests with Mom and Dad. Parents and their adult children are not staring at one another over the chasm of a "generation gap," but likely share similar tastes in music, movies, and, in many households, politics. That infamous gap was a product of the disjunctures that separated the generation that came of age in World War II from their boomer children, and it loomed large. But it has not emerged in succeeding generations: The Rolling Stones and Bob Dylan perform to sell-out crowds with gray hairs and twenty-somethings in the audience.

Still, we should not overemphasize the role of taste in spurring the trend toward accordion families. There is an unmistakable structural engine at work. International competition is greater than it once was, and many countries, fearful of losing markets for their goods and services, are responding by restructuring the labor market to cut the wage bill. Countries that regulated jobs to ensure they were full time, well paid, and protected from layoffs now permit part-time, poorly paid jobs and let employers fire without restriction. That may serve the interests of businesses—a debatable low-road strategy—but it has destroyed the options for millions of new entrants to the labor market throughout advanced postindustrial societies.

Japanese workers who once looked forward to lifetime employment with a single firm have gone the way of the dinosaur. American workers have seen the emergence of contingent labor (part-time, part-year, and short-term contracts), downsizing, offshoring, and many other responses to globalization that have exposed the American work force to wage stagnation and insecurity. European labor is arguably facing a very rocky future as the global consequences of the current financial crisis weaken the economies of the European Union and threaten the social protections that made them the envy of the developed world.

Eventually, those conditions will envelop the entire work force. For the time being, though, they are most evident in the lives of the least powerful: new entrants to the labor market, immigrants, and low-skilled workers. The generation emerging from college in the first decade of this century has been struggling to find a foothold in a rapidly changing economy

that cannot absorb its members as it once did, while housing prices—foreclosure epidemics notwithstanding—are making it hard for them to stake a claim to residential independence.

They fall back into the family home because, unless they are willing to take a significant cut in their standard of living, they have no other way to manage the life to which they have become accustomed. Moreover, if they aspire to a professional occupation and the income that goes with it, a goal their parents share for them, it is going to take them a long time and a lot of money to acquire the educational credentials needed to grab that brass ring. Sheltering inside an accordion family leaves more money to pay toward those degrees.

So what's the big deal? In earlier eras, people lived at home until they married. Is there anything new here? Yes and no. For several decades now, middle-class people in the United States, at least, expected to see their children live independently for a number of years before they married, and parents expected to have empty nests once their kids passed the magical mark of 18.

That formation was so widespread that it became a national norm, and it was made possible by a rental housing market and patterns of cohabitation (romantic, roommates) that made independence affordable. And for many, it still is. Yet increasingly the forces of labor-market erosion and rising housing and educational costs have combined to put independence out of reach.

Societal norms—the expectations that people bring to the table when social change is in the air—matter for how parents around the world view these new family formations. In Japan, where I found that parents expect discipline and order, this new trajectory is disturbing and tends to be defined as personal failure. Italian families, by contrast, report that they enjoy having their grown children live with them, however vexing it may be for their government.

Spanish parents and their adult children are angry at their government for facilitating lousy labor contracts that have damaged the children's prospects, but they know that it can be a joy to be near the younger generation.

In America, we deploy a familiar cultural arsenal in crafting meaning: the work ethic and the hope of upward mobility. If Joe lives at home because it will help him get somewhere in the long run, that's fine. If he's hiding in the basement playing video games, it's not fine. The accordion family has to be in the service of larger goals or it smacks of deviance.

All of these adaptations are responses to central structural forces beyond the control of any of us. Global competition is taking us into uncharted waters, reshaping the life course in ways that would have been scarcely visible only 30 years ago. It's a brave new world, and the accordion family is absorbing the blows as best it can.

Critical Thinking

1. What does the author mean by the terms "delayed departure," "boomerang arrangement," and "accordion family?"

2. Do you live with your parents now or anticipate moving back home after college? If so, why? What kinds of

problems or challenges come with living with your parents as an adult?

3. List some historical, economic, cultural, and social factors contributing to "accordion families."

4. What are some ground rules that adult children and their parents should set around their living arrangement?

Create Central

www.mhhe.com/createcentral

Internet References

AARP Blog: Boomerang Kids
  http://blog.aarp.org/tag/boomerang-kids

National Council on Family Relations
  www.ncfr.com

Article

Prepared by: Patricia Hrusa Williams,
University of Maine at Farmington

Daddy Issues
Why Caring For My Aging Father Has Me Wishing He Would Die

SANDRA TSING LOH

Learning Outcomes

After reading this article, you will be able to:

- Identify the financial and emotional burdens adult children face in caring for their aging parents.

- Describe how role reversal in parent–child relationships alters family dynamics.

- Identify supports needed by adult children caring for their aging parents.

Recently, a colleague at my radio station asked me, in the most cursory way, as we were waiting for the coffee to finish brewing, how I was. To my surprise, in a motion as automatic as the reflex of a mussel being poked, my body bent double and I heard myself screaming:

"I WAAAAAAAANT MY FATHERRRRRR TO DIEEEEE!!!"

Startled, and subtly stepping back to put a bit more distance between us, my coworker asked what I meant.

"What I mean, Rob, is that even if, while howling like a banshee, I tore my 91-year-old father limb from limb with my own hands in the town square, I believe no jury of my peers would convict me. Indeed, if they knew all the facts, I believe any group of sensible, sane individuals would actually roll up their shirtsleeves and pitch in."

As I hyperventilated over the coffee-maker, scattering Splenda packets and trying to unclaw my curled fingers, I realized it had finally happened: at 49, I had become a Kafka character. I am thinking of "The Judgment," in which the protagonist's supposedly old and frail father suddenly kicks off his bedclothes with surprisingly energetic—even girlish—legs and, standing ghoulishly tall in the bed, delivers a speech so horrifying, so unexpected, and so perfectly calculated to destroy his son's spirit that his son—who until this point has been having a rather pleasant day writing a letter to a friend, amidst a not unpleasant year marked by continuing financial prosperity and a propitious engagement to a well-placed young woman—immediately *jumps off a bridge.*

Clearly, my nonagenarian father and I have what have come to be known as "issues," which I will enumerate shortly. By way of introduction, however, let us begin by considering *A Bittersweet Season,* by Jane Gross. A journalist for 29 years at *The New York Times* and the founder of a *Times* blog called The New Old Age, Gross is hardly Kafkaesque. An ultra-responsible daughter given to drawing up to-do lists for caregivers and pre-loosening caps on Snapple bottles, Gross undertook the care of her mother in as professional a way as possible. She was on call for emergencies and planned three steps ahead by consulting personally with each medical specialist. Like the typical U.S. family caregiver for an elder (who is, statistics suggest, a woman of about 50), Gross worked full-time, but (atypically) she was unencumbered by spouse or children. She had the help, too, of her child-free brother, a calm, clear-headed sort given to greeting his sister with a quiet, reassuring "The eagle has landed." What could go wrong?

Plenty. As Gross herself flatly describes it, in her introduction:

> In the space of three years ... my mother's ferocious independence gave way to utter reliance on her two adult children. Garden-variety aches and pains became major health problems; halfhearted attention no longer sufficed, and managing her needs from afar became impossible. ... We were flattened by the enormous demands on our time, energy, and bank accounts; the disruption to our professional and personal lives; the fear that our time in this parallel universe would never end and the guilt for wishing that it would. ... We knew nothing about Medicaid spend-downs, in-hospital versus out-of-hospital "do not resuscitate" orders, Hoyer lifts, motorized wheelchairs, or assistive devices for people who can neither speak nor type. We knew nothing about "pre-need consultants," who handle advance payment for the funerals of people who aren't dead yet, or "feeders," whose job it is to spoon pureed food into the mouths of men and women who can no longer hold a utensil.

However ghoulish, it is a world we will all soon get to know well, argues Gross: owing to medical advancements, cancer deaths now peak at age 65 and kill off just 20 percent of older Americans, while deaths due to organ failure peak at about 75 and kill off just another 25 percent, so the norm for seniors is becoming a long, drawn-out death after 85, requiring ever-increasing assistance for such simple daily activities as eating, bathing, and moving.

This is currently the case for approximately 40 percent of Americans older than 85, the country's fastest-growing demographic, which is projected to more than double by 2035, from about 5 million to 11.5 million. And at that point, here comes the next wave—77 million of the youngest Baby Boomers will be turning 70.

Quick back-of-the-envelope calculation, for Baby Boomers currently shepherding the Greatest Generation to their final reward? Hope your aged parents have at least half a million dollars apiece in the bank, because if they are anything like Mama Gross, their care until death will absorb every penny. To which an anxious (let's say 49-year-old) daughter might respond: But what about long-term-care insurance? In fact, Gross's own mother had purchased it, and while it paid for some things, the sum was a pittance compared with a final family outlay of several hundred thousand dollars. But how about what everyone says about "spending down" in order to qualify for Medicare, Medicaid, Medi-Cal, or, ah—which exactly is it?

Unfortunately, those hoping for a kind of *Eldercare for Dummies* will get no easy answers from *A Bittersweet Season*. Chides Gross: "Medicaid is a confusing and potentially boring subject, depending on how you feel about numbers and abstruse government policy, but it's essential for you to understand." Duly noted—so I read the relevant section several times and . . . I still don't understand. All I can tell you is that the Medicaid mess has to do with some leftover historical quirks of the Johnson administration, colliding with today's much longer life expectancies, colliding with a host of federal and state regulations that intertwine with each other in such a calcified snarl that by contrast—in a notion I never thought I'd utter—public education looks hopeful. Think of the Hoyer lift that can be delivered but never repaired, or the feeder who will not push, or the pusher who will not feed.

But it gets worse. Like an unnaturally iridescent convalescent-home maraschino cherry atop this Sisyphean slag heap of woe, what actually appears to take the greatest toll on caregivers is the sheer emotional burden of this (formless, thankless, seemingly endless) project. For one thing, unresolved family dynamics will probably begin to play out: "Every study I have seen on the subject of adult children as caregivers finds the greatest source of stress, by far, to be not the ailing parent but sibling disagreements," Gross writes. Further, experts concur, "the daughter track is, by a wide margin, harder than the mommy track, emotionally and practically, because it has no happy ending and such an erratic and unpredictable course." Gross notes, I think quite rightly, that however put-upon working parents feel (and we do keeningly complain, don't we—oh the baby-proofing! oh the breast-pumping! oh the day care!), we can at least plan employment breaks around such relative foreseeables as pregnancy, the school year, and holidays. By contrast, ailing seniors trigger crises at random—falls in the bathroom, trips to the emergency room, episodes of wandering and forgetting and getting lost. Wearied at times by the loneliness of the daughter track, Gross writes, in a rare moment of black humor:

> I know that at the end of my mother's life I felt isolated in my plight, especially compared to colleagues being feted with showers and welcomed back to work with oohs and aahs at new baby pictures. I was tempted, out of pure small-mindedness, to put on my desk a photo of my mother, slumped in her wheelchair.

Those seeking a more hopeful take on this bittersweet season might turn, for momentary comparison, to *Passages in Caregiving,* by Gail Sheehy. Reading Sheehy is always a boost—even when she's rewriting some Passage she predicted 10 or 20 or 30 years ago, as is necessarily (and, given our ever-increasing life spans, probably will continue to be necessarily) the case. From her intro (as swingingly nostalgic—isn't it, almost?—as Burt Bacharach):

> In my books and speeches since 1995, when I published *New Passages* [the first update of the original *Passages*], I keep predicting liberation ahead—the advent of a Second Adulthood, starting in one's midforties and fifties. At that proud age, having checked off most "shoulds," people generally feel a new sense of mastery. Haven't you done your best to please your parents, your mentor, your boss, and your mate, and now it's time for you? The children are making test flights on their way to piloting solo. Your parents have become giddy globetrotters, piling up frequent-flier miles and e-mailing playful photos of themselves riding camels. . . . Now you can finally earn that degree, start your own business, run for office, master another language, invent something, or write that book you keep mulling.

Ominous new paragraph—to reflect tire-screeching 21st century update:

Then you get The Call.

In Sheehy's case, The Call was a cancer diagnosis for her husband, Clay Felker, which kicked off an almost two-decade period of medical battles before his death (which was actually not, in the end, from cancer). Although Sheehy offers her book as an umbrella guide for all caregivers, weaving her personal experience together with a demographically wide range of case studies, it strikes this caregiver as less than universal. For one thing—and in fact this is a tribute to how engagingly Sheehy tells her story—even with a tube in his stomach (for which sympathetic chefs blended gourmet food at Paris bistros, whereupon he continued to charm dinner guests as usual in his handsome navy-blue blazer), Clay Felker, on the page anyway, is still pretty great company. And then, to further vanquish the blues, Sheehy and Felker rented a houseboat, spent the summer in France . . . (How is it that, no matter what, Boomers always seem to be having more fun?)

And while there is some aesthetic appeal to Sheehy's mandala-like formulation of the caregiver's journey being not a straight path but a labyrinth (whose eight turnings are Shock and Mobilization, the New Normal, Boomerang, Playing God, "I Can't Do This Anymore!", Coming Back, the In-Between Stage, and the Long Goodbye), this taxonomy feels more descriptive than helpful. Also, her take on what one learns when caring for one's failing loved one is, if not quite a Hallmark card, certainly the best possible case:

> It opens up the greatest possibilities for true intimacy and reconnection at the deepest level. The sharing of strengths and vulnerabilities, without shame, fosters love. And for some caregivers, this role offers a chance in Second Adulthood to compose a more tender sequel to the troubled family drama of our First Adulthood. We can become better than our younger selves.

Jane Gross also believes spiritual growth is possible, but her take, predictably, is far less rosy, even verging on Old Testament:

> Here we are, not just with a herculean job but with a front-row seat for this long, slow dying. We want to do all we realistically can to ease the suffering, smooth the passing, of our loved ones. But we also have the opportunity to watch what happens to our parents, listen to what they have to say to us, and use that information to look squarely at our own mortality and prepare as best we can for the end of our own lives.

For herself, insists Gross: "I can tell you now that it was worth every dreadful minute, a transformative experience." And the inspiring lesson? Here it is, as expressed in a sere opening quotation by May Sarton: "I have seen in you what courage can be when there is no hope."

Clearly, various ruminations on the meaning of the caregiver's "journey" will continue, as ever more literature is added to the caregiving genre, as ever more of us spend ever more of our days belaying loved ones in Hoyer lifts like stricken beef cattle. That said, while I do carry a datebook festooned with soothing nature photography and the proverbs of the Buddhist nun Pema Chödrön (the sort of curious artifact 50-ish women like myself receive as Christmas gifts, along with very tiny—to reduce calories—lavender-and-sea-salt-infused gourmet chocolates), I myself have yet to see any pitch for the spiritual benefit of this grim half-million-dollar odyssey that is remotely inviting. To quote Amy Winehouse, who didn't want to go to rehab: No, no, no!

No . . . No . . . No. What I propose instead is seeking comfort in what I like to call, borrowing in part from Kafka's German, *Elderschadenfreude*. On the one hand, sure, here we stand around the office coffeemaker in middle age, mixing flax into our Greek yogurt and sharing more and more tales about our elderly parents, tales that are dull ("Mom slipped in the shower—at first she said it was nothing"), slow-moving ("And then I took her to the foot doctor, but then, right there in the parking lot, she insisted she had to go to the bathroom—but the door is on the *north* side while we were on the *south*—"), and in the end, well, depressingly predictable (we already know which colleges our wards are getting into—NONE). On the other

hand, I believe it is by enduring this very suffering and tedium that one can eventually tease out a certain dark, autumnal, delightfully-bitter-as-Fernet-Branca enjoyment, best described by some dense and complicated noun-ending German word.

Elderschadenfreude is the subtle frisson of the horror tale that always begins so simply ("Mom slipped in the shower—at first she said it was nothing") but makes listeners raise eyebrows, nod knowingly, begin microwaving popcorn. It is the secret pleasure of hearing about aging parents that are even more impossible than yours. Prepare to enjoy.

My father's old age began so well. Back in his 70s, to prepare for his sunset years, this Chinese widower had taken the precaution of procuring (after some stunning misfires) his retirement plan: an obedient Chinese-immigrant wife, almost 20 years younger than himself, who, in exchange for citizenship, would—unlike American women—accept the distinctly nonfeminist role of cutting up his fruit and massaging his bunions. In addition to doing all that, said Chinese wife, Alice, helped my dad run the informal Craigslist-peopled boarding house he had turned our family home into, for which her reward would be a generous inheritance upon his death, and the right to live in the house until hers. It is a measure of my dad's frugality that he didn't even buy health insurance for Alice until she turned 65—he rolled the statistical dice against the premiums, and won! With $2,000 a month from renters, on top of a Social Security check of $1,500, he and Alice were actually *making* money. What with their habit of taking buses everywhere and a shared love of Dumpster diving, they could star in their own reality show about thrift.

This is not to say my father has been completely "well." After age 78, if you asked him "How are you?" he would exclaim: "I'm dying!" At his 80th-birthday party, when he tremulously lifted his centimeter of red wine while watching my girlfriends dance, I mourned his visible frailty. At 82, he was passing out on bus benches, hitting his head, causing his doctors to insist on a pacemaker (which he refused). By 85, battling Parkinson's, he was still hobbling down to the beach to attempt rickety calisthenics and swimming, but "he's barely *swimming* in those two feet of water," my older sister worried. "It's more like falling." By 89, he was so slowed, like a clock winding down, that, never mind going to the beach, one morning he couldn't even get out of bed.

That was when he called me, in fear and confusion, for help. A pulse-pounding hourlong drive later, arriving at his bedside, I found to my panic that I could not rouse him. He lay in that waxy, inert, folded-up pose that looks unmistakably like death (I had seen it when my mother died, of early Alzheimer's, at 69). "This is it—it's really it—Papa's dead," I wept over the phone, long-distance, to my sister. And I remember, as the dust motes danced in the familiar golden light of our family home, how my sister and I found ourselves spontaneously, tumblingly observing to each other how we were sad . . . and yet oddly at peace.

Yes, my history with this man has been checkered: in my childhood, he had been cruelly cheap (no Christmas, no heat);

in my teens, he had been unforgivably mean to my mother; in my 20s, I rebelled and fled; in my 30s, I softened and we became wry friends—why not, he couldn't harm me now; in my 40s, sensing that these were the last days of a fading elder, the memories of whom I would reflect on with increasing nostalgia, the door opened for real affection, even a kind of gratitude. After all, I had benefited professionally from using him as fodder for my writing (as he had benefited financially for years by forging my signature so I ended up paying his taxes—ah, the great circle of life).

In short, there was real grief now at seeing my father go, but I was a big girl—actually, a middle-aged woman, with some 1,000 hours of therapy behind me—and, chin up, I would get through it. Unlike in the case of my mother, who had left too early, my business here was done. I had successfully completed my Kübler-Ross stages.

The conundrum that morning in the dining room (where my father's bed was), however, was that although my father wasn't rouseable, he wasn't actually dead. (He has a lizard-like resting pulse of 36, so even in his waking state, he's sort of like the undead.) I called the Malibu paramedics, who carted him to the emergency room and stuck an IV in. An hour later, the surprisingly benign diagnosis? Simple dehydration.

With a sudden angry snort, my father woke up. I won't say I wish I had hit him over the head with a frying pan to finish the job when it seemed we were so, so close. But I will say that when my dad woke up that day, my problems really began. Because what this episode made clear was that, while nothing was wrong with my dad, although he was 89—89!—something was wrong with Alice, who was supposed to be taking care of him. Her penchant for gibbering Chinese was not, as we'd imagined, a symptom of her English skills' plateauing after 15 years in America, but of the early or middle stages of dementia. This, I hadn't expected, because, as I remind you, she is much younger than my father. Alice's age is . . . drum-roll . . . 72.

So now, aside from neglecting my elderly father, the formerly mild-mannered Alice is starting to disturb the tenants: waving butcher knives at them, hurling their things into the street. (What a fun life they're having—my father believes some of the more sturdy renters can pitch in and "help shower" him. Best to think twice before renting a room off Craigslist!) Alice is increasingly found wandering at 2 A.M. on freeways in places like Torrance (50 miles away), and is ever more routinely brought home in the dead of night by various police officers and firemen (your tax dollars at work!). And in contrast to her formerly frugal ways, Alice no longer understands money. At one point, my father called the police because she was hitting him—not to have her arrested but, as my dad says, just to "scare" her. To evade capture, she ran away with a duffel bag stuffed with their passports, marriage certificate, immigration papers, and two small, tightly packed envelopes, one with exactly 13 crisp $1 bills inside it and another with a Keystone Kops–type mélange of Chinese money, Turkish money, and . . . as I said, upon discovery, to my sister: "I didn't know Bill Nye the Science Guy *had* his own currency!"

When I gave Alice the bag (returned by the police), she accused me of stealing $2,000 from it. Meanwhile, forensic

analysis reveals she had withdrawn $13,000, gone to a bank in Chinatown, and purchased a useless universal life-insurance policy, an event she cannot recall. My father does not want Alice to move to assisted living, however, because he enjoys her cooking. So the solution for Alice is a full-time Mandarin-speaking female companion. At $5,000 a month, this service is a relative bargain if it keeps Alice from withdrawing, and flinging to the winds, her next $50,000. (And who knows *where* all these mysterious accounts are? I'm trying to find out, I'm trying!) Meanwhile, armed with his own capable full-time Filipino male nurse (another $5,000 a month), my father has roared back with formidable energy. As long as he's hydrated, it appears that no bacterium can fell him—remember, he has been eating out of Dumpsters (we're talking expired sushi) for *several decades already*. (Who knows if he hasn't morphed into another life form, possibly amphibian?) Which is to say, now I have a wheelchair-bound but extremely active 91-year-old who greatly enjoys getting bathed and diapered and fed ice cream and crashing UCLA science lectures and, oh, by the way—every day he calls me now: he wants SEX. He proudly needs only 1/16th of a Viagra pill for SEX. Because Alice is no longer complying (she is unfortunately not quite that crazy), and because I have not—yet?—caved (although if one Googles this issue, one will find to one's horror the phrase *healing hands*!), my father has started to proposition Alice's lady nurse, trying to grab her breasts, begging her to touch him. Which he can't do himself, as he can barely clasp his hand around a spoon.

What would Gail Sheehy call this particular new Passage, aside from, peppily, "The New Normal"? Outdoing the "giddy globetrotters" in Sheehy's midlife Boomertopia, my father would park his wheelchair on top of the camel, then get pitched headfirst from the camel, then probably try to molest the camel. Eternally leaping up, like a ghoul, he is the über-Kafka father.

But there's more. My father's care demands an ever-changing flotilla of immigrant caregivers, of whom the chief one is Thomas. Because my father is so difficult, it's not atypical for new caregivers to quit before noon. The miraculously tolerant Thomas is the only nurse who has stuck with my father, which means that my sister, brother, and I basically work for Thomas. We've co-signed on an apartment for him and his wife and four children, who just emigrated from the Philippines; we've fixed up a beater car for him (which I've spent many a weekday smogging, re-smogging, insuring, handicapped-plating). We do all this because Thomas does an excellent job, always trying to raise the standard of my dad's care. Which is a good thing. Or is it?

Thomas is concerned about my dad's regularity. The cranberry pills and stool softeners I regularly deliver from Costco have worked to a point, yes, but now Thomas has hit upon something better: milk of magnesia. Problem is, the product is so effective that when my father is given it before bed, *although* he has finally consented to wearing an adult diaper at night, within four hours he is at capacity and begins fouling his sheets. Hence, Thomas has started finishing his 10-hour day by sleeping in my father's room at night, for which, of course, he must be given a raise, to $6,500 a month.

Thomas is optimistic. He ends conversations about the overflowing diapers with this cheerful reassurance: "I will get your Papa to 100!"

Oh my God—how could he *say* such a horrible thing? I am hyperventilating again. Okay. Never mind the question of whether, given that they have total freedom and no responsibilities, we are indulging our elders in the same way my generation has been famously indulging our overly entitled children. Never mind the question of whether there is a reasonable point at which parents lose their rights, and for the good of society we get to lock them up and medicate them.

The question that really haunts me, and that I feel I must raise now, is: At these prices, exactly how much time do I have to spend *listening to stories about my dad defecating*?

I rant to myself: He is taking everything! He is taking all the money. He's taken years of my life (sitting in doctors' offices, in pharmacies, in waiting rooms). With his horrid, selfish, grotesque behavior, he's chewed through every shred of my sentimental affection for him. He's taken the serenity I fought for—and won—in 1,000 hours of therapy centered on my family. In fact, he's destroyed my belief in "family" as a thing that buoys one up. Quite the opposite: family is like the piano around Holly Hunter's ankle, dragging me implacably down.

I have to ensure Hilton-level care for my barely Motel 6 father, the giant baby, as well as for his caregiver, the big-baby nurse, all caught up with the high-pitched drama of feeding and diapering and massaging. That's right: my family is throwing all our money away on powdering our 91-year-old dad's giant-baby ass, leaving nothing for my sweet little daughters, with their thoughts of unicorns and poetry and dance, my helpless little daughters, who, in the end, represent me! In short, on top of everything else he has taken from me, he has taken away my entire sense of self, because at age almost-50, it appears that I too have become a squalling baby!!!

The other day, my writer friend Laura was doing her own woeful monologue—and how they all just continue, like leaves falling—about her dad.

"He has learned *nothing* in 78 years. He has no wisdom. He has no soul. He insults me. He ignores his grandchildren. How much longer do I need to keep having a relationship with him?"

We were walking in the hills above Griffith Park, which turn into the grassy slopes of Forest Lawn, which put me in mind of the ending of one of the best memoirs I have ever read—and, come to think of it, perhaps the only book one will ever need—about difficult parents, Bernard Cooper's *The Bill From My Father*. The title comes from the day Cooper received a bill from his lawyer father, typed on his customary onionskin paper, demanding immediate reimbursement for parenting outlays (including an entire childhood's worth of groceries and clothing) in the amount of $2 million. Cooper Sr. escalated the pain, upon his other sons' deaths, by not just sending their widows bills but filing actual lawsuits against them.

Still, Cooper continues to have an on-again, off-again relationship with Cooper the Elder (whose history with his sons can be summed up by the progression of painted signs on the front of his law-office door, as telling as a piece of concrete poetry: COOPER; COOPER & COOPER; COOPER, COOPER & COOPER; COOPER, COOPER, COOPER & COOPER; COOPER, COOPER & COOPER; COOPER & COOPER; COOPER). Their relationship eventually drew the interest of a publisher—did Cooper want to write a book about his father? As Cooper recalls:

It would be foolish to refuse her offer because . . . Well, because money was involved, but also because the rest of my family was gone forever and Dad was all I had left, though I wasn't sure what constituted "all." Or "Dad" for that matter.

He quotes from John Cheever's short story "Reunion": " 'My father,' thinks the son, 'was my future and my doom.' " The memoir concludes with a wonderful Forest Lawn cemetery scene (his father's punchy epitaph: YOU FINALLY GOT ME).

I almost don't know what I envy Bernard Cooper for more—his incomparable literary genius or the fact that his father is *dead*. (Anti-*Elderschadenfreude*.)

The paradox is, I can't miss the good things about my father while he is alive, but I will of course miss him . . . when he is dead. By the same token—and perhaps this is the curious blessing—if my mother were alive today (what would she be, 84?), she would be driving me *insane*!!!

But then, inevitably, comes (at least in my Pema Chödrön calendar) yet another day. And indeed, inspired by my Buddhist stationery, what I decide I will let go of today is any of the previous ideas I had about future planning—the college tuitions, paying off the house, putting together some kind of retirement. . . .

Then again, in the new America, shouldn't the wealth be re-equalized from generation to generation? Is it not somewhat fitting that the Loh family's nest egg should be used to put not our children but Thomas's through college, as Andrew Carnegie advocated? ("I will get your Papa to 100!") Is that really the worst use of this money? Indeed, I muse slyly, perhaps, unlike my own Western daughters, jazz shoes and drawing pads (how useless!) spilling out of their bags, Thomas's children will actually buckle down and get real majors, leading to real jobs—doctor, engineer, or, most lucrative of all . . . *geriatric nurse*.

So I feel a little calmer today, as I deliver my raft of pills. And I find it is a rare calm day at my father's house as well. The various triaging schemes are holding. Thomas has the house smelling soapy, white sheets cover sagging couches, vases hold artificial flowers, medications are arranged on various bureaus in proud and almost spectacular displays. For today, Thomas's beater car runs. For today, Alice is medicated, and therefore pleasant. She serves a mysterious bell-pepper dish that—aside from being wildly spicy—is edible. My father's hair has never been more poofy—or black. He too is vaguely fragrant. Could be his lucky day. SEX.

I have to acknowledge, too, that in traditional China, with its notions of filial responsibility, my elders would be living with me in my home, or I in theirs. So the beautiful oh-so-Western thing is that, for today, I can drive away. And as I drive down PCH—dipping celery into Greek yogurt sprinkled with flax, dropping it all over my sweatpants—I realize that because things are not actually terrible (no cops, no paramedics, no $13,000 bank withdrawals), today qualifies as a fabulous day.

I can no longer think of my dad as my "father." But I recognize in him something as familiar to me as myself. To the end, stubborn, babyish, life-loving, he doesn't want to go to rehab, no, no, no.

Critical Thinking

1. Why does the author sometimes wish her elderly father would die? Is she being selfish in saying this? Why or why not? Do you think other adult children feel this way but do not say anything?

2. What are some of the financial and emotional burdens adult children face in caring for their aging parents?

3. How does the reversal in roles that occurs when children become caregivers for their parents alter family and relationship dynamics?

4. What types of supports do adult children need as they try to meet the needs of their own families and their aging parents?

Create Central

www.mhhe.com/createcentral

Internet References

National Center on Caregiving
    www.caregiver.org
National Council on Aging
    www.ncoa.org
Alzheimer's Association
    www.alz.org

SANDRA TSING LOH is the author, most recently, of *Mother on Fire*.

Unit 4

UNIT

Prepared by: Patricia Hrusa Williams,
University of Maine at Farmington

Challenges and Opportunities

Stress is life and life is stress. Sometimes stress in families gives new meaning to this statement. When a stressful event occurs in families, many processes occur simultaneously as families and their members cope with the stressor and its effects. One thing that can result is a reduction in family members' ability to act as resources for each other. Indeed, a stressor can overwhelm the family system, and family members may be among the least effective people in coping with each other's behavior. In this unit, we consider a wide variety of stressful life events and crises that families may experience. Some are normative, stressful life events which occur as families evolve and change. Families add and lose family members. Family members age, and one's health can fail. Individuals experience changes in employment and the need to balance work-family concerns as families develop and change.

There are also other non-normative, stressful life events and crises which many families experience. Marriages can break up.

A family member may be called on to serve their country and be separated from their family for a period of time. Children and adults in the family can be diagnosed with chronic illnesses or health problems. Personal, economic, relationship, and social strains can result in maladaptive coping strategies such as drug and alcohol use, mental health crises, violence, and infidelity.

The articles in this unit explore a variety of family crises, stresses, and strains. Among them are the impact of family violence, substance abuse, mental health challenges, infidelity, and economic concerns. The nature of stress resulting from life-threatening and chronic illness, disability, loss, grief, the many crises of war, as well as family challenges and adaption for single-parent and divorced families are also considered. Throughout this unit, the focus is not only on understanding the challenges these factors present to families, but also on understanding how to best support families as they navigate the stresses of life.

Article

Prepared by: Patricia Hrusa Williams,
University of Maine at Farmington

Terrorism in the Home

Eleven myths and facts about domestic violence

VICTOR M. PARACHIN

Learning Outcomes

After reading this article, you will be able to:

- Identify the signs of domestic violence.

- Understand several causes or factors associated with the occurrence of domestic violence.

- Explain strategies which may be effective in reaching out to and assisting victims.

If anything is truly equal opportunity, it is battering. Domestic violence crosses all socioeconomic, ethnic, racial, educational, age, and religious lines.

— K. J. Wilson, *When Violence Begins At Home*

Sadly, a U.S. Department of Justice study indicates that approximately one million violent crimes are committed by former spouses, boyfriends, or girlfriends each year, with 85 percent of the victims being women. For domestic violence to be defeated, it must begin with information. Here are 11 myths and facts about domestic violence.

Myth 1: Domestic violence is only physical.

Fact: Abusive actions against another person can be verbal, emotional, sexual, and physical.
There are four basic types of domestic violence:

- Physical (shoving, slapping, punching, pushing, hitting, kicking, and restraining)
- Sexual (when one partner forces unwanted, unwelcome, uninvited sexual acts upon another)
- Psychological (verbal and emotional abuse, threats, intimidations, stalking, swearing, insulting, isolation from family and friends, forced financial dependence)
- Attacks against property and pets (breaking household objects, hitting walls, abusing or killing beloved pets)

Myth 2: Domestic violence is not common.

Fact: While precise statistics are difficult to determine, all signs indicate that domestic violence is more common than most people believe or want to believe. Here's one example: due to lack of space, shelters for battered women are able to admit only 10 to 40 percent of women who request admission. Another example is from divorced women. Though they make up less than 8 percent of the U.S. population, they account for 75 percent of all battered women and report being assaulted 14 times more often than women still living with a partner. Whatever statistics are available are believed to be low because domestic violence is often not reported.

Myth 3: Domestic violence affects only women.

Fact: Abuse can happen to anyone! It can be directed at women, men, children, the elderly. It takes place among all social classes and all ethnic groups. However, women are the most targeted victims of domestic violence. Here are some statistics:

- One in four American women report being physically assaulted and/or raped by a current or former spouse, cohabiting partner, or date at some time in their life.
- According to the FBI, a woman is beaten every 15 seconds.
- In 1996, 30 percent of all female murder victims in the United States were slain by their husbands or boyfriends.
- Around the world, at least one in every three women has been beaten, coerced into sex, or otherwise abused in her lifetime.
- While men are victims of domestic abuse, 92 percent of those subjected to violence are women.

Myth 4: Domestic violence occurs only among lower class or minority or rural communities.

Fact: Domestic violence crosses all race and class lines. Similar rates of abuse are reported in cities, suburbs, and rural areas, according to the Bureau of Justice. Abusers can be found living in mansions as well as in mobile homes. Susan Weitzman,

Ph.D., is author of the book *Not to People Like Us: Hidden Abuse in Upscale Marriages.* In her book, Dr. Weitzman presents case-by-case studies of domestic violence in families with higher than average incomes and levels of education.

Myth 5: Battered women can just leave.

Fact: A combination of factors makes it very difficult for the abused to leave. These include: family and social pressure, shame, financial barriers, children, religious beliefs. Up to 50 percent of women with children fleeing domestic violence become homeless because they leave the abuser. Also, many who are abused face psychological ambivalence about leaving. One woman recalls: "My body still ached from being beaten by my husband a day earlier. But he kept pleading through the door. 'I'm sorry. I'll never do that to you again. I know I need help.' I had a 2-week-old baby. I wanted to believe him. I opened the door." Her abuse continued for two more years before she gained the courage to leave.

Myth 6: Abuse takes place because of alcohol or drugs.

Fact: Substance abuse does not cause domestic violence. However, drugs and alcohol do lower inhibitions while increasing the level of violence, often to more dangerous levels. The U.S. Department of Health and Human Services estimates that one-quarter to one-half of abusers have substance abuse issues.

Myth 7: They can just fight back or walk away.

Fact: Dealing with domestic violence is never as simple as fighting back or walking out the door. "Most domestic abusers are men who are physically stronger than the women they abuse," notes Joyce Zoldak in her book *When Danger Hits Home: Survivors of Domestic Violence.* "In the case of elder abuse, the victims' frail condition may limit their being able to defend themselves. When a child is being abused, the adult guardian is far more imposing—both physically and psychologically—than the victim."

Myth 8: The victim provoked the violence.

Fact: The abuser is completely responsible for the abuse. No one can say or do anything which warrants being beaten and battered. Abusers often try to deflect their responsibility by blaming the victim via comments such as: "You made me angry." "You made me jealous." "This would never have happened if you hadn't done that." "I didn't mean to do that, but you were out of control." Victims need to be assured that the abuse is not their fault.

Myth 9: Domestic abuse is a private matter and it's none of my business.

Fact: We all have a responsibility to care for one another. Officials at the National Domestic Violence Hotline offer this advice to people who see or suspect domestic violence: "Yes, it is your business. Maybe he's your friend, your brother-in-law, your cousin, co-worker, gym partner, or fishing buddy. You've noticed that he interrupts her, criticizes her family, yells at her,

or scares her. You hope that when they're alone, it isn't worse. The way he treats her makes you uncomfortable, but you don't want to make him mad or lose his friendship. You surely don't want to see him wreck his marriage or have to call the police. What can you do? Say something. If you don't, your silence is the same as saying abuse is OK. He could hurt someone, or end up in jail. Because you care, you need to do something—before it is too late."

Myth 10: Partners need couples counseling.

Fact: It is the abuser alone who needs counseling in order to change behavior. Social Worker Susan Schechter says couples counseling is "an inappropriate intervention that further endangers the woman." Schechter explains her position: "It encourages the abuser to blame the victim by examining her 'role' in his problem. By seeing the couple together, the therapist erroneously suggests that the partner, too, is responsible for the abuser's behavior. Many women have been brutally beaten following couples counseling sessions in which they disclosed violence or coercion. The abuser alone must take responsibility for assaults and understand that family reunification is not his treatment goal: the goal is to stop the violence."

Myth 11: Abusers are evil people.

Fact: "Anyone can find himself or herself in an abusive situation, and most of us could also find ourselves tempted to be abusive to others, no matter how wrong we know it to be," notes Joyce Zoldak. Abusers are people who may be strong and stable in some areas of their lives but weak, unreasonable and out of control in other ways. This does not excuse their behavior, because abuse is always wrong. Abusers need to be held accountable for their actions and encouraged to seek help promptly by meeting with a psychologist, psychiatrist, therapist, or spiritual leader. Abusers can also receive help from The National Domestic Violence Hotline 1-800-799-7233 or via their website: http://www.thehotline.org.

With an informed community, and with the help of family and friends, the cycle of abuse can be broken.

Critical Thinking

1. What are some impediments or reasons why women do not report domestic violence?
2. What are some reasons why domestic violence occurs in couple relationships and in families?
3. Explain why it can be difficult to identify and assist victims.
4. Why do you think some of these myths about domestic violence persist?
5. Given the information in the article, what do you think may be effective strategies which can be used to reach out to and assist victims of domestic violence?

Create Central

www.mhhe.com/createcentral

Internet References

Futures Without Violence
www.futureswithoutviolence.org
National Coalition Against Domestic Violence
www.ncadv.org
National Network to End Domestic Violence
www.nnedv.org

National Resource Center on Domestic Violence
www.nrcdv.org

VICTOR M. PARACHIN writes from Tulsa, Oklahoma.

Article

Prepared by: Patricia Hrusa Williams,
University of Maine at Farmington

Anguish of the Abandoned Child

CHARLES A. NELSON III; NATHAN A. FOX AND CHARLES H. ZEANAH, JR.

The plight of orphaned Romanian children reveals the psychic and physical scars from first years spent without a loving, responsive caregiver.

Learning Outcomes

After reading this article, you will be able to:

- Understand the political, social, and economic reasons behind the "orphan problem" in Romania.

- Explain reasons why children become orphans worldwide.

- Identify how early experiences of deprivation impact child development and later outcomes.

- Define and explain the term "sensitive period."

In a misguided effort to enhance economic productivity, Nicolae Ceauşescu decreed in 1966 that Romania would develop its "human capital" via a government-enforced mandate to increase the country's population. Ceauşescu, Romania's leader from 1965 to 1989, banned contraception and abortions and imposed a "celibacy tax" on families that had fewer than five children. State doctors—the menstrual police—conducted gynecologic examinations in the workplace of women of child-bearing age to see whether they were producing sufficient offspring. The birth rate initially skyrocketed. Yet because families were too poor to keep their children, they abandoned many of them to large state-run institutions. By 1989 this social experiment led to more than 170,000 children living in these facilities.

The Romanian revolution of 1989 deposed Ceauşescu, and over the next 10 years his successors made a series of halting attempts to undo the damage. The "orphan problem" Ceauşescu left behind was enormous and did not disappear for many years. The country remained impoverished, and the rate of child abandonment did not change appreciably at least through 2005. A decade after Ceauşescu had been removed from power, some government officials could still be heard saying that the state did a better job than families in bringing up abandoned children and that those confined in institutions were, by definition, "defective"—a view grounded in the Soviet-inspired system of educating the disabled, dubbed "defectology."

Even after the 1989 revolution, families still felt free to abandon an unwanted infant to a state-run institution. Social scientists had long suspected that early life in an orphanage could have adverse consequences. A number of mostly small, descriptive studies that lacked control groups were conducted from the 1940s to the 1960s in the West that compared children in orphanages with those in foster care and showed that life in an institution did not come close to matching the care of a parent—even if that parent was not the natural mother or father. One issue with these studies was the possibility of "selection bias": children removed from institutions and placed into adoptive or foster homes might be less impaired, whereas the ones who remained in the institution were more disabled. The only way to counter any bias would require the unprecedented step of randomly placing a group of abandoned children into either an institution or a foster home.

Understanding the effects of life in an institution on children's early development is important because of the immensity of the orphan problem worldwide (an orphan is defined here as an abandoned child or one whose parents have died). War, disease, poverty and sometimes government policies have stranded at least eight million children worldwide in state-run facilities. Often these children live in highly structured but hopelessly bleak environments, where typically one adult oversees 12 to 15 children. Research is still lacking to gain a full understanding of what happens to children who spend their first years in such deprived circumstances.

In 1999, when we approached Cristian Tabacaru, then secretary of state for Romania's National Authority for Child Protection, he encouraged us to conduct a study on institutionalized children because he wanted data to address the question of whether to develop alternative forms of care for the 100,000 Romanian children then living in state institutions. Yet Tabacaru faced stiff resistance from some government officials, who believed for decades that children received a better upbringing in institutions than in foster care. The problem was exacerbated because some government agencies' budgets were funded, in part, by their role in making institutional care arrangements. Faced with these challenges, Tabacaru thought that scientific evidence about putative advantages of foster care for young children over state institutions would make a convincing case for reform, and so he invited us to go ahead with a study.

Infancy in an Institution

With the assistance of some officials within the Romanian government and especially with help from others who worked for SERA Romania (a nongovernmental organization), we implemented a study to ascertain the effects on a child's brain and behavior of living in a state institution and whether foster care could ameliorate the effects of being reared in conditions that run counter to what we know about the needs of young children. The Bucharest Early Intervention Project was launched in 2000, in cooperation with the Romanian government, in part to provide answers that might rectify the aftereffects of previous policies. The unfortunate legacy of Ceauşescu's tenure provided a chance to examine, with greater scientific rigor than any previous study, the effects of institutionalized care on the neurological and emotional development of infants and young children. The study was the first-ever randomized controlled study that compared a group of infants placed in foster care with another raised in institutions, providing a level of experimental precision that had been hitherto unavailable.

We recruited, from all six institutions for infants and young children in Bucharest, a group of 136 whom we considered to be free of neurological, genetic and other birth defects based on pediatric exams conducted by a member of the study team. All had been abandoned to institutions in the first weeks or months of life. When the study began, they were, on average, 22 months old—the range of ages was from six to 31 months.

Immediately after a series of baseline physical and psychological assessments, half the children were randomly assigned to a foster care intervention our team developed, maintained and financed. The other half remained in an institution—what we called the "care as usual" group. We also recruited a third group of typically developing children who lived with their families in Bucharest and had never been institutionalized. These three groups of children have been studied for more than 10 years. Because the children were randomly assigned to foster care or to remain in an institution, unlike previous studies, it was possible to show that any differences in development or behavior between the two groups could be attributed to where they were reared.

Because there was virtually no foster care available for abandoned children in Bucharest when we started, we were in the unique position of having to build our own network. After extensive advertising and background checks, we eventually recruited 53 families to foster 68 children (we kept siblings together).

Of course, many ethical issues were involved in conducting a controlled scientific study of young children, a trial in which only half the participants were initially removed from institutions. The design compared the standard intervention for abandoned children—institutional rearing—with foster care, an intervention that had never been available to these children. Ethical protections put in place included oversight by multiple Romanian- and U.S.-based institutions, implementation of "minimal risk" measures (all used routinely with young children), and noninterference with government decisions about

changes in placement when children were adopted, returned to biological parents or later placed in government-sponsored foster care that at the outset did not exist.

No child was moved back from foster care to an institution at the end of the study. As soon as the early results became available, we communicated our findings to the Romanian government at a news conference.

To ensure high-quality foster care, we designed the program to incorporate regular involvement of a social work team and provided modest subsidies to families for child-related expenses. All foster parents had to be licensed, and they were paid a salary as well as a subsidy. They received training and were encouraged to make a full psychological commitment to their foster children.

Sensitive Periods

The study set about to explore the premise that early experience often exerts a particularly strong influence in shaping the immature brain. For some behaviors, neural connections form in early years in response to environmental influences during windows of time, called sensitive periods. A child who listens to spoken language or simply looks around receives aural and visual inputs that shape neural connections during specific periods of development. The results of the study supported this initial premise of a sensitive period: the difference between an early life spent in an institution compared with foster care was dramatic. At 30, 40 and 52 months, the average IQ of the institutionalized group was in the low to middle 70s, whereas it was about 10 points higher for children in foster care. Not surprisingly, IQ was about 100, the standard average, for the group that had never been institutionalized. We also discovered a sensitive period when a child was able to achieve a maximum gain in IQ: a boy or girl placed in a home before roughly two years of age had a significantly higher IQ than one put there after that age.

The findings clearly demonstrate the devastating impact on mind and brain of spending the first two years of life within the impersonal confines of an institution. The Romanian children living in institutions provide the best evidence to date that the initial two years of life constitute a sensitive period in which a child must receive intimate emotional and physical contact or else find personal development stymied.

Infants learn from experience to seek comfort, support and protection from their significant caregivers, whether those individuals are natural or foster parents—and so we decided to measure attachment. Only extreme conditions that limit opportunities for a child to form attachments can interfere with a process that is a foundation for normal social development. When we measured this variable in the institutionalized children, we found that the overwhelming majority displayed incompletely formed and aberrant relationships with their caregivers.

When the children were 42 months of age, we made another assessment and found that the children placed in foster care displayed dramatic improvements in making emotional attachments. Almost half had established secure relationships with another person, whereas only 18 percent of the institutionalized children had done so. In the community children, those never institutionalized, 65 percent were securely attached. Children placed into foster care before the end of the 24-month sensitive period were more likely to form secure attachments compared with children placed there after that threshold.

These numbers are more than just statistical disparities that separate the institutionalized and foster groups. They translate into very real experiences of both anguish and hope. Sebastian (none of the children's names in this article are real), now 12, has spent virtually his entire life in an orphanage and has seen his IQ drop 20 points to a subpar 64 since he was tested during his fifth year. A youth who may have never formed an attachment with anyone, Sebastian drinks alcohol and displays other risk-prone behaviors. During an interview with us, he became irritable and erupted with flashes of anger.

Bogdan, also 12, illustrates the difference that receiving individualized attention from an adult makes. He was abandoned at birth and lived in a maternity ward until two months of age, after which he lived in an institution for nine months. He was then recruited into the project and randomized to the foster care group, where he was placed in the family of a single mother and her adolescent daughter. Bogdan started to catch up quickly and managed to overcome mild developmental delays within months. Although he had some behavioral problems, project staff members worked with the family, and by his fifth birthday the foster mother had decided to adopt him. At age 12, Bogdan's IQ continues to score at an above-average level. He attends one of the best public schools in Bucharest and has the highest grades in his class.

Because children raised in institutions did not appear to receive much personal attention, we were interested in whether a paucity of language exposure would have any effect on them. We observed delays in language development, and if children arrived in foster care before they reached approximately 15 or 16 months, their language was normal, but the later children were placed, the further behind they fell.

We also compared the prevalence of mental health problems among any children who had ever been institutionalized with those who had not. We found that 53 percent of the children who had ever lived in an institution had received a psychiatric diagnosis by the age of four and a half, compared with 20 percent of the group who had never been institutionalized. In fact, 62 percent of the institutionalized children approaching the age of five had diagnoses, ranging from anxiety disorders—44 percent—to attention-deficit hyperactivity disorder (ADHD)—23 percent.

Foster care had a major influence on the level of anxiety and depression—reducing their incidence by half—but did not affect behavioral diagnoses (ADHD and conduct disorder). We could not detect any sensitive period for mental health. Yet relationships were important for assuring good mental health. When we explored the mechanism to explain reduced emotional disorders such as depression, we found that the more secure the attachment between a child and foster parent, the greater probability that the child's symptoms would diminish.

We also wanted to know whether first years in a foster home affected brain development differently than living in an institution. An assessment of brain activity using electroencephalography (EEG)—which records electrical signals—showed that infants living in institutions had significant reductions in one

component of EEG activity and a heightened level in another (lower alpha and higher theta waves), a pattern that may reflect delayed brain maturation. When we assessed the children at the eight-year mark, we again recorded EEG scans. We could then see that the pattern of electrical activity in children placed in foster care before two years of age could not be distinguished from that of those who had never passed time in an institution. Children taken out of an orphanage after two years and those who never left showed a less mature pattern of brain activity.

The noticeable decrease in EEG activity among the institutionalized children was perplexing. To interpret this observation, we turned to data from magnetic resonance imaging, which can visualize brain structures. Here we observed that the institutionalized children showed a large reduction in the volume of both gray matter (neurons and other brain cells) and white matter (the insulating substance covering neurons' wire-like extensions).

On the whole, all the children who were institutionalized had smaller brain volumes. Placing children in foster care at any age had no effect on increasing the amount of gray matter—the foster care group showed levels of gray matter comparable to those of the institutionalized children. Yet the foster care children showed more white matter volume than the institutionalized group, which may account for the changes in EEG activity.

To further examine the biological toll of early institutionalization, we focused attention on a crucial area of the genome. Telomeres, regions at the ends of chromosomes that provide protection from the stresses of cell division, are shorter in adults who undergo extreme psychological stresses than those who escape this duress. Shorter telomeres may even be a mark of accelerated cellular aging. When we examined telomere length in the children in our study, we observed that, on the whole, those who had spent any time in an institution had shorter telomeres than those who had not.

Lessons for All

The Bucharest Early Intervention Project has demonstrated the profound effects early experience has on brain development. Foster care did not completely remedy the profound developmental abnormalities linked to institutional rearing, but it did mostly shift a child's development toward a healthier trajectory.

The identification of sensitive periods—in which recovery from deprivation occurs the earlier the child begins to experience a more favorable living environment—may be one of the most significant findings from our project. This observation has implications beyond the millions of children living in institutions, extending to additional millions of maltreated children whose care is being overseen by child-protection authorities. We caution readers, however, not to make unwarranted assumptions that two years can be rigidly defined as a sensitive period for development. Yet the evidence suggests that the earlier children are cared for by stable, emotionally invested parents, the better their chances for a more normal development trajectory.

We are continuing to follow these children into adolescence to see if there are "sleeper effects"—that is, significant behavioral or neurological differences that appear only later in youth or even adulthood. Further, we will determine whether the effects of a sensitive period we observed at younger ages will still be observed as children enter adolescence. If they are, they will reinforce a growing body of literature that speaks to the role of early life experiences in shaping development across one's life span. This insight, in turn, may exert pressure on governments throughout the world to pay more attention to the toll that early adversity and institutionalization take on the capacity of a maturing child to traverse the emotional hazards of adolescence and acquire the needed resiliency to cope with the travails of adult life.

More to Explore

Cognitive Recovery in Socially Deprived Young Children: The Bucharest Early Intervention Project. Charles A. Nelson III et al. in Science, vol. 318, pages 1937–1940; December 21, 2007.

Effects of Early Intervention and the Moderating Effects of Brain Activity on Institutionalized Children's Social Skills at Age 8. Alisa N. Almas et al. in Proceedings of the National Academy of Sciences USA, vol. 109, Supplement no. 2, pages 17, 228–17,231; October 16, 2012.

Scientific American Online

For a video that details more about the importance of early-life caregiving, visit http://ScientificAmerican.com/apr2013/orphans.

Critical Thinking

1. Why did Romania experience an "orphan problem?"
2. Is it possible that children could receive a better upbringing in a state-run institution than they could in foster care or the care of their parents? Why or why not?
3. What do you see as ethical issues in randomly placing children to be cared for either in state-run institutions or foster families?
4. Describe some of the issues experienced by children who spent their early years in a state institution.
5. What is the best strategy to use to provide care for orphans? What should we do in situations when there are not enough foster families available to care for orphans or abused/maltreated children?

Create Central

www.mhhe.com/createcentral

Internet References

Scientific American
http://www.scientificamerican.com/article.cfm?id=orphans-how-adversity-affects-young-children

Child Rights Information Network
www.crin.org

Child Welfare Information Gateway
www.childwelfare.gov

CHARLES A. NELSON III is professor of pediatrics and neuroscience and professor of psychology in psychiatry at Harvard Medical School. He has an honorary doctorate from the University of Bucharest in Romania.

NATHAN A. FOX is Distinguished University Professor in the Department of Human Development and Quantitative Methodology at the University of Maryland, College Park.

CHARLES H. ZEANAH, JR. is professor of psychiatry and clinical pediatrics at Tulane University and executive director of the university's Institute of Infant and Early Childhood Mental Health.

Article

Prepared by: Patricia Hrusa Williams,
University of Maine at Farmington

We Are Family: When Elder Abuse, Neglect, and Financial Exploitation Hit Home

JEANNIE JENNINGS BEIDLER

Learning Outcomes

After reading this article, you will be able to:

- Identify the characteristics of elder abuse.
- Explain the practical, legal, financial, and emotional complexities and difficulties encountered in trying to intervene to protect elderly family members.

Research and popular press report alarming instances of familial elder abuse, neglect, and financial exploitation. The House of Representatives Select Committee on Aging found that older adults are at the greatest risk for abuse, and that in more than two-thirds of substantiated cases, the perpetrator is a family member in a caregiving role—usually an adult child (Elder Serve Act of 2009).

Often there are other contributing factors that fuel elder abuse, which include substance abuse (on the part of the abuser or the victim) and diminished capacity of the elder due to conditions such as dementia (Spencer and Smith, 2000). The following true story illustrates what can happen when these factors come into play.

The Visit

In October 2005, police were dispatched to my grandparents' home following a dispute between my parents and my uncle. My uncle, my grandparents' unemployed adult son who was living in the home, became infuriated when my parents arrived for an unscheduled visit and he refused to let them in. Hearing the commotion, my grandmother appeared and insisted that my parents stay, which further exacerbated my uncle's anger. In an effort to keep my grandmother inside, there was a scuffle: several glass panes of a door were broken, and my grandmother and my mother sustained cuts. My father called the police.

When law enforcement arrived, they observed that my grandmother and the home were in poor condition, and that my uncle appeared agitated, inebriated, and unclean. My grandparents were reportedly uncooperative, also unclean, and disoriented. They expressed no concerns about endangerment and declined to press charges.

The exterior of my grandparents' home was in terrible shape, with shattered windows, overgrown landscaping, and broken fencing. Inside, it was filthy and littered with trash. There was little food in the house, but an abundance of alcohol. The police officers insisted this was a case of self-neglect—not of criminal action or intent; they did not create a case or make any further investigation (the only record of the incident was the 911 call that summoned the police). Upon learning that law enforcement would not intervene, my parents, though terrified of my uncle's retribution, reported their concerns to Adult Protective Services (APS).

Soon thereafter, an APS worker made a home visit. Again, my grandparents denied that their welfare was in jeopardy and refused any offers for assistance. The APS worker made the same observations as did the law enforcement officers: My grandparents were clearly oblivious to the dangers of their environment and required immediate medical attention.

After being persuaded by family, law enforcement, and APS, my grandparents were transported to two different local hospitals. My grandfather was treated for various nonlife-threatening conditions and was discharged within a few days, while my grandmother remained hospitalized for nearly three weeks. I visited often and regularly communicated with the hospital staff about her care. Later, I, along with my parents, uncle, and grandfather, attended a "family meeting" in preparation for my grandmother's discharge. During the meeting, it became apparent that my grandfather was confused about his wife's condition and the level of care she would require; he was beginning to show signs of dementia. My uncle agreed to tend to such tasks as transporting his parents to medical appointments, ensuring that prescriptions would be filled in a timely manner, and providing adequate food and water. He also admitted that he had been unemployed for a long time and was working on his sobriety (a glaring "red flag" to me).

Unable to ignore my concerns, I requested a competency evaluation for my grandmother and strongly recommended that she not return home but be assessed for placement in an assisted living facility. I expressed that it was unlikely that my grandparents would receive the care they required should they return home to their son's care. Nonetheless, it was determined that my grandmother would be discharged to home.

The Struggle

I called frequently in the following weeks. Initially, my grandmother would participate in conversations with some degree of awareness, but this capability slowly faded. More often than not, calls placed would go unanswered. Within months, ensuring my grandparents' welfare could only be accomplished by contacting authorities to request a check on their welfare. Ultimately, the rest of my family was forced to trust the APS worker, who had promised to closely monitor the situation.

Over the next four years, my grandparents' home continued to deteriorate. Countless times, concerned neighbors reported suspicious activities to the authorities and APS. My uncle continued to live in the home and, because of unaddressed substance abuse issues, he remained unemployed.

On July 24, 2010, my great-uncle and my husband made an unscheduled visit to my grandparents' home. The house was in deplorable condition. Despite repeated shouts into the house, there was no response. They called 911. The police arrived quickly and confirmed my grandparents and uncle were inside. They warned my great-uncle and husband that they wouldn't "last long" when they went inside the house because of the filth and stench, and suggested they call APS. The police made no attempt to rescue my grandparents or confront my uncle. Stunned, my great-uncle and husband left the premises briefly, returning moments later: they were afraid they would not see my grandparents alive again.

Upon seeing them, my uncle was irate and an explosive dispute ensued. Despite my uncle's unyielding hostility, my great-uncle insisted on seeing my grandparents. He found my grandfather scantily dressed, emaciated and weak, dirty, and lying in his own waste. Down the hall, he found my grandmother, dressed in soiled men's clothing, immobile, and confined to a tattered mattress. My grandparents were oblivious to their circumstances, and responded pleasantly to my great-uncle.

My uncle became increasingly violent toward my great-uncle and husband. Feeling fearful and helpless, with no support from the police, they left. That afternoon, I learned of the situation. Immediately, I made calls to the police, APS, and the crisis hotline. I called for days before a crisis worker agreed to visit my grandparents. To my amazement, the worker believed my grandparents were not in acute danger. Shocked and frustrated, I questioned her perception of acute danger. Couldn't she see that my grandparents were suffering and that they had no food, water, heat, or air-conditioning? The supposed top defenders of the defenseless were now my top source of disappointment.

The Intervention

The following morning, I called the police, APS, the crisis hotline, and miscellaneous advocacy groups. I ended each call saying, "My grandparents are going to die if they aren't helped. What is your name, so I can document that you knew and did nothing!" It was now forty-eight hours since the 911 call on July 24; I feared that my grandparents would die before help reached them. The next day, an APS worker informed me that an intervention was planned for that afternoon and would include her supervisor, paramedics, and the police. I was asked to accompany them, and arrived to find a fleet of ambulances, police cruisers, and official government cars in front of my grandparents' home.

When my great-uncle and husband had described to me the conditions they had found, they had spared me the worst details: black mold covered the walls and ceilings; and it was difficult to breathe due to the intense stench of feces, urine, and rotting trash. The cupboards were bare, the refrigerator inoperative, and there was no running water for drinking, bathing, or cleaning. With no operable HVAC system, the sweltering heat was unbearable. The once-beautiful brick home was now a complete eyesore.

I found my grandparents just as my great-uncle had described. My grandfather was wearing the same undergarment and was sitting in the same urine-saturated chair. Paramedics immediately removed him from the home—against his will—and transported him to the ER. He was in a life-threatening condition and unable to maintain consciousness due to extremely high blood pressure. My grandmother was curled up in the fetal position upon a rotting mattress. Maggots were swarming in the waste that she was forced to lie in. Oblivious to the horror of her environment, my grandmother greeted me with enthusiasm.

For hours, the intervention team and I tried to persuade my grandmother to go to the hospital. She refused, stating there was nothing wrong with her. When the APS workers informed her she could not live in such conditions, my grandmother was grossly offended. She told the worker that she had a beautiful home and scolded her for being so critical. Then, at 5:00 p.m., the APS workers prepared to depart. Panicking, I pleaded with them not to leave, but their day was over. They left. Dismayed, I called the afterhours crisis unit.

The crisis worker was familiar with the case because of my many calls over the past four days. She expressed frustration that APS had made no attempt to get an emergency custody order and had passed the case off. Once at the house, the worker quickly surveyed the premises and looked in on my grandmother. Promising that the "nonsense" would end, within an hour she obtained an emergency custody order and instructed paramedics to remove my grandmother from her home. Though my grandmother was hysterical, I was relieved. Both of my grandparents were finally safe.

In the following days, I acquainted myself with the hospital staff in order to help monitor my grandparents' conditions and to protect them from my uncle. One day, a nurse informed me that my uncle had visited, and it appeared that my grandmother was signing checks for him. While my grandparents were fighting for their lives, my uncle was still using their funds.

The Court Case

I hastened to make a plan for my grandparents' discharge and to institute a measure of protection for them from my uncle. I felt like a sitting duck, appearing calm and cool on the water's surface, but paddling like mad underneath.

Despite making phone calls for a full day, nothing was accomplished. During my final call, I was referred to an Assistant Commonwealth's Attorney (ACA) who was known as a staunch elder advocate. Expecting to reach her voicemail, I was elated when she answered in person. She listened as I explained the situation and my concerns, instructing me to come to the courthouse the next morning and bring any photos and documentation: she would arrange a hearing to request an order of protection for my grandparents. I thanked her and began preparing for the unconventional court appearance (so called because in the eyes of the law, I had no legal authority to request a protective order). Luckily, while at my grandparents' house during the intervention, I had used my cell phone to take photographs and video recordings; and I prepared a succinct presentation of the circumstances.

The next morning, I met briefly with the ACA who helped me muster the courage to go before the judge.

The judge listened to my story, but explained that I could not ask for this kind of protective order against my uncle on behalf of my grandparents. He said that such an order could only be solicited by the person in need of protection, the next of kin (if the person is unable to make such a petition), or the legal guardian. I stated that none of these parties were able to make the request, and that my grandparents were in grave danger. The judge, with some hesitation, granted a temporary protective order and explained that I should return in two weeks for another hearing to determine if a permanent protective order was necessary.

The judge then asked why my uncle had not been arrested. The ACA clarified that my family had been making reports for years, and that APS was involved, but that a case was never created. Dissatisfied with this, the judge directed the ACA to call the police to get a warrant for my uncle's arrest. He also advised that I should take the necessary steps to become the legal guardian and conservator for my grandparents. He allowed that this would cost me thousands of dollars in legal fees and require proving my grandparents' legal incapacity, but would give me the authority to represent my grandparents' best interests. Finally, he informed me that in order to represent my grandparents at the permanent protective order hearing in two weeks, I would have to confirm that I had initiated this complex legal process.

By mid-afternoon, I had been interviewed by several police officers and a warrant against my uncle was obtained. He was arrested and incarcerated. The sergeant in charge apologized that his unit had failed my family and assured me that he would do whatever necessary to be of assistance. Though saddened by the measures taken that day, I felt victorious—and exhausted; I

knew this undertaking would be all-consuming. Upon returning home, I contacted my employer to request an extended leave of absence (which later led to my resignation).

My mission was to care for my grandparents. Although I lacked the legal authority to act on their behalf, my family respected my wishes, for no one else was similarly involved. I decided to relocate my grandparents to a nursing home near me and hired legal representation for the guardian/conservatorship proceedings. I worked closely with the ACA and investigators to prosecute my uncle for abusing and neglecting my grandparents. My uncle remained incarcerated, with his requests for bond denied three times.

The Aftermath

Trying to put together the pieces of my grandparent's lives was difficult since both were diagnosed with Alzheimer's-type dementia. I discovered dozens of delinquent accounts that had gone to collection—tens of thousands of dollars in debts. I found out that every day my uncle would persuade my grandmother to write him a check, telling her the money was for household bills. He would cash the check at a convenience store, buy a case of beer, and drink it while sitting in my grandparents' driveway. He also abused a variety of prescription drugs.

Further investigation revealed that the city's building inspector was aware of the situation: the inspector had made multiple visits to the property and had left numerous citations for the hazardous environmental conditions. Unfortunately, no action was taken to report these findings to the authorities, despite the fact that the inspector knew an elderly couple resided in the home with their son. Within two weeks of the intervention, the property was condemned. The home, once valued at $175,000, was reappraised and reassessed. With the permission of the Commissioner of Accounts, I sold the house to an investor for its true value of $32,000, in order to pay my grandparents' debts and mounting medical expenses.

Through numerous court appearances and continuances over an eight-month period, my uncle avoided going to trial. With an overwhelming amount of evidence, he eventually pleaded guilty to two felony charges of the abuse and neglect of an incapacitated adult. He was sentenced to ten years on each charge and mandated to serve three years incarcerated and seventeen on probation.

My grandfather passed away four months after the intervention and my grandmother joined him eleven months later. Though a tragic story, I find great peace in knowing that they were well cared for and happy during their final months of life. This was my life's most challenging and demanding period, but it was also the most meaningful. I will forever cherish my memories of my grandparents.

Conclusion

In retrospect, there were ample opportunities for professionals to intervene. In order to prevent elder abuse and neglect in the future, there must be better inter-agency communication, more personal responsibility taken by agency staff members, collaboration between well-trained professionals, and increased community awareness. Focused research, preventative programs, reformed policies and practices, and increased social awareness of what constitutes elder abuse can help to protect older people and, ultimately, eradicate this heartbreaking problem.

References

Elder Serve Act of 2009, H. R. 973, 111th Cong. (2009). www.gpo .gov/fdsys/pkg/BILLS-111hr973ih/pdf/BILLS-111hr973ih.pdf. Retrieved July 2012.

Spencer, C., and Smith, J. 2000. "Elder Abuse & Substance Abuse: Making the Connection." *Nexus,* a publication for NCPEA affiliates. www.preventelderabuse.org/nexus/spencersmith.html. Retrieved July 2012.

Critical Thinking

1. The article states that two-thirds of cases of elder abuse are perpetrated by family caregivers. Why do you think this is the case?

2. Why can it be so difficult to intervene on behalf of an elderly family member who you suspect may be being abused or taken advantage of?

3. How does elder abuse within a family alter family roles and family dynamics?

4. What can be done to prevent elder abuse?

Create Central

www.mhhe.com/createcentral

Internet References

National Council on Aging
   www.ncoa.org
National Center on Elder Abuse
   www.ncea.aoa.gov
Alzheimer's Association
   www.alz.org

Article

Prepared by: Patricia Hrusa Williams,
University of Maine at Farmington

Alcohol and Drug Misuse: A Family Affair

A shift in the way we understand addiction problems towards a family-inclusive focus has the potential to benefit millions—both those engaging in problematic consumption and those impacted by their behaviour.

ALEX COPELLO

Learning Outcomes

After reading this article, you will be able to:

- Identify the types of harm associated with alcohol and drug misuse.

- Explain the types of supports needed by families affected by substance abuse.

- Describe three different types of family interventions that can be used with individuals and their families affected by addiction.

Alcohol and drug problems tend to be conceptualised as difficulties experienced by an individual, with attention centred on the impact of consumption on the substance user. The predominant focus tends to be either physical symptoms (e.g. signs of tolerance or withdrawal) or psychological factors (motivational, behavioural and/or cognitive). The main belief is that if the therapist or counsellor can make an impact on these factors, it will lead to improvements in the substance-related problem. The resulting help tends to be individually tailored, and occurs within the confines of the treatment or counselling room. While individual work has benefited numerous people experiencing addiction problems, I would like to argue that the adoption of a social focus, involving 'thinking family', can make a significant contribution to the practice and to improved outcomes in this field.

The way in which the concept of harm reduction has been mostly applied is somewhat narrow, stressing mainly the physical aspects of the reduction of harm. Yet the social and family harm that arises when an addiction problem develops is significant, and there is much potential for reducing this harm, even when the substance user is not in contact with services, or has not yet engaged in behaviour change. The facts that engagement in treatment of the substance user can be triggered when working with affected family members, and that substance misuse outcomes are at least as good (and more often superior)

when using family-based approaches, strengthen the argument for an increased family focus in services and interventions.

In order to move along the track of family-based approaches, we need to move away from an individualistic view of addiction problems, and to conceive of them instead as problems that have a significant social component—that both impact upon and are to a great extent influenced by the social environment of the substance user. Social interaction can help to shape behaviour, and families and social networks can influence the process of treatment entry as well as addictive behaviour change.

The Impact of Addiction on Families

When an addiction problem develops, those close to the person with the substance problem (mostly family members, but also friends) tend to be significantly affected. Time and again, studies exploring stress in family members living with someone with an addiction problem show high levels of physical and psychological symptoms resulting from this stress, and on a par with those experienced by people approaching mental health services due to anxiety and depression.[1-3] The actual experience of living with and being concerned about someone with an alcohol or drug problem has been described in some detail.[4] It has the nature of severe stress, threat, and abuse, and involves multiple sources of threat to the self and the family—emotional, social, financial, and health and safety-related. Family members also report that it can have a significant impact on children, and that worry is a prominent feature. Attempting to cope creates difficult dilemmas, and there is no guidance on the subject. While social support for the family is needed, it often tends to fail, and professionals who might help are often badly informed at best, and sometimes unhelpfully critical.

When interviewed about their experience of living with someone with a substance misuse problem,[4] family members report two separate, yet related, needs. First, they need to understand the problem they are facing, and to receive support in their own right—which involves receiving accurate information about addiction problems and their effects. Second, they tend to want to contribute to the treatment of their substance-misusing relative if possible, which in some cases may involve helping to promote the substance user's entry into treatment.

Family-Based Interventions: The Research Evidence

A number of intervention approaches have been developed to involve family members in addiction treatment, some of which focus on the family members' own needs.

Two reviews of the academic literature[5,6] have summarised social and family addiction treatments.

These concluded that when all strands of evidence are considered, there is a compelling case to recommend implementation of family intervention approaches in routine clinical practice. Recent NICE guidance on psychosocial interventions for drug misuse has recommended an approach based on working with couples: behavioural couple therapy,[7] and also stresses the need to respond to families in their own right when they approach routine drug services.[8]

Family interventions are of three types:

- those that aim to involve family members in the treatment of the substance user
- those that work with families to promote the entry into treatment of the substance user
- those focused on the needs of family members in their own right.

Involving Family Members in Treating the Substance User

Most interventions that have been reported in the research literature relate to involving family members in the treatment of the substance misuser. This category includes approaches that involve working with the family (and in some cases wider social networks) and substance user together, where the main focus is on the substance user and improvement of the substance user's behaviour. A secondary positive outcome may be a benefit for the family members involved, but, on the whole, the approaches are driven by the aim of reducing substance-related behaviour. Most approaches that have been evaluated are based on cognitive and behavioural models. However, there is some tradition of family therapy, particularly with drug problems. Two examples of evaluated interventions of this type are described below.

Behavioural couple therapy (BCT) is a well established and researched approach to working with couples in which one spouse has an alcohol or drug problem. Recently recommended for implementation by NICE, this approach uses a range of cognitive and behavioural strategies. BCT aims to engage the family's support for the client's efforts to change by working on couple and family interactions in a way that promotes a stable relationship that supports stable abstinence.[7]

Social behaviour and network therapy (SBNT)[9,10] is a family and social network approach that was originally developed for the UK Alcohol Treatment Trial (UKATT). The model drew from a range of evidence-based approaches with a social and

family focus. The central idea is that social support is key in facilitating and supporting change in people with alcohol and drug problems. In the language of SBNT, this is called 'social support for a positive change in substance use'. The approach was tested in UKATT,[11] and found to be as effective and as cost-effective as the more established motivational enhancement therapy (MET). Both treatments led to positive outcomes for those receiving them, including significant reductions in alcohol consumption and mental health problems.

SBNT involves a range of different themes and strategies. In the early stages of the intervention, therapists are encouraged to draw a network diagram in order to identify the important people in the problem substance user's social environment. This usually helps both the focal client (a term used in SBNT to denote the person with the alcohol or drug problem) and the therapist to start what we describe as 'thinking network' (i.e. begin understanding the problem as influencing and being influenced by the problem drinker's social environment). At this stage, network members may be invited to join treatment sessions if this is considered appropriate by both client and therapist. Efforts can then focus on strengthening the network, through discussing themes of communication, coping, sharing information, and joint activities. Therapists are trained to work through a coherent set of strategies, driven by the overall aim of developing social support either for a change in substance use or for the maintenance of previous gains. A further important aspect is that the SBNT therapist or counsellor can continue to work with any part of the network that remains engaged in the treatment process. This can help, for example, in cases where the substance user lapses, or has a setback, and temporarily stops attending. Work can continue with network members to support re-engagement of the substance user at this difficult time, as well as to explore the impact of the relapse on network members.

Working with Families to Promote Treatment Entry of the User

Examples of interventions that focus on working with family members as a way of triggering treatment entry include community reinforcement and family training[12] (CRAFT) and the pressures to change (PTC) approach.[13] Both approaches were developed to enable services to respond when family members approach asking for help with a substance misuse situation. Both are structured, and involve some initial exploration of the family member's circumstances, followed by a discussion to explore ways of promoting treatment entry by the user. This can sometimes take place through the family member making a direct request, which can be planned and practised during therapy sessions.

Focusing on the Needs of Family Members

Interventions that involve working directly with family members and seeing them as people with needs in their own right are the least developed in terms of research. The 5-step intervention[14,15] constitutes one example, based on a 'stress-strain-coping-support' model of addiction and the family. An important principle of the

5-step model is that living with a highly stressful experience, such as the impact of an addiction problem in the family, may lead to psychological and physical symptoms of ill-health for family members other than the substance user. Family members in this predicament try to respond to the situation by employing a range of 'coping' behavioural strategies. Coping behaviours, along with available social support, can influence the extent of the stress experienced by family members, as well as the course and development of the addiction problem. As part of the 5-step intervention, family members receive support that is structured around five steps, covering the following specific areas: listening nonjudgmentally; providing relevant information; exploring ways of responding and interacting with the substance misuser; discussing the family member's available and potential social support; and establishing the need for further help. The 5-step intervention has been evaluated in a number of studies in primary care[16,17] and specialist settings,[18] and shown significant promise for reducing physical and psychological stress symptoms. Other approaches focused on family members include programmes for parents of substance misusing adolescents, such as behavioural exchange systems training[19] (BEST); and parent coping skills training.[20] Although the underlying model of the approaches discussed so far is very different, there are some obvious parallels with mutual-aid groups for affected family members, including Al-Anon.[21]

Moving Towards Family-Focused Services

From a research point of view, a number of family interventions have shown enough promise that they can be recommended with confidence for routine service provision. However, beyond the application of specific techniques is the more fundamental issue of impacts on the family and wider social network. Addressing this involves the development of a family-focused way of working and thinking in every case; incorporating a range of strategies to help families dealing with addiction problems; and moving towards the development of family-focused routine addiction services.

In our recent research work with addiction teams,[22] we have found that a combination of the 5-step approach and SBNT can be used flexibly in order to provide a framework for services to increase family-focused and family-inclusive practice into routine, mainstream addiction work. In these studies, whole teams have received training in the 5-step and SBNT methods in workshop format, followed by regular monthly team consultancy and supervision meetings with the researchers over 10–12 months in order to facilitate the development of family-focused practice. Services can then be responsive to family members in their own right, using the 5-step method, or run joint SBNT sessions, including the focal client and their family and network members, if this is considered appropriate and helpful by all involved. Some examples of the type of work conducted by teams as part of this project are summarised in Table 1.

Working in a family-focused way brings challenges to service providers and therapists. The traditional way of thinking about substance-misusing individuals and problems has to give

Table 1 Examples of Family-Focused Work Conducted by Teams

Some examples of the diversity of relationships between the focal client and their family members and wider support network

- Wife
- Husband
- Fiancée
- Mother and father of 18-year-old client
- Wife, sister and brother-in-law
- A friend
- Two neighbours

Some examples of the diversity of therapeutic work with family members

- Focal client and daughter for one session
- Three sessions with a couple, followed by sessions with the client alone
- Client alone, with mother once, then with father once
- One session with the client and their partner, followed by a large family meeting
- Home detoxification, involving five joint sessions with the client's spouse and sometimes other family members

Some examples of the diversity of gains from family/network involvement

- Family members feel calmer
- Conflict handled in the safer environment of the therapy session
- Support for the family after the client has died
- Reassurance after relapse
- Improvement in communication and mutual understanding
- All have a clear goal and plan

way to a broader view of addiction as a family and social problem affecting more than one person. In our experience, this requires a shift in thinking. Existing policies may need to be revised; ways of recording work reviewed; and contracts for services based on individual approaches closely examined.

In introducing the SBNT approach to teams of therapists in our research, we have found that initial concerns regarding the involvement of family members and friends (eg regarding client choice, family members taking over meetings, conflicts arising in sessions, and issues of confidentiality) give way to a more positive view and a problem-solving approach over time. As practitioners gain experience of working in this way, they report developing a clearer picture of the problem through the involvement of concerned and affected others; being able to extend the impact of the work beyond the actual session; and improved relationships between the client with the alcohol or drug problem and affected family members, which can then increase mutual support. Such therapists are better able to see and communicate the benefits of involving families in routine addiction practice, both to clients and their family members, and to the service as a whole.

References

1. Svenson, L., Forster, D., Woodhead, S., Platt, G. *Individuals with a chemical-dependent family member. Does their health care use increase?* Canadian Family Physician. 1995; 41:1488–1493.

2. Ray, G., Mertens J, Weisner C. *The excess medical cost and health problems of family members of persons diagnosed with alcohol or drug problems.* Medical Care. 2007; 45:116–122.

3. Ray, G., Mertens, J., Weisner C. *Family members of people with alcohol or drug dependence: health problems and medical cost compared to family members of people with diabetes and asthma.* Addiction. 2009; 104:203–214.

4. Orford, J., Natera, G., Copello A et al. *Coping with alcohol and drug problems: the experiences of family members in three contrasting cultures.* London; Taylor and Francis; 2005.

5. Copello, A., Velleman, R., Templeton, L. *Family interventions in the treatment of alcohol and drug problems.* Drug and Alcohol Review. 2005; 24:369–385.

6. Copello, A., Templeton, L., Velleman, R. *Family intervention for drug and alcohol misuse: is there a best practice? (invited review).* Current Opinion in Psychiatry. 2006; 19:271–276.

7. O'Farrell, TJ., Fals-Stewart, W. *Behavioral couples therapy for alcoholism and drug abuse.* New York: Guilford Press; 2006.

8. National Collaborating Centre for Mental Health. *Drug misuse: psychosocial interventions. Commissioned by National Institute for Health and Clinical Excellence (NICE). National clinical practice guideline number 51.* London: The British Psychological Society/The Royal College of Psychiatrists; 2008.

9. Copello, A., Orford, J., Hodgson, R., Tober, G., Barrett, C. *On behalf of the UKATT Research Team (2002). Social behaviour and network therapy: basic principles and early experiences.* Addictive Behaviors. 2009; 27:345–366.

10. Copello, A., Orford, .J, Hodgson, R., Tober, G. *Social behaviour and network therapy for alcohol problems.* London: Brunner-Routledge; 2009.

11. UKATT Research Team. *Effectiveness of treatment for alcohol problems: findings of the randomised UK alcohol treatment trial.* British Medical Journal. 2005; 331:541–544.

12. Meyers, R., Miller, W., Hill, D., Tonigan J. *Community reinforcement and family training (CRAFT): engaging unmotivated drug users in treatment.* Journal of Substance Abuse. 1999; 10:291–308.

13. Barber, JG., Crisp, BR. *The 'pressures to change' approach to working with the partners of heavy drinkers.* Addiction. 1995; 90:269–276.

14. Copello, A., Orford, J., Velleman, R., Templeton, L., Krishnan, M. *Methods for reducing alcohol and drug related family norm in non-specialist settings.* Journal of Mental Health. 2000; 9:329–343.

15. Copello, A. *Responding to addiction in the family: natural and assisted change in coping behaviour.* PhD thesis, University of Birmingham; 2003.

16. Copello, A., Templeton, L., Krishnan, M., Orford, J., Velleman, R. *A treatment package to improve primary care services for relatives of people with alcohol and drug problems.* Addiction Research. 2000; 8:471–484.

17. Copello, A., Templeton, L., Velleman, R et al. *The relative efficacy of two primary care brief interventions for family members affected by the addictive problem of a close relative: a randomised trial.* Addiction. 2009; 104:49–58.

18. Templeton, L. *Use of a structured brief intervention in a group setting for family members living with substance misuse.* Journal of Substance Use. 2009; 14:223–232.

19. Toumbourou, J., Blyth, A., Bamberg, J., Forer, D. *Early impact of the BEST intervention for parents stressed by adolescent substance abuse.* Journal of Community and Applied Social Psychology. 2001; 11:291–304.

20. McGillicuddy, NB., Rychtarik, RG., Duquette, JA., Morsheimer ET. *Development of a skill training program for parents of substance-abusing adolescents.* Journal of Substance Abuse Treatment. 2001; 20:59–68.

21. Humphreys, K. *Circles of recovery: self-help organizations for addictions.* Cambridge: Cambridge University Press; 2004.

22. Orford, J., Templeton, L., Copello, A., Velleman, R., Ibanga, A., Binnie C. *Increasing the involvement of family members in alcohol and drug treatment services: the results of an action research project in two specialist agencies.* Drugs: Education, Prevention and Policy. 2009; 16:1–30.

Critical Thinking

1. What is meant by the concept of "harm reduction?" What kinds of harm might alcohol and drug misuse bring to the individual and family?

2. Why is there such an individualistic view of addiction problems?

3. How might the involvement of the family in treatment promote recovery? What problems or issues might arise when families are involved?

Create Central

www.mhhe.com/createcentral

Internet References

Substance Abuse and Mental Health Services Administration
www.samhsa.gov

National Institute of Alcohol Use and Alcoholism
www.niaaa.nih.gov

ALEX COPELLO is Professor of Addiction Research at The School of Psychology, University of Birmingham, and Consultant Clinical Psychologist with the Birmingham and Solihull NHS Foundation Trust addiction services. His career has combined clinical and academic work, and his special areas of interest include the study of the impact of addiction on families, and the development and evaluation of family and social network-based interventions.

Acknowledgements—This article draws on research that I have been involved in, working with close collaborators over the years, in particular Lorna Templeton, Jim Orford, and Richard Velleman.

Article

Prepared by: Patricia Hrusa Williams,
University of Maine at Farmington

Impact of Family Recovery on Pre-Teens and Adolescents

Virginia Lewis and Lois Allen-Byrd

Learning Outcomes

After reading this article, you will be able to:

• Describe the Family Recovery Project.

• Identify the developmental recovery stages.

• Summarize the effects of recovery on pre-teens and adolescents.

• Identify treatment recommendations.

When discussing parental alcoholism, it is often assumed that the parent's entry into recovery will resolve all problems. However, our research, which examined the impact of family recovery from alcoholism, shows that rather than being a unifying force for all family members, this process is traumatic, with pre-teens and adolescents frequently becoming the "forgotten" members of the family. The effects upon these forgotten members can be explained and understood in the context of recovery stages and family types. The purpose of this article is threefold: (1) to present a very complex process called family recovery, (2) to describe its traumatic impact on pre-teens and adolescents, and (3) to provide treatment suggestions for supporting young people.

The Family Recovery Project

In 1989, Drs. Stephanie Brown and Virginia Lewis were the first researchers to study the processes of family recovery from alcoholism. This research marked a dramatic shift from understanding how alcoholism affects all family members, to identifying the dynamics of family recovery and its influence on all aspects of family and individual functioning.

There were three questions of interest to this project: 1) What happens to the family when one or both parents stop drinking? 2) Is there a normal developmental process of recovery? and 3) What allows some alcoholic families to maintain recovery while others relapse (often repeatedly)?

Methodology

The research methodology was a cross-sectional design, studying 54 volunteer families who ranged in sobriety from a few months to 18 years. The study was multi-perspective (participants' data and researchers' observations) and multi-level (tests that measured individual, dyad, and family dynamics) in order to obtain a comprehensive picture of family recovery dynamics. In addition, two types of data analysis were used—qualitative (research team analyzing video tapes to determine individual and family functioning) and quantitative (a battery of paper/pencil measures administered to each family member). (Specific information on research methodology and results can be found in Brown & Lewis, 1995, 1999; Brown, Lewis, & Liotta, 2000; Petroni, Allen-Byrd, & Lewis, 2003; Rouhbakhsh, Lewis, & Allen-Byrd, 2004.)

Due to the focus of this research, the drinking stage and its impact upon family members were studied retrospectively. Families were asked to describe the drinking years which, when combined with the data collected, provided a before and after sobriety perspective. Although painful for many, this journey into the past was necessary as family recovery cannot be fully understood without knowing what life was like, individually and systemically, during the drinking years.

Important Findings

Information from this research revealed that: a) there are normal developmental stages of recovery, b) there are different types of recovering families, and c) the early years of recovery are very traumatic. These latter two findings were surprising and clinically significant. For example, we found that the type of recovering family impacts stage development and requires different treatment approaches for both type of family and stage of recovery. The concept that the early years of recovery were traumatic came from the families' descriptions that this time was very disruptive, frightening, and dynamic. However, rather than being a negative, this "trauma" was normal, allowing for the disequilibrium and collapse of the addictive processes at the individual and system levels. In its place was a void without a map of how to navigate this necessary state. In time, the void was replaced with new knowledge, coping skills, and real-time functioning, providing the parents stayed in recovery through participation in 12-step programs, remained abstinent, and used various treatment modalities (individual, marital, familial) at different times during the recovery journey.

The early years of recovery are very traumatic.

These findings led to the emergence of two theoretical models: The Family Recovery Model and The Family Recovery Typology Model. Both models are briefly discussed below.

The Family Recovery Model

The Family Recovery Model captures the complex nature of family recovery. This complexity is critical for clinicians to understand because *rather than being the end point, abstinence is the beginning of a long and arduous journey that affects all functioning within a family.*

The Family Recovery Model has two dimensions: time and domain. Time is noted by four developmental stages: (1) drinking, (2) transition, (3) early recovery period, and (4) ongoing recovery period. Each domain is examined at three levels: the environment (family atmosphere); the system (family functioning—roles, rules, routines, communication patterns); and the individual (all family members, their emotions, cognitions, behaviors). The three domains are described in detail in *The Alcoholic Family in Recovery* (Brown & Lewis, 1999).

Developmental Recovery Stages

The following is a brief discussion of the three developmental recovery stages. See Box 1 for a summary of this information.

Transition Stage. This stage, which is characterized by the individual moving from drinking to abstinence, can last for several years during which there may be frequent shifts by the alcoholic between drinking and sobriety. The alcoholic feels completely out of control and the family system is in total chaos. The abstinence sub-stage is referred to as the "trauma of recovery"— there is the relief of sobriety and the utter terror of relapse. For example, although the adults in the family are feeling confused, frightened, and out of control, they are attempting to attend meetings and learning that recovery is possible. Their children, however, typically have no one available to them for support, information, or guidance, leaving them also feeling frightened and confused.

Early Recovery Stage. In this stage, the learning curve is steep for the parents as they are learning self-responsibility and self-care, and are slowly acquiring non-addictive lifestyles. It is a time of tremendous acquisition and application of knowledge. The alcoholic and co-alcoholic (spouse) are breaking addictive interactive patterns and learning to "separate" in order to develop their own individuality. Children and adolescents may cope by withdrawing, acting-out, "adopting" a friend's family, or attending 12-step meetings.

Ongoing Recovery Stage. In this stage, the process of recovery is becoming internalized. Recovery has become a central organizing principle (main force of focus) for the alcoholic and co-alcoholic. Life feels manageable and healthy. Problems, when they do occur, are addressed and resolved whenever possible. Parents can tolerate hearing about their children's pain and anger during the drinking and early recovery years. There is a process of healing between the parents and their now late adolescent or adult children.

Family Recovery Typology Model

The second theoretical model with significant implications for understanding recovery emerged from the finding that there were three types of families who differed dramatically from one another in terms of their recovery process. There were families who, regardless of time in recovery, seemed successful in their recovery processes while others appeared trapped in their dysfunctional patterns despite abstinence by the alcoholic.

Box 1
Family Recovery Model: Three Developmental Recovery Stages

	Transition	**Early Recovery**	**Ongoing Recovery**
Drinking			
Alcoholic/Spouse	Alcoholic moves from drinking to abstinence; may involve frequent shifts between drinking and sobriety, lasting several years.	Alcoholic and spouse are breaking addictive interactive patterns.	The family recovery process is becoming internalized.
Children	Alcoholics' children typically have no supports, information, or guidance available at this time. They are left feeling frightened and confused.	Alcoholics' children may be left to cope by withdrawing, "acting out," "adopting" a friend's family, or attending 12-step meetings.	By this point, most children are now adult age. A possible healing process between the parents and children may begin.

The "successful" family style was the Type I family—both spouses were in recovery attending 12-step programs, accepting responsibility for change, and participating in therapy at different points in time. They practiced their sobriety, and recovery was a central organizing principle. The more rigid, stuck, and dysfunctional styles were found in the Type II and Type III families. In the Type II family, only one spouse was in recovery (typically the alcoholic who attended AA meetings), and the family environment and system retained the alcoholic dynamics, influences, and tensions. The alcoholic straddled two worlds: individual recovery and marital/family non-recovery. In the Type III family (of which there were only a few and the alcoholics were all males with short-term recovery), the alcoholics just quit drinking without participation in any 12-step program. Although they "looked" the best on the tests (probably due to denial of any problems), they were the most rigid and stilted in the interviews.

Effects of Recovery on Pre-Teens and Adolescents

Recovery is a life-long process for families that is very complex, traumatic, and utterly confusing in the early years. One major and disheartening discovery in our research was that pre-teens and adolescents were generally ignored in recovery (similar to their experiences during the drinking years). When one or both spouses became sober and began participating in 12-step programs, they became immersed in working at staying sober. For example, they attended meetings, spoke a new language (recovery terms), and developed new relationships. They were told that their number one focus was to stay abstinent. The result was that their children lacked much-needed effective and active parenting.

For pre-teens and adolescents, the early years of recovery were often worse than the drinking years. For example, they had learned how to "function" in the alcoholic system while the alcoholic was drinking; but with recovery, everything changed with no understanding of what was happening to their family. According to several adult children in the study, they "preferred" the drinking period to early recovery for a variety of reasons. For example, they had learned how to read some of the "signs" associated with drinking, (such as the alcoholic going on a binge, the first drink of the day), and, consequently, knew how to affect damage control. Initial recovery, on the other hand, was fraught with unpredictable, traumatic and out-of-control dynamics resulting in uncertainty on the part of the adolescent on how to deal with these new issues.

The following vignettes demonstrate the impact of alcoholism and recovery on adolescents.

Vignette 1

In one family, the oldest adolescent overdosed on over-the-counter medication (an attempt to break the denial that there was a problem). As she was going to the hospital, she handed her mother a note saying, "Please go to AA, you are an alcoholic." Initially her mother refused, but in time she became sober, both parents went into recovery, and they became a Type I family. For the first few months in the Transition Stage, the teens would come home, find no food on the table, and become angry. "Our parents got their own place (e.g., AA and AlAnon) and new 'parents' (sponsors), and we lost the parents we knew." Six months later, the youngest child left home as he found the changes and abandonment too painful. When this family was interviewed, they were in the Ongoing Recovery Stage and the parents had developed close relationships to their now adult children. This closeness and healing was hard-earned, requiring individual, couple, and family therapy at different times in the recovery years.

Vignette 2

A late adolescent child in the study became very anxious during the research interview. His parents had been in recovery for years and were a Type I family in the Ongoing Recovery Stage. While they were describing the drinking years, he became aware of how much he had denied that there was a problem in the family while growing up. His mother (who kept her alcohol stash in a closet in his room) would frequently drive him to school functions while drunk—behavior he would say was normal or not his problem. He began to frequently stay over at his friend's house thus "adopting" another set of parents in his early teens. Since no one commented, he thought it was normal. As the interview progressed, he said, "This is making me question my reality checks, my perceptions of life." What had been his constructed reality of himself and his family was being shattered. This is threatening for young people launching into adulthood as it questions their identity and their ability to understand reality and their place in the family system. His father said that there was one regret in recovery—that they had abandoned their son to meetings and new people (sponsors, AA members, etc.), and did not help him understand what was happening or how important he was to his parents. This was a common regret expressed by parents who had years of recovery and the ability to reflect on the past (Brown & Lewis, 1999).

Vignette 3

This last vignette is adapted from Lewis and Allen-Byrd (in press) as a brief portrayal of what an adolescent may experience in the transition/early periods of recovery.

Kayla, the oldest child, was the identified caregiver in the family and was gratefully supported by the non-alcoholic parent. She assisted in household decisions and duties, provided parental guidance to the younger children, and had special privileges because of her elevated role and status in the family system. When the parents/family went into recovery, Kayla was, in essence, demoted because as the recovering parent became more actively involved in the family, Kayla's role and functions were no longer needed. Her sense of worth and power, her identity and understanding of her family's reality were taken away when her parents went into recovery leaving Kayla feeling resentful, angry, and bewildered. Without appropriate intervention, adolescents in situations similar to Kayla's will typically act out and/or withdraw from the family.

Treatment Suggestions to Support Young People

With the awareness that family recovery is difficult for pre-teens and adolescents, positive and therapeutic action can be taken. Practitioners can play a vital role in helping children make the transition from drinking into early family sobriety. They can educate the parents, normalize the process of recovery, and provide a safe place for young people to express their fears and feelings. Box 2 provides a number of examples.

The family type will dictate how practitioners can approach parents and provide parenting guidelines. The Type I family will be open and receptive to new ideas and knowledge as both parents are in recovery and accept responsibility for change, growth, and the hope of a healthy family. In the early years, they will require a great deal of external support in the form of sponsors, 12-step members, and therapists.

The Type II and III families present additional issues. In the Type II family, one member is in recovery while the family system remains alcoholic. There is chronic marital and environmental tension that, while unnamed, is typically experienced by the children. For example, the recovering alcoholic

becomes the scapegoat as a way to explain problems and tension in the family, or splitting may occur when the adolescent aligns with one parent against the other. Initially the therapist can effect change by working at the marital level and educating the adults on family recovery (e.g., the three domains of recovery, how every member in the family is impacted by alcoholism, and the danger for relapse when only one parent is in recovery).

Hopefully, with intervention, the Type II family will transition into a Type I family. If the "non-alcoholic" parent refuses marital treatment in order to change the alcoholic system into a recovery system, he/she could join a group that educates families about family recovery.

Pre-teens and adolescents may join another group to become educated about family recovery, to find alternative ways to cope with the tensions and changes, and to acquire healthy ways to begin the separation and individuation process. Frequently, without appropriate intervention, the adolescents in Type II and Type III families become involved in the rebellious, acting-out phase of life.

The Type III families (who were typically in therapy for parent–child issues because their children were identified as the "cause" of the family problems) presented unique challenges. Although the alcoholic stopped drinking, nothing else changed. The alcoholic may have cognitive rigidity (black and white thinking), emotional intolerance, and be on a collision course with the adolescent who is acting out and/or attempting to break away from a stifling, straight jacket, family dynamic. During our research Type III families remained the least clear because of their defensive stance in the interviews and paper-pencil measures. For them, the first step is to break individual and systemic denial. The least threatening approach is an educational format where the adults can attend a parent group to learn about the impact of alcoholism on family members, even though no one is currently drinking, and learn healthier parenting skills (e.g., learn what the developmental needs of the pre-teen and adolescent are). There could be a parallel education group for pre-teens and adolescents wherein they could learn the effect alcoholism had on their lives and the toll it took on their personality development, as well as help them become empowered to alter internalized alcoholic processes and develop healthy choices for their future.

Box 2
Strategies for Facilitating Adolescents' Healthy Transition from Family Drinking to Early Family Sobriety

- Work with parents on basic parenting skills, inform them of the importance of these skills for abating turmoil within the pre-teen and/or adolescent.
- Explain alcoholism and recovery to the pre-teen and adolescent in age-appropriate terms.
- Educate parents on the needs of adolescents who are developmentally leaving the family and may not be interested in becoming involved in the new recovery family structure and dynamics.
- Provide safe parental substitutes for their children.
- Provide opportunities for children and adolescents to become involved in Alateen, Alakid, Alatot.
- Let children know they are not responsible for their parents' alcoholism, recovery, or relapse.
- Encourage parents to ask for help before parent–child problems become a crisis.
- Refer pre-teens and adolescents for individual therapy with a therapist who understands the recovery process and can help the young person navigate through the bewildering and newly emerging family system. The therapy focus should be on helping teens define their own individuality; work through new roles, rules, boundaries; and find their own voice.

(Adapted from Lewis & Allen-Byrd, in press)

Limitations

There were several limitations to the study, noted by the following: (1) the participants were all volunteers; (2) they were educated (high school graduates to all levels of college degrees); (3) they were predominantly Caucasians (multiple attempts were made to recruit a greater ethnic diversity), and (4) small sample size. Further contribution to family recovery could be made by studying single-parent families, court-ordered families, and families from other cultures.

Summary

Family recovery from alcoholism is still an unfamiliar concept in the field of addictions and treatment (Lewis & Allen-Byrd, in press; Brown & Lewis, 1995, 1999). The more knowledgeable practitioners are in the dynamics of recovery, the more effective they will be in helping families and their children move through the normal developmental processes of recovery and launching young people into healthy adulthood.

Practitioners are on the front lines providing vital and appropriate treatment plans and referrals for recovering families with children. Their understanding of the normal processes in the stages of recovery and the knowledge of the different types of families can assist them in creating more successful interventions while minimizing family relapses and preventing adolescents from acting out or withdrawing. Pre-teens and adolescents need a voice and therapists can provide a safe and knowledgeable format for them to be heard and to help guide them through the bewildering times of adolescence in general, and in family systems of recovery, in particular.

References

Brown, S. (1985). *Treating the Alcoholic: A Developmental Model of Recovery*. New York: Wiley.

Brown, S., & Lewis, V. (1995). The alcoholic family: A developmental model of recovery. In S. Brown (Ed.), *Treating Alcoholism* (pp. 279–315). San Francisco: Jossey-Bass.

Brown, S., & Lewis, V. (1999). *The Alcoholic Family in Recovery: A Developmental Model*. New York: Guilford Press.

Brown, S., Lewis, V., & Liotta, A. (2000). *The Family Recovery Guide*. Oakland, CA: New Harbinger Publications.

Lewis, V., & Allen-Byrd, L. (2001). Family recovery typology: A new theoretical model. *Alcoholism Treatment Quarterly, 19*(3), 1–17.

Lewis, V., & Allen-Byrd, L. (in press). Coping strategies for the stages of family recovery. *Alcoholism Treatment Quarterly*, special edition.

Lewis, V., Allen-Byrd, L., & Rouhbakhsh, P. (2004). Understanding successful family recovery: Two models. *Journal of Systemic Therapies, 23*(4), 39–51.

Petroni, D., Allen-Byrd, L., & Lewis, V. M. (2003). Indicators of the alcohol recovery process: Critical items from Koss-Butcher and Lachan-Wrobel analysis of the MMPI-2. *Alcoholism Treatment Quarterly, 21*(2), 41–56.

Rouhbakhsh, P., Lewis, V., & Allen-Byrd, L. (2004). Recovering alcoholic families: When normal is not normal and when is not normal healthy. *Alcoholism Treatment Quarterly, 22*(2), 35–53.

Critical Thinking

1. What are some of the differences between adolescents with substance abuse problems and adults?

2. Looking back at the three vignettes, what would be some advice for families coping with substance abuse?

3. List some of the important concepts in the article that you feel are essential for therapists to know, and explain why you feel they are important.

4. From a research perspective, what do you think about the limitations mentioned? Would the recommendations fit other cultures?

Create Central

www.mhhe.com/createcentral

Internet References

Substance Abuse and Mental Health Services Administration
www.samhsa.gov

National Institute of Alcohol Use and Alcoholism
www.niaaa.nih.gov

VIRGINIA LEWIS, PHD, is co-founder and co-director of the Family Recovery Project and a Senior Research Fellow at the Mental Research Institute (MRI) in Palo Alto, California. **LOIS ALLEN-BYRD, PHD,** is a Research Associate at MRI. Dr. Lewis has co-authored two books on family recovery and both she and Dr. Allen-Byrd have published numerous articles on the subject.

From *The Prevention Researcher*, November 2006, pp. 14–17. Copyright © 2006 by Integrated Research Services, Inc. Reprinted by permission. www.tpronline.com.

Article

Prepared by: Patricia Hrusa Williams,
University of Maine at Farmington

A Guide in the Darkness

When a life starts to unravel, where do you turn for help?

JOHN LELAND

Learning Outcomes

After reading this article, you will be able to:

- Identify the legal, medical, financial, family, and practical challenges faced by families as they navigate the mental health system.

- Explain how having a mentally ill person in the family affects family dynamics.

Melissa Klump began to slip in the eighth grade. She couldn't focus in class, and in a moment of despair she swallowed 60 ibuprofen tablets. She was smart, pretty and ill: depression, attention deficit disorder, obsessive-compulsive disorder, either bipolar disorder or borderline personality disorder.

In her 20s, after a more serious suicide attempt, her parents sent her to a residential psychiatric treatment center, and from there to another. It was the treatment of last resort. When she was discharged from the second center last August after slapping another resident, her mother, Elisa Klump, was beside herself.

"I was banging my head against the wall," the mother said. "What do I do next?" She frantically called support groups, therapy programs, suicide prevention lines, anybody, running down a list of names in a directory of mental health resources. "Finally," she said, "somebody told me, 'The person you need to talk to is Carolyn Wolf.'"

That call, she said, changed her life and her daughter's. "Carolyn has given me hope," she said. "I didn't know there were people like her out there."

Carolyn Reinach Wolf is not a psychiatrist or a mental health professional, but a lawyer who has carved out what she says is a unique niche, working with families like the Klumps.

One in 17 American adults suffers from a severe mental illness, and the systems into which they are plunged—hospitals, insurance companies, courts, social services—can

be fragmented and overwhelming for families to manage. The recent shootings in Newtown, Conn., and Aurora, Colo., have brought attention to the need for intervention to prevent such extreme acts of violence, which are rare. But for the great majority of families watching their loved ones suffer, and often suffering themselves, the struggle can be boundless, with little guidance along the way.

"If you Google *'mental health lawyer,'*" said Ms. Wolf, a partner with Abrams & Fensterman, "I'm kinda the only game in town."

On a recent afternoon, she described in her Midtown office the range of her practice.

"We have been known to pull people out of crack dens," she said. "I have chased people around hotels all over the city with the N.Y.P.D. and my team to get them to a hospital. I had a case years ago where the person was on his way back from Europe, and the family was very concerned that he was symptomatic. I had security people meet him at J.F.K."

Many lawyers work with mentally ill people or their families, but Ron Honberg, the national director of policy and legal affairs for the *National Alliance on Mental Illness,* said he did not know of another lawyer who did what Ms. Wolf does: providing families with a team of psychiatrists, social workers, case managers, life coaches, security guards and others, and then coordinating their services. It can be a lifeline—for people who can afford it, Mr. Honberg said. "Otherwise, families have to do this on their own," he said. "It's a 24-hour, 7-day-a-week job, and for some families it never ends."

Many of Ms. Wolf's clients declined to be interviewed for this article, but the few who spoke offered an unusual window on the arcane twists and turns of the mental health care system, even for families with money. Their stories illustrate how fraught and sometimes blind such a journey can be.

One rainy morning last month, Lance Sheena, 29, sat with his mother in the spacious family room of her Long Island home. Mr. Sheena was puffy-eyed and sporadically inattentive; the previous night, at the group home where he has been living since late last summer, another resident had been screaming incoherently and was taken away by the police. His mother, Susan Sheena, eased delicately into the family story.

"I don't talk to a lot of people because they don't get it," Ms. Sheena said. "They mean well, but they don't get it unless they've been through a similar experience. And anytime something comes up, like the shooting in Newtown, right away it goes to the mentally ill. And you think, maybe we shouldn't be so public about this, because people are going to be afraid of us and Lance. It's a big concern."

Her son cut her off. "Are you comparing me to the guy that shot those people?"

"No, I'm saying that anytime there's a shooting, like in Aurora, that's when these things come out in the news."

"Did you really just compare me to that guy?"

"No, I didn't compare you."

"Then what did you say?"

"I said that when things like this happen, one of the first things you hear about is somebody being mentally ill." She added that her son, like most people with mental illness, has never been violent.

Ms. Wolf, a neighbor who attended the same synagogue, was one of the few people Ms. Sheena talked to about her son. Ms. Wolf started her career as a hospital administrator, then after law school represented hospitals in commitment hearings. Families of mentally ill people, she said, heard about her and began to turn to her for help.

A popular, athletic child, Lance started showing signs of obsessive-compulsive disorder at age 11 and began using drugs around the same age.

"I never had trouble buying drugs because I sold drugs," Mr. Sheena recalled. "And when I wasn't buying drugs I got them from the doctor. Valium, Xanax, Adderall, Ritalin, Seroquel. Finished a bottle of Adderall in 12 hours once. That's like 30 pills, 20 mg each. I was lying under the air-conditioner listening to my heart beat. Finally I woke up, took some Xanax."

Eight years ago, after taking "a lot of prescription drugs and Ecstasy," he said, he landed in the psychiatric ward at North Shore Hospital in a state of drug-induced psychosis. It was the first of several such stays, some by his volition, others against his will. Three years ago, Ms. Sheena came home to find him in the woods behind the house, wearing only shorts and a T-shirt in the January cold.

"The level of life I had in me that was productive was so low," he said. "I was almost homeless, I was a complete bum, and I decided to clean the woods. It was the only thing I could do."

Finally, at a psychiatric hospital upstate, he received a diagnosis of schizophrenia.

"It was tearing us apart," Ms. Sheena said. Her son's three younger brothers were angry at him for the turbulence in their home, she said. His youngest brother, who is now in high school, had never known a normal home life. After that hospitalization three years ago Lance Sheena stopped using drugs—for his mother, he said.

Mr. Sheena returned to school and earned an associate's degree. But his illness follows its own agenda. Last summer, he became flooded with thoughts of death and was hospitalized twice in quick succession, the second time against his will. He left his mother angry messages, which she saved.

"Nasty messages," she said. "'I hate you. Get me out of here.' Nasty."

"Why'd you save them?" he asked.

"I don't know."

"No really, why?"

During that time, Ms. Sheena began turning to Ms. Wolf for help. Ms. Wolf said she could petition to have Mr. Sheena released from the hospital and into a different kind of supervised involuntary commitment, known as assisted outpatient treatment, that would be less restrictive. But she also advised the Sheenas not to let their son move back into the family home.

"We were at a breaking point," Ms. Sheena said. "He would come home and we'd be back in the same roles where I'm looking to see if he's going to his meetings, if he's taking his medicine. What is he doing? Is he sleeping? Is he bouncing off the walls all night?"

It was too much, Ms. Wolf said. "I try to get people off of that, because I have found over these 20-plus years that it works better when you put the professionals in place and the family members go back to being the loved ones," she said.

Ms. Wolf helped Mr. Sheena move to a group home, where he has a case manager and social worker and takes the bus to court-mandated therapy appointments and group meetings. Now, when he returns home to visit, "there's a real sense of calmness in the house," his mother said. "It's wonderful, it's peaceful, it's loving, he sleeps home often on Friday night. And he's doing better because he's not as stressed, because we're not watching him like that."

Mr. Sheena said he was unhappy about not being allowed to move back home. But his life is more stable, he said, and he has started to write about his experiences, with help from his mother.

"Now, he's the best he's been in the last 10 years," she said. "He's come to accept that he's mentally ill, that he has an illness and that it needs to be treated. And I hope he can be better than he is now, but who knows?"

Not all of Ms. Wolf's clients can report even that much hope.

In a Midtown financial services office, a consultant whose son suffers from bipolar schizoaffective disorder described an almost unbroken series of setbacks, with his son now living in an efficiency hotel in Georgia, refusing to take medications or acknowledge that he needs care. To avoid causing more pain to family members, the father would be identified only by his first initial, J., and his son by the initial R.

"It tears your heart out as a parent, believe me," J. said.

J. first met Ms. Wolf more than a decade ago at New York-Presbyterian Hospital, where he was visiting his son and she was representing the hospital in commitment hearings. By that time, R., who is now in his early 40s, had been hospitalized involuntarily several times, each time ceasing treatment after he was released. He lost apartment after apartment, sometimes for harassing the owners or other residents.

Then he took a bigger step, going to the home of a film executive and harassing the man's wife. When he was arrested and charged, his father called Ms. Wolf.

"The D.A. wanted to put him in jail for two years," J. said. His son's criminal lawyer was ready to take a plea deal, which would involve prison time, the father said.

Instead, Ms. Wolf negotiated with the prosecution to allow him to be committed involuntarily to Bellevue Hospital Center. When R. petitioned to go home, saying he did not need treatment, Ms. Wolf argued that he was still a danger to himself and others.

"She went to court for us every Tuesday," the father said, "and we were able to show cause why he should be kept there. And the doctors helped us, but only because Carolyn spoke to them and assisted us."

After nine months in Bellevue, R. was finally discharged, against the efforts of Ms. Wolf and his father. Ms. Wolf engaged a psychiatrist, a case manager, and someone to live with R. to make sure he took his medications. But soon he stopped complying again; nothing was different.

Now, J. would like to see his son in a residential psychiatric center or a hospital. But R. will not go voluntarily, and unless he commits a serious crime, the courts will not commit him long-term.

"I've gone through a fortune, and the system stinks," J. said. "It can be shown by some of these recent killings in Sandy Hook and in Aurora. Or Virginia Tech. These are people who are mentally ill and they've proved that they're mentally ill, who the court system fails and the mental health system fails. You can see the glary, starey eyes of this killer from Aurora in court. I've seen that expression from my son when he's been locked up. And it's because he's totally psychotic."

The day Melissa Klump, now 28, tried to kill herself, in April 2011, she woke with a sense of overwhelming serenity, knowing what she wanted to do. She had fought with her brother the day before, when he blamed her for destroying their parents' marriage.

"I was calm," she said. "I went upstairs, I showered, I did my hair, I put on a nice little cute outfit, I wrote a letter to my grandmother apologizing for what I was about to do, and I wrote that I wanted to be cremated. I lined up all my pills and took a picture and sent it to my brother and I said, Happy Easter. And I downed 20 Xanax and 10 Trazodone, and took it all with a warm Corona.

"Just then my dad started pounding on the door. I opened the door and said, 'This is what you guys wanted, so here you go.' I threw my bottles down the stairs."

At a recent appointment in Manhattan, she arrived early, with polished nails and crisp eye makeup, eager to talk—about her suicide attempt, about her future, about her serial medication regimens: Lexapro, Effexor, Cymbalta, Xanax, Trazodone, Prozac, Klonopin, Lamictal, Ativan. She showed the delicate script tattoos on her wrists, reading "Carpe Diem" on one arm and "La Bella Vita" on the other, covering the places where she'd cut herself with a hot safety pin.

After she was sent home from the treatment center for slapping another resident, her mother took her to see Ms. Wolf, who asked her what her goals were.

"I didn't think she would ask me that," Melissa Klump said. "It seemed nice that she was interested in me as a person. She said she had someone who could help. She also said I was one of her few clients who have goals and plans."

Ms. Wolf arranged for a care manager and a life coach to see Ms. Klump several times a week at her grandmother's house.

Christopher Mooney, the care manager, said he was working with her to meet her goals: to pay down her five-figure credit card debt—the result of a few manic sprees—to set a budget, to make a financial plan; then they will start to look for apartments. "She's got the capability, but she needs someone there to help her make it happen," he said.

Mr. Mooney bills $150 an hour for his time. The life coach, who meets with Ms. Klump more regularly, charges $50 an hour. Ms. Wolf would not discuss her fees.

It adds up, Elisa Klump said, especially on top of all the other expenses. "We're coming to the point where there's going to be no more money left," she said. And still she knows that her daughter could slide back, as could any of the others. Their lives remain subject to powerful forces, both internal and external, for which a lawyer can do only so much.

"We're in baby steps," Elisa Klump said. "She's lost many years of her life. Carolyn put her down the right road. We'll see where she goes."

Critical Thinking

1. What do you see as the greatest challenge faced by families where a member has a mental illness? Why?

2. How can we work with families and patients so they feel safe and not stigmatized?

3. How can we best support families struggling with mental health issues? How might the strategy or approach differ by the patient's age, mental health problem, and the characteristics of their family?

4. Using information gained from this article, describe an intervention or support program that could be developed to facilitate the positive development of families struggling with mental illness.

Create Central

www.mhhe.com/createcentral

Internet References

Substance Abuse and Mental Health Services Administration
   www.samhsa.gov
National Alliance on Mental Illness
   www.nami.org

Prepared by: Patricia Hrusa Williams,
University of Maine at Farmington

Article

From Promise to Promiscuity

HARA ESTROFF MARANO

Learning Outcomes

After reading this article, you will be able to:

- Describe how people cheat on their partners.
- Identify why people cheat.
- Explain what happens to a relationship after infidelity.

As devastating experiences go, few events can match the emotional havoc following the discovery that one's partner is having an affair. Atop a suddenly shattered world hover pain and rejection, doubts about one's worth, and, most searingly, the rupture of trust. For Deanna Stahling, discovery struck in a hallucinatory moment that forever fractured time into Before and After. She had just stepped off a plane from the Caribbean after a week's vacation with a family friend and picked up a copy of the city's leading newspaper. There, in the lifestyles section, was a profile of a top woman executive whose name Deanna had heard a lot lately—her husband worked with the woman. Deanna had even met her—introduced by her husband a few weeks earlier at a corporate function. The exec, it was reported, was leaving the company so that she could ethically pursue a relationship with a colleague.

Deanna doesn't remember the trip home from the airport, but the house was empty and her husband's belongings were gone. A denuded bookshelf highlighted now-missing Giants memorabilia. A note on the kitchen table advised her—after 25 years, two newly fledged kids, and the recent purchase of a joint cemetery plot—to refer any questions to his attorney.

The next morning found Deanna sobbing in a therapist's office. Together they began the search for the source of the sudden defection. Like most therapists (and indeed, most everyone else), they subscribed implicitly to a deficit model of affairs: the presumption that there were fatal problems in the relationship.

Over the past several years, however, leading thinkers have begun to abandon such a pathologizing approach. No one doubts that a straying partner is alone responsible for the often disastrous decision to engage in infidelity. But a new, more nuanced perspective that puts far more emphasis on contextual and situational factors has sparked a revolution in understanding and handling affairs. The new approach encourages as a matter of course what happens now only by chance—complete recovery without any feelings being swept under the rug and even fortification of the couple bond.

The Shifting Landscape of Illicit Love

No one knows for sure just how common affairs are. Social desirability and fear of disclosure skew survey responses significantly. In 1994, 77 percent of 3,432 people constituting a representative sample of Americans declared that extramarital sex is always wrong (although the vast majority of people also have fantasies of engaging in an affair). And the number is actually growing. Today, over 90 percent of respondents deem sexual straying unacceptable—and expect sexual monogamy.

Still, decades of studies show that affairs are common, and, at least historically, more so among men than women: Among American couples, 20 to 40 percent of heterosexual married men and 10 to 25 percent of heterosexual married women will have an affair during their lifetime. In any given year, 1.5 to 4 percent of married individuals engage in an affair.

The newest surveys also reveal a very notable shift in the demographics of deception. Among younger cohorts—those under 45—the rates of infidelity among men and women are converging. Psychologists and sociologists attribute the development to huge changes in sheer opportunity, particularly the massive movement of women out of the home and into the workplace; studies show that the majority of individuals engaged in an affair met their lover at work. The rising financial power of women renders them less risk-averse, because they are less dependent on a spouse for support. As for a longstanding belief that men are more instinctually inclined to sexual infidelity than women are? Well, it's now far more of an open question.

That doesn't mean there are no gender differences in affairs. For women, infidelity is thought to be driven more by emotional needs and is most likely when they are not satisfied in their marital relationship, especially when it is not a partnership of equals. For men, infidelity has long been more independent of the state of the marital relationship. The pioneering psychologist Shirley Glass first reported in 1985 that among individuals engaging in infidelity, 56 percent of men and 34 percent of women rate their marriage as "happy" or "very happy." However, some of these differences may be disappearing, too. In 2003, just before she died, Glass reported that 74 percent of men were emotionally (as well as sexually) involved with their affair partner.

While the landscape of illicit love has been shifting, the therapeutic world has remained fairly fixed in the belief that affairs occur because something is radically wrong with the marriage. Make no mistake—most couples stay and want to stay together after a partner has strayed, despite the enormous psychic trauma to the uninvolved spouse. And indeed, 70 percent of couples choose to rebuild the relationship after infidelity, although they may not know how. Even couples for whom the violation is so painful or incomprehensible that divorce seems the only alternative often later regret a decision made in the highly disorienting days after discovery.

Studies indeed show that relationship dissatisfaction is associated with engaging in extramarital sex. But there's evidence that in almost two-thirds of cases, marital problems are the *effect,* not the cause, of extramarital involvements. Further, affairs themselves skew perceptions of the marriage. Once infidelity has occurred, partners tend to look back on their primary relationship and see it as having been flawed all along—an attempt to reduce cognitive dissonance.

Focusing attention exclusively on relationship flaws, say the field's leading thinkers, encourages couples to get psychologically stuck, brooding on the emotional betrayal and assigning blame. There is no statute of limitations on the hurt and anger that follow a partner's affair. But for the sake of dampening emotional volatility, injured partners are often rushed into "moving on," burying distrust and resentments that fester underground, sometimes for decades, forever precluding restoration of closeness.

Context, Context, Context

Affairs, says Washington, D.C., psychologist Barry McCarthy, are "the absolutely best example of behavior being multicausal, multidimensional. There are many contributing factors. Sometimes they have nothing to do with the marriage. The most common reason for an affair is high opportunity. People fall into affairs rather than plan them." Another very common cause of affairs, he observes, is that "people do not feel desired and desirable in their marriage, and they want to see if they can be desired and desirable outside it." For others, he notes, the affair is a symptom of a mental health problem like alcohol abuse or bipolar disorder. But unless all contributing elements are openly discussed and their meaning evaluated by both partners together, injured partners cannot regain the sense of security that allows them to forgive a straying spouse and rebuild trust in their mate. "The reality is that it takes two people to continue a marriage but only one to terminate a marriage," says McCarthy.

By far the biggest predictor of affairs, experts agree, is sheer opportunity—how people vary in access and desirability to others. And the workplace is the great benefactor, providing large numbers of people with constant contact, common interests, an income to camouflage the costs of socializing outside the office, and an ironclad excuse.

In a study of more than 4,000 adults, reported in the *Journal of Family Psychology,* Donald Baucom and colleagues found that both income and employment status are indices of opportunity for affairs. "Income may not be the critical variable in itself," they offer. "Individuals with higher incomes might be considered to have higher status, to travel more, or to interact professionally with more appealing individuals." In their study, those who worked but whose spouses did not were the most likely to report being unfaithful. Opportunity at the office is most ominous when it mixes with a disparity in relationship power at home.

Travel is way up there, researchers find, especially work related travel. "Lots of elements go into that," says Kristina Coop Gordon, professor of psychology at the University of Tennessee. "You're away from your partner, maybe even missing your mate, and you're in situations where you're encountering

---

The Other Woman

She might be history's most reviled female. Or most misunderstood. She isn't all she's cracked up to be. Sex with her is generally no better than sex in the marriage. And she's not likely to be a bombshell. The most you can say for sure is that she's different from the wife, and that may be all some cheaters need. Most male affairs, which is to say most affairs, are excursions of opportunity with little emotional investment. Worth crying over, yes. But not necessarily worth bringing the house down. Fewer than 25 percent of cheaters leave a marriage for an affair partner, and those relationships are statistically extremely unlikely to endure.

However much the mystery woman incites rage and envy and dreams of malevolence, she falls short of the self-destructive comparisons made against her.

Usually, says University of Tennessee psychologist Kristina Coop Gordon, fixation on the other woman and desire for details about her are not what they seem. "It's really a test of the straying spouse by the wounded one: 'Will you be open with me about the affair?' They really don't want to know the gory details; either it will spark a fight or make them feel bad. The wounded spouse just wants proof that she's important enough."

Sometimes, however, the other woman won't let go. She may threaten retaliation or self-harm. On the other hand, the involved spouse may do a miserable job of setting firm boundaries and not make a clean break of it. "Some men are not quite letting go themselves," Gordon finds. "And they're sending mixed messages to the other woman, which both she and the wife pick up on. That may be one reason a wounded wife can become obsessed with the other woman; there's a continuing threat."

—H. E. M.

plenty of people," Gordon explains. "It certainly facilitates one-night stands." Companies that employ large cohorts of young people, especially those who socialize together after work, create an environment for affairs.

No one profession has a lock on infidelity, Gordon maintains. Most relevant is the culture within a company. "Really macho cultures, which often exist in drug enforcement and police work, can involve a 'player' phenomenon where you need to show how virile you are. They are the clearest examples of work environments that foster infidelity that I've seen."

Duplicity also has a downtown address. Living in the midst of a city abets infidelity. Not only is there exposure to large numbers of potential partners, there's more opportunity to escape detection. The larger the city one lives in, researchers have found, the greater the likelihood of an affair.

Attending religious services is generally a deterrent to infidelity, perhaps because it embeds people in a social network that promotes accountability. But it helps only those who are already happy in their relationship. If the primary relationship is less than ideal, then dissatisfaction overrides religious values. Rates of infidelity do not differ by denomination.

Education increases the propensity to infidelity. It may be a marker for more liberal attitudes toward sexuality and permissive attitudes toward adultery. Ditto a history of divorce, or having parents who divorced, especially if either one had an extramarital involvement. Women with more education than their husbands have more affairs, perhaps because they are less dependent on a spouse.

Friendships are a factor in infidelity. Peer groups may sanction or even encourage it, researchers have found. Those who engage in extramarital involvements estimate a higher prevalence of affairs in their community than those who don't and believe their friends would be relatively approving. Separate his and her friendship networks are especially risky. One way of avoiding infidelity is to share a spouse's social network. Befriending a partner's family proves particularly protective. In one study it was linked to a 26 percent decrease in the odds of sexual infidelity.

Personality differences between partners play a role as well. Spouses who are comfortable with conflict and more or less matched on that trait are less likely to have affairs, perhaps because they are most open to airing marital concerns and dissatisfactions with each other.

In general, openness is protective and a characteristic of non-cheaters. Associated with intelligence, creativity, curiosity, and insightfulness, openness makes partners more satisfied with the relationship and better able to express feelings, including love. Some researchers believe that openness is essential to commitment to and enduring satisfaction in a relationship.

Low levels of agreeableness (the tendency to be compassionate and cooperative) bode poorly for monogamy. More important, however, is whether couples are matched on that trait. Spouses who see themselves as more agreeable than their mate believe themselves to be more giving, feel exploited by their partner, and seek reciprocity through outside relationships. Many studies show that a high level of neuroticism also inclines individuals to infidelity, independent of a partner's personality.

Psychological problems factor in, too. Affairs, associated with insecurity and having low self-esteem, can be a way of seeking reassurance of desirability or of combating depression. An affair certainly provides an arousing stimulus that is an antidote, however temporary, to feeling down. Then, too, affairs are also linked to high self-regard, a sense of one's own attractiveness or entitlement, or maybe the accompaniment to narcissism.

Situations that deplete self-control—exposure to alcohol, an exhausting day of travel, doing highly challenging work—raise the risk of infidelity. They disable sexual restraint, psychologists Roy Baumeister and Matthew Gailliot have found. The two manipulated self-control by giving subjects cognitively demanding or simple word puzzles before presenting them with purely hypothetical scenarios testing their willingness to engage in infidelity. The more demanding the tasks, the more depleted self-control, the more subjects were unable to inhibit their inclination to infidelity or to stifle sexual thoughts. Of course, hypothetical infidelity is a long way from landing in bed with someone.

Hypocrisy or Hormones?

The very make-up of the human brain contributes to affairs, too, observes anthropologist Helen Fisher. She has shown in brain-imaging studies that there are separate neural systems for sex drive, romantic love, and attachment, and they can operate independently. "Everyone starts out in marriage believing they will not have an affair. Why do data from around the world consistently show that infidelity occurs even among people who are happy in their marriage? You can feel deep attachment to a partner but also feel intense romantic love for someone else while also feeling a desire for sex with other partners," she observes.

The attachment system, fueled by the neurohormones oxytocin in females and vasopressin in males, drives animals, including humans, to pair-bond to rear their offspring as a team. Both hormones are triggered by orgasm, and both trigger dopamine release in reward regions of the brain. But all animals cheat, even when they form pair bonds.

In most mammals, the bond lasts only as long as it takes to rear the young. Among prairie voles, science's favorite model of monogamy, knocking out the gene that codes for vasopressin receptors abolishes their penchant for pair-bonding. And implanting it in their notoriously promiscuous cousins, the mountain voles, leads the males to fixate on a specific female partner even when alluring others are abundantly available.

More recently, in a study of over 500 men, Swedish researchers found that variations in a gene that codes for vasopressin receptors in humans influences the very ability to form monogamous relationships. Men with two copies of a specific gene variant scored significantly lower on a questionnaire known as the Partner Bonding Scale and reported twice as many marital crises in the past year. Those with two copies of the variant were also twice as likely to be involved in outside relationships and far less likely to have ever been married than those not carrying the allele.

"Monogamy does not mean sexual fidelity. That is a separate issue," says Fisher. In fact, scientists increasingly speak of "social monogamy" to distinguish promise from promiscuity. If we are monogamous, we are also just as predictably adulterous. What's more, people jeopardize their family, their health, their safety, their social standing, their financial well-being for affairs—and violate their own strong beliefs.

Monogamy may be the norm in human culture, but it is only part of the human reproductive repertoire, contends Fisher. "We humans have a dual reproductive strategy," she argues. "We regularly appear to express a combination of lifelong (or serial) social monogamy and, in many cases, clandestine adultery."

Despite its many risks, and sometimes because of them, there are big payoffs for infidelity, Fisher argues. For men especially, genetic variation is the most obvious. But she believes that women benefit, too. Infidelity may provide a "back-up mate" to offer protection and resources when the regular guy is not around. And women may use affairs as away of "trading up" to find a more desirable partner. It's possible, too, that infidelity can serve a positive role in relationships—as a way to gain attention from one's primary partner or to signal that there are problems in the relationship that need attending to.

In a study reported in 2010 in *PLoS One,* Justin Garcia, a postdoctoral fellow at Binghamton University, outlined another payoff—pure, passionate thrill. He found that individuals with a variant of a dopamine receptor gene were more likely than those without it to have a history of "uncommitted sex, one-night stands, and adultery." The motivation, he says, "stems from a system of pleasure and reward." Fisher suspects that's just the tip of the infidelity iceberg, and more biological contributors are likely to be identified in future studies.

From Angry Victim to Proud Survivor

One of the great facts of infidelity is that it has such a wildly different emotional impact on the marital partners. The uninvolved partner is deeply traumatized and emotionally distraught over the betrayal, and desperately trying to piece together what happened. The straying partner, often because of deep shame, may get defensive and shut down or blame the spouse for not moving on, only compounding the hurt. One needs to talk about what happened; the other can't bear to. "It's as if one of them is speaking German, the other is speaking Greek, and they're not speaking English to each other," McCarthy says.

Getting them on the same track of understanding is the key to recovery from affairs, says Gordon, who along with Baucom and Douglas Snyder, professor of psychology at Texas A&M, has sparked the revolution in treating infidelity not only by focusing on the many contributing factors but by developing the first empirically validated model of recovery. As detailed in their book, *Getting Past the Affair,* the first step is for both spouses to recognize the huge emotional impact on the uninvolved partner. Gordon and company have found a powerful device: After encouraging the partners to make no decisions about the future in the immediate aftermath of discovery or disclosure, they ask that the cheated-on partner write a letter to the spouse describing what the hurt feels like.

"The cheating partner must hear, no matter how discomfiting it is," says Gordon. "The experience is very intense and usually a turning point. Partners begin to soften towards each other. It's a demonstration to the injured partner that he or she really matters."

Then together the spouses search for the meaning of the affair by exploring how the choice was made and what contributed to it. Everything is fair game—attitudes and expectations about marriage that each partner has, conflicts and anything else going on in the relationship, hidden desires, personal anxieties and insecurities, needs for excitement, the closeness and distance they feel, job demands, work ambience, flirtations, opportunities, the people and pressures around them at home and outside it. The approach short-circuits the often misguided inclination to focus on The Other Person.

From understanding flows forgiveness, which allows partners to become close again. Wild as the reaction to discovery of a partner's affair can be in the beginning, Gordon welcomes it. "At least it provides the opportunity to interact around the pain. What often happens with the 'nice' couples," she says, "is they stay together but lead parallel lives marked by great distance. There's no bond anymore."

Renewing Romance

Barry McCarthy gives the revolution in recovery from affairs another twist all his own—re-eroticizing the marriage. "A couple has to develop a new sexual style" that facilitates sexual desire both in and out of the bedroom, he says. The point is to abolish the inclination to compare marital sex with affair sex—a hopeless cause as affair partners don't have to contend with sick kids and other realities of life, and the illicitness of the liaison intensifies excitement—but to compare marital sex before the affair and after it.

For the vast majority of American couples today, sexual satisfaction plummets at the birth of the first child and reemerges, if at all, after the last child leaves home. Of course, it doesn't have to be that way. Admittedly, McCarthy says, "it's a balancing act for partners to maintain their sense of who they are as individuals, their sense of being a couple, and being parents and sexual people." But in the long run, it's in everyone's best interest. Most contemporary couples, he laments, treat sexuality with benign neglect—until an affair sets off a crisis.

In healthy marriages, sex plays what he deems "a relatively small part, a 15 to 20 percent part"—but it energizes the whole bond and allows each partner to feel desired and desirable. When couples abandon sex, they wind up draining the entire relationship of its vitality. "You not only lose the marriage connection but your sense of self," McCarthy finds. "An affair can be an attempt to regain a sense of self."

So McCarthy puts great effort into reconnecting partners both emotionally and physically. He focuses on "non-demand pleasure." "We try to reintroduce the idea of touching inside and outside the bedroom, clothed and not clothed, valuing sensual and playful touch. It can be a bridge to intercourse, but there's no demand that it has to go to intercourse." He encourages couples to find a mutually acceptable level of intimacy and come up with their own erotic scenarios.

Pacts of Prevention

Because good intentions do not prove good enough, McCarthy takes post affair repair one step further—asking couples to create an explicit pact to prevent future infidelity by either of them. Together, they lay out the terms for disclosing when their interest is straying. Having painfully reached an understanding of the complex personal, marital, and situational vulnerabilities that led to an affair, couples draft a relapse prevention agreement.

The purpose is to rob any future affair of its spontaneity and its emotional and sexual secrecy. Both partners are encouraged to articulate the types of situation, mood, and person that could draw them into an affair—and to share that information with each other.

Then they commit to alert the spouse if they are in a high-risk situation and to discuss it rather than act on it. As an incentive, the agreement, drawing on recent experience, spells out the emotional costs to both parties of an affair. Because the secrecy and cover-up of infidelity are often more damaging than the defection itself, partners agree that, if there is a sexual incident, they will disclose it within 72 hours. And it works, McCarthy finds.

The pact of prevention embodies a principle Helen Fisher enunciates most succinctly: "Predisposition isn't predestination."

Six years after her disorienting discovery, Deanna is remarried; her new husband shares her taste for travel and adventure. She can talk dispassionately (with close friends) about the thin spots that likely existed all along in her first marriage. She understands how her frequent travels as a consultant, although they never tempted *her* to stray, carried intimations of abandonment for her more anxious ex. And how, under the circumstances, his conversations with an attentive female coworker could have evolved from the collegial to the confidential almost imperceptibly over the course of a year. But there's one question that still nags at her: Why, when their marriage was about to blow apart, did her husband insist that they share eternity by purchasing a joint burial plot? She'll probably never know.

Critical Thinking

1. The article refers to infidelity as a "multicausal, multidimensional behavior." Explain what this means.
2. Who is most likely to cheat in a relationship? Why?
3. What factors contribute to cheating behavior? In what situations is someone more likely to cheat on a spouse and why?
4. What, if anything, can be done to prevent or lessen the likelihood that a spouse will cheat?

Create Central

www.mhhe.com/createcentral

Internet Reference

American Association for Marriage and Family Therapy: Infidelity
www.aamft.org/imis15/content/Consumer_Updates/Infidelity.aspx

Article

Prepared by: Patricia Hrusa Williams,
University of Maine at Farmington

Financial Infidelity

Lying About Money and Finances Can Result in Strained Relationships, Sometimes Divorce

ALEXIA ELEJALDE-RUIZ

Learning Outcomes

After reading this article, you will be able to:

- Define "financial infidelity."
- Explain how financial infidelity affects marital relationships.

Of all the ways to cheat on your spouse or partner, fibbing about finances may seem like the least of all evils. After all, is it anyone's business that you carry mountains of old credit card debt? Do you really need to disclose how much money you lose on sports bets? Wouldn't it cause more harm to reveal that after a bad day you seek solace in $300 shoes?

But checkbook cheating often reflects a deeper problem in the relationship, and the consequences can be as dire as those of an affair, some experts say. Even when those shopping bags stashed in your trunk don't lead to financial ruin, which they sometimes do, the conscious deception or omission chips away at intimacy and erodes trust.

"I call financial infidelity the No. 1 relationship wrecker," said Bonnie Eaker Weil, a New York psychotherapist and author of the book *Financial Infidelity* (Hudson Street Press; $24.95). "Because it's subtle, and many people don't think they're doing anything wrong, it can escalate and lead to other things."

A third of American couples with combined finances say they have committed financial infidelity, with both sexes lying to their partners in equal numbers, according to a Harris Interactive poll released in January. Sixty-seven percent of those couples had arguments as a result, and 42 percent said it caused less trust in the relationship. But the fallout can be much more severe. In 16 percent of cases, the lying led to divorce, and in 11 percent it caused a separation.

Transparency Crucial

While people shouldn't have to clear every purchase with their spouse or partner, they must be transparent about all income, spending and saving, a habit couples should establish at the beginning of the relationship, divulging in the first few dates what each person makes and who is expected to pick up the restaurant checks, Eaker Weil said. That may seem like a no-brainer, but many couples have difficulty discussing finances.

"People lie about money because they don't feel safe talking about money," said Eaker Weil, whose book guides couples in using "Smart Heart" dialogue to empathetically and constructively talk about finances.

The roots of secret spending can go deep: Money can be a form of control when you're feeling insecure in the relationship, or a form of revenge when you feel you've been betrayed, Eaker Weil said. People also hide spending when they fear that the other person won't approve, to fill a void in their lives or to get a thrill.

Financial infidelity can be a gateway drug to a romantic affair, especially when a person gets a high from their secret spending, because they may be tempted to push the limits of what they can get away with, Eaker Weil said.

Other times, it's a byproduct of living in a selfish culture in which everyone feels entitled to whatever they want, said John Wagner, a psychotherapist based in Winter Park, Fla. That works if you're single but not if you're in a committed relationship, when "ours" needs to be more important than "mine" and "yours."

"In our marriage, if we're going to spend more than $100, we check in with the other person," Wagner said. "Not out of control but out of respect."

Discovering a spouse's financial deceit can bring on feelings similar to those wrought by adultery: pain, distrust and not knowing what's coming next, Wagner said. If you're lying about money, your partner likely wonders what else you might lie about, he said.

The financial problems rarely can be fixed without first addressing the core relationship issues, Wagner said. An important part of the healing is to agree to a "contract" describing how the couple will handle finances, including a spending threshold, above which each partner will check in with the other before making a purchase.

Gone unchecked, money lies can destroy credit and marriages.

A man walked into credit counselor Jackie Goff's office after he received a letter from his mortgage company alerting him that his mortgage was two-years delinquent. The man thought his wife had been paying the mortgage, but it turned out she had been intercepting the mail and hiding the delinquency letters. She also had been opening credit cards in his name without telling him. The couple owed, all told, $100,000.

"He was just blindsided because he trusted her," said Goff, senior assistant director at Consumer Credit Counseling Service of North Central West Virginia. The man had to file for bankruptcy, and the couple divorced.

When It Gets Awkward

Credit counselors say it is not uncommon to see couples driven deep into debt because one person was financially cheating on the other.

"It's always a very awkward counseling session," said Claire Gray, credit counselor at Apprisen Financial Advocates in Columbus, Ohio.

Gray remembers one married couple, in their mid-50s, who came to her after being sued by a creditor. The husband had racked up some $50,000 on credit cards he opened behind his wife's back, which the wife discovered only when she tried to refinance their home and was denied a loan.

To make matters worse, the couple made the mistake of going through a debt settlement company, hoping that by putting off payment, the creditors would settle for a lesser payment, but the company's fees swelled their debt to $80,000 without producing a settlement. With both husband and wife already working full time and unable to cover the minimum payments, their only option was to file for bankruptcy, Gray said.

Gray said these crises could be avoided if everyone took ownership of the family finances. Even if just one person is doing the check writing and check balancing, both partners should look at the monthly bank statements and free annual credit reports (annualcreditreport.com).

A couple should have a budget they both agree on, and they should go over what they're making and spending every payday or at least once a month, Gray said. Even if you have personal debt that you plan to pay off yourself, it's wise to disclose it to your spouse, Goff said. With the job market precarious, you never know if you might suddenly find yourself without income. Also, if you have to file for bankruptcy and you co-own a home with your spouse, you're both going down.

"People need to be truthful," Goff said. "Eventually it will catch up with you."

Clandestine Cash

Thirty-one percent of Americans with combined finances have lied to their spouse about money, according to a Harris Interactive survey of 2,019 adults, commissioned by Forbes Woman and the National Endowment for Financial Education. Among the offenders:

- 58 percent hid cash
- 54 percent hid a minor purchase
- 30 percent hid a bill
- 16 percent hid a major purchase
- 15 percent hid a bank account
- 11 percent lied about debt
- 11 percent lied about earnings

Critical Thinking

1. What is "financial infidelity?"
2. Which is worse for the relationship—financial infidelity, or sexual infidelity? Why?
3. What are some strategies couples should utilize in order to improve family resource management and financial practices so they do not have detrimental effects on their marital relationships?

Create Central

www.mhhe.com/createcentral

Internet References

Oprah: Personal Finance for Couples
    www.oprah.com/money/Personal-Finance-for-Couples
The Ohio State University Extension Manage Your Money Course
    http://ohioline.osu.edu/mym

Article

Prepared by: Patricia Hrusa Williams,
University of Maine at Farmington

International Perspectives on Work-Family Policies: Lessons from the World's Most Competitive Economies

ALISON EARLE, ZITHA MOKOMANE, AND JODY HEYMANN

Learning Outcomes

After reading this article, you will be able to:

- Identify family-friendly work policies.

- Understand the differences between the United States' and other nations' work-family policies.

- Discuss the challenges parents have in dividing time between work and family.

In the majority of American families with children today, all parents are employed. In 67 percent of families with school-age children, 64 percent of families with preschool-age children, and 60 percent of families with children age three and younger, the parents are working for pay.[1] As a result, the workplace policies that parents face—such as how many hours they need to be away from home, the leave they can take to care for a sick child, and the work schedules that determine whether and when they are able to visit a son's or daughter's school—shape not only their income but also the time they have available for childrearing.

U.S. policies on parental leave, sick leave, vacation days, and days of rest are often in sharp contrast to other developed and developing countries, but those who want to make these policies more supportive of parents and their children face stiff opposition from those who say such policies will harm the United States' ability to compete economically with other countries. This article takes an international perspective to evaluate whether having workplace policies that support parents' ability to be available to meet their children's needs is compatible with economic competitiveness and low unemployment. We analyze a unique global database of labor legislation, focusing specifically on those measures dealing with parental availability in the first year of life, when caregiving needs are particularly intensive; parental availability to meet children's health needs; and their availability to meet their children's developmental needs.

We first review the evidence on the relationship of parental working conditions to children's outcomes. Second, we discuss the claims made in the public debates regarding the potential costs and benefits of family-supportive labor policies to individual employers and national economies, and review the academic literature on this topic. We then use new cross-national data to examine the extent to which highly competitive countries and countries with low unemployment rates do or do not provide these policies. Finally, we summarize the implications of our findings for U.S. policy.

Relationship of Parental Working Conditions to Children's Outcomes

Research in the United States and in other developed as well as developing countries suggests that workplace policies that support parents' ability to be available for their children at crucial periods of their lives have measurable effects on children's outcomes.

Paid Parental Leave

Research shows that the availability of paid leave following childbirth has the potential to improve infant and child health by making it affordable and feasible for parents to stay home and provide the intensive care newborns and infants need, including breast-feeding and a high caregiver-to-infant ratio that most child-care centers are unable to match.[2] Parental leave can have substantial benefits for child health. Christopher Ruhm's examination of more than two decades of data from sixteen European countries found that paid parental leave policies were associated with lower rates of infant and child mortality after taking into account per capita income, the availability of health services and technology, and other factors linked with child health. Ruhm found that a ten-week paid maternity leave was associated with a reduction in infant mortality rates of 1–2 percent; a twenty-week leave, with a 2–4 percent reduction; and a thirty-week leave, with a 7–9 percent reduction.[3]

Sasiko Tanaka reaffirmed these findings in a study that analyzed data from Ruhm's sixteen European countries plus the United States and Japan. The data covered the thirty years between 1969 and 2000 including the period between 1995 and 2000 when several significant changes were made in parental leave policies.[4] Tanaka found that a ten-week extension in paid leave was associated with a 2.6 percent decrease in infant mortality rates and a 3.0 percent decrease in child mortality rates. Maternity leave without pay or a guarantee of a job at the end of the leave had no significant effect on infant or child mortality rates in either study.

One of the most important mechanisms through which paid parental leave can benefit infants is by increasing a mother's ability to initiate and sustain breast-feeding, which a wealth of research has shown to be associated with a markedly lower risk of gastrointestinal, respiratory tract, skin, ear, and other infections; sudden infant death syndrome; and overall mortality.[5] Health benefits of breast-feeding have also been reported for mothers, including reduced risk of premenopausal breast cancer and potentially reduced risks of ovarian cancer and osteoporosis.[6]

Generous maternity leave benefits available across European countries make it possible for mothers to breast-feed their infants for a lengthy period of time without having to supplement feedings with formula. In some cases the leave is long enough that mothers can exclusively breast-feed for at least six months, as recommended by the World Health Organization; and in countries with more than half a year of leave, mothers can continue breast-feeding (while also adding appropriate solid foods).[7] In contrast, in countries with less generous maternity leave, such as the United States, working women are less likely to start breast-feeding their babies, and those who do breast-feed stop sooner, on average, than mothers in countries with these supportive policies.[8] Lacking paid maternity leave, American mothers also return to work earlier than mothers in most other advanced countries, and research has found that early return to work is associated with lower rates of breast-feeding and immunizations.[9]

While far less research has been conducted on the impact of paternity leave policies, there is ample reason to believe that paternal leave can support children's healthy development in ways parallel to maternal leave, with the obvious exception of breast-feeding. Although fathers can take time off under parental leave policies that can be used by one or both parents, they are more likely to stay at home to care for a new child when paternity leave is available.[10]

The longer the period of leave allowed, the more involved with their infants and families fathers are.[11] Moreover, longer leaves increase the probability that fathers will continue their involvement and share in child care even after the leave ends.[12] The benefits of fathers' engagement for children's social, psychological, behavioral, emotional, and cognitive functioning are significant.[13] In short, paternity leave policies are associated with greater gender equity at home and, through fathers' increased involvement with their infants, with positive cognitive and social development of young children.

Leave for Children's Health Needs

Four decades of research have documented that children's health outcomes improve when parents participate in their children's health care, whether it is a treatment for an acute illness or injury or management of a chronic condition.[14] As Mark Schuster, Paul Chung, and Katherine Vestal discuss in this volume, children heal faster and have shorter hospital stays when parents are present and involved during inpatient surgeries and treatments as well as during outpatient medical procedures.[15] Parents' assistance is especially important for children with chronic conditions such as diabetes and asthma, among others.[16] Parents can help improve children's health outcomes in many ways including by maintaining daily medical routines, administering medication, and providing emotional support as children adjust to having a chronic physical or mental health problem.[17]

If children are sick and parents do not have any schedule flexibility or paid leave that can be used to address a family member's health issue, children may be left home alone, unable to get themselves to a doctor or pharmacy for medication or to a hospital if a crisis occurs. Alternatively, parents may have no choice but to send a sick child to school or day care. The contact with other children and teachers contributes to the rapid spread and thus high incidence of infectious diseases in day-care centers, including respiratory infections, otitis media, and gastrointestinal infections.[18]

Research has also documented how significantly parental availability influences the level of preventive care children receive. Getting a child to a clinic or doctor's office for a physical exam or immunizations usually requires parents or other caregivers to take time off work. Working parents in a range of countries have cited schedule conflicts and workplace inflexibility as important obstacles to getting their children immunized against preventable childhood diseases.[19] One study of a large company in the United States found that employees who faced difficulties taking time off from work were far more likely to report that their children were not fully immunized.[20]

In contrast to the vast majority of countries around the globe, the United States has no federal policy requiring employers to provide paid leave for personal illness, let alone to address family members' health issues. (The Family and Medical Leave Act covers only serious health issues of immediate family members and is unpaid.) Only 30 percent of Americans report that their employer voluntarily offers paid sick leave that can be used for family members' care.[21] As a result, many parents are unable to be present to attend to their children's health needs. Parents whose employers provide paid sick days are more than five times as likely to be able to personally provide care to their sick children as parents whose employers do not offer paid sick days.[22] Working adults with no paid leave who take time off to care for ill family members are at risk of losing wages or even their job.[23] The risk of job loss is even greater for parents whose child has a chronic health problem, which typically involves more visits to the doctor or the hospital and more days of illness. In a longitudinal study of working poor families in the United States, we found that having a child with health problems was associated with a 36 percent increase in job loss.[24]

Leave and Availability for Children's Educational and Developmental Needs

When parents are involved in their children's education, whether at the preschool, elementary, or secondary level, children perform better in school.[25] Parental involvement has been linked with children's improved test scores in language and math, fewer emotional and behavioral problems, lower dropout rates, and better planning for and transitions into adulthood.[26] Greater parental involvement in schools appears to improve the quality of the education received by all students in the school.[27] Research has found that fathers' involvement, like that of mothers, is associated with significantly better exam scores, higher educational expectations, and higher grades.[28]

Parental participation and assistance can improve school outcomes for at-risk children.[29] Educational outcomes for children with learning disabilities improve when parents are involved in their education both at school and helping at home with homework in math as well as reading.[30] Low-income children can also benefit markedly when their parents are involved in their classrooms and with their teachers at school.[31] Studies suggest that low-income children benefit as much or more when their parents also spend time assisting their children in learning skills and material outside the classroom; training or instructing parents in providing this assistance further boosts the gains of time spent together.[32]

Parents' working conditions can markedly affect their ability to play an active role in their children's education. Active parental involvement often requires the flexibility to meet with teachers or consult with specialists during the workday. To be able to help with homework, parents need to have a work schedule that allows them time with their children after school and before children go to sleep. Our national research on the availability of paid leave and schedule flexibility among parents of school-age children in the United States shows that parents whose children were struggling academically and most needed parental support were at a significant disadvantage. More than half of parents who had a child scoring in the bottom quartile on math assessments did not have consistent access to any kind of paid leave, and nearly three-fourths could not count on schedule flexibility. One in six of these parents worked during evening hours, and more than one in ten worked nights, making it impossible to help their children routinely. Families in which a child scored in the bottom quartile in reading had equally challenging working conditions.[33]

Economic Feasibility of Workplace Policies Supporting Parents

Despite substantial evidence that children gain when parents have adequate paid leave and work flexibility, the economic costs and benefits of providing this leave and flexibility are still the subject of great contention in the United States. Each time legislation to guarantee parental leave, family medical leave, and related policies has been brought to Congress, the debate has revolved around questions of financial feasibility. In particular, legislators and others have questioned whether the United States can provide these benefits and still remain economically competitive.

For example, the proposed Healthy Families Act would guarantee a minimum of seven paid sick days—a small number by international standards—to American workers so they could stay home when they or family members fall ill. At a hearing in 2007 on the legislation, G. Roger King, a partner at the Jones Day corporate law firm, summarized the general argument raised against the legislation, saying that the Healthy Families Act, or any similar "regulations" to protect employees, would diminish U.S. competitiveness in the global economy. "Employers in this country are already burdened by numerous federal, state and local regulations which result in millions of dollars in compliance costs," King stated in his written testimony. "These mandated and largely unfunded 'cost of doing business' requirements in certain instances not only hinder and impede the creation of new jobs, but also inhibit our nation's employers from competing globally."[34]

We report findings from our recent research that examines the relationship between work-family legislation and national competitiveness and unemployment rates. First, however, we briefly summarize some of the evidence on costs and benefits to employers from policies that support families.

A series of studies including data from the United States, Japan, and the United Kingdom show that women who receive paid maternity leave are significantly more likely to return to the same employer after giving birth.[35] Increased employee retention reduces hiring and training costs, which can be significant (and include the costs of publicizing the job opening, conducting job interviews, training new employees, and suboptimal productivity among newly hired workers during the period just after they start).

There is no research known to us about the costs or benefits to individual American employers related to paid leave for children's health issues, most likely because this type of leave is uncommon in the United States. To the extent that the leave allows parents to ensure their children have time to rest and recuperate and avoid exacerbating health problems that could result in additional lost workdays in the future, parents' productivity could increase and absenteeism be reduced.

Similarly, while we are not aware of any studies that examine the costs and benefits to employers of legislation guaranteeing time off for employees to be with children, recent studies showing that long hours are associated with lower productivity suggest that similar productivity losses may exist for employees who work for long periods of time without a substantial block of time away from work or, in the shorter term, for those who work without a weekly day of rest. A study of eighteen manufacturing industries in the United States over a thirty-five-year period found that for every 10 percent increase in overtime hours, productivity declined 2–4 percent.[36] Although small in absolute size, in the context of a forty-hour workweek, these productivity losses suggest that employers may be able to increase productivity by guaranteeing regular time off.

A study of highly "effective" employers by the Families and Work Institute found that many report a series of economic benefits resulting from their flexibility policies that include paid leave for new mothers and time off for caregiving among other scheduling and training policies.[37] Benefits cited by employers include "increasing employee engagement and retention; reducing turnover; reducing absenteeism and sick days; increasing customer satisfaction; reducing business costs; increasing productivity and profitability; improving staffing coverage to meet business demands; [and] enhancing innovation and creativity."[38]

The centrality of the economic arguments in policy debates calls for further examination of the empirical evidence on workplace policies important to parents and their children. We examine two important indicators of economic performance. The first is a measure of global economic competitiveness, a concept encompassing productivity, a country's capacity for growth, and the level of prosperity or income that can be attained. This indicator is of particular salience to businesses and is used by international organizations such as the World Economic Forum (WEF). The second is the national unemployment rate, the indicator more often cited as being of high concern in the public's mind.

To evaluate the claim that nationally mandating paid leave would cause a reduction in jobs or loss of competitiveness, one ideally would have evidence from a randomized or natural experiment where the policy in place is not associated with other country or state characteristics that could influence the outcome. That approach is not possible, because there have been no such experiments. However, to test whether policies supporting working families inevitably lead countries to be uncompetitive or to have high unemployment, it is sufficient to find counterexamples. To that end, we ask a straightforward question: Are paid leave and other work-family policies that support children's development economically feasible?

To answer this question, we developed a global database of national labor policies and global economic data on competitiveness and unemployment in all countries that belong to the United Nations. The database includes information from original legislation, labor codes, and relevant amendments in 175 countries, as well as summaries of legislation for these and additional countries. The vast majority of the legislation was gathered from NATLEX, the International Labour Organization's (ILO) global database of legislation pertaining to labor, social security, and human rights from 189 countries. Additional sources included global databases that compile and summarize national legislation.[39]

Public Policies Supporting Working Families in Highly Competitive Countries

Using our global labor policy database, we set out to assess whether the countries that have consistently been at the top of the rankings in economic competitiveness provide working conditions that give employed parents the ability to support their children's healthy development. To identify these "highly competitive" countries, we use data from the business-led WEF.[40] Its annual Global Competitiveness Report includes

country "competitiveness" rankings based on dozens of indicators of institutions, policies, and other factors that WEF members judge to be the key drivers of economic competitiveness. These factors include, among others, the efficiency of the goods market, efficiency of the labor market, financial market development, technological readiness, market size, business sophistication, innovation, infrastructure, and the macroeconomic environment.[41] We define "highly competitive" countries to be those that were ranked among the top twenty countries in competitiveness in at least eight of the ten years between 1999 and 2008. Fifteen countries meet this definition: Australia, Austria, Canada, Denmark, Finland, Germany, Iceland, Japan, the Netherlands, Norway, Singapore, Sweden, Switzerland, the United Kingdom, and the United States. Although India and China are not among the fifteen, we also present data on their family-supportive policies for two reasons. First, the press and laypersons often single out China and India as U.S. "competitors," and second, they have the two largest labor forces in the world.[42]

Paid Parental Leave

Paid leave for new mothers is guaranteed in all but one of the fifteen most competitive countries (Table 1). The exception is the United States, which has no federal policy providing paid leave for new parents. (As noted, leave provided under the federal Family and Medical Leave Act is unpaid.) Australia's paid leave policy took effect starting in January 2011; under the Paid Parental Leave Act, all workers—full time, part time, or casual—who are primary caregivers and earn $150,000 or less a year are guaranteed eighteen weeks of leave paid at the federal minimum wage. All of the most competitive countries with paid leave for new mothers provide at least fourteen weeks of leave, counting both maternity and parental leave, as recommended by the ILO. The norm of six months or more far exceeds the recommended minimum. China offers eighteen weeks (ninety working days) of leave for new mothers at full pay; India offers twelve weeks.

Table 1 also shows that although the duration of paid leave for new fathers is far less than for mothers, almost all highly competitive countries provide this type of leave. Switzerland is the lone top-ranked nation that provides paid leave to new mothers but not to new fathers. Neither India nor China has paid leave for new fathers.[43]

Breast-Feeding Breaks

Guaranteeing new mothers a breast-feeding break during the workday is the law in about half of the highly competitive countries, including Austria, Germany, Japan, the Netherlands, Norway, Sweden, Switzerland, and the United States (Table 2). India mandates two breaks a day in the child's first fifteen months. China guarantees new mothers breast-feeding breaks totaling an hour a day for the baby's first year.

Leave for Children's Health Needs

Unpaid leave from work to address children's health needs is ensured in every highly competitive nation (see Table 2). All but four of the fifteen most competitive countries provide paid leave for this purpose; the exceptions are Finland, Switzerland, the United Kingdom, and the United States.

Table 1   Parental Leave Policies in Highly Competitive Countries

Country	Paid Leave for Mothers			Paid Leave for Fathers		
	Availability	Duration (Weeks)	Wage Replacement Rate (%)	Availability	Duration (Weeks)	Wage Replacement Rate (%)
Australia	Yes	18	flat rate	Yes	18	flat rate
Austria	Yes	81–146	100, flat rate	Yes	65–130	flat rate
Canada	Yes	50	55	Yes	35	55
Denmark	Yes	50–58	80–100	Yes	34–42	80–100
Finland	Yes	164	25–90	Yes	154	25–70
Germany	Yes	66–118	33–100	Yes	52–104	33–67
Iceland	Yes	26	80	Yes	26	80
Japan	Yes	58	30–60	Yes	44	30–40
Netherlands	Yes	16	100	Yes	0.4	100
Norway	Yes	90–100	80–100, flat rate	Yes	87–97	80–100, flat rate
Singapore	Yes	14	100	Yes	2	100
Sweden	Yes	69*	80, flat rate	Yes	67*	80, flat rate
Switzerland	Yes	14	80	No	n.a.	n.a.
United Kingdom	Yes	39	90	Yes	2	90
United States	No	n.a.	n.a.	No	n.a.	n.a.

Notes: In the database and all tables, data reflect national policy. Coverage conditions such as firm size, sector, and duration of employment vary by country. Paid leave for mothers includes paid leave for women only (maternity leave) and parental leave that is available to women. Paid leave for fathers includes paid leave for men only (paternity leave) and parental leave that is available to men. The table presents data on the maximum amount of leave available to the mother if she takes all of the maternity leave available to mothers and all of the parental leave available to either parent. Parallel data are presented for fathers. The minimum and maximum (as a range) are presented to reflect that country's policy of providing parents with a choice between a shorter leave at a higher benefit level (percentage of wages or flat rate) and a longer leave at a lower benefit.

Source: Based on updated data from Jody Heymann and Alison Earle, *Raising the Global Floor: Dismantling the Myth That We Can't Afford Good Working Conditions for Everyone* (Stanford University Press, 2010).

n.a. = Not applicable.

*Sweden's parental leave policy also allows parents to take part-time leave with partial benefits for a longer duration.

Table 2   Leave Policies to Attend to Children's Health Care in Highly Competitive Countries

Country	Breast-Feeding Breaks	Age of Child When Breast-Feeding Breaks End	Break Time of At Least One Hour a Day	Leave to Care for Children's Health Needs	Leave Is Paid
Australia	No	n.a.	n.a.	Yes	Yes
Austria	Yes	For duration	Yes	Yes	Yes
Canada	No	n.a.	n.a.	Yes	Yes
Denmark	No	n.a.	n.a.	Yes	Yes
Finland	No	n.a.	n.a.	Yes	No
Germany	Yes	For duration	Yes	Yes	Yes
Iceland	No	n.a.	n.a.	Yes	Yes
Japan	Yes	1 year	Yes	Yes	Yes
Netherlands	Yes	9 months	Yes	Yes	Yes
Norway	Yes	For duration	Yes	Yes	Yes
Singapore	No	n.a.	n.a.	Yes	Yes
Sweden	Yes	For duration	Yes	Yes	Yes
Switzerland	Yes	1 year	Yes	Yes	No
United Kingdom	No	n.a.	n.a.	Yes	No
United States	Yes	1 year	Yes	Yes	No

n.a. = Not applicable.
Source: See Table 1.

Leave and Availability for Children's Developmental and Educational Needs

Neither paid vacation leave nor a day off each week is designed specifically for parents; these rest periods benefit all working adults. Yet weekly time off and vacations do provide an important assurance that working parents can spend time with their children and be available to support their educational, social, and emotional development. All of the most highly competitive countries except the United States guarantee paid annual or vacation leave (Table 3). The vast majority of these countries provide generous amounts of leave at full pay. Half provide more than four weeks a year: Austria, Denmark, Finland, Germany, Iceland, Norway, Sweden, and the United Kingdom. China's labor laws guarantee five days of paid leave after one year of service, ten days after ten years on the job, and fifteen days after twenty years. In India workers are provided one day of paid leave for every twenty days worked during the previous year.

Virtually all highly competitive nations also guarantee at least one day of rest a week. The exceptions are the United States and Australia (see Table 3). Both China and India guarantee workers a day of rest a week.

Labor legislation is relatively less common around a small number of issues that are receiving attention as a result of recent economic and technological developments. Countries are still adjusting their labor policies in response to the rise of the "24/7" schedule that has come about as global trade, communications, and sourcing of products have increased. Policies either to restrict or compensate for work at times when school-age children in particular benefit from a parent's presence—evenings and nights—exist in many highly competitive countries. Guaranteeing a wage premium increases the likelihood that a wide range of workers will volunteer for night work and decreases the likelihood that parents will need to work at night merely because of limited seniority. Finland, Norway, and Sweden have passed laws placing broad restrictions on night work for all workers. Germany, Japan, and Switzerland instead guarantee a wage premium for those who are required to work at night. Over half of the highly competitive nations allow night work but restrict or ban it for workers who might be harmed by it: children, pregnant or nursing women, or employees with medical conditions that make them unable to work at night (see Table 3). China bans night work for pregnant women. Although India bans night work for all women, some states have lifted it for women working in information technology and telecommunications.

Not new to parents but to some policy makers is the need for adults to occasionally take time off during the day to address a child's academic, social, or behavioral issue, or to attend a school event. Although leave during the day to meet with a teacher or attend an event typically does not involve a great deal of the employee's time in any given period, only four of the fifteen countries provide leave explicitly for such purposes. Labor laws in Denmark and Sweden require employers to provide leave to attend to "children's needs" including educational issues. Switzerland takes a different approach, requiring

Table 3 Policies on Paid Annual Leave, a Day of Rest, and Night Work in Highly Competitive Countries

Country	Availability of Paid Annual Leave	Duration of Paid Annual Leave (Weeks)	Weekly Day of Rest	Premium for Night Work	Ban or Broad Restrictions on Night Work	Ban or Restriction for Children, Pregnant or Nursing Women, or Medical Reasons
Australia	Yes	4.0	No	No	No	No
Austria	Yes	5.0	Yes	No	No	Yes
Canada	Yes	2.0	Yes	No	No	Yes
Denmark	Yes	5.5	Yes	No	No	Yes
Finland	Yes	4.4	Yes	No	Yes	No
Germany	Yes	4.4	Yes	After 11 P.M.	No	Yes
Iceland	Yes	4.4	Yes	No	No	No
Japan	Yes	1.8	Yes	After 10 P.M.	No	Yes
Netherlands	Yes	4.0	Yes	No	No	Yes
Norway	Yes	4.2	Yes	No	Yes	Yes
Singapore	Yes	1.3	Yes	No	No	No
Sweden	Yes	5.0	Yes	No	Yes	No
Switzerland	Yes	4.0	Yes	After 11 P.M.	No	Yes
United Kingdom	Yes	5.1	Yes	No	No	Yes
United States	No	n.a.	No	No	No	No

n.a. = Not applicable.
Source: See Table 1.

employers to structure work schedules and rest periods keeping in mind employees' family responsibilities including attending to the educational needs of children up to age fifteen. In addition, Switzerland also requires employers to provide a lunch break of at least an hour and a half to parents if requested. Parents in Singapore can take leave for their children's educational needs under the country's family leave law. Neither India nor China provides paid leave for general family needs and issues or for children's education.

Public Policies Supporting Working Families in Low Unemployment Countries

As an additional check, we also examined whether it was possible to have relatively low unemployment rates while guaranteeing a floor of working conditions that help parents care for children. We looked specifically at members of the Organization for Economic Cooperation and Development (OECD). The OECD definition of unemployment is comprehensive, including employment in formal and informal jobs.[44] We defined low unemployment countries as those OECD members ranked in the better half of countries in terms of unemployment at least 80 percent of the time in the decade between 1998 and 2007. Thirteen countries fit these criteria: Austria, Denmark, Iceland, Ireland, Japan, Republic of Korea (South Korea), Luxembourg, Mexico, the Netherlands, Norway, Switzerland, the United Kingdom, and the United States. Overall, do these countries provide working conditions that can help parents support children's healthy development? In short, yes.

Paid Parental Leave

Every low unemployment country but one, the United States, has national legislation guaranteeing paid leave for new mothers. The length of the leaves ranges from twelve weeks in Mexico to more than a year in Austria, Japan, Norway, and South Korea. In the middle are Iceland and Ireland, where new mothers receive six months, and Luxembourg and the United Kingdom, with nine months. All but one of those with paid leave replace 80 percent or more of wages, and seven guarantee 100 percent.

Paid leave for new fathers, whether in the form of leave for fathers only or leave that can be used by either parent, is not universally available but is provided in nine of the thirteen low unemployment countries. Ireland, Mexico, Switzerland, and the United States do not provide this type of leave. New fathers are entitled to take between six months and a year in Denmark, Iceland, Japan, and Luxembourg, and more than a year in Austria, Norway, and South Korea.

Breast-Feeding Breaks

Ten of the thirteen countries ensure that new mothers can continue breast-feeding for at least six months after they return to work, and eight of those ten ensure this right for a year or until the mother chooses to stop.

Leave for Children's Health Needs

Guaranteed leave to address children's health needs is the norm; all but two low unemployment countries—Mexico and South Korea—provide either paid or unpaid leave of this type. The leave is paid in Austria, Denmark, Iceland, Ireland, Japan, Luxembourg, the Netherlands, and Norway and unpaid in Switzerland, the United Kingdom, and the United States.

Leave and Availability for Children's Developmental and Educational Needs

Every low unemployment country except the United States guarantees workers a weekly day of rest and a period of paid vacation leave once a year. Mexico and Japan guarantee from one to two weeks while nine of the thirteen guarantee four weeks or more. As noted earlier, labor laws in Denmark and Switzerland also require employers to provide leave to address "children's needs," which in the Swiss legislation explicitly include educational issues.

These findings show that mandating workplace policies that support parents' ability to ensure their children's healthy development does not inevitably lead to high job loss or high unemployment rates. As this discussion shows, many OECD countries kept unemployment rates relatively low while passing and enforcing legislation that supports parents. In fact, the majority of consistently low unemployment countries have adopted nearly all the policies shown to be important for children's health and well-being. Whether these nations would have had somewhat lower or higher unemployment in the absence of family support policies is not known. But our research clearly shows that it is possible for a nation to guarantee paid leave and other policies that provide parents with time to address their children's needs and at the same time maintain relatively low unemployment.

Summary of Findings

Longitudinal data are not available that would enable researchers to determine conclusively the immediate and long-term impact on national economic outcomes of changing guarantees of parental leave and other family-support policies. However, an examination of the most competitive economies as well as the economies with low unemployment rates makes clear that ensuring that all parents are available to care for their children's healthy development does not preclude a country from being highly competitive economically. Moreover, as noted, evidence from decades of research on parents' roles during children's infancy and in caring for children's health and education makes clear that policies enabling working fathers and mothers to provide that care are likely to have substantial positive effects on the health and developmental outcomes of American children.

Few of the policies that would help working parents raise healthy children are guaranteed in the United States. As noted, the federal Family and Medical Leave Act allows new parents to take unpaid time off without fear of job loss when they adopt or give birth, or to attend to a parent or child suffering from a serious illness. Half of Americans are not covered by the act because of the size of the firms in which they work, the number of hours they have worked, or a recent job change, and many of those who are covered cannot afford to take all the leave they are entitled to because it is unpaid. Only in 2010 did the United States pass federal legislation requiring employers to provide breast-feeding breaks and facilities for breast-feeding (as part of the health care reform bill and without much public awareness). Paid parental leave and child health care leave policies are the norm in the countries that have been highly competitive and those that have maintained low unemployment for a decade. The analysis of global data presented here suggests that guaranteeing paid parental leave as well as paid leave when a child is sick would be feasible for the United States without jeopardizing its highly competitive economy or low unemployment rates in the future.

The overwhelming majority of countries guarantee paid parental leave through a social insurance system. While many countries provide some kind of tax credit or stipend at the birth of a child, next to none rely only on this for paid parental leave. A critical step that European countries have increasingly followed is to guarantee that a percentage of the leave is dedicated to fathers as well as some dedicated solely to mothers. This approach ensures that men have in practice, and not just on paper, an equal chance of using the leave.

The countries that guarantee paid sick leave finance it through a variety of means ranging from requiring employers to pay employees benefits (that is, continue to pay salary or wages during the leave) to establishing a social security system whereby some combination of employees, employers, and government pay into a fund out of which payments are made to individuals while they are unable to work. One two-stage model requires employers to pay wages for short periods of illness but provides benefits from the social insurance system for longer leaves associated with major illnesses. Reasonably short employer liability periods—seven to ten days a year—make it feasible for the employer to reimburse wages at a high rate and keeps administrative costs low, while ensuring that paid leave covers most common illnessess that adults and children suffer. Covering longer illnesses through social insurance ensures that employers will not be overburdened with long-term payments.

The overwhelming majority of countries around the world guarantee all working women and men some paid annual leave and a weekly day of rest. In these nations the right to reasonable work hours is built into employers' labor costs and is often seen as a sensible, basic human right that also enhances productivity.

Considering policy change is always difficult, and recommending programs with public and private sector budgetary implications is particularly difficult when the United States is only now recovering from the Great Recession. That said, many of the country's most important social and labor policies date from the Great Depression. While periods of economic duress raise understandable questions about the feasibility of change, they also naturally focus attention on how critical safety nets are to American of all ages. As articles throughout this issue of the *Future of Children* demonstrate, guaranteeing a floor of decent working conditions and social supports is essential not only to working parents but also to the healthy development of their children. We believe that evidence is equally compelling that such guarantees are economically feasible for the United States.

Notes

1. U.S. Bureau of Labor Statistics, "Employment Characteristics of Families, Table 4: Families with Own Children: Employment Status of Parents by Age of Youngest Child and Family Type, 2008–09 Annual Averages" (www.bls.gov/news.release/archives/famee_05272010.htm); U.S. Bureau of the Census, "Women in the Labor Force: A Databook" (2009 ed.), Table 7, "Employment Status of Women by Presence and Age of Youngest Child" (March) (www.bls.gov/cps/wlftable7.htm).

2. Lawrence Berger, Jennifer Hill, and Jane Waldfogel, "Maternity Leave, Early Maternal Employment and Child Health and Development in the U.S.," *Economic Journal* 115, no. 501 (2005): F29–F47; Sheila B. Kamerman, "Maternity, Paternity, and Parental Leave Policies: The Potential Impacts on Children and Their Families (rev. ed.)," in *Encyclopedia on Early Childhood Development (online),* edited by R. E. Tremlay, R. G. Barr, and R. D. Peters (Montreal: Centre of Excellence for Early Childhood Development, 2005) (www.child-encyclopedia.com/documents/KamermanANGxp_rev-Parental.pdf).

3. Christopher J. Ruhm, "Parental Leave and Child Health," *Journal of Health Economics* 19, no. 6 (2000): 931–60.

4. Sasiko Tanaka, "Parental Leave and Child Health across OECD Countries," *Economic Journal* 115, no. 501 (2005): F7–F28.

5. Richard G. Feachem and Marge A. Koblinsky, "Interventions for the Control of Diarrhoeal Diseases among Young Children: Promotion of Breast-feeding," *Bulletin of World Health Organization* 62, no. 2 (1984): 271–91; Kathryn G. Dewey, M. Jane Heinig, and Laurie A. Nommsen-Rivers, "Differences in Morbidity between Breastfed and Formula-Fed Infants. Part 1," *Journal of Pediatrics* 126, no. 5 (1995): 696–702; Peter W. Howie, and others, "Protective Effect of Breast-feeding against Infection," *British Medical Journal* 300, no. 6716 (1990): 11–16; Philippe Lepage, Christophe Munyakazi, and Philippe Hennart, "Breastfeeding and Hospital Mortality in Children in Rwanda," *Lancet* 319, no. 8268 (1982): 403; M. Cristina Cerqueiro and others, "Epidemiologic Risk Factors for Children with Acute Lower Respiratory Tract Infection in Buenos Aires, Argentina: A Matched Case-Control Study," *Reviews of Infectious Diseases,* suppl. 8, no. 12 (1990): S1021–28; Christopher J. Watkins, Stephen R. Leeder, and Richard T. Corkhill, "The Relationship between Breast and Bottle Feeding and Respiratory Illness in the First Year of Life," *Journal of Epidemiology and Community Health* 33, no. 3 (1979): 180–82; Anne L. Wright and others, "Breast-feeding and Lower Respiratory Tract Illness in the First Year of Life," *British Medical Journal* 299, no. 6705 (1989): 946–49; Michael Gdalevich and others, "Breast-Feeding and the Onset of Atopic Dermatitis in Childhood: A Systematic Review and Meta-Analysis of Prospective Studies," *Journal of American Academy of Dermatology* 45, no. 4 (2001): 487–647; Jennifer Baxter, "Breastfeeding, Employment and Leave: An Analysis of Mothers Growing Up in Australia," *Family Matters* no. 80 (2008): 17–26; Amanda R. Cooklin, Susan M. Donath, and Lisa H. Amir, "Maternal Employment and Breastfeeding:

Results from the Longitudinal Study of Australian Children," *Acta Paediatrica* 97, no. 5 (2008): 620–23; Gustaf Aniansson and others, "A Prospective Cohort Study on Breast-Feeding and Otitis Media in Swedish Infants," *Pediatric Infectious Disease Journal* 13, no. 3 (1994): 183–88; Burris Duncan and others, "Exclusive Breast-Feeding for at Least 4 Months Protects against Otitis Media," *Pediatrics* 91, no. 5 (1993): 867–72; Cody Arnold, Susan Makintube, and Gregory Istre, "Daycare Attendance and Other Risk Factors for Invasive Haemophilus Influenzae Type B Disease," *American Journal of Epidemiology* 138, no. 5 (1993): 333–40; Stanley Ip and others, "Breastfeeding and Maternal and Infant Health Outcomes in Developed Countries," Agency for Healthcare Research and Quality, AHRQ Publication 07-E007 (April 2007).

6. Ip and others. "Breastfeeding and Maternal and Infant Health Outcomes in Developed Countries" (see note 5).

7. Adriano Cattaneo and others, "Protection, Promotion and Support of Breast-Feeding in Europe: Current Situation," *Public Health Nutrition* 8, no. 1 (2005): 39–46.

8. Sylvia Guendelman and others, "Juggling Work and Breastfeeding: Effects of Maternity Leave and Occupational Characteristics," *Pediatrics* 123, no. 1 (2010): e38–46; Baxter, "Breastfeeding, Employment and Leave" (see note 5); Cooklin, Donath, and Amir, "Maternal Employment and Breastfeeding" (see note 5).

9. Berger, Hill, and Waldfogel, "Maternity Leave, Early Maternal Employment and Child Health and Development in the U.S." (see note 2).

10. Berit Brandth and Elin Kvande, "Flexible Work and Flexible Fathers," *Work, Employment and Society* 15 no. 2 (2001): 251–67.

11. Ruth Feldman, Amy L. Sussman, and Edward Zigler, "Parental Leave and Work Adaptation at the Transition to Parenthood: Individual, Marital and Social Correlates," *Applied Developmental Psychology* 25, no. 4 (2004): 459–79; Rudy Ray Seward, Dale E. Yeatts, and Lisa K. Zottarelli, "Parental Leave and Father Involvement in Child Care: Sweden and the United States," *Journal of Comparative Family Studies* 33, no. 3 (2002): 387–99.

12. Linda Haas and Phillip Hwang, "The Impact of Taking Parental Leave on Fathers' Participation in Childcare and Relationships with Children: Lessons from Sweden," *Community, Work and Family* 11, no. 1 (2008): 85–104; Lindy Fursman and Paul Callister, *Men's Participation in Unpaid Care: A Review of the Literature* (Wellington: New Zealand Department of Labour 2009) (www.dol.govt.nz/publication-view.asp?ID=289).

13. According to Catherine S. Tamis-LeMonda and others, "Fathers and Mothers at Play with Their 2- and 3-Year-Olds: Contributions to Language and Cognitive Development," *Child Development* 75, no. 6 (2004): 1806–20, one example is resident fathers who engage their children in more cognitive stimulation have children with higher mental development (that is, memory skills, problem-solving skills, vocalization, language skills) at twenty-four months (as measured by the Bayley Scales of Infant Development, Second Edition Mental Development Index). For a brief summary of this research, see Andrew Kang and Julie Weber, "Opportunities for Policy Leadership on Fathers," Policy Briefing Series 20 (Sloan Work and Family Research Network, Chestnut Hill, Mass., 2009) (www.wfnetwork.bc.edu). See also Ann M. Taubenheim,

"Paternal-Infant Bonding in the First-Time Father," *Journal of Obstetric, Gynecologic, and Neonatal Nursing* 10, no. 4 (1981): 261–64; Per Nettelbladt, "Father/Son Relationship during the Preschool Years: An Integrative Review with Special Reference to Recent Swedish Findings," *Acta Psychiatrica Scandinavica* 68, no. 6 (1983): 399–407. Although the bulk of the literature has focused on the bonds between mothers and infants, no evidence exists to suggest that bonding with fathers is any less significant to children.

14. Inger Kristensson-Hallstrom, Gunnel Elander, and Gerhard Malmfors, "Increased Parental Participation in a Pediatric Surgical Daycare Unit," *Journal of Clinical Nursing* 6, no. 4 (1997): 297–302; Mervyn R. H. Taylor and Peter O'Connor, "Resident Parents and Shorter Hospital Stay," *Archives of Disease in Childhood* 64, no. 2 (1989): 274–76; Patricia A. LaRosa-Nash and Jane M. Murphy, "An Approach to Pediatric Perioperative Care: Parent-Present Induction," *Nursing Clinics of North America* 32, no. 1 (1997): 183–99; Alan George and Janice Hancock, "Reducing Pediatric Burn Pain with Parent Participation," *Journal of Burn Care and Rehabilitation* 14, no. 1 (1993): 104–07; Sarah J. Palmer, "Care of Sick Children by Parents: A Meaningful Role," *Journal of Advanced Nursing* 18, no. 2 (1993): 185; Perry Mahaffy, "The Effects of Hospitalization on Children Admitted for Tonsillectomy and Adenoidectomy," *Nursing Review* 14 (1965): 12–19; John Bowlby, *Child Care and the Growth of Love* (London: Pelican, 1964); James Robertson, *Young Children in Hospital* (London: Tavistock, 1970).

15. See also Taylor and O'Connor, "Resident Parents and Shorter Hospital Stay" (see note 14); Kristensson-Hallstrom, Elander, and Malmfors, "Increased Parental Participation in a Pediatric Surgical Daycare Unit" (see note 14).

16. Annete M. LaGreca and others, "I Get By with a Little Help from My Family and Friends: Adolescents' Support for Diabetes Care," *Journal of Pediatric Psychology* 20, no. 4 (1995): 449–76; Barbara J. Anderson and others, "Family Characteristics of Diabetic Adolescents: Relationship to Metabolic Control," *Diabetes Care* 4, no. 6 (1981): 586–94; Kim W. Hamlett, David S. Pellegrini, and Kathy S. Katz, "Childhood Chronic Illness as a Family Stressor," *Journal of Pediatric Psychology* 17, no. 1 (1992): 33–47; Clara Wolman and others, "Emotional Well-Being among Adolescents with and without Chronic Conditions," *Adolescent Medicine* 15, no. 3 (1994): 199–204; Cindy L. Hanson and others, "Comparing Social Learning and Family Systems Correlates of Adaptation in Youths with IDDM," *Journal of Pediatric Psychology* 17, no. 5 (1992): 555–72.

17. LaGreca and others, "I Get By with a Little Help from My Family and Friends" (see note 16); Wolman and others, "Emotional Well-Being among Adolescents with and without Chronic Conditions" (see note 16); Hamlett, Pellegrini, and Katz, "Childhood Chronic Illness as a Family Stressor" (see note 16); Stuart T. Hauser and others, "Adherence among Children and Adolescents with Insulin-Dependent Diabetes Mellitus over a Four-Year Longitudinal Follow-Up: II. Immediate and Long-Term Linkages with the Family Milieu," *Journal of Pediatric Psychology* 15, no. 4 (1990): 527–42; E. Wayne Holden and others, "Controlling for General and Disease-Specific Effects in Child and Family Adjustment to Chronic Childhood Illness," *Journal of Pediatric Psychology* 22, no. 1 (1997): 15–27; Katrina Johnson, "Children with Special

Health Needs: Ensuring Appropriate Coverage and Care under Health Care Reform," *Health Policy and Child Health* 1, no. 3 (1994): 1–5; Timothy A. Waugh and Diane L. Kjos, "Parental Involvement and the Effectiveness of an Adolescent Day Treatment Program," *Journal of Youth and Adolescence* 21 (1992): 487–97; J. Cleary and others, "Parental Involvement in the Lives of Children in Hospital," *Archives of Disease in Childhood* 61 (1986): 779–87; C. P. Sainsbury and others, "Care by Parents of Their Children in Hospital," *Archives of Disease in Childhood* 61, no. 6 (1986): 612–15; Michael W. L. Gauderer, June L. Lorig, and Douglas W. Eastwood, "Is There a Place for Parents in the Operating Room?" *Journal of Pediatric Surgery* 24, no. 7 (1989): 705–06.

18. Isabelle Diehl, "The Prevalence of Colds in Nursery School Children and Non-Nursery School Children," *Journal of Pediatrics* 34, no. 1 (1949): 52–61; Peggy Sullivan and others, "Longitudinal Study of Occurrence of Diarrheal Disease in Day Care Centers," *American Journal of Public Health* 74, no. 9 (1984): 987–91; Merja Möttönen and Matti Uhari, "Absences for Sickness among Children in Day Care," *Acta Paediatrica* 81, no. 11 (1992): 929. Frank A. Loda, W. Paul Glezen, and Wallace A. Clyde Jr., "Respiratory Disease in Group Day Care," *Pediatrics* 49, no. 3 (1972): 428–37; K. Strangert, "Respiratory Illness in Preschool Children with Different Forms of Day Care," *Pediatrics* 57, no. 2 (1976): 191; Anna-Beth Doyle, "Incidence of Illness in Early Group and Family Day-Care," *Pediatrics* 58, no. 4 (1976): 607; Ron Haskins and Jonathan Kotch, "Day Care and Illness: Evidence, Costs, and Public Policy," *Pediatrics* 77, no. 6, (1986): 951–80; Muriel Oyediran and Anne Bamisaiye, "A Study of the Child-Care Arrangements and the Health Status of Pre-School Children of Employed Women in Lagos," *Public Health* 97, no. 5 (1983): 267; Susan D. Hillis and others, "Day Care Center Attendance and Diarrheal Morbidity in Colombia," *Pediatrics* 90, no. 4 (1992): 582; Centers for Disease Control and Prevention, "National Immunization Program: "Estimated Vaccination Coverage with Individual Vaccines and Selected Vaccination Series among Children Nineteen to Thirty-Five Months-of-Age by State" (Atlanta: 2001); World Health Organization (WHO), *WHO Vaccine Preventable Diseases: Monitoring System* (Geneva: WHO Department of Vaccines and Biologicals, 2000); Kim Streatfield and Masri Singarimbun, "Social Factors Affecting the Use of Immunization in Indonesia," *Social Science and Medicine* 27, no. 11 (1988): 1237–45.

19. Centers for Disease Control and Prevention, "National Immunization Program" (see note 18); World Health Organization, *WHO Vaccine Preventable Diseases* (see note 18).

20. J. E. Fielding, W. G. Cumberland, and L. Pettitt, "Immunization Status of Children of Employees in a Large Corporation," *Journal of the American Medical Association* 271, no. 7 (1994): 525–30.

21. Vicky Lovell. *No Time to Be Sick: Why Everyone Suffers When Workers Don't Have Paid Sick Leave* (Washington: Institute for Women's Policy Research, 2004) (www.iwpr.org/pdf/B242.pdf).

22. S. Jody Heymann, Sara Toomey, and Frank Furstenberg, "Working Parents: What Factors Are Involved in Their Ability to Take Time Off from Work When Their Children Are Sick?" *Archives of Pediatrics and Adolescent Medicine* 153, no. 8 (1999): 870–74; Jody Heymann, *The Widening Gap: Why America's Working Families Are in Jeopardy and What Can Be Done about It* (New York: Basic Books, 2000).

23. National Alliance for Caregiving and American Association of Retired People, "Caregiving in the U.S." (Bethesda: 2004); Heymann, *The Widening Gap* (see note 22).

24. Alison Earle and S. Jody Heymann, "What Causes Job Loss among Former Welfare Recipients? The Role of Family Health Problems," *Journal of the American Medical Women's Association* 57 (2002): 5–10.

25. Charles Desforges and Alberto Abouchaar, "The Impact of Parental Involvement, Parental Support, and Family Education on Pupil Achievement and Adjustment: A Literature Review," *DfES Research Report* 433 (Chelsea: Department for Education and Skills, 2003) (http://publications.dcsf. gov.uk/eOrderingDownload/RR433.pdf); Arthur Reynolds, "Early Schooling of Children at Risk," *American Educational Research Journal* 28, no. 2 (1991): 392–422; Kevin Callahan, Joyce A. Rademacher, and Bertina A. Hildreth, "The Effect of Parent Participation in Strategies to Improve the Homework Performance of Students Who Are at Risk," *Remedial and Special Education* 19, no. 3 (1998): 131–41; Timothy Z. Keith and others, "Does Parental Involvement Affect Eighth-Grade Student Achievement? Structural Analysis of National Data," *School Psychology Review* 22, no. 3 (1993): 474–76; Paul G. Fehrmann, Timothy Z. Keith, and Thomas M. Reimers, "Home Influences on School Learning: Direct and Indirect Effects of Parental Involvement on High School Grades," *Journal of Educational Research* 80, no. 6 (1987): 330–37.

26. Leon Feinstein and James Symons, "Attainment in Secondary School," *Oxford Economics Papers* 51, no. 2 (1999): 300–21. This study found that parental interest had a much stronger effect than either in-school factors such as teacher-student ratios or social factors such as the family's socioeconomic status and parental educational attainment. See also Arthur J. Reynolds, "Comparing Measures of Parental Involvement and Their Effects on Academic Achievement," *Early Childhood Research Quarterly* 7, no. 3 (1992): 441–62; James Griffith, "Relation of Parental Involvement, Empowerment, and School Traits to Student Academic Performance," *Journal of Educational Research* 90, no. 1 (1996): 33–41; Sandra L. Christenson, Theresa Rounds, and Deborah Gorney, "Family Factors and Student Achievement: An Avenue to Increase Students' Success," *School Psychology Quarterly* 7, no. 3 (1992): 178–206; Deborah L. Miller and Mary L. Kelley, "Interventions for Improving Homework Performance: A Critical Review," *School Psychology Quarterly* 6, no. 3 (1991): 174–85; James P. Comer, "Home-School Relationships as They Affect the Academic Success of Children," *Education and Urban Society* 16, no. 3 (1984): 323–37; John W. Fantuzzo, Gwendolyn Y. Davis, and Marika D. Ginsburg, "Effects of Parental Involvement in Isolation or in Combination with Peer Tutoring on Student Self-Concept and Mathematics Achievement," *Journal of Educational Psychology* 87, no. 2 (1995): 272–81; Tracey Frigo and others, "Australian Young People, Their Families, and Post-School Plans" (Melbourne: Australian Council for Educational Research, 2007).

27. James P. Comer and Norris M. Haynes. "Parent Involvement in Schools: An Ecological Approach," *Elementary School Journal* 91, no. 3 (1991): 271–77; Griffith, "Relation of Parental Involvement, Empowerment, and School Traits to Student Academic Performance" (see note 26); Arthur J. Reynolds and others, "Cognitive and Family-Support Mediators of Preschool Effectiveness: A Confirmatory Analysis," *Child Development* 67, no. 3 (1996): 1119–40.

28. National Center for Education Statistics, "Father's Involvement in the Children's Schools," NCES 98-091 (U.S. Department of Education, 1997); Christine Winquist Nord, DeeAnn Brimhall, and Jerry West, "Dads' Involvement in Their Kids' Schools," *Education Digest* 63, no. 7 (March 1998): 29–35; Michael E. Lamb, "The Emergent American Father," in *The Father's Role: Cross-Cultural Perspectives,* edited by Michael E. Lamb (Hillsdale, NY: Lawrence Erlbaum Associates Publishers, 1987); Rebecca Goldman, *Fathers' Involvement in Their Children's Education* (London: National Family and Parenting Institute, 2005).

29. Desforges and Abouchaar, "The Impact of Parental Involvement, Parental Support, and Family Education on Pupil Achievement and Adjustment" (see note 25); Reynolds, "Early Schooling of Children at Risk" (see note 25); Callahan, Rademacher, and Hildreth, "The Effect of Parent Participation in Strategies to Improve the Homework Performance of Students Who Are at Risk" (see note 25).

30. F. Davis, "Understanding Underachievers," *American Education* 20, no. 10 (1984): 12–14; M. Gajria and S. Salend, "Homework Practices of Students with and without Learning Disabilities: A Comparison," *Journal of Learning Disabilities* 28 (1995): 291–96; S. Salend and J. Schliff, "An Examination of the Homework Practices of Teachers of Students with Learning Disabilities," *Journal of Learning Disabilities* 22, no. 10 (1989): 621–23; H. Cooper and B. Nye, "Homework for Students with Learning Disabilities: The Implications of Research for Policy and Practice," *Journal of Learning Disabilities* 27, no. 8 (1994): 470–79; S. Salend and M. Gajria, "Increasing the Homework Completion Rates of Students with Mild Disabilities," *Remedial and Special Education* 16, no. 5 (1995): 271–78.

31. Arthur J. Reynolds, "A Structural Model of First Grade Outcomes for an Urban, Low Socioeconomic Status, Minority Population," *Journal of Educational Psychology* 81, no. 4 (1989): 594–603; C. S. Benson, E. A. Medrich, and S. Buckley, "The New View of School Efficiency: Household Time Contributions to School Achievement," in *School Finance Policies and Practices: 1980's Decade of Conflict,* edited by James W. Guthrie (Cambridge, Mass.: Ballinger Publishers, 2005); Reginald M. Clark, "Why Disadvantaged Students Succeed: What Happens Outside Schools' Critical Period," *Public Welfare* (Spring 1990): 17–23.

32. Joyce L. Epstein, "Parent Involvement: What Research Says to Administrators," *Education in Urban Society* 19, no. 2 (1987): 119–36; Ray T. J. Wilks and Valerie A. Clarke, "Training versus Non-Training of Mothers as Home Reading Tutors," *Perceptual and Motor Skills* 67 (1988): 135–42; United Nations Children's Fund (UNICEF), *The State of the World's Children 2001* (New York: 2001); R. Myers, *The Twelve Who Survive: Strengthening Programmes of Early Childhood Development in the Third World* (London and New York: Routledge in cooperation with UNESCO for the Consultative Group on Early Childhood Care and Development, 1992); Linda P. Thurston and Kathy Dasta, "An Analysis of In-Home Parent Tutoring Procedures: Effects on Children's Academic Behavior at Home and in School and on Parents' Tutoring Behaviors," *Remedial and Special Education* 11, no. 4 (1990): 41–52.

33. Heymann, Toomey, and Furstenberg, "Working Parents" (see note 22); Heymann, *The Widening Gap* (see note 22).

34. G. Roger King, "The Healthy Families Act: Safeguarding Americans' Livelihood, Families and Health with Paid Sick Days," Testimony before the U.S. Senate Committee on Health, Education, Labor, and Pensions, February 13, 2007.

35. Berger, Hill, and Waldfogel, "Maternity Leave, Early Maternal Employment and Child Health and Development in the U.S." (see note 2); Susan Macran, Heather Joshi, and Shirley Dex, "Employment after Childbearing: A Survival Analysis," *Work, Employment, and Society* 10, no. 2 (1996): 273–96.

36. Edward Shepard and Thomas Clifton, "Are Longer Hours Reducing Productivity in Manufacturing?" *International Journal of Manpower* 21, no. 7 (2000): 540–52.

37. Defined as meeting six criteria: job autonomy, learning opportunities, decision making, involvement, coworker/supervisor support, and flexibility.

38. Ellen Galinksy, Sheila Eby, and Shanny Peer, "2008 Guide to Bold New Ideas for Making Work Work from the 2007 Winners of the Alfred P. Sloan Awards for Business Excellence in Workplace Flexibility" (New York: Families and Work Institute, 2008) (http://familiesandwork.org/3w/boldideas.pdf).

39. For a full description of the adult labor database, see Jody Heymann and Alison Earle, *Raising the Global Floor: Dismantling the Myth That We Can't Afford Good Working Conditions for Everyone* (Stanford: Stanford University Press, 2010).

40. The World Economic Forum (WEF) is an international organization made up primarily of business leaders, as well as government officials and academic researchers. Its aims are to be "the foremost organization which builds and energizes leading global communities; the creative force shaping global, regional and industry strategies; [and] the catalyst of choice for its communities when undertaking global initiatives to improve the state the world." WEF primarily gathers together business leaders at summits, conferences, and meetings to discuss and develop solutions to global issues (www.weforum.org).

41. From 1987 to 2005 the WEF published the Growth Competitiveness Index, which ranked each nation according to its score on thirty-five variables that represent three conceptual areas: the macroeconomic environment, the quality of public institutions, and technology. Beginning with the 2006 report, this report was renamed the Global Competitiveness Index. The WEF reported rankings based on each nation's scores on more than ninety competitiveness indicators organized into nine areas: institutions; infrastructure; macroeconomy; health and primary education; higher education and training; market efficiency; technological readiness; business sophistication; and innovation. Many of the data used in the competitiveness reports are obtained through a global network of 104 research institutions and academics that partner and collaborate with WEF, as well as from a survey of 11,000 business leaders in 131 nations. The categories are weighted to account more accurately for levels of development in measuring each indicator's impact on competitiveness.

42. World Bank, World Development Indicators, "Labor Force, Total, 2009" (http://data.worldbank.org/indicator/SL.TLF.TOTL.IN?order=wbapi_data_value_2009+wbapi_data_value+wbapi_data_value-last&sort=asc).

43. China has no national standard, but leave is available in certain circumstances in some provinces.

44. The agreed definition of "unemployed" is working-age individuals who are not working and are available for and actively seeking work. The unemployment rate is then equal to the number of unemployed persons as a percentage of civilian employees, the self-employed, unpaid family workers, and the unemployed. For further information on the selection and development of this unemployment definition, see Eurostat Internet site (http://europa.eu.int/comm/eurostat). The original data from each individual country that are merged to create the OECD unemployment database are either "registered" unemployment from administrative data sources or are from national household surveys (for example, the U.S. Census Bureau's Current Population Survey). In the early 1990s almost all OECD nations agreed to use a common set of criteria for classifying individuals as "unemployed" based on common household survey information. The only variations that still exist are the age group included in the calculation of the unemployment rate and the definition of an "active" job search. Over the past two decades (the time period from which our data come), the consistency, quality, and comparability of the OECD data have increased. In addition to consensus on the definitions, data collection and processing methods have converged.

Critical Thinking

1. Is it incompatible for a country to be economically competitive and family friendly in its workplace and leave policies?

2. How do work-family policies in the United States compare with those in 15 economically competitive nations?

3. What are the two work-family policies that you feel are most important to family well-being? Why are these policies important and needed?

Create Central

www.mhhe.com/createcentral

Internet References

Families and Work Institute
   www.familiesandwork.org

Modern Family or Modernized Family Traditionalism?: Master Status and the Gender Order in Switzerland
   www.sociology.org/content/vol006.004/lwk.html

Sociological Perspectives of Work and Family
   www.scribd.com/doc/24528839

ALISON EARLE is a principal research scientist at Northeastern University. **ZITHA MOKOMANE** is a senior research specialist at the Human Sciences Research Council of South Africa. **JODY HEYMANN** is the founding director of the Institute for Health and Social Policy at McGill University.

Article   Prepared by: Patricia Hrusa Williams,
University of Maine at Farmington

Behind Every Great Woman

CAROL HYMOWITZ

Learning Outcomes

After reading this article, you will be able to:

- Explain why women are becoming primary breadwinners in families.

- Describe the challenges faced by families where mothers are employed outside of the home and fathers assume primary responsibility for childrearing.

- Identify how parents can balance their time spent with their family and their career.

Among the 80 or so customers crammed into Bare Escentuals, it's easy to spot Leslie Blodgett. It's not merely her six-inch platform heels and bright magenta-and-blue dress that set her apart in the Thousand Oaks (Calif.) mall boutique, but her confidence. To the woman concerned she's too old for shimmery eye shadow, Blodgett swoops in and encourages her to wear whatever she wants. With a deft sweep of a brush, she demonstrates a new shade of blush on another customer's cheek. And when she isn't helping anyone, she pivots on her heels for admirers gushing about her dress, made by the breakout designer Erdem.

Blodgett, 49, has spent the past 18 years nurturing Bare Escentuals from a startup into a global cosmetics empire. She sold the company for $1.7 billion to Shiseido in March 2010 but still pitches products in stores around the world and chats incessantly with customers online. Scores of fans post daily messages on Blodgett's Facebook page, confessing details about their personal lives and offering opinions on her additive-free makeup. She only wishes her 19-year-old son, Trent, were in touch with her as frequently as he is with her husband, Keith. In 1995, at 38, Keith quit making television commercials to raise Trent, freeing up Leslie to build her business. She'd do it all again, but she's jealous of her husband's relationship with her son. Trent, a college sophomore, texts his father almost every day; he often goes a week without texting her.

"Once I knew my role was providing for the family, I took that very seriously. But there was envy knowing I wasn't there for our son during the day," says Blodgett. "Keith does everything at home—the cooking, repairs, finances, vacation planning—and I could work long hours and travel a lot, knowing he took such good care of Trent. I love my work, but I would have liked to have a little more balance or even understand what that means."

Blodgett's lament is becoming more familiar as a generation of female breadwinners look back on the sacrifices—some little, some profound—required to have the careers they wanted. Like hundreds of thousands of women who have advanced into management roles in the past two decades—and, in particular, the hundreds who've become senior corporate officers—she figured out early what every man with a corner office has long known: To make it to the top, you need a wife. If that wife happens to be a husband, and increasingly it is, so be it.

When Carly Fiorina became Hewlett-Packard's first female chief executive officer, the existence of her househusband, Frank Fiorina, who had retired early from AT&T to support her career, was a mini-sensation; nine years later, this arrangement isn't at all unusual. Seven of the 18 women who are currently CEOs of Fortune 500 companies—including Xerox's Ursula Burns, PepsiCo's Indra Nooyi, and WellPoint's Angela Braly—have, or at some point have had, a stay-at-home husband. So do scores of female CEOs of smaller companies and women in other senior executive jobs. Others, like IBM's new CEO, Ginni Rometty, have spouses who dialed back their careers to become their powerful wives' chief domestic officers.

This role reversal is occurring more and more as women edge past men at work. Women now fill a majority of jobs in the U.S., including 51.4 percent of managerial and professional positions, according to U.S. Census Bureau data. Some 23 percent of wives now out-earn their husbands, according to a 2010 study by the Pew Research Center. And this earnings trend is more dramatic among younger people. Women 30 and under make more money, on average, than their male counterparts in all but three of the largest cities in the U.S.

During the recent recession, three men lost their jobs for every woman. Many unemployed fathers, casualties of layoffs in manufacturing and finance, have ended up caring for their children full-time while their wives are the primary wage earners. The number of men in the U.S. who regularly care for children under age five increased to 32 percent in 2010 from 19 percent in 1988, according to Census figures. Among those fathers with preschool-age children, one in five served as the main caregiver.

Even as the trend becomes more widespread, stigmas persist. At-home dads are sometimes perceived as freeloaders, even if they've lost jobs. Or they're considered frivolous kept men— gentlemen who golf. The househusbands of highly successful women, after all, live in luxurious homes, take nice vacations, and can afford nannies and housekeepers, which many employ at least part-time. In reaction, at-home dads have launched a spate of support groups and daddy blogs to defend themselves.

"Men are suddenly seeing what it's been like for women throughout history," says Linda R. Hirshman, a lawyer and the author of *Get to Work,* a book that challenges at-home moms to secure paying jobs and insist that their husbands do at least half the housework. Caring for children all day and doing housework is tiring, unappreciated work that few are cut out for—and it leaves men and women alike feeling isolated and diminished.

There's some good news about the at-home dads trend. "By going against the grain, men get to stretch their parenting abilities and women can advance," notes Stephanie Coontz, a family studies professor at Evergreen State College in Olympia, Wash., and author of *Marriage: a History.* And yet the trend underscores something else: When jobs are scarce or one partner is aiming high, a two-career partnership is next to impossible. "Top power jobs are so time-consuming and difficult, you can't have two spouses doing them and maintain a marriage and family," says Coontz. This explains why, even as women make up more of the workforce, they're still a small minority (14 percent, according to New York-based Catalyst) in senior executive jobs. When they reach the always-on, all-consuming executive level, "it's still women who more often put family ahead of their careers," says Ken Matos, a senior director at Families and Work Institute in New York. It may explain, too, why bookstore shelves and e-book catalogs are jammed with self-help books for ambitious women, of which *I'd Rather Be in Charge,* by former Ogilvy-Mather Worldwide CEO Charlotte Beers, is merely the latest. Some, such as Hirshman's top-selling *Get to Work,* recommend that women "marry down"—find husbands who won't mind staying at home—or wed older men who are ready to retire as their careers take off. What's indisputable is that couples increasingly are negotiating whose career will take precedence before they start a family.

"Your wife's career is about to soar, and you need to get out of her way." That's what Ken Gladden says his boss told him shortly before his wife, Dawn Lepore, was named the first female CIO at Charles Schwab in 1994. He was a vice-president at Schwab in computer systems. Lepore's promotion meant she'd become his top boss. "I married above my station," Gladden jokes.

Gladden moved to a job at Visa. When their son, Andrew, was born four years later in 1998, Gladden quit working altogether. He and Lepore had tried for years to have a child and didn't want him raised by a nanny. Being a full-time dad wasn't the biggest adjustment Gladden made for Lepore's career. That came later, when Seattle-based drugstore.com recruited Lepore to become its CEO in 2004.

Gladden had lived in the San Francisco Bay Area for 25 years and wasn't keen to move to a city where it rains a lot and he didn't know anyone. He rejected Lepore's suggestion that she commute between Seattle and San Francisco, and after some long discussions he agreed to relocate—on the condition that they kept their Bay Area home. They still return for holidays and some vacations. "To do what I'm doing, you've got to be able to say 'my wife's the breadwinner, the more powerful one,' and be O.K. with that. But you also need your own interests," says Gladden, who has used his computing skills to launch a home-based business developing software for schools.

The couple's five-bedroom Seattle home overlooks Lake Washington. Gladden, 63, is chief administrator of it and their children, who now are 9 and 13. While they're in school, he works on his software. From 3 P.M. until bedtime, he car-pools to and from sports and music lessons, warms up dinners prepared by a part-time housekeeper, and supervises homework. Lepore, 57, is often out of town. She oversaw the sale of drugstore.com to Walgreens last year, for $429 million. As CEO, she was rarely home before 8 or 9 P.M. and traveled several days a week. Now, as a consultant to several startups and a director at eBay, she still travels frequently. If Gladden envies anything, it's the ease with which his wife can walk into a room filled with well-known executives like Bill Gates and "go right up to them and start talking. I don't feel like I can participate," he says.

Lepore wishes her "biggest supporter" would get more recognition for everything he does at home. When an executive recently told her "having an at-home husband makes it easy for you to be a CEO," she responded, "No, not easy. He makes it possible." Lepore advises younger women to "choose your spouse carefully. If you want a top job, you need a husband who isn't self-involved and will support your success," even if you go further than him. There are tradeoffs, she warns: "I've missed so much with my kids—school plays, recitals, just seeing them every day."

For Lepore and Gladden, the role reversal paid off, and, as one of the few couples willing to go public about their domestic arrangement, they're a rare source of inspiration for those who are still figuring it out. Like Gladden, Matt Schneider, 36, is an

A Changing Landscape

	1970	Now
Percentage of employees who are women	35%	49%
Percentage of college graduates who are women	36%	54%
Share of husbands whose wives' income tops theirs	4%	23%
Contribution of wives' earnings to family income	27%	36%
The number of Fortune 500 CEOs who are women	0	18

at-home dad. A former technology company manager and then a sixth grade teacher, he cares for his sons Max and Sam, 6 and 3, while his wife, Priyanka, also 36, puts in 10-hour days as chief operating officer at a Manhattan real estate management startup. He feels "privileged," he says, to be with his sons full-time "and see them change every day," while allowing that child care and housework can be mind-numbing. He uses every minute of the 2½ hours each weekday when Sam is in preschool to expand the NYC DADS Group he co-founded, 450 members strong. Members meet for play dates with their kids, discuss parenting, and stand up for at-home dads. "We're still portrayed as bumbling idiots," Schneider says. He rails against a prejudice that moms would do a better job—if only they were there. "Everyone is learning from scratch how to change diapers and toilet-train," he says, "and there's no reason to think this is woman's work."

Schneider and his wife, who met as undergraduates at University of Pennsylvania's Wharton School of Business, decided before they wed that she'd have the big career and he'd be the primary parent. "It's her name on the paycheck, and sure, we've thought about the precariousness of having just one breadwinner. But she wouldn't earn what she does if I wasn't doing what I do," he says. Which is not to say that he doesn't wonder "whether I can get back to a career when I want to and build on what I've done before."

At-home moms have snubbed him at arts and crafts classes and on playgrounds. "Men, even those of us pushing strollers, are perceived as dangerous," Schneider says. He was rejected when he wanted to join an at-home neighborhood moms' group, which prompted him to blog more about the similarities among moms and dads. "I've met moms *and* dads who are happy to give a screaming kid a candy bar to get him to settle down, and moms *and* dads who show up at play dates with containers filled with organic fruit," he says. "The differences aren't gender-specific."

It's no different for gay couples. Brad Kleinerman and Flint Gehre have taken turns being at-home dads for their three sons, now 19, 18, and 10. When their sons—biological siblings they adopted through the Los Angeles County foster care system—were young, Kleinerman and Gehre relied first on a weekday nanny and then a live-in one while both worked full-time. Kleinerman, 50, was an executive in human resources at Walt Disney and NASA. Gehre, 46, was a teacher and then director of global learning and communications at Disney. Five years ago, they decided they no longer wanted to outsource parenting. "We always wanted to have dinner together as a family, but by the time we got home, the nanny had fed our kids," says Gehre. "Our kids were at pivotal ages—the two oldest about to go to high school and the youngest to first grade. We wanted to be the ones instilling our values and be there when they needed help with homework or had to get to a doctor."

In 2007 the couple moved from Los Angeles to Avon, Conn., where they were able to get married legally and find better schools for their kids. Kleinerman became the full-time dad and Gehre kept his Disney job, working partly from home and traveling frequently to Los Angeles. A year later they switched: Gehre quit Disney to parent full-time and Kleinerman found a new job as a human resources director at Cigna Healthcare.

Gehre says he's never felt discriminated against as a gay dad or a stay-at-home dad. "No one has ever said to me, 'Why would you stay home with the kids?' Where we're discriminated is when we pay taxes. We don't qualify for the marriage deduction, we have to file as single people," he says. If he has one regret about being at home, it's the lack of adult conversation and stimulation: "I worked in a very high-intensity atmosphere with very intelligent and hard-driving people, and that keeps you sharp." Any dullness doesn't make Gehre doubt his decision. Having consciously chosen to have a family, he and Kleinerman felt they had not only to provide the essentials, but also to be present.

Is there an alternate universe where both parents can pursue careers without outsourcing child care? The five Nordic countries—Iceland, Norway, Sweden, Finland, and Denmark—are noted leaders in keeping moms, in particular, on the job. "These countries have made it possible to have a better division of labor both at work and at home through policies that both encourage the participation of women in the labor force and men in their families," says Saadia Zahidi, co-author of the World Economic Forum's *Global Gender Gap Report.* The policies Zahidi refers to include mandatory paternal leave in combination with maternity leave; generous, federally mandated parental leave benefits; gender-neutral tax incentives; and post-maternity reentry programs.

There were no such programs or precedents for Jennifer Granholm and Dan Mulhern. When the two met at Harvard Law School, she grilled him about what he expected from a wife. Mulhern accepted that Granholm would never be a homemaker like his mother, but he never expected her to run for political office. "When I was young," he says, "I thought *I'd* be the governor"—not married to the governor. Granholm was governor of Michigan from 2003 through 2010, and her election forced Mulhern to walk away from the Detroit-based consulting business he founded, which had numerous contracts with state-licensed health insurance companies, municipalities, and school districts. Once that happened, he felt "in a backroom somewhere" and in a marriage that was "a lot more give than take."

Mulhern understood that his wife faced "extraordinary pressure" during her two terms, including a $1.7 billion budget deficit and the bankruptcies of General Motors and Chrysler. She had limited time for their three children, who were 6, 11, and 14 when she was elected, and even less for him. "I didn't want to say, 'hey, you missed my birthday' or 'you haven't even noticed what happened with the kids,' but I sometimes felt resentful," he says.

Mulhern says he complained to his wife that they spent 95 percent of the little time they had together talking about her work. He missed the attention she used to give him but felt humiliated asking for it. He gradually changed his expectations. He stopped waiting for Granholm to call him in the middle of the day to share what had happened at meetings they'd spent time talking about the prior evening. And he realized he couldn't re-create for her all the memorable or awkward moments he had with their children—like the time he found his daughter and her high school friends in the outdoor shower, "ostensibly with their clothes on. I had to call all the parents and tell them, as a courtesy, 'I want you to know this happened at the Governor's mansion,'" he says. "While my wife was battling the Republican head of the State Senate, I had a teenage daughter who was a more formidable opponent."

When Granholm left office and was asked "what's next?", she said, "it's Dan's turn." As a former governor, though, she's the one with more obvious opportunities. Later this month, Granholm launches a daily political commentary show on Current TV. She's also teaching at the University of California at Berkeley, where Dan has a part-time gig thanks to his wife.

"The employment opportunities that come my way—and my salary potential—aren't what my wife's are now," says Mulhern. He plans to continue to teach, write, and do some consulting, while also taking care of their 14-year-old son. "Someone has to be focused on him every day," he says.

The experiences and reflections of powerful women and their at-home husbands could lead to changes at work so that neither women nor men have to sacrifice their careers or families. "There's no reason women should feel guilty about achieving great success, but there should be a way for success to include professional and personal happiness for everyone," says *Get to Work* author Hirshman. "If you have to kill yourself at work, that's bad for everyone."

Kathleen Christensen agrees. As program director at the Alfred P. Sloan Foundation, she has focused on work and family issues and says we're back to the 1950s, only "instead of Jane at home, it's John. But it's still one person doing 100 percent of work outside the home and the other doing 100 percent at home." Just as we saw the Feminine Mystique in the 1960s among frustrated housewives, Christensen predicts, "we may see the Masculine Mystique in 2020."

The children of couples who have reversed roles know the stakes better than anyone. One morning last year, when Dawn Lepore was packing for a business trip to New York, her nine-year-old daughter burst into tears. "I don't want you to travel so much," Elizabeth told her mother. Lepore hugged her, called her school, and said her daughter would be staying home that morning. Then she rescheduled her flight until much later that day. "There have been times when what Elizabeth wants most is a mom who stays home and bakes cookies," she says.

Lepore is sometimes concerned that her children won't be ambitious because they've often heard her complain about how exhausted she is after work. But they're much closer to their father than kids whose dads work full-time, and they have a different perspective about men's and women's potential. When a friend of her daughter's said that fathers go to offices every day, Lepore recalls, "Elizabeth replied, 'Don't be silly, dads are at home.'"

Critical Thinking

1. Why are more women becoming the primary breadwinners in their families?

2. What strategies do families use to create work-family balance?

3. When husbands leave their careers to man the home front, what effect does this role reversal have on children, marriages, and families?

4. What types of supports are needed for families where dads serve as primary caregivers?

Create Central

www.mhhe.com/createcentral

Internet References

Families and Work Institute
www.familiesandwork.org

Modern Family or Modernized Family Traditionalism?: Master Status and the Gender Order in Switzerland
www.sociology.org/content/vol006.004/lwk.html

Sociological Perspectives of Work and Family
www.scribd.com/doc/24528839

Article

Prepared by: Patricia Hrusa Williams,
University of Maine at Farmington

Homeless in the Suburbs

Jenny Deam

Learning Outcomes

After reading this article, you will be able to:

- Explain the reasons why families are homeless.

- Describe how homelessness affects parenting.

- Understand supports needed to assist homeless families.

E leven-year-old Devin Bodiford's eyes blink open in the back room of a suburban Denver church. The clock reads 5 A.M. when his mother whispers that it's time to get up. His little sister and brother stir in their cots next to him. Two trash bags filled with the family's clothes are stashed in the corner; a tube of toothpaste, an alarm clock, a bottle of shampoo, and schoolbooks line the only table. For five days this has been home. In three more he will move again, to another church, to another cot in another room.

"Being homeless," the fifth-grader explains, "means you don't stay in one spot and have to move around a lot. It gets kind of confusing."

A lot of people think they know what homelessness in this country looks like. They see an urban image of the downtrodden sleeping in alleys and pleading for spare change. Yet as the economy worsens and joblessness soars, there's a new and equally troubling picture emerging: Homelessness is creeping into the once-protected enclaves of the suburbs, but it remains a mostly hidden phenomenon. By day, families fade easily into the landscape; by night, they sleep in shelters, in shabby motels, or on the couches of relatives and friends. "Suburban homelessness is among the most invisible because it doesn't fit our stereotypes," says Barbara Duffield, policy director for the National Association for the Education of Homeless Children and Youth, in Washington, DC.

Devin attends school in middle-class Jefferson County, CO, where the number of identified homeless students is double that of the nearby Denver city school district. School officials say they saw a 100 percent increase the first two months of the 2008 school year. Duffield says 330 school districts across the country identified at least the same number, or more, of homeless students in the *beginning* of the 2008–2009 school year as in the entire previous year.

Families make up nearly 40 percent of the homeless population—and that doesn't even fully reflect the recent economic downturn.

Counting homeless children and families is complicated. The Department of Housing and Urban Development defines homelessness in the traditional way: living in shelters, in cars, or on the streets. It estimates that in 2007 more than 341,000 children lived in a shelter at least once over a 12-month period.

But the Department of Education, mandated to gather data so schools can provide support for homeless families, expands the traditional definition to include parents and children living in motels and "doubling up," or staying with friends and families because of lost housing. Its preliminary statistics estimate there were nearly 800,000 homeless students in the 2007–2008 school year, a 15 percent increase from the previous year.

Others say even those numbers are too low. The National Center on Family Homelessness, a nonprofit advocacy group, released a report in March that estimated 1.6 million, or about 1 in 50, children in the United States experienced homelessness at least one day between 2005 and 2006. "No one knows the real number in the suburbs because the communities don't want to know," says Laura Flynn, a housing services administrator for a Salvation Army family shelter in Olathe, KS, a suburb of Kansas City, MO, and county seat of one of the most affluent counties in the nation.

What everyone can agree on, though, is that the face of homelessness is changing. Ellen Bassuk, PhD, president of the National Center on Family Homelessness, says that when she began studying homelessness in the 1980s, families with children made up less than 1 percent of the homeless population. Today they are nearly 40 percent—and experts say the numbers don't even fully reflect the recent economic downturn, since there's often a lag between financial trouble and homelessness.

The long-term prognosis for these kids is not good. Research shows that homeless children who live in chaotic settings or change schools often are more likely to be at least a grade level behind in math and reading. They also are more likely to repeat a grade. They have behavioral and emotional problems three times as often as other children, and more than half will not graduate high school. Worse, suburban homelessness is also the hardest to fight. Suburbs rarely have the kind of social-service infrastructure found in cities. Public transportation is more difficult, distances are farther, and shelters are rare. The stigma is also greater. But all the statistics and research in the world can never really explain what it's like to live in a place filled with four-bedroom houses, and none to call your own. You have to see it through the eyes of those who've experienced it. Here, three families offer a glimpse into their lives:

The Bodiford-Gettle Family
Jefferson County, CO

Devin pads sleepily into the church fellowship hall to fill a cereal bowl and finish a book report. He didn't get his homework done the evening before because it was shower night. Every other night the family is driven by church volunteers to a neighborhood rec center so they can use the locker rooms.

The friendly boy with cropped blond hair and piercing eyes has switched schools eight times since kindergarten, moving from apartments to motels to shelters to friends' houses. He doesn't much like school, except for math. He wishes he could have sleepovers like the other kids.

His mother, 31-year-old Heather Bodiford, came to Colorado with her three kids from Arkansas in 2004 after filing for divorce from her children's father. She moved with family friend David Gettle, who had landed a construction job. They became a couple and the kids soon started calling him Dad. But both had trouble finding steady work. They would fall behind on the rent, get evicted, and have to move. Gettle was at a party raided by police and spent six months in jail on a drug charge. Landlords won't look at them now without a large down payment, and the waiting list for subsidized housing is three months to two years. Gettle works construction jobs when he can. Bodiford dreams of owning her own restaurant. She recently applied for a job at Taco Bell. So did 72 others. Gettle sells his plasma at a blood bank for $35 a couple of times a week.

"The church is okay, but I wish we had a house," Devin says. He longs for a room to decorate with sports posters. His 9-year-old sister, Sierra, sometimes gets scared when they move; his 6-year-old brother, Conner, gets clingy. A program called Interfaith Hospitality' Network of Greater Denver lets them stay at different suburban churches every week while they save for an apartment. The catch is that they have to be out every morning by 7 A.M. and can't return until after 5 P.M. Bodiford likes the suburbs. She says the city shelters frighten her: "I know, being homeless, I can't be too choosy, but I can choose to keep my children safe."

Just before 6 A.M. the family of five steps into the predawn darkness to catch the series of buses that will take the kids to school. It is 75 minutes each way. Bodiford gets off the bus with her kids at school to make sure they are on time. She has never missed a parent-teacher conference. After school she'll be there again.

"Sometimes I feel like a really bad mother," Bodiford says. "If I can't provide a house for my kids, there must be something wrong with me." She tries to push aside such feelings because she does not want them to seep into her children. "I tell them bad things happen to lots of people. It doesn't make you a bad person. My main goal in life is to make sure my kids grow up to be compassionate, responsible, contributing adults." She tries to keep her kids connected with old friends and maintain as much consistency in their lives as possible: Bedtimes are strict no matter where the bed. "The one thing we make sure of," she says, "is that the kids know no matter what, we are a family."

The Marshall Family
Johnson County, KS

Robert Marshall knows how to scrape by. At 17, he lived on the street for six months after being cut loose from the foster-care system. At 24, he lived for a while in a singlemen's shelter. But this time, after losing his job and a place to live, it's different. This time he's a single father raising a 3-year-old son. "It's kind of scary. It's not just me anymore," the 29-year-old says.

In April, Marshall and his son, Robert Jr., moved into a 1940s-era motel that has been converted into a ten-room family shelter in the affluent Kansas City, MO, suburb of Olathe, KS. It is the only homeless shelter in the county, and there is a waiting list of more than 50 families.

Sometimes the little boy seems confused. "I want to go home," he whines.

"This is home for now," Marshall explains. "I'm sorry, son. Daddy's trying. Everything will be better soon."

Marshall and his son's mother broke up when the baby was only a few months old. Marshall felt he could be the better parent to Robert Jr., so he took parenting classes, met with social workers, and made a plan to take accounting classes at a vocational college so he could become a bookkeeper. He had steady work at a metal foundry, making $8 an hour. Just after his son's first birthday, Marshall was awarded sole custody. Soon he and Robert Jr. were living happily with Marshall's new girlfriend. He was working hard and taking those accounting classes.

Then his world crashed again. His foundry job evaporated when the company went out of business; then he lost his next job, at The Home Depot, for missing too much work following hernia surgery. Finally, after two years together, Marshall and his girlfriend broke up. For the next few months, father and son drifted among friends and family. No one could take them in for long, and Marshall couldn't get a new job because he had no childcare. He was flunking out of school because he could no longer get to class. "Maybe the shelter wouldn't be so bad," he decided. He called every day for weeks until there was an opening. "I feel embarrassed because I know I can do better," he says.

Still, he clings to a stubborn optimism that has gotten him through hard times before. He remembers how excited he felt just before Robert Jr. was born, buying tiny outfits and toys for his baby boy. His life seemed on track. He thinks about that now, when he folds his hands before dinner or in the stillness of his room late at night. "Hey Lord, what's going on?" he asks. "Am I doing something wrong?"

He tries to stay practical, too. As soon as he can get child-care worked out, he will return to school. A degree, he figures, will lift him out of the cycle of temporary jobs.

A single father in a homeless shelter is a rarity. But he says it's wrong to think fathers can't be there for their children just as surely as mothers can. "I really believe I'm a good dad," he says. Together, father and son play kickball or climb the play-ground equipment at the shelter. They work on numbers and ABC's. "He can count to twenty, no problem," Marshall boasts. They eat dinner in a group hall with the other families. The little boy has panicked in the middle of the night, when he's woken and not been able to see his father in the dark: "Daddy? Daddy? Where are you?"

"I'm right here," Marshall's called back softly.

Marshall hopes they can be back on their feet soon. Maybe they'll even have a house and a fenced yard where the little boy can have friends over. "I want my son to have the life I never had," he says.

The Wega Family
Seminole County, FL

"This is forever," Rhonda Wega said, trying to keep the panic from her voice as she told her daughters to go through their closets and decide what to save and what to leave behind.

The family had lived in their mobile home for ten years, but on October 18, 2008, a notice to vacate was tacked to the door. Their home was now in foreclosure, and in less than 24 hours it would be padlocked and eventually bulldozed. The family of five quickly packed as much of their lives as would fit into the back of a borrowed truck.

The kids in the family—three girls ages 11 to 16—would hold up a toy or a book or a medal won, and ask their mom: "Can I take this?" They were moving things to a storage unit, but there wasn't room for everything.

"I was sad and scared," remembers 14-year-old Kacy. "I was like, 'Where are we going to live?'"

Richard Wega had worked as a cement contractor for a swimming-pool company. During the housing boom, he could make $1,500 per job. His annual income was close to $80,000—but then the housing market in Florida collapsed. In March 2007 he was laid off, and worked odd jobs when he could find them. His wife had chronic kidney problems, which led to a trans-plant in December 2007. By spring they were behind on their $600-a-month mortgage and foreclosure proceedings had begun.

"I was totally heartbroken," Richard says. "Everything I had worked so hard on for my kids was totally trashed. I didn't feel like a dad."

They drove away in the truck at 1 A.M., Rhonda still wear-ing the pajamas she'd slept in the night before because she'd forgotten to grab clothes for herself. She was mostly worried about her kids. She also forgot the baby pictures, which are now gone for good.

For six months the family crashed with friends—eight peo-ple in a double-wide trailer. Rhonda slept on a mattress on the floor; Macy, 16, slept on a couch; Kacy, on a loveseat; Richard and Summer, 11, slept in a camper out back.

How to Help

- **Find the People Who Need You** Each school district is required to have a Local Homeless Edu-cation Liaison. To locate yours, call your district or visit the National Center for Homeless Education at SERVE site at *Serve.org/nche.* Click on State/Local Resources (many states have their own web-sites, which you can link to from here). You can also contact local churches or search for area shelters at *Homelessshelterdirectory.org.* Ask what they need donated, and have your kids help you gather items.

- **Volunteer with a Local Group** The National Coalition for the Homeless has a directory of homeless and housing advocacy groups (go to *Nationalhomeless .org,* then click on Resources). Think about exper-tise you can lend, especially if money's tight. Some shelters might need people to babysit or to help job hunters with writing résumés.

- **Donate to the Cause** You might consider contribut-ing to the National Center for Family Homelessness, which is dedicated specifically to helping homeless families. Plus, if you start at their site (*Familyhome-lessness.org*) and shop at certain online stores (like *Amazon.com*), the organization will receive a dona-tion at no cost to you. Another good option: At the site for the National Association for the Education of Homeless Children and Youth (*Naehcy.org*), you can donate to a scholarship fund.

The strain took its toll. "We argued more, especially about money," says Rhonda. They weren't exactly guests, but they didn't really live there, either. "It's not your stuff; it's not your place. You don't feel secure," she says.

Macy's grades started slipping, and at least once a week she would make up excuses to stay home from school. She would lash out in a fury her parents had never seen before. When they told her to do something, she would snap: "Yeah? Well, you told me we weren't going to lose our house, either." She started going to anger-management therapy.

The younger girls never wanted their mother out of their sight. Summer seemed to burst into tears for no reason; Kacy stopped telling people where she lived.

But in March, things started to turn around. The family was able to move into an apartment in a low-income complex, thanks to assistance from Families in Transition, a Seminole County school-based assistance program. They had no furni-ture, though: At first, they didn't have the money to retrieve what had been in storage since the foreclosure.

Richard now has a $7.21-per-hour telemarketing job and is trying to pick up some cement work. Rhonda is looking for a part-time job as she continues to recover from her surgery. The Wegas are cautiously optimistic. The apartment manager gave them an old couch, and someone else brought them a table. "We were able to sit together as a family for the first time in a long time," Rhonda says. "We can be ourselves again. The kids are still sleeping on a mattress, but it's *their* mattress. They are happy again."

Critical Thinking

1. What factors are contributing to an increase in homeless families in the United States?
2. Is homelessness only an urban problem? Why or why not?
3. What are some challenges for children, parents, and families in adapting in the face of residential instability and homelessness?
4. What supports are needed by families to prevent homelessness? To ensure child and family well-being while homeless?

Create Central

www.mhhe.com/createcentral

Internet References

The National Center on Family Homelessness
www.familyhomelessness.org
National Alliance to End Homelessness
www.endhomelessness.org/pages/families

JENNY DEAM is a former newspaper reporter who now writes about children and family issues for national magazines.

Article

Prepared by: Patricia Hrusa Williams,
University of Maine at Farmington

The Positives of Caregiving: Mothers' Experiences Caregiving for a Child with Autism

MICHAEL K. CORMAN

Learning Outcomes

After reading this article, you will be able to:

- Identify challenges experienced by mothers caring for children with autism.

- Explain the benefits mothers experience in caring for a child with autism.

- Identify the ways in which professionals can work with families who have children with autism.

The documentation and representation of the experiences of caregivers of children with autism and other developmental disabilities has been one dimensional at best, with a pervasive focus on the stresses, burdens, and parental coping associated with caregiving (Grant, Ramcharan, McGrath, Nolan, & Keady, 1998). Much of this focus is warranted. For example, sources of stress (stressors) for caregivers of these children are numerous and might include the autistic traits themselves (DeMyer, 1979; Tomanik, Harris, & Hawkins, 2004), social stigmas from the general public and health practitioners (Gray, 1998, 2002a, 2002b), and the social support system that is intended to alleviate stress (Corman, 2007a; DeMyer, 1979; Gray, 1998).

This multitude of stressors can have an immense effect on individuals in the family, including parents and siblings (DeMyer, 1979; Kaminsky & Dewey, 2001; Schopler & Mesibov, 1994), extended family members (Gray, 1998), and, depending on how caregivers cope, the possible life gains that the individual with autism can make (Schopler & Mesibov, 1994). For example, parents often experience a combination of emotional problems (such as depression, isolation, and feelings of being a failure as a parent), physical problems (fatigue, ulcers, headaches, fluctuation in weight, dermatitis, and other physical health conditions), career problems (limited or no employment—specifically for mothers and career changes), and negative effects on the marriage (marital discord often

ending in divorce; Gray, 1998, 2002a). Parents also report feelings of guilt, isolation, doubts of their ability to care for their child, anger toward the symptoms of autism, increased physical and psychological tensions, frustrations, lack of life satisfaction, and feelings of exhaustion and old age (DeMyer, 1979; Gray, 2002b). Last, because of the unique and often complex symptomatology associated with autism, such as a lack of verbal communication, variant cognitive functioning, and severe behaviors, comparative studies have reported that the burden of caregiving for children with autism is greater than that of parenting a child with other disabilities (Weiss, 2002), such as mental retardation, Down's syndrome, cystic fibrosis, and chronic and fatal physical illness.

Caregiving for a child with autism is stressful! But what about the positive side of caregiving? The narrow focus on the stressful and negative aspects of the caregiving experience offers only partial insights into the experiences of caregiving for children with chronic conditions. There is a need for research to examine the other side of the spectrum, the positive and often joyous side of parenting children with disabilities. The purpose of this article is to provide insight into that positive side by exploring the experiences of mothers of children with autism through in-depth interviews. Although these mothers portrayed an experience that was often stressful, they also discussed many joys of caregiving. This article attempts to strike a balance with the majority of research that focuses on the negatives of caregiving; it will show that caregiving for children with autism is not solely stressful. These findings have theoretical and practical implications. First, this article provides a brief overview of the literature on the positives of caregiving for individuals with chronic conditions.

Literature Review

Most caregiving research focuses solely on the negative aspects of the experience (Chappell, Gee, McDonald, & Stones, 2003), which may be indebted to the pathological models of stress that guide such inquiries. For instance, Pearlin, Lieberman,

Menaghan, and Mullan's (1981) framework of the stress process focuses on the stressors (antecedents to stress) associated with caregiving and pays specific attention to the many related relationships, and the developing and changing nature of these relationships over time, that eventually lead to stress (see also Pearlin, Mullan, Semple, & Skaff, 1990). Lazarus and Folkman (1984) offered a framework that focuses on the more individual and psychological components of what they called the *stress-coping process*. They suggested that it is how stressors are appraised, in addition to individual resources, that determines whether or not an event is stressful (Lazarus & Folkman, 1984). Although these conceptualizations are useful for exploring the stressful aspects of caregiving and how individuals cope, they are limited in that they fail to address any positives of caregiving in a systematic way; positives have been left by the wayside (Kelso, French, & Fernandez, 2005). As Grant et al. (1998) suggested, such a singular view fails to account for other important dimensions.

Research on caregiving has only recently considered gratification and the role of positives in the caregiving experience. For example, in Susan Folkman's (1997) seminal study of caregiving for men with HIV/AIDS, she discussed how positive states of mind can co-occur with negative states. She reported that "despite high levels of distress, people also experience positive psychological states during caregiving and bereavement" (p. 1207). Folkman described four psychological states associated with coping: (a) positive reappraisal, (b) goal-directed problem-focused coping, (c) spiritual beliefs and practices, and (d) the infusion of ordinary events with positive meaning. All four states have an underlying characteristic, that is, the appraisal of positive meanings occurring within a stressful event, which she referred to as *meaning-based coping*.

Grant et al. (1998) explored the positives of caregiving by interviewing 120 caregivers of individuals with intellectual disabilities. They described rewards and caregiver gratification as emerging from three sources: (a) the relationship between caregiver and care receiver, (b) intrapersonal characteristics of the caregiver, and (c) the desire for positive outcomes or the avoidance of negative affect. They also found that many of the gratifications expressed by caregivers were related to, or a product of, successful coping strategies, supporting Folkman's (1997) findings.

More recently, Chaya Schwartz (2003) defined caregiver gratification as "fulfilling parental duties, a better idea of 'what's important in life', learning about inner strengths, aware of personal limitations, learning to do new things, satisfaction from doing what's right, personal growth, [and] becoming more self-confident" (p. 580). In her study of 167 primary caregivers of individuals with mental, developmental, or physical disabilities, she found that caregivers who were younger, unemployed, and had poor health were more likely to experience caregiver gratification. In addition, she found the only characteristics of the child that factored into experiencing gratification were the age of the child (younger children) and the type of disability (having a physical rather than a mental disability). Last, subjective (perceived stress) rather than objective burden (the level of care required) was associated with less caregiver gratification

(Schwartz, 2003). Schwartz speculated that the gratification parents experienced might be a product of how they perceived or created meaning in their caregiving role.

In the field of autism, research has only provided marginal insights into the more rewarding aspects of caregiving. For instance, in a study about narratives published on the Internet by parents, Amos Fleischmann (2004) found that in addition to the demanding aspects of caregiving, a majority of Websites focused on the positive essence of individuals with autism and the caregiving experience, with an emphasis on parents' positive relationship with their child and joyous experiences derived from caregiving. Fleischmann's study is supported by other research on the contributions people with disabilities make to their families: families might benefit in terms of strengthened family ties, compassion and fulfillment, and happiness (Pruchno, 2003).

Despite the shortcomings of Pearlin et al. (1981, 1990) and Lazarus and Folkman's (1984) models, they allow for a scope that looks beyond adjustment and toward positives (Kelso et al., 2005). This is apparent in Folkman's (1997) work on caregiving for individuals with HIV/AIDS (see also Folkman & Moskowitz, 2000a, 2000b). Using these insights, the positives of caregiving are defined in this article as experiences or events that caregivers appraise as positive and sometimes joyous. It is important to note that if this definition seems ambiguous, it is because the positives of caregiving remain relatively uncharted, lacking conceptual clarification (Grant et al., 1998). Based on mothers' reflections, this article explores the positives of caregiving for a child with autism. In doing so, a more complete understanding of these parents' lived experiences emerges, with important contributions to the broader constellation of caregivers of children with chronic conditions.

Method
Participants
Results reported in the next section were drawn from a larger study that explored mothers' experiences of caregiving for a child with autism, before and after their child was placed outside of the home (either in foster care, a group home setting, or a treatment-care facility, hereafter referred to as *placed* or *placement*). Interviews occurred between November 2005 and February 2006. Nine mothers participated in total; 6 lived in British Columbia, and 3 lived in Alberta, Canada. The average age of mothers was 46, with a range between 35 and 62 years old. For 7 out of the 9 mothers, family income ranged between $30,000 and more than $100,000. One mother responded "middle class," and another chose not to answer. As of the first interview, the children with autism were between the ages of 8 and 18, with the average being 14 years old. The age of these children at the time of placement was 6–15, with an average of 11 years old. Mothers were purposely chosen because they are usually the primary caregivers (Gray, 2003) and are therefore more likely to be involved in the day-to-day ups and downs of caregiving. Furthermore, a unique sample of mothers was chosen; their experiences were so stressful that their child was ultimately placed outside of the home (see Corman, 2007a). Although this

study did not aim to be generalizable, it was assumed that if this sample experienced positives, caregivers in less stressful circumstances (e.g., caregivers of a child with less severe autistic characteristics and other disabilities) would also experience them. Therefore, these findings are potentially transferable to other constellations of caregivers.

A diagnosis of autism was reported by 7 out of the 9 mothers during the initial contact, with the remaining 2 mothers reporting a diagnosis of pervasive developmental disorder (PDD) and PDD not otherwise specific (PDD-NOS). Mothers also reported co-occurring conditions, including Landau-Kleffner syndrome, obsessive compulsive disorder, mental handicap, epilepsy (for three children), and Down's syndrome. Two of the mothers had a female child, and 7 had a male child. Although I refer to a generalized *autism*, it is important to note that there is no all-or-nothing form of autism but rather a continuum of severity, known as autism spectrum disorders (Wing, 1988). Based on mothers' descriptions, these children would most likely fall within the moderate to severe end of the spectrum.

Research Design

In-depth, semistructured interviews were conducted based on transcendental phenomenology (Moustakas, 1994), a qualitative research strategy and philosophy that allows researchers to identify the essence of experience as it relates to certain phenomena as described and understood by participants of a study (Creswell, 2002). Mothers were interviewed at their homes and asked to retrospectively talk about their caregiving experiences. Questions were geared toward exploring the positives and joys of caregiving, the demands of caregiving, and how mothers coped, focusing on the times before and after out-of-home placement. The portion of the interviews reported in the analysis below are based on the questions that explored the positives during the early years prior to placement (approximately 0–8 years of age, depending when the placement process was activated) and after their child left home. Interviews lasted on average 2.24 hours with a range of 1.5–3 hours. The interviews and the numbers of mothers interviewed continued until sufficiency and saturation of information were reached.

Interviews were transcribed in their entirety and analyzed based on a modified approach offered by Moustakas (1994), specifically intended for the analysis of qualitative data. Eight steps were followed: (1) identifying patterns in the data based on the lived experiences of participants, (2) reducing the data by identifying unique aspects of experience, (3) organizing the data into core themes that represent the experience of participants, (4) validating step 3 by reviewing the complete transcript of participants, (5) constructing an individual textural description of the experience presented by each participant, (6) based on step 5, constructing a clear account of the dynamics of the experience, (7) combining steps 5 and 6 to create a textural-structural description of each participant that incorporated the experiences of participants, and (8) combining individual textual descriptions of each participant into one that represents the experience presented by the group as a whole.

To assist in the process just described, insights offered by Moerer-Ur-dahl and Creswell (2004) were followed. Initially, significant statements within each participant's transcripts were identified, with a primary focus on understanding how individuals viewed different aspects of their experiences as they related to the positives and joys of caregiving. The goal here was to ground or contextualize the positives of caregiving to gain a better understanding of the distinct character of positives as described by mothers. The data were then broken down into themes based on the experiences of mothers. Once themes were developed, a detailed description of the experience of each mother as it related to the themes that emerged was provided. Conclusions were then drawn in accordance with the lived experiences expressed by participants. The product of this process was the grouping of statements into the themes discussed in the next section.

Results
Pockets of Child Development

All parents expressed the positives during the early years of their child's development as "pockets" because they were "kind of few and far between." Positives discussed by mothers included their child developing, seeing their child happy, times devoid of negative autistic traits or maladaptive behaviors (as perceived by the mother) that are often associated with autism, spending time with their child, unique and/or positive personality traits of their child, and knowing or discovering what was wrong with their child. I discuss each in the following paragraphs.

Developmental Gains

With a diagnosis on the autism spectrum, parents are often left in ambiguity because of the nature of the disability; they do not know how much their child will develop in the years to come. As a result, mothers described feelings of joy when their child started to make developmental gains. For example, one mother discussed how she was "very pleased" when her child progressed in developmental areas, such as "when he started to speak." Another mother commented on her child's success in learning new tasks; "Oh yeah, his success still makes me feel good, no matter what. Like I remember when he learned how to wave good-bye. That made me cry that day [laugh]." Another mentioned the "little milestones that parents take for granted, I think are tremendous."

Another mother discussed how watching her child was "hugely satisfying . . . it makes it all worth it when you start to see a little bit of language or a behavior, or a skill emerge." For some mothers, this gave them hope for their child's future. One mother explained, "I think . . . a little bit of joy with a child that's seriously handicapped goes a long way. It gives you a lot of hope."

Child Being Happy

All mothers experienced positives derived from seeing their child happy. Although this might seem like a common experience of all parents, it is important to contextualize this side of caregiving in that many mothers viewed their child as being chronically unhappy. One mother put it best, "just to see him happy, because all through his life he's lived either withdrawn or anxious, or afraid of doing things." When mothers saw their child happy, they were especially happy. For example, joy arose for one mother when she watched her child enjoy his favorite activity. She explained:

> You see this bright-eyed little boy at the top of the slide, that was his favorite activity was going down the slides. So when you see him at the top of the slide with this big grin on his face, those kinds of times were really exciting for me. . . . I just knew that he enjoyed that.

Seeing her child happy made her feel "really good. . . . That is sort of what we hope our kids are going to feel." Another mother described, "when he's happy and having a really good time, then I'm happy. It's like I'm just a normal parent."

Times Devoid of Negative Autistic Traits or Maladaptive Behaviors

Mothers also talked about times devoid of negative behaviors (negative autistic traits), which they thought of as "normal" times. For instance, one mother described how when her child "didn't throw his food . . . [or] didn't have any feces smearing in the bathroom," these were more positive times. Others experienced positives when their child "hadn't pinched another child or hit another child." One mother went on to explain, "So any time he was cooperating . . . times that he was being and not bothering anybody. . . . If I heard that he sat for five minutes in his desk, or he sat in circle time without poking the next person." During these times, some mothers expressed being "really happy."

Spending Time with Your Child

Despite many of the difficulties, all mothers described the positives of spending time with their child. For instance, one mother discussed how she and her child would go swimming together and go down to the beach to spend time together. Her child "loved it" and always "liked hanging off me." She described how there were so many "nice times" that they spent together. Another mother described how she felt "just connected" to her child because of the times they spent together, specifically "the caregiving part . . . being hands on, physically connected." She talked about how she "really enjoyed" the connection she had with her child: "We're connected on a different level." This mother concluded:

> I guess having a child with autism, you connect with them on a completely different level than I think you would with other children because you don't have language. He's also mostly nonverbal, so physical connections are really important; it's the way you communicate that's beyond words I guess, so I think that's part of it.

For this mother, what might be viewed as a demanding aspect of caregiving was in fact very joyous for her.

Unique and/or Positive Personality Traits of Their Child

Individuals with autism often have a variety of challenges, including maladaptive behaviors, difficulty in communicating with others, difficulty listening and following directions, and other co-occurring medical conditions. However, individuals who have autism are heterogeneous; the severities of impairments vary from person to person (Gray, 2003; Seltzer, Shattuck, Abbeduto, & Greenberg, 2004). Nonetheless, the positive side of this uniqueness often goes unrecognized. All mothers in this study recognized the uniqueness of their child. In doing so, they expressed many positives derived from the unique personality traits of their child.

For example, mothers discussed how their child was "real sweet" and showed affection. Another mother talked about her child being a "very warm individual. . . . We were blessed that way, I guess; very cuddly, quite attached to your close family members." Other personality traits included being "very funny, like she's got a good sense [of humor] . . . she's quite a little monkey," and being "a very good-natured kid . . . he still has a happy disposition." Despite the negative traits mothers dealt with throughout their caregiving experience, which sometimes worsen or change as their child ages into adulthood (Gray, 2002a), mothers described the many unique personality traits of their child as a positive side of caregiving.

Knowing or Discovering What Was Wrong with Their Child

Common perceptions of receiving a diagnosis on the autism spectrum suggest that the experience is devastating, and often it is (Mansell & Morris, 2004). In fact, for many of the mothers in this study, the autism diagnosis represented the loss of the child that was or could have been. One mother explained how "the day that I found out [I was floored] because there's nothing like that in my family, and we've always been high achievers . . . and I don't know where that [diagnosis] came from."

Although some mothers described receiving the diagnosis of autism as very burdensome—"it was sad, it's pretty devastating, to have a child who's not typical"—for others, the receipt of the diagnosis was not a stressful experience but a positive one. With a diagnosis, mothers were relieved to finally know what was wrong with their child after having entered into multiple systems of care in search for answers and supports. For example, after receiving a diagnosis, one mother described how "all of a sudden you know . . . because up until this point everybody's been asking me 'Why is he doing this? What's he doing?' And I'd be going 'I don't know; I don't know.' I really had no answers for anybody." With a diagnosis, answers started "coming out." With these answers, mothers described a positive experience derived from knowing and understanding.

Furthermore, the receipt of a diagnosis allowed the mother to gain access to specialized services and supports for her child, such as intervention therapy, and herself, such as respite, and set out a pathway of care for her child.[1] The ability to take action was positive, and often a relief, because now the mother was able to help her child. One mother expanded upon this point:

> I'm very much a doer, and so when you have a diagnosis, then you can look at putting the pieces together to move forward and do something; especially I hear so

much about early development and early intervention. It was right around the time that the money was being made available for early intervention, and I didn't want to waste a minute, especially knowing that that money would dissolve when he was 6.

The Impacts of Positives

Parents did not just describe the positive side of caregiving, they also discussed how the positives interacted with negative and stressful experiences (i.e., their stress-coping process). For example, the positives associated with their child developing gave mothers hope. One mother, like many parents of children with autism, worried about her child's future (Ivey, 2004). When her child started to make developmental milestones, she began to have a more positive outlook for her child's future. This hope impacted the concerns and worries she had for her child's future. She went on to explain how the positives "are the things that keep you going . . . a little bit of joyful experience gives you . . . the ability to go on."

On a more general note, one mother described how the positives of caregiving had an impact on her stress-coping process.

> Well they (the positives) kept me going . . . it wasn't all negative. It kind of gave me hope to continue on, like every day is a new day kind of thing. . . . It gave me a reason to get up in the morning so I wouldn't be waking up going "oh no, I have to deal with another day" sort of thing . . . any time you have any kind of joy or positive feelings then that . . . just gives you a really good feeling that you can continue over the next period of time.

Another mother explained:

> [The positives] just keep you going. Without the moments of comic relief, without the joys, without those moments of connection where he catches your eye directly for 1 minute and you actually have his gaze directly, without those things, you'd go stir crazy. Those are the things that feed you. I get a huge amount of strength from the tiniest little things.

Despite the demands of caregiving, mothers experienced a multitude of positives during their caregiving years, many of which brought joy to their lives.

Positive Reflections on Their Overall Caregiving Experience

All mothers spoke about personal transformation as a result of their caregiving years. This transformation included learning from their experience and growing as a person. It is important to note that these positive reflections are not linked to any specific event but were a product of their caregiving experience as a whole. Furthermore, it is important to contextualize this positive side of caregiving: All mothers eventually placed their child with autism due to a number of factors, including their child's maladaptive behaviors increasing drastically, "getting more intense" and more difficult to deal with over time, a failure in the support system that was intended

to alleviate stress, and a general inability to cope with the demands of caregiving, leading to mothers experiencing severe distress and feeling that they "couldn't go on" (Corman, 2007a). However, despite this experience of severe distress, all mothers ultimately reflected positively on their caregiving experience as a whole.

For example, one mother explained the learning involved in caregiving where she not only "learned a lot about autism, but I learned a lot about people, and I would have missed that . . . it was a really wonderful thing." Another explained how "the biggest positive is just the learning that came out of that for us as a family, but for me in particular as a person. But I think it's shaped all of us, it certainly has shaped [my husband and daughter] as well as me."

Others described caregiving as making them stronger as a person. One mother mentioned how she "became a fighter, just kind of like an advocate for the family but also for [my child with autism]. . . . So, yeah, definitely it makes you stronger. And it makes you tougher in a way." Her experience also made her realize what is "important. . . . So, you realize what's really important and don't sweat the small stuff." Another mother described her child with autism as being one of her greatest teachers in life:

> I mean, I don't even know who I would be if I hadn't had May . . . it's kind of a weird thing, but in my life, she's been kind of one of my key teachers. She's kind of forced me to kind of examine parts of myself that I don't know if I ever would have got to if I didn't have her. And, she forced [my husband] and I to kind of deal with issues that might have taken us years. . . . It's been a struggle, and sometimes I've hated her for it, [but] nobody has taught me so much.

Mothers also discussed how the caregiving experience made them more empathetic:

> My husband and I were asked one time about the biggest thing that we got from Sam. I think it was the gift of patience 'cause I have patience unlimited, you know . . . 'cause once somebody's dumping milk out in your front yard [laugh], it's amazing how much patience you have.

Discussion and Conclusion

Despite the demanding aspects of caregiving for children with autism, and it is often very demanding, caregivers experience many positives and joys from their role as caregivers. However, the majority of research focuses on the negative and more stressful aspects of the caregiving experience. Breaking away from this preponderance of research in the field of autism, this article highlights some of the positives of caregiving that mothers experienced during the early years of their child's development and overall reflections on their caregiving experience after their child left home. When asked to discuss the positives of caregiving, all mothers expressed a multitude of positives directly related to their caregiving role (Chappell et al., 2003; Folkman, 1997; Grant et al., 1998; Schwartz, 2003). Others derived positives from finding the "positive essence" in their child (Fleischmann, 2004) and achievements of their child (Grant et al., 1998). More unique positives included discovering what was wrong with their child in the face of not knowing.

Implications for Practice

Many practical implications arise from this study. Although caregiving for children with autism is demanding, this article suggests that the positives and joys that emerge from this role are not only important but also have a specific function. Whereas current research describes the positives of caregiving as a *product* of successful coping—the adaptational function of positives (see Folkman, 1997; Grant et al., 1998)—parents in this study discussed how positives had an impact *on* their stress-coping process, rather than being simply a product of it. In other words, positives also occur outside of the stress-coping process, and interact with it, affecting how mothers experience stressors and negative outcomes, potentially impacting their ability to cope at different times. This finding expands on the function of positives within the caregiving experience; they go beyond adaptational function to being a core aspect of caregivers' experiences.

Furthermore, the importance and function of the positives and joys of caregiving is most apparent when they are not present. In the larger study that contributed to this article, all mothers described severe distress and solely negative outcomes during the time leading up to and immediately following the placement of their child, a time devoid of any positives or joys of caregiving. One mother described it best: "When the stresses got to be too much, the joy of everything started to disappear." Does a lack of positives impact caregiver well-being and a caregiver's ability to cope? Cummins (2001) explained that most caregivers are able to describe positives derived from their caregiving role; when they are unable to do so, the demands of their role are likely to be intolerable. Grant et al. (1998) further explained that without the positives of caregiving, it may not be possible for caregivers to feel as if they are able to continue encountering the stressful circumstances corollary to their role. As such, it might be concluded that the positives of caregiving are an integral part of parents' ability to cope, to the point that when they are not present, parents may not be able to continue caregiving. Policy and practice implications directly follow from these findings in that a lack of positives might be an indicator of the current state of a caregiver's well-being or lack of well-being. It might be an indicator for professional services and supports that additional supports are needed to proactively assist those in crisis or on the brink of crisis. Furthermore, policies need to be developed that are proactively geared toward preventing a crisis or assisting those on the brink of a crisis rather than solely intervening once the crisis emerges. Of equal importance, this examination of positives provides future families of children with autism and other disabilities a better understanding of the experience of caregiving as a whole—an experience that is very demanding at times but also has many positives.

How families cope with the demands associated with caring for a child with autism not only influences the well-being of the family but also possible life gains that an individual with autism can make (Schopler & Mesibov, 1994). Current research on caregiving for children with autism attempts to promote the use of successful coping strategies and resources to improve the quality of life of the caregiver and care receiver (Dunn, Burbine, Bowers, & Tantleff-Dunn, 2001; Gray, 1994, 1998). One practical implication that might inform research, policy, and practice on successful coping is the need to promote and draw attention to the positives of caregiving both within service agencies and for those caregiving for children with autism and other disabilities. If services and supports are able to enhance the positive aspects of caregiving by drawing attention to them, parents might be able to cope more successfully with the difficulties of caregiving. In addition, it might be beneficial for services and supports to facilitate the joys of caregiving by drawing attention to the strengths of the caregiver and the positive contribution their child with a disability makes to their family (Pierpont, 2004). The strengths-based perspective and active interviewing are two resources that service providers might draw upon to help facilitate and draw attention to the positives of caregiving.

The strengths-based perspective is one orientation that might assist those whose work intersects with individuals with disabilities and their families in drawing attention to and facilitating the identification of the positive and joyous aspects of caregiving. This perspective shifts away from pathological conceptions of persons with disabilities and the experiences of caregiving to more qualitative and holistic understandings, aligned with the positives of caregiving discussed earlier. By focusing on strengths (see Cohen, 1999; Early, 2001), this perspective has the potential to assist service providers in gaining a more complete understanding of the caregiving experience and perceiving their experiences in a more positive light, which has the potential to increase caregivers' quality of life and the quality of care they provide (Berg-Weger, Rubio, & Tebb, 2001).

In addition to the strengths-based perspective, and complementary to it, insights offered by the reflexive and linguistic turns in sociology could be of use to service providers and researchers alike as a resource or tool to draw upon to explore the positives of caregiving and draw attention to them. One approach aligned with this shift is "the active interview," which is a methodological and analytical approach to interviewing that conceptualizes the interview as an active meaning-making process between interviewee and interviewer, who both participate in the coproduction of knowledge. The interviewer (i.e., service provider), in the context of exploring the positives of caregiving, might invite or "incite" the interviewee (i.e., caregiver) to talk about and reflect on the positives of caregiving. Traditionally, this approach might be viewed as leading the respondent, resulting in a social desirability bias (Esterberg, 2002; see also Cummins, 2001). However, the active interview suggests that interviewers are inevitably embedded and implicated in the meaning-making processes of respondents. Holstein and Gubrium (2002) explained:

This is not to say that active interviewers merely coax their respondents into preferred answers to their questions. Rather, they converse with respondents in such a way that alternate considerations are brought into play . . . encouraging respondents to develop topics in ways relevant to their own everyday lives . . . to provide an environment conducive to the production of the range and complexity of meanings that address relevant issues. (pp. 120–121)

Furthermore, in the context of the positives of caregiving, the active interview is not solely concerned about the positives; it suggests that there is usefulness in inviting individuals to think about the positives and honor participants in the meaning-making process. As such, I suggest that this approach can provide a more fruitful examination of the caregiving experience as a whole by assisting researchers and service providers in exploring and gaining a better understanding and appreciation of the positives of caregiving. This process might also facilitate families and caregivers in talking about and reflecting upon their experiences in a more positive and joyous light (Berg-Weger et al., 2001).

Directions for Future Research

The findings from this study suggest that future research should focus on the factors that lead to positives of caregiving, which might identify and assist in the development of services, supports, and specific interventions that will potentially facilitate improved outcomes for individual caregivers, care receivers, and the family as a whole. As such, there is a need to explore links among positives, social supports, coping, and appraisal processes of caregivers of children with autism and other chronic conditions. Furthermore, future research should investigate these links to determine how the facilitation of positives might affect caregivers' lived experiences. Also, as mentioned earlier, it is important to examine positives and joys not only in relation to stressors but also as a significant factor throughout the entire stress-coping process.

Last, this study focused on the retrospective experience of mothers whose children were under 18 years old. However, for the first time in history, large numbers of people with autism are reaching old age (National Advisory Council on Aging, 2004; Seltzer et al., 2004). As a result, parents now "face a lifetime of caregiving responsibilities" (Kim, Greenberg, Seltzer, & Krauss, 2003, p. 313). However, very little is known about this constellation of caregivers and care receivers. There is need to explore the experiences of individuals with autism, their caregivers, and families as they age over the life course.

Note

1. In British Columbia and Alberta, for instance, institutional services and supports are attached to a diagnosis of autism (see Corman, 2007b).

References

Berg-Weger, M., Rubio, D., & Tebb, S. (2001). Strengths-based practice with family caregivers of the chronically ill: Qualitative insights. *Families in Society: The Journal of Contemporary Human Services, 82*(3), 263–272.

Chappell, N., Gee, E., McDonald, L., & Stones, M. (2003). *Aging in contemporary Canada.* Toronto, Canada: Pearson Educational Publishers/Prentice Hall.

Cohen, B. (1999). Intervention and supervision in strengths-based social work practice. *Families in Society: The Journal of Contemporary Human Services, 80*(5), 460–466.

Corman, M. K. (2007a). *Primary caregivers of children with autism spectrum disorders—An exploration of the stressors, joys, and parental coping before and after out-of-home placement.* (Masters Thesis, University of Victoria, Canada, 2007). Available from the Electronic Theses and Dissertations Website: http:// hdl.handle.net/1828/1227.

Corman, M. K. (2007b, August). *Panning for gold—An institutional ethnography of health relations in the process of diagnosing autism in British Columbia.* Paper presented at the meeting of The Society for the Study of Social Problems, New York.

Creswell, J. (2002). *Research design: Qualitative, quantitative, and mixed methods approaches* (2nd ed.). Thousand Oaks, CA: Sage Publications.

Cummins, R. (2001). The subjective well-being of people caring for a family member with a severe disability at home: A review. *Journal of Intellectual & Developmental Disability, 26*(1), 83–100.

DeMyer, M. (1979). *Parents and children in autism.* Washington, DC: V. H. Winston & Sons.

Dunn, M., Burbine, T., Bowers, C., & Tantleff-Dunn, S. (2001). Moderators of stress in parents of children with autism. *Community Mental Health Journal, 37*(1), 39–52.

Early, T. (2001). Measures for practice with families from a strengths perspective. *Families in Society: The Journal of Contemporary Human Services, 82*(2), 225–232.

Esterberg, K. G. (2002). *Qualitative methods in social research.* Boston: McGraw-Hill.

Fleischmann, A. (2004). Narratives published on the Internet by parents of children with autism: What do they reveal and why is it important? *Focus on Autism and Other Developmental Disabilities, 19*(1), 35–43.

Folkman, S. (1997). Positive psychological states and coping with severe stress. *Social Science & Medicine, 45*(8), 1207–1221.

Folkman, S., & Moskowitz, J. T. (2000a). Positive affect and the other side of coping. *American Psychologist, 55*(6), 647–654.

Folkman, S., & Moskowitz, J. T. (2000b). Stress, positive emotion, and coping. *Current Directions in Psychological Science, 9*(4), 115–118.

Grant, G., Ramcharan, P., McGrath, M., Nolan, M., & Keady, J. (1998). Rewards and gratifications among family caregivers: Towards a refined model of caring and coping. *Journal of Intellectual Disability Research, 42*(1), 58–71.

Gray, D. (1994). Coping with autism: Stresses and strategies. *Sociology of Health & Illness, 16*(3), 275–300.

Gray, D. (1998). *Autism and the family: Problems, prospects, and coping with the disorder.* Springfield, IL: Charles C. Thomas Publisher.

Gray, D. (2002a). Ten years on: A longitudinal study of families of children with autism. *Journal of Intellectual & Developmental Disability, 27*(3), 215–222.

Gray, D. (2002b). 'Everybody just freezes. Everybody is just embarrassed': Felt and enacted stigma among parents of children with high functioning autism. *Sociology of Health & Illness, 24*(6), 734–749.

Gray, D. (2003). Gender and coping: The parents of children with high functioning autism. *Social Sciences & Medicine, 56,* 631–642.

Holstein, J. A., & Gubrium, J. F. (2002). Active interviewing. In D. Weinberg (Ed.), *Qualitative research methods* (pp. 112–126). Oxford, UK: Blackwell.

Ivey, J. (2004). What do parents expect? A study of likelihood and importance issues for children with autism spectrum disorders. *Focus on Autism and Other Developmental Disabilities, 19*(1), 27–33.

Kaminsky, L., & Dewey, D. (2001). Sibling relationships of children with autism. *Journal of Autism and Developmental Disorders, 31*(4), 399–410.

Kelso, T., French, D., & Fernandez, M. (2005). Stress and coping in primary caregivers of children with a disability: A qualitative study using the Lazarus and Folkman process model of coping. *Journal of Research in Special Educational Needs, 5*(1), 3–10.

Kim, W., Greenberg, S., Seltzer, M., & Krauss, W. (2003). The role of coping in maintaining the psychological well-being of mothers of adults with intellectual disability and mental illness. *Journal of Intellectual Disability Research, 47*(4–5), 313–327.

Lazarus, R., & Folkman, S. (1984). *Stress, appraisal, and coping.* New York: Springer Publishing.

Mansell, W., & Morris, K. (2004). A survey of parents' reactions to the diagnosis of an autistic spectrum disorder by a local service: Access to information and use of services. *Autism, 8*(4), 387–407.

Moustakas, C. (1994). *Phenomenological research methods.* Thousand Oaks, California: Sage Publications.

Moerer-Urdahl, T., & Creswell, J. (2004). Using transcendental phenomenology to explore the "ripple effect" in a leadership mentoring program. *International Journal of Qualitative Methods, 3*(2), 1–28.

National Advisory Council on Aging. (2004). *Seniors on the margins: Aging with a developmental disability.* Canada: Minister of Public Works and Government Services Canada.

Pearlin, L., Lieberman, M., Menaghan, E., & Mullan, J. (1981). The stress process. *Journal of Health and Social Behavior, 22*(4), 337–356.

Pearlin, L., Mullan, J., Semple, S., & Skaff, M. (1990). Caregiving and the stress process: An overview of concepts and their measures. *The Gerontologist, 30*(5), 583–594.

Pierpont, J. (2004). Emphasizing caregiver strengths to avoid out-of-home placement of children with severe emotional and behavioral disturbances. *Journal of Human Behavior in the Social Environment, 9*(1/2), 5–17.

Pruchno, R. (2003). Enmeshed lives: Adult children with developmental disabilities and their aging mothers. *Psychology and Aging, 18*(4), 851–857.

Schopler, E., & Mesibov, G. (1994). *Behavioral issues in autism.* New York: Plenum Press.

Schwartz, C. (2003). Parents of children with chronic disabilities: The gratification of caregiving. *Families in Society: The Journal of Contemporary Human Services, 84*(4), 576–584.

Seltzer, M., Shattuck, P., Abbeduto, L., & Greenberg, J. (2004). The trajectory of development in adolescents and adults with autism. *Mental Retardation and Developmental Disabilities Research Reviews, 10*(4), 234–247.

Tomanik, S., Harris, G., & Hawkins, J. (2004). The relationship between behaviours exhibited by children with autism and maternal stress. *Journal of Intellectual & Developmental Disability, 29*(1), 16–26.

Weiss, M. (2002). Hardiness and social support as predictors of stress in mothers of typical children, children with autism, and children with mental retardation. *Autism, 6*(1), 115–130.

Wing, L. (1988). The continuum of autistic characteristics. In E. Schopler & G. Mesibov (Eds.), *Diagnosis and assessment in autism* (pp. 91–110). New York: Plenum Press.

Critical Thinking

1. How can the positives outweigh the negatives in caring for those with autism?

2. Have you personally witnessed examples of positive as well as negative caregiving? If so, did one experience outweigh the other?

3. What do you think can be learned from the experience of caring for those with autism?

Create Central

www.mhhe.com/createcentral

Internet References

Family Caregiver Alliance National Center on Caregiving
http://caregiver.org

Federation for Children with Special Needs
www.fcsn.org

Michael K. Corman, MA, is a doctoral student in the Department of Sociology at the University of Calgary and a part-time faculty member in the Department of Sociology & Anthropology at Mount Royal College in Calgary, Alberta. His research and teaching interests include the sociology of health and illness, aging, institutional ethnography, caregiving and autism spectrum disorders, health care work, and critical research strategies. Correspondence regarding this article can be sent to the author at mkcorman@ucalgary.ca or University of Calgary, Department of Sociology, Social Sciences 913, 2500 University drive NW, Calgary, AB, T2N 1N4 Canada.

Author's note—I would like to thank Dr. Neena L. Chappell for her continued support throughout the larger study that contributed to this article and the preparation of this manuscript.

Article

Prepared by: Patricia Hrusa Williams,
University of Maine at Farmington

The Coming Special Needs Care Crisis

MICHELLE COTTLE

Learning Outcomes

After reading this article, you will be able to:

- Identify the daily challenges experienced by families raising special needs children.

- Explain the concerns and needs of families with special needs children as they become adults.

Eli Toucey has seizures and social issues that make it all but impossible to leave him with a random baby-sitter. What could really save Hillary Toucey's life is a personal-care attendant to help with her 7-year-old son, Eli. Dark-haired, fair-skinned, and fragile, Eli suffers from a raft of health problems: cerebral palsy, celiac disease, epilepsy, asthma, and what his mom calls "pretty severe" autism.

His speech is "kind of garbled"; he has leg braces and a wheelchair; seizures render him incontinent at night; and he has acute sensory sensitivities. He cannot bear to touch Styrofoam or the paper wrappings on crayons. Loud music sends him into a panic. When his first-grade class took a field trip this Christmas to see The Cajun Nutcracker, "we lasted three minutes," says Toucey.

Eli is extremely attached to his mother. Toucey spends as much time with him as possible, but since her divorce, the 32-year-old Louisianan has been attending nursing school in the hopes of escaping her hand-to-mouth existence. When her husband left in November 2009 (two weeks before their 10th anniversary and four days after Toucey had surgery for a thyroid tumor), he took the car with him. Toucey isn't sure when she'll be able to afford another one.

Eli's seizures and social issues make it all but impossible to leave him with a random babysitter. "There's only a handful of people he can be with," says Toucey. Having one of the state's personal-care attendants (PCAs) come in for 30 hours a week would make a world of difference: the attendant could take him to therapy, help him practice life skills like brushing his teeth and showering, watch him while Toucey studied. Maybe then she could give more attention to her other kids: 11-year-old Jonah, himself diagnosed with Asperger's, who cries easily and doesn't have many friends; and Charlotte, "a perfectly healthy, wonderful, brilliant" 9-year-old who her mom fears will fall

through the cracks. "I feel horrible," says Toucey. "I really have to carve out time for her." Toucey has been told that the PCA bureaucracy can take "forever," and she calls the agency constantly to make sure the process hasn't stalled. Taking care of the essentials is pretty much all she can handle these days. Says Toucey matter-of-factly, "I have no life."

Now and again, the spotlight falls on the challenges of raising special-needs children. In 2008 Sarah Palin captured public attention with her son Trig, who has Down syndrome. This election cycle, Rick Santorum did so with heartbreaking stories about 3-year-old Bella, who suffers from Trisomy 18. Dramatic parenting moments often take the spotlight: stories of diagnosis, acute health crises, surprise breakthroughs.

But for most parents, it's the day-to-day stuff that consumes them: the hours of therapy, the doctor visits, the financial pressures, and the grinding anxiety that comes with it all. It is a rough, often isolating road. And one that promises to become even more challenging as our society enters a new, more complicated era of caregiving. That era is coming in part because many of the medical and social advances that have improved the lives of special-needs individuals have also increased the burden of caring for them. For instance, people with Down syndrome were once lucky to survive to age 30; today, the average lifespan is 55. This presents parents (and society more broadly) with the challenge of somehow providing for an adult child decades after their own deaths, a situation complicated by the fact that the Down population develops Alzheimer's at a rate of 100 percent, typically in their 40s or 50s.

Then there is the 800-pound gorilla in the room: autism. In late March, the Centers for Disease Control issued an estimate that 1 in 88 children now fall on the autism spectrum. While debate rages over the roots of the "epidemic," this swelling population is placing increasing strains on our health-care, education, and social-services systems. A study released last month put the annual cost of autism in the U.S. at $126 billion, more than triple what it was in 2006. The bulk of those expenses are for adult care. Geraldine Dawson, chief science officer for the advocacy group Autism Speaks, calls the situation "a public-health emergency." And if you think things are tough now, she cautions, just wait until autistic teens start aging out of the education system over the next few years. "We as a nation are not prepared."

Saya Barkdoll doesn't remember much about the meeting at which a grim-faced neurosurgeon told her that the kindest thing to do was to let her newborn daughter die. The baby, Taylor, had been born with multiple malformations, and her prognosis was grim. "They took us into this room—it was really intense, with about 20 doctors and nurses—to show us the result of this MRI," recalls the 32-year-old massage therapist. "It was not good. They sat us down and drew us pictures. They were basically saying Taylor had little to no brain mass."

"I didn't believe them," says Barkdoll. "I had not even held her yet, but I could see life in her." Her girlish voice takes on a hard edge: "We fired that neurosurgeon."

Seven years later, Taylor is an outgoing first-grader thriving at her local public school in Silver Springs, Md. She's big into dress-up, Monster High dolls, and Taylor Swift. And though the little girl's health remains delicate and she can neither run nor write clearly, Taylor suffers no cognitive delays. "She's totally there," Barkdoll beams.

Getting Taylor this far, however, has exacted a steep toll on her mom. For the first few years, Barkdoll did nothing but tend to her daughter as Taylor underwent multiple surgeries and extensive therapy. Barkdoll and Taylor's dad, Kevin, originally opted not to marry so as not to risk a combined household income that could jeopardize their daughter's government benefits. By the time Taylor was 3, the relationship had crumbled under the strain of constant caregiving. "We lost sight of each other," says Barkdoll sadly.

It is perhaps unsurprising that the pressures of parenting special-needs children prove too much for many couples. There is a commonly cited statistic that the divorce rate among the parents of autistic children is 80 percent. (Toucey mentioned it during our talk.) Recent studies have debunked this figure, yet it persists among parents because it feels so true. "Based on my and my friends' experience, that stat makes complete sense," asserts journalist Hannah Brown, the mom of a teenage boy with autism and the author of a new novel, *If I Could Tell You*, about the challenges of parenting autistic children. Of her son's condition, she says, "I tried to fight it, but it completely took over my life." Brown recalls that when she and her husband split up, she was initially embarrassed to tell the staff at her son's school. As it turned out, she chuckles, "they were really good at dealing with it because they deal with it all the time!"

Even when marriages survive, such long-term caregiving can have a corrosive impact on parents' well-being. Research indicates that the mothers of special-needs children have higher stress levels and poorer health than other parents. One 2009 study found that the mothers of older autistic children had levels of the stress-related hormone cortisol similar to those found in combat soldiers and sufferers of post-traumatic stress disorder.

Part of the problem is that the experience is so isolating. Not only are parents overwhelmed by the practical matters of caregiving, they often have a tough time relating to people with "normal" children. "When people call you and are like, 'Oh, I'm so stressed out, my plans for Disney are falling through, blah blah blah,' I can't relate to that," says Toucey. "I'm like, 'My kid stopped eating three weeks ago and is on a liquid diet, and we're wondering if we're going to have to put a feeding tube in him.'"

For parents whose children have behavioral problems, the situation can be even trickier. "When my son was younger and his behavior less manageable, people didn't invite us over that much," says Brown. "And I can't really blame them."

The arrival of a special-needs child brings an onslaught of warnings about risks and limitations rather than the usual fantasies of a baby's limitless promise. "You receive an overwhelming amount of information, and most of it is talking about everything that may go wrong," says Rep. Cathy McMorris Rodgers, whose 4-year-old son, Cole, has Down syndrome. Soon after Cole's delivery, the doctor briefed the Washington state congresswoman and her husband on Cole's increased risk for leukemia, hearing difficulties, vision problems, and thyroid issues. "It was a long list," she says, and more than a little dispiriting.

Rodgers colleague, Mississippi Rep. Gregg Harper, faced a similar litany when his 22-year-old son, Livingston, was diagnosed at age 4 with Fragile X syndrome, the most common inherited mental disability. But the couple pushed on. "We threw away a lot of the stuff and said, 'We're not going to accept that,'" says Harper's wife, Sidney.

Like many parents of special-needs children, Sidney found herself swallowed up by her child's condition. "Your whole life revolves around figuring out what to do to help him," she says. Quitting her nursing job, Sidney drove Livingston to endless therapy sessions (with his infant sister, Maggie, in tow), enrolled him in an early-intervention program, and put him in a mothers-day-out class to help his socialization. Told that Livingston would never swim or ride a bike, his mom signed him up for swim lessons and literally strapped him to a specially outfitted bicycle until he could ride like a pro. "The more they told me he wouldn't do something, the more I took him to do it," she says.

Both Harpers get misty-eyed talking about their son's achievement. "Our goal was to have him graduate from high school," says Sidney. "That was it: get him through the 12th grade." Today, Livingston is enrolled in a pilot program at Mississippi State University designed for students with intellectual disabilities. Gushes the congressman: "He's living in a dorm, eating in the cafeteria, going to classes. He's living the life!"

And yet . . . for all Livingston's progress, his future remains a question mark. The hope is that after two or three years at college, he can find some sort of job (he has experience working at a family friend's restaurant) and, with a little luck and more oversight, live basically on his own. But as his father softly acknowledges, "We don't know what the long term is."

Part of what makes special-needs parenting so daunting is that the load often does not lighten with time—that golden day when one's child is more or less self-sufficient never arrives. In fact, many parents report that the school years are by far the easiest. Autism Speaks' Dawson says she frequently hears the shift out of school described as "falling off a cliff, because so few services are available after you exit high school." In the wake of high school, she says, about 40 percent of these young adults have no activity outside the home, and the same percentage have no social activity.

Finding appropriate housing for an adult child with special needs is one of the biggest challenges. Residential facilities are in short supply, even for the well off and well connected. Just ask Rep. Pete Sessions. The Texas Republican has an 18-year-old son, Alex, with Down syndrome, who attends 10th grade at a special school in Dallas. Alex will never be able to live on his own, says Sessions, and the programs for young adults with Alex's needs tend to be full and/or prohibitively expensive. Instead, the congressman hopes to "cobble together" an unofficial group home with a few other families—an increasingly popular choice. "Generally what happens is a group of parents who all have the same needs get together and buy a community house or find an apartment," Sessions explains. "Alex can have a bright, bright future," he says hopefully.

For her part, Hillary Toucey assumes she will be Eli's caregiver for the rest of her life—and she hates to think about what will happen when she's gone. "It's very scary what the future holds," she says. "Right now my plan is to be around as long as possible and to save as much money as possible."

Maybe a little later, when she's not "struggling just to make ends meet," she will be able to focus more on long-term planning. But for now, she has more pressing concerns, like getting Eli to therapy, keeping an eye on his schooling, trying not to flunk her classes, and, of course, calling to find out when that PCA might arrive. And so she waits—and tries to keep her head above water.

Critical Thinking

1. Why does the author of the article believe there is a special needs care crisis on the horizon?

2. What do you think is the hardest part of having a child with special needs when they are young? How might the challenges be different as children grow older and enter adulthood?

3. What types of supports are needed for families with special needs children across the lifespan?

Create Central

www.mhhe.com/createcentral

Internet References

Federation for Children with Special Needs
www.fcsn.org
Family Caregiver Alliance National Center on Caregiving
http://caregiver.org

Article

Prepared by: Patricia Hrusa Williams,
University of Maine at Farmington

Family Members' Informal Roles in End-of-Life Decision Making in Adult Intensive Care Units

JILL R. QUINN, RN, PHD, CS-ANP ET AL.

Learning Outcomes

After reading this article, you will be able to:

- Understand the types of decisions that need to be made when a family member is critically ill.
- Identify the different formal and informal roles family members take in the decision making process.
- Explain how family dynamics are influenced when someone is critically ill.

Background To support the process of effective family decision making, it is important to recognize and understand informal roles that various family members may play in the end-of-life decision making process.

Objective To describe some informal roles consistently enacted by family members involved in the process of end-of-life decision making in intensive care units.

Methods Ethnographic study. Data were collected via participant observation with field notes and semistructured interviews on 4 intensive care units in an academic health center in the mid-Atlantic United States from 2001 to 2004. The units studied were a medical, a surgical, a burn and trauma, and a cardiovascular intensive care unit.

Participants Health care clinicians, patients, and family members.

Results Informal roles for family members consistently observed were primary caregiver, primary decision maker, family spokesperson, out-of-towner, patient's wishes expert, protector, vulnerable member, and health care expert. The identified informal roles were part of families' decision making processes, and each role was part of a potentially complicated family dynamic for end-of-life decision making within the family system and between the family and health care domains.

Conclusions These informal roles reflect the diverse responses to demands for family decision making in what is usually a novel and stressful situation. Identification and description of these informal roles of family members can help clinicians recognize and understand the functions of these roles in families' decision making at the end of life and guide development of strategies to support and facilitate increased effectiveness of family discussions and decision making processes.

Health care clinicians in settings such as intensive care units (ICUs) are part of an institutional social system and are linked through a variety of relationships. They fill formal roles (eg, nurse, physician), exercise rights and privileges, and are expected to discharge obligations and responsibilities in conformity with established values, norms, and rules for behavior.[1] Similarly, persons in a family comprise a small social system; they function in a different sociocultural domain. They occupy formal roles (eg, mother, son), exercise rights and privileges, and discharge obligations and responsibilities in conformity with established family values, norms, and rules for behavior. When a member of a family becomes a patient in the ICU, members of these 2 domains come into dynamic interaction with each other. Family members are often involved in decision making for withdrawal of life-sustaining treatment.[2]

Sometimes a family member has been named the legally designated surrogate end-of-life decision maker (health care proxy or agent) for an ICU patient who has lost capacity; this formal role has been studied extensively.[3-8] Although 1 family member is asked or expected to be the "voice" for the patient by clinicians involved with the patient's care, often several family members become involved in the process of end-of-life decision making. Under these circumstances, the complexity of the end-of-life decision making process can escalate. This increased complexity not only affects the level of tension associated with end-of-life decision making, but also the satisfaction of family members involved.[9,10] To understand and support the process of effective family decision making, it is important to understand the informal roles that various family members may play in the end-of-life decision making process.

The findings reported here are part of a larger study of the sociocultural contexts for end-of-life decision making in ICUs.[11] In an earlier article,[11] we focused on variation in cultures of different ICUs related to end-of-life decision making; the focus of this article, that emerged from the data, is on the various informal family roles that are expected of and engaged in by family members during end-of-life decision making in an ICU.

Formal family roles are not culturally defined to address every circumstance, or to accommodate the personal characteristics of families and their individual members. Families functioning in an ICU context are not in a usual setting for family life. Informal roles emerge in the context of situational demands and describe how people actually behave in particular situations, rather than how they are expected to behave.[12] Informal roles can reflect responses to the common situational demands of any small system, including families, and a number of these roles have been previously identified. They include the scapegoat, who may be seen as the problem when negative emotions threaten the system, and the deviant, whose behavior helps clarify system boundaries by challenging norms.[13] The emergence of informal roles of clinicians specific to the developing small system of the health care team also has been studied.[14]

Study of informal role behavior is particularly useful in the situation of family members in the ICU because family members have no agreed-upon normative "script" for their behavior. Informal roles emerge in this context to help fill the gaps in how family members respond to the novel challenge of end-of-life decision making.[15–18] Recognizing and understanding the informal roles that family members may play in this setting can help guide clinicians in their strategies for working with family members in end-of-life decision making.

Design and Methods

This ethnographic study was prospective. Data were collected on 4 ICUs in an academic health center in the mid-Atlantic United States from 2001 to 2004. The units studied were a medical ICU, a surgical ICU, a burn and trauma ICU, and a cardiovascular ICU.

The university institutional review board for human subjects protection approved the study. All interviewed participants signed informed consent forms. A full description of the study design has already been published.[11]

Participants

Participants included health care clinicians, patients, and patients' family members interviewed in relation to specific cases or in general on end-of-life decision making. When possible, we interviewed clinicians and patients or family members involved in the same situation. If decision making continued for several days, participants were approached for another interview to assess changes and explore questions raised by field observations and earlier interviews. The total number of interviews conducted was 157, with 130 participants. The interviews were with the following categories of

participants: 46 interviews with 30 physicians; 60 interviews with 48 nurses; 13 interviews with 10 other providers such as clergy, social worker, ethicist, and pharmacist; 4 interviews with 4 patients; and 34 interviews with 38 family members. Field notes were included in the analysis, along with recordings from 22 family meetings.[11]

Methods

A 6-member research team used participant observation, field notes, and semistructured interviews to examine the end-of-life decision making process from different participants' perspectives. The semistructured interviews were audiotaped and lasted from 15 to 60 minutes. For this analysis, we focused on interview questions specific to the participation of family members, including questions related to their relationships with the patient, with other family members, and with health care clinicians; their involvement in the decision making; and problems or disagreements related to the decision making process. Information from the medical record was used to identify some circumstances of decision making, for example, the patient's condition and availability of advance directives.

Procedure

Data were collected for approximately 5 hours a day, 5 to 7 days a week for 7 months on each unit sequentially (>700 hours per unit). Once a potential end-of-life decision making situation was identified, the attending physician was asked for permission for a research team member to contact the patient and/or the patient's family. Data collection began as soon as possible. Patients were followed up by the research team until the patient's death or discharge from the ICU.

Data Analysis

All the tapes were transcribed verbatim and reviewed for accuracy. Transcribed corrected interviews, family meetings, field notes, and chart data were dated and entered into the ATLAS.ti program.[19] Analysis, using an ethnographic approach,[20,21] began at the time of the first observation and continued throughout the study.

Small group and family dynamics theories[12,13,14] informed the understanding of family members' informal roles in end-of-life decision making in ICUs that were identified in data analysis. In the analysis for this article, we used data coded as "Roles-Family," which was defined as various key roles that family members played in end-of-life decision making. This general code was generated in our early analysis and subsequently was divided into subcodes for the specific informal roles of family members in end-of-life decision making that consistently emerged as data analysis progressed.

Results

Eight informal roles that family members engaged in during the end-of-life decision making process in these ICU settings were identified: primary caregiver, primary decision maker, family spokesperson, out-of-towner, patient's wishes expert, protector, vulnerable member, and health care expert.

The Primary Caregiver

If family caregiving was involved before ICU admission, the primary caregiver was a role of the family member who had spent the most time caring for the patient before hospitalization. One spouse said:

> After she had the stroke I took care of her naturally. I'm her husband. I did everything for her or whatever. I made sure that she's had therapy . . . I mean, I've looked out for her best care the best I could. I don't know . . .

When a loved one was admitted to the ICU, the primary caregiver was confronted with the reality that it was no longer possible for him or her to care for the ill family member. This previously important role was relinquished in the hospital setting. The same spouse explained:

> "I'm using his [doctor's] judgment [now]. That's why I brought her. I can't take care of her. I can't—I've gotta use their judgment . . ."

The primary caregiver often experienced great angst over relinquishing this role to hospital personnel. Often clinicians expected a quick shift of the primary caregiver into the role of primary decision maker for treatment decisions in the ICU. A family member of another patient stated:

> He [doctor] did say go with the way you feel but he also said if that was my wife or my daughter, I would remove life support, and I said but I can't do that. Something in my heart is saying we've got to give her more time.

The Primary Decision Maker

As others[3,7,22] have described, the role of the primary decision maker emerges in families as a response to the demands for surrogate end-of-life decision making. Sometimes a family member fulfilling this role was formally designated (eg, in the patient's advance directive). Whether this had occurred or not, ICU clinicians sought 1 individual to become the primary decision maker, a family role viewed by clinicians as central to the end-of-life decision making task when the patient was incapacitated. As 1 social worker described this role:

> Probably the people I work with the most in these situations are the decision makers, you know, the primary people in the family that are there the most and taking the lead and initiative to make the decisions that provide the care. Often families had multiple decision makers rather than 1 primary decision maker as preferred by the clinicians.

The primary decision maker frequently conversed with other family members in the decision making process, and the burden of decision making could be shared informally among family members. Family language around decision making often contained "we" as the referent, reflecting this shared decision making process. A striking example from the field notes illustrates this process of sharing in the decision making and in the decision itself. The family acted in concert to support the primary decision maker.

> [The physician] gets the DNR [do not resuscitate] order sheet out and goes over the entire form with the family. He then asks which one is the proxy. [A daughter] says she is; he asks her to sign. [Another daughter] says, "We all want to sign, we don't want only [named proxy] to feel like she's the one who did this." [Two sons] immediately agree; and [one daughter] hugs [the other daughter] who is teary. [The physician] says there is room for everyone to sign. They all sign the form.

If multiple decision makers were not acceptable to clinicians or family members, either 1 clear primary decision maker emerged or the primary decision maker's role was contested.

On the other hand, discussion could become too inclusive, as shown in the following example from a family meeting, where family friends exerted their own opinion in the decision making process.

> [Friend of family]: Maybe he [patient] won't do it [recover] as quickly as a 20-year-old. But they want their father, and she wants her husband. And that's what we should be focusing on, rehabilitation, getting him up and getting him going.

> Physician: Well, I think it's always important and the thing I was asking [his wife] about. I think there's nobody in the whole world better able to speak to the desire of her husband than she. And I think sometimes families forget that what they really want is what's best for their loved one.

Family Spokesperson

One informal family role, family spokesperson, was encouraged by clinicians because of the clinician's wish to address families' needs for information efficiently and to facilitate the decision making processes. Despite the complexity of many families' internal decision making processes, many clinicians preferred to deal with 1 family spokesperson, as reflected in the following staff quotation: "The problem often is that we do not have a family spokesperson but a spokesgroup." The nurse manager of 1 ICU spoke of the formal process expected on their unit to be followed to identify the family spokesperson.

> What we ask is . . . there be a family spokesperson that we can give information to, and we ask that that family spokesperson disseminate the information to the other family members . . . if somebody calls in, it needs to be the spokesperson. . . .

At least 3 ICUs had this role formally identified in the visitor brochure they provided, which included visitation policy and asked for an individual name with contact information to be placed in the medical record and care plan. Some units were inconsistent with identifying and documenting an individual family member for this role. Further, although this was constructed on several units as a formal role for 1 family member, we found that some families would informally evolve this role to include other members. Although the tendency was for the hospital staff to combine the roles of spokesperson and primary decision maker, it was observed that a family member who acted as a spokesperson with hospital staff was not necessarily the primary decision maker (eg, an adult child as spokesperson for a parent who was making final decisions).

Families, especially when there was disagreement among members, often were reluctant to identify just 1 member as the sole spokesperson. Regardless of whether the unit had a formal process of identifying the spokesperson, clinicians and staff tried to seek one out when a problem arose. However, at times, we observed that any family member who was convenient, at the bedside or in a visitor waiting area, was approached by a clinician and offered information or asked questions about the patient. This clinician's behavior conveyed a message that any family member present could be a spokesperson, but this was also seen as contrary to the formal rule regarding identification of 1 family spokesperson. One nurse expressed this situation well:

> Some nurses will talk to all—a lot of different family members about what's going on. That makes it very, very difficult. I think . . . that it's very important to have it be [the] family spokesperson. Just 1 person should be the proxy to whom that information is going. . . .

The Out-of-Towner

Complex family dynamics of decision making were apparent through other informal roles of family members that were identified. One such role was the out-of-towner, a family member who had not been involved in the daily care giving and may not have been engaged during the early ICU stay and, therefore, often brought a different perspective to the in-town family's end-of-life decision making discussions. End-of-life decisions often were put on hold until in-town family members could communicate with out-of-town relatives and they could be part of the discussion about the patient's condition and the status of decision making thus far. Because they were from out of town, they often also had time limits on their ability to be physically present in the situation and, if present, might be eager to have a firm decision made before their departure. Consequently, their involvement added complexity to the decision making process and could create conflict within the patient's family and with clinicians. An example of this is a brother who described his perspective on his out-of-town sister's role in decision making about their father:

> My sister was—you have to take a lot of things into consideration. She is the child from out of town. She is the one that feels that she has to have this whole thing fixed before she can go home. She is the one that doesn't have the time to wait it out. This illness is a wait out. . . . She is trying to get this whole thing fixed before she goes home. She has to go home and I understand that. She just has to leave and trust that it's gonna happen correctly. . . .

> Especially where family members may not all be in the same city. So, they have not seen mom or dad, [and] you will be in a family meeting and, the one [local] daughter will say, "Look, I'm with Mom all the time; I know what she wants. You see her twice a year. How do you know what she wants?"

This example illustrates another emergent family informal role related to decision making, when the family had not achieved consensus about what the dying family member's wishes might have been as a guide to that decision making.

The Patient's Wishes Expert

Being primary decision maker was difficult, but family members were much more likely to come together in support of a primary decision maker and collectively to feel confident they were following the patient's wishes in the context of known preferences of the patient. In the context of unknown preferences, decision making was often much more difficult for the primary decision maker, and other family members were much more open to differing interpretations of what the patient would have wanted. The patient's wishes experts were family members who claimed that their interpretations of the patients' wishes were the correct interpretations.

> [Son]: You have to listen to everything my father says . . . it's like his living will. I read it, and I know what my mother and sister said, and I said wait a minute, my father doesn't want to be intubated, I understand that. Okay, if he is brain dead, he doesn't want to be intubated; but he is alive, he can get better. My father wants to live; he is afraid to die. This is something that has been on his mind for 10 years.

When this role was enacted by several family members with different interpretations of the patient's wishes, end-of-life decision making was often prolonged and inconclusive.

The Protector and the Vulnerable Family Member

In this situation, a family member who might typically be expected to be the primary decision maker was viewed as vulnerable for some reason, and another family member asserted family decision making authority to protect the vulnerable family member. Commonly, these paired roles emerged when adult children believed they needed to protect an older parent (eg, spouse of the ill family member) from the stress of end-of-life decision making. An example was a daughter who was concerned about her mother being expected to decide about withdrawal of mechanical ventilation from her husband, resulting in end of life too quickly for the mother to handle emotionally. The daughter stated, "Taking him off the respirator is only going to change things by hours, and I think that that would be way too painful for my mom given the rapidity of this event." If the vulnerable member did not accept that role, it caused family conflict that made the decision making process more difficult and delayed the decision making process.

Occasionally, patients had at least some capacity for decision making. However, in such circumstances they could be identified by family members as the vulnerable member. The quotation below is about a dying woman who was intubated but aware. Her husband had been very involved in the decision making and wanted her included in any decision about reintubation if extubation failed. However, some negative information about her condition, known to her husband, had been withheld from her at the husband's request. He questioned whether she would be able to make a decision about reintubation, especially when she did not have all of the relevant clinical information.

> [Husband]: I'm trying to—I'm trying to think if her choice would be a real choice, to her. Because I would be okay with whatever her choice was, so I'm trying to think, would it be a real choice? Would she know that that's a real choice and her deciding, and it might be . . . because she doesn't like that and maybe she had enough of it and she doesn't want it. Or maybe she'd say, "Yup, if I start to lose it, put it back in."

Even though in this rare ICU situation, the patient had the capacity to participate, her protector family member saw her as vulnerable, remained in charge of the family end-of-life decision making process, and asked clinicians to withhold some information about her condition from her.

Another field note observation illustrates the patient's wishes expert and the paired set of family informal roles of protector and vulnerable member roles occurring in the context of a clinician looking for consent to perform a procedure. He said:

> They [mother and father, father is the patient] have been married for 52 years. He [father] never let her [mother] make a decision in 52 years. You are gonna let her [mother] cut her teeth on this one? No, she is not cutting her teeth on life or death. I'll do that. I will give mom my feelings on that and I'm not gonna subject her [mother] to making that decision. I think I know what he [father] wants, so that's what I told her [mother].

In this example, the son claims his own expertise in knowing his father's preferences (or wishes). He also was prepared to protect his mother from having to make a life and death decision about her husband. He saw his mother as vulnerable because, in his view, she had never made decisions during 52 years of marriage.

The Health Care Expert

The health care expert was a family member who could influence decision making in the family system through a claim of clinical expertise by virtue of some connection to the health care domain (eg, nurses, physicians). Family members and sometimes clinicians viewed this role as one that had the potential to facilitate the decision making process. The health care expert might use resources to bridge the gap between the 2 domains, whereas family members who lacked this expertise struggled more with the

situation and with end-of-life decision making. Family members often relied heavily on the family health care expert for direction in the end-of-life decision making process. The quotation that follows illustrates the role of the health care expert, in this case a daughter who was a licensed practical nurse:

> [Daughter]: My brothers and sisters never thought of the antibiotics and you know, I think sometimes you have a little more knowledge. Whether you understand things better, which is why they [my family members] put me down as the spokesperson. Which is why she put me down as her [proxy]. . . .

Clinicians' reactions to family health care experts could be mixed: on the one hand, sometimes they were viewed as able to understand medical situations and expected to be "reasonable" about the treatment decisions or more in line with the clinicians' way of thinking. An example of this is expressed by a registered nurse:

> I think her mother deferred to her [daughter] the physician. . . . It is definitely nice when the family is so knowledgeable about what is going on that, you know, they realize as you realize, at almost the same time, that this is . . . that CPR would be futile.

Other family health care experts challenged the thinking and recommendations of the ICU clinicians, as well as the quality of care that their family members were receiving, stimulating conflict between the family and clinicians. A good example of this from the field notes is when a group of nurses talked one day about a patient's son-in-law, who was a physician. On the phone he had yelled at one of the nurses and then had hung up. From the nurse's perspective, he had conveyed that the nurses were all incompetent. When family health care experts did not agree with the clinicians, there was an element of surprise and frustration expressed, as this resident physician viewed it: "Granted that her son-in-law is a physician, but we are still not getting through."

The situation got even more complicated when more than 1 family member could claim a role as health care expert, and the different "experts" were not in agreement. Family members could also "call in" friends who were health care clinicians to play the role of health care expert for the family or some subgroup of the family; again, calling in multiple experts could complicate the decision making process.

Discussion

As illustrated in these results, the identified informal roles were intricately tied to the family's decision making process, and each helped to create a potentially complicated family dynamic for end-of-life decision making within the family system, and between the family and health care domains. In their expectations for end-of-life decision making, clinicians, on the other hand, often pushed for 1 family member to be both primary decision maker and family spokesperson to facilitate communication and decision making. However, our findings suggest that this often did not happen and made the process more complicated than desired by clinicians.

These 8 informal roles did not all emerge in every family. More than 1 role might be assumed by a single family member (eg, the out-of-towner could also be the health care expert) or the informal roles might be shared among multiple family members. Whether these informal roles facilitated decision making or escalated family conflict or family/clinician conflict depended on the family context (ie, family history and culture around difficult decision making).

In situations where other family members interacted to support a single member both as primary decision maker and family spokesperson, consensus within families was more easily achieved. In other families where there was less cohesion, as more family members became involved there was a greater proliferation of informal roles in the decision making process, potentially more conflict and disagreement, and a more difficult time with making end-of-life decisions. When no consensus was reached among family members around end-of-life decision making, informal roles might be used to leverage a decision in a way that advanced the role of the person in the family system, for example by claiming to be a protector or health care expert.

Jockeying for position in the family system can be viewed as a consequence of the removal, by life-threatening illness, of a member of the system and a scramble for a new status in that altered system. Thus, for example, with the removal of an ill parent, adult children might move to claim status and authority in the system previously held by that parent.

In either circumstance of cohesive or conflict-prone family decision making processes, ICU clinicians who attempted direct communication through identification of a family spokesperson often found that there was a "spokesgroup" of family members playing differing informal roles but all wanting input into the decision making process either directly or indirectly. As others who have studied family involvement with end-of-life decision making have found, the decision to withdraw or withhold treatment generally includes multiple family members,[23] and communication needs for families often go unmet.[9,24,25]

Recognizing and understanding the roles that family members play within the family unit during critical decision making is important in facilitating more effective interaction and consensus among family members and reducing conflict among family and clinicians. Interventions limiting conflict and strengthening family supports should be a major goal, but the manner in which this is done needs to incorporate the cultural differences of families and the expertise of clinicians. Family meetings with clinicians, when held, can make these complex roles involved in family end-of-life decision making visible.

Family meetings can also reduce conflict between clinicians and family members regarding frustration with not having 1 person as family spokesperson and/or primary decision maker.[25] More recently, emphasis has increased on conducting effective family meetings within critical care as well as use of other services, such as palliative care services, that may be called to consult if the process of decision making becomes problematic.[26] Awareness of the potentially complicated dynamics associated with some of these family informal role processes may assist clinicians to seek earlier consultation.

Limitations

Although the purpose of qualitative research is not to make broad generalizations but to examine the depth of individual experience in a phenomenon such as end-of-life decision making, this study had some limitations. First the study was conducted in 1 setting, a university medical center, although different types of ICUs were included to capture cultural differences regarding end-of-life decision making among the units.[11] The data were collected some time ago; however, the nature of the data and analyses reported here, as well as the results, concerning informal roles in family decision making processes in critical care situations, are not likely to "age" quickly, as family systems processes such as the decision making processes identified are fundamental to family life. The approach taken to analysis is theoretically informed, drawing on a rich body of theoretical literature related to informal roles in family systems, family crisis responses, and small group functioning, which became relevant as we explored the data.

The presence of the researchers and the process of audiotaping during family meetings and interviews could have influenced the responses. We describe the results only of participants who agreed to participate, although few potential participants who were approached refused to participate. Finally, we do not claim to have exhausted potentially identifiable informal family roles. There may be other informal roles that did not emerge in these data either because we missed them in our analyses, they are infrequent, or they do not play as prominent a role in the end-of-life decision making process.

Conclusions

End-of-life decision making for patients in ICUs involves an intersection of both the health care domain and the family domain. Promoting family responses to end-of-life questions that honor the wishes of the patient requires an understanding of informal family roles such as those observed and described, as well as an awareness of how these roles may be enacted. Strategies should be developed to facilitate smooth resolution of conflicting views and decisions among family members and between clinicians and family members that foster effective decision making processes. Potentially fruitful areas for further exploration include the identification of other important informal family roles that may be less prominent or less frequently portrayed but may be equally important in some end-of-life decision making, and the role of advance directives in family end-of-life decision making processes. A closer examination of family meetings as a way to foster effective family end-of-life decision making and the role of hospital-based palliative care services in supporting effective family end-of-life decision making processes are vital areas for further study.[27]

Notes

Financial Disclosures

1. This study was supported by grants from the National Institutes of Health/National Institute of Nursing Research (RO1NR04940 and 1R15NR012147).

eLetters

1. Now that you've read the article, create or contribute to an online discussion on this topic. Visit **www.ajcconline.org** and click "Submit a response" in either the full-text or PDF view of the article.

2. To purchase electronic or print reprints, contact The InnoVision Group, 101 Columbia, Aliso Viejo, CA 92656. Phone: (800) 899-1712 or (949) 362-2050 (ext 532); fax: (949) 362-2049; e-mail: reprints@aacn.org.

3. ©2012 American Association of Critical-Care Nurses

References

1. Breitborde LB. *Rebuttal Essay. Int J Soc Lang. 1983;39: 161–177.*

2. Search Google Scholar Kirchhoff KT, Kowalkowski JA *Current practices for withdrawal of life support in intensive care units. Am J Crit Care. 2010;19:532–541.*

3. Abstract/FREE Full Text Tilden VP, Tolle SW, Nelson CA, et al. *Family decision making to withdraw life-sustaining treatments from hospitalized patients. Nurs Res. 2001;50:105–115.*

4. CrossRefMedline Arnold RM, Kellum J. *Moral justifications for surrogate decision making in the intensive care unit: implications and limitations. Crit Care Med. 2003;31:S347–S353.*

5. CrossRefMedline Berger JT, DeRenzo EG, and Schwartz J. *Surrogate decision making: reconciling ethical theory and clinical practice. Ann Intern Med. 2008;149:48–53.*

6. Medline Evans LR, Boyd EA, Malvar G, et al. *Surrogate decision makers' perspectives on discussing prognosis in the face of uncertainty. Am J Respir Crit Care Med. 2009;179:48–53.*

7. Abstract/FREE Full Text Heyland DK, Cook DJ, Rocker GM, et al. *Decision making in the ICU: perspectives of the substitute decision-maker. Intensive Care Med. 2003;29:75–82.*

8. Medline Luce JM *End-of-life decision making in the intensive care unit. Am J Respir Crit Care Med. 2010;182:6–11.*

9. Abstract/FREE Full Text Radwany S, Albanese T, Clough L, et al. *End-of-life decision making and emotional burden: placing family meetings in context. Am J Hosp Palliat Care. 2009;26:376–383.*

10. Abstract/FREE Full Text Westphal DM, McKee SA. *End-of-life decision making in the intensive care unit: physician and nurse perspectives. Am J Med Qual. 2009;24:222–228.*

11. Abstract/FREE Full Text Baggs JG, Norton SA, Schmitt MH, et al. *Intensive care unit cultures and end-of-life decision making. J Crit Care. 2007;22:159–168.*

12. CrossRefMedline Dunphey DC. *The Primary Group: A Handbook for Analysis and Field Research. New York, NY: Appleton-Century-Crofts; 1972.*

13. Search Google Scholar Mills TM. *The Sociology of Small Groups. Englewood Cliffs, NJ: Prentice-Hall; 1984.*

14. Search Google Scholar Farrell MP, Schmitt MH, and Heinemann GD. *Informal roles and the stages of interdisciplinary team development. J Interprof Care. 2001;15:281–295.*

15. CrossRefMedline Abbott KH, Sago JG, Breen CM, et al. *Families looking back: one year after discussion of withdrawal or withholding of life-sustaining support. Crit Care Med. 2001;29:197–201.*

16. CrossRefMedline Bartels DM, Faber-Langendoen K. *Caring in crisis: family perspectives on ventilator withdrawal at the end of life. Fam Syst Health. 2001;19:169–176.*

17. CrossRef Johnson N, Cook D, Giacomini M, et al. *Towards a "good" death: end-of-life narratives constructed in an intensive care unit. Cult Med Psychiatry. 2000;24:275–295.*

18. CrossRefMedline Norton SA, Tilden VP, Tolle SW, et al. *Life support withdrawal: communication and conflict. Am J Crit Care. 2003; 12:548–555.*

19. Abstract/FREE Full Text *ATLAS.ti: The Knowledge Workbench [computer program]. Version 5.0. Berlin, Germany: Atlas.ti; 2004.*

20. Munhall PL, Boyd CP, and Germain CP. *Ethnography: the method. In: Munhall PL, Boyd CP, eds. Nursing Research: A Qualitative Perspective. New York, NY: National League for Nursing; 1993:237–268.*

21. Search Google Scholar Morse JM, Field PA. *Qualitative Research Methods for Health Professionals. Thousand Oaks, CA: Sage; 1995.*

22. Search Google Scholar White DB, Malvar G, Karr J, et al. *Expanding the paradigm of the physician's role in surrogate decision making: an empirically derived framework. Crit Care Med. 2010;38:743–750.*

23. CrossRefMedline Wiegand D. *In their own time: the family experience during the process of withdrawal of life-sustaining therapy. J Palliat Med. 2008;11:1115–1121.*

24. CrossRefMedline Hsieh HF, Shannon SE, Curtis JR. *Contradictions and communication strategies during end-of-life decision making in the intensive care unit. J Crit Care. 2006;21: 294–304.*

25. CrossRefMedline Norton SA, Bowers BJ. *Working toward consensus: providers' strategies to shift patients from curative to palliative treatment choices. Res Nurs Health. 2001;24:258–269.*

26. CrossRefMedline Norton SA, Hogan LA, Holloway RG, et al. *Proactive palliative care in the medical intensive care unit: effects on length of stay for selected high-risk patients. Crit Care Med. 2007; 35:1530–1535.*

27. CrossRefMedline Daly BJ, Douglas SL, O'Toole E, et al. *Effectiveness trial of an intensive communication structure for families of longstay ICU patients. Chest. 2010;138:1340–1348.*

Critical Thinking

1. What are some formal roles that family members take when making decisions about someone who is critically ill? How do you think the decision is made regarding who will formally represent the family?

2. Do you agree with the statement made in the article that health care providers often feel that they "do not have a spokesperson but a spokesgroup?"

3. The study identified a variety of different, informal roles that family members may take on when someone is critically ill. Have you witnessed anyone in your family take on these types of roles or responsibilities?

4. What can be done to support families as they are making important decisions about a critically ill family member?

Create Central

www.mhhe.com/createcentral

Internet References

Family Caregiver Alliance National Center on Caregiving
  http://caregiver.org
Hospice Foundation of America
  www.hospicefoundation.org

JILL R. QUINN is an associate professor, MADELINE SCHMITT is a professor emerita, SALLY A. NORTON is an associate professor, MARY T. DOMBECK is a professor, and CRAIG R. SELLERS is an associate professor of clinical nursing at the University of Rochester School of Nursing in Rochester, New York. JUDITH GEDNEY BAGGS is a distinguished professor at Oregon Health & Science University School of Nursing in Portland.

Corresponding author: Jill R. Quinn, RN, PhD, CS-ANP, University of Rochester School of Nursing, 601 Elmwood Avenue, Box SON, Rochester, NY 14642 (e-mail: jill_quinn@urmc.rochester.edu).

Acknowledgments—We thank the patients, families, and clinicians who made this study possible. We also thank Dr. Nancy Press for her review of this manuscript.

Article Prepared by: Patricia Hrusa Williams,
University of Maine at Farmington

Military Children and Families

Strengths and Challenges during Peace and War

The gathering of military men should be thanking their children, their fine and resourceful children, who were strangers in every school they entered, thanking them for their extraordinary service to their country, for the sacrifices they made over and over again. . . . Military brats . . . [spend] their entire youth in service to this country and no one even [knows]. (Conroy, 1991)

NANSOOK PARK

Learning Outcomes

After reading this article, you will be able to:

- Describe the adaptability and resilience of military families.

- Identify how children cope with their parents' deployment.

- Summarize the strengths and challenges faced by military families.

A common saying in the military is that when one person joins, the whole family serves. Military families may often be in the background of public discourse on the military, but they are critical to its success. Although aspects of military life can be difficult for families, positive family functioning boosts a service member's morale, retention, and ability to carry out missions (Shin-seki, 2003). According to a recent report, service members reported positive family relationships as a source of resilience and problems at home as a source of stress and interference (Mental Health Advisory Team 6, 2009). Any efforts to build a strong, effective, and sustainable military force must also consider military families, improving the relationships of the soldier with his or her family members and strengthening the family itself (cf. Gottman, Gottman, & Atkins, 2011).

Since the start of the Global War on Terror, military children and families have faced multiple tests associated with unprecedented lengthy and multiple deployments; shorter stays at home between deployments; and greater risks of death, injury, and psychological problems among service members. Although many military children and families rise to the occasion and do well (Wiens & Boss, 2006), these challenges can take a toll on their health and well-being (Chandra, Burns, Tanielian, Jaycox, & Scott, 2008; Flake, Davis, Johnson, & Middleton, 2009).

Despite urgent needs to better understand the impact of deployment on military children and families and to provide appropriate support for them, there is a dearth of research. Programs and interventions exist, but definitive conclusions about what really works are by and large lacking.

Programs that try to assist military children and families often focus only on the prevention or reduction of problems. As important as it is to address problems, it is just as important to recognize the strengths and assets of military children and families and to promote and bolster them. A full and accurate picture of military children and families is needed upon which to base interventions. One of the best ways to prevent or solve problems is to identify what goes well and to use this as the basis of intervention (Park, 2004, 2009; Park & Peterson, 2008; Park, Peterson, & Brunwasser, 2009; Peterson & Park, 2003).

Over the years, studies of military children and families by psychologists have been isolated from and neglected by mainstream psychology. Most studies are done by researchers who are present or former members of the military or immediate members of military families. Studies are too rarely published in the mainstream psychology journals. This state of affairs needs to change to meet the surging needs of military children and families.

This article describes what is known about military children and families: their demographics, their challenges, and their strengths, during both peace and war times. Also addressed are issues and gaps in the existing research and practice. The thesis is that greater attention to the strengths and assets of military children and families is needed in order to design and implement effective programs to support them. This approach echoes the premise of the U.S. Army Comprehensive Soldier Fitness (CSF) program described elsewhere in this special issue (Cornum, Matthews, & Seligman, 2011). The fitness of soldiers extends beyond mere physical prowess to include psychosocial well-being, a key component of which is the well-being of their families (Peterson, Park, & Castro, 2011; Rohall, Segal, & Segal, 1999). Currently, collaborative efforts between psychologists and the U.S. Army are extending the CSF program to family members.

The Changing Demographics of the Modern U.S. Military Family

In the United States today, there are several million men and women wearing the uniform of the country's military. In broad terms, this is a young (50 percent below age 25) and male (85 percent) population, with individuals from rural, less affluent, and ethnic minority (African American and Latino/a) backgrounds overrepresented (U.S. Department of Defense, Defense Manpower Data Center, 2008). Almost all have a high school degree or equivalent, and 70 percent have at least some college credits. About half of them are married, with about 10 percent of the armed forces in dual-career marriages (i.e., married to another member of the military).

In contrast to the U.S. population as a whole, members of the military tend to marry earlier, a fact that researchers need to take into account in comparing military and civilian families because marriage at a younger age can be associated with more problems than marriage at an older age (Amato, Booth, Johnson, & Rogers, 2007). Among married individuals in the armed forces, more than 70 percent have one or more children, and there are at least 1.85 million children with one or both parents in the military (65 percent active duty and 35 percent Reserves or National Guard; Chandra et al., 2008; Segal & Segal, 2004).

Research on military families as well as formal programs to support them often uses a narrow definition of what a *family* entails: mother and father—one of whom wears a uniform—and their biological children. The so-called nuclear family is not the only type that exists, especially in the contemporary United States. Single-parent families have increased in recent decades, as well as blended families and intergenerational families. With the increase of women in the military, dual-career military families have increased (Segal & Segal, 2004). Each type of family has unique difficulties and assets.

In this article, the phrase *military children and families* is used to refer broadly to all individuals who are connected to a military family—traditional and nontraditional families, extended and binuclear families, spouses and significant others, sons and daughters, stepsons and stepdaughters, brothers and sisters, parents and grandparents, and so on. The focus is on military-connected children, but the functioning of all family members bears on the well-being of these children.

Strengths and Challenges among Military Children and Families

Military life presents both challenges and opportunities to grow for children and families (Hall, 2008). To provide effective services for military children and families, we need a better understanding of these challenges and strengths framed in terms of the culture and function of the military during peace and during war.

During Peace

Even during peaceful times, military children and families face recurrent separations, frequent and often sudden moves, difficult reunions, long and often unpredictable duty hours, and the threat of injury or death of the military service member during routine training and peaceful missions (Black, 1993). On average, active duty military families move every two to three years within the United States or overseas (Croan, Levine, & Blankinship, 1992). Secondary school-age students move three times more often than their civilian counterparts do (Shinseki, 2003). These frequent relocations disrupt children's schoolwork, activities, and social networks, requiring ongoing adjustment to new schools and cultures. Children can grow up feeling rootless and may have difficulties building deeper relationships or maintaining long-term commitments (Wertsch, 1991). Especially during adolescence, interruption of peer relationships can be detrimental to a child's psychosocial development (Shaw, 1979). Also, separation from a parent because of military assignments can have negative impacts on a child's school performance and mental health (Jensen, Grogan, Xenakis, & Bain, 1989). Due to different school and state requirements for course credits and course materials, frequent moves pose additional challenges for academic achievement and graduation by transferring students. These problems are especially pronounced for students with special needs (Hall, 2008).

Nevertheless, the available evidence suggests that military children typically function as well as or even better than civilian children on most indices of health, well-being, and academic achievement. They have similar or lower rates of childhood psychopathology, lower rates of juvenile delinquency, lower likelihood of alcohol or drug abuse, better grades, and higher median IQs than do their civilian counterparts (Jensen, Xenakis, Wolf, & Bain, 1991; Kenny, 1967; Morrison, 1981). According to a large-scale survey of military adolescents (Jeffreys & Leitzel, 2000), military children are in general healthy, have good peer relationships, are engaged in school and community, do well at school, and are satisfied with life. On average, military children report high optimism and positive self-images (Watanabe, 1985).

Compared with civilian children, military children have greater respect for authority and are more tolerant, resourceful, adaptable, responsible, and welcoming of challenges, and they have a greater likelihood of knowing and befriending someone who is "different" (Hall, 2008); they engage in fewer risky behaviors (Hutchinson, 2006); they exhibit greater self-control (Watanabe, 1985); and they show lower levels of impatience, aggression, and disobedience and higher levels of competitiveness (Manning, Balson, & Xenakis, 1988). Most military children are happy to embrace the term *military brat* and one or another of its backronyms such as "brave, resilient, adaptable, and trustworthy."[1]

Difficult life events do not automatically lead to problems in children. In some cases, challenges provide an opportunity to grow. For instance, relocation can be a positive experience. Children and families have the opportunity to meet new people and make new friends, to visit different places, and to experience diverse cultures (O'Connell, 1981).

If families have positive attitudes toward relocation, social support, previous relocation experience, and active coping styles, they do better when they move (Feldman & Tompson, 1993; Frame & Shehan, 1994). As stressful as parental separation can be, military children are afforded the opportunity to take on responsibilities and to be more independent and mature. Although the inherent hierarchy and structure of military culture can produce resentment among some military children and decrease their independent thinking, it can also foster discipline. Furthermore, military values that emphasize service, sacrifice, honor, teamwork, loyalty, sense of purpose, sense of community, and pride can work as resilience factors to overcome the difficulties of military life (Paden & Pezor, 1993).

During War

The major challenge for military children and families during war is a lengthy deployment of the uniformed family member to a combat zone. Children not only miss the deployed parent, but they also experience obvious uncertainty surrounding his or her safety, especially in single-parent or dual-career families. There are other issues as well. Children may be asked to take on greater responsibilities, and daily routines may change (Pincus, House, Christenson, & Adler, 2001). Families may move to be closer to other relatives. Unlike relocation during times of peace, war-time relocation of families may require them to move off base into the civilian community where they lose the existing military support system (MacDermid, 2006).

Nearly 900,000 U.S. children have had at least one of their parents deployed since 2001, and currently 234,000 children have one or both parents at war (Zoroya, 2009). Long and frequent deployments of service members put military children and families at risk for psychosocial problems (American Psychological Association, Presidential Task Force on Military Deployment Services for Youth, Families, and Service Members, 2007). According to U.S. Department of Defense data, between 2003 and 2008 the number of military children receiving outpatient mental health care doubled, and during that period inpatient visits by military children increased by 50 percent, with a 20 percent jump from 2007 to 2008 ("Department of Defense Reaches Out to Children of Soldiers," 2009). This indicates potentially a cumulative toll of parental deployments on military children and urgent needs for proper mental health services for this population.

Although scarce, several studies have looked at the impact of parental deployment on children during current wars. Although military children and families cope relatively well with shorter separations (less than six months), longer and multiple deployments create measurable distress (Chandra et al., 2010; Flake et al., 2009). Parental deployment can affect physical health, academic performance, behavior problems, depression, and anxiety of military children. Adolescent children of deployed parents show significantly higher levels of stress, systolic blood pressure, and heart rate than their civilian counterparts (Barnes,

Davis, & Treiber, 2007). Children of deployed service members also show decreases in their academic performance, school engagement, and overall school adjustment (Engel, Gallagher, & Lyle, 2010). More than one third of school-age children showed high risk for psychosocial difficulties during parental deployment, 2.5 times the national norm (Flake et al., 2009). Children of deployed parents, especially older youth and girls, reported more problems with school, family, and mental health. The longer the parental deployment is, the greater these problems are, during and after deployment (Chandra et al., 2010).

Risk factors exacerbating the negative effects of deployment on military children and families include a history of family problems, younger families, less educated families, foreign-born spouses, families with young children, those with lower pay grades or reduced income, those without a unit affiliation such as National Guard and Reserve families, families with children who have disabilities, families with pregnancies, single-parent families, and families with mothers in the military (American Psychological Association, Presidential Task Force, 2007).

Although military deployment poses risks, especially for some families, it is equally important to remember that many military children and families show resilience and growth. During the deployment of a family member, parents report that their children are closer to family and friends, and that they are more responsible, independent, and proud. Seventy-four percent of the spouses of service members report personal growth, despite also reporting increased loneliness, stress, and anxiety (U.S. Department of Defense, Defense Manpower Data Center, 2009b).

Resilience plays an important role in all phases of deployment. Resilience mitigates stress and improves adjustment to deployment by children and families. Families that function most effectively are active, optimistic, self-reliant, and flexible (Jensen & Shaw, 1996; Wiens & Boss, 2006). Families that function well find meaning in military life and identify with the work of their uniformed family member (Hammer, Cullen, Marchand, & Dezsofi, 2006; Marchant & Medway, 1987). Family preparedness for deployment as well as community and social support lead to better adjustment (Wiens & Boss, 2006).

Huebner (2010) found that adolescents who adapted well during parental deployment showed the ability to put the situation in perspective; positive reframing; the embracing of change and adaptation as necessary; effective coping skills; and good relationships with family, friends, and neighbors. For example, one adolescent reported, "I have really good neighbors that understand the situation going on. And I'm always welcome at my neighbors" (Huebner, 2010, p. 14).

During deployment, the well-being of military children needs to be approached not just at the level of the individual child but also in terms of larger social systems—the extended family, neighborhoods, schools, and communities. The community environment affects children's adjustment and coping during wartime deployment, and parental stress strongly relates to a military child's psychosocial functioning during deployment (Flake et al., 2009; Huebner, Mancini, Bowen, & Orthner, 2009). The challenges faced by military children are exacerbated by family and community inability to recognize and provide proper support and assistance. If the family as a whole adjusts well to deployment, then so do children. If we care about military children's well-being, it is imperative to ensure family well-being because they are so closely connected.

All things considered, military families on average have done well and show resilience during peace and even war. Problems of course exist for some military families, but rarely to a greater extent than among civilian families. Contrast this conclusion with the notion of the *military family syndrome,* which refers to a constellation of out-of-control offspring, authoritarian fathers, and depressed mothers (Lagrone, 1978). This alleged syndrome has been refuted repeatedly by relevant evidence (e.g., Jensen, Gordon, Lewis, & Xenakis, 1986; Jensen et al., 1991; Morrison, 1981), but it seems to be as resilient as the healthy military family that it fails to acknowledge. The fact that military families overall have done well in the past deserves greater dissemination in the present than seems to occur in today's popular media. If nothing else, the historical strength of the military family can serve as a source of pride and inspiration.

Strengths-Based Approaches

Military children and families often do well, but they are not invulnerable (Cozza, Chun, & Polo, 2005). Rather, they do well because they have compensating strengths and assets (Bowen, Mancini, Martin, Ware, & Nelson, 2003: Palmer, 2008). It behooves us to identify what these may be, to enhance them, and to use what is learned to design interventions for all military children and families, those with or without problems. As noted, one way to prevent or solve problems is to base interventions on what is going well.

The previous section reviewed the strengths and assets of military children and families. More family support programs that address strengths as well as problems are needed. Existing programs need not be replaced but expanded. A focus on what goes well does not mean that what goes poorly should be ignored. Indeed, strengths-based interventions complement and extend problem-focused interventions (Park, 2004, 2009; Park & Peterson, 2006, 2008; Park et al., 2009; Peterson & Park, 2003). A comprehensive approach to the support of military families may be more effective than a problem-focused strategy, and it would certainly reduce the stigma that surrounds the seeking of "mental health" care.

Programs and resources, formal and informal, already exist in both military and civilian sectors to support military children and families. Targeted programs and services are helpful, but we need further assistance, support, and engagement of the broader community.

The *Military Child Education Coalition* (MCEC) programs to support military children are worthy of attention. They embody the strengths-based focus advocated here. MCEC has been working directly with different branches of the military, school districts, and parents to facilitate transition of transferring military children (MCEC, 2001). MCEC offers regular training for school counselors and teachers, involves civilian students in their programs, and makes available relevant information to schools as well as parents. Underlying all of the MCEC programs is the assumption that military families are resilient and resourceful, but that accessible information, consistent school rules, and support help reduce the annoyances associated with student relocation.

The Student 2 Student program of MCEC is a unique student-led, school-based program for transitioning students from military families. This program provides social as well as instrumental support for students relocating to and from different schools. A team of advisors, volunteer students, and school liaison officers from each school are trained to develop and implement specific plans that fit their particular school setting and to implement, recruit, and train others at their school. These programs benefit all transitioning students, military connected or not.

As another example, MCEC's initiative "Living in the New Normal: Helping Children Thrive through Good and Challenging Times" engages and empowers the whole community. It is designed to reach everyone involved with military-connected children. It provides resources and trains adults to help children with deployment-related challenges to develop resilience. Further, the program brings together all sectors of the community to identify the unique assets of that community and to develop specific plans to utilize those assets to provide sustained support not only for military children and families but also for all community members. The MCEC programs stand in contrast to many other interventions for military families, which are often brief and highly targeted, because they involve larger social units (schools and communities) on an ongoing basis.

Issues and Recommendations

There is a significant shortage of evidence-based programs. Indeed, many programs for military children and families are not evaluated at all. In the absence of evidence for their effectiveness, they are but well-intended interventions. When resources are limited and demands are great, it is even more critical to identify programs that are effective and efficient, and to understand the active ingredients that make programs successful (Lester, McBride, Bliese, & Adler, 2011). Following appropriate evaluation, successful programs can be disseminated with confidence, and ineffective programs can be modified or eliminated. A better job needs to be done coordinating and disseminating information about existing programs, increasing their accessibility to the entire military community, and reducing stigma associated with seeking mental health care.

More generally, the research literature on military children and families is too scant, especially in light of contemporary concerns with their well-being while the United States is at war. Several observations about this literature are offered, followed by recommendations for further research and interventions.

Much of the relevant research on military families is not methodologically rigorous. Studies are often hampered by small and nonrepresentative samples and often lack appropriate comparison groups. They are often cross-sectional and starkly descriptive. Potential confounds are often not measured and thus cannot be taken into account, leaving studies inconclusive.

Studies of military children need to use multiple informants. Studies usually depend on what the nonmilitary parent says and may reflect a reporting bias. Consider that one investigation found greater problems among military children than among civilian children according to parental report but *not* according to the direct report of the children (Jensen et al., 1991). Chandra et al. (2010) noted similar discrepancies between conclusions based on parental report and child report.

The lack of explicit theory is conspicuous, although there is an important exception: the cycle of deployment model, which distinguishes different phases through which military families pass when a family member is deployed: (a) predeployment (from notification to departure), (b) deployment (from departure to return), (c) reunion (termed *redeployment* in the military), and (d) postdeployment. Each phase has its own characteristics and requirements (Pincus et al., 2001).

Research on the effects of deployment on military children and families usually focuses only on the period of actual deployment. Redeployment and postdeployment are poorly understood and in need of greater explication. Although reunion can be joyous, it also requires changes and adjustments in roles and routines for all family members, and these can be stressful and confusing (American Psychological Association, Presidential Task Force, 2007). Furthermore, many families have to start preparing for the next deployment again. For both families and service members alike, the postdeployment stage is particularly long and complex (MacDermid, 2006). Many returning service members experience combat-related mental health problems, injuries, and disabilities. These can burden children and families. There is simply not enough research about the long-term effects on children and families of living with a parent who is experiencing such difficulties and how to help them. Longitudinal studies are needed.

Also, a developmental perspective should be utilized in understanding the effect of deployment on children in order to provide developmentally appropriate services. Children at various developmental stages face different developmental tasks and have different levels of cognitive, emotional, and social skills. As a result, children may respond quite differently at each deployment cycle depending on their developmental stages (Paden & Pezor, 1993).

As already noted, most military family studies assume a traditional family and thus do not adequately sample the relevant populations. Considering the diversity of military family types, future studies should examine the impact of military life, especially deployment, on children from different types of families. Future studies should also compare the effects on children of maternal versus paternal deployment.

Although studies have been done spanning different military eras, they rarely use the same measures or procedures, precluding strong conclusions about similarities and differences among different military cohorts (e.g., those serving during Vietnam, Somalia, Desert Storm, and Operation Iraqi Freedom/Operation Enduring Freedom versus those serving during more peaceful times). Military families, no less than their civilian counterparts, are complex. The challenges they face are likely not across the board but rather are influenced by a host of interacting factors—branch of service, age, education,

ethnicity, pre-existing problems and assets, community integration (e.g., living on base or off base), exposure to combat, and number of deployments—that are rarely studied in terms of their interactions.

Studies making direct comparisons across branches of the service are also rare, although those studies that do exist often find differences in family functioning across Army, Navy, Air Force, Coast Guard, and Marines. Another neglected contrast related to family functioning is whether the uniformed family member is active duty or Reserve or National Guard. As is well known, a large number of Reserve and National Guard members currently serve; almost 700,000 members of the Reserve and National Guard have been activated since 9/11, parents of about 35 percent of military children (U.S. Department of Defense, Defense Manpower Data Center, 2009a). Reserve and National Guard families live off base among civilians and are less integrated into a military community, factors that limit their access to military support systems and programs. Many have either left or put on hold their civilian careers because of their "suddenly military" status. The effects on children and families are largely unknown, although one suspects that they include notable instability and stress.

Recent reports suggest that Reserve children and families may be at greater risk for mental health and adjustment issues (Chandra et al., 2008; Mental Health Advisory Team 6, 2009). Children from Reserve families report a lack of understanding and support from their peers and teachers more than children from active-duty families. And what about the children and families of civilian contractors and Federal Agency employees serving in war zones, so heavily relied upon during the current wars? No study has addressed the challenges they face.

There are members of the military family who are often neglected in research and intervention. Siblings can play an important role in bolstering the well-being and resilience of military children and deployed service members. Sibling relationships in general are among the most crucial in a person's life (Bank & Kahn, 1982). Increased attention to military children who do or do not have siblings would be important. Given frequent relocations, siblings may be even more important for military children than for civilian children, providing stability, familiarity, and support not readily available elsewhere.

Another glaring absence in the literature is consideration of the brothers and sisters of service members. The siblings of service members are of course affected by the deployment, injury, or death of those who serve, but virtually nothing is known about challenges they face and how to help them. Studies of civilians make clear that sibling loss adversely affects health and well-being. Surviving siblings often experience anxiety, guilt, sadness, and anger (Bank & Kahn, 1982). They report health that is even worse than that of surviving spouses (Hays, Gold, & Pieper, 1997).

"Siblings of troops often are forgotten mourners" (Hefling, 2009). According to a recent report, there are several thousand surviving siblings from current wars. Many are in their 20s or 30s (Hefling, 2009), but considering that many service members who have lost their lives were young, a large number of surviving siblings are also in their teens or even younger—children themselves. When a service member dies, the spouse, the children, and the parents are generally expected to be most affected. Sibling death may be overlooked as a significant loss (Moss, Moss, & Hansson, 2001). As a result, siblings may not receive the support they need.

Finally, more research is needed to understand the impact of deployment and grief on military parents and grandparents (Rando, 1986). Their coping and adjustment are important for their own sake as well as in terms of the impacts on the health and well-being of all other family members (Fry, 1997).

CSF Program for Military Family Members

Currently, a major effort is under way to extend the CSF program to all Army family members. Psychologists and the U.S. Army are collaborating to enhance the resilience and well-being of military family members. This project is based on the premise that family members play an important role in the soldier's performance, resilience, and well-being. Parallel to the CSF for soldiers, the family CSF program will include both assessment and program modules built on a strengths-based approach.

The Global Assessment Tool for families, now under development, measures a person's strengths and problems in four life domains: emotional, social, familial, and spiritual (Peterson et al., 2011). The contents of assessment and training modules for families are designed to address both common personal and family-related issues with special attention to unique challenges and experiences faced by military families. The assessment tool is planned to be available through a military website for family members, and the outcome will be confidential. Upon completion of the survey, participants will receive instant feedback on strengths and issues in each life domain. Depending on the results, tailored information and various training modules, from self-development online programs to more intensive group or personal interventions, will be made available.

At this early stage of the project, the target participants are adults in the military family—spouses or caretakers of military children. Strengths and problems among military children will be measured by the caretaker's report, and separate training modules are planned to provide adults with tools to promote the resilience and well-being of military children. A larger community of military family members will be reached in an efficient and cost-effective way with computer technology in conjunction with other strategies to deliver assessment and programs (Gottman et al., 2011). The family component of the CSF program has just begun. The initiative will be revised on the basis of the results of ongoing research and evaluation. It is conceivable that in the future, additional direct assessment and programs for military children will be added to the CSF program.

Conclusion

Throughout history, military children and families have shown great capacity to adapt to and grow from challenges, during peace or during war. However, with U.S. involvement in current wars, military families face multiple challenges that put them at high risk of distress and mental health problems. Their needs are greater than ever. The well-being of military children and families is desirable in its own right and as a means to many other valued ends, for individuals and the larger society.

There is an urgent need for better understanding of both the challenges and the strengths and assets of military children and families to help them not only survive but also thrive. Studies and programs need to take a comprehensive approach that is strengths based *and* problem focused. Studies and programs must focus not just on the individual but also on larger social contexts. We need more high-quality research and more evidence-based programs. Programs need to be rigorously evaluated and better disseminated to reach all those who are in need. Current efforts to expand the CSF program to military family members are another example of a systematic collaboration between psychology and the military to achieve the goal of a healthy, resilient, and productive military community.

Psychology as a field is in a unique position to accomplish all of these goals (Seligman & Fowler, 2011). Military children and families deserve sustained attention from psychology. One hopes that more psychologists will join and indeed help lead this worthy endeavor. About one third of the population has a direct relationship with someone in the military, and virtually everyone has an indirect relationship (Black, 1993). Military families live in our neighborhoods. Their children go to our schools. Much can be learned from them. Building and sustaining healthy, resilient, and thriving military children and families will bring benefits not just to them but ultimately to all Americans. The military family *is* the American family.

References

Amato, P. R., Booth, A., Johnson, D. R., & Rogers, S. J. (2007). *Alone together: How marriage in America is changing.* Cambridge, MA: Harvard University Press.

American Psychological Association, Presidential Task Force on Military Deployment Services for Youth, Families, and Service Members. (2007). *The psychological needs of U.S. military service members and their families: A preliminary report.* Washington, DC: American Psychological Association.

Bank, S., & Kahn, M. (1982). *The sibling bond.* New York, NY: Basic Books.

Barnes, V. A., Davis, H., & Treiber, F. A. (2007). Perceived stress, heart rate, and blood pressure among adolescents with family members deployed in Operation Iraqi Freedom. *Military Medicine, 172,* 40–43.

Black, W. G. (1993). Military-induced family separation: A stress reduction intervention. *Social Work, 38,* 273–280.

Bowen, G. L., Mancini, J. A., Martin, J. A., Ware, W. B., & Nelson, J. P. (2003). Promoting the adaptation of military families: An empirical test of a community practice model. *Family Relations, 52,* 33–44. doi: 10.111 l/j.1741-3729.2003.00033.x

Chandra, A., Burns, R. M., Tanielian, T., Jaycox, L. H., & Scott, M. M. (2008). *Understanding the impact of deployment on children and families: Findings from a pilot study of Operation*

Purple Camp participants [Working paper]. Santa Monica, CA: Rand Corporation.

Chandra, A., Lara-Cinisomo, S., Jaycox, L. H., Tanielian, T., Burns, R. M., Ruder, T., & Han, B. (2010). Children on the homefront: The experience of children from military families. *Pediatrics, 125,* 16–25.

Conroy, P. (1991). Introduction. In M. E. Wertsch, *Military brats: Legacies of childhood inside the fortress* (p. xix–xxvii). St. Louis, MO: Brightwell.

Cornum, R., Matthews, M. D., & Seligman, M. E. P. (2011). Comprehensive soldier fitness: Building resilience in a challenging institutional context. *American Psychologist, 66,* 4–9. doi:10.037/a0021420

Cozza, S. J., Chun, R. S., & Polo, J. A. (2005). Military families and children during operation Iraqi Freedom. *Psychiatric Quarterly, 76,* 371–378. doi:10.1007/slll26-005-4973-y

Croan, G. M., Levine, C. T., & Blankinship, D. A. (1992). *Family adjustment to relocation* (Technical Report No. 968). Alexandria, VA: U.S. Army Research Institute for the Behavioral and Social Sciences.

Department of Defense reaches out to children of soldiers. (2009, October 22). *U.S. Medicine.* Retrieved from www.usmedicine.com/articles/Department-of-Defense-Reaches-Out-to-Children-of-Soldiers.html

Engel, R. C, Gallagher, L. B., & Lyle, D. S. (2010). Military deployments and children's academic achievement: Evidence from Department of Defense education activity schools. *Economics of Education Review, 29,* 73–82.

Feldman, D. C, & Tompson, H. B. (1993). Expatriation, repatriation, and domestic geographical relocation: An empirical investigation of adjustment to new job assignments. *Journal of International Business Studies, 24,* 507–529. doi: 10.1057/palgrave.jibs.8490243

Flake, E. M., Davis, B. E., Johnson, P. L., & Middleton, L. S. (2009). The psychosocial effects of deployment on military children. *Journal of Developmental and Behavioral Pediatrics, 30,* 271–278. doi: 10.1097/ DBP.0b013e3181aac6e4

Frame, M. W., & Shehan, C. (1994). Work and well-being in the two-person career: Relocation stress and coping among clergy husbands and wives. *Family Relations, 43,* 169–205. doi: 10.2307/585323

Fry, P. S. (1997). Grandparents' reactions to the death of a grandchild: An exploratory factor analysis. *Omega: Journal of Death and Dying, 35,* 119–140.

Gottman, J. M., Gottman, J. S., & Atkins, C. (2011). The Comprehensive Soldier Fitness program: Family skills component. *American Psychologist, 66,* 52–57. doi:10.1037/a0021706

Hall, L. K. (2008). *Counseling military families: What mental health professionals need to know.* New York, NY: Routledge.

Hammer, L. B., Cullen, J. C, Marchand, G. C, & Dezsofi, J. A. (2006). Reducing the negative impact of work-family conflict on military personnel: Individual coping strategies and multilevel interventions. In C. A. Castro, A. B. Adler, & T. W. Britt (Eds.), *Military life: The psychology of serving in peace and combat* (Vol. 3, pp. 220–242). Westport, CT: Praeger Security International.

Hays, J. C, Gold, D. T., & Pieper, C. F. (1997). Sibling bereavement in late life. *Omega: Journal of Death and Dying, 35,* 25–42.

Hefling, K. (2009). *Siblings of troops often are forgotten mourners.* Retrieved October 21, 2009, from www.armytimes.com/news/2009/09/ap_military_grieving_siblings_092409

Huebner, A. J. (2010, January). *Impact of deployment on children and families: Recent research updates.* Presentation at the National Guard Professional Development Conference: Family Program Professional Development, Orlando, FL.

Huebner, A. J., Mancini, J. A., Bowen, G. L., & Orthner, D. K. (2009). Shadowed by war: Building community capacity to support military families. *Family Relations, 58,* 216–228. doi: 10.111 l/j.1741-3729. 2008.00548.x

Hutchinson, J. W. (2006). Evaluating risk-taking behaviors of youth in military families. *Journal of Adolescent Health, 39,* 927–928. doi: 10.1016/j.jadohealth.2006.05.015

Jeffreys, D. J., & Leitzel, J. D. (2000). The strengths and vulnerabilities of adolescents in military families. In J. A. Martin, L. N. Rosen, & L. R. Sparacino (Eds.), *The military family: A practice guide for human service providers* (pp. 225–240). Westport, CT: Praeger.

Jensen, P. S., Gordon, G. A., Lewis, R. L., & Xenakis, S. N. (1986). The military family in review: Context, risk, and prevention. *Journal of the American Academy of Child Psychiatry, 25,* 225–234. doi: 10.1016/ S0002-7138(09)60230-2

Jensen, P. S., Grogan, D., Xenakis, S. N., & Bain, M. W. (1989). Father absence: Effects on child and maternal psychopathology. *Journal of the American Academy of Child and Adolescent Psychiatry, 28,* 171–175. doi:10.1097/00004583-198903000-00004

Jensen, P. S., & Shaw, J. A. (1996). The effects of war and parental deployment upon children and adolescents. In R. J. Ursano & A. E. Norwood (Eds.), *Emotional aftermath of the Persian Gulf War: Veterans, families, communities, and nations* (pp. 83–109). Washington, DC: American Psychiatric Press.

Jensen, P. S., Xenakis, S. N., Wolf, P., & Bain, M. W. (1991). The "military family syndrome" revisited: "By the numbers." *Journal of Nervous and Mental Disease, 179,* 102–107. doi: 10.1097/00005053199102000-00007

Kenny, J. A. (1967). The child in the military community. *Journal of the American Academy of Child Psychiatry, 6,* 51–63. doi:10.1016/S0002-7138(09)61289-9

Lagrone, D. M. (1978). The military family syndrome. *American Journal of Psychiatry, 135,* 1040–1043.

Lester, P. B., McBride, S., Bliese, P. D., & Adler, A. B. (2011). Bringing science to bear: An empirical assessment of the Comprehensive Soldier Fitness program. *American Psychologist, 66,* 77–81. doi: 10.1037/a0022083

MacDermid, S. M. (2006). *Multiple transitions of deployment and reunion for military families.* Retrieved from the Military Family Research Institute, Purdue University website: www.cfs.purdue.edu/mfri/DeployReunion.ppt

Manning, D. T., Balson, P. M., & Xenakis, S. N. (1988). Prevalence of type A behavior in American combat soldiers and their children. *Military Medicine, 153,* 358–360.

Marchant, K. H., & Medway, F. J. (1987). Adjustment and achievement associated with mobility in military families. *Psychology in the Schools, 24,* 289–294. doi:10.1002/1520-6807(198707)24:3<::AID-PITS2310240315>3.0.CO;2-A

Mental Health Advisory Team 6. (2009, November 6). *Mental Health Advisory Team (MHAT) 6 Operation Enduring Freedom 2009 Afghanistan* (Report chartered by the Office of the Command Surgeon US Forces Afghanistan

(USFOR-A) and Office of the Surgeon General United States Army Medical Command). Retrieved from www. armymedicine.army.mil/reports/mhat/mhat_vi/MHAT_VI-OEF_Redacted.pdf

Military Child Education Coalition. (2001). *United States Army secondary education transition study.* Arlington, VA: Military Family Resources Center.

Morrison, J. (1981). Rethinking the military family syndrome. *American Journal of Psychiatry, 138,* 354–357.

Moss, M. S., Moss, S. Z., & Hansson, R. O. (2001). Bereavement and old age. In M. S. Stroebe, R. O. Hansson, W. Stroebe, & H. Schut (Eds.), *Handbook of bereavement research: Consequences, coping, and care* (pp. 241–260). Washington, DC: American Psychological Association, doi: 10.1037/10436-010

O'Connell, P. V. (1981). *The effect of mobility on selected personality characteristics of ninth and twelfth grade military dependents* (Unpublished doctoral dissertation). University of Wisconsin, Milwaukee.

Paden, L. B., & Pezor, L. J. (1993). Uniforms and youth: The military child and his or her family. In F. W. Kaslow (Ed.), *The military family in peace and war* (pp. 3–24). New York, NY: Springer.

Palmer, C. (2008). A theory of risk and resilience in military families. *Military Psychology, 20,* 205–217. doi: 10.1080/08995600802118858

Park, N. (2004). Character strengths and positive youth development. *Annals of the American Academy of Political and Social Science, 591,* 40–54. doi:10.1177/0002716203260079

Park, N. (2009). Building strengths of character: Keys to positive youth development. *Reclaiming Children and Youth, 18,* 42–47.

Park, N., & Peterson, C. (2006). Moral competence and character strengths among adolescents: The development and validation of the Values in Action Inventory of Strengths for Youth. *Journal of Adolescence, 29,* 891–910.

Park, N., & Peterson, C. (2008). Positive psychology and character strengths: Application to strengths-based school counseling. *Professional School Counseling, 12,* 85–92.

Park, N., Peterson, C, & Brunwasser, S. M. (2009). Positive psychology and therapy. In N. Kazantzis, M. A. Reinecke, & A. Freeman (Eds.), *Cognitive and behavioral theories in clinical practice* (pp. 278–306). New York, NY: Guilford Press.

Peterson, C, & Park, N. (2003). Positive psychology as the evenhanded positive psychologist views it. *Psychological Inquiry, 14,* 141–146.

Peterson, C, Park, N., & Castro, C. A. (2011). Assessment for the U.S. Army Comprehensive Soldier Fitness program: The Global Assessment Tool. *American Psychologist, 66,* 10–18. doi:10.1037/a0021658

Pincus, S. H., House, R., Christensen, J., & Adler, L. E. (2001). The emotional cycle of deployment: A military family perspective. *Journal of the Army Medical Department, 4/5/6,* 615–623.

Rando, T. (1986). Death of the adult child. In T. Rando (Ed.), *Parental loss of a child* (pp. 221–238). Champaign, IL: Research Press.

Rohall, D. E., Segal, M. W., & Segal, D. R. (1999). Examining the importance of organizational supports on family adjustment to military life in a period of increasing separation. *Journal of Political and Military Psychology, 27,* 49–65.

Segal, D. R., & Segal, M. W. (2004). America's military population. *Population Bulletin, 59,* 1–40.

Seligman, M. E. P., & Fowler, R. D. (2011). Comprehensive Soldier Fitness and the future of psychology. *American Psychologist, 66,* 8286. doi:10.1037/a0021898

Shaw, J. A. (1979). Adolescents in the mobile military community. In D. X. Freedman et al. (Eds.), *Adolescent psychiatry* (Vol. 7, pp. 191–198). Chicago, IL: University of Chicago Press.

Shinseki, E. K. (2003). *The Army family* (White paper). Retrieved from www.whs.mil/library/Dig/AR-M620U_20080912.pdf

U.S. Department of Defense, Defense Manpower Data Center. (2008). *The changing profile of the Army 1985–2008.* Alexandria, VA: Author.

U.S. Department of Defense, Defense Manpower Data Center. (2009a). *Reserve components: Noble Eagle/Enduring Freedom/Iraqi Freedom.* Alexandria, VA: Author.

U.S. Department of Defense, Defense Manpower Data Center. (2009b). *2008 surveys of military spouses: Impact of deployments on spouses and children.* Alexandria, VA: Author.

Watanabe, H. K. (1985). A survey of adolescent military family members' self-image. *Journal of Youth and Adolescence, 14,* 99–107.

Wertsch, M. E. (1991). *Military brats: Legacies of childhood inside the fortress.* St. Louis, MO: Brightwell.

Wiens, T. W., & Boss, P. (2006). Maintaining family resiliency before, during, and after military separation. In C. A. Castro, A. B. Adler, & T. W. Britt (Eds.), *Military life: The psychology of serving in peace and combat* (Vol. 3, pp. 13–38). Westport, CT: Praeger Security International.

Zoroya, G. (2009, June 25). Troops' kids feel war toll. *USA Today.* Retrieved from www.usatoday.com/news/military/2009-06-24-military-kids_N.htm

Note

1. The origin of the term *military brat* is not agreed on, although some have traced it to an acronym for British Regiment Attached Traveler (i.e., a soldier's child).

Critical Thinking

1. What are some of the strengths and challenges military families face?

2. How do children cope when a parent is deployed more often and for greater lengths of time?

3. What can friends of these families do to help them cope?

4. Why do you think that children have more trouble coping?

Create Central

www.mhhe.com/createcentral

Internet References

Substance Abuse and Mental Health Services Administration
www.samhsa.gov

National Military Family Association
www.militaryfamily.org

Military OneSource
www.militaryonesource.mil

I would like to acknowledge Daniel Fifis, retired school psychologist at Fort Jackson Schools, Columbia, South Carolina, whose generosity and dedication to military children and families have touched so many, including me. I thank Christopher Peterson, Albert Cain, Mary Keller, Jennifer Kirkpatrick, and Joyce Hodson for their help during preparation of this article. Special thanks go to Patricia K. Shinseki, who shared valuable insights and resources about military children and families and provided inspiration through her deep concerns and caring for them.

Correspondence concerning this article should be addressed to Nansook Park, Department of Psychology, University of Michigan, 530 Church Street, Ann Arbor, MI 48109-1043. E-mail: nspark@umich.edu

Article

Prepared by: Patricia Hrusa Williams,
University of Maine at Farmington

Evaluating the Needs of Military and Veterans' Families in a Polytrauma Setting

Objective: To examine the perceived importance of needs and the extent to which they are met among a sample of family members in an inpatient polytrauma setting. *Method:* The Family Needs Questionnaire was administered to 44 family members of patients at the Polytrauma Rehabilitation Center at McGuire Veterans Affairs Medical Center over a 30-month period. *Results:* Families rated health information needs as most important and most frequently met. conversely, family members rated emotional support and instrumental support needs as least important and most frequently unmet. *Conclusion:* Preliminary data suggest that the similarity between family needs in military and civilian settings is noteworthy, and provide direction for development of empirically based family intervention models for polytrauma settings.
Keywords: traumatic brain injury, polytrauma, military family needs, family needs questionnaire

KATHRYN P. WILDER SCHAAF, ET AL

Learning Outcomes

After reading this article, you will be able to:

- Understand the challenges faced by military families when their service member is severely injured.

- Identify the support needs of military families who have a service member who is severely injured.

Impact and Implications

- This study represents the first empirically based research that specifically examines met and unmet family needs in a military/veteran inpatient rehabilitation setting.

- This study provides a comparison of family needs in military/veteran rehabilitation settings to family needs in civilian inpatient rehabilitation settings reported in the literature.

- This study provides an empirical basis to inform future research and clinical interventions with family members in military/veteran rehabilitation settings.

Introduction

Skilled in providing comprehensive medical, surgical, and rehabilitation care for severe and complex polytraumatic injuries, the Polytrauma System of Care emerged, within the U.S. Department of Veterans Affairs, in response to conflicts in Iraq and Afghanistan (Sigford, 2008). The Polytrauma System of Care is a vast network that includes five Polytrauma Rehabilitation Centers (PRCs), or comprehensive inpatient rehabilitation programs, and over 100 additional polytrauma programs that provide an array of outpatient services to veterans nationwide. Polytrauma, defined as "two or more injuries to physical regions or organ systems, one of which may be life threatening, resulting in physical, cognitive, psychological, or psychosocial impairments and functional disability" (VHA Handbook, p. 3), includes amputations, fractures, burns, hearing loss, and traumatic brain injury (TBI) (Friedemann-Sánchez, Sayer, & Pickett, 2008). TBI is often cited as the most common component of polytraumatic injuries, with reported rates among returning veterans varying from 12%–23% (Schneiderman, Braver, & Kang, 2008; Terrio et al., 2009). Sequelae of TBI are cognitive, behavioral, emotional, and psychosocial in nature (Draper, Ponsford, & Schönberger, 2007; Riggio, 2010; Ruttan, Martin, Liu, Colella, & Green, 2008).

The long-term effect of brain injury on family members in civilian settings has been well documented. The consequences can include mood disturbance (Schönberger, Ponsford, Olver, & Ponsford, 2010), elevated anxiety and depression (Ponsford & Schönberger, 2010), poor family functioning (Kreutzer, Gervasio, & Camplair, 1994; Schönberger et al., 2010; Winstanley, Simpson, Tate, & Myles, 2006), social isolation (Marsh, Kersel, Havill, & Sleigh, 2002), and reduced life satisfaction (Livingston et al., 2010).

In comparison to family members in civilian settings, family members in veterans or military hospital settings often face a number of additional daunting challenges. First, polytrauma sequelae can add substantially to preexisting stresses arising from multiple deployments and extended separation from family members. Prior to the injury, some PRC families deal with typical deployment stressors such as role reorganization and anticipatory fear. Although families may be aware that their loved one could be harmed, few anticipate providing long-term care to rehabilitate a complex injury (Collins & Kennedy, 2008). In addition, because there are only five PRCs in the United States, family members must often travel significant distances to be bedside with the patient, often leaving behind jobs, children, other family members, and community support systems (Collins & Kennedy, 2008). Finally, family members are often tasked with providing long-term support and care to service members with complex conditions, including severe burns, traumatic amputations, psychological trauma, and other combat-related injuries (Collins & Kennedy, 2008). Blast-related polytraumatic injuries have been described as more clinically complex than typical injuries seen in civilian inpatient rehabilitation. In fact, a study examining PRC provider perspectives noted that the complexity of injury in the PRC was often more consistent with subacute care rather than inpatient rehabilitation (Friedemann-Sánchez et al., 2008).

Regardless of setting, families face complex and difficult challenges after brain injury. Understanding family needs is crucial to developing effective, well utilized family support and education services, yet there is little quantitative information about family needs in polytrauma settings. Clinical researchers in civilian settings have used the Family Needs Questionnaire (FNQ; Kolakowsky-Hayner, Miner, & Kreutzer, 2001; Kreutzer, 1988; Kreutzer, Serio, & Berquist, 1994; Witol, Sander, & Kreutzer, 1996). One of the most consistent findings using the FNQ is that family members identify health information as one of their most important needs (Kolakowsky-Hayner et al., 2001; Kreutzer, Serio, & Berquist, 1994; Moules & Chandler, 1999; Nabors, Seacat, & Rosenthal, 2002; Serio, Kreutzer, & Gervasio, 1995; Witol et al., 1996). Specifically, within the health information domain, family members cite needs including: (a) having questions answered honestly, (b) complete information about the patient's cognitive, medical, and psychological status, (c) reassurance that the staff respects patients' wishes, and (d) having information communicated in terms that are clear and understandable. In many studies, emotional and instrumental support needs are often cited as both less important and least likely to be met (Kreutzer, Serio, & Berquist, 1994; Moules & Chandler, 1999; Nabors et al., 2002; Serio et al., 1995). That is, family members did not see needs pertaining to their own lives, such as help keeping the house clean, reassurance about negative feelings, and spending time with friends, to be as salient as needs pertaining to the patient (Kreutzer, Serio, & Berquist, 1994; Witol et al., 1996).

There is a great deal of literature within the civilian demographic documenting the tremendous impact of brain injury on both the injured person and their family. However, there is little precedence for what is known about the needs of polytrauma patients' family members. Anecdotal evidence suggests that family members often assume the primary caregiving role once patients are discharged. Furthermore, some have suggested that meeting family members' needs allows them to be more effective caregivers. Given family members' important supporting role, the present study focused on family members in a PRC setting with the following specific objectives: (a) to examine the perceived importance of their needs and (b) to examine the extent to which needs designated as important are perceived as met.

Method
Participants
Data were derived from 44 family members of patients admitted to the PRC at Hunter Holmes McGuire Department of Veterans Affairs Medical Center in Richmond, Virginia. The final sample consisted of parents (48%), spouses (34%), siblings (9%), adult children (2%), and others (7%), including other blood relatives and unrelated persons listed as having power of attorney. Mean age was 42.9 years old ($SD = 14.50$) and ranged from 19–68 years old; most (75%) were married. Respondents were primarily female (70%), employed full time (46%), and White (84%). Of patients admitted during the recruitment window, 30% of families enrolled. Seven patients had two or more family members participate, representing 17 enrolled subjects. Reasons for not enrolling included: lack of family present (there are only five such facilities in the United States and travel can prohibit families from visiting) and families visiting outside of business hours (research assistants were only available during their specified tour of duty). Thus, reasons for nonparticipation were, in part, related to lack of family member availability.

Patients sustained multiple physical, cognitive, and/or emotional impairments consequent to trauma. The admissions team judged all to have the potential to benefit from rehabilitative care. The research team strongly considered requesting patient data. Ultimately, the decision was made not to request this data because the intended focus of family needs as well as a number of compelling reasons related to patient and family concerns. The following aggregate clinical data were available regarding patients admitted to the PRC during the data collection period. Patients were predominantly men (97%), most had sustained a TBI (81%), and had a mean age of 30 years ($SD = 9.4$). All patients treated at the PRC were either active duty military or veterans. Nearly half (45%) were injured in Operation Enduring Freedom or Operation Iraqi Freedom; the remainder were injured while deployed to other locales or injured within the continental United States.

Materials and Procedure
Demographics questionnaire. Information was collected about participants' race and ethnicity, sex, age, marital status, relationship to the patient, and employment. Questions were asked about their perceptions of patients' injury severity, where, geographically, the patient was injured, and how much time had elapsed since injury.

Family Needs Questionnaire. The Family Needs Questionnaire (FNQ) is a commonly used 40-item self-report instrument designed to characterize family members' perceived needs after brain injury (Hauber & Jones, 2002; Kim & Moon, 2007; Kreutzer, Serio, & Berquist, 1994; Kreutzer et al., 2009; Moules & Chandler, 1999; Murray, Maslany, & Jeffery, 2006). The items address commonly identified psychosocial and educational needs. Family members first indicate the extent to which needs are perceived as important on a scale ranging from 1 (*not important*) to 4 (*very important*). Then they rate the extent to which they perceive each need has been met (*not met, partly met,* or *met*). Researchers have provided evidence of content and construct validity as well as internal consistency (Spearman-Brown split-half reliability = 0.75; Kreutzer, Serio, & Berquist, 1994). Six factor analytically derived scales have been identified (Serio, Kreutzer, & Witol, 1997): Health Information, Emotional Support, Instrumental Support, Professional Support, Community Support Network, and Involvement with Care.

Procedure

From July 2007 through January 2010, family members of PRC patients presenting for treatment were approached and invited to participate in a study of family needs during rehabilitation. Participants were selected after having been identified by a licensed clinical psychologist as part of the established patient treatment process. Family members were approached while visiting the PRC and consent was addressed by trained research assistants not affiliated with patient care. The purpose of the study was fully explained, and informed consent was obtained. Respondents were asked to complete the paper-and-pencil study measures, and each was given as much time as needed for completion; subjects completed the measures anonymously. This study was reviewed by the McGuire institutional review board (IRB) and the Chesapeake IRB (on behalf of the Henry M. Jackson Foundation for the Advancement of Military Medicine). In addition, a U.S. Department of Defense administrative review was conducted by the United States Army Medical Research and Materiel Command at Fort Detrick, as required by the Defense and Veterans Brain Injury Center.

The first set of analyses identified family members' most and least important needs as well as their perceptions of the extent to which needs were met. First, the percentage of respondents who rated each need as important or very important was calculated to determine the most important needs. Subsequent analyses focused on the extent to which needs were perceived as met. Using the strategy used by Kreutzer, Serio, & Berquist (1994), only needs rated as important or very important by PRC family members were included in the met or not met analyses. Specifically, the mean percentage of met needs was calculated by dividing the sum of needs rated as met by the number of needs rated as important or very important. The mean percentage of not met needs was calculated similarly.

Results
Importance Ratings

To identify the needs most often perceived as important, the percentage of respondents who rated each need as important or very important was calculated. Across items, percentages

ranged from 34%–100%, with a mean of 83.1% (SD = 14.0%). Nine of the 40 needs were endorsed as important or very important by all (100%) PRC family members (see Table 1). Nearly all of the items unanimously endorsed as important were drawn from the Health Information domain.

Ratings of the Extent to Which Needs Are Met

To assess the extent to which participants perceived their needs as met, the percentage of needs rated as met and not met were calculated separately. Participants' met ratings were only included in the analysis if they were also rated as important or very important. Across items, the percentage of important needs rated by respondents as met ranged from 23%–83%, with a mean of 55.4% (SD = 26.7%). Table 1 provides a list of needs most frequently rated as met. Needs in the Health Information domain were most frequently represented.

Finally, the percentage of needs rated by respondents as not met ranged from 0%–27%, with a mean of 7.6% (SD = 9.7%). Needs in the Emotional Support and Instrumental Support domains were most frequently rated as not met (see Table 2). Ten of the 40 FNQ items did not receive a single (0%) not-met rating.

Discussion

The current study represents the first effort to empirically evaluate family needs after brain injury in a military or veteran setting. The findings provide a foundation for development of intervention programs by identifying needs rated as most important and met. Given the unique demands that many military and veteran families face, some might speculate that their needs differ from those families in civilian rehabilitation settings. However, findings from the present study regarding the types of needs rated as important and met were largely consistent with previous family needs studies in civilian settings (Kolakowsky-Hayner et al., 2001; Kreutzer, Serio, & Berquist, 1994; Moules & Chandler, 1999; Nabors et al., 2002; Serio et al., 1995; Witol et al., 1996).

Analyses of the FNQ reveal that families dealing with tragic, life-changing circumstances prefer that professionals convey honest, current, and complete health information. The analysis of needs met ratings shows that rehabilitation providers seem to be effective at delivering injury-related information. In contrast, analysis of needs rated most often as not met (instrumental and emotional support) indicates that family members are likely to be struggling with their day-to-day duties outside of the hospital, and they may not have family or friends who understand what they are going through.

This research provides an empirical foundation for designing military/veteran interventions. Given PRC family members' reports of unmet emotional and instrumental needs, development of programs to help family members to request support when needed, to discuss concerns with loved ones, and to find ways to share concerns with the patient's friends and extended family members should be a priority. In addition, given the importance placed on health information, attention to effective and family-friendly methods for providing information and a standardized information delivery system to address families' needs at different time points should also take precedence.

Table 1 Needs Most Frequently Rated as Important and Met by the PRC Samples

FNQ item	Scale	% PRC endorsement (important)	% PRC endorsement (met)
To have complete information on the patient's problems in thinking (e.g., confusion, memory, communication)	Health Information	100%	56%
To have my questions answered honestly	Health Information	100%	77%
To be assured that the best possible medical care is being given to the patient	Health Information	100%	65%
To have a professional to turn to for advice or services when the patient needs help	Support Network	100%	77%
To have complete information on the patient's physical problems (e.g., weakness, headaches, dizziness, problems with vision or walking)	Health Information	100%	58%
To have information on the patient's rehabilitative or educational progress	Health Information	100%	52%
To be shown that medical, educational, or rehabilitation staff respect the patient's needs or wishes	Health Information	100%	74%
To have enough resources for the patient (e.g., rehabilitation programs, physical therapy, counseling, job counseling)	Professional Support	100%	56%
To have complete information on the medical care of traumatic injuries (e.g., medications, injections, surgeries)	Health Information	100%	55%
To be told about all changes in the patient's medical status	Health Information	98%	63%
To have explanations from professionals given in terms I can understand	Health Information	98%	83%
To have different professionals agree on the best way to help the patient	NA[a]	98%	74%
To be told why the patient acts differently, is difficult, or acts strangely	NA[a]	91%	67%
To give my opinions daily to others involved in the patient's care, rehabilitation, or education	Involvement with Care	81%	68%
To discuss openly my feelings about the patient with other friends or family	Support Network	77%	70%

Note. FNQ = Family Needs Questionnaire; PRC = polytrauma rehabilitation center; NA = not applicable.

[a] This item is one of three that did not factor into one of the six factors analytically derived FNQ scales (Serio, Kreutzer, & Witol, 1997).

Table 2 Needs Most Frequently Rated as Not Met by the PRC Sample

FNQ item	Scale	% PRC endorsement
Help preparing for the worst	Emotional Support	27%
To have help keeping the house (e.g., shopping, cleaning, cooking)	Instrumental Support	25%
To get a break from my problems and responsibilities	Instrumental Support	23%
To discuss my feelings about the patient with someone who has gone through the same experience	Emotional Support	21%
To spend time with friends	Instrumental Support	20%
To have my significant other understand how difficult this is for me	Emotional Support	19%
Help getting over my doubts and fears about the future	Emotional Support	18%
To get enough rest or sleep	Instrumental Support	18%
To be shown what to do when the patient is upset or acting strangely	Professional Support	16%
To have the patient's friends understand his/her problems	Support Network	15%

Note. FNQ = Family Needs Questionnaire; PRC = polytrauma rehabilitation center.

Study Limitations

The limitations of the present study are worthy of consideration. The design was cross-sectional, and it relied exclusively on quantitative measures. Participants were drawn from a single inpatient polytrauma setting, one of five operating in the United States. Furthermore, the sample size was modest. Given these limitations, results should be considered preliminary; additional research is needed. Future research should use repeated measures and longitudinal designs, allowing for better appreciation of the changes in needs over time. To address concerns about sample size, future research should study family needs in a number of polytrauma inpatient and outpatient settings. Concurrent, prospective studies using a combination of qualitative and quantitative measures are encouraged to thoroughly evaluate similarities and differences. Qualitative methodology should be used to further explore unique themes that may emerge with family members in military or veteran settings.

Conclusion

To date, there is little or no systematically derived empirical information about the unique needs of families in polytrauma settings and what interventions may be effective in supporting their coping. Clinical researchers in polytrauma settings are encouraged to consider evaluating and adapting interventions shown to be effective in civilian rehabilitation settings.

References

Collins, R. C., & Kennedy, M. C. (2008). Serving families who have served: Providing family therapy and support in interdisciplinary polytrauma rehabilitation. *Journal of Clinical Psychology, 64*, 993–1003. doi:10.1002/jclp.20515

Department of Veterans Affairs Veterans Health Administration. (2005). Polytrauma rehabilitation procedures. *VHA Handbook*. Retrieved from www1.va.gov/vhapublications/ViewPublication.asp?pub_ID=1317

Draper, K., Ponsford, J., & Schönberger, M. (2007). Psychosocial and emotional outcomes 10 years following traumatic brain injury. *The Journal of Head Trauma Rehabilitation, 22*, 278–287. doi:10.1097/01.HTR.0000290972.63753.a7

Friedemann-Sánchez, G., Sayer, N. A., & Pickett, T. (2008). Provider perspectives on rehabilitation of patients with polytrauma. *Archives of Physical Medicine and Rehabilitation, 89*, 171–178. doi:10.1016/j.apmr.2007.10.017

Hauber, R. P., & Jones, M. L. (2002). Telerehabilitation support for families at home caring for individuals in prolonged states of reduced consciousness. *Journal of Head Trauma Rehabilitation, 17*, 535–541. doi:10.1097/00001199-200212000-00005

Kim, J. W., & Moon, S. S. (2007). Needs of family caregivers caring for stroke patients: Based on the rehabilitation treatment phase and the treatment setting. *Social Work in Health Care, 45*, 81–97. doi:10.1300/J010v45n01_06

Kolakowsky-Hayner, S. A., Miner, K. D., & Kreutzer, J. S. (2001). Long-term life quality and family needs after traumatic brain injury. *The Journal of Head Trauma Rehabilitation, 16*, 374–385. doi:10.1097/00001199-200108000-00007

Kreutzer, J. S. (1988). *Family Needs Questionnaire*. Medical College of Virginia: Richmond, VA.

Kreutzer, J. S., Gervasio, A. H., & Camplair, P. S. (1994). Primary caregivers' psychological status and family functioning after traumatic brain injury. *Brain Injury, 8*, 197–210. doi:10.3109/02699059409150973

Kreutzer, J. S., Serio, C., & Berquist, S. (1994). Family needs following brain injury: A quantitative analysis. *The Journal of Head Trauma Rehabilitation, 9*(3), 104–115. doi:10.1097/00001199-199409000-00009

Kreutzer, J. S., Stejskal, T. M., Ketchum, J. M., Marwitz, J. H., Taylor, L. A., & Menzel, J. C. (2009). A preliminary investigation of the brain injury family intervention: Impact on family members. *Brain Injury, 23*, 535–547. doi:10.1080/02699050902926291

Livingston, L. A., Kennedy, R. E., Marwitz, J. H., Arango-Lasprilla, J. C., Rapport, L. J., Bushnik, T., & Gary, K. W. (2010). Predictors of family caregivers' life satisfaction after traumatic

brain injury at one and two years post-injury: A longitudinal multi-center investigation. *NeuroRehabilitation, 27*, 73–81. doi:10.3233/NRE-2010-0582

Marsh, N. V., Kersel, D. A., Havill, J. A., & Sleigh, J. W. (2002). Caregiver burden during the year following severe traumatic brain injury. *Journal of Clinical and Experimental Neuropsychology, 24*, 434–447. doi:10.1076/jcen.24.4.434.1030

Moules, S., & Chandler, B. J. (1999). A study of the health and social needs of carers of traumatically brain injured individuals served by one community rehabilitation team. *Brain Injury, 13*, 983–993. doi:10.1080/026990599120990

Murray, H. M., Maslany, G. W., & Jeffery, B. (2006). Assessment of family needs following acquired brain injury in Saskatchewan. *Brain Injury, 20*, 575–585. doi:10.1080/02699050600664590

Nabors, N., Seacat, J., & Rosenthal, M. (2002). Predictors of caregiver burden following traumatic brain injury. *Brain Injury, 16*, 1039–1050. doi:10.1080/02699050210155285

Ponsford, J., & Schönberger, M. (2010). Family functioning and emotional state two and five years after traumatic brain injury. *Journal of the International Neuropsychological Society, 16*, 306–317. doi:10.1017/S1355617709991342

Riggio, S. (2010). Traumatic brain injury and its neurobehavioral sequelae. *Psychiatric Clinics of North America, 33*, 807–819. doi:10.1016/j.psc.2010.08.004

Ruttan, L., Martin, K., Liu, A., Colella, B., & Green, R. E. (2008). Long-term cognitive outcome in moderate to severe traumatic brain injury: A meta-analysis examining timed and untimed tests at 1 and 4.5 or more years after injury. *Archives of Physical Medicine and Rehabilitation, 89*(12 Supp.), S69–S76. doi:10.1016/j.apmr.2008.07.007

Schneiderman, A. I., Braver, E. R., & Kang, H. K. (2008). Understanding sequelae of injury mechanisms and mild traumatic brain injury incurred during the conflicts in Iraq and Afghanistan: Persistent postconcussive symptoms and posttraumatic stress disorder. *American Journal of Epidemiology, 167*, 1446–1452. doi:10.1093/aje/kwn068

Schönberger, M., Ponsford, J., Olver, J., & Ponsford, M. (2010). A longitudinal study of family functioning after TBI and relatives' emotional status. *Neuropsychological Rehabilitation, 20*, 813–829. doi:10.1080/09602011003620077

Serio, C., Kreutzer, J. S., & Gervasio, A. (1995). Predicting family needs after traumatic brain injury: Implications for intervention. *The Journal of Head Trauma Rehabilitation, 10*(2), 32–45. doi:10.1097/00001199-199504000-00005

Serio, C. D., Kreutzer, J. S., & Witol, A. D. (1997). Family needs after traumatic brain injury: A factor analytic study of the Family Needs Questionnaire. *Brain Injury, 11*, 1–9. doi:10.1080/026990597123764

Sigford, B. J. (2008). "To care for him who shall have borne the battle and for his widow and his orphan" (Abraham Lincoln): The Department of Veterans Affairs polytrauma system of care. *Archives of Physical Medicine and Rehabilitation, 89*, 160–162. doi:10.1016/j.apmr.2007.09.015

Terrio, H., Brenner, L. A., Ivins, B. J., Cho, J. M., Helmick, K., Schwab, K., . . . Warden, D. (2009). Traumatic brain injury screening: Preliminary findings in a US Army Brigade Combat Team. *The Journal of Head Trauma Rehabilitation, 24*, 14–23. doi:10.1097/HTR.0b013e31819581d8

Winstanley, J., Simpson, G., Tate, R., & Myles, B. (2006). Early indicators and contributors to psychological distress in relatives during rehabilitation following severe traumatic brain injury: Findings from the brain injury outcomes study. *The Journal of Head Trauma Rehabilitation, 21,* 453–466. doi:10.1097/00001199-200611000-00001

Witol, A., Sander, A. M., & Kreutzer, J. S. (1996). A longitudinal analysis of family needs following traumatic brain injury. *NeuroRehabilitation, 7,* 175–187. doi:10.1016/1053-8135(96)00190-4

Critical Thinking

1. What is meant by the term "polytrauma?" Have you ever known someone who has faced these types of injuries? What were some of the challenges faced by them and their families?

2. How do the experiences of military families and civilian families with severely injured family members differ?

3. What strategies are most effective in assisting military families coping with trauma?

4. Using information gained from this article, describe an intervention or support program that could be developed to facilitate the positive development of military families where a family member has sustained a severe injury.

Create Central

www.mhhe.com/createcentral

Internet References

Substance Abuse and Mental Health Services Administration
www.samhsa.gov

National Military Family Association
www.militaryfamily.org
Military OneSource
www.militaryonesource.mil

Kathryn P. Wilder Schaaf, Department of Physical Medicine and Rehabilitation, Virginia Commonwealth University; Jeffrey S. Kreutzer, Department of Physical Medicine and Rehabilitation, Department of Neurosurgery, and Department of Psychiatry, Virginia Commonwealth University; Steven J. Danish, Department of Psychology, Virginia Commonwealth University; Treven C. Pickett, Department of Physical Medicine and Rehabilitation and Department of Psychiatry, Virginia Commonwealth University, and McGuire VA Medical Center, Richmond, Virginia; Bruce D. Rybarczyk, Department of Psychology, Virginia Commonwealth University; and Michelle G. Nichols, McGuire VA Medical Center and Defense and Veterans Brain Injury Center, Washington, DC.

No commercial party having direct financial interest in the results of the research supporting this article has or will confer a benefit upon the authors or upon any organization with which the authors are associated. Supported in part by the Department of Veterans Affairs Office of Academic Affiliations, National Institute on Disability and Rehabilitation Research, Office of Special Education and Rehabilitative Services, U.S. Department of Education (Grant Nos. H133A070036, H133P090013), the Defense and Veterans Brain Injury Center, and the Henry M. Jackson Foundation for the Advancement of Military Medicine. We thank Angela Satariano, Tiffany Amos, and Tiffany Lewis who are research assistants with the Defense and Veterans Brain Injury Center.

Correspondence concerning this article should be addressed to Kathryn Wilder Schaaf, PhD, Department of Physical Medicine and Rehabilitation, VA Commonwealth University, Box 980542, Richmond, VA 23298-0542. E-mail: wilderkp@vcu.edu

Article

Prepared by: Patricia Hrusa Williams,
University of Maine at Farmington

Why Do Marriages Fail?

JOSEPH N. DUCANTO

Learning Outcomes

After reading this article, you will be able to:

• Identify some common reasons why couples divorce.

• Consider strategies to decrease the frequency of divorce in the United States.

After 56 years as a divorce lawyer, people may assume that I know a lot about marriage and, therefore, can easily answer the inevitable question "why do marriages fail?" Indeed, a divorce lawyer can relate much about his/her personal observation respecting this issue, anticipating that many will take exception to at least one or more of the following views.

Increased Life Span

I blame medical science for a significantly large percentage of failed marriages! During the past 100 years, the average life span of humans in the Western world has increased nearly 60 percent from the start of the 20th century (average 49 years) to 2010 (average 78 years). This increase alone has had an overpowering impact upon marriage, which is a static institution remaining unchanged from the dawn of time. It remains to be seen what civil union marriage will do to both the state of marriage (now at an all-time low) and the absolute numbers of divorce (without reference to customary marriages—as opposed to civil unions), which have fallen in recent years because of increasing disinterest by the young to legally engage in such relationships.

In past centuries, the young married very young, parallel-ing the onset of puberty, produced numerous children (many of whom died during their infancy), and departed life in their 30's and 40's. Perhaps the greatest love story of all time, Romeo and Juliet, exemplifies this phenomenon with Juliet 14, and Romeo 16, yearning for the nuptial couch. They clearly were not unique in their era, and in many places throughout the world, such early teenage marriages continue as acceptable and are endorsed by cultural principals and religious adherence.

Quite clearly, a marriage duly made "until death do us part," that could be reasonably expected to endure 20 to 25 years at most, is a far different commitment made today, where joint lifespan can see marriages endure for 50, 60, and even 70 years! Clearly, then, medical science, which has so effectively increased the lifespan of people, must bear some responsibility for the proven fact that marriages of long duration enlarge inordinately the number of prospective clients who ultimately find their way to a divorce lawyer's office. Divorce among the "Metamucil Generation" is no longer an unusual event.

Individual Changes Over the Years

Accompanying the incredibly long duration of marriages today is the unhappy fact that married people do not always mature and grow at the same rate and quality over the longer period of years people are married today. She is involved in her career and he is consumed by his occupation. Inevitably—particularly as the kids age and leave home—the parties metamorphose in their interest, attitudes, and aspiration in ways that do not necessarily correlate with the essential unity of the original underlying basis of the marriage. For example, her involvement with professional requirements could create conflicts with the lifestyle adopted over time by him and his colleagues as sports become a passion. Conflict here is inevitable and divorce often a certainty, as neither can abandon the pillars of support each has erected in terms of his or her own individual desires and concerns.

Exacerbation of Pre-Existing Strains

Kids are beautiful and, for many, life would not be worth living without them. Little is said, however, of the disruptive problems that the appearance of children may inflict upon a marriage already experiencing some irritation and doubts. Over my years of practice, I have observed that pre-existing strains in a marriage are strongly exacerbated by additional adverse events which, surprisingly, can often be the appearance of a newborn or, worse, the death of a child, the loss of a job or a business, or the purchase of a new home. Any existing cracks in an otherwise placid marriage will often produce significant fractures when such events occur, thus leading to divorce. These customary strains upon a marriage are intensified when one or both of the parents begin to indulge in escape from drudgery by excessive use of alcohol or drugs, or seek out others to escape from marital unhappiness.

Boredom

Boredom in a relationship is often insidious and corrosive of the marriage bonds. Repetitive behavior, even if initially enjoyed, can soon pale and become irritating. Think, I tell my friends, of eating oatmeal every morning for 40 years and tell me what you believe your reaction would be? Indeed, many marriages are destroyed by boredom and the need or necessity by one of the parties to exit the doldrums of their life for some excitement—any excitement—good or bad—known or unknown.

Life Changes

Virtually nothing has been written relating to the role that menopause plays in leading ultimately to a divorce. Much is known and published that describes the onset and symptoms of menopause in women, which appears around the age of 50 in normal development. With menopause there are numerous psychological and emotional symptoms that present themselves, which can include rapid mood shifts, irritability, and loss of libido.

Many men find these newly-emerging symptoms difficult, and their presence in a wife of many years may lead to emotional and physical withdrawal by both parties. From the female's point of view, many former "quirks" possessed by her husband or supposed personal strengths and long-held opinions may become intolerable during this period, leading to increasing tension and endless arguments between the parties. The husband, if experiencing his wife's coldness or withdrawal altogether from sex, could find easy excuses for infidelity with younger women who "understand and appreciate me" when his wife has failed to do so.

Any meaningful change in the marital relationship coincidentally occurring with the arrival of menopause, such as becoming "empty nesters," a change of occupation or retirement, unemployment, financial instability, plus the unavoidable onset of old age may tip the marital scales toward separation and, inevitably, a mid-life divorce.

Another Man or Woman

The often-supposed "reason" for divorce attributed to the appearance or presence of the other man or woman in the life of one of the partners is simply a symptom of a pre-existing desire to escape the malaise of a moribund relationship. One may seek solace in the other man/woman relationship with the prime purpose of re-injecting life or purpose in an existence that may seem to have become barren. It is not uncommon in my experience that one of the parties to a meretricious relationship will operate with a certainty of detection by the other party, thus motivating the otherwise "innocent" spouse to move for the courthouse door!

Personality Changes

As life goes on, we all undergo personality changes. None of us by age 50 can truthfully believe we are the same person we were at 25. We learn, educate, grow, and change at uneven rates that are heavily dependent upon many variables—including intelligence, receptivity, and intensity of experiences. Uneven growth between spouses is common, and unless great pain is taken to assure continuing effective communication, the marriage can fail. A mother with a high-school education who is housebound for 20 years talking to three-foot-high people over those years may not be expected to maintain a close communion and relationship with an ever-working husband who has acquired several advanced degrees, travels the world over in his occupation, and consorts with the intellectual opinion makers of the world.

Limited Marriage Contract

I have in the past, partially in jest, suggested that there actually be a "marriage contract"—as opposed to a prenuptial one—in which the marriage has a finite term; say five years. At or near the end of that time, the parties are called upon to renew or rewrite their agreement or proceed to divorce. Such a shocking requirement requires a balancing of what is good in the relationship as opposed to that which is destructive. A "time out" to reconstitute the ongoing basis of the marriage is clearly preferable to an inevitable drift toward ending the relationship. Remember, a "civil union" complete written contract is not limited to homosexual relationships, but can be extended to a man/woman relationship that falls outside of the usual bounds of matrimony.

It is imperative, if the marriage is to continue, that both parties commit themselves to a course of re-bonding and enhancement of communication with each other. With kids, it is often difficult but essential that there be frequent "time outs" where a couple can recommit to one another, compare notes so to speak, and plan for their future as a couple in addition to that as a family. A failure to work on the changing nature of a relationship over time is to be confronted by the inescapable fact that the marriage may be dead and, unfortunately, in need of a decent burial!

Critical Thinking

1. With our increased life spans, is it realistic to think that marriages will last "until death do us part?"
2. Of the factors listed as contributing to divorce, which do you see as more important? Why?

3. Given the list of factors that the author states contribute to divorce, what can be done to help couples sustain marriages?

4. What can be done as couples enter marriage to better prepare them for the challenges ahead?

Create Central

www.mhhe.com/createcentral

Internet References

HelpGuide: Children and Divorce
www.helpguide.org/mental/children_divorce.htm

HelpGuide: Divorce and Remarriage
www.helpguide.org/topics/breakup_divorce.htm

Ducanto, Joseph N. From *American Journal of Family Law,* vol. 26, no. 4, Winter 2013, pp. 237–239. Copyright © 2013 by Wolters Kluwer Law & Business. Reprinted by permission.

Prepared by: Patricia Hrusa Williams,
University of Maine at Farmington

Article

Helping Children Endure Divorce

Marlene Eskind Moses

When in the midst of a divorce, it is understandable for a party to become entrenched in what is felt to be a personal battle and preoccupied with details such as where to live, how to maximize the financial settlement, and how to pay the legal fees. Sometimes, this preoccupation leads to losing sight of what is going on with one's children, who are unquestionably also directly affected by that parent's decision to divorce.

Learning Outcomes

After reading this article, you will be able to:

- Describe the impact of divorce on children.
- Summarize how the parent–child relationship survives divorce.
- Explain how divorce can happen without devastating the children involved.

If the divorce practitioner receives little feedback from a client about the children, it is all too easy to focus exclusively on meeting the client's personal goals with minimal awareness of how doing so will truly affect the client's children. However, it is up to us to actively solicit feedback from our clients about their children and educate our clients about how to help their children navigate the transition. We should remain mindful that our clients' children are "shadow clients,"[1] and we should strive to fine-tune our advice and strategies accordingly.

The Effects of Divorce on Children

There has been an abundance of research concluding that growing up in a single-parent household is less than ideal and can be detrimental to a child's well-being. Even in low-conflict divorces, children can suffer in a myriad of ways. The obvious immediate repercussion is the disruption of life as they have known it. Children not living with both biological parents are more likely to experience psychological struggles and academic problems.[2] Long-term effects of divorce on children can include increased susceptibility to substance abuse. Teenagers with divorced parents are 50 percent more likely to drink alcohol than those with married parents.[3] Children of divorce also are more likely to experience divorces of their own down the road.[4]

Research shows that the effects of divorce on a child depend to some extent on the age of the child at the time of divorce, the child's gender and personality, and the degree of conflict between the parents. Infants may react to changes in parents' energy level and mood by losing their appetite or spitting up more. Preschool-aged children often blame themselves for their parent's divorce, viewing it as the consequence of their own misbehavior. They may regress and exhibit behavior such as bedwetting and may become uncooperative or aggressive. School-aged children are old enough to understand that they are hurting because of their parents' separation. They may feel rejected by the parent who left. It is not uncommon for children in this age group to exhibit psychosomatic symptoms such as headaches or stomachaches. Adolescents may become excessively moody, withdrawn, depressed or anxious. They may favor one parent, blaming the other for the divorce.[5]

Some research even suggests gender differences. Certain studies have found that children raised primarily by a parent of the same sex tend to have greater success adjusting to the divorce than those who are raised primarily by a parent of the opposite sex.[6] Although there is little correlation between the sheer amount of time that divorced fathers spend with their children and those children's overall adjustment, children of divorce whose fathers spend quality time actively engaged in their lives and activities tend to perform better in school and exhibit fewer behavioral problems.[7] Father involvement has been linked to children feeling less at the mercy of the world and more willing to behave responsibly.[8]

The quality of a child's relationship with the primary parent is a particularly strong indicator of the child's successful adjustment following a divorce. It also goes without saying that day-to-day involvement of both parents lets a child know that he or she is loved. This does not mean, however, that an equal or near-equal division of parenting time is necessarily the best option. For instance, preschool-aged children may feel they are being punished when they are moved from one household to another. Older children, too, may dislike this type of arrangement if it intrudes on their daily lives. Some parents with equal or near-equal division of time, or who engage in multiple transfers of the children back and forth in a short period of time, fight more often because they are in constant contact, which in turn causes the children to suffer.[9] A child's well-being is particularly affected by the amount and intensity of conflict between the parents. Marital conflict is associated with increased anxiety and depression, and poorer overall social and academic adjustment in children.[10]

So, how can we use this research to educate our clients with the goal of helping ensure that their children adjust with minimal side-effects to the divorce?

Guidelines for Helping Children

1. *Telling children about the divorce:*

   Ideally, children should be told about the divorce as soon as a definite decision has been made to get divorced. Children need to be told before any changes occur, and they should be informed of the changes to expect, such as moving to a new house or school, or beginning a parenting schedule. If possible, both parents should tell the children together, with the parents agreeing on the details of the explanation ahead of time. It is important to present a united front as much as possible.[11]

   Children are entitled to know why their parents are divorcing, and the reasons given should be simple and honest. Telling children that it is too complicated to explain or that they would never understand the reasons could leave them wondering whether they might be able to change their parents' plans. Blanket reassurances do not always work, and children will likely need an opportunity to talk about why they feel at fault for the divorce, oftentimes on more than one occasion. Parents need to acknowledge the reasons for the child's concerns, such as "Yes, you are right that your father and I do argue about how much time we each feel you should spend on the computer or with friends or watching television, and I can see why this makes you worried that the divorce is your fault." Then, words of reassurance need to follow immediately, such as: ". . . but you didn't cause the breakup . . ." If a child's concerns are not cavalierly dismissed but are instead truly heard and discussed, without the parents becoming defensive or dismissive, the child is more likely to feel assured that indeed he or she was not the cause of the parents' divorce. The child who feels at fault could also feel responsible for fixing the problem. Therefore, children need a clear statement from each parent that they cannot prevent or reverse the divorce.[12] They also need to be reassured that while parents and their children do not always get along, they do not stop loving each other and do not get divorced from each other.[13]

   Finally, it may be tempting to place blame on the other parent for the divorce, but such defensiveness sends a message that the children need to take sides, which only serves to increase their anxiety, guilt and stress.[14]

2. *Encouraging a relationship with the other parent:*

   Because of the inherently adversarial nature of divorce, it may seem counter-intuitive to a litigant not to seek to limit the other parent's time with the children. The "winner" gets the kids, and the "loser" does not. In fact, a better legal strategy may be to encourage and facilitate time and a continuing relationship with the other parent. Tennessee's custody statute requires the court to consider, in making a custody determination, "each parent's past and potential . . . willingness and ability . . . to facilitate and encourage a close and continuing parent–child relationship between the child and both of the child's parents, consistent with the best interest of the child. In determining the willingness of each of the parents . . . to facilitate and encourage a close and continuing parent–child relationship between the child and both of the child's parents, the court shall consider the likelihood of each parent . . . to honor and facilitate court ordered parenting arrangements and rights, and the court shall further consider any history of either parent or any caregiver denying parenting time to either parent in violation of a court order."[15]

   In addition to what the law tells us, social research tells us that children are better off with the influence and presence of both parents in their lives, absent extraordinary circumstances. It is important for both parents to be mindful of this and to strive to create a parenting plan that provides this for their children.

   Hand-in-hand with encouraging and facilitating a meaningful relationship with the other parent is showing respect for the other parent. It is harmful to a child for either parent to make derogatory remarks about the other parent. The child can be made to feel as if he or she is expected to take the side of the parent who is disparaging the other parent. This behavior by a parent violates the statutory standard parenting rights set forth in all Tennessee parenting plans. Such rights include "the right to be free of unwarranted derogatory remarks made about the parent or his or her family by the other parent to the child or in the presence of the child."[16] Acting contrary to this mandate can lead to a finding of contempt and sometimes even a change of custody in extreme circumstances.

3. *The parenting schedule.*

   It is usually best for each parent's time with the children to be scheduled at regular and predictable times.[17] Once the schedule is created, it is important that it be honored. Children may see missed visits, especially without notification, as rejection.[18] Children crave consistency, and routines provide a sense of security and may help ease fears of abandonment. If possible, the parents should work together to ensure that the same routines and rules are followed at each home. It is important to resist the temptation to spoil the children during or following a divorce by not enforcing limits or allowing children to break rules.[19]

   Handovers between the two households can be particularly stressful for children, let alone parents. Children often feel guilty and are reluctant to admit to one parent that they are thinking about or missing the other parent. As a result, children are often anticipating the emotional turmoil of the handover back to the other parent instead of enjoying the time remaining before the transfer.[20] The divorce practitioner can counsel clients to minimize the number of handovers each week. Furthermore, it may help for the handovers to occur at a neutral location such as the child's school, as this is likely to cause less stress than handovers occurring on either parent's home turf. The parents will need to commit to making handovers free of arguments and hostility.

Although the typical parenting plan mentions only in passing that each parent has the statutory "right to unimpeded telephone conversations with the child at least twice a week at reasonable times and for reasonable durations,"[21] it may be worthwhile to be proactive and help clients work through the logistics. For instance, it can be wise to avoid phone calls at emotionally charged and more intrusive times such as meal time or bedtime.[22] It is not uncommon for a parent to feel that the ex-spouse is interfering with the phone calls in a multitude of ways, so a word to the wise: address these potential issues before they arise.

Finally, in crafting the parenting schedule, thinking outside the box can make for much more meaningful periods of parenting time. When children have been asked what they would change about their scheduled times with each parent, some have responded that they do not necessarily care to be shuffled back and forth with their siblings as a group. Children enjoy and benefit from one-on-one time with each parent. However, frequently, for the purposes of organizing the schedule, children are indeed "lumped together as a homogenous group, irrespective of their ages and needs."[23] Tennessee's standard parenting plan form treats the children as a group, so we lawyers need to be more proactive and consider suggesting to our clients that separate parenting times for each child be carved out if feasible for the family.

Conclusion

Given the proof that parents have the power to affect their children's reactions to divorce, it is necessary that parents put their children's welfare ahead of their own conflict with their spouse or former spouse. We as divorce practitioners also have the power to influence our clients' behavior by educating them and helping them craft parenting plans that minimize as much as possible the negative effects of divorce on our clients' children.

Notes

1. Sammons, William A.H., and Lewis, Jennifer M. (1999), *Don't Divorce Your Children*.
2. Pendergrast, Val (1997), "Sheathing Solomon's Sword," http://www.weeklywire.com/ww/08-04-97/knox_feat.html.
3. *Family Matters: Substance Abuse and the American Family,* The National Center on Addiction and Substance Abuse at Columbia University (March 2005), http://www.casacolumbia.org/articlefiles/380-Family percent20Matters.pdf.
4. Nuri, Banister, "Children of Divorced Parents Are More Likely to Themselves Divorce," *Journal of Young Investigators,* vol. 23, issue 3, March 2012, http://www.jyi.org/news/nb.php?id=352.
5. Temke, Mary (1998), "The Effects of Divorce on Children," University of New Hampshire, Cooperative Extension, http://extension.unh.edu/Family/Documents/divorce.pdf.
6. *Id.*
7. Nowinski, Joseph (2011), "The New Grief: Helping Children Survive Divorce: Three Critical Factors," http://www.psychologytoday.com/blog/the-new-grief/201110/helping-children-survive-divorce-three-critical-factors.
8. Biller H., Solomon R.S. (1986), *Child Maltreatment and Paternal Deprivation: A Manifesto for Research, Treatment, and Prevention.*
9. Temke, *supra.*
10. Nowinski, *supra.*
11. Ferrer, Millie and McCrea, Sara (2002), *Talking to Children about Divorce,* University of Florida, IFAS Extension.
12. Sammons, *supra.*
13. Block, Jocelyn; Kemp, Gina; Smith, Melinda; Segal, Jeanne (2012), "Children and Divorce: Helping Kids Cope with Separation and Divorce," http://www.helpguide.org/mental/children_divorce.htm.
14. Sammons, *supra.*
15. *Tenn. Code Ann.* § 36-6-106(a)(10).
16. *Tenn. Code Ann.* § 36-6-101(a)(3)(A).
17. Sammons, *supra.*
18. Gold-Bikin, Lynne Z. and Kolodny, Stephen (2003), *The Divorce Trial Manual: From Initial Interview to Closing Argument.*
19. Block, *supra.*
20. Sammons, *supra.*
21. *Tenn. Code Ann.* § 36-6-101(a)(3)(A).
22. Sammons, *supra.*
23. *Id.*

Critical Thinking

1. Do you think divorce is always something children merely endure? What do you think they are aware of during the process?

2. Can divorce ever be beneficial or helpful to children? Are the results always negative?

3. The author makes several recommendations regarding how parents can help their children through a divorce. Do you agree with them? Why or why not?

4. Using information gained from this article, describe an intervention or support program that could be developed to facilitate the positive development of children from families where parents are divorcing.

Create Central

www.mhhe.com/createcentral

Internet References

HelpGuide: Children and Divorce
www.helpguide.org/mental/children_divorce.htm

HelpGuide: Divorce and Remarriage
www.helpguide.org/topics/breakup_divorce.htm

MARLENE ESKIND MOSES is the principal and manager of MTR Family Law PLLC, a family and divorce law firm in Nashville. She is currently serving as a vice president of the International Academy of Matrimonial Lawyers. She has held prior presidencies with the American Academy of Matrimonial Lawyers, Tennessee Board of Law Examiners, Lawyer's Association for Women, and the Tennessee Supreme Court Historical Society. She has also served as vice president for the United States Chapter of the International Academy of Matrimonial Lawyers and first vice president of the Nashville Bar Association. Selected as a Diplomate in the American College of Family Trial Lawyers, she is the only one in the College from Tennessee. The Tennessee Commission on Continuing Legal & Specialization has designated Moses as a Family Law Specialist; she is board certified as a Family Law Trial Specialist in addition to holding certifications in mediation, arbitration, and collaborative law.

Prepared by: Patricia Hrusa Williams,
University of Maine at Farmington

Article

Strengthening Fragile Families

Sara McLanahan et al.

Learning Outcomes

After reading this article, you will be able to:

- Define the term "fragile family."

- Identify challenges faced by unmarried parents.

- Describe policies and support for unmarried parents.

The rise of fragile families—families that begin when a child is born outside of marriage—is one of the nation's most vexing social problems. In the first place, these families suffer high poverty rates and poor child outcomes. Even more problematic, the very groups of Americans who traditionally experience poverty, impaired child development, and poor school achievement have the highest rates of non-marital parenthood—thus intensifying the disadvantages faced by these families and extending them into the next generation.

Nonmarital births have increased precipitously in the past forty years, especially among minorities and the poor, the groups of greatest concern. Today more than 70 percent of black children, 50 percent of Hispanic children, nearly 30 percent of white children, and 40 percent of all children are born outside marriage, assuring the persistence of poverty, wasting human potential, and raising government spending. Reducing nonmarital births and mitigating their consequences should be a top priority of the nation's social policy.

Social science aims to illuminate the choices available to policy makers both by promoting better understanding of social problems and by providing reliable information about the effects of potential solutions. And yet, until a decade ago, social scientists had accumulated little data about nonmarital childbearing and its consequences for parents, children, and communities. Recognizing the need for such data, in the late 1990s researchers at Princeton and Columbia universities organized the first large-scale study of nonmarital childbearing and its consequences. The researchers randomly sampled parents of approximately 5,000 newborns (including 3,600 nonmarital births) in twenty of the nation's largest cities. For the past decade, the research team has been following the parents and children to learn more about their capabilities and experiences. The findings of this research, known as the Fragile Families Study, have been reported in numerous academic articles, newsletters, and books. Now the most important findings have been pulled together in the new volume of the journal *The Future of Children*. Here we provide a brief overview of those findings and draw from them what we believe to be the most important policy recommendations.

The Fragile Families Study Findings

Four findings in particular stand out. The first, a big surprise when it was first published, is that a large majority of unwed parents have close and loving relationships at the time of their child's birth. A little more than half the unmarried couples were living together when their child was born, and an additional 32 percent were in dating relationships. One-night stands these were not. The couples talked readily about marriage, with 87 percent of the fathers and 72 percent of the mothers giving their relationship at least a 50/50 chance of leading to marriage.

The second, more sobering, finding is that unwed parents have a host of demographic and human capital characteristics that complicate getting good jobs, forming stable families, and performing successfully as parents. Unwed parents in the sample were much younger than the married parents—the mothers almost six years younger, and the fathers, four. Only about 4 percent of the married mothers, but 26 percent of the unwed mothers, were teenagers. And even though the unwed parents were younger than their married counterparts, about three times as many had a previous birth with another partner, leaving many of the children in these households to deal with a parent figure (the mother's new boyfriend or husband) inside their home and a biological parent outside the home, an arrangement that can be stressful for all involved.

The human capital and health differences between the two groups are equally striking. Unwed mothers were more than twice as likely to lack even a high school degree, while married mothers were nearly fifteen times more likely to have graduated from college. In part as a result of their educational advantages, married mothers on average earned more than twice as much as unwed mothers, about $25,600 compared with $11,100. The lower earnings of unwed mothers contributed to a poverty rate that was more than three times as high (43 percent) as that of married mothers (14 percent). The differences between unwed and married fathers were similar. Unwed parents also differed in health status and behaviors detrimental to health.

They were more likely to report being in poor or fair health, more likely to have a health-related limitation, and much more likely to use illegal drugs. Nearly 8 percent of unwed mothers reported heavy drinking, about four times the rate among married mothers.

A final difference in human capital between the two groups is of special concern. More than 36 percent of the unmarried fathers had a prison record, five times the share of married fathers who ever spent time in prison. Research shows that incarceration disrupts fathers' relationships with their families, requires a difficult (and thus often unsuccessful) transition back to life in the community, and greatly reduces the chance of finding employment. Even when these fathers do find employment, they work less and have lower wages. As if these disadvantages were not enough, research consistently shows that recidivism rates are high, deepening even further the disadvantages associated with having spent time in prison.

The third set of findings is equally sobering. Relatively few of the unwed couples were able to form stable relationships. At five years after the birth of their child, only about 35 percent were still together. Breakups were less likely among couples in which fathers had higher earnings, mothers had more education, attitudes about marriage were positive, and relationship quality was good.

Relationship dissolution is only the first step toward household instability. Once the couple splits, both of the unwed parents usually go on to form new relationships and often to have additional children by other partners. Over the five years of the study, over a quarter of unwed mothers lived with a new partner, and a fifth had a child with a new partner. Changes in dating partnerships were even more common. Nearly 60 percent of mothers who were single at birth experienced three or more relationship transitions over the five years.

The parental split reduces substantially the contact between the children and their fathers. By year five, only 51 percent of the fathers involved in splits saw their child even once a month. In effect, when couples break up, within five years half the children are destined to have little contact with their father. It would seem very difficult for a father who sees his child once a month or less to provide effective parenting.

Finally, and most important, these differences in demography, human capital, health, and household stability are associated with negative developmental outcomes for children born to unwed parents. Relationship instability in particular is linked with both poor test performance and behavioral problems in children, especially boys. With unstable and increasingly complex home environments, and with children's development already moving off track by age five, it is difficult to be optimistic that most of the children of unwed parents will grow into flourishing adults.

Policies to Address the Fragile Families Findings

The Fragile Families Study has clearly fulfilled its goal of providing abundant information about couples whose children are born outside marriage and about those children. With 40 percent of the nation's children—including a disproportionate number of poor and minority youngsters—now being born to unwed parents, the Fragile Families Study should raise grave concerns among policy makers about the problems faced by these families and their children. Although the Fragile Families Study was not designed to test the effectiveness of programs to help these families, we think, based on the Fragile Families Study and other studies, that four policy initiatives are justified.

Because few social interventions produce major or immediate improvements in the problems they address, there can be little doubt that nonmarital births and their attendant problems will still be with us for several generations. Thus the nation needs to maintain and even strengthen its safety net for single parents. We doubt that the safety net will ever provide these parents and children with enough cash and in-kind benefits to maintain a decent lifestyle, so the nation should, for both custodial and noncustodial single parents, strengthen its welfare policy emphasis on work and public work supports such as cash earnings supplements and child care. The federal government and the states should also work with noncustodial parents to create child support payment levels that they could be reasonably expected to meet. We are especially concerned about the weakness in the cash benefits part of the safety net revealed by the current recession. States must find ways to balance strong work and child support requirements with cash benefits and adjustments in child support for those who cannot find work.

The second policy initiative is preventing nonmarital pregnancies. Policy simulations in the new *Future of Children* volume show that mass media campaigns that encourage men to use condoms, teen pregnancy prevention programs that discourage sexual activity and educate teens about contraception use, and Medicaid programs that subsidize contraception all reduce pregnancy rates among unmarried couples—in the process saving more than enough public dollars to cover their costs. Happily, the federal government is now at various stages of implementing policies that are responsive to two of the three findings from the policy simulations. The Obama administration's plan to expand teen pregnancy programs, now funded by Congress and being aggressively implemented, holds great promise for further reductions in teen pregnancy rates. In addition, a provision in the new health care legislation gives states the option to cover additional women with family planning services without the need for a waiver as required under current law. This reform is consistent with the simulation's finding that additional Medicaid family planning coverage for women would be cost beneficial. With two of the three reforms recommended by the simulations already being implemented, only the third recommendation—media campaigns encouraging men to use condoms—has not already been addressed by policy makers. Given the evidence from the simulation of this policy, we think spending about $100 million a year on a social marketing campaign would be good policy and would pay for itself.

A third area needing policy reform is the U.S. prison system. The Fragile Families Study found that unwed fathers are more than five times as likely to serve prison sentences as married fathers are, with profoundly negative effects on their life after prison. So serious are the consequences for employment, integration into community life, and subsequent imprisonment that a prison sentence has come to be the modern equivalent of the scarlet "A." And yet good studies find that many long prison sentences in the United States—which has one of the highest incarceration rates in the world—are the result of victimless drug crimes and recommitment for minor parole offenses.

Rethinking sentencing policy is especially urgent because research shows how difficult it is to rehabilitate men once they have served prison terms. A key goal should be to revise mandatory sentencing laws in accord with the recommendations of the United States Sentencing Commission—in this case, to shorten the sentences of nonviolent minor drug dealers, or even to address their offenses outside of prison. The fall 2008 issue of *The Future of Children*, edited by Lawrence Steinberg, reviewed impressive evidence that community programs that worked with adolescents and their parents were not only more effective than imprisonment in preventing subsequent crimes, but also were more cost-effective. Policy makers should make every effort to modify federal and state mandatory sentencing laws to keep young offenders out of prison.

The final pressing policy issue that directly affects fragile families involves the $100 million a year federal healthy marriage grant program and the $50 million a year fatherhood grant program, both initiated during the administration of George W. Bush. The two programs are scheduled to be reauthorized in 2010, although the demands of Congressional business will likely cause the legislation to slip until 2011.

Regardless of the timing, the Obama administration has joined the issue on what is arguably the most important provision in federal law on marriage and fatherhood. The marriage grant program provides an average of $610,000 for five years to 125 community-based marriage projects. Grantees include churches, postsecondary schools, county and state governments, nonprofit and for-profit entities, and faith-based organizations. Most of the programs provide marriage education for low-income couples, but some conduct marriage education for high school students, others provide divorce reduction programs, and still others combine educational activities with public advertising campaigns on the value of healthy marriage and the availability of services. Similarly, the fatherhood grant program funds 100 projects that promote responsible fatherhood by helping community-based organizations and others run programs that provide healthy marriage, responsible parenting, and economic stability services, including employment or skills training assistance, as well as encouraging fathers to make their child support payments.

The Obama administration would replace these networks of marriage and fatherhood programs with a "Fatherhood, Marriage, and Families Innovation Fund." Rather than making grants to community-based organizations, the federal government would allocate funds to states or coalitions of states for two types of programs: "comprehensive responsible fatherhood initiatives" and "comprehensive family self-sufficiency demonstrations [that] address the employment and self-sufficiency needs of parents." The Obama proposal would end funding for the current marriage and fatherhood programs and set in motion the new state-run programs. Thus, it appears that the emphasis on couple relationships and marriage in the Bush programs would give way to an emphasis on fatherhood and self-sufficiency, although marriage programs would be allowed. The Obama initiative also would focus much more on assessing program effectiveness than the Bush marriage and fatherhood grants, which have received virtually no evaluation.

Since the Obama administration announced its innovation fund proposal last winter, a program designed by the Bush administration as part of its marriage initiative has begun publishing results that bear directly on marriage and fatherhood programs. A random-assignment evaluation of Bush's Building Strong Families (BSF) demonstrations in eight sites was mounted to test the effects of marriage education and services on young unwed parents. More than 5,000 couples participated either in a control group that received no services or in a treatment group that received three types of services: marriage education group sessions; support from a family coordinator who encouraged participation in the group sessions and provided ongoing emotional support to the couples; and referral for services such as job search, mental health, and child care. The marriage education sessions were guided by curriculums designed specifically for low-income couples to teach skills including effective communication, showing affection, managing conflict, co-parenting, and family finances. The curriculums offered between thirty and forty-two hours of group sessions.

Interim results fifteen months after couples had applied for the program can be summarized in four points. First, averaged across all eight sites, there were no differences between control and program couples on any of the major outcomes. Second, the programs nonetheless had positive effects on black couples, who improved their ability to manage conflicts and avoid destructive behaviors, reduced infidelity and family violence, and increased effective co-parenting. Third, the Oklahoma City site produced a host of positive impacts, including keeping couples together, increasing their happiness, and helping them express support and affection and use constructive rather than destructive behaviors during conflict, among others. The positive results for black couples appear to be driven primarily by the Oklahoma program. Fourth, couples in the Baltimore program experienced some negative impacts, including fewer couples maintaining their romantic involvement, lower expression of support and affection, more severe violence against women, lower quality of co-parenting, and less father involvement.

It is disappointing that the BSF program had no effects overall, and the Baltimore results are disturbing. We urge further study of the Baltimore site, but note that the couples there were the most disadvantaged of all participants, and their relationships were more tenuous, which suggests that there could be thresholds below which participation in marriage education programs is not advisable. But despite these disappointments, the finding of benefits for black couples and the positive effects found in Oklahoma imply that a program serving black couples—who have the highest rates of unwed parenting—built on the Oklahoma model could produce similar positive effects. Moreover, initial evaluations of many social programs produce findings not unlike those reported in the BSF evaluation; indeed, findings are often even more discouraging. From this perspective, the early findings showing a range of benefits for the biggest subgroup (blacks) and for the biggest individual program (Oklahoma) seem relatively encouraging. It would be premature to use the BSF results to conclude that marriage education programs for unwed couples don't work, or to abandon research and demonstration programs that attempt to promote healthy relationships between couples in fragile families.

A compromise along these lines with the Obama proposal lies readily at hand. The criticism that the Bush network of 125 marriage projects has provided virtually no evaluation evidence is entirely correct. As a result, no one has any idea whether these programs are working. We recommend that the Obama administration open a new round of marriage-promotion grants, allowing the 125 existing programs to apply if they so choose, but basing decisions about funding in the new round on the quality of the new proposals and on the reliability of the evaluation plan that would be required for every proposal. Projects should also be required to report a standard set of results that include the types of measures reported in the BSF evaluation.

The administration is proposing to spend $500 million over three years on its initiative. We would recommend spending about $50 million of the $500 million specifically on marriage education projects that attempt to replicate and expand the approach taken in the Oklahoma program. This would leave $450 million of the $500 million for the fatherhood and self-sufficiency programs favored by the administration. Projects that bring fatherhood programs and marriage programs into a close working relationship to promote child well-being would be especially welcome. The key point is to follow up on what has been learned from the BSF evaluation and evaluations of fatherhood programs in recent years.

Although the administration should consult widely to learn more about the program characteristics that may have played a role in producing the negative impacts in Baltimore and the positive impacts in Oklahoma and among black couples, we think two unique characteristics of the Oklahoma program are especially important. The two characteristics are involving married couples as well as fragile families in the marriage education groups and focusing strongly on attendance. Average attendance in the Oklahoma program was far superior to that in the other programs. About 55 percent of participants in Oklahoma received at least 60 percent of the marriage curriculum. In Indiana, where attendance was next best, 33 percent of participants reached that rather low bar. In the remaining six programs, an abysmal average of 14 percent did so. Half the participants in four of the eight programs failed to attend even a single session. A fair test of the marriage curricula requires that ways be found to boost attendance—as was in fact achieved by the Oklahoma program.

The most important conclusion from the Fragile Families Study is that these families play a central role in boosting the nation's poverty rate and that they and their children contribute disproportionately to many other serious social problems. Our policy recommendations would in all likelihood have only modest effects on poverty and other social problems, but until more disadvantaged children live in stable households with both of their biological parents sharing healthy relationships, the negative effects of unwed births will continue to trouble the nation. Meanwhile, policy makers should strengthen the safety net that provides cash and in-kind support to custodial and noncustodial parents and helps them find work; continue to aggressively implement and even expand the prevention policies that have been shown to reduce nonmarital births and save money; revise criminal sentencing laws and experiment with policies designed to help men avoid prison and integrate back into their communities when prison cannot be avoided; and refuse to give up on healthy marriage programs that have shown at least some promise in achieving the stability and positive parent relationships that could prove helpful for these couples, their children, and the nation.

Additional Reading

Natasha J. Cabrera, Jacqueline D. Shannon, and Catherine Tamis-LeMonday, "Fathers' Influence on Their Children's Cognitive and Emotional Development: From Toddlers to Pre-K," *Applied Developmental Science* 11, no. 4 (2007): 208–13.

Department of Health and Human Services, Office of Child Support Enforcement, "Questions and Answers on Fatherhood, Marriage, and Families Innovation Fund" (www.acf.hhs.gov/programs/cse/pubs/2010/Fatherhood_Marriage_and_Families_ Innovation_Fund_QA.html [accessed on July 8, 2010]).

Kathryn Edin and Maria Kefalas, *Promises I Can Keep: Why Poor Women Put Motherhood before Marriage* (University of California Press, 2007).

Paula England and Kathryn Edin, editors, *Unmarried Couples with Children* (New York: Russell Sage, 2007).

Ron Haskins and Isabel Sawhill, *Creating an Opportunity Society* (Washington: Brookings Institution Press, 2009), chapter 10.

Sara McLanahan and Gary Sandefur, *Growing Up with a Single Parent: What Hurts, What Helps* (Harvard University Press, 1997).

Ronald B. Mincy, editor, *Black Males Left Behind* (Washington: Urban Institute, 2006).

Daniel Patrick Moynihan, Timothy M. Smeeding, and Lee Rainwater, editors, *The Future of the Family* (New York: Russell Sage, 2006).

Daniel P. Moynihan, *The Negro Family: The Case for National Action* (Washington: U.S. Department of Labor, March 1965).

Laurence Steinberg, "Introducing the Issue," *The Future of Children* 18, no. 2 (Fall 2008).

William J. Wilson, *The Truly Disadvantaged: The Inner City, the Underclass, and Public Policy* (University of Chicago Press, 1987).

Robert G. Wood and others, *Strengthening Unmarried Parents' Relationships: The Early Impacts of Building Strong Families* (Princeton, N.J.: Mathematica Policy Research, Inc., May 2010).

Critical Thinking

1. What is the goal of the Fragile Families Study?
2. What is meant by the term "fragile family?" What are some negative connotations of the term?

3. What challenges are experienced by unmarried parents? Why do most unmarried parents not remain together?

4. What policies are needed to support fragile families and promote children's positive developmental outcomes?

Create Central

www.mhhe.com/createcentral

Internet References

The Future of Children

www.futureofchildren.org

SARA MCLANAHAN is editor-in-chief of the journal, The future of Children.

Unit 5

UNIT

Prepared by: Patricia Hrusa Williams,
University of Maine at Farmington

Families, Now and into the Future

What is the future of the family? Does the family even have a future? These questions and others like them are being asked. Many people fear for the future of the family. As previous units of this volume have shown, the family is an institution that continues to evolve and change. Still, certain elements of family appear to be constant. The family is and will remain a powerful influence in the lives of its members. This is because we all begin life in some type of family, and this early exposure carries a great deal of weight in forming our social selves—who we are and how we relate to others. From our biological families we are given our basic genetic makeup. In the context of daily routines and rituals we also learn how to care for ourselves and attend to our health. In families, we are given our first exposure to values, and it is through families that we most actively influence others. Our sense of commitment and obligation begins within the family, as does our sense of what we can expect of others.

Much that has been written about families has been less than hopeful, focusing on ways of avoiding or correcting "maladaptive" behaviors and patterns. The articles in this unit take a positive view of family and how it influences its members. Through its diversity, rituals, traditions, history, and new ways of establishing connections, the family still remains a vital structure in which we work, play, love, and adapt.

The articles in this unit explore the different shapes and forms families come in and the rituals and celebrations that link them. Articles also consider how technology and changes in societal norms and values are altering how we procreate, relate, marry, and parent the next generation. A goal is to explore the family now and as it might be as we venture into the future, considering its role as a healthy, supportive place for personal growth.

Article

Prepared by: Patricia Hrusa Williams,
University of Maine at Farmington

Meet My Real Modern Family

As a gay man, the author never expected to have children. Now he and his husband have four between them. How science, friendship, and love created an unconventional clan.

ANDREW SOLOMON

Learning Outcomes

After reading this article, you will be able to:

- Discuss some of the variations between families.
- Describe how the author used his own unconventional family.
- Apply the concept of unconventional families.

Children used to make me sad. With the happy children in my adult life, I felt guilty, even mean, about being sad. The origin of that sadness was opaque, but I think it came most from how the absence of children in the lives of gay people had been repeatedly held up as my tragedy. When I came out, the prevailing view was that I was shortsightedly choosing sexual fantasies over producing a family. I was encouraged by my parents and the world to marry a woman and procreate. I spent years drifting between relationships with men and with women; I was mildly bisexual in a fluid era, but if children hadn't been part of the equation, I wouldn't have bothered with the other half. Even though I was in love with some of the women I dated, I felt mildly fraudulent in those intimacies. While I was becoming true to myself, the world changed. What I couldn't know then was whether I truly wanted children, or whether I just wanted to prove wrong everyone who had pitied me.

Shortly after I met John, who is now my husband, we ran into his friends Laura and Tammy and their toddler, Oliver, at the 2001 Minnesota State Fair. John and Laura had been co-workers, and Laura had observed him for years before she and Tammy had asked him to be their child's biological father. Though not especially close to them, he had agreed, signing legal documents in which he foreswore paternal rights and they foreswore claims to support. He had offered to be in the child's life to the extent he was able, if the child so wished, but in deference to Tammy's position as adoptive mother, he had so far remained uninvolved. Nevertheless, the women asked him to be a sperm donor again, and Lucy was born in 2004, by which time John was living with me in Manhattan.

The question of having biological children in unorthodox ways was familiar to me. A few years before I met John, during a trip to Texas, I attended a dinner that included my college friend Blaine. I had adored her for more than 20 years, but then, everyone adores Blaine; she is serenely beautiful and poised, and I had never felt indispensable to her as I do with more difficult friends. Blaine had divorced and shortly thereafter lost her mother, and she alluded to her yearning to become a mother herself. I said I'd be thrilled to father her child. The idea that she might actually want to have a baby with me was unimaginable; I suggested it with the rhetorical politesse with which I'd invited new acquaintances in remote countries to stop by for a drink if they ever found themselves in Greenwich Village. When I got home, however, I wrote her a letter, saying that I thought she would be a glorious mother, and that if she didn't have a child with me, I hoped she'd have one with someone.

When Blaine came to my 40th birthday party in New York three years later, in 2003, we realized that we both wanted to have that child together. I wasn't ready to tell John, who was still living in Minneapolis. When I did tell him, he exploded. He had been a sperm donor, he argued; I would have a child who would bear my last name. I would be involved in an ongoing, profound relationship with Blaine that he feared would lethally triangulate our own. I did not know how hard it is to reinvent family, and he could not envision how fulfilling this particular reinvention might be. I nearly backed out but felt I couldn't renege on my word, based on a wish I could likewise not forsake. John, whose benevolence invariably triumphs, finally relented, and Blaine and I conceived through IVF. Blaine, meanwhile, had met her partner, Richard, putting a reasonable if unusual balance in place.

I did not know how hard it is to reinvent family, and he could not envision how fulfilling this particular reinvention might be.

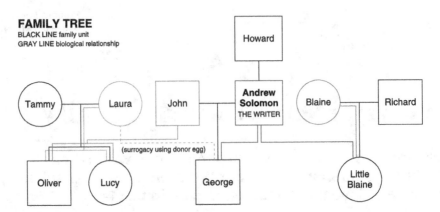

FAMILY TREE
BLACK LINE family unit
GRAY LINE biological relationship

(surrogacy using donor egg)

CLOCKWISE FROM UPPER LEFT   Tammy (she and Laura are mothers to Oliver and Lucy; Andrew's partner, John, is the biological father of both children); **Laura** (she was also the surrogate for Andrew and John's son, George); **Andrew** (married to John, he is the biological father of little Blaine and George); **little Blaine** (the daughter of Andrew and his college friend Blaine, who conceived through **IVF**); **Blaine** (Andrew's college friend and the mother of little Blaine); **Oliver** (Laura and Tammy's son; John's biological child); **Richard** (Blaine's partner); **Howard** (Andrew's father); **George** (Andrew and John's son, whom Laura carried; Andrew is the biological father); **John** (Andrew's partner, George's dad, and the biological father of Oliver and Lucy); **Lucy** (daughter of Tammy and Laura; John's biological child).

Falling in love with John had meant not only the discovery of great happiness, but also the elimination of great unhappiness. Marrying him was my way of acknowledging our love as more a presence than an absence, which was especially urgent as we moved forward with the Blaine plan. I am a dual national, and Britain had recently passed an encompassing civil-partnership law, so we had a June ceremony in the English countryside, presided over by a registrar, a minister, and a rabbi. In my wedding toast, I said, "The love that dared not speak its name is now broadcasting." If all my gay childhood traumas had led me to this day, I thought, maybe they were not so bad as they had seemed. Oliver, then 7, served as John's ring bearer. Blaine, four months pregnant with our child, came with Richard, and John ventured that we'd had the first gay shotgun wedding.

John and I headed to Texas for little Blaine's delivery, by Caesarean section, on Nov. 5, 2007. I watched the obstetrician pull my child out of her mother, and was the first person to hold her, and was as shocked as I was elated. I had to affirm paternity before my name went on the birth certificate; the hospital clerk advised me, as an unmarried father, to ask for genetic testing, referring knowingly to the "love child." I spared him the details.

Little Blaine was to live in Texas with her mother, and we were to visit each other often. I was grateful that John welcomed the daughter he had dreaded—grateful, too, that he and Blaine had come to cherish each other. Blaine's 86-year-old father, whose values I had thought this might challenge, accepted me as a son; my father was overjoyed by his granddaughter. My pleasure in fatherhood aligned with the satisfaction of giving scope to Blaine's genius for motherhood. Blaine had my own mother's elegance of thought and appearance, echoed her ability to find hilarity in the dailiness of life, demonstrated the same madcap imagination largely hidden by discretion and obdurate reserve, and shared her gene for intelligent empathy tinged with sadness.

Still, I wanted a child in my own house with John. It's good news that being gay is no longer crazy (removed from the DSM, psychiatry's bible, in 1973) or illegal (fully decriminalized in 2003), but we carry the legacy of its being both, and couldn't have children to assert progress, social or personal. John had wanted to marry; I hadn't, particularly; and then the reality had entranced me. I exacted a child as fair trade, believing John, too, would end up entranced. John said, "How much happier do you need to be?" I said, "If we don't have a child because you've vetoed the idea, it will infect the rest of our marriage." The conversation stalled there, but John's compassion ultimately carried the day. For my birthday six months later, in October 2007, he gave me a carved antique cradle tied up with a bow, and said, "If it's a boy, can we call him George, after my grandpa?"

A lawyer laid out the advantages of having one woman provide the egg and another the womb, so that neither would have full claim as mother, and we began the blind-dating egg hunt. Our first choice was a charming woman who, several months into preparations, tested positive for cocaine. Even as I championed another prospect, whose egg we finally used, I felt sorry that I would never see what might come of mixing John's genes with my own. I was thankful we could get an egg, but sad that neither of us could produce one; glad we could have a child at all, and regretful about the aura of manufacturing that clung to the venture. Children are always products of emotion and biology, but it's disorienting when those elements become asynchronous.

John had proposed that I be biological father of this child and said that he might sire the next, if there were one. When we told Laura and Tammy our plan, Laura said, "We couldn't have had Oliver and Lucy without you, and we'll never be able to thank you enough for that, but I could be your surrogate to show how much you mean to us." There followed medical screenings of Laura, the egg donor, and me; samples (the bright hospital room, the leatherette briefcase of dated girlie magazines provided by the staff); fertility treatments for Laura; embryo transfers; and ultrasounds. Children had been a buffer for Laura against pain and fear, giving purpose to her calm authority; now, she bravely converted that vulnerability into generosity.

We got pregnant on our second IVF protocol. Pregnancy supersedes irony; you never know anyone as admiringly as you do when she is carrying your child, and I marveled at the way Laura wove the life she was building for us into the life she had built for herself. Through the proceeding, we drew inexorably closer to Laura and Tammy and the kids. Oliver and Lucy referred to the expected baby as their brother, and I was shy of their enthusiasm. However, I liked Oliver's zaniness and Lucy's exuberance, and I loved how John's wit and gentleness echoed in them. We went to Minneapolis for the late stages of the pregnancy and ended up staying a month, seeing them every day. When Oliver and Lucy learned that little Blaine called us Daddy and Papa John, they said they wanted to call us Daddy and Papa, too. I was not prepared for the idea that all of these children were in various degrees mine, but the generosity with which John had come to embrace an inclusive notion of family and celebrate the Blaines modeled my path to acceptance. Having set out to have two children, I was suddenly contemplating four. To bring us closer had been part of Laura's purpose in helping us, and it worked. By little Blaine, by the imminent George, by Oliver and Lucy, I had been changed, and children made me happy.

On April 9, 2009, at 9:45 P.M., at Abbott-Northwestern Hospital in downtown Minneapolis, we got a view of George's pate, and then Laura pushed six times, and out he popped, into John's arms. I cut the cord. We summoned Oliver and Lucy from the waiting room; we called Blaine and my father. John was instantly enraptured, as I knew he would be. For nine months, we'd felt the favor Laura did us almost as though someone had offered to carry an increasingly heavy bag of groceries up an increasingly steep staircase, but that day we understood that she had made a life for us. We saw clearly for the first time something wild and heroic in her, an acreage of heart and valor beyond anything our male experience had taught us.

Planning to have a baby had been my department; caring for one was John's. I had taught him about determination, about doing things instead of simply imagining them; now he taught me about experiencing those things. We had been advised that if the Defense of Marriage Act were repealed, we should have a marriage legally recognized where we live, so we had a second wedding in Connecticut, two years after our English one. We incorporated a naming ceremony for George, appointing godparents and honorary aunts. It was momentous to hear the Danbury city clerk declare us "husband and husband" and just as consequential to have all four children together for the first time. I keep on my iPhone a portrait from that day, a visual aid for elucidating how we are all related. I wrote this story to usurp that image.

When John and I were invited to the White House Easter Egg Roll last spring, we explained that we were an extended nuclear family, and the whole lot of us went. When my stepsister got married in October, all four children were pages or bridesmaids.

We spent most of December together in the candyland of a New York Christmas, and it was revisionist Rockwell, the four kids around the tree at my father's house. Loving John had helped me to become whole, and loving these children rooted me in that wholeness. I had feared ahead of time that I might not love my children enough: now I am enthralled by George's fascination with the moon; by little Blaine announcing, when she saw that I had cut my finger, "You need a mommy," and fetching a Band-Aid; by Oliver and Lucy debating whether to leave a ginger cookie for Santa or give it to John and me.

Little Blaine has learned to say, soulfully, "I miss you, Daddy," even when we are together, which used to break my heart. During a vacation in June, I took her for a walk, leaving Blaine and Richard in a restaurant with John and George. As I was pointing out sights, she said, "Oh, Daddy, I'm so happy," and when I picked her up, she leaned her head on my collarbone and said, "I miss you." The next morning, out on a boat, she threw her arms around her mother, and said, "I miss you," and I realized that for her, "miss" and "love" meant one idea. I have come to use the words interchangeably myself. I miss my children even when I'm beside them, and acknowledging that ache seems the best way to contain it. Although he would never forsake the kids we have, John maintains that he could have been happy without children, but now that I know this joy, I feel I could not. I dwell too much in abstraction and the future, and parenting has taught me the present time that children require, where contentment, even rapture, reside.

All happy families are the same, and yet, when my brother says he loves his wife and children, everyone is delighted; when I speak of loving my family, people are often shocked and occasionally disgusted. Our affection becomes political—thrilling in a way, but I'd prefer to have intimacy untainted by purpose. That photo on the iPhone often seems euphemistic, because what it shows looks easy. It is exhilarating to be Christopher Columbus landing on the wilder shores of love, but sometimes one would prefer to live where the luxury hotels have already been built and Internet access is wireless. Most people expect to have children, and there are susceptibilities attached to that; I had expected not to have children, and the reversal contains stranger ones. I have had to separate the relief of escaping that tragic childlessness to which my parents gave so much airtime and the reality of human beings for whom I am variously responsible. It must be easier when there is a script.

Once George arrived, the urgent question arose of how all these relationships might constellate. John and I have complete charge of George; Blaine and I had agreed in advance that we would make the major decisions about little Blaine together; Laura and Tammy have separate parental authority, and we do not set the course for Oliver and Lucy, nor Laura and Tammy for George. The three arrangements are different, and as most parents suppress sibling rivalry, we struggle to avoid situational comparison. I would not obscure the frictions sparked by conflicting priorities and boundaries, disparate resources, myriad parenting styles—but they are dwarfed by the fact that it all somehow functions. We have earned the familial relationships into which others stumble, and there is a veteran's peace in our mutual devotion.

John and I sent out birth announcements that included a picture of us with George. One of John's cousins returned it with a note that said, "Your lifestyle is against our Christian values. We wish to have no further contact." Some people scorn the idea of calling five adults and four children in three states a family, or believe that the existence of our family undermines theirs. I do not accept competitive models of love, only additive ones. I espouse reproductive libertarianism, and would propose that when everyone has the broadest choice, love itself expands. I would never want to be smug about the affection we all found in one another. It is not a better love than others, but it is another love, and just as species diversity is crucial to sustain the planet, this diversity strengthens the ecosphere of kindness.

I espouse reproductive libertarianism, and would propose that when everyone has the broadest choice, love itself expands.

Even the most liberal courts note, apparently in approval, that gay people do not make their children gay. If one suggests that black people should be able to reproduce so long as the kids are white, one sees how much prejudice is enmeshed in even ostensibly pro-gay arguments about family. It's disorienting to recognize that the more conventional our choices are, the more radical we are, that my days of party hopping and sexual adventuring were tolerable, but that our arguing about how much to babyproof, thinking about preschools, buying a swing set, and joining a church constitute an assault on family values. There's a bizarre and hateful inversion in this. American modernity is built on our liberation from a pernicious 1950s model of the nuclear family that was never true in the first place, and those who attempt to preserve that model are not conservatives, but regressives.

The change has already happened; it's only the law that lags. The road less traveled, as it turns out, leads to pretty much the same place.

Critical Thinking

1. How would you compare your family to the author's "unconventional family?"

2. What do you think the author means by "unconventional?"

3. Why is there so much variation in families?

Create Central

www.mhhe.com/createcentral

Internet References

World Family Map
http://worldfamilymap.org/2013

Australian Institute of Family Studies
www.aifs.gov.au

Feminist Perspectives on Reproduction and the Family
http://plato.stanford.edu/entries/feminism-family

Kearl's Guide to the Sociology of the Family
www.trinity.edu/MKEARL/family.html

SOLOMON'S last book, *The Noonday Demon*, won the National Book Award; his new book on extraordinary families, *Far From the Tree*, will be out in 2012.

Article

Prepared by: Patricia Hrusa Williams,
University of Maine at Farmington

Relative Happiness

Your family may not be storybook, but you can cheer up the house by breaking bread, finding fun, and following a few proven plotlines.

AMY ROSENBERG

Learning Outcomes

After reading this article, you will be able to:

• Consider what it means to be "happy."

• Recognize the attributes of happy families.

• Describe how families can be happier.

When I was a child, I loved the *All-of-a-Kind Family* books. Five sisters sharing a bedroom in a small New York apartment at the turn of the last century—what could be more fun? To me, growing up in the suburbs with an older brother with whom I was never very close, and with parents who were active in numerous clubs and organizations that often kept them out of the house, the idea of a large family doing things together was extremely appealing. I envied even a housecleaning scene in which the girls' mother hid buttons for them to find as they dusted the living room. Everything was tackled with team spirit, and so everything—even the chores—seemed like play. The family possessed an infectious energy that you couldn't help but absorb through the books' pages. Simply put, they were happy.

Of course, the current era demands a different kind of family life. You and your partner may both be working long hours while staying electronically tethered to the office afterward. Your kids, too, are probably deep into their devices. On the weekends, homework—your kids' or your own—takes over, and errands swallow up whatever time is left. Then, when you finally manage to corral the whole clan for some quality time together, someone is too exhausted to enjoy it, someone else resents the forced fun, and no one really knows how to talk to anyone else.

It's hard to feel in control when you're busy managing the daily scramble. But you should at least be cognizant of the power you have to set the tone of your home, even if it's most often set by default, by all those electronic interferences. For starters, you can impose limits on interruptions

and distractions. And then, on top of that, you can consciously decide to do what came naturally to the *All-of-a-Kind Family,* one that constantly shared adventures, despite being poor. Because they were steeped in Jewish culture, they adhered to family rituals that further increased warmth and closeness. Happiness wasn't their goal; it was a by-product of their lifestyle.

> **You have the power to set the tone of your home, even if it's most often set by default.**

Tolstoy wrote that all happy families are alike, but an unhappy family is unhappy after its own fashion. This may or may not be true, but happy families share certain behaviors and that unhappy ones can change. Examining what works for others might help you figure out ways to start increasing the levels of joy among your own clan.

A truly happy family supports and encourages the growth of each of its members. Reaching that ideal state requires the group to respect one another's space while simultaneously fostering togetherness. Such a family paradoxically provides predictable comfort and dramatic highs and lows, both of which come from caring deeply for the people under your own roof.

Communicate Well and Often

Catie and Kevin O'Keefe, a couple in their late 50s who live in Washington, D.C., where they raised their three children, swear that effective communication is the key. When their kids, now 26, 23, and 19, were younger, Catie and Kevin (who, incidentally, own a communications company together) emphasized the importance of interacting with one another. "We ate dinner together every night," says Kevin. "That was a given. We asked each other, 'What did you do today?' We had discussions about everyday kinds of things. It brought us closer together."

Barbara Fiese, a psychologist who studies family routines and health at Syracuse University, finds that "eating together helps open up the lines of communication. Concerns leak out, and it becomes an opportunity to solve problems as a team."

The Landsgaards, a large clan living in a small town in Mississippi, also insist on eating together—no easy feat with six children ranging in age from 3 to 10 years old. "Everyone feels free to express themselves around the table," says Kristen Landsgaard, mother of the family, "even the babies. I homeschool the older kids, so I have breakfast and lunch with all of them, and my husband always joins us for dinner. We all connect that way."

Eating together is an opportunity for families to solve problems as a team.

For Naomi Pabst and Don Daly, who live in lower Manhattan with their 3 children—Anatola, 11, Ian, 4, and Ariana, 1, one-on-one time with each child is as crucial as group sessions. "Maintaining five different schedules in a chaotic city means we really have to take the opportunity to have one-on-one time when it arises," Naomi says. "We have to make the in-between moments count." She often has her most heartfelt conversations with her elder daughter while walking with her from one activity to another.

The O'Keefes also encouraged their kids to verbally resolve conflicts. "We let our kids talk things out among themselves," Kevin explains. And when talking was hard, they found other ways. "Our middle child always found it easier to write letters than to speak. When she was a teenager and we set a curfew for her, she disagreed with our rules. She wrote us a letter that made a great argument for a later curfew, and we changed our minds."

The letter episode demonstrates one of the most important aspects of communication in any relationship: listening with an open mind and letting each person communicate in his or her own way. It's tempting, as a parent trying to maintain a sense of authority or avoid unwanted precedents, to set hard and fast rules and stick to them unwaveringly. But truly understanding others' points of view is crucial. As clinical psychologist and family dynamics expert Ellen Weber Libby points out, "You have to have confidence that other family members, even kids, have healthy instincts about what they need for themselves."

"For us," Kevin says, "it was about respect. We were able to communicate well with our kids because we respected them as individuals, and they, in turn, respected us. Because we listened to them and told them exactly what we expected of them, they didn't want to disappoint us."

Now that their children are older and living away from home, daily dinner-table communication is not an option for the O'Keefes, but the family still finds ways to stay connected. They speak on the phone often and get together for holidays. As the eldest, Patrick, puts it, "We always ask each other about our activities when we talk. We rely on one another to tell when big events are coming up and then we do our best to remember to ask about it the next time we talk."

Build Rituals

For Dave Nuscher and Dave Sullivan, of Belmont, Massachusetts, regular rituals are the glue that holds their family together. Rituals lend structure to the Nuscher-Sullivans' days, creating a framework to support communication and respect.

The two Daves adopted their 9-year-old son, Perry, when he was just under a year old. As a non-traditional family, they had to work perhaps harder than others to get the ball rolling; simply starting the international adoption process was a test of their commitment to the idea of having a family. But they had already been together for five years and they knew they had a strong enough foundation. "We felt confident that we'd be good dads," says Nuscher, "and we wanted to provide a child with the same kind of happiness we both had growing up."

When they brought their son home from Cambodia, all the established habits and roles had to undergo adjustment, just as with any new parents. "From the very beginning, we found that having a routine helped Perry get settled and it helped us, too," says Nuscher. "From the time he was 9 months old until he was 2 or 3, we sang him the same two songs and read him the same two books every single night."

Now that Perry is older, the daily routine maps out a division of labor in which each family member knows what's expected of him, and the logistics of each day run as smoothly as possible. Nuscher, director of editorial and creative services at Tufts University, manages all the finances. As a computer science instructor at Harvard and Boston Universities, Sullivan has a slightly more flexible schedule; he helps Perry get ready for school and out the door. Perry, for his part, knows exactly what jobs he must complete each morning (prepare for school, feed the guinea pigs) in order to earn 30 minutes of video-game time.

Other, more special rituals give them quality time together. Once a week, they take turns choosing a restaurant to go to for dinner. On Saturdays, Perry and Nuscher go to the library and play sports; on Sundays, Perry and Sullivan go to church together. And equally important is the alone-time built into the daily structure. "We can predict when we'll have time together and when we'll have time to ourselves," says Nuscher. "That's really important to us." It's important in general, according to Feise. "You want everyone in the family to have a sense of place and individual identity," she says. "That is what lends each person the belief that they have something to contribute."

The Landsgaard family also relies on daily routine to sustain a sense of security. "For us," Kristen says, "the most important ritual is saying the rosary together every night before bedtime. We're all together in the same room at the same time then, and everyone is quiet. There's a real sense that we're all there for each other."

Some families hold fast to less frequent, often more elaborate traditions that are equally effective for creating a sense of closeness and shared excitement. Larry Rosen, a professor of psychology at California State University, Dominguez Hills, and author of *Rewired: Understanding the iGeneration and the Way They Learn,* offers as an example his family's construction of an extravagant gingerbread house each year. Twenty years ago, he says, when he had two teenagers, a preteen, and a baby, he cut out a newspaper article about the art of edible homes, and he and his kids got to work. It became a project central to the family's holiday experience, starting about a month or so before Christmas with a group discussion about possible themes and designs. "Now," Rosen says, "it's become an invio-lable thing." His children, ranging in age today from 18 to 35, all return home during the holidays, and everyone sets aside a full 48 hours to complete the house. "It's not really about the house, though," observes Rosen. "It's about the fact that we spend two days a year together as a family. Our closeness is partly grounded in the ritual."

Stay Flexible

As important as routine is, *too* rigid families with inflexible attitudes suffer under the weight of predictability. The Pabst-Dalys keep a mind-bogglingly complex schedule. Three days a week, Naomi Pabst commutes three hours round-trip between Manhattan and New Haven, Connecticut, where she is a profes-sor of African-American studies at Yale University. Don Daly, who owns his own real estate business, usually oversees getting the children to school and day-care. Anatola, a serious gymnast, has four-hour practices four evenings a week and weekly com-mitments with a performing arts group. And Daly and Pabst insist on having dinners all together each night, even if it means late bedtimes. "It takes a lot of order and precision to coordi-nate each day, and we have to organize things meticulously," Pabst says. "But within that, we're spontaneous. We think of ourselves as orderly, but never regimented. It's crucial for us to be able to go with the flow."

While the family has rituals, such as celebrating every holi-day and having a pancake brunch together every weekend, they make a point of also doing things on the spur of the moment. They might, for example, hop in their car for an unplanned weekend trip to Vermont or accept an impromptu invitation to a friend's house, even when doing so disrupts the usual eve-ning, homework, or morning routine. "We like to keep a sense of adventure and fun," says Pabst. "It's part of working to keep the family dynamic alive, fresh, and bright."

Be confident that family members, even kids, have healthy instincts about what they need for themselves.

Focusing on that dynamic allows Pabst and Daly to keep their own relationship vibrant. "Our secret ingredient," Pabst says, "is that Don and I are madly in love with each other. We have a deep regard for one another, and we work hard to keep

ourselves emotionally available. Even if I'm taxed to my limit, I'll still take the time to pay attention to him in loving ways, and he'll do the same. The spontaneity is part of that."

Therein, according to Ellen Weber Libby, lies one of the keys to creating a happy family. "The parents' relationship is the beginning. Children mirror tensions they see and feel in their parents, and those tensions affect their relationships with one another. When they see their parents loving each other and committing to each other, the whole family is strengthened."

Nevertheless, Libby says, if parents are no longer com-mitted to each other, it doesn't make sense to project a false love, or to stay together for the sake of trying to keep chil-dren happy. "Kids feel so much more relaxed when a house isn't filled with unspoken tension," she says. "If parents are not working well together, their children may be better off if they separate." Divorced parents can still express respect for their ex-spouses, respond honestly and openly to their kids' needs, and engage in fun activities with their kids, she points out. "Being from a single-parent family does not have to mean being unhappy."

Have Fun and Reach Out Together

Another essential ingredient in a happy family life is taking the time to do new things together—even if doing so means drag-ging reluctant teenagers along. "When you enjoy each other," says Libby, "you create joint experiences that serve as a bond. You get to know each other as individuals, and kids learn impor-tant things like compromise and respect for others' desires."

As Patrick O'Keefe explains, "When you're young, it's hard to tell your friends that you're going out of town for the weekend with your parents and sisters. We went often, and I always felt like I was missing out on things. Most of the time though, it ended up being really fun. On our boat we had no TV, no friends, and no video games, so we would entertain each other and get rest. Each weekend made us closer, and I think the seclusion from the rest of our confusing adolescent worlds was crucial to the growth of all of us individually and as a unit."

Doing things as a family also gives parents a chance to impart values to kids and to model appropriate behaviors through their own behavior. As Richard Weissbourd, a child and family psy-chologist at Harvard University, argues, parents today tend to *overemphasize* their children's happiness. "What would really be helpful to kids is seeing their parents caring for others; that should he a priority. That's how kids themselves learn to care for others." Choosing activities you can do together that will benefit others—volunteering at a soup kitchen, for example, or helping in a community cleanup—allows kids to see par-ents caring about the world around them, and also gives them a sense of their own place in that world.

For Pabst and Daly, that kind of togetherness is inspiring, and helps them keep their own senses of wonder while reinforc-ing the sense of wonder in their kids. "We always want them to have a feeling of abundance in the world, and to be grateful for that abundance, and to give freely to others because of it," Pabst says. "When they're older, we plan to figure out ways to enjoy time together while also contributing to the communities around us. That just feels like the right thing for a family to do."

Critical Thinking

1. How would you describe your own family's happiness?
2. What kind of attributes have you identified from the article that are in your family?
3. Do you agree with the author's opinion on happiness in families? Why or why not?
4. In thinking about happy families, are there any attributes that are missing from the author's list?
5. Are all families who are happy alike? Why or why not?

Create Central

www.mhhe.com/createcentral

Internet References

University of Pennsylvania Positive Psychology Center
www.ppc.sas.upenn.edu

Kearl's Guide to the Sociology of the Family
www.trinity.edu/MKEARL/family.html

AMY ROSENBERG is a writer living in New York City.

From *Psychology Today*, July/August 2010, pp. 62–69. Copyright © 2010 by Sussex Publishers, LLC. Reprinted by permission.

Prepared by: Patricia Hrusa Williams,
University of Maine at Farmington

Article

Back to the Dinner Table

MARY BETH McCAULEY

Learning Outcomes

After reading this article, you will be able to:

- Explain the positive effect that rituals like family meals have on family ties.

- Discuss the sense of togetherness that rituals like family meals provide.

- Identify the ways that rituals like family meals provide families with intergenerational processes.

Sociology

Most nights, the American family dinner is anything but haute. There are the peas fed to the dog; the fibs fed to the parents; the thing that looks like grace but really is heads bowed, hands fervently texting. Mom's on a diet. The diorama due tomorrow is half done. No wonder the evening meal, once a no-brainer, drifted over recent decades from the diningroom table to the kitchen counter to the minivan.

But lately, family dinner has gone upscale. In one of the most "duh" iterations of everything-old-is-new-again, dinner has regained the allure Mom always suspected it should have.

Bolstered by scientific data and an intensifying popular buzz, the family dinner has returned full force as the most important time of the day for many, and as the defining—nay, sacred—family activity. The ritual of breaking bread together creates family identity even as it conveys it. Soccer practice seems so yesterday.

Studies show that roughly half of families eat together most nights. And while that number holds fairly steady, as a movement, family dinner seems to be reaching critical mass. Opinion leaders—like Tiger Mother Amy Chua, TV personality Cynthia McFadden, medical ethicist Ezekiel Emanuel—now dish about their personal experiences in *The New York Times. The Huffington Post* suggests table talk topics. "An Inconvenient Truth" documentary producer Laurie David takes the style elements up a notch in her book *The Family Dinner*. Facebook chief operating officer Sheryl Sandberg breaks from motherhood's don't-ask-don't-tell policy to fess up: She's always left work at 5:30 to eat with her children. Actress Gwyneth Paltrow spills in *Harper's Bazaar* that she's doing dinner for her husband and kids. The food-conscious Obamas share their own family dinner habits.

The "new" family dinner has a designated day—Sept. 24 this year—along with corporate funding and recipes. Some communities have weekly activity-free nights to clear time for family dinner. Pediatricians are recommending the practice, as are authors, bloggers, and celebrity chefs. And now that dinner has gone, well, Hollywood, a meat-and-potatoes aesthetic has yielded to artfully folded table linens in Brooklyn, vintage monastery tables in Levittown, and, everywhere, the possibility of kelp.

Who could ever question the communal breaking of bread? If nothing else, it simultaneously meets life's needs for physical, social, and spiritual nourishment. Until about 30 years ago, everybody got that. But the microwaves that enabled single-serving feeding converged in the 1980s with a woman-working/keep-kids-busy ethos. The result? A generation of picky eaters made more so by specially marketed kiddie foods served up by tired parents unwilling to pick a fight with kids they hadn't seen all day.

This, plus the idea of enforcing a family dinner routine when there might be a budding gymnastics superstar in the house bordered on, well, bad parenting. Didn't it?

Not anymore. In recent years, the family dinner has been returned to the manual of best parenting practices; and if you're not doing it, you know you probably should, says Miriam Weinstein, author of *The Surprising Power of Family Meals*.

"It's become almost an article of faith that it's the right thing to do," says Ms. Weinstein. The tide began to turn, she says, with 2005–06 data from the National Center on Addiction and Substance Abuse (CASA) at Columbia University in New York linking family dinner to a host of good outcomes for children. Other studies reinforced the link. Today, frequent family dinners—the magic number seems to be at least five times a week—are associated with lower teen use of alcohol, tobacco, and marijuana; lower risk of obesity, eating disorders, and teen pregnancy; and improved nutrition, physical and mental health, grades, and relationships with parents.

Today, more than half of families with children eat dinner together at least three to five times a week, according to Marlene Schwartz of the Rudd Center for Food Policy & Obesity at Yale University. US Census data suggest that the number may be creeping up, and advocates think the number may rise as those who schedule kids' activities clear time for families.

Some believe that the recession years' data may also boost the numbers of families eating together because unemployment leaves more time for cooking, and hard times spawn more appreciation for end-of-the-day togetherness.

"A positive spin" on the bad economy, Marshall Duke, professor of psychology at Emory University in Atlanta, calls it.

Census data suggest that family meals are most frequent in Hispanic households and in two-parent homes, and least frequent when a parent is divorced. The higher the parents' educational level, the less frequent the practice: Those who have not completed high school are the most likely to eat together, and those with advanced degrees the least.

Experts say the benefits accrue whether the food is organically grown or taken out of a pizza box, whether the conversation follows a take-turns ritual or a more free-for-all format, whether it's actually family breakfast instead of family dinner that's being had.

And kids of all ages benefit. Even teenagers, stereotypically the most I'm-out-of-here bunch, think family dinner is important. A recent CASA poll reports that 58 percent of teens eat dinner with their families at least five times a week, and that 54 percent say they value the conversation as well as the food.

Professor Duke believes that the practice is more vital now than ever because family stories told at the table build the resilience kids need to navigate a recession-weary, post-9/11 world.

"The more that kids know about their family background, the more resilient they are. And not just about the positives, but about the times the family had trouble and people came through," he explains. They learn that relatives have made mistakes and recovered, and so can they; and that family identity can help them resist temptation, says Duke.

If it's resilience that kids need, it's prodding to take charge of their families that Mom and Dad need, says Weinstein, who often speaks to parent groups.

"Parents are feeling so incompetent, it's sad. . . . So many pick up the kids at day care, go through the drive-through, and eat in the car. I say 'why don't you take home the bag and eat [the food] on the table?' " says Weinstein.

Feeding a family is empowering for parents, say experts.

"There's a confidence about sharing something with your family, that you can provide something for your family, that your family can be together without having to send out for something," Weinstein explains.

But many just don't know how: They have no food in the house, no skills to prepare a meal, no confidence to turn off the TV and start a conversation. The feeling of incompetence afflicts the affluent and well-educated as well as the poor. Many are intimidated by what could be perceived as a need to be perfect—a standard suggested by celebrity chefs and by the call

Dinner is the Dalmass Family's Main Dish

MOORESTOWN, NJ.

Right after "American Idol" one recent weeknight, three of Kelly and Chris Dalmass's four children perform what looks like a well-practiced ballet of table setting, milk pouring, and arranging of chairs. The plates and the kitchen floor are well worn, the cups neon plastic.

It's 9:15 by the time their brother has finished practice and comes in the back door of their rambling home. Quickly, Nate, age 12, and his dad take their places at the table with Kelly as well as Kiera, 14; Julia, 11; and Johnny, 10. They join hands and begin a lightning round of a grace, to which each is expected to contribute. Thanks go up for everything from a new baby cousin to—simply—lacrosse, before Dad brings things to a close, as he does every night since 9/11, with a prayer for America and for the troops. The table, which Chris made himself, has gotten a bit snug for their six, his wife explains, but she likes it "because we're close."

As pork chops are passed, the meal takes on a kind of generic dinnertime feel. Wrapped in happy chatter are encouragements and admonishments, mini rebellions and micro corrections, gibes, jokes, banter, and barbs. In this house, you don't have to finish all the food on your plate; but you do have to wear your shirt, take off your hat, mind your manners. Everybody shares the same food. The day's events are replayed, and clarifications sought.

All the while Kelly, a lawyer, and her husband, whose company makes artificial limbs, nudge the family's understanding of the day toward the good: good manners, good schoolwork, good eating habits, good ways to say things, good ways to handle things. So by the time the conversation moves to the next day's schedule, the kids have received a Mom-and-Dad-filtered perspective of the day, a Dalmass reality check—whether they realize it or not.

By 9:45 plates are cleared and kids are off to shower, and their parents catch up with each other over the dishes.

The family finds time to eat together every night, even if, as happens, somebody's practice goes as late as 9, or, as on one weekend recently, there are 20 games on the schedule. Kids are big into lacrosse and soccer—summer leagues, club leagues, winter leagues—and that's not counting the random choir practice, religious ed class, volunteer activity, and such.

The parents share cooking and driving duties, divvying things up daily based on whose schedule allows for which tasks. The first one home cooks, having pulled something out of the freezer in the morning, and the last one home does the carpooling. On many Sundays, the extended family—anywhere from 10 to 35 people total—gather for what everyone considers the real family dinner.

If Kelly and Chris wind up sacrificing some of their own togetherness while they build their family, they consider it temporary and worth it.

Says Kelly: "[Dinner together is] to help our kids grow into adulthood. . . . I want my kids to love life and to have fun."

—Mary Beth McCauley

to wholesomeness and the home grown, to the requisite recipes, conversation starters, and let's-cook-together pressures.

But, actually, family dinner can be a balm for adults as well as kids, Weinstein says, citing an IBM study showing that, no matter how many hours they worked, employees who got home for dinner felt better about their families and jobs. Older studies, she says, have shown that even in homes of an alcoholic, the meal gave a sense that there was a family to hold onto.

The nonprofit Family Dinner Project, in Watertown, Mass., aims to shore up the practice. (See the story later in this article.) At its community dinners, mentors provide hands-on practice to families in preparing food, dining, conversing, and cleaning up. College students visit schools at lunch to model table manners during small-group dining. The project's website highlights families who've intentionally tapped dinner's therapeutic value to bond and counter discord.

The Gallegoses' Ttradition: Tortillas and Togetherness

SAN YSIDRO, CALIF.

On the most southwesterly street in the United States, inside a shade-dappled tract house, Rosa Gallegos is in the kitchen preparing *gorditas de chicharrón* on a recent Saturday afternoon. Her husband, Jesus, and grown kids, Ailin and Omar, hover nearby waiting to help slice strips of cheese and stuff the little tortilla pouches with a spicy filling of pork rinds, tomatoes, and chilies.

For now, though, the kitchen is Rosa's domain. She reaches into a bowl of *masa* (corn dough), shapes a golf-ball-sized sphere, flattens it into a disc with a tortilla press, and cooks it on the *comal* (tortilla griddle).

"My mother used to make the *masa* at home from scratch," she says in Spanish, cocking her chin toward 85-year-old Manuela Marín, who is watching a black-and-white movie on TV "But I just buy this from the *tortillería*."

US Census data show that among the 10 million Latino households in America—like the Gallegoses—family dinners are more common than in the general population. More than 84 percent of Latino parents with kids under age 6 report having daily meals together.

Four generations wait hungrily for Rosa's *gorditas* today, including Omar's wife, Mary, and their infant son, Carlo; Ailin and her daughter, Paulette, 7; and cousin Melanie Diaz, 5.

'People [in the US] aren't used to eating together. . . . [B]ut if you sit and eat alone, you keep your stress inside.'

— Jesus Gallegos, patriarch of a Mexican-American family that eats together daily

---

Store-bought *masa* is but a minor tweak of a family tradition that has remained unchanged for generations.

Rosa learned this recipe at Manuela's skirts. Manuela learned it from her mother back in Durango, Mexico. Manuela's memories are fuzzy, but thinking of her own mother's cooking induces reverie over *buñuelos* (sweet, fried dough).

When the *gorditas* are done, the kids are called to put down their iPods and Barbies and come to the table. Extra stools are pulled in, and raspberry lemonade is poured. The conversation touches on borderland topics—how long was the wait at *la linea* (the border) today?—but is dominated by Paulette, who speaks animated Spanish, with occasional English words like "report card."

Afterward, Omar helps his grandmother to the couch and returns to linger at the table with Jesus. Mary and Ailin argue good-naturedly about who will wash dishes. The little girls scamper to the kitchen and plunge their hands into the bowl of *masa* to press *gorditas* for leftovers.

Later, Jesus wanders into his toy-strewn backyard. Not far beyond the back wall, the vibrant chaos of his native Tijuana rises over a trio of border fences festooned with concertina wire. In Jesus' 1960s childhood, there was no fence, and he recalls sneaking across the border to snatch tomatoes and cucumbers from farms on the US side before his grandmother called him and his cousins into the house for dinner.

"People here aren't used to eating together," he says. "Kids come home after school and they eat what they want. They don't wait for everybody to sit together. With Latino customs, there's more communication; you feel more relaxed with the support of your family. If someone has a problem, you can vent about it; but if you sit and eat alone, you keep your stress inside."

—**Maya Kroth** / Contributor

'These are the good moments life is giving us. . . .'

A Cornell University study questions whether the benefits to teens may be due to family environment, not dinner itself. In fact, whether family dinner as a practice actually produces successful children or simply reflects parental ability to organize a home and family is a matter of ongoing debate.

"It could be a bellwether of how stable family life is overall," says Ashley Merryman, coauthor of the book "NurtureShock." The character-builders inherent in the family meal—structure, ritual, commitment, discipline, sacrifice—are well-established parenting positives, but the interpretations are individual.

Even what appears bad can be a plus, says Ms. Merryman. If yours is an arguing family, maybe you'll be good at getting raises from the boss someday. If you're complainers, maybe you'll be good at effecting change. Resist the temptation to bring out the good china and instead lower your standards, she advises parents. It's the predictability that's key.

The Rev. Leo Patalinghug, whose "Grace Before Meals" Web-based cooking show, website, and cookbook aim to promote family dinner, says all religions consider food a central element in bringing people together. He points to the parable of the prodigal son, where it was literal starvation that prompted the son's return to his father, who fed him lavishly. The Roman Catholic priest advises parents to aim to "be faithful, not perfect" in their meals, and to recognize the spiritual role they play: "Feeding his children is how God shows his love for us. In the simple act of feeding their own children," parents echo the divine love.

Ms. Schwartz of Yale, along with many others, praises the health benefits of the meal: "If you have dinner as a family, it's more likely that someone [at home] made the meal, and meals are more healthy when made at home." There tend to be more fruits, vegetables, and whole grains; less added sugar, fat, and sodium; and smaller servings than restaurant-prepared meals, she explains. In her own house, Schwartz says, togetherness is the tastiest ingredient. "There aren't other opportunities for everyone to sit down together, to have the feeling that we are a family."

"These are the good moments life is giving us," says producer and author Ms. David. Her family dinner began as soon as her now-teenage daughters could sit at the table, and has

Dinner for 17: How Many Meatloaves did Mom Make?

DEVON, PA.

There are plenty of Walsh family dinner stories. That's because there are plenty of Walsh kids—15 of them, born between 1949 and 1968 to Barbara, a former runway model, and Bill, a World War II veteran and insurance company executive, who married in 1948.

But for Barbara, the stories meld into an overall sense of having spent a great deal of her life at the kitchen sink. A family friend once observed that she and her husband were affectionately known as "Mommy Barbara" and "Mr. Walsh." And that's pretty much how it worked—she oversaw the food and he, a former naval officer, made sure things didn't get out of hand.

Barbara's kitchen, in a huge, 10-bedroom house on Philadelphia's Main Line, was big enough to hold a giant picnic table, with room for extra chairs on the ends. There was always at least one high chair and often a bassinet. The six left-handed children sat along one side. Though Barbara says she likes to think that she instilled formal table manners in her brood, their number precluded a single conversation. Plus, the group was usually in some kind of spilled-milk minicrisis.

But the older siblings helped little ones, and everyone learned over time. As their mother puts it, "I think when they went out they knew how to behave."

During the heavy sports years, there were two seatings in the big kitchen—early for the babies, who couldn't wait, and late for the athletes who had after-school practice.

"I'd have to sort of pace the food," Barbara says. Though she recalls being tired at night, she loved family life. "We were all in the kitchen together, and it was nice having everyone there." Even with 15 mouths to feed,

she says, the only time she felt over-whelmed was the day she brought her first baby home.

Meals weren't fancy. Milk came from giant metal milk drums. Hot dogs with SpaghettiOs—the far and away favorite dinner—was served weekly. There was meatloaf—always an extra in the freezer to send to another family "in case someone died"—and a weekly eight boxes of cookies. "When they were gone, they were gone," says Barbara.

On Sundays, the children's friends were invited for a barbecue. And from their earliest days, Barbara and Bill went out to dinner by themselves once a week. "Half the time we could barely afford it," she recalls, but she strongly advocates it still with her own children now that they are parents. "The two of you were there first," she reminds them.

The Walsh family dinners have long outgrown the dinner hour. They number at least 50 now, and require at least five tables. They'll gather over the July 4 weekend for Bill's 90th birthday for what promises to be four days and 15 families' worth of songs, skits, video presentations, and athletic events. One night, they have 45 tickets to the Phillies. Their matriarch will be back at her kitchen sink—in a manner of speaking—soaking up what she most loves in life: "It's the together thing."

—**Mary Beth McCauley**

been one of her life's great pleasures ever since. Dinner sometimes includes her ex-husband, "Seinfeld" co-creator Larry David. As a parent coming down the homestretch with her kids, she gives credit to the family dinner tradition for her close relationships with her daughters, and with helping prevent them from "falling through the cracks" of an affluent, busy culture. And she credits it with helping her feel successful in her parenthood. "All this happened because I did this ritual," she says. "It's comforting to know I did this thing right."

But what happens when the couscous dries out or the preteen storms off or there are last-minute Lakers tickets?

Well that's kind of the point, experts say. Life—especially family life, and even in Hollywood—rarely goes according to script. But, as Ms. David puts it, "The great thing is you get to try again tomorrow."

Can You Teach the Family Dinner Ritual?

LYNN, MASS.

The iconic American family dinner may look very right and natural as portrayed on TV (think Mrs. Cleaver's casserole) and in art (think Norman Rockwell's "Freedom from Want").

But for some households, a family dinner is an improbable and unrealistic occurrence.

In the Boston area, one organization is trying to change that by modeling the tradition. The Family Dinner Project—a grass-roots organization that bills itself as a "movement of food, fun, and conversation about things that matter"—aims to promote the benefits of the family dinner and connect families with the resources they need to start a family dinner tradition of their own.

"We're trying to orient kids to a meal, to interest them in conversation," says executive director John Sarrouf. "We want everyone to come to the table to be together, to communicate, to ask questions of each other, to have fun, and to make memories."

Many researchers say that families who break bread together regularly may have lower rates of underage substance abuse, teen pregnancy, depression, and problems in school. So the project holds outreach programs promoting the dinner concept at local schools.

At one such event—held recently at the Robert L. Ford School in an impoverished area of Lynn, Mass.— volunteers set up a half-dozen cafeteria tables, each set with real flat-ware and plates, and candles. As families trickled in, the kids were invited to make centerpieces using flowers and rocks.

As one little boy in bright plaid manhandled a plate of cracker hors d'oeuvres, Mr. Sarrouf attempted a kindly redirect, explaining the etiquette of touching only the thing you want to eat.

Socioeconomic factors can definitely affect the ability of families to set aside time for dinner together, explained Claire Crane, principal at the school, where most students qualify for free lunches. "Most families here . . . work two or three jobs," Dr. Crane said. "[F]or some of the families here, this is the first opportunity they have had to do this. When I was a little girl, we ate at 5. We need to go back to that."

Over aluminum trays of lasagna, children chattered and parents talked. Jennifer Paulino brought her two children and three stepchildren to the event without her husband, who had to work. Ms. Paulino looked tired, but happy to be at the dinner. She said she'd recently found a job and was hoping eventually to go back to school. The biggest challenge to dinner in her family is scheduling a time when neither parent is at work, she said.

At another table, Pam Taylor was waging a losing battle against the stubborn tomato sauce adorning her young grandson's face. The mother of six grown kids who now has custody of her three grandchildren, Ms. Taylor suddenly has a new brood to feed.

"But I'm used to having a lot going on," she said. She makes her grandchildren sit down to dinner now. "We make a point of having them sit with us, say grace. The TV goes off. If the phone rings, I just let it ring. . . . I'm fortunate because I am home, and they're young enough that they can't say, 'I'm taking off to go hang out with friends.' "

As the evening wound down, children helped clear the plates and clean the tables. Salvatore, age 4, the youngest of Taylor's grandchildren, finally sat still long enough for her to wipe his face. His favorite part of the dinner? Making whipped cream for dessert.

—**Meredith Bennett-Smith**
Correspondent

Critical Thinking

1. What are some benefits of families eating dinner together?

2. Some are advocating for family meals as a "parenting best practice." Describe some of the reasons why families may not share a meal together. Describe some things that can get in the way of this ritual.

3. Do you think some of the benefits attributed to family meals are overstated? Why or why not?

4. After reading the case studies of the different families, identify similarities and differences in how different families carry out the ritual of a family meal.

Create Central

www.mhhe.com/createcentral

Internet References

The Family Dinner Project
   http://thefamilydinnerproject.org
The Power of Family Meals
   http://poweroffamilymeals.com

Prepared by: Patricia Hrusa Williams,
University of Maine at Farmington

Article

Goy Meets Girl

ANNA WEAVER

Learning Outcomes

After reading this article, you will be able to:

- Define interfaith and interchurch marriages.
- Discuss the challenges faced by couples who do not share the same religious faith experience.
- Describe some ways interfaith and interchurch couples negotiate religious differences and conflicts.

Before Juliann Richards met Neal Levy, she didn't doubt that she'd marry a fellow Catholic someday. After all, Richards was raised Catholic, attended Catholic school, grew up mostly around fellow Catholics, and knew she wanted her children raised with the same faith.

"For many years, I told myself (and others) that I was going to the nearby Catholic college so I could meet a nice Catholic boy and get married," Richards recalls.

But when she met Levy—who is Jewish—the two quickly became friends and eventually started dating. Fast-forward several years: Richards and Levy, both 27, are newlyweds who married in a Jewish-Catholic ceremony.

Such marriages—interfaith (between a Catholic and a non-Christian) and interchurch (between a Catholic and another Christian)—have been on the rise for the past 30 years.

In fact, a 2007 survey on marriage by the Center for Applied Research in the Apostolate (CARA) revealed that marrying another Catholic is a low priority for young Catholics. Of never-married Catholics, only 7 percent said it was "very important" to marry someone of the same faith.

"We realize that this is a major pastoral issue," says Sheila Garcia, associate director of the U.S. Conference of Catholic Bishops' Secretariat on Laity, Marriage, Family Life, and Youth.

Good Foundation

Garcia says that while supporting these couples pastorally, the church also is concerned with making sure the Catholic in a mixed-religion marriage continues to practice his or her faith and that the couple takes seriously the Catholic party's pledge to raise their children Catholic.

Despite these challenges, Garcia believes that mixed marriages offer an opportunity for "peace and understanding, and, where possible, unity."

"The Catholic Church is moving towards how to support the interchurch/interfaith couple," Garcia says. "Mixed religion couples can live out Christ's call to be one."

One of the landmark changes in how the church approaches interfaith and interchurch engaged couples came with the 1983 revision to the Code of Canon Law, around the same time many of the millennials getting married today were born. Before the revision, the non-Catholic party had to sign a document saying they agreed that their children would be raised Catholic. Post-revision, the Catholic spouse pledges to maintain his or her faith and "to do all in her or his power so that all off-spring are baptized and brought up in the Catholic Church." The non-Catholic is informed of that pledge.

"We've changed quite a bit of stuff since Vatican II," says Claretian Father Greg Kenny. "I don't think allegiance to one church or one faith should keep you from the most basic command, that you should love one another."

Kenny says the way the Catholic Church should deal with the growing number of interfaith marriages is on a grassroots level, one couple at a time, with parish and diocesan programs.

"If we can get across to people that religion is not getting in the way, that religion is there to help, that makes so much more sense to me," he says. "Marriage preparation becomes a possible moment of grace."

A Nice Catholic Boy

Despite the rise in interfaith and interchurch marriages, they're not at an all-time high. According to CARA, the highest rate of interfaith marriages took place in the 1970s and 1980s, when young Catholics dispersed from East Coast and Midwestern cities into areas of the country where there were fewer Catholic enclaves.

But as Ohio couple Richards and Levy illustrate, attraction and love can trump proximity to potential partners of the same faith. While Richards' Ohio hometown has three Catholic churches and a majority Christian populace, once she met Levy all her plans for a "nice Catholic boy" disappeared.

As they dated, the two made sure big issues like how their children would be raised or what religious traditions were important to them were discussed respectfully and resolved early on without either forgoing their faith.

When the two decided to get married, the prospect of planning for a Jewish-Catholic ceremony and, more importantly, a marriage got easier when they found an understanding priest, Father David Bline, pastor of St. Francis de Sales Parish in Akron, Ohio. Bline had worked with Rabbi Susan Stone on another interfaith marriage and put the couple in touch with her.

Richards and Levy went through both Catholic and Jewish pre-marital counseling and were surprised at how "refreshingly similar" the advice they received from both sides was. "It was good to know that the same things were being asked of us," Richards says.

They plan to raise their children Catholic, but they both say their kids will be well aware of their Jewish heritage, and they were encouraged to raise them as such by Bline.

Respect for both of their beliefs extended into their wedding ceremony, which was led by both the priest and the rabbi. There were readings from the Hebrew scriptures and the New Testament, signing of an interfaith *ketubah* (a Jewish marriage contract), drinking from a *kiddush* cup, and the couple stood under a *chuppah*, or canopy during the ceremony. All the ceremony components were explained to guests in an extensive program.

Richards and Levy say being rasised in "very open and accepting families," has helped support them throughout their relationship.

Family Conflict

Things went differently for Midwesterners Sarah and Mike Miles (not their real names), who were surprised at just how much tension their own Jewish-Catholic union churned up in Mike's family.

This is Sarah's second marriage. In her first, which lasted about three years, she married a fellow Jew. "It was important for me to marry someone Jewish at that time," she says, adding that her mother was also a big advocate of marrying someone of the same faith.

Mike was raised Catholic, in what he calls a "very religious family." He went to a Catholic school and attends Mass regularly.

"When I started dating and when I met Sarah, religion wasn't a factor," he says. "I wasn't marrying someone because of her religion. I was marrying Sarah because she was who she was."

I wasn't marrying someone because of her religion. I was marrying Sarah because she was who she was.

When they got engaged, both Sarah and Mike took interfaith marriage preparation classes, which helped with tough discussions they had about raising kids, celebrating holidays, and dealing with family dynamics.

The classes suggested they pick one religion for their future children. "We chose Judaism early on because it was the root of all Christianity, and there was nothing in my religion that Mike couldn't understand," Sarah says.

It wasn't until after they were married and the topic of children came up that Mike's parents voiced their disagreement with how their grandchildren would be raised. They also complained that the Jewish traditions had overshadowed the Catholic traditions at the Miles' wedding.

Sarah and Mike decided to go to an interfaith marriage counselor and tried to talk with Mike's parents. But face-to-face conversations, letters, and phone calls didn't seem to help.

Several years later, Sarah and Mike have a distant relationship with Mike's parents. But the difficulties have only brought them closer, they say.

"We'd like [his parents] to be a part of [our lives], and we welcome that opportunity, but only if we can get these issues resolved."

Ecumenical Glue

Even with a common Christian background, interchurch couples have issues to resolve in order to make their marriages work. For Lena and Luke Glover, the bond that holds their marriage together goes beyond Sunday church services. Lena, 35, is Catholic, and Luke, 34, is a nondenominational Christian.

When the two were first married there were tensions, such as when they would attend Mass together and Luke couldn't receive communion, including at their own nuptial Mass. "It highlights our divisions," Luke says.

What helped the Glovers find common ground was the ecumenical charismatic group People of Praise. "It's kind of the glue for our marriage," Luke says. "It focuses on the similarities of our life together."

"It gives us something to do together as a family and as a couple that's kind of bigger than church," Lena says. "If we went round and round about our differences we would spend all our time arguing!"

The couple believes that the differences they have in faith aren't major but that the things they do hold in common, such as their belief in Christ and the gospel, are.

"Now I wouldn't want to change [our religions] for the world," Lena says. "It doesn't bother me anymore because I feel like we experience a level of ecumenism more acutely than those couples that are of the same denomination, and I'm so grateful for that."

The couple now lives in Portland, Oregon and has four children, ages 11, 9, 6, and 5, all of whom are being raised Catholic. For a while the Glovers would attend both a Catholic and a Protestant service on Sundays plus the People of Praise community meetings. But being in church all day was difficult with young kids. Luke decided he'd choose going to Mass with the family.

"We do raise them Catholic, but we give that a little caveat and say we are raising them in a very ecumenical home," Lena says.

Their older two kids are asking more questions now, like why Luke doesn't take communion—he receives a blessing—or why some people pray the rosary. "We teach that there are Christians that emphasize different things," Lena says.

She's proud that her children are learning about different denominations. . . .

The USCCB's Sheila Garcia says that ecumenical and interfaith couples are the grassroots version of what the Catholic Church hopes to accomplish in its ecumenical and interfaith statements, dialogues, conferences, and outreach.

"What these couples are living out in their own lives is what these dialogues are trying to accomplish," Garcia says.

One Family Table

No matter how much interchurch couples such as the Glovers work toward unity, there's a clear and highly visible sign of their disunity—communion.

Bonnie Mack, who works for the Archdiocese of Cincinnati's Marriage and Family Life Office, says, "For nearly every Catholic-Protestant couple that I've talked to, there is pain from not receiving communion together.

"There are some who would say, 'I don't think Jesus would do that. I think he'd call anyone forward.'"

And in fact she has seen some young couples from the marriage preparation classes she teaches go up and receive communion together despite one not being Catholic. "Their way of handling church teachings is much different today," she says. "It's no big deal to them."

Over the years she's seen pastors try to balance the pastoral side and the church-teaching side of the issue. One pastor who has long dealt with the issue is Claretian Father Kenny. He has worked with interfaith and interchurch couples in the Northeast and now at his present assignment in the South as pastor emeritus of Corpus Christi Parish in Stone Mountain, Georgia.

Kenny says that in his area interchurch marriages are very common since Catholics are only the third largest denomination in the region, outnumbered by Baptists and Methodists.

"What I now explain is why the church is so stringent on that issue. There needs to be unity of worship, unity of belief, of dogma, and unity of conduct and morality to receive communion."

But he adds, "If you could say that this was the only way to get the spiritual nourishment you seek, follow your conscience. I can't tell you not to follow your conscience."

Sometimes what begins as an interchurch relationship ends with one person joining the Catholic Church. Matt and Jessica Williams are one such couple who found their faith backgrounds coming together even before they were married. Jessica, 32, was baptized Lutheran but was not raised practicing that faith.

Jessica first met Matt, 43, through a mutual friend. About three or four months into their relationship, Matt, a cradle Catholic, invited Jessica to attend Mass with him at his parish, St. Margaret Mary in Winter Park, Florida.

"It really helped strengthen our relationship . . . to go to church together," Matt says. "It was just a very important part of the week for us."

He also recalls being surprised when, a few months into going to church together, Jessica turned to him and said, "All you have to do is ask me to convert."

Matt says he'd been careful not to put any pressure on her, but was delighted. Jessica enrolled in RCIA, where the director, Dominican Sister Rosemary Finnegan, double-checked that, as Jessica puts it, "Your heart was in it, and that you were not just converting because it was 'the right thing to do.'"

When the pair married in 2010, two months after Jessica became Catholic, it was at a Mass at St. Margaret Mary. The Williamses say that a mutual Catholic faith has served as a strong base when they face challenges.

"It's nice to have that extra support system in place," Jessica says. And as they look into the future at having kids, she says she's happy that they won't be one of those families she'd observed at church with an absentee or non-Catholic parent.

"I wanted our kids to grow up being raised in the faith, praying with them, and trying to educate them on the faith wherever we can," Jessica says.

Matt says he never felt "locked into" the idea of marrying another Catholic. "But now that it's a reality, it's very important to me," he says. "And looking back, maybe it's more important than I realized."

Belief Differences

It's one thing for a couple to come from a common Christian background, or to at least share a religious foundation, but Bonnie Mack says it's another thing when one person has no faith.

"One, you can't draw on commonalities, and two, those couples tend to drift away from church altogether," she says.

Christie and Peter Wood disagree. The 27-year-old couple met while attending the University of Maryland. They dated for four years before Peter proposed while stargazing in Christie's backyard. They married in 2010, at Peter's home parish, St. Paul in Damascus, Maryland.

Christie was raised Methodist but now considers herself an agnostic. Peter describes himself as a "pretty hard-core" Catholic.

The newlyweds' marriage parallels Peter's parents' relationship. Peter's dad was raised Methodist but didn't practice his faith as an adult, and Peter's mom is Catholic. His father was active in helping out with church and community projects and never converted to Catholicism.

"My dad showed me that it really matters more that you walk the walk as opposed to talk the talk," Peter says. "I was able to see that a marriage like that could work. I have a good model and good support in my parents."

Christie says that when they began dating, she found Peter's faith appealing. "I kind of admired it actually. I felt it was a lot of who he is," she says. "It was that level of dedication [to his faith] that was impressive, and it was also obvious to me that his faith is what made him such a good person. I could see that reflected in his everyday actions.

"We have the same morals. We still agree on most issues and how we run our life," Christie adds.

The Woods admit that it will be more difficult once they have kids and want to send a consistent message to them about religion.

On the Web

For more tips on how to prepare for an interfaith or interchurch marriage, visit *uscatholic.org*.

"The most difficult thing will probably be when our [child] starts asking questions, but before they're old enough to understand that Peter and I have different views," she says. "For example, I'm sure the question of, 'Why doesn't mommy go to church?' will come up. It's a complicated answer that Peter and I understand, but one that will be trickier to explain to a little child."

However, Peter adds, "I feel like it would be a lot more challenging if we had different religious perspectives that were competing with one another or trying to steal time from each other."

Sheila Garcia notes that even Catholics who marry Catholics often have faith differences. A regular Mass-goer in a relationship with a twice-a-year Catholic is "practically a mixed marriage in and of itself," she says.

What's key, Garcia believes, is that every couple has to address and explore the differences in their religious beliefs because the issues won't resolve themselves. And diocesan and parish programs should support them in their faith explorations.

Critical Thinking

1. What is the difference between an interfaith marriage and an interchurch marriage?

2. How much does a potential partner's religion factor into mate selection and marriage decisions?

3. What challenges are faced by couples who are part of interfaith and interchurch marriages?

4. This article explores the challenges of unions between Catholics and non-Catholics. Do you think interfaith or interchurch marriages between different groups are more or less challenging?

5. What supports are needed for couples contemplating interfaith and interchurch marriages?

Create Central

www.mhhe.com/createcentral

Internet References

Combined Jewish Philanthropies: Interfaith Couples and Families
www.cjp.org/interfaith-couples-and-families.aspx
Families Forever: Strengthening Interfaith Marriages
http://foreverfamilies.byu.edu/Article.aspx?a=146

ANNA WEAVER is a Hawaii-born writer now living in Washington, D.C.

Article   Prepared by: Patricia Hrusa Williams,
                                   University of Maine at Farmington

Where Is Marriage Going?

ANTHONY LAYNG

Learning Outcomes

After reading this article, you will be able to:

- Discuss the evolution of marriage in today's American society.
- Explain some common beliefs around marriage.
- Synthesize the nature of martial relationships.

It was bad enough when the divorce rate in the U.S. reached epidemic proportions and single parenting became commonplace. Now, more and more Americans are developing a tolerance for same-sex marriage. New York recognizes such marriages, and the California and Connecticut Supreme Courts struck down those states' laws banning marriage for same-sex couples, allowing them to join Massachusetts in accepting homosexual unions. Even though Californians recently voted to stop granting marriage licenses to same-sex couples, the sanctity of marriage seriously seems to be undermined and in danger of further deterioration.

Most Americans believe that marriage is an inherently sacred institution, the purpose of which is procreation and the socialization of children. That is why the idea of same-sex marriage, the prevalence of single mothers raising children, and the frailty of modern marriages are considered such a threat to "proper" marriage. Such pessimism particularly is prevalent among biblical literalists and other Christian fundamentalists who feel that any alteration of traditional marriage constitutes a moral decline, and many others agree.

However, examining the history of marriage encourages quite a different conclusion. The ethnographic study of tribal societies suggests what marriage meant to our ancestors thousands of years ago. Obviously, having children is an ancient concern, but most tribal people did not view marriage as something sacred. Many tribes had no ritual to acknowledge the start of a marriage, nothing we would equate to a wedding. Among the traditional Cheyenne, courtship involved a girl allowing a suitor to sleep with her in her parents' tepee, entering stealthfully after dark and leaving before the others in the tepee awakened. All the couple needed to do to be considered married was to have the young man sleep late enough to be discovered by her parents. Similarly, some Pacific islanders, such as the Ulithi, allowed couples to "announce" that they wished to be considered married simply by cohabiting. Coming-of-age rituals were far more common in tribal societies than weddings, and yet marriage was, with very few exceptions, the norm in all these societies.

Somehow, the belief that marriages are arranged in heaven, an extremely romantic idea, has become equated with considering marriage as sacred. Again, taking a historical perspective as provided by our knowledge of traditional societies, marriages frequently were arranged by parents or other relatives. Among the Sambia of New Guinea and the Tiwi of northern Australia, many marriages involved infant brides. In numerous warlike tribes such as the Yanomamo of Venezuela, men obtained wives by capturing them from enemy villages.

Granted, marriage in this country often is associated with religious concepts and usually initiated with a sacred ritual. Yet, from the perspective of the history of humanity, this is a rather recent development. Even newer are our present matrimonial motives. Instead of marrying to ensure that our offspring will care for us when we are too old to provide for ourselves, we now consciously limit the number of children to how many we can afford. No longer does marrying and having children provide assurance that the elderly will be cared for. Understandably, most modern couples, for a variety of reasons, choose to limit their fecundity to one or two children or remain childless. Unlike tribal people, those of us who elect to avoid marriage nevertheless may be admired and influential. However, our tribal ancestors structured their lives around marriage. Who you were, your role in society, and your prestige all largely were determined by your place in the kinship system. Whom you and your kin married could ensure or alter your status in society. One rose and fell in the social order by strategic marriage. Of course, infant marriage and marriage by capture no longer are acceptable. Arranged marriages remain legal, but are considered unsuitable. Now, it seems, the only legitimate motivation for marriage is romantic love and seeking emotional fulfillment. Marriage to enhance status still occurs, but generally is frowned upon. We are quite critical of the wealthy senior socialite who marries her young tennis instructor, or the twenty something beauty who marries a famous elderly celebrity. Such unions are considered laughable or crass.

Tribal people married to gain prestige by having many children (hopefully, several sons) to ensure their future welfare. Additionally, given the strict sexual division of labor in these societies, at least one man and one woman were necessary components of a normal household. This had been the case since our ancestors lived as hunters and gatherers. Even in traditional agrarian societies, the labors of men and women produced very different things, and both were required for running a successful household and providing for children. Now that men and women are obtaining nearly equal educations and more and more couples are, of necessity, gainfully employed, any domestic division of labor likely is to be dictated by personal inclinations and circumstances rather than gender. No longer is the husband inevitably the breadwinner and the wife a stay-at-home mother. Marriage in the U.S. is a very flexible institution today. The nature of a marital relationship is not determined primarily by custom but is left to each couple to work out according to personal needs and preferences. It no longer necessarily involves a hierarchical arrangement between spouses. Contemporary husbands and wives frequently consider themselves to be equal partners. Even parenting has lost its imperative tie to marriage since it has become acceptable for single people to raise children today.

The nature of a marital relationship is not determined primarily by custom but is left to each couple to work out. . . .

It is under these circumstances, given how marriage has evolved to its present form, that homosexual men and women have begun to find same-sex marriage attractive. Clearly, each marriage is an ever-adapting relationship, altering over time as circumstances change. Similarly, the institution of marriage has evolved and will continue to do so. Since the earliest marriages in very primitive societies, this custom has taken various forms, always adjusting as society evolved. That process particularly is evident today because social change has been accelerating. Current legislative attempts to prohibit such change are understandable, but unsuitable and unlikely to succeed, as our technology, beliefs, and customs have a long dynamic history, and marriage is subject to the same forces of social change as the rest of our culture.

Critical Thinking

1. How do you view marriage in today's society?
2. What has changed in marriage?
3. What has had the greatest impact on marriage?
4. How does society impact marriage?
5. What are the common beliefs around marriage, and how do media impact those beliefs?

Create Central

www.mhhe.com/createcentral

Internet References

Coalition for Marriage, Family, and Couples Education
   www.smartmarriages.com
National Council on Family Relations
   www.ncfr.com
Kearl's Guide to the Sociology of the Family
   www.trinity.edu/MKEARL/family.html

Anthony Layng is professor emeritus of anthropology at Elmira (N.Y.) College.

Article

Prepared by: Patricia Hrusa Williams,
University of Maine at Farmington

The Child's Advocate in Donor Conceptions: The Telling of the Story

Kris A. Probasco

Learning Outcomes

After reading this article, you will be able to:

- Define the term "donor conception."

- Understand the ethical and personal dilemmas faced by parents who conceive via donor conception.

- Recognize how issues about family, adoption, and biological heritage can be addressed with children in a developmentally appropriate way.

Traditionally, to create a child, there is a joining of a woman's egg and a man's sperm via sexual intercourse. When, by choice or by happenstance, this process is not available, modern persons have access to additional methods. These methods stem from the donation of materials originating in others, a donated egg, donated sperm, or more recently, a donated fertilized frozen embryo. The donations range from easily obtained material (sperm) to complexly obtained material (eggs) to material created via a large sum of money and effort by the donors (embryo) (see Figure 1). As in traditional adoption, the donor procedure of creating a child involves a minimum of two parties, one in whom the gamete material was created and one who accepts this material to obtain a child.

> **Donated Egg:** Transfer of preovulatory oocytes from voluntary donor to a suitable host. Oocytes are collected through an invasive procedure, fertilized in vitro, and transferred to the host.
>
> **Donated Sperm:** Collection of ejaculated sperm from voluntary donor used to fertilize egg in human host or in vitro.
>
> **Donated Embryo:** Embryo that has been created through in vitro fertilization in excess of what was used by the gestating woman. Often frozen for further use, recent trend to donate for adoption by others.

Figure 1. Definitions

The history of donor conception dates back to 1884, when the first case of donor insemination was documented. At that time, physicians were using their own sperm for conception (Snowden, 1983). The first documented case of egg donation was in 1983 (Buster et al., 1983), and embryo placement and adoption began in 1997 ("Embryo adoption becoming the rage," 2009). Donor conceptions are provided for couples with male or female infertility, individuals who have a genetic disorder they do not want to pass on to a child, second marriages where there was a vasectomy in the first marriage, single women, and the lesbian and gay population. Estimates are that thousands of children are born by donor conception each year in the United States, more than the number of infants placed in traditional adoptions.

This article suggests the assistance families will need in sharing the stories of their children's beginnings with them. This author believes that keeping origins secret can be detrimental to a child's mental health, and that open donation, similar to open adoption, is most helpful in the healthy family system.

Preparing for Parenthood

Unlike the traditional method of pregnancy in which one-third of all pregnancies are unplanned, using donor material takes some intention. An essential step in the process is coming to terms with the choice to use donor material. Parents must accept that this chosen alternative is different. Grieving the loss of personal ability to create the genetic offspring, the loss of the biological child or a marriage or relationship that would create a genetic child is an important factor in being prepared to parent children through a donor conception. Mental health therapists have found through experience as counselors to families that without preparation of the parents through education and courses, the losses tend to become the responsibility and burden of the child. Mental health therapists believe a child should be born into a family without having to cure the situation that brought donor conception to the family. For many, a history of infertility has preceded the decision for a donor conception. Acknowledgement and acceptance of all losses connected to the infertility struggle is a part of parenting preparation.

Young Children (Ages 3 to 10)

How I Began: The Story of Donor Insemination, by N.S.W Infertility Social Workers Group, J. Paul, (Ed.), 1988, Port Melbourne, Australia: The Fertility Society of Australia.

Let Me Explain: A Story About Donor Insemination, by J. Schnitter, 1995, Indianapolis, IN: Perspectives Press.

Mommy, Did I Grow in Your Tummy? Where Some Babies Come From, by E. Gordon, 1992, California: E.M. Greenberg Press, Inc.

My Story/Our Story, by Donor Conception Network, 2002, London: Donor Conception Network.

Phoebe's Family: A Story about Egg Donation, by L. Stamm, 2010, Niskayuna, NY: Graphite Press.

Sometimes It Takes 3 to Make a Baby: Explaining Egg Donation to Young Children, by K. Bourne, 2002, Melbourne, Australia: Melbourne IVF.

The Family Book, by T. Parr, 2003, New York: Little, Brown & Co.

Before You Were Born, Our Wish for a Baby, by J. Grimes, 2004, Webster, IA: X, Y, and Me.

Older Children (12 and Older)

Behind Closed Doors: Moving Beyond Secrecy and Shame, by M. Marrissette, 2006, New York: Be-Mondo Publishing Inc.

Who Am I? Experiences of Donor Conception, by A. McWhinnie, 2006, Warwickshire, UK: Idreos Education Trust.

Nurses and Parents

Building a Family with the Assistance of Donor Insemination, by K. Daniels, 2004, Wellington, New Zealand: Dunmore Press.

Choosing to be Open about Donor Conception: Experiences of Parents, by S. Pettle and J. Burns, 2002, London Donor Conception Network.

Experience of Donor Conception: Parents, Offspring & Donors through the Years, by C. Lorbach, 2003, London: Jessica Kingsley Publishers.

Families Following Assisted Conception: What Do We Tell Our Child? by A. McWhinnie, 1996, Dundee, UK: University of Dundee.

Telling and Talking about Donor Conception: A Guide for Parents, by Donor Conception Network, 2006. London: Donor Conception Network.

Third Party Assisted Conception Across Cultures: Social, Legal & Ethical Perspectives, by E. Blyth and R. Landau, 2003, London: Jessica Kingsley Publishers.

Truth & the Child 10 Years On: Information Exchange in Donor Assisted Conception, edited by E. Blyth, M. Crawshaw, and J. Speirs, 1998, Birmingham, UK: British Association of Social Workers.

Lethal Secrets, The Psychology of Donor Insemination Problems and Solutions, by A. Baron and R. Pannor, 2008, Las Vegas, NV: Triadoption Publications.

Mommies, Daddies, Donors, Surrogates: Answering Tough Questions and Building Strong Families, by D. Ehrensaft, 2005, New York: Guilford Press.

Figure 2.   Readings

Note: Many of these publications are available through the Infertility Network (www.InfertilityNetwork.org).

The Donor Sibling Registry www.donorsiblingregistry.com
Infertility Network www.InfertilityNetwork.org
Embryo Adoption Awareness Center www.embryoadoption.org
Adoptive Families (magazine) www.adoptivefamilies.com
American Society for Reproductive Medicine www.asrm.org

Figure 3.   Websites of Interest

For couples planning to parent a child by donor conception, it is vital that both individuals emotionally accept the decision for a donor. The infertile couple needs assistance from others to make the conception medically possible. The nature vs. nurture debate has been illuminated by years of adoption research (Bouchard, Lykken, McGue, Segal, & Tellegan, 1989) that who we become is approximately 50% nature and 50% nurture. Those who choose sperm or egg donation must accept the significance of the genetic component in their child's life. For an embryo placement, the child's complete genetics are connected to another family. Thus, it is important that parents learn as much as they can about the donors they are 'inviting into their home,' accept that another person or family is helping to conceive the child, and that the child may have life-long genetic, social, and emotional connections to that family.

Earlier in my career as a social worker in the infertility and donor world, there was very little information, if any, provided regarding the anonymous donors. Sperm and eggs came privately or with very basic medical information. This has now changed. Resources are now available to select a donor's genetic material based on social, psychological, and medical information, including pictures, videos, and audio tapes, and identified donors who can be available for medical emergency and as social contacts at a later date. In embryo placement, there are open arrangements so the genetic family and prospective adoptive family know about each other and continue to be a resource for both families as their children grow in understanding their particular stories.

Education

Whether traditional adoption, donor conception, or embryo placement, education of prospective parents is mandatory. Educational resources are increasingly available, including books, children's books, the Infertility Network from Canada, and the Donor Sibling Registry (see Figures 2 and 3). All of these resources have Internet connections for those in the decision-making process and families who are parenting children, and also include messages from those who came to a family by donor conception. It is important to learn from those who have come before us so parents can become effective advocates for their children.

In adoption, it is positive for families to announce their decision to their family and friends to gain their support. Because a donor conception includes a pregnancy in the family, the question of whether to go public is more difficult. While families deserve some privacy regarding personal decisions, it is well known from family systems theory that secrets cause problems. From my clinical experience, it is generally best that couples who are successful with a donor conception share with family and friends. It benefits the family to celebrate the unique arrival of this child and to share in the celebration because this will be a very important part in the child's story.

Legal Issues

Legal issues with donor conception are evolving. Many states have legislation regarding sperm donor insemination, few states have legislation regarding egg donation, and only one state has legislation regarding embryo placement. In the Kansas City area, both Kansas and Missouri have legislation for sperm donation. There is no legislation for egg donation or embryo placement. In my practice, we recommend a stepparent adoption in egg donation and a full adoption for embryo placement with an adoption decree. Recognizing what legal liabilities are present for a child born by donor conception in the state of residency provides for the child's security.

The Child's Story
Beginning the Story

The basic need of a child brought to any family is a positive attitude about his or her conception, birth, and family. Accepting the child as an individual with a unique, genetic history is a crucial factor for donor conceptions. The parents' decision to bring a child into their family by donor represents the first step for creating a positive story. As in traditional adoption, it is the parents' job to tell all they know regarding their donor conception to help the child understand. There is an attachment process during the child's growing years, which is enhanced by honest stories about how the child came to be. We want a child/adult to say they do not remember being told because they always knew how they came into the family.

Infancy

During the child's infancy is a time for parents to practice talking to their child with positive language and feelings. "We so wanted to be parents. We were meant to be your parents. We are so happy that we got help. Many people assisted us in your coming to our family, especially our donor." Tone of voice communicates pride, love, and celebration, explaining, "We have so much to tell you and we are so excited for you to understand how you came into our family." Continue the positive language and talk basically throughout the child's growing years.

Early Childhood

Some details can be helpful in the understanding process for the child in early childhood. Children in this stage are more aware of the world around them and basically understand the concept of "family." By this age, children will be able to tell you who their family members are and how they are related to each other. They do this by family experiences and being exposed to different families.

This is a great time to start reading storybooks, and many are available. The Web site www.XYandMe.com contains a series of 16 books that begin and end the same, with not being able to have a biological child, to the joy of having a child. The middle section describes the child's particular reproduction method for coming to the family.

It is also a good idea to put a beginning book together of pictures of the child coming home. These pictures should include parents wanting a child, waiting for a positive pregnancy test, the clinic where the parents received assistance or picture of the sperm bank and/or egg facility, the doctor's office, pictures of the donor and/or genetic family, and pictures throughout the pregnancy and birth. This book will start the child from his or her beginning, which includes the parents' decision, individuals from whom they received assistance, and the helper/donor who gave his or her genetics for the child's life. For a known donor situation, actual pictures of the family member, friend, or extended family can also be provided in the book. The message is clear, that "we wanted to have children in our family, we worked really hard for our children to arrive, and we accepted and celebrated the assistance of many people."

This is also a time to look for opportunities to point things out to children as they learn about the world around them. For example, "This is a fire station, where firemen help people when they are in an emergency." "This is where we went when we needed help for you to come into our family." "This is the hospital where you were born." Showing the child these places provides images and concrete facts along the way. This is also an excellent time to be talking to the child about the many ways that children come into a family. Todd Parr (2003) has authored many books about families and the importance of the love they share with each other.

Middle Childhood

During the middle years, as in adoptions, children have many questions. These can occur when driving the car, seeing a pregnant woman, or standing in line at a grocery store. Parents are wise to "go with the flow" in terms of these questions. Parents do well to keep the conversations active in bringing up the subject from time to time. The healthy message is that this is a comfortable subject to talk about, and it is okay to ask questions. Girls tend to ask questions earlier than boys. As children move into the questions of how babies are made, more factual information can be shared. Generally during this time, the "ah-ha" moments will occur, and children will figure out what "donor" actually means and then understand this genetic connection to another.

Sex education received from parents and schools is now starting to make more sense: They have inherited genes from the donor and may now begin to question who their "real" parent(s) are. The questions "What is real?" and "Who is real?" come into their thoughts. The realization of who they are and who their identity is to become is not a shock because of all the early telling. However, there is some sadness when children actually understand that one or both of their parents is not genetically connected to them.

During this time, the child will ask lots of questions, and the parents will provide them with information. It is best to share most of this information before the adolescent years. In this way, children can put the puzzle pieces together as they work on identity formation. In our experience, girls are more likely to ask lots of questions; boys tend not to want to be different and may not display curiosity. All extremes are possible from not wanting to talk about it to talking about it frequently.

The best parental stance is to keep the communication lines open and answer questions with as much factual information as possible. If the child asks a question about the donor, and the parent does not have the information, it is best to have empathy for the child and say, "I wish I could answer that question. If I were you, I would want to know, too." In an open, identified donor or a known donor situation, it may be helpful to write the questions down so the value of the child's curiosity is validated. The parent can assure the children these questions can be asked of the donor.

Adolescence

As children move into their teenage years, they will learn about science, reproduction, and deoxyribonucleic acid (DNA) in school. For some children, this will simply be academic information. However, donor children will identify these scientific concepts with themselves. In teenage years, everything is fair game for challenges and questions. Most adults remember when, as adolescents, they thought, "Parents don't really know anything. I am so different from them." The psychological task in adolescent years, as discussed by Erikson (1968), is to individuate, to become a person with individualized needs, tasks, and freedoms. Teens want to find out how they are similar and different from their parents and how they became a unique individual. Donor-conceived children also have to figure out how they are similar and different from the genetic donor. These questions will often challenge the non-genetic parents' authority, which may produce anxiety for parents. The adolescent may say things like "You are not my real parents." It is best for parents to understand the teenager's quest for identity without becoming defensive. Parents need to continue to distinguish between the facts of the teen's conception from the normal responsibilities of parenting.

A teenager who now chooses to share information with his or her peers may cause concern for parents because not everyone will understand (or approve of) how the child came to their family. This is a very fine detail because parents want to ensure their teen has pride in him or herself. Some parents might have chosen to maintain more privacy about the methods used for conception. The child, however, is really in charge of who is told, and there may be some surprises along the way.

Summary

Parents who use donor gametes should feel firm and entitled to say they are this child's parents. Health care providers (doctors, nurses, and social workers) must help these parents. Their decision to bring a child into the world creates continuous consequences for the whole family. The parents' responsibility is to attach, parent, and educate, and the child's responsibility is to ask questions to form an identity and find ways to feel secure about the individual he or she is becoming. Participating as the child's advocate presents many joys and celebrations, as well as many challenges. Pediatric nurses can help families resolve infertility issues and obtain education about donor conception. This advocacy provides the freedom for parents to be proud of their decision, attach to the process, and rejoice for the child who comes to their family. This is a true blessing for everyone.

References

Bouchard, T.J., Jr., Lykken, D.T., McGue, M., Segal, N.L., & Tellegan, A. (1990). Sources of human psychological differences: The Minnesota Study of Twins Reared Apart. *Science 250*(4978), 223–228.

Buster, J.E., Bustillo, M., Thorneycroft, I.H., Simon, J.A., Boyers, S.P., Marshall, J.R., . . . Louw, J.A. (1983) Non-surgical transfer of an invivo fertilized donated ovum to an infertility patient. *The Lancet, 1*(8328), 816–817.

"Embryo adoption becoming the rage." (2009, April 19). *The Washington Times*. Retrieved from http://www.washingtontimes.com/news/2009/apr/19/embryo-adoption-becoming-rage.

Erikson, E. (1968). *The stages of psychosocial development*. New York: Norton.

Parr, T. (2003). *The family book*. New York: Little, Brown & Co.

Snowden, R., Mitchell, G.D., & Snowden, E.M. (1983). *Artificial reproduction: A social investigation*. London: George Allen & Unwin.

Critical Thinking

1. If you were conceived via donor conception, what questions would you have about your donor biological parent, if any? How would it feel if there was no way to have your questions answered?

2. The article suggests that parents who conceive through donor conception share this information with family and friends. Do you agree or disagree with this piece of advice? Why or why not?

3. Explain how children's questions or concerns about their biological heritage may change as they grow up.

4. The article provides advice for parents about how to address issues related to donor conception with children at different ages. Do you agree with the article's advice? Why or why not?

Create Central

www.mhhe.com/createcentral

Internet References

Adoptive Families
www.adoptivefamilies.com

American Society for Reproductive Medicine
www.asrm.org
Society for Assisted Reproductive Technology
www.sart.org
Adelaide Center for Bioethics and Culture
www.bioethics.org.au

Kris A. Probasco, LSCSW, LCSW, is Executive Director, Adoption & Fertility Resources, A Division of Clinical Counseling Associates, Inc., Liberty, MO, and Overland Park, KS.

Author's Note: *I would like to dedicate this article to my mentors, Annette Baron (author of* The Adoption Triangle *and* Lethal Secrets*) and Sharon Kaplan Rozia (author of* The Open Adoption Experience*). Annette and Sharon have taught me to speak the truth and to encourage parents to speak the truth to their children for the benefit of their children.*

Reprinted from *Pediatric Nursing*, 2012, vol. 38, no. 3, pp 179–182. Reprinted with permission of the publisher, Jannetti Publications, Inc., East Holly Avenue/Box 56, Pitman, NJ 08071-0056; (856) 256-2300; FAX (856) 589-7463; Web site: www.pediatricnursing.net. For a sample copy of the journal, please contact the publisher.

Article   Prepared by: Patricia Hrusa Williams,
                             University of Maine at Farmington

Family Unplugged

SHAWN BEAN

Learning Outcomes

After reading this article, you will be able to:

- Identify some different ways that parents, children, and families utilize technology.

- Explain how technology use influences family interaction.

- Describe some benefits of families taking a "digital sabbatical."

For five days, I broke up with my BlackBerry. And my iPad. Oh yeah, my computer, too. I even ditched my TV (it isn't you, it's me). Perhaps not so surprisingly, I discovered that disconnecting my family is actually the best way to make a connection.

Red. It's the color of love, of passion. It's also the color of the little blinking light on my BlackBerry.

Oh, blinky red light. Your allure is so magnetic. It doesn't matter if I'm at a traffic light, with my firstborn, Jackson, at the playground, or watching Tanner sing at his preschool graduation. That red light (paired with the titillating purr of a couple of vibrations) draws me in. Technology is my mistress.

Technology is also the medicine, the babysitter, the emergency contact. On numerous occasions, I've calmed a sibling squabble with a 50-milligram dose of *Supah Ninjas. He-Man* clips on YouTube have bought me extra minutes to meet a deadline. Then, of course, there was the time I got lost in the spaghetti-loop vortex of Disney World's highway system. There I was, an iPad open on my lap, stealing glances at MapQuest as I navigated through the Mouse Trap.

1 in 4 people would consider a completely tech-free day for their family.

It's not only me, of course. Our collective whatever-ness about technology has become a smidge scary. Roughly one in five adults admits to poor mobile etiquette but continues the behavior because everyone else is doing it. Forty-two percent of children think their parents need to disconnect when they're at home. "iParents" (digitally connected moms and dads) are twice as likely as regular parents to neglect their responsibilities because they're on Facebook and Twitter, according to a study by Retrevo. And it's not just that we've all been there. We *are* there.

59 percent of kids have seen their parent use a mobile device while driving.

The Disney World moment was a real wakeup call. I'm sure I would have made a smarter decision had the boys been in the car. (Right?) I need to rediscover undivided attention, eye contact, stillness, the nothings that happen between the somethings.

My whatever-ness is officially over. It's time to break up with the blinky red light.

Shawn Bean Just Met a Modern Dad Who Checks His E-mail at the Public Library

William Powers's version of whatever-ness ended just before Labor Day 2007. At his family's home in Cape Cod, there were three sets of eyes, and three screens: His then 9-year-old son, William, was playing a game online, his wife, Martha Sherrill, was on a laptop doing research, and Powers was on his own computer. "We were exchanging silent glances," recalls Powers. "That's when I realized something, anything, had to be done."

That something, anything, was the Internet Sabbath: From bedtime on Friday to sunrise on Monday, all plugged-in devices (laptops, smartphones, etc.) were off-limits. If someone absolutely, positively had to get online, they could use one of the computers at the public library. It was this experience—and the lessons learned—that inform his book, *Hamlet's BlackBerry: A Practical Philosophy for Building a Good Life in the Digital Age.*

I tell Powers about my plan: I'm taking my boys on a digital sabbatical. For five days, we'd forgo all technology. No *Supah Ninjas.* No YouTube. No MapQuest. No more trysts with the blinky red light.

"Expect that your house will feel slightly different," he says. "You won't know exactly what to do. We also had to relearn the art of sustained conversation with eye contact." (An interesting point. See how long your next parent–child conversation goes before a device interrupts. Technology has a wicked case of attention deficit disorder.)

One more thing: "You'll be shocked at the tics you've developed. You'll realize how often you reach for a tech fix." Powers says the first two months "were a real struggle. There was unbelievable withdrawal. I can't lie—there were tears."

Shawn Bean Is Off the Grid, and Has No Idea What He Will Do to Fill the Time

Before unplugging on Day One, I put a status update on Facebook about my experiment: "About to embark on a digital sabbatical with the boys. See you on the other side!" Comments included "Good luck!" and "Emme would die without her *Phineas and Ferb* fix."

I did not forewarn the boys that we were doing this, nor did I plan anything. It's easy to unplug when you've got a dozen distractions lined up. I want to face the analog world unarmed. Surprisingly, Jackson is on board from the get go, and wonders why we are only doing it for five days. I write up a contract: "Daddy, Jackson, and Tanner will not watch TV or play on the computer." I sign my name, Jackson writes "Jackson B," and Tanner squiggles a line resembling a seismograph reading.

Without a plan of attack, we quickly find ourselves doing, well, everything. Fishing poles come out of the garage, and we dig for earthworms in the front yard. We break out a bubble machine, left unopened from a recent birthday. We remix boring items into something new, from tinfoil (police badges) to plastic bottles in the recycling bin (test tubes). But I realize I'm going about this all wrong. I'm making our activities fast-paced, high-energy, and visually stimulating. Why am I re-creating television?

I also notice tingling in my phantom limb. More than twice, I mindlessly feel my pants pocket for my BlackBerry. Each time I pass the nightstand, I look for the blinky red light. There it is, blinking. Sweet, beautiful blinking. *Don't worry, baby. We'll be together again soon.*

42 percent of kids think their parents need to disconnect more at home.

Shawn Bean just Scared a Woman in Portland with Talk of Cell Phones Causing Cancer

Even with newborn Casey in her arms, Ellen Currey-Wilson was momentarily distracted by something else she loved: *The Price Is Right*. As she was rolled through the maternity ward,

Tech-Free Fun

A list of the unplugged activities my boys and I created out of thin air.

1. Built a ninja obstacle course using sofa cushions and pillows.
2. Repurposed empty plastic bottles in the recycling bin as test tubes. We filled them with water and added food coloring.
3. Created a mosaic sidewalk by coloring in the bricks with chalk.
4. Invented a "mocktail" using the fruit juices and drinks we already had in the refrigerator.
5. Played "airport." I gave them plane tickets and empty suitcases to pack. I also played the security agent who screened their luggage.

she caught Bob Barker on a wall-mounted screen, then quickly returned to her son's gaze.

"Television was my other parent," says Currey-Wilson. "I grew up with a single mom." B.C. (Before Casey), television was "a companion, an escape, a drug, a procrastinator's dream." Life was a series of sitcoms and game shows (creating a bridal registry, for example, reminded her of *Let's Make a Deal*). But A.D. (After Delivery), it was an obsession she did not want to pass on to her child. So she went cold turkey, to mixed results. She details her journey in *The Big Turnoff: Confessions of a TV-Addicted Mom Trying to Raise a TV-Free Kid*. Like Powers, she had a tough transition. She hid a television in the storage room upstairs and snuck in viewings of *Three's Company* while her baby napped.

During my funny and insightful conversation with Currey-Wilson, I catch glimpses of the nervous, hyper-analyzing mother from *The Big Turnoff*: the mom who acted as a human shield to block *Sesame Street* during a playdate, the mom who worried that her son would be ostracized at school for not knowing the theme song to *SpongeBob SquarePants*. After a quick introduction, we discuss the ways technology affects our kids. (Currey-Wilson conducted an informal survey of the students in her fourth-grade class and discovered that those who watched the most TV were the least focused.) We then chat about recent findings connecting cell-phone use to cancer. How ironic, I say: Here we are, both on cell phones, discussing cell-phone use and cancer. The line goes quiet. She politely asks if I can call her back on the landline.

For so many new moms, who feel isolated by their new 24-hour job, technology is a way to connect. Roughly 35 percent of moms consider a mother they met on a message board a friend, according to a *Parenting*-BlogHer survey. Seventy-three percent talk about sensitive issues like their children's behavior and development on message boards; about 43 percent do the same on Facebook.

"With technology, you can instantly interact with real people," Currey-Wilson explains. "Even watching a TV show made me feel like I was part of the conversation. I was lonely without it."

How did she change after breaking up with the boob tube? "I learned to face my problems more quickly, skipping over the hours of TV I usually needed to watch before attempting to deal with anything challenging or unpleasant," she says. "I also became closer to my husband. We fought more, too, much to his dismay. It was a big adjustment for him to learn to deal with a wife who wasn't zoned out anymore."

49 percent of parents prohibit their kids from having a computer in their bedroom.

"To have a deep relationship, you have to spend time and focus," Powers explains. "It's hard to be present when one part of your mind is wondering what's happening out in the world."

At the end of Day Three, my wife, Brandy, and I tuck the boys into bed and head out to the porch. The stars are out—faint, winking gemstones—but tonight I don't use *Star Walk* on my iPad to discover what corner of the sky is getting filleted by Orion's Sword. A few minutes later, Jackson walks out and curls up on my lap. We sit quietly. Across the lake, milky blue light flickers inside a living room. "They're watching TV," Jackson says.

Shawn Bean is Watching His Son Catch His First Wave

Four years later; Powers and his family still observe their Internet Sabbath. "When I come back to the digital world on Monday morning, I'm reminded of how great it is," he says. "I love it more because I've had a break." He adds that his son, William, has a huge fort at the back of the property. "He convinces his friends to leave their phones in the house."

By Day Five, Jackson had not only caught an earthworm and a smallmouth bass, but his first wave on a longboard during a trip to the beach. He yells like a banshee as I push him into the swirling meringue of the breaking wave. He falls. He bobs to the surface. He wants to do it again.

Of course, these activities are not exclusive to the analog world. But we know that in the digital world, children 6 and under spend two hours a day using screen media, and adults spend more than five hours a day online. That's two days every week without sustained eye contact or conversation. The digital sabbatical gives us that time back. It's no longer the blinky red light versus your son's question about the food on Mars. As it should be, a ridiculous debate about lunch in outer space wins every time.

"It's not about turning against technology," Powers notes, "but designing our lives the way we want them."

I open Microsoft Word to begin writing this story, and there it is: the cursor. It's blinking impatiently, waiting to move forward, like a runner jogging in place at a red light. That's when it hits me: Technology is about next. Family is about now.

Critical Thinking

1. What are some challenges for families as technology becomes an ever-present force in our lives?

2. What are some benefits of unplugging and giving our family a "digital sabbatical?"

3. What guidelines can you develop for families regarding computer and cell-phone use?

Create Central

www.mhhe.com/createcentral

Internet References

Family Online Safety Institute
  www.fosi.org
Pew Internet and American Life Project: Networked Families
  www.pewinternet.org/Reports/2008/Networked-Families.aspx